To be encouraged to put one's own preaching into broad historical context, beginning with the apostles, is a rare treat. This is a book for all preachers and not only those who have a liking for church history. The various authors provide a comprehensive examination of the context and method of preaching through the ages. Those of us who preach—especially those who preach without a carefully examined philosophy of preaching or a constantly reviewed biblical hermeneutics—can only be enriched and encouraged by these studies.

GRAEME L. GOLDSWORTHY, was lecturer in Old Testament and biblical theology at Moore Theological College

The apostle Paul commanded, "Preach the word." This book introduces some of the most influential preachers from the first through the eighteenth centuries and offers fascinating studies of how they responded to Paul's mandate with great diversity of doctrine and methodology.

JOEL R. BEEKE, president, Puritan Reformed Theological Seminary, Grand Rapids, Michigan

What an incredible work. I was so impressed by the thoughtfulness and care the editors put into their selections. To have so many of Christian history's great preachers and teachers of God's Word sampled and collected in one location makes reading these volumes an incredible delight, not to mention an invaluable resource. If you want to be blessed by, and mentored by, some of the most anointed teachers in history, this great work is where to begin! I'm excited to add it to my library and hope every serious student of God's Word will do the same.

J. D. GREEAR, pastor, The Summit Church, Raleigh-Durham, North Carolina

Paul said, "follow my example, as I follow the example of Christ." Discipleship always works best when the Christian life is modeled for others. The same truth also applies in preaching. My advice to preachers young and old is to stay committed to the Word and learn from those who preach well. Sitting at the feet of history's greatest preachers is a great honor that will enrich your soul, enliven your flock, and enhance your ministry. If this is your desire, then read this book. It tells the tales of history's greats and relates to you a legacy that will inspire you to, like Paul, "boldly ... proclaim the mysteries of the gospel."

DR. TONY EVANS, senior pastor, Oak Cliff Bible Fellowship; president, The Urban Alternative

It is well-known that the Reformers and their heirs regarded faithful preaching of the Scriptures as a mark of a true church. In these two volumes we have a rich exploration of the way in which God has indeed blessed his people with such preaching ever since the apostolic era. Given the unique biographical focus of these essays, these two volumes also remind us that preaching is always mediated through distinct personalities, hence the differences in exegetically-sound preaching over the years. In sum, what we have here is a treasure trove for all who love the preaching of the Word and for all called to this central task in the church's life.

MICHAEL A. G. HAYKIN, professor & chair of church history, The Southern Baptist Theological Seminary

"How did you learn to preach?" is one of the more frequent questions I'm asked. In addition to practice (trial and error!), I can honestly say that I learned much in terms both of what to do and not to do by studying great preachers from the past and present. Virtually all effective preachers will admit that in some sense they stand on the shoulders of someone who has preceded them, from whose method and style and understanding of Scripture they have drawn. That is certainly true of me. These volumes are a treasure trove of homiletical insights from the greatest of preachers in the history of the Christian church. It is a wonderful resource that I am extremely happy to recommend.

SAM STORMS, Bridgeway Church, Oklahoma City, Oklahoma

For most pastors—maybe for all—becoming a better preacher is a lifelong quest. And on that quest, few things are more beneficial than spending quality time with more gifted preachers. Reading *A Legacy of Preaching* affords an unprecedented opportunity for all kinds of pastors to learn from a legion of men and women who are widely regarded as among the best preachers in history, from Peter and Paul to Billy Graham and Gardner Taylor. Hearing their life stories, learning their homiletical theology, and listening to their gospel proclamation will help any pastor fulfill the high calling of preaching the gospel of Jesus Christ.

PHILIP RYKEN, president, Wheaton College

A *Legacy* OF PREACHING

VOLUME TWO

ENLIGHTENMENT TO THE PRESENT DAY

BENJAMIN K. FORREST, KEVIN L. KING,
BILL CURTIS, AND DWAYNE MILIONI

To Reagan, Hudson, and Graham—I pray that
you spend your lives proclaiming the glories of the
risen Christ, as well as listening to the preaching
of the Spirit through the written Word.
BKF

To Daylee, Walter, Sebastian, Solomon, Kevin, Sharin,
and Julianna—you are gifts from the Father that have
added immeasurably to my life. As the homiletical
luminaries in this volume continue to illuminate the
Word, may your lives continue to bear witness to the
life-changing message of the gospel of Jesus Christ.
KLK

For my mentor, Dr. Wayne McDill, who birthed
in me a love for preaching and preachers.
BC

This book is dedicated to Kay, my wife and dear sister
in the faith, and to my students whom I desire to know
preaching history so they will carry on the legacy.
DM

Contents

Abbreviations

ABD	All but dissertation
BD	bachelor of divinity
DBWE	Dietrich Bonhoeffer Works English Edition
DPHIL	Doctor of Philosophy
FBI	Florida Bible Institute
MACCH	Manuscripts of Robert Murray M'Cheyne
MTP	*Metropolitan Tabernacle Pulpit*
NBC	National Baptist Convention
NPS	*New Park Street Pulpit*
SBC	Southern Baptist Convention
SBTC	Southern Baptists of Texas Convention
SBTS	*Southern Baptist Theological Seminary*
SEE	*Spurgeon's Expository Encyclopedia*
SS	Charles Haddon Spurgeon: Preacher, Author, Philanthropist, with anecdotal reminiscences
ST	*The Sword and the Trowel*
STD	Doctor of Sacred Theology
TBN	Trinity Broadcasting Corporation
YFC	Youth for Christ

Foreword

For the word of God is quick, and powerful, and sharper than any twoedged sword, piercing even to the dividing asunder of soul and spirit, and of the joints and marrow, and is a discerner of the thoughts and intents of the heart.

Hebrews 4:12 KJV

From the Protestant Reformers to the evangelist Billy Graham, evangelical preachers have often affirmed their belief that Holy Scripture, the infallible Word of God, possesses great power and bears great and glorious spiritual fruit. Martin Luther was one such preacher. In his *Exhortation to the Clergy of Augsburg* (1530), Luther crafted a "Reformation report card" of sorts (our term). It described the advance of the Evangelical Gospel from 1517, when he had posted his epochal "Ninety-Five Theses," until 1530.[1] But in the latter year, Luther was concerned that "people have forgotten what the world was like before my teaching began."[2] Luther wanted them for their comfort sake to see "what great and glorious fruit the Word of God has produced."[3]

Before 1517, Luther lamented that the "best work" of doctors at the universities "was in despising Holy Scriptures and letting them lie under the bench. 'Bible, Bible,' said they. 'The Bible is a heretics' book! You must read the doctors! There you find what is what!' I know that I am not lying about this, for I grew up among them and have heard and seen all this from them."[4] By contrast, Luther

---

1. Martin Luther, *Works of Martin Luther: The Philadelphia Edition* (Grand Rapids: Baker, 1982), 4:329–82.
2. Ibid., 336.
3. Ibid.
4. Ibid, 347.

and other Reformers extolled the mighty spiritual power of Scripture alone (*sola scriptura*). Said Luther about Scripture: "The Bible is alive, it speaks to me; it has feet, it runs after me; it has hands, it lays hold of me."[5]

In his "Reformation report card," Luther observed he would begin "where my doctrine began, that is, with the indulgences."[6] Luther humbly confessed that it was the decisive power of the Word of God and not his own personal efforts that had "released" people from that spiritually deadening system:

> If our Gospel had done nothing else than release men's consciences from the shameful abomination and idolatry of the indulgences, that alone would be enough to show that it was the Word and power of God. For the whole world must admit that no human wisdom could have done this, since no bishop, no chapter, no monastery, no doctor, no university, not I myself, in short, no human reason, understood or knew this abomination; still less did any know how to check or attack it; everyone had to approve it and let it pass as good and wholesome doctrine and the dear bishops and the pope got money out of it, and let it go on richly.[7]

Luther wanted the truth to be known that he had been incapable of attacking the indulgence system in a successful fashion. By contrast, he also wanted people to remember that the power of the preached Word of God was fully up to the task. On another occasion, Luther observed that even while he slept or drank beer with a colleague, the Word of God did everything in advancing the gospel.

The Reformer John Calvin also believed that the power of the Word of God brought forth "great and glorious" fruit. Calvin worried, however, that some preachers did not seek in their preaching to see the Word of God do this. Rather, they tried to induce compliments from parishioners regarding how well they had preached. Quite simply, they failed to preach with the import of Hebrews 4:12 framing their sermons.

Calvin bemoaned the vacuous nature of the preaching of contemporary preachers who evinced this mindset:

> What preaching is it, I beseech you, that they would have? They wish that the doctrine might hang in suspense, and be like a flint, as Ezekiel makes

---

5. Mary Ann Jeffreys, "Colorful Sayings of Luther," *Christian History Magazine* 34 (Carol Stream, IL: Christianity Today, 1992). https://www.christianitytoday.com/history/issues/issue-34/colorful-sayings-of-colorful-luther.html

6. Luther, *Works of Martin Luther*, 4:336.

7. Ibid., 336–67.

the comparison, so that we might hear no other words but these.'"Oh, he preached very well. Oh, that was a good sermon." And how? Without any profit or edifying the hearers. And yet this is what a great number seek nowadays. And this proverb, "To preach according to the text," means nothing else but this: that the Word of God no longer has any use nor virtue among us, that we be there as if in hiding, and that God would no longer enlighten us (Heb 4:12). But on the contrary, it is said let the Word of God be a two-edged sword, let there be neither marrow nor bone nor thoughts nor affections that are undiscovered or fail to be sought and searched by God as if he were taking our souls apart. And moreover, as it is said in another text, that the office of the Word of God is to feel us even to the bottom, and to bring to light the things that we want to keep hidden (Luke 8:17), as it is also said, that as it is God who searches the hearts (Acts 1:24; 1 Cor 2:15), and that matter belongs to him, so also he wants virtue "to be in his word."[8]

Nearly half a millennium after the Reformation, the evangelist Billy Graham (1918–2018) clearly indicated he too embraced the full authority of Scripture as the infallible Word of God. Moreover, he counted on the power of the Word of God under the influence of the Holy Spirit to energize and impact his preaching. But in 1949, just before his famous Los Angeles Revival tent meetings, he experienced serious doubts about the authority of Scripture. At Forest Home campground in the mountains surrounding Los Angeles, Graham walked into the woods and put his open Bible on a stump. He later recalled that he began to pray: "The exact wording of my prayer is beyond recall, but it must have echoed my thoughts: 'O God! There are many things in this book I do not understand'... I was trying to be on the level with God, but something remained unspoken. At last the Holy Spirit freed me to say it: 'Father, I am going to accept this as Thy Word—by faith!'... I sensed the presence and power of God as I had not sensed it in months."[9]

Billy Graham indicated that his embrace of the authority of Holy Scripture was the very "secret" of his ministry. Over and over again during his lengthy preaching career he would declare: "The Bible says." Moreover, he likewise referenced Hebrews 4:12 in describing Scripture's power to penetrate even the hardened hearts of unbelieving listeners: "The people were not coming to hear great oratory, nor were they interested in my ideas. I found they were desperately

---

8. John Calvin, *Sermons on 1 Timothy, Volume 2*, eds. Ray Van Neste and Brian Denker (Jackson, TN: CreateSpace, 2016), 147–48.

9. Billy Graham, *Just as I Am: The Autobiography of Billy Graham* (San Francisco: Harper-San Francisco, 1997), 139.

hungry to hear what God had to say through His Holy Word. I felt as though I had a rapier in my hand, and through the power of the Bible was slashing deeply into men's consciences, leading them to surrender to God. Does not the Bible say of itself, 'For the word of God is quick, and powerful, sharper than any two-edged sword, piercing even to the dividing asunder of soul and spirit, and of the joints and marrow, and is a discerner of the thoughts and intents of the heart' (Heb. 4:12 KJV). I found that the Bible became a flame in my hands. That flame melted away unbelief in the hearts of people and moved them to decide for Christ. The word became a hammer breaking up stony hearts and shaping them into the likeness of God. Did not God say, 'I will make my words in thy mouth fire' (Jer. 5:14 KJV) and 'is not my word like as a fire? . . . and like a hammer that breaketh the rock in pieces?'" (Jer 23:29 KJV).[10]

In today's spiritually starved world, the need is patent for preachers of unimpeachable integrity who preach with full confidence in the authority and power of the Word of God and who desire to witness Scripture's "great and glorious fruit" poured out. May we be encouraged and inspired in this regard by reading the stories and counsel of the leading preachers recounted in this volume. May we likewise remember that those preachers who were blessed of the Lord often humbly confessed that it was the power of Scripture, God's Word, that produced the "good and glorious fruit" in their ministries, and not they themselves. Rather, as Dr. J. I. Packer observed so wisely, preaching is God's work: "Holy Scripture, the inspired Word (message) of the living God may truly be described as God preaching . . . Only as God himself is perceived to be preaching in our sermons can they have genuine spiritual significance and God will be perceived to speak through us [preachers] only as we are enabled to make plain the fact that it is really the Bible that is doing the talking."[11]

JOHN D. WOODBRIDGE, Research Professor of Church History and the History of Christian Thought at Trinity Evangelical Divinity School in Deerfield, Illinois.

---

10. Billy Graham, "Biblical Authority in Evangelism," *Christianity Today* 1, no. 1 (October 1956).
11. Quoted on page 543 of the present volume.

Acknowledgments

Ben, Kevin, Bill, and Dwayne would like to first thank all the contributing authors who gave of their time, study, and expertise to pass along wisdom from the past for the future training up of preachers—who will eventually leave their own legacy of preaching. Most of these contributing authors responded to a random email from an unknown "colleague." Their gracious response made this project something that we hope will have a long-lasting impact on the field of preaching. We would also like to thank Sarah Funderburke for first seeing the potential in this book many years ago. Laura Sipple, Cheryl Job, Heather Bradly, and Jesse Welliver, although connected to this project only for a short while, were extremely helpful—we appreciate your encouragement and assistance. A special thanks to Joshua Erb, graduate assistant extraordinaire, who worked behind the scenes on several occasions, looking up footnotes, editing bibliographical information, and becoming quite proficient in editing along the way.

We also must (and want to heartily) thank the entire team at Zondervan for bringing this project to fulfillment. Dr. Stan Gundry, Ryan Pazdur, Jesse Hillman, Josh Kessler, Kim Tanner, and a host of others worked behind the scenes to bring this idea to fruition. Thank you for your assistance and friendship along the way. It is a great blessing to be considered a Zondervan author! Here, we would also like to thank Dr. Ed Hindson for encouraging us to submit this project to Zondervan in the first place. He is and has been a great advocate for his faculty—and we appreciate his leadership!

I (Ben) would like to thank all the pastors and preachers who have influenced my life. There are too many to name individually, but (hopefully) you know who you are. The proclamation of the gospel from these many pulpits has contributed to my own understanding of the call to "preach the word" (2 Tim 4:2). Specifically, I would like to thank Nathan Smith (and Heritage Baptist Church) for being an encouragement and an example of faithfulness to the biblical text. To my wife, Lerisa—thank you for being an example of a woman who "preaches" Christ with your life daily. Each morning when you get out of bed to meet with Jesus, you remind me of whose we are and where we want to invest our lives. To Reagan, Hudson, and Graham—look at the example set by your mother, and follow it! We love you and hope your lives are committed to following Jesus as his disciples. Share him with those you meet along the way—share with life and love, deed and word! To Will and Greg—thank you for being great examples, even as younger brothers. I will continue to pray that the church you plant in Seattle will "fearlessly make known the mystery of the gospel" (Eph 6:19). Dad and Mom, thank you for training me up in the way I should go, for teaching me from Scripture, and encouraging me toward holiness—the fruit of your discipleship is reflected in all my work. To my students, Landon, Sri, Josh, Patrick, AJ, Sean, and Torrey, hold high the Word of God. I am encouraged by your heart, passion, and desire to faithfully proclaim the gospel as good news. Lastly, I want to thank my coeditors—Kevin, Bill, and Dwayne. Thank you all for your friendship and mentorship. I look up to you and appreciate the ways you have let me partner with you in ministry.

I (Kevin) would like to thank Ben Forrest, whose inspiration, creativity, and persistence brought this project from its inception to its completion. It has been a great pleasure to work alongside you these few years at Liberty University. I thank God for your leadership and friendship. I also want to thank my two other coeditors, Bill Curtis and Dwayne Milioni. Your expertise and passion for preaching and preachers is contagious. You push me to greater exploration in the field as I try just to "keep up." To Joy, my girlfriend and wife of over thirty-three years—it was in church we first met, and it is in the church we serve together. I do appreciate the weekly sermon critiques you provide between the services. Your desire to see my preaching improve pushes me to strive for excellence, as I am privileged each week to preach the "incomparable riches of his grace, expressed in his kindness to us in Christ Jesus" (Eph 2:7). To my children, Daylee (and her husband Wal Ter and son Sebastian), Kevin Jr. (and his wife Sharin), and Julianna—you are a great blessing to me, and I rejoice to see your commitment to our Savior as you serve in his church. To my students—I am privileged to share in your journey. As I have had the occasion to share with you what has been shared with me, I await with great anticipation and expectation that the world will one day say of you as you step out into service of our King, they have been with Jesus (Acts 4:13). This book is a continuation of our conversation on preaching. Preach the Word!

I (Bill) would like to thank my coeditors for their work on this project. Ben, Dwayne, and Kevin made this a journey that was both enriching and enjoyable.

I would also like to thank the elders at Cornerstone Baptist Church, Darlington, South Carolina, for their ongoing support of my investment in academia. Despite the heavy load of my pastoral ministry, they encourage me to teach and to write. What a blessing to shepherd God's church with these men! Finally, I would like to thank my amazing wife, Lyla, for her patience and sacrifice. She makes countless sacrifices so I can fulfill God's calling through the proclamation of the Word and the production of works that strive to bring him glory.

I (Dwayne) would like to thank my wife, Kay, for her love, devotion, and sacrifice of time while I wrote and edited this project. I would also like to thank the elders and pastoral staff of Open Door Church in Raleigh for their encouragement. Finally, thanks to the faculty and administration of Southeastern Baptist Theological Seminary, who allow me to teach History of Preaching courses to graduate and PhD students. I hope this volume may benefit my students and many others in the decades to follow.

Contributor Bios

JOHN N. AKERS (PhD, University of Edinburgh) served as personal assistant to the Reverend Billy Graham. Formerly he was Academic Dean of Montreat College and is author of *Montreat & Evangelists: From Billy Sunday to Billy Graham*.

DANIEL L. AKIN (PhD, University of Texas at Arlington) is President and Professor of Theology and Preaching at Southeastern Baptist Theological Seminary in Wake Forest, North Carolina. His speaking, writing, and leadership emphases have been on expository preaching, marriage and family, and the Great Commission. He has authored or coauthored several books, including *God on Sex*, *Engaging Exposition* (with Stephen Rummage and Bill Curtis), and *I Am Going* (with Bruce Ashford). He is the editor of a systematic theology textbook, *A Theology for the Church*, and a series editor (with David Platt and Tony Merida) of the *Christ-Centered Exposition Commentary Series*.

DAVID L. ALLEN (PhD, University of Texas at Arlington) is Dean of the School of Preaching, Distinguished Professor of Preaching, Director of the Center for Expository Preaching, and holds the George W. Truett Chair of Pastoral Ministry at Southwestern Baptist Theological Seminary in Fort Worth, Texas. Some of his books include *The Extent of the Atonement: A Historical and Critical Review*; *Hebrews* in the New American Commentary Series; *1–3 John: Fellowship in God's Family* in the Preaching the Word Series; and *Text-Driven Preaching*.

KRISTOPHER K. BARNETT (PhD, Southwestern Baptist Theological Seminary) is Associate Dean of the Clamp Divinity School at Anderson University.

TERRIEL BYRD (PhD, The Union Institute) is Professor of Urban Christian Ministry at Palm Beach Atlantic University. He was 2012–2013 President of the African American Caucus of the Academy of Homiletics of North America. His books include *I Shall Not Be Moved: Racial Separation in Christian Worship*; *By This Shall We Be Known: Interpreting the Voice, Vision and Message of*

Martin Luther King Jr.; and *Let the Church Be the Church: The Social Teaching of the Christian Church.*

ROBERT W. CALDWELL III (PhD, Trinity Evangelical Theological Seminary) is Associate Professor of Church History at Southwestern Baptist Theological Seminary. His research focuses on the history and theology of evangelicalism in North America, with specialties in American awakenings and the theology of Jonathan Edwards. He is the author of *Theologies of the American Revivalists: From Whitefield to Finney* (IVP Academic, 2017).

KEITH W. CLEMENTS (PhD, Bristol University) is a graduate of Cambridge, Oxford, and Bristol University. He is an ordained Baptist minister, and taught for thirteen years at Bristol Baptist College and in the Department of Theology and Religious Studies at Bristol University. Five of his titles are on Bonhoeffer, his latest being *Dietrich Bonhoeffer's Ecumenical Quest* (World Council of Churches, 2015). He was a member of the Editorial Board for the recently completed *Dietrich Bonhoeffer Works* (English) Series, and was editor of Volume 13, London 1933–1935.

BILL CURTIS (PhD, Southeastern Baptist Theological Seminary) is Assistant Professor of Homiletics at Southeastern Baptist Theological Seminary and pastor of Cornerstone Baptist Church in Darlington, South Carolina. His newest book is *Gypsy Smith: The Forgotten Evangelist.*

ANIL SOOK DEO (PhD, Johns Hopkins University) is a church planter with Global Outreach Mission. He has been a Foreign Affairs Deputy Director in Africa, as well as a former President of Oval College (Cape Town, South Africa). He has published articles and reviews in *Journal of Ethic Studies, Raconteur, Journal of Modern Africa Studies, Latin American Research Review,* and *Early America Online.* His dissertation was published as Freedom, Festivals, and Caste in Trinidad after Slavery (Xlibris, 2000).

MICHAEL DUDUIT (PhD, Florida State University) is Professor of Christian Ministry and the founding Dean of the College of Christian Studies and the David T. Clamp Graduate School of Christian Ministry at Anderson University. He is also founder and director of the National Conference on Preaching and the International Congress on Preaching.

CHARLES A. FOWLER (PhD, Mississippi State University) serves as Senior Pastor at Germantown Baptist Church in Germantown, Tennessee. Prior to coming to Germantown Baptist Church, he completed almost sixteen years of service at Union University as Senior Vice President for University Relations and Professor of Christian Ministries.

AARON FRIESEN (PhD, University of Wales) is Community Life and College Pastor at Eugene Faith Center. He is adjunct professor at George Fox

University and Life Pacific College. His research and writing focus on Pentecostal history and theology.

CHARLES W. FULLER (PhD, Southern Baptist Theological Seminary) is Associate Professor of Christian Studies and Director of the Honors Program at Anderson University (South Carolina). He contributes regularly to *Preaching* magazine, and his most recent book publication was *The Trouble with "Truth through Personality": Phillips Brooks, Incarnation, and the Evangelical Boundaries of Preaching.*

ALFONZA W. FULWOOD (DMin, PhD, Southeastern Baptist Theological Seminary) is Pastor of Riley Hill Baptist Church in Wendell, North Carolina. He has taught preaching at Shaw University Divinity School as well as at Southeastern Baptist Theological Seminary. He is a contributor to *Baptist Informer,* and his dissertation was titled "A Study of Gardner C. Taylor's Theology of Preaching as a Decisive Factor Shaping His Theory of Preaching: Implications for Homiletical Pedagogy."

ROGER J. GREEN (PhD, Boston College) is Emeritus Professor of Biblical and Theological Studies at Gordon College. He is the recipient of The Salvation Army's rarely bestowed Order of the Founder, and of an honorary degree from William and Catherine Booth College (now Booth University College). In addition to his work published in journals and his contributions to several editions of the Bible, he is the author of a bookshelf's worth of volumes about The Salvation Army, including *War on Two Fronts: The Redemptive Theology of William Booth, The Life and Ministry of William Booth,* and *Catherine Booth: A Biography of the Co-Founder of The Salvation Army.* He is the coeditor of *Word & Deed: A Journal of Salvation Army Theology & Ministry.*

BENJAMIN HERNÁNDEZ (MDiv, Gordon-Conwell Theological Seminary) is the Lead Pastor of Cross Pointe Church in Sioux Falls, South Dakota, and a PhD student at Southeastern Baptist Theological Seminary.

EDWARD E. HINDSON (DMin, Westminster Theological Seminary; DPhil, University of South Africa) is the founding Dean of the School of Divinity and Distinguished Professor of Religion at Liberty University. He is author of forty books, including *Introduction to Puritan Theology, Illustrated Bible Survey, Essence of the Old Testament,* and the Gold Medallion Book Award–winning *Knowing Jesus Study Bible.*

ROBERT MATZ (PhD, Liberty University) is Assistant Professor of Christian Studies at Midwestern Baptist Theological Seminary. He is coeditor of *Four Views on Divine Impassibility* (with A. Chadwick Thornhill).

DENNIS R. MCDONALD (PhD, Dallas Theological Seminary) is Assistant Pastor at Allen Chapel Baptist Church in Dallas, Texas. His dissertation research was focused on the theology of Martin Luther King Jr.

DWAYNE MILIONI (PhD, Southeastern Baptist Theological Seminary) is Assistant Professor of Preaching and coordinator for the PhD in Preaching program at Southeastern Baptist Theological Seminary. He is also Lead Pastor of Open Door Church in Wake Forest, North Carolina.

THOMAS J. NETTLES (PhD, Southwestern Baptist Theological Seminary) is Senior Professor of Church History at the Southern Baptist Theological Seminary. He is author of *Living by Revealed Truth: The Life and Pastoral Theology of Charles Haddon Spurgeon.*

R. SCOTT PACE (PhD, Southeastern Baptist Theological Seminary) serves as Associate Professor of Preaching and Pastoral Ministry and Associate Director for the Center for Preaching and Pastoral Leadership at Southeastern Baptist Theological Seminary. He is author of *Preaching by the Book* and coauthor of *Pastoral Theology* (with Daniel L. Akin).

GREGG L. QUIGGLE (PhD, Open University) is the D. L. Moody Professor of Theology and Dean of Study Abroad Programs at Moody Bible Institute. His research interests include the history of religion in America.

LELAND RYKEN (PhD, University of Oregon) is Professor of English Emeritus at Wheaton College. His research interests include teaching the Bible, Bible translation, and literature. He has published fifty-five books and served as the literary stylist for the English Standard Version of the Bible, published by Crossway. One of his recent works was a biography, *J. I. Packer: An Evangelical Life* (Crossway, 2015).

GREG R. SCHARF (DMin, Trinity Evangelical Divinity School) is chair of the Pastoral Theology Department and Professor Emeritus of Homiletics and Pastoral Theology at Trinity Evangelical Divinity School. He is also a former President of the Evangelical Homiletics Society and learned from John Stott as a student at Trinity and as an intern and curate at All Souls, Langham Place in London. He has written *Prepared to Preach: God's Work and Ours in Proclamation* and *Let the Earth Hear His Voice: Strategies for Overcoming Bottlenecks in Preaching God's Word.*

ROBERT SMITH JR. (PhD, Southern Baptist Theological Seminary) is Professor of Christian Preaching and holds the Charles T. Carter Baptist Chair of Divinity at Beeson Divinity School. Dr. Smith is a contributing editor for a study of Christian ministry in the African American church, *Preparing for Christian Ministry,* and is coeditor of *A Mighty Long Journey* and *Our Sufficiency Is of God: Essays on Preaching in Honor of Gardner C. Taylor.* His publications include *Doctrine That Dances: Bringing Doctrinal Preaching and Teaching to Life,* recipient of 2008 and 2009 preaching book awards, and *The Oasis of God: From Mourning to Morning—Biblical Insights from Psalms 42 and 43,* along with articles and essays on preaching and racial reconciliation.

JORDAN MARK STONE (PhD, Southern Baptist Theological Seminary) is pastor at Redeemer Presbyterian Church in McKinney, Texas. His dissertation was titled *A Communion of Love: the Animating Principle behind the Christocentric Spirituality of Robert Murray M'Cheyne.*

JERRY SUTTON (PhD, Southwestern Baptist Theological Seminary) invested thirty years as a Senior Pastor. He has taught at Southwestern, Southern, Liberty, and Midwestern Seminaries. In his first stint at Liberty, he was Associate Professor of Christian Proclamation and Pastoral Theology. At Midwestern, he served as Vice President of Academic Development and Dean of the Faculty. Presently, he teaches Church History at Liberty University. He is known for his books, *The Baptist Reformation: The Conservative Resurgence in the Southern Baptist Convention; A Matter of Conviction: A History of the Ethics and Religious Liberty Commission;* and *A Primer on Biblical Preaching.*

CARL TRUEMAN (PhD, University of Aberdeen) is Paul Woolley Chair of Church History at Westminster Theological Seminary, the William E. Simon Visiting Fellow in Religion and Public Life at Princeton University, and Pastor of Cornerstone Presbyterian Church (OPC) in Ambler, Pennsylvania. He was editor of *Themelios* for nine years, has authored or edited more than a dozen books, and has contributed to multiple publications, including the *Dictionary of Historical Theology, The Cambridge Companion to Reformation Theology, John Owen: Reformed Catholic Rennaissance Man,* and *Luther on the Christian Life: Cross and Freedom.*

WILLIAM H. WILLIMON (STD, Emory University) a United Methodist bishop, retired, is Professor of the Practice of Christian Ministry, Duke Divinity School. He is the author of many books on pastoral theology in addition to *The Early Preaching of Karl Barth* (Westminster John Knox, 2009), *Conversations with Barth on Preaching* (Abingdon, 2010), and *How Odd of God: Chosen for the Curious Vocation of Preaching* (Westminster John Knox, 2015).

DANTE D. WRIGHT I (DMin, Liberty University; PhD, ABD Midwestern Baptist Theological Seminary) is Senior Pastor of Sweet Home Baptist Church in Texas. In 2014, he was inducted into the Martin Luther King Jr. Board of Preachers at Morehouse College. He serves on the Board of Trustees at Criswell College and currently serves as the Vice President of the Southern Baptists of Texas Convention (SBTC).

HERSHAEL W. YORK (PhD, Mid-America Baptist Theological Seminary) is the Victor and Louise Lester Professor of Christian Preaching at The Southern Baptist Theological Seminary and Senior Pastor of the Buck Run Baptist Church in Frankfort, Kentucky.

DARRELL YOUNG (MA, Ambrose Seminary in Calgary, Alberta) is Director of International Workshops for the Charles Simeon Trust.

Introduction

"Preach the word; be prepared in season and out of season" (2 Tim 4:2). This book is about the seasons of preaching history and the preachers who proclaimed the eternal riches of God's grace and truth. Our goal is to present a historical, theological, and methodological introduction to the history of preaching. This approach to the history of preaching is one of this volume's unique markers. Instead of teaching the history of preaching from a perspective of movements and eras, our goal is to aid the reader in the exploration of preaching history, with a biographical and theological examination of its most important preachers. Therefore, each contributing author will tell the story of a preacher in history, allowing these preachers from the past to come alive and instruct us about their lives, theologies, and methods of preaching.

Our intent is not to focus *only* on the history of preaching as a past event, but to consider how to best move forward in our own pulpits and in the training of future preachers. To accomplish this goal, we have looked backward in order to explore how theology intersects with and informs the practice of preaching *in context*. By telling the stories of these preachers, we provide a stage for understanding how their theology informed their practice and how they methodized the task of approaching the Scriptures for the proclamation of the gospel. It will be evident that preachers throughout history have done this differently. Some preachers have a very robust theology *of* preaching, while others have a theology *for* preaching.

This book details how great pulpiteers in history have approached their task of preaching as pastor-theologians. This book doesn't teach *how* biblical preaching is done; it demonstrates how it *has* been done. Our hope is that this approach will yield fruit for present and future preachers as they formulate their own understanding of how to be a practicing theologian from the pulpit.

There has been a great legacy of research in the area of the history of preaching. It is our goal to stand on the shoulders of this research, much like the figures in this book have stood on the shoulders of the preachers who have gone before them.

CHOOSING THE PREACHERS

Choosing which preachers to include for a book such as this is an imperfect process, and some readers may be disappointed in who was left out. When this project was birthed over breakfast at Cracker Barrel, we only had a vague notion about whom to include. A later discussion over lunchtime pizza gave our list more clarity, but it was still imperfect. Our final product is still lacking, but it is an attempt to give a voice to those whose impact must certainly be remembered and to those with a unique methodology or theological perspective on preaching that we believed was significant enough to include. We hope that readers will commit to researching those important preachers who were not included and yet deserve a place among those who have preached from history's most influential pulpits.

As will soon be readily apparent, we did not include preachers whose ministries are still alive, active, and vibrant—even though some of them have stepped down from their weekly trek to the pulpit. We did not want to write a historical epitaph on preachers whose ministries are still being defined, albeit in a different, unique, or professorial context. Individuals that could have been included had we opened up this list to the living are John Piper, Ravi Zacharias, Chuck Swindoll, John McArthur, Tony Evans, Rick Warren, Barbara Brown Taylor, William H. Willimon, or James Earl Massey. Certainly, all of these preachers have had a great impact on their culture *and* the world. However, the scope of their influence is still being established, and we did not want to come across as summarizing a ministry that is still greatly influential. Haddon Robinson and R. C. Sproul would have certainly been included in the project had we started our table of contents today, yet at our beginning point several years ago, they were still engaged in ministry and ministering. As you read on, you will see that this list is not exhaustive, but we hope that our attempt at a big-tent approach to the history of preaching is evident. We want readers to be encouraged and edified by the various veins and styles found in the history of preaching.

ORGANIZATION OF TEXT

Each chapter in this book has been written by a different author who is a scholar of the preacher under consideration. We left room for each author to express their particular voice, while maintaining consistency throughout the book.

Each chapter will start with the "historical background" of the preacher. The length and scope of the biographical section varies based on how much background information is needed to clarify their social and ministerial context. Following this section, each author will explore theological aspects of the preacher's approach to preaching. First, they will articulate either the preacher's theology *of* preaching or their theology *for* preaching. Second, there will be an analysis of the preacher's homiletical methodology. As you might imagine, some preachers were very precise in their sermon development methodologies, while others were more extemporaneous. Third, the preacher's overall contribution to the field of preaching will be considered, including a sermon excerpt so that readers can hear the voice of the preacher in their own words.

OUR CHALLENGE

Our challenge to readers is threefold, and there is a nuance in our challenge to you, depending on why you have come to this book.

If you're an inquisitive pastor wanting to learn from the great preachers of history, then our hope for you is that you will find comradery and encouragement in the strengths of these preachers. We also hope you find solidarity as you recognize (perhaps very intimately) their challenges. At some point in your ministry as a pastor, you will find yourself in a situation where looking back may just help you to move forward. As you look back on these pulpiteers, I hope you see their resolve, their commitment to the ministry of the Word, and their pursuit *for* the church. As you observe this, we hope you will be refreshed and encouraged to press in and on to your calling.

If you find yourself reading this book as a student, we hope you will find several heroes, or at least some examples to imitate. Just as George Whitefield was inspired by Matthew Henry, we hope you will find an example and hero for yourself. No preacher is perfect, and what is written here is not hagiography; it is deferential. Do not look to anyone but Christ to find the perfect role model for ministry. Yet as you sit at the feet of these preachers, view them as examples of preachers who sought to follow Christ, love the church, and preach the Word. Let this be how you read this book. Recognize your own imperfections and learn from those who have gone before you.

If you find yourself reading this book as you prepare to teach in the field of homiletics, history, or practical theology—we hope you will enjoy these chapters and the research your colleagues have provided. For those you disciple in ministry, encourage them to be students of the Word. Inspire them to observe the study and teaching practices of history's great preachers. Challenge them with the reality that sermon preparation is never done—that life is constantly preparing us for the next sermon. Prod them with examples from your own life about the challenges and joys of drinking the Word personally and sharing it with a thirsty flock. For those you disciple in the classroom, urge them to compare those in history with those we are familiar with today. Embolden them with a vision that places the proclamation of the gospel at the summit of seminary preparation. Share with them the stories of your own heroes from the pulpit. Your hero may be found in a chapter in this book, or it may be a pastor barely known to history. After all, you will likely have students that will go on to have ministries that make a visible impact, while others will remain largely unseen until eternity. Let them know that both of these epitaphs are to be celebrated. Do not set before students the goal of being remembered by history. Rather, let them see that faithfulness to the gospel through the proclamation of Christ is what counts when considering *a legacy of preaching!*

Soli Deo Gloria!

Benjamin K. Forrest
Kevin L. King
Bill Curtis
Dwayne Milioni

PART *One*

Nineteenth-Century European Preaching

In the study of history, there are moments that become symbols for movements. One such moment that symbolized a movement was the French Revolution of 1789. As the crowd that gathered outside the Bastille in Paris on July 14 turned into a tumultuous mob, that moment represented a movement that saw the changing of the historical tides on the continent of Europe. As the eighteenth century was drawing to a close, a revolutionary movement was dawning in Europe that would touch every facet of life as the nineteenth century drew near. The French Revolution, followed by the Napoleonic Wars and the succeeding political revolutions, would touch virtually all of the European continent until about midcentury. Historians have referred to these revolutions as democratic revolutions. These democratic revolutions laid the groundwork for the contemporary understanding of the modern state.

As tumultuous as the political unrest was, so was the economic revolution that was well under way in the nineteenth century. The Industrial Revolution changed the economic landscape of Europe. European countries became economic powerhouses. Social mobility due to wealth and not due to birth, changed the social dynamic within many European countries. The social elites who held their privilege by birth had to make room for those who climbed the social ladder because of their entrepreneurial expertise. Accompanying the economic boon was the bust in terms of labor unrest. Workers were exploited. Low wages, poor working conditions, and long work hours were grievances that led to riots. It was in this context that Karl Marx and Friedrich Engels promulgated their view of economics that capitalism would be replaced by socialism and then communism.

Imperialism and colonization became prominent features of the nineteenth century. As the Industrial Revolution increased the coffers of European countries, their ever-expanding appetite for more resources led them to expand across the globe in their search to satisfy those appetites. Great Britain, under the long reign of Queen Victoria, embodied the very notion of imperialism, as can be seen in the motto "Rule Britannia." While it was true that the sun never set on the British Empire, similar claims could be made by other European countries, including France, Belgium, and Germany.

The motif of revolution in the nineteenth century continued in the areas of philosophy and theology. Philosophy, now living in a post-Kantian world, saw, in relative terms, a revolt against the cold rationalism of the Enlightenment, to romanticism (German idealism), which then moved to existentialism. Prominent among the philosophical thinkers of the century were Johann Fichte, Friedrich Schelling, and Georg Hegel (German idealism) and Søren Kierkegaard, Fyodor Dostoyevsky, and Friedrich Nietzsche. In the theological world, Friedrich Schleiermacher stands at the forefront of Protestant liberalism. This movement would eventuate the attacking and undermining of historic Christian convictions that ran the gamut of theological pronouncements. While not written to specifically challenge Christianity, Charles Darwin's *On the Origin of Species* became one of the most monumental challenges that Christianity faced during the nineteenth century and on into the twentieth. One bright spot in a theological sense was the continuing expansion of missions. Mission societies in Europe grew rapidly to meet the expanding opportunities.

If one were to try and summarize and put the revolutionizing movements into two words, they might be *modernization* and *secularization*. The world changed dramatically with the technological advances that occurred during this century. The steam engine made traveling easier in general (rail and sea travel). It not only changed the production of goods, but also revolutionized the transportation of those goods to market. With more people moving into the large cities of Europe, the small villages no longer dominated the physical and social space of the population. In those villages, located most often in or near the center, was a church. The church served as the hub of the social, intellectual, and political life of the village. With the rise of large cities, that would be forever changed. As the central space was no longer occupied by the village church, secularization seemed to fill the vacated space. The combination of modernization, philosophical attacks, and liberal theological attacks on historic Christianity contributed to a general drift away from and reliance on Christianity. It is in this milieu of revolution that the preachers in this section ministered. We now turn to their notable contributions in the field of preaching.

In a century that saw incredible change in all spheres of life, **Charles Simeon** (1759–1839) stands as a testimony to persistence. Just as the lighthouse stands as a reference point to protect and guide ships safely along the coast, the ministry of

Charles Simeon shines a light on the persistence and dedication that are needed for pastoral ministry. Overcoming great opposition that lasted for years, Simeon was dedicated to making "Bible Christians." Simeon's contribution to preaching is immense and can be found in his *Horae Homileticae*. Whereas Charles Simeon was privileged to have a very long ministry, **Robert Murray M'Cheyne** (1813–1843), who died before he was thirty and served just six years in ministry, leaves us an example of Christ-centered preaching and pastoral accountability. He combined a shepherd's love for his flock with an evangelist's burning passion to see souls come to faith in the Lord Jesus Christ.

Among the many contributions of **Alexander Maclaren** (1826–1910) is his unwavering commitment to his calling to the ministry. An outgrowth of his calling was a deep commitment to learn the original languages so as to become skilled in biblical exposition. Maclaren's skill at expositing the different literary genres of the Bible is a gift to contemporary preachers. Maclaren's discipline and skill as an expositor lead to application. In trusting the sufficiency of the Word, Maclaren shows great skill in applying the principle in very practical ways.

William and **Catherine Booth** (1829–1890) founded the "The Christian Mission" in 1865. This mission eventually matured into The Salvation Army. While William and Catherine were both active in the preaching ministry within The Salvation Army, it was Catherine's preaching that has been recognized and remembered both far and wide as she emphasized holiness and the role of the Spirit for equipping people for the works of ministry.

Charles Haddon Spurgeon (1834–1892) is probably one of the most well-known preachers of all time. The incredible expansion of his ministry is remarkable for any age. Spurgeon's sermons were published and could be found in diverse places around the globe. By the end of his life, it would take sixty-three volumes to house his sermons. Though Spurgeon was celebrated for his remarkable gifts, commitment, and vision for ministry, it came at a price. Spurgeon endured failing health, bouts of depression, and the stress of the "Downgrade Controversy." But his consistent proclamation of the gospel is a reminder to preachers that wherever they find themselves in the text, they are to make a beeline to the cross.

While Charles Spurgeon is one of the most well-known preachers in the history of the church, **Rodney "Gypsy" Smith** (1860–1947) may be one that is less familiar. Even so, the ministry Gypsy Smith had is one that was not only long and durable—it lasted seventy years—but was also global in scope. While having no formal theological training, Smith was adept at speaking to the heart of people. Gypsy Smith reminds us that the gospel is not an essay or a lecture, nor is it entertainment. Rather, the gospel is the good news of Jesus Christ that is the difference between heaven and hell.

Charles Simeon

Preaching That Humbles the Sinner, Exalts the Savior, and Promotes Holiness

DARRELL YOUNG

For modern preachers, some of the details of Charles Simeon's life (1759–1839) are legendary. In this modern era, five years is considered a long tenure as a pastor. Simeon stayed in his pulpit for fifty-four. In two different seasons over that period, key people attempted to remove him from his role. For years, the pews were locked so that newcomers had to sit in the aisles. Despite these obstacles, Simeon carried out a lively pulpit ministry while training and encouraging hundreds of younger preachers. He had an inspiring tenacity and a belief that God would build the church through an unwavering ministry of the Word.

HISTORICAL BACKGROUND

Charles Simeon was born in 1759 in Reading, in the county of Berkshire, England.[1] His father, Richard, fostered respect for religion, but not a genuine belief in the Christian faith.[2] For school Simeon was enrolled at Eton, where by the account of several others, he was athletic and a skilled horseman. By his own account, he would look back on these years with "the deepest shame and horror" because of his unruly behavior.[3] Though he did have one brush with repentance while there. In 1776, during the American War, a national day of fasting was held. The need to humble himself before God fell heavily upon Simeon. When his friends noticed a change in him, they mocked him until "they soon dissipated my good desires, and reduced me to my former state of thoughtlessness and sin."[4]

1. Handley Moule, *Charles Simeon, Pastor of a Generation* (Fern, Ross-shire, Great Britain: Christian Focus, 1997), 7.

2. Ibid., 9.

3. William Carus, ed., *Memoirs of the Life of the Rev. Charles Simeon, M.A.* (London: Hatchard & Son, 1848), 3–4.

4. Moule, *Charles Simeon*, 10–11.

Simeon's rough behavior, however, did not prevent him from eventual acceptance at King's College, Cambridge, in 1779. On only the third day after his arrival, he had another, more lasting spiritual experience. He was informed that in three weeks' time he would be required to attend a service of the Lord's Supper. He was overwhelmed with the idea that Satan was as fit to attend the Lord's Supper as he. He purchased a book called *The Whole Duty of Man* and pored over it.[5] Soon he was calling out to God for mercy and would later write, "From that day to this, blessed, forever be blessed, be my God, I have never ceased to regard the salvation of my soul as the one thing needful."[6]

This was followed by three years of intense growth as a Christian. Soon Simeon was ordained in the Church of England as a deacon in 1782, and then as a priest in 1783. He then set about looking for an appointment in a pulpit. An early opportunity came at St. Edwards Church near King's College, when he was asked to fill in for the vicar, Christopher Atkinson.[7] Over the seventeen weeks that he substituted for Mr. Atkinson, he drew great crowds with his preaching. He also drew much good will as he visited the church folk from house to house. When the vicar returned, the church clerk was relieved at the prospect of things returning to normal. He said, "Oh, sir, I am so glad you are come; now we shall have some room!"[8]

It was in these years that Simeon had a friendly exchange with another minister about the doctrine of election. He was convinced of the doctrine, but then in what would foreshadow some thoughts he would later develop, reflected, "But I soon learned that I must take the Scripture with the simplicity of a little child, and to be content to receive on God's testimony what he has revealed, whether I can unravel all the difficulties that may attend it or not. . . . This, I am persuaded, is the way in which we should receive instruction from God; and if we will do so, I verily believe, that we shall in due time see a beauty and harmony in many things."[9]

During his days at Cambridge, Simeon would sometimes walk past Trinity Church and think of how he would rejoice if God were to allow him to preach there. His life was changed when the minister there, Henry Therond, died in October of 1782. Simeon was given the appointment, and thus began a fifty-four-year ministry in one pulpit.[10]

While the bishop quickly and decisively appointed Simeon as minister, the congregation, for the most part, was very much against him. They preferred the

---

5. Ibid., 19
6. Carus, *Memoirs*, 6–7.
7. Moule, *Charles Simeon*, 27–28.
8. Ibid., 31.
9. Carus, *Memoirs*, 25–26.
10. Moule, *Charles Simeon*, 32–33.

assistant curate, a Mr. Hammond. The bishop stood firm, so their only recourse was to elect Hammond as lecturer. This gave Hammond the right to preach at the Sunday afternoon service and limited Simeon to the Sunday morning service. With the bishop's support, he preached his first sermon at Trinity Church on November 10, 1782.[11]

This uncomfortable arrangement with Hammond carried on for five years until another minister took on this role for seven more years. In addition, during the Sunday morning services, the prominent owners of the pews locked the pew doors and remained absent, leaving only the aisles for the people to gather in. When Simeon purchased chairs and placed them in any open spot he could, the church officers threw them into the churchyard. This hostility was not limited to Sundays; many in the congregation would not open their homes to the new minister throughout the week.[12]

To say this was difficult and awkward would be an obvious understatement. From the beginning, however, Simeon chose to be gentle, civil, and to trust the Lord, as exemplified in the postscript of a letter written to a friend: "I forgot to tell you that my churchwardens have shut my church-doors against me, and prevented my continuing an evening lecture, which I had established, and which was well attended. Their behaviour has been highly displeasing to the whole parish. . . . May God bless them with an enlightening, sanctifying, and saving grace: I shall renew the lecture next summer."[13] This kind of gentle resolve carried Simeon through decades of ministry.

Over the years, he began to gather his sermons for his magnum opus, the *Horae Homileticae.* In it he desired to unfold key parts of the Old and New Testaments in such a way that divine truth would be exemplified in a simple and edifying way.[14] He explained in the dedication of the *Horae* that he saw a deficit in the preparation of ministers in the church. Education in the universities was available for areas such as medicine and law. These fields offered appropriate levels of study to qualify students in these professions. But there were no institutions established for preparing gospel preachers to be pastors in the life of the church. He felt that this led to the discouragement of younger clergy when they began their pastoral duties.[15]

In the preface to the *Horae,* Simeon provided outlines to the biblical texts, which he referred to as "skeletons." He saw them as something between an essay

11. Ibid., 35.
12. Ibid., 35–36.
13. Carus, *Memoirs*, 59.
14. Charles Simeon, *Horae Homileticae, Vol. 1, Genesis to Leviticus* (London: Holdsworth & Ball, 1832), 19.
15. Ibid., 17–18.

and a complete sermon.[16] He compressed his material in these skeletons, for if
he had not, by his own estimation, his sermons would have filled one hunded
volumes. He also pointed out that if one were to read one sermon every day, it
would take seven years.[17] His idea was not to show every rule of organizing and
constructing sermons, but to display one general rule, and that was to demonstrate how texts should be treated naturally. All of this was born out of his own
experience. He had no formal instruction in homiletics, and was so discouraged
early in his ministry that he considered quitting. He said that for the first seven
years he "did not know the head for the tail of a sermon."[18]

Simeon was also very concerned about his preaching colleagues. James
Houston asserted that Simeon was the first preacher in the Church of England
to understand that it was necessary and possible to teach other pastors to preach
well.[19] He would gather a number of young men from Cambridge on a weekly
basis to go over sermon outlines and to discuss issues related to the Christian
faith and life.[20] In this way, Simeon came to exert a major influence over younger
ministers and missionaries in the Church of England. Eventually, over 1,100
Anglican clergy came under his guidance.[21]

THEOLOGICAL FOUNDATIONS

Something that becomes very apparent to one who reads Simeon's thoughts on
preaching is that he was a pastor who wanted his sermons to make a real difference to his listeners. He tested his own work in the pulpit with a set of three
questions, putting it this way: "Does it uniformly tend to humble the sinner,
to exalt the Saviour, and to promote holiness? If in one single instance it lose
sight of any of these points, let it be condemned without mercy."[22] He desired to
develop what he termed "Bible Christians." He was, himself, very much a Bible
Christian, rising every morning at 4:00 a.m. to pray and meditate on the Scriptures. He would conclude at 8:00 a.m.[23] After beginning the day with four hours
of devotional study and prayer, he would call in a friend and a servant and then
have "family prayer." Moule suggests that in this piety was the secret of Simeon's

---

16. Ibid., v.

17. Ibid., xxviii.

18. Carus, *Memoirs*, 37.

19. James Houston, ed. *Evangelical Preaching: An Anthology of Sermons by Charles Simeon* (Portland:
Multnomah, 1986), xv.

20. Alexander C. Zabriskie, "Charles Simeon: Anglican Evangelical," *Church History* 9, no. 2 (June
1940): 103–119.115.

21. Hugh Evan Hopkins, *Charles Simeon, Preacher Extraordinary* (Cambridge: Grove, 1979), 33.

22. Simeon, *Horae*, vol. 1, *Genesis to Leviticus*, xxi.

23. Zabriskie, "Charles Simeon: Anglican Evangelical," 105.

great grace and spiritual strength. It both comforted him in his difficulties and prepared him for his many duties.[24]

As a Bible Christian himself, and trying to develop other Bible Christians, Simeon's goal in the ministry of the Word was to be focused simply on the text at hand. His main interest was to derive his faith and practice from the Bible, and to be faithful to the whole message of the Bible.[25] This was clearly seen in his approach to some of the theological controversies of his day—for example, the Calvinist/Arminian debate. He claimed to be "no friend to systematizers in Theology."[26]

Simeon believed that a devout Arminian and a devout Calvinist, when on their knees in prayer, were actually pretty close to each other. The Arminian would acknowledge his total dependence on God while the Calvinist would acknowledge his responsibility to God. This is the posture he hoped to achieve in his study. So he expected to be approved by both sides and criticized by both. His fear was that both sides would be overly sensitive by grasping notes in his work that opposed their preferred system and assuming that, in them, his entire view was represented.[27]

Simeon believed that issues like this were difficult to reconcile, mainly due to limited human capacity. At the same time, maybe these points were not as opposite as generally imagined. He felt it was possible that the truth would be found not in an exclusive acceptance of one view over another or in some muddled middle ground, "but in the proper and seasonable application of them both."[28] This he considered "rightly dividing the word of truth." This would likely be unsatisfying to both Calvinists and Arminians, but he hoped that both sides would accept his emphasis on the truth of Scripture.[29]

So Simeon proposed something novel. Instead of attempting to downplay one side over the other, or to reach a soft middle ground, texts should be expounded and taken to their conclusion. Biblical passages should be preached to their conclusions, whether they lean more to one side or the other. Of course it was possible, he affirmed, for either of these points to be poorly expressed and applied.[30] So if the doctrine of election is stated in such a way as to undermine people's free agency, and to make them passive in salvation, then it is not stated in accord with articles of the church. And if the doctrine of free will is stated in

---

24. Moule, *Charles Simeon*, 67.
25. Zabriskie, "Charles Simeon: Anglican Evangelical," 105.
26. Simeon, *Horae*, vol. 1, *Genesis to Leviticus*, xxiii.
27. Ibid., xxiv.
28. Ibid., xv.
29. Ibid., xvi.
30. Simeon, *Horae*, vol. 1 of *Genesis to Leviticus*, xviii.

such a way as to undermine the honor of God in salvation, then it is not stated in accord with teaching of the established church or the clear teaching of the Bible. Simeon's point was that both perspectives should be taught as they were encountered in Scripture.[31]

In effect, this means that each doctrine should be taught to its fullest sense, to the edges of it, instead of a diplomatic center. In this way, every passage could be treated faithfully in its own context and congregants could be challenged or comforted without equivocation. Texts would not be softened out of concern for a system or theological framework. In fact, he felt that the truth is not in the middle, and not in one extreme, but in both extremes. To a friend he wrote, "Today I am a strong Calvinist; tomorrow a strong Arminian . . . so that if extremes please you, I am your man; only remember, it is not *one* extreme that we are to go, but *both* extremes."[32] This is not to say that Simeon did not believe there was a system in the Scripture. He did, after all, ascribe to the Thirty-Nine Articles of the Church of England. Truth could not be inconsistent with itself. But while he believed in the need to systematize Scripture, he feared the development of a rigid system that did not allow the truth of each text to be freshly heard.[33] This is why he encouraged the development of Bible Christians, not system Christians.

Therefore, "he has endeavoured to derive from Scripture alone his views of religion: and to them it is his wish to adhere with scrupulous fidelity; never wresting a word of God to favour a particular opinion, but giving to every part of it that sense which it seems to him to have been intended by its Great Author to convey."[34] A sense of Simeon's theological conviction regarding the Bible can be gained from sermon 1933 on 1 Corinthians 2:2. Here he asserted that, over time, God revealed himself in different ways: through visions, voices, and the Holy Spirit to the minds of individuals. "But since the completion of the sacred canon, he has principally made use of his written word, explained and enforced by men, whom he has called and qualified to preach his Gospel; and though he has not precluded himself from conveying again the knowledge of his will in any of the former ways, it is through the written word only that we are now authorized to expect his gracious instructions. This, whether read by ourselves or published by his servants, he applies to the heart, and makes effectual for the illumination and salvation of men."[35]

---

31. Ibid.

32. Carus, *Memoirs*, 600.

33. Simeon, *Horae*, vol. 1 of *Genesis to Leviticus*, xv.

34. Ibid., xxiii.

35. Charles Simeon, *Horae Homileticae, Vol. 16, 1 & 2 Corinthians* (London: Holdsworth & Ball, 1832), 32–33.

Citing the example of Philip speaking to the Ethiopian eunuch, Simeon went on to emphasize that the Lord "chiefly uses the ministry of his servants, whom he has sent as ambassadors to a guilty world."[36]

A few points can be made here regarding Simeon's theology concerning the Bible and its practical implications for preaching. First, he sees the canon as complete, and thus is not looking outside of the Bible for further revelation. This is not to say God could not make use of the earlier forms of revelation, but Simeon is not counting on or looking for them. Today, the gracious instructions from the Lord can be expected only from the texts of the Bible. Then these instructions are applied to the heart by the Lord. These applications can be achieved by reading the Bible for oneself, or by its being "published" by one of his servants. Simeon seems to mean that the primary way the Lord conveys his instructions to his people is through the ministry of his people. This gives insight into the priority Simeon gave to the ministry of preaching the Bible and to investing in younger men training to be preachers. The whole effort results in the truth of the Bible being effectual for illumination and salvation. The stakes for this work are high.

This commitment to the Scriptures and the truth found in them are expressed in this well-known quote by Simeon: "My endeavour is to bring out of Scripture what is there, and not to thrust in what I think might be there. I have a great jealousy on this head; never to speak more or less than I believe to the mind of the Spirit in the passage I am expounding."[37] This conviction is a simple but profound principle for modern preachers to consider and apply in their own pulpits.

In sermon 2257 in the *Horae*, on 2 Timothy 3:16–17, Simeon explains more about his understanding of Scripture as it relates to preaching. He is clear that both the Old and New Testaments were given by the inspiration of God. He believed there is such continuity in the "system of revelation" that if one part were overthrown, the whole would be overthrown.[38] Two key issues arise out this confidence. One is that the Scriptures are able to establish sound doctrine. He perceived that in the Bible are found ample means of discovering truth and refuting error. The second is that they are useful for promoting holy practice. The many evils in the world are condemned in the Bible. The works of the flesh and the fruit of the Spirit are portrayed with such precision that there is no excuse for ignorance.[39]

---

36. Ibid.
37. Moule, *Charles Simeon*, 79.
38. Charles Simeon, *Horae Homileticae, Vol. 19, 2 Timothy to Hebrews* (London: Holdsworth & Ball, 1832), 73.
39. Ibid.

In sermon number 2258 on 2 Timothy 4:2, Simeon discusses the charge to "preach the Word." He writes, the minister "is not at liberty to amuse the people with the fancies and conceits of men, but must declare simply the mind and will of God. He is sent of God for that very end. He is an ambassador from God to man."[40] The Christian minister is appointed to an "order of men" that instructs humankind and advances the Christian faith in the world. It is necessary for the happiness of man.[41] Such is the importance Simeon placed on the work of preaching.

In sermon 1891 on Romans 10:12–15, he mentions again "the order of men" who have been appointed to preach. In fact, he asserts that without human agents there would be no hope that the message of salvation would be spread throughout the world.[42] The point is that people are sinners and need to be reminded that a Savior has been provided, and the salvation he provides is offered freely to all. Simeon called the declaration of this message the ministry of reconciliation, because the purpose of it is to proclaim "that God was in Christ reconciling the world unto himself, not imputing their trespasses to them."[43] According to Simeon, there is no subject in the universe as important as this, and it falls to this "order of men" to carry it out.[44]

METHODOLOGY FOR PREACHING

Charles Simeon intended from the beginning of his pulpit ministry to be simple and direct. He rejected the putting on of airs, opting instead for a natural and unaffected approach. An example from one of his Friday sermon groups with the young men of Cambridge is instructive. As he recited his outline, one of them said, "Amidst the tumult of Israel the son of Amram stood unmoved." Simeon asked him, "The son of Amram, who was he?" "I meant Moses," the young man replied. "Then why not say Moses? What ordinary congregation carries in their memories the genealogies ready for use?"[45]

Restricted to preach on Sunday mornings at Holy Trinity, Simeon welcomed opportunities in nearby communities. These additional opportunities helped in his composition of sermons. He would take the sermons he preached in his own pulpit and revise them to make them clearer to enhance his illustrations.[46]

---

40. Ibid., 76–77.
41. Ibid., 76.
42. Simeon, *Horae*, vol. 15, *Romans*, 392.
43. Ibid., 390.
44. Ibid.
45. Moule, *Charles Simeon*, 72.
46. Carus, *Memoirs*, 60–61.

This also helped him in his arrangement of the material, which would be helpful to him later as he developed the skeletons for the *Horae Homileticae.*

Even so, he struggled to settle on a method for putting his sermons onto paper. He tried writing them out in full. This had the drawback of sounding heavy and dull when read. In later years, he would reflect on his early clumsiness: "When I began to write at first, I knew no more than a brute how to make a sermon—and after a year or so, I gave up writing and began to preach from notes. But I so stammered and stumbled that I felt this was worse than before—and so I was obliged to take to a written sermon again."[47] But reading from a full manuscript again proved difficult, so that he was tempted to "give up preaching altogether."[48]

Eventually, Simeon settled on using "notes," a less detailed, more skeletal approach. He put much effort into preparing to preach. He felt he could not expect the Lord to bless his work otherwise. So he copied every sermon by hand and then read over it repeatedly until he felt he had mastered it. This allowed him to deliver it with "perfect ease and his usual animation."[49]

In the preface to the *Horae,* he suggested that younger ministers write their sermons out in full during their early years. This will train them in expressing their thoughts with clarity. And while Simeon felt it was never acceptable to deliver an "unpremeditated harangue," there was a middle ground between "extemporaneous effusions" and "servile adherence" to what was written down.[50] He thought this less precise approach should only be taken after delivering hundreds of sermons. But it had the advantage of giving the minister the ability to speak more effectively to the "hearts of men, and of addressing himself to their passions, as well by his looks and gesture, as by his words."[51]

This passion, it turns out, was at least partially responsible for the opposition he encountered at Holy Trinity. He wrote, "My parish, after two or three years, made a formal complaint against me to the bishop; they complained that I preached so as to alarm and terrify them, and that the people came and crowded the church."[52] According to Simeon's detractors, the chaos that came from the larger crowds did not offset any perceived benefits. He admitted later that in his pulpit work he tried to please the Lord by being faithful and zealous, but did not carry himself in a judicious way. He was too bold, a mistake he felt was common among younger ministers. During these years, he thought, he was ill-informed,

---

47. Ibid., 62.
48. Ibid.
49. Ibid., 63.
50. Simeon, *Horae,* vol. 1, *Genesis to Leviticus,* xii.
51. Ibid.
52. Carus, *Memoirs,* 64.

and made the subjects of death, judgment, heaven, and hell too prominent in every sermon. He compared his approach to assault and battery. He was focused too much on what he was able to say and not enough on what the people were able to receive.[53]

After preaching for a decade, he came across an essay by Jean Claude (1619–1687) called "Essay on the Composition of a Sermon." He was pleased that he had been practicing for years all the rules set out for preaching in this essay. It confirmed for him that both he and Claude had discovered these rules in nature, "since he himself had learned them from nature."[54] He took them and adopted and adapted them for his own lectures, amending them at a few points he thought necessary. In general, though, his skeletons served as a complement to these rules.[55]

In the preface to the *Horae*, Simeon addresses the manner in which sermons are constructed. He does this through a series of questions. The first is: "What is the scope and meaning of the text?"[56] To this line Simeon adds the following footnote in capital letters: "I BEG EVERY YOUNG MINISTER VERY ESPE-CIALLY TO REMEMER THIS." He uses Jeremiah 31:18–20 as an example, suggesting this passage is a speech by the Lord, expressing what is going on in Ephraim's mind. Having determined the limits of the preaching text, nothing else is to be added into the sermon that does not enlighten the main subject.[57]

The second question is: "Of what parts does the text consist, or into what parts may it most easily and naturally be resolved?"[58] He sees in this Jeremiah passage an obvious division between the thoughts of the Lord and those of Ephraim. Then these two parts must be taken in order, and a heading assigned to each. He emphasizes that the headings should not be so general that they could be taken from any number of passages. Instead, they should be specific enough that listeners would have precise knowledge of this passage.[59]

The third question to be asked in working on a sermon is: "What are the particular reflections which God noticed in the penitent before us?"[60] Simeon here describes his discussion of the particulars of the passage. Here he is arrang-ing what he is going to say. Other relevant biblical passages may be brought to bear, and each of his major points are developed to form the major content of the sermon.

---

53. Ibid.
54. Ibid., 61.
55. Ibid., 62.
56. Simeon, *Horae*, vol. 1, *Genesis to Leviticus*, vi.
57. Ibid.
58. Ibid.
59. Ibid.
60. Simeon, *Horae*, vol. 1, *Genesis to Leviticus*, vi–vii.

This is followed by the fourth area, this time not framed as a question. After the (1) scope and meaning are determined, (2) the passage is divided and (3) discussed, then (4) "we proceed to the application."[61] The nature of the application will be shaped by the passage and what is discussed therein, and on the makeup of the congregation. If most in the congregation are Christians, it will be necessary to give them some attention and to speak to them "in part" in how they are convicted, consoled, or encouraged. If it is known that most in the congregation are walking "in the broad way," then the application should be directed to them "alone." After these parts of the sermon are constructed, then the introduction is to be written.[62]

Simeon saw many benefits to using those five steps in preparing a sermon. It would preserve unity and clarity in the sermon. It would also keep the audience's attention by the better use of simple observations. And then the listeners would be more able "to discern beauties in the Scripture when they peruse it in their closets."[63] Here, again, can be seen Simeon's concern to raise up Bible Christians.

Anticipating criticism that his approach might cramp the mind, he asserts that it allows the mind great liberty. Another advantage to this method is that the skeletons, as he has formed them, will last about half an hour if read aloud. This will, in turn, give the preacher greater knowledge of the Scriptures since the skeletons contain many supporting Scripture references.

Simeon concludes his description of the use of the formation and use of the skeletons with two cautions. First, since the skeletons contain many supporting Scripture references, if they were all read or quoted, they "would make the sermon a mere rhapsody, a string of texts that could not fail to weary and disgust the audience. On the other hand, if they are merely glanced at and interwoven with the minister's own thoughts, they will add richness and variety to the talk."[64]

The second caution anticipates our modern reality of the vast supply of sermons available on the internet. Some of Simeon's friends feared that the skeletons being published in the *Horae Homileticae* could encourage sloth and idleness. He counters this by suggesting that these are not ready-made sermons. They cannot just be taken up and preached. He also was confident that true preachers would want to do the work to produce their own sermons for their own congregations.[65]

As noted above, Simeon asked three questions of his own work in the pulpit: Does it humble the sinner? Exalt the Savior? Promote holiness? He was very

---

61. Ibid., vii.
62. Ibid.
63. Ibid., viii.
64. Simeon, *Horae*, vol. 1, *Genesis to Leviticus*, x.
65. Ibid.

aware of the need to set the gospel clearly before those from outside the faith who may have entered his church building on a Sunday morning. He even expected at times that his congregation was "almost entirely composed of persons walking in the broad way of worldliness and indifference."[66] This passion to preach to those outside the church may have been the fuel behind his efforts to organize and send countless chaplains to India under the influential Church Missionary Society.[67]

Of course, Simeon was focused on preaching Christ. He hoped that 1 Corinthians 2:2, "For I resolved to know nothing while I was with you except Jesus Christ and him crucified," would be inscribed on his memorial at Trinity Church. It was.[68] This was his abiding desire: to preach the glories of Christ from every text of Scripture. This is made clear upon a reading of his sermons.

This commitment to preach Christ was connected in his sermons to the call on Christians to live holy lives, which would be realized through a dependence on the Holy Spirit. In sermon 2337 on Hebrews 12:14, he explained the importance and nature of sanctification: "Holiness is a conformity of heart and life to the revealed will of God. . . . Sanctification is a progressive work. A child of God arrives not at full stature but by degrees: he is constantly growing in grace."[69]

Simeon's life was not easy. In both his personal and public life he experienced difficulties, arising both from the attacks of others and from his own faults. But he did characterize the ideals of one who would grow and mature as he got older, exemplifying the very aims that arose from his preaching ministry.[70]

CONTRIBUTIONS TO PREACHING

Chris Armstrong states that "by the close of his life Charles Simeon had almost single-handedly renewed an Anglican Church in danger of losing all the benefit it had gained from John Wesley and John Newton."[71] Alexander Zabriskie believes Simeon was the central figure among the pastors who were part of the evangelical movement in the Church of England toward the end of the nineteenth century. This movement intended to awaken a largely inert and indifferent population through the preaching of sin and judgment and of forgiveness and eternal life.[72]

---

66. Ibid., viii.

67. Chris Armstrong, *Patron Saints for Postmoderns* (Downers Grove, IL: InterVarsity Press, 2009), 130.

68. J. F. Clayton, "The Centenary of Charles Simeon," *Modern Churchman* 26, no. 9 (December 1936): 500–504.

69. Simeon, *Horae*, vol. 19, *2 Timothy to Hebrews*, 466–67.

70. Armstrong, *Patron Saints for Postmoderns*, 146.

71. Armstrong, *Patron Saints for Postmoderns*, 130.

72. Zabriskie, "Charles Simeon: Anglican Evangelical," 103.

This renewal was needed during these years when most sermons were dry, academic talks. They were often fully-written manuscripts that were either memorized or simply read. Many preachers even read sermons written by others. People were expected to listen to these sermons and think about them, but there was little expectation that they would apply them to their lives or deepen their spiritual experiences in any real way.[73] Simeon took a very different approach. He wrote his own sermons, often taking up to twelve hours to prepare. And he targeted not just the mind but also the heart. His delivery was passionate and dramatic. Over time, attendance at Holy Trinity Church grew to over one thousand.[74]

Simeon's huge impact was enhanced by the location of his church in Cambridge. About half of the graduates of the university were pastoral candidates, and by 1817, up to half of his congregation were undergraduate students.[75] The renewal of church life in the country was fueled by the supply of pastors from Cambridge to the churches. Many of these young men had spent time with Simeon in his sermon classes, which took place on Sundays after church. He continued this for over forty years. Each term, fifteen to twenty pastoral students would gather weekly to sit under Simeon's instruction.[76] He described the process this way: "I give the text for the elucidation of each distinct topic. They treat the text; and I make my remarks on their compositions, pointing out what I conceive to be the more perfect way."[77]

He wanted to pursue this avenue because of the lack of formal training offered to ministers in their pastoral and preaching duties. In the dedication of the *Horae*, Simeon noted with regret that while universities laid a good foundation in the preparation of pastors, "there is no subsequent instruction given us to fit us for the employment of the ministry."[78] None of these kinds of institutions existed at that time.

The Sunday meeting was augmented by the Friday conversation parties in his own lodgings, commonly attended by fifty to sixty students. He gave this description of this meeting: "I have an open day, when all who choose it come to take their tea with me. Everyone is at liberty to ask what questions he will, and I give to them the best answer I can."[79] By investing himself in these young men

---

73. Richard H. Schmidt, *Glorious Companions: Five Centuries of Anglican Spirituality* (Grand Rapids: Eerdmans, 2002), 164.
74. Ibid., 164–65.
75. Gary Jenkins, *A Tale of Two Preachers: Preaching in the Tradition of Simeon-Stott* (Cambridge: Grove, 2012), 3.
76. Ibid., 4.
77. Carus, *Memoirs*, 642.
78. Simeon, *Horae*, vol. 1, *Genesis to Leviticus*, 1.
79. Carus, *Memoirs*, 641.

over many years, Simeon helped to shape the pulpits in England for generations. As these men fanned out into pulpits across England, the church was revitalized. Carrying out such a ministry in a large church for a long time allowed Simeon to have a significant impact.

One notable preacher who felt Simeon's influence was John Stott. He was introduced to Simeon during his undergraduate years at Cambridge. It was Simeon's uncompromising commitment to Scripture as the Word of God to be obeyed and expounded that captured Stott's admiration. Stott called him "one of the greatest and most persuasive preachers the Church of England has ever known."[80]

The spirit of Simeon's intent to train preachers in the ministry of the Word is carried on today by a number of organizations working around the world.[81] They gather pastors to encourage them in their efforts and to equip them with the tools and principles they need. They operate under the command from Paul to Timothy. In discussing the ministry of the Word in the church community, he charged in 1 Timothy 4:15: "Be diligent in these matters; give yourself wholly to them, so that everyone may see your progress." Surely this captures the heart of the work of Charles Simeon.

Sermon Excerpt

Paul's Love to the Church at Rome (Romans 1:9–12)[82]

It has been thought by some, that it would have been better for the Church if the Gospels only had been transmitted to posterity, and the Epistles had perished to oblivion. This impious sentiment originates altogether in men's hatred of the truth; and it argues as much ignorance of the Gospels, as it does ingratitude to God. The Gospels contain all the same truth as the Epistles; but the Epistles render them more clear. Never should we have had so complete a view of the correspondence between the Jewish and Christian dispensations, as we are favoured with in the Epistle to the Hebrews: nor would the doctrine of justification by faith alone have been so clearly defined, or so incontrovertibly established,

---

80. John Stott, "Charles Simeon: A Personal Appreciation," in *Evangelical Preaching: An Anthology of Sermons by Charles Simeon*, James Houston, ed. (Portland: Multnomah, 1986), xxvii.

81. An example is the Charles Simeon Trust, which exists to promote the growth of the gospel of Jesus Christ throughout the world by training an emerging generation of biblical expositors. See http://www.simeontrust.org.

82. Simeon, *Horae*, vol. 15, *Romans*, 5–6.

if the Epistle to the Romans and the Galatians had never existed. We are moreover indebted to the Epistles for a much clearer insight into practical religion, than we ever should have been without them. It is true, that the example of Christ is perfect, and that the precepts he has given us are perfect also; but we should never have known what heights of piety are attainable by "men of like passions with ourselves," if we had not known more of the Apostles than what is recorded of them in the Gospels. In the Acts of the Apostles we behold much of their zeal and diligence; but in the Epistles, the full portrait of a minister is drawn with a minuteness and accuracy which we should in vain look for in any other place. To go no further than the words before us—what an exalted idea have we of the love which a minister should bear towards his people, in the solemn declaration of St Paul! ◆

BIBLIOGRAPHY*

Armstrong, Chris. *Patron Saints for Postmoderns.* Downers Grove, IL: InterVarsity Press, 2009.

Carus, William, ed., *Memoirs of the Life of the Rev. Charles Simeon, M.A.* London: Hatchard & Son, 1848.

Clayton, J. F. "The Centenary of Charles Simeon." *Modern Churchman* 26, no. 9 (December 1936): 500–504.

Hopkins, Hugh Evan. *Charles Simeon, Preacher Extraordinary.* Cambridge: Grove, 1979.

Houston, James, ed. *Evangelical Preaching: An Anthology of Sermons by Charles Simeon.* Portland: Multnomah, 1986.

Jenkins, Gary. *A Tale of Two Preachers: Preaching in the Tradition of Simeon-Stott.* Cambridge: Grove, 2012.

Moule, Handley. *Charles Simeon, Pastor of a Generation.* Fern, Ross-shire, Great Britain: Christian Focus, 1997.

Schmidt, Richard H. *Glorious Companions: Five Centuries of Anglican Spirituality.* Grand Rapids: Eerdmans, 2002.

Simeon, Charles. *Horae Homileticae.* Vol. 1, *Genesis to Leviticus.* London: Holdsworth & Ball, 1832.

_____. *Horae Homileticae.* Vol. 15, *Romans.* London: Holdsworth & Ball, 1832.

_____. *Horae Homileticae.* Vol. 16, *1 & 2 Corinthians.* London: Holdsworth & Ball, 1832.

_____. *Horae Homileticae.* Vol. 19, *2 Timothy to Hebrews.* London: Holdsworth & Ball, 1832.

Zabriskie, Alexander C. "Charles Simeon: Anglican Evangelical." *Church History* 9, no. 2 (June 1940): 103–19.

*Brief quotations have not been included in the bibliographies of this volume but are included in the footnotes.

Robert Murray M'Cheyne

Preaching the Love of God in Jesus Christ

JORDAN MARK STONE

Robert Murray M'Cheyne (1813–1843) passed into glory two months before his thirtieth birthday. Few preachers have died so young and yet left as long-lasting a legacy as M'Cheyne. He was a minister committed to the church, to holiness, to prayer, and to Christ. He labored to point people to the love of Christ and to lead them to show love to Christ in return. Affection for Christ was the pulsating power behind his piety and preaching. His life story offers a worthy model of grace, and his ministerial pattern a model for service.

HISTORICAL BACKGROUND

Born on May 21, 1813, to Adam and Lockhart M'Cheyne, Robert Murray M'Cheyne was the youngest of five children. He displayed obvious intellectual gifts and a winsome personality from the start. At the age of four, while laid up sick, he memorized the Greek alphabet "as an amusement."[1] Poetry, sketching, and gymnastics were among his most cherished pursuits. He regularly won awards in school, cultivating deep friendships along the way.[2]

Although he was committed to church attendance and catechism classes in his teenage years, M'Cheyne's biographer said he "regarded these as days of ungodliness—days wherein he cherished a pure morality, but lived in heart a Pharisee."[3] His conversion from sin to faith in Christ came through tragedy. In July 1831, Robert's oldest brother, David, died suddenly from a serious fever. David was an earnest Christian and had often counseled Robert to consider the

---

1. L. J. Van Valen, *Constrained by His Love: A New Biography on Robert Murray McCheyne* (Fearn, Scotland: Christian Focus, 2002), 16.
2. Alexander Smellie, *Biography of R. M. McCheyne* (1913; repr., Fearn, Scotland: Christian Focus, 1995), 31.
3. Andrew Bonar, ed., *Memoir and Remains of the Rev. Robert Murray M'Cheyne* (Dundee: Middleton, 1845), 2.

state of his soul. David's death, at the age of twenty-seven, struck a spiritual blow from which Robert never recovered. Years later, Robert wrote to a parishioner on the anniversary of David's death, "This day eleven years ago, I lost my loved and loving brother, and began to seek a Brother who cannot die."[4]

After coming alive to Christ, M'Cheyne devoted himself to the Lord's service. His poetry and letters reveal a growing concern for the things of God. He began ministering in his church's Sabbath school, voraciously reading God's Word, and attending evangelical preaching wherever it could be found.

M'Cheyne decided to pursue the gospel ministry soon after his conversion. In November 1831, he matriculated into the thriving Divinity Hall at the University of Edinburgh. There he came under the spell of Thomas Chalmers, a renowned professor who "was at the height of his amazing influence; no one since the days of John Knox had been held in such deep veneration."[5] Chalmers taught courses on divinity and endorsed a ministerial pattern that M'Cheyne came to personify. The professor mentored M'Cheyne, inviting the young student to join an exclusive "Exegetical Society" that met weekly during the term. Gathering on Saturdays at 6:30 a.m., members of the Society presented papers and interacted on their interpretations. The meetings served to sharpen the participants' theological and biblical insight, and offer a glimpse into M'Cheyne's growing ability to explain Scripture. He had a profound grasp of Hebrew and delighted in reading the original languages each day. M'Cheyne also joined the Visiting Society at the Divinity Hall, which purposed "to set apart an hour or two every week for visiting the careless and needy in the most neglected portions of the town."[6] His early visiting efforts uncovered a den of sin and misery he had never before encountered. Such experiences awoke in him an earnest compassion for the lost. He later declared, "I think I can say, I have never risen a morning without thinking how I could bring more souls to Christ."[7]

M'Cheyne matched an increasing piety to his growing earnestness in Bible study, theology, and evangelism. His diary entries while at the Divinity Hall reveal a consistent longing for greater conformity to Christ, for he recognized that the heart and the head must be wedded together for Christian maturity. He wrote: "Oh that heart and understanding may grow together, like brother and sister, leaning on one another!"[8] His goal in this growth to maturity was for

---

4. Ibid., 9.

5. Marcus L. Loane, *They Were Pilgrims* (Sydney: Angus & Robertson, 1970; repr., Edinburgh: Banner of Truth, 2006), 142.

6. Bonar, *Memoir and Remains*, 22.

7. Robert Murray M'Cheyne, *A Basket of Fragments* (1848; repr., Inverness, Scotland: Christian Focus, 1975), 77.

8. Bonar, *Memoir and Remains*, 16.

"more abundant longings for the work of the ministry. Oh that Christ would but count me faithful, that a dispensation of the gospel might be committed to me!"[9] In order to accomplish these goals pushing him toward holiness and effectiveness in ministry, he reflected on his role as steward over the time given to him, saying, "What right have I to steal and abuse my Master's time? 'Redeem it,' He is crying to me."[10] Elsewhere he wrote, "And yet these four-and-twenty hours must be accounted for."[11] M'Cheyne's focus on redeeming the time is noteworthy as he died young, at twenty-nine years old. His intentionality to use every moment for Christ is one reason why a life that failed to reach its fourth decade continues to influence many people today.

In July 1835, just months after graduating, M'Cheyne accepted a call to labor as John Bonar's assistant in the united parish of Larbert and Dunipace. M'Cheyne's brief ministry as Bonar's assistant forged his ministerial passions in two areas: preaching and visitation. He often preached three different sermons every Lord's Day in either Larbert or Dunipace, or at one of five preaching stations surrounding the parish. He spent the rest of the week visiting parishioners, offering words of exhortation and prayer to all who opened their door. He told his mother he enjoyed visitation more than any other aspect of ministry at his first ministerial charge.

By the spring of 1836, M'Cheyne was growing restless for more gospel opportunities. He confided to his father, "I sometimes feel the lack of not having the full powers of a minister of God, for that reason alone I would desire an exchange."[12] Such an opportunity arrived speedily. A few months later, the leaders of St. Peter's Church Dundee invited M'Cheyne to preach as a candidate to become their first minister. After preaching his sermon, the congregation of St. Peter's unanimously called M'Cheyne to be their first pastor in August 1836, and he was ordained to the gospel ministry on November 24, 1836. M'Cheyne took Isaiah 61:1–3 as his first sermon text, a passage he used in following years to commemorate the anniversary of his first Sabbath as pastor. From the start, a dependence on God's Spirit characterized his labor.

M'Cheyne sought to minister in common and creative ways at St. Peter's. He continued the practice of diligent visitation learned under Chalmers and Bonar. He preached three times each Sunday, and the congregation's 1,100 seats were full from the start. He installed ten elders. With the church's support, he introduced a Thursday night prayer meeting that soon overflowed with eight

---

9. Ibid., 17.
10. Ibid., 12.
11. Ibid.
12. MACCH 2.6.27.

hundred participants. During the summer months he held weekly "meetings for singing," which intended to improve the congregation's singing ability. Other innovative practices included increasing Communion seasons from two to four times per year. In 1837, M'Cheyne started a Sabbath school to reach young children, and over three hundred students soon enrolled. Recognizing that older children required specific instruction, he began a Tuesday evening class attended by some two hundred and fifty young people.[13]

In the winter of 1838–1839, sickness struck M'Cheyne and laid him aside from the work of ministry. Thinking a change in climate would aid his health, M'Cheyne's friends and doctors urged him to join a deputation from the Church of Scotland that was soon to depart for the Holy Land. The "Mission of Inquiry" aimed to discern how the Church might best evangelize the Jewish people in Palestine and throughout Europe.[14] Leaving St. Peter's in the hands of William Chalmers Burns, M'Cheyne left in April 1839. He returned seven months later to a congregation in the throes of revival.[15] The awakening spirit first came upon St. Peter's through Burns's powerful preaching in early August. When M'Cheyne returned and preached to his people, he wrote, "I never preached to such an audience, so many weeping, so many waiting for the words of eternal life. I never heard such sweet singing anywhere, so tender and affecting, as if the people felt that they were praising a present God."[16] The revival lasted into the summer of 1840, and M'Cheyne promoted its continuing value throughout Scotland. A more expansive preaching ministry marked M'Cheyne's final years, as he contributed to "preaching raids" throughout Scotland, Ireland, and England.

In March 1843, M'Cheyne contracted typhus fever and passed into glory on March 25 at the age of twenty-nine.[17] James Hamilton captured the common sentiment regarding M'Cheyne's life and legacy by writing, "I never knew one so instant in season and out of season, so impressed with the invisible realities, and so faithful in reproving sin and witnessing for Christ. . . . Love to Christ was the great secret of all his devotion and consistency, and since the days of Samuel Rutherford, I question if the Church of Scotland has contained a more seraphic mind, one that was in such constant flame of love and adoration toward Him that liveth and was dead."[18]

---

13. Van Valen, *Constrained by His Love*, 150.

14. See Andrew Bonar and Robert Murray M'Cheyne, *Narrative of a Mission of Inquiry to the Jews from the Church of Scotland in 1839* (Edinburgh: William Whyte & Co., 1842).

15. Bonar, *Memoir and Remains*, 114.

16. Smellie, *Biography of R. M. McCheyne*, 146–47.

17. Bonar, *Memoir and Remains*, 165.

18. James Hamilton, quoted in Smellie, *Biography of R. M. McCheyne*, 173.

THEOLOGY OF PREACHING

M'Cheyne's Presbyterian tradition articulated the significance of preaching in the Westminster Shorter Catechism 89 by asking, "How is the word made effectual to salvation?" The answer follows, "The Spirit of God maketh the reading, but especially the preaching, of the word, an effectual means of convincing and converting sinners, and of building them up in holiness and comfort, through faith, unto salvation." M'Cheyne happily ministered in such a heritage, being convinced that as "weak and foolish as it may appear, [preaching] is the grand instrument which God has put into our hands, by which sinners are to be saved, and saints fitted for glory."[19] He called preaching the minister's "grand business."[20]

M'Cheyne's homiletical theology was grounded in the firm yet warm theology of the Westminster Standards—the Confession of Faith, and Larger and Shorter Catechisms. He subscribed to the Standards at his ordination and never deviated from his vows. Always intent on communicating truth to the simplest hearer, M'Cheyne summarized his theology for preaching as an appropriation of Rowland Hill's three Rs: "ruin by the fall, righteousness by Christ, and regeneration by the Spirit."[21] A close examination of M'Cheyne's sermons uncovers four main theological motifs in his preaching ministry.

Proclaiming the Father's Sovereignty

A complete Calvinism saturated M'Cheyne's theology. He took the Father's sovereign grace in the salvation of sinners to be a certainty. "It was a mercy that made Him give His only begotten Son," M'Cheyne said. "It was mercy that made Him choose, awaken, and draw any sinner to Christ. He never saved any but out of free sovereign mercy."[22] M'Cheyne's preaching offered hearers a regular confrontation with God's grace. His declarations regarding election sounded forth with sweet intent, for he believed that the doctrine glorified God and humbled humanity. He announced, "Salvation is by grace. When a man chooses an apple off a tree, he generally chooses the ripest, the one that promises best. It is not so with God in choosing the soul He saves. He does not choose those that have sinned least, those that are most willing to be saved; He often chooses the vilest of men, 'to the praise of the glory of his grace.'"[23] The good news of grace was, in M'Cheyne's mind, no deterrent to wooing sinners to Christ; rather, it was

---

19. Bonar, *Memoir and Remains*, 360.
20. Ibid., 359.
21. Ibid., 360.
22. Robert Murray M'Cheyne, *Helps to Devotion* (Glasgow: Free Presbyterian, 1988), 12.
23. Ibid., 41.

truth that undercut the possibility of someone contributing anything to their own salvation, leading them to cling to Christ alone for redemption.

Announcing Humanity's Depravity

M'Cheyne knew it is only through a clear sense of sin that a person is awakened to God's grace in Jesus Christ. James Gordon writes of M'Cheyne's preaching: "If a soul was to be awakened to 'its perilous condition,' then an honest statement of the spiritual facts was in order"—namely, the terrifying reality of sin.[24] M'Cheyne never shied away from bold declarations regarding sin's pollution and penalty. He knew that discovering the depths of one's sinful condition is essential to a true understanding of the gospel, for "the more you feel your weakness, the amazing depravity of your heart . . . the more need have you to lean on Jesus."[25] For M'Cheyne, a deeper clarity regarding the heinousness of sin only increases one's adoration of Christ's love.

Such convictions resulted from his own self-examination. M'Cheyne regularly probed his heart and discovered a depth of iniquity that caused him to feel "broken under a sense of my exceeding wickedness."[26] He wrote to his good friend the Reverend Dan Edwards, urging, "Pray for more knowledge of your own heart—of the total depravity of it—of the awful depths of corruption that are there."[27] This self-examination was not merely advice for others but a discipline of his practice, for he recognized and wrote in his diary about his own besetting sins, which were pride and the lust for people's praise.[28]

Declaring the Savior's Beauty

M'Cheyne's proclamation of the good news was that of an *experienced* gospel. As Bonar writes, "From the first he fed others by what he himself was feeding upon. His preaching was in a manner the development of his soul's experience. It was a giving out of the inward life. He loved to come up from the pastures wherein the Chief Shepherd had met him—to lead the flock entrusted to his care to the spots where he found nourishment."[29] M'Cheyne believed proper preaching cannot be done any other way. He knew that it is only when a pastor makes personal discoveries of Christ that the preacher can then "speak with power, holy admiration, and urgency."[30]

---

24. James M. Gordon, *Evangelical Spirituality* (London: SPCK, 1991; repr., Eugene, OR: Wipf & Stock, 2006), 127.

25. Bonar, *Memoir and Remains*, 526–27.

26. Ibid., 56.

27. Ibid., 242.

28. Bonar, *Memoir and Remains*, 63.

29. Ibid., 34–35.

30. M'Cheyne, *New Testament Sermons*, 155–56.

The place where M'Cheyne dwelled most in preaching was the greatness and glory of Christ—for Christ is the main thing in the gospel. He said, "The chief object of the Bible, [is] to show you the work, the beauty, the glory, the excellency of this High Priest."[31] M'Cheyne preached a full-orbed Christ, resisting any Christology that minimized aspects of Christ's person and work. With unrelenting passion, he proclaimed a Christ who is Lord, Savior, Judge, and Friend. His sermons magnify Christ in all his comeliness, loveliness, preciousness, sweetness, freeness, and fitness.[32]

If M'Cheyne's Christ-centered preaching had a main theme, it undoubtedly was the Savior's love. M'Cheyne said Christ's love for sinners led the Son to obey God's law in our stead, become the sacrificial substitute for sinners, undergo the horror of God's wrath for sin, and unite us to his person.[33] Such "divine love" is the supreme argument that "persuades sinners now to believe on him."[34] A ruling elder at St. Peter's recalled, "How beautifully affectionate were M'Cheyne's addresses! He *draws* you to Christ."[35] According to James Gordon, "M'Cheyne seemed to have a heightened awareness of the reality and near presence of Christ, and sensed in him a fragrance and loveliness that was breathtaking in power and attraction. The suffering of the crucified Christ kindled an ardor and devotion he could sometimes barely contain."[36] Parishioners often noted how whenever M'Cheyne's sermons went longer than usual, it was because of the fullness of his love for Christ.[37]

Emphasizing the Spirit's Efficacy

M'Cheyne extolled the Holy Spirit as the "greatest of all the privileges of a Christian," adding, "It is sweet to get the love of Christ; but I will tell you what is equally as sweet—that is to receive the Spirit of Christ."[38] He said the sweetness of the Spirit's ministry is its focus on regeneration and sanctification. It is the Spirit who is God's agent unto conversion, who works through the preached Word to bring peace to sinners, and who brings the new birth. Further, the "Spirit of Grace" is the one who comes in and renovates the soul.[39] M'Cheyne

---

31. Robert Murray M'Cheyne, *Sermons on Hebrews* (Edinburgh: Banner of Truth, 2004), 87.

32. M'Cheyne, *New Testament Sermons*, 49.

33. M'Cheyne, *Sermons on Hebrews*, 22.

34. Robert Murray M'Cheyne, *Comfort in Sorrow* (Fearn, Scotland: Christian Focus, 2002), 140–41.

35. William Lamb, *M'Cheyne from the Pew: Being Extracts from the Diary of William Lamb,* ed. Kirkwood Hewat (1898; repr., Belfast: Ambassador, 1987), 31 (emphasis original).

36. Gordon, *Evangelical Spirituality,* 128–29.

37. Bonar, *Memoir and Remains,* 66.

38. Robert Murray M'Cheyne, *Old Testament Sermons* (Edinburgh: Banner of Truth, 2004), 74.

39. Robert Murray M'Cheyne, *From the Preacher's Heart* (1846; repr., Fearn, Scotland: Christian Focus, 1993), 226.

consistently extolled the Spirit's Christ-centered ministry by saying the Spirit redeems and renews by making the sinner "look to a pierced Christ."[40]

Much of M'Cheyne's teaching on pneumatology emphasizes the Spirit's "tender desire" to make God's people holy. M'Cheyne taught that no sinner comes to Christ in their own power, nor can they advance in Christlikeness apart from the Spirit. He said, "In the sanctification of the people of God, though means are used, yet the word is not by might, nor by power, but by God's Spirit."[41] Just as M'Cheyne was careful to preach the expansive role of Christ, so too was he diligent to communicate the Spirit's full ministry.

THEOLOGY FOR PREACHING

M'Cheyne's emphases of God's sovereignty, humanity's depravity, the Son's beauty, and the Spirit's efficacy ultimately came together in his free offer of the gospel. The best way to describe M'Cheyne's homiletical identity is to call him *a preacher of the free offer of Christ's love for sinners*. Annotations on the free offer fill his earliest notebooks from the Divinity Hall. He referred to it as "the stamina of good preaching."[42] The free offer of Christ's love grounded his pulpit ministry because he believed ministerial faithfulness depended on it: "A faithful watchman preaches a free Saviour to all the world. This was the great object of Christ's ministry."[43]

M'Cheyne acknowledged the difficulty in reconciling God's election with the freeness of the gospel, yet he believed both because he found both in the Bible. He taught that Christ nowhere invites "the elect" to come but everywhere invites all people to faith and repentance. A typical invitation from M'Cheyne sounded as follows: "The free offer of Christ is the very thing that pierces you to the heart. You hear that He is altogether lovely—that He invites sinners to come to Him—that He never casts out those who do come."[44] Christ's freely offered love is what enables a sinner to come to Christ and grow in Christ, and M'Cheyne preached accordingly.

The free offer of Christ was a doctrine not only for M'Cheyne's pulpit but also for the hymnal. One of his better-known hymns sings forth,

> *When free grace awoke me, by light from on high,*
> *Then legal fears shook me, I trembled to die;*

---

40. M'Cheyne, *From the Preacher's Heart*, 228.
41. M'Cheyne, *Old Testament Sermons*, 168.
42. MACCH 1.6, 112.
43. Bonar, *Memoir and Remains*, 536.
44. Ibid., 370.

No refuge, no safety in self could I see, —
Jehovah Tsidkenu my Saviour must be.

My terrors all vanished before the sweet name;
My guilty fears banished, with boldness I came
To drink at the fountain, life-giving and free, —
Jehovah Tsidkenu is all things to me.[45]

M'Cheyne's theology for preaching was rooted in the knowledge of God's free love in Christ. "Nothing is more wonderful than the love of Christ," he said. Everyone must therefore "learn the freeness of the love of Christ."[46] William Blaikie has articulated best the essence of M'Cheyne's theology by saying that M'Cheyne "brought into the pulpit all the reverence for Scripture of the Reformation period; all the honour for the headship of Christ of the Covenanter struggle; all the freeness of the Gospel offer of the Marrow theology; all the bright imagery of Samuel Rutherford; all the delight of the Erskines in the fulness of Christ."[47]

METHODOLOGY FOR PREACHING

M'Cheyne preached the gospel at a time when "the old evangelical sermon" thrived in Scotland.[48] This homiletical school—influenced largely by Thomas Chalmers—employed hermeneutics "as the springboard" for "doctrinal discourses."[49] M'Cheyne's hermeneutical approach to Scripture is best described as "a doctrinal-typological method." Under Chalmers's tutelage, M'Cheyne imbibed a doctrinal approach to preaching. Chalmers advised preachers not to tarry on linguistic arguments or exegetical precision but to arrive speedily at the text's main doctrine. He said, "The very utterance of your text will generally be enough for gaining their assent to the doctrine which it enunciated, or, at the most, the concurrence of a few decisive testimonies from other parts of Scripture, will abundantly suffice in the way of argument."[50]

M'Cheyne's sermons show how he adapted Chalmers's instruction. After brief exegetical comments, M'Cheyne stated his main doctrine and then wove

---

45. Ibid., 583.

46. M'Cheyne, *From the Preacher's Heart*, 168.

47. William G. Blaikie, *The Preachers of Scotland: From the Sixth to the Nineteenth Century* (1888; repr., Edinburgh: Banner of Truth, 2001), 294.

48. William Gerald Enright, "Preaching and Theology in Scotland in the Nineteenth Century: A Study of the Context and the Content of the Evangelical Sermon" (PhD thesis, University of Edinburgh, 1968), 207–12.

49. Ibid., 234.

50. Quoted in Enright, "Preaching and Theology in Scotland in the Nineteenth Century," 238.

his subsequent exposition into extended exhortations and applications. The main doctrinal force of each sermon was christological, as M'Cheyne anchored his messages on the Redeemer's love for sinners.

A second facet of M'Cheyne's hermeneutical method was its esteem for typology. M'Cheyne ransacked the Scriptures for typological portrayals of Christ, including Abraham's offering of Isaac, the Passover Lamb, Moses and Joshua, the tabernacle's furniture and features, the cities of refuge, and the temple. His notebooks contain his typological comments on numerous other types of Christ. Although M'Cheyne ordinarily spoke on christological types, he also elaborated on types of the covenant of grace, the devil, the church, the Holy Spirit, eternal rest, and Pentecost. His typological outlook was so pervasive that a sermon on Christ's healing of the deaf and mute man was an extended commentary on how the event is a "type of the way in which Jesus saves a poor sinner."[51]

M'Cheyne married a simple homiletical model to his doctrinal-typological hermeneutic. His standard practice was to state the sermon's central doctrine and then proceed to illuminate its truth along a series of headings. One hearer observed, "The heads of his sermons were not the mile stones that tell you how near you are to your journey's end, but they were nails which fixed and fastened all he said. Divisions are often dry; but not so *his* divisions—they were so textual and so feeling, and they brought out the spirit of a passage so surprisingly."[52] Further, his preaching was specific in its application, with exhortations directed distinctly at the lost, the awakened, the backslider, the afflicted, and the true believer. Bonar notes how M'Cheyne's applications flowed naturally from his doctrine: "[His sermon manuscripts] may convey a correct idea of his style and mode of preaching doctrine. But there are no notes that give any idea of his affectionate appeals to the heart and searching applications. These he seldom wrote; they were poured forth at the moment when his heart filled with his subject; for his rule was to set before his hearers a body of truth first—and there was always a vast amount of Bible truth in his discourses—and then urge home the application. His exhortations flowed from his doctrine, and thus had both variety and power."[53]

M'Cheyne's method of sermonic delivery evolved throughout his ministry. While at the Divinity Hall, he learned to write out his sermons in full. From a lecture on "Composition of Sermons," he carefully notes, "The extemporaneous is a good temptation to indolence and is apt to lead you always into the same strain of preaching. The bulk of your parish preparations should be in writing,

---

51. M'Cheyne, *New Testament Sermons*, 42–51.
52. Bonar, *Memoir and Remains*, 64 (emphasis original).
53. Ibid., 65.

but in a rapid style of writing."[54] M'Cheyne took the instruction to heart and began his ministry by writing out his sermons and lectures at length, yet never falling into the practice of merely reading his message. He worked to memorize the essential substance of his manuscript and then preach with relative liberty. A crucial moment for change came one "Lord's Day . . . as he rode rapidly along to Dunipace, his written sermons were dropped on the wayside. This accident prevented him from having the opportunity of preparing in his usual manner; but he was enabled to preach with more than usual freedom. For the first time in his life, he discovered that he possessed the gift of extemporaneous composition, and learned, to his own surprise, that he had more composedness of mind and command of language than he believed."[55]

As he matured, and as preaching opportunities increased significantly, M'Cheyne's manuscripts inevitably became more concise. The shorter notes reveal an unyielding concern for order. He wrote, "Nothing is more needful for making a sermon memorable and impressive than a logical arrangement."[56] M'Cheyne also stressed clarity of purpose in preaching. He critiqued Andrew Bonar's habit of being unclear, telling his friend, "Study to express yourself very clearly. I sometimes observe obscurity of expression. Form your sentences very regularly. . . . It sometimes strikes me you begin a sentence before you know where you are to end it, or what is to come in at the end."[57] Such attention to articulation did not produce in M'Cheyne's preaching the veneer of polished rhetoric. Instead, what marked his preaching was natural eloquence joined to evident sincerity.

A notable feature in M'Cheyne's preaching is how tenderness flooded his sermons. Marcus Loane's conclusion is representative of most memorials: "The great secret of his success in the pulpit was his combination of faithfulness to the Word of God with tenderness for the souls of men."[58] "The new element he brought to the pulpit," Blaikie concludes, "or rather which he revived and used so much that it appeared new, was *winsomeness*."[59]

While he possessed an innately tender disposition, M'Cheyne nonetheless believed that Scripture mandated that preachers show forth Christ with tones of tenderness. In one journal entry, he penned, "Large meeting in the evening. Felt very happy after it, though mourning for *bitter speaking of the gospel*. Surely it is a gentle message, and should be spoken with angelic tenderness, especially by such

---

54. MACCH 1.6, 107.

55. Bonar, *Memoir and Remains*, 38.

56. Ibid., 29.

57. Quoted in Marjory Bonar, ed., *Reminiscences of Andrew A. Bonar, D.D.* (London: Hodder & Stoughton, 1895), 7.

58. Loane, *They Were Pilgrims*, 172–73.

59. Blaikie, *The Preachers of Scotland*, 294–95 (emphasis original).

a needy sinner."[60] He said a minister must reflect the Holy Spirit, who empowers the preacher: "Ah! brethren, if the Spirit, whose very breath is all gentleness and love—whom Jesus hath sent into the world to bring men to eternal life—if he begins his work in every soul that is to be saved by convincing of sin, why should you blame the minister of Christ if he begins in the very same way?"[61]

A final facet of M'Cheyne's methodology was his willingness to announce the doom that accompanies unbelief. M'Cheyne stated, "The deepest place in hell will be for . . . [anyone who] is not ravished with [Christ's] beauty, and attracted to Him by His loveliness."[62] M'Cheyne knew the Bible is a "blessed book full of the clearest declarations of God's wrath against sin."[63] He preached in kind. His preaching of sin's certain punishment was persistent enough that some in his congregation urged him to lessen his emphasis on judgment. "Sometimes you wonder at our anxiety for you," he told St. Peter's. "Sometimes you say, 'Why are you so harsh?' O poor soul! It is because the house is on fire. . . . Every day that passes is bringing you nearer to the judgment-seat."[64] Heralding such truth usually led to a simple exhortation: "Ah! dear souls, flee now the wrath to come!"[65]

With the love of Christ and plight of sinful humanity always in view, a sense of urgency filled M'Cheyne's preaching. Sinners stood on the precipice of eternity, soon to find God's judgment falling on them. How could a faithful preacher not warn them? M'Cheyne's love led him to strive for the salvation of lost sinners in danger of judgment. He proclaimed, "Learn that it is in love we beseech you. Am I become your enemy, because I tell you the truth? When we speak of sins, your lost condition, the wrath that is over you, the hell beneath you, it is in love."[66] Additionally, in M'Cheyne's estimation, the truth of God's judgment served to magnify, not minimize, Christ's love to sinners—for Christ endured the torrent of God's wrath in his people's place.

CONTRIBUTIONS TO PREACHING

Through the power of the Spirit, M'Cheyne's pulpit ministry was like a hammer that broke the hard-hearted, a fire that warmed the weary, an ointment that soothed the hurting, and a light that guided the lost. Three realities empowered M'Cheyne's preaching and are worthy of emulation today.

---

60. Bonar, *Memoir and Remains*, 42 (emphasis original).
61. M'Cheyne, *From the Preacher's Heart*, 310.
62. M'Cheyne, *New Testament Sermons*, 102.
63. M'Cheyne, *Old Testament Sermons*, 60.
64. M'Cheyne, *Basket of Fragments*, 80.
65. M'Cheyne, *New Testament Sermons*, 152.
66. Ibid., 277.

Plead for the Centrality of Christ

M'Cheyne's preaching centered on Christ—crucified, buried, resurrected, and glorified. In every sermon, he set forth Christ, calling people to look and live. He believed that ministerial fidelity depends on saturating a sermon with Christ, because "the more ministers have Christ in their sermons, the more they faithfully preach."[67] The Savior's beauty, not cultural or political polemics, should preoccupy every pulpit. M'Cheyne did not try to answer every specific objection, question, or need that lay before him on the Lord's Day. He wisely dealt with the most obvious concerns and then sprinted to Calvary, convinced that Christ alone is the answer to every concern and the remedy for every ailment: "O yes, my friends, we have utterly failed in our preaching of Jesus if we have not set Him forth to you as 'a feast of fat things, of wines on the lees refined.'"[68]

Further, M'Cheyne's sermons were not presentations of Christology, but proclamations of Christ. As Bonar noted, "It was not *doctrine* alone that he preached; it was *Christ*, from whom all doctrine shoots forth as rays from a centre. He sought to hang every vessel and flagon upon him."[69] M'Cheyne hinted at this nuance when he recorded after one Lord's Day service: "It is strange how sweet and precious it is to preach directly about Christ, compared with all other subjects of preaching."[70] He rightly understood that it is possible to proclaim essential evangelical truths—faith, repentance, and obedience—in a way that relegates Christ from being the magnetic center of all truth. And so, he did not call St. Peter's merely to hold fast to Christ's blessings or benefits but to cling to Christ himself.

Another key feature in M'Cheyne's preaching was how his proclamations always included fervent pleading. He critiqued most Scottish evangelical preaching as being weak on pleading: "I would observe what appears to me *a fault in the preaching of our beloved Scotland*. Most ministers are accustomed to set Christ before the people. They lay down the gospel clearly and beautifully, but they do not urge men to enter in. Now God says, Exhort,—beseech men,—persuade men; not only point to the open door, but compel them to come in. Oh, to be more merciful to souls, that we would lay hands on men and draw them in to the Lord!"[71]

M'Cheyne's example also calls ministers to have a healthy self-forgetfulness in the pulpit. He confessed, "*I see that a man cannot be a faithful minister, until*

---

67. M'Cheyne, *Basket of Fragments*, 28.
68. M'Cheyne, *New Testament Sermons*, 4.
69. Bonar, *Memoir and Remains*, 65 (emphasis original).
70. Ibid.
71. Ibid., 362 (emphasis original).

he preaches Christ for Christ's sake—until he gives up striving to attract people to himself, and seeks only to attract them to Christ. Lord, give me this!"[72] Every preacher knows the battle to which M'Cheyne refers. In an age that pursues personality-based platforms, M'Cheyne reminds us that only one person—Jesus Christ—is to be the subject of true preaching.

Emphasize the Necessity of Personal Piety

M'Cheyne admitted, "I feel there are two things it is impossible to desire with sufficient ardour—personal holiness, and the honour of Christ in the salvation of souls."[73] It is on the first point that M'Cheyne is typically remembered. And rightly so. He believed growth in holiness is the essence of what it means to love Christ. He also said a zeal for holiness is a mark—and point—of God's saving grace. He wrote to a church member, "I trust you feel real desire after complete holiness. This is the truest mark of being born again. It is a mark that he has made us meet for the inheritance of the saints."[74] He exhorted believers to "seek advance of personal holiness. It is for this that the grace of God has appeared to you."[75]

Because holiness is the reason Christ chose his people, died for them, and converted them, M'Cheyne was unflinching in calls to pursue personal godliness. He was especially persistent in requiring that ministers be people of holiness. In an ordination sermon for a pastor, he proclaimed, "Oh! study universal holiness of life. Your whole usefulness depends on this. Your sermon on Sabbath lasts but an hour or two—your life preaches all the week."[76]

Not long before he died, M'Cheyne penned a small document entitled "Secret Reformation." In the first section, he concentrated on "Personal Reformation," saying, "I am persuaded that I shall obtain the highest amount of present happiness, I shall do most for God's glory and the good of man, and I shall have the fullest reward in eternity, by maintaining a conscience always washed in Christ's blood, by being filled with the Holy Spirit at all times, and by attaining the most entire likeness to Christ in mind, will, and heart, that it is possible for a redeemed sinner to attain to in this world."[77]

M'Cheyne proceeded to delineate a scheme for personal holiness that would enable him to live in increasing communion with Christ. The plan included strategies for confessing sin, reading Scripture, applying Christ to the conscience,

---

72. Ibid., 43 (emphasis original).
73. Bonar, *Memoir and Remains*, 242.
74. Ibid., 248.
75. Ibid., 255.
76. Ibid., 365.
77. Bonar, *Memoir and Remains*, 151.

being filled with the Spirit, growing in humility, fleeing temptation, and meditating on heaven, as well as studying specific christological subjects. He knew that no one drifts into godliness. He thus exhorted every minister to plan for and diligently pursue Christlikeness through the ordinary means of grace.

Piety in the ministry waxes and wanes—even in M'Cheyne's life. His journal regularly reveals dissatisfaction with his own growth in Christ. Only months before his death, he wrote a letter to Horatius Bonar asking for help in how to better study the Bible.[78]

M'Cheyne is a compelling example of sincere godliness. Love for Christ—which increases through the Word, sacrament, and prayer—is the mature expression of holiness. Christ's love is what makes the heart holy, and growth in love for Christ demonstrates increasing holiness. This christological love, M'Cheyne taught, is what propels faithfulness and fruitfulness in ministry. His life and ministry offer a clarion call for today's ministers to heed the apostle Paul's promise that "those who cleanse themselves ... will be instruments for special purposes, made holy, useful to the Master and prepared to do any good work" (2 Tim 2:21).

Focus on the Priority of Prayer

Throughout his life M'Cheyne often lay in bed for weeks on end, battling sickness. He used these times for examination, believing the affliction was the Father's loving discipline. M'Cheyne's typical conclusion was that God laid him aside to learn the value of prayer. For example, he exhorted a newly ordained minister: "Give yourself to prayer and to the ministry of the Word. If you do not pray, God will probably lay you aside from your ministry, as he did me, to teach you to pray."[79] To another friend he wrote, "I am persuaded that I have been brought into retirement to teach me the value and need of prayer. Alas! I have not estimated aright the value of near access to God."[80]

In the second section of his "Secret Reformation," M'Cheyne focused on "Reformation in Secret Prayer." He committed himself to the earnest use of all kinds of prayer—adoration, confession, thanksgiving, and intercession. His prayer plan included regular intercession for no less than twenty-five different groups or agencies. He wrote,

I ought to pray before seeing anyone. Often when I sleep long, or meet others early, and then have prayer, and breakfast, and forenoon callers, often it is eleven or twelve o'clock before I begin secret prayer. This is a

---

78. Ibid., 274.
79. Ibid., 366.
80. Ibid., 172.

wretched system. It is unscriptural. Christ rose before day, and went into a solitary place. David says, "Early I will seek thee; thou shalt early hear my voice." Mary Magdalene came to the sepulchre while it was yet dark. Family prayer loses much of its power and sweetness; and I can do no good to those who come to seek me. The conscience feels guilty, the soul unfed, the lamp not trimmed. Then, when secret prayer comes, the soul is often out of tune. I feel it is far better to begin with God—to see his face first—to get my soul near him before it is near another.[81]

Prayer was essential to M'Cheyne's spirituality because he viewed it as the minister's "noblest and most fruitful employment, and is not to be thrust into any corner."[82] He was certain that ministers should be standard-bearers when it comes to their personal piety—especially in prayer.

M'Cheyne's example not only commends personal prayer but also promotes public prayer. At the Divinity Hall, he helped lead a Saturday prayer meeting in Thomas Chalmers's vestry. He began a corporate prayer time on Thursday evenings soon after his ordination at St. Peter's, and it grew to over eight hundred regular attendees. He also initiated a Dundee ninety-minute ministerial prayer meeting on Monday mornings. Additionally, M'Cheyne and his brother pastors covenanted to pray for one another on Saturday evenings because they knew faithful preaching required the Spirit's power—which comes through prayer. He was once asked if the busyness of parish life crowded out prayerful preparation on Saturday. He responded, "What would my people do if I were not to pray?"[83] "If a minister is to thrive in his own soul, and be successful in his work," M'Cheyne said, "he must be the half of the time on his knees."[84]

CONCLUSION

M'Cheyne's ministry continues to captivate ministers and church members. The secret of his ongoing influence is found in his exaltation of Jesus Christ. M'Cheyne's ardent pursuit of personal holiness was the overflow of his love for Christ. The good news of Christ's love saturated his preaching; with earnestness and enthusiasm, he presented the freeness and fullness of a Savior who longs to save sinners and sanctify saints. M'Cheyne offers to us today a winsomely compelling example of how to preach nothing but "Jesus Christ and him crucified" (1 Cor 2:2).

---

81. Bonar, *Memoir and Remains*, 158.
82. Ibid., 159.
83. Ibid., 51.
84. M'Cheyne, *Basket of Fragments*, 119.

Sermon Excerpt

Follow Jesus[85]

Jesus said, "Follow me." That little word reached [Matthew's] heart. We often make great mistakes—often make use of long arguments to bring people to Christ. Often we make use of long high-sounding words, and expect them to be blessed; whereas it is the simple exhibition of Christ that is carried home by the Spirit. If we could only set before you Him who is love embodied, and if the Spirit but breathe on the word, these little words, "Follow Jesus," would break your soul away from all the world to follow Him. Speak for Christ. One little word may be blessed. "Follow Jesus," may win a soul.

The soul that has once seen the loveliness of Christ, leaves all for Him.

I doubt not that Jesus gave Matthew a glimpse of His excellency. He felt the savour of Divine Love. He saw the gold—the pearl. What is all the world to him now? He cares not for its gain, its pleasures, its reproaches. In Christ he sees what is sweeter than all.

Matthew *made a great feast*, and brought publicans. When he found that Jesus was so precious to a publican, he went and gathered all his fellow-sinners to meet with Jesus. . . . You who have been called by Christ, can you do nothing to bring others to Him? You know that is possible for such to be *saved*. You may have helped them in sin. Can you not *now* bring them to meet with Jesus? How many contrivances you might fall upon, if you had the compassion of Jesus.

Oh that Christians had more mercy, more of the bowels of Paul—of the spirit of Christ!

BIBLIOGRAPHY

Blaikie, William G. *The Preachers of Scotland: From the Sixth to the Nineteenth Century.* 1888. Repr., Edinburgh: Banner of Truth, 2001.

Bonar, Andrew A., ed. *Memoir and Remains of the Rev. Robert Murray M'Cheyne.* Dundee: Middleton, 1845.

Bonar, Marjorie, ed. *Reminiscences of Andrew A. Bonar.* London: Hodder & Stoughton, 1895.

Enright, William Gerald. "Preaching and Theology in Scotland in the Nineteenth Century: A Study of the Context and the Content of the Evangelical Sermon." PhD thesis, University of Edinburgh, 1968.

Gordon, James M. *Evangelical Spirituality.* London: SPCK, 1991. Repr., Eugene, OR: Wipf & Stock, 2006.

Lamb, William. *M'Cheyne from the Pew: Being Extracts from the Diary of William Lamb.* Edited by Kirkwood Hewat. 1898. Repr., Belfast: Ambassador, 1987.

---

85. Robert Murray M'Cheyne, *The Believer's Joy* (1858; repr., Glasgow: Free Presbyterian, 1987), 83–85 (emphases original). From M'Cheyne's sermon on Matthew 9:9–13, titled "Follow Jesus."

Loane, Marcus L. *They Were Pilgrims*. Sydney: Angus & Robertson, 1970. Repr., Edinburgh: Banner of Truth, 2006.

MACCH: Manuscripts of Robert Murray M'Cheyne, New College Library, Edinburgh.

M'Cheyne, Robert Murray. *A Basket of Fragments*. 1848. Repr., Inverness, Scotland: Christian Focus, 1975.

_____. *The Believer's Joy*. 1858. Repr., Glasgow: Free Presbyterian, 1987.

_____. *Comfort in Sorrow*. Fearn, Scotland: Christian Focus, 2002.

_____. *From the Preacher's Heart*. 1846. Repr., Fearn, Scotland: Christian Focus, 1993.

_____. *Helps to Devotion*. Glasgow: Free Presbyterian, 1988.

_____. *New Testament Sermons*. Edinburgh: Banner of Truth Trust, 2004.

_____. *Old Testament Sermons*. Edinburgh: Banner of Truth Trust, 2004.

_____. *Sermons on Hebrews*. Edinburgh: Banner of Truth Trust, 2004.

Smellie, Alexander. *Biography of R. M. McCheyne*. 1913. Repr., Fearn, Scotland: Christian Focus, 1995.

Van Valen, L. J. *Constrained by His Love: A New Biography on Robert Murray McCheyne*. Fearn, Scotland: Christian Focus, 2002.

Alexander Maclaren

The Art of Hermeneutics for the Practice of Homiletics

R. SCOTT PACE

Alexander Maclaren (1826–1910) is generally regarded as one of the most prolific expositors in the history of the Christian pulpit. Maclaren's dedication to exegeting the original text was a lifelong hallmark. This commitment is evidenced in his most recognized work, *Expositions of Holy Scripture*, which demonstrates his remarkable proficiency in biblical exposition and his intense dedication to a careful handling of the sacred text. His convictions required preachers to recognize their obligation toward personal holiness, dedicated preparation, and faithful proclamation. His example also reveals his view of spiritual devotion and sanctification that helped influence his commitment to sound biblical exposition and practical application. Furthermore, Maclaren's expositions identify much of what made him such a powerful instrument in the hand of God, an ability to apply God's Word with contemporary relevance while remaining faithful to the original text and biblical author's intent.

HISTORICAL BACKGROUND

Alexander Maclaren[1] was born in Glasgow, Scotland, on February 11, 1826, and he was raised in a Christian home.[2] His family was actively involved in Hope Street Baptist Chapel, where he was deeply influenced by his pastor, Reverend James Patterson.[3] Alexander was converted in a revival meeting where he sur-

---

1. There is a variety of spellings used for "Maclaren," but as Atkins points out in *The Best of Alexander Maclaren*, "In general, he signed himself McLaren, but penciled under or over the signature Maclaren. The "McL" he thought looked ugly in print. The *Manchester Guardian* always printed "McLaren" (ix). The dominant use of the spelling "Maclaren" in the sources examined for this essay leads to the use of "Maclaren" for this chapter.

2. Leslie R. Keylock, "Alexander Maclaren: In Christ, in Peace, in Hope," *Fundamentalist Journal* 8, no. 1 (January 1989): 56.

3. Clyde E. Fant Jr. and W. M. Pinson Jr., *20 Centuries of Great Preaching, Volume 5, 1826–1912* (Waco, TX: Word, 1971), 3–4.

rendered to Christ and, in his words, found "peace and power in believing that Christ is the savior."[4] He was baptized on May 17, 1840.[5]

His family moved to London in 1842, and Alexander enrolled at Stepney College, a Baptist institution, as a candidate for the Baptist ministry.[6] Immediately following his graduation, he accepted the call to Portland Chapel in Southampton, England, where he ministered for twelve years. The little church prospered and grew during his ministry. In 1858, after repeated requests from multiple churches, he accepted the pastorate of the Union Baptist Chapel in Manchester. He ministered there faithfully for forty-five years until he retired in 1903.[7] During his ministry he also served twice as the president of the Baptist Union of Great Britain and became the first president of the Baptist World Alliance in 1905.[8]

Maclaren was a consummate pastor whose ministry and devotion was marked by the certainty of his calling: "I cannot ever recall any hesitation as to being a minister . . . it just had to be."[9] Harwood Pattison recognized the corresponding impact this conviction had on Maclaren's ministry: "The strong persuasion that he was called to be a messenger and that the place where that message was to be proclaimed was the pulpit, has made Doctor Maclaren the preacher that he is; and his pulpit has radiated an influence which goes far to justify the bounds which he has put to his work."[10]

Although there are many noteworthy aspects of his ministry to be celebrated and emulated, Maclaren's legacy as a preacher and his primary contribution to the history of preaching is his unwavering commitment to biblical exposition combined with relevant application for his listeners. By considering his approach to relevant interpretation, preachers today can determine some practical guidelines for applying the timeless truths of Scripture for contemporary audiences. Examining several of Maclaren's expositions can establish some practical guidelines, but a preliminary overview of his theological framework for preaching will help to provide the basis for understanding his expositional approach to application.

THEOLOGY OF PREACHING

There are a variety of formative influences and experiences that helped shape Maclaren's theology and preaching philosophy. The early influence of his family,

---

4. Gaius G. Atkins, ed. *The Best of Alexander Maclaren* (Manchester: Ayer Composition, 2002), xiii.

5. Keylock, "Alexander Maclaren," 56.

6. Atkins, *Best of Alexander Maclaren*, viii.

7. E. C. Dargan, *A History of Preaching* (New York: Hodder & Stoughton, 1912), 2:574.

8. David L. Larsen, *The Company of the Preachers* (Grand Rapids: Kregel, 1998), 580.

9. Atkins, *Best of Alexander Maclaren*, viii.

10. T. Harwood Pattison, *The History of Christian Preaching* (Philadelphia: American Baptist, 1903), 344.

particularly of his father, is noticeable in a variety of aspects of Maclaren's ministry. Alexander's father, David Maclaren, was a Glasgow city merchant who, though he never served as a vocational pastor, displayed expositional gifts as a lay preacher. He was renowned for his clarity, rational thought, humility, and a strong work ethic, all of which became trademarks of his son's ministry as well.[11] Most importantly, his father's expositional approach to preaching provided a template that Alexander adopted and advanced.

In addition to his family, Maclaren had some prominent ministerial influences that helped inspire his approach to ministry and helped cement his commitment to exposition. His childhood pastor had a personal impact on his life that was formative in his pastoral leadership.[12] Yet, in his own estimation, the most profound ministerial influence in his development as a preacher was Dr. Thomas Binney.[13] Binney, a pastor for over forty years of King's Weigh-House Chapel in London, was known as a "forceful biblical preacher" who preached without notes, used textual divisions as his sermon structure, and skillfully communicated biblical truth.[14] Maclaren began to model these same characteristics as he absorbed his homiletic training through consistent exposure to Binney's preaching.[15]

Maclaren's academic experience was also instrumental in his formation as an expositor. While studying at Stepney, David Davies, the eminent Hebrew scholar, inspired Maclaren's passion for the biblical languages.[16] His commitment to studying Scripture "in the original" is evident through his careful textual expositions, keen insights, and controlled manner of his preaching.[17] The impact his education had on his preaching is also obvious in his counsel to young preachers: "You can be what many churches wish, a popular preacher—if that be the height of your ambition—with little Greek and less Hebrew; but you can neither be what the churches need nor a faithful steward if you neglect the prime responsibility of your stewardship here, and pass from these walls without having bent yourself to learn, so as to use and love the tongues in which the Spirit of God has spoken to man."[18]

The collective influence of his education, his family, and mentoring ministers culminated to produce a preacher whose "theological position was candidly

11. Ibid., vii.

12. Fant and Pinson, *20 Centuries of Great Preaching*, 5:4.

13. Dargan, *History of Preaching*, 573.

14. Larsen, *Company of the Preachers*, 453.

15. Atkins, *Best of Alexander Maclaren*, ix.

16. Dargan, *History of Preaching*, 573.

17. Ibid., viii–ix.

18. Alexander Maclaren, *Counsels for the Study and the Life* (Louisville: The Review & Expositor, 1925), 6. This book is the recorded form of an address that was delivered before the students and friends of Rawdon College and was published by Maclaren at their request.

and thoughtfully evangelical."[19] He was unwavering in his conservative convictions even in the face of the evolving trends of liberalism in his day and especially in opposition to the textual-critical approach to Scripture.[20] His doctrinal commitments ultimately proved to be foundational in establishing his approach to preaching, and three in particular were especially significant: his view of Scripture, the transforming power of the gospel, and a preacher's personal holiness.

Scripture as Divine Revelation

Maclaren's passion for the Scriptures and his renowned commitment to the original languages, derived from his understanding of Scripture as divine revelation. Ultimately, this theological conviction became the decisive factor in his devotion to expository preaching. To Maclaren, preaching was the exposition of the eternal divine thought.[21] As E. C. Dargan noted, "A keen, trained, disciplined intellect, accurate knowledge of the original languages, easy acquaintance with the best Biblical scholarship, and, above all, an ardent love for the Bible, made him an incomparable explorer into its storehouse of truth and a wonderful expounder of that truth to others."[22]

In what is commonly referred to as the "golden-age of preaching,"[23] Maclaren was highly regarded by his preaching colleagues. Most notably, Charles Spurgeon called him "a tower of strength to the evangelical faith." Spurgeon also noted, "He above all his contemporaries has faithfully interpreted Scripture."[24] Spurgeon spoke of Maclaren's profound influence as an expositor, stating, "Our belief is that Dr. Maclaren, more than any other, except [F. W.] Robertson, has altered the whole manner of preaching in England and America, and that immeasurably for the better."[25]

---

19. Dargan, *History of Preaching,* 573.

20. Fant and Pinson, *20 Centuries of Great Preaching,* 5:5.

21. Alexander Maclaren, "An Appreciation" in *Expositions of Holy Scripture,* vol. 17, ed. W. Robertson Nicoll (Grand Rapids: Baker, 1974), xii.

22. Dargan, *History of Preaching,* 576.

23. Regarding the unparalleled preaching of the nineteenth century, Dargan notes, "The pulpit of (the nineteenth century) ranks high in comparison with the past. In fact, this era marks one of the four great culminating points in the history of the Christian pulpit after the apostles. The three preceding culminations were those of the fourth, the thirteenth, and the sixteenth centuries. While the preaching of the nineteenth century was not marked by any one or two outstanding characteristics, but rather exemplifies the heightening of power in all directions, it is perhaps on that very account to be regarded as the greatest of the four epochs mentioned." Ibid., 350–51.

24. Pattison, *History of Christian Preaching,* 341. Other prominent religious leaders also commented on Maclaren's influence on them. Speaking on a public occasion, the bishop of Manchester said, "Thirty years ago I was studying with great profit the published sermons of the man we honor today; and I will say this, that in any age which has been charmed and inspired by the sermons of Newman, and Robertson of Brighton, there were no published discourses which, for profundity of thought, logical arrangement, eloquence of appeal, and power over the human heart, exceeded in merit those of Doctor Maclaren."

25. Ibid., 343.

In specifically describing Maclaren's preeminence as an expositor, Robertson Nicoll remarked, "A man who reads one of Maclaren's sermons must either take his outline or take another text!"[26] Nicoll further described his gift of analyzing a text as "extraordinary," elaborating with, "he touched [the text] with a silver hammer, and immediately it broke up into natural and memorable divisions, so comprehensive and so clear that it seemed wonderful that the text should have been handled in any other way."[27]

Maclaren's reputation as an expositor reflected his careful handling of the biblical text. But, perhaps more significantly, his uncompromising commitment to faithful interpretation ultimately reveals and confirms his conviction regarding Scripture as divine revelation. Maclaren's reverence for God's Word and the preacher's corresponding responsibility to handle it properly (2 Tim 2:15) undoubtedly served as the primary building blocks in the theological foundation of his preaching.

Gospel Transformation

While his commitment to the Scriptures as divine revelation established the foundation for his devotion to biblical exposition, Maclaren also operated under the theological conviction that the gospel had the power to transform lives. As Nicoll noted, "All the wisdom of the world was to him contained in the Bible, but his business was to apply the Bible to life and his whole effort was to bring Bible truth into effective contact with the human heart."[28] The ministerial and social context in which he lived cemented this conviction even further and helps explain his attention to contemporary relevance in his sermons.

The political, social, and intellectual advancements of the nineteenth century are, in many ways, unparalleled in human history. The rapid and wide-ranging progress of the time affected every aspect of culture, including religion and preaching.[29] And yet Maclaren's preaching seemed, in large part, to be free from its influence. His expositions avoided the popular trend of biblical criticism that became so common in his day, and his sermons rarely addressed the cultural plagues that enamored other preachers. This differentiated him from many of his contemporaries who were often eager to address the social and political controversies.[30]

He explicitly summarized his understanding of a preacher's social impact, "I have been so convinced that I was best serving all the varied social, economical,

26. Dargan, *History of Preaching*, 576.
27. Maclaren, *Expositions of Holy Scripture*, xiii.
28. Maclaren, *Expositions of Holy Scripture*, xii–xiii.
29. Dargan, *History of Preaching*, 350.
30. Atkins, *Best of Alexander Maclaren*, x.

and political interests that are dear to me by preaching what I conceived to be the gospel of Jesus Christ, that I have limited myself to that work."[31] In other words, he was concerned about moral and social issues, but he put no confidence in social institutions or their ability to change people and the culture. He believed that social righteousness would derive from the power of the gospel to produce personal holiness. If individuals were spiritually transformed, then society would be as well. If Christians would submit to the demands of the gospel, social evils would disappear.[32] As a result, Maclaren grounded his preaching in the biblical text and applied it to the lives of his hearers, both as Christians and as citizens.[33]

This is where the pragmatic elements of his sermons became so distinct. Maclaren saturated his messages with personal applications for everyday Christians called to engage their culture.[34] Maclaren's consistent inclusion of application reflects his understanding of the Christian's role in society. But it also reveals the underlying theological premise that he believed in the life-transforming power of the gospel. Therefore, he did not have to be a political or social activist; he could focus on preaching and applying God's Word, trusting the Lord to work through it to transform people, and in turn their culture.[35] Ernest Jeffs in his *Princes of the Modern Pulpit* recalls Maclaren's mixture of application within his expositions well: "The charm of Maclaren's preaching was intellectual and artistic. It lay in the logical closeness and firmness of his exposition, the architectural culmination of proof and argument, the warmth and richness of his metaphor and illustration; and under all this was the stern challenge to righteousness and repentance, bringing into the sunshine, so to speak, when the emphasis changes from the God who judges to the Jesus who redeems."[36]

The Preacher's Holiness

Maclaren's conviction regarding the power of the gospel to transform culture stemmed from the personal testimony of his own transformed life. He believed strongly in God's ability to use those who are "instruments for special purposes, made holy, useful to the Master" (2 Tim 2:21). As a result, he was

---

31. Pattison, *History of Christian Preaching,* 344–45.
32. Fant and Pinson, *20 Centuries of Great Preaching,* 5:5.
33. Ibid., 5:6.
34. Ibid., 5:10.
35. Leslie Keylock quotes Maclaren's deeper thoughts relative to a Christian's cultural interaction and his role in preaching to equip them for engagement. She records Maclaren's words in "Maclaren: In Christ, in Peace, in Hope": "If Christian people think that they have done all their duty, in regard of clamant and common inquiries, by simply abstaining from them and presenting a noble example, they have yet to learn one very important chapter of their duty. . . . For Christ has sent us here in order, amongst other things, that we may bring Christian principles to bear upon the actions of the community, and not be afraid to speak when we are called upon by conscience to do so." (57)
36. John Pitts, "Alexander Maclaren: Monarch of the Pulpit," *Christianity Today* (5 June 1964): 8.

firmly committed to his own spiritual growth and intimacy with Christ and challenged other preachers with this truth. "I have always found that my own comfort and efficiency in preaching have been in direct proportion to the depth of my daily communion with God. I have no way in which we can do our work but in fellowship with God, in keeping up the habits of the student's life, which needs some power of saying 'No' and by conscientious pulpit preparation. The secret of success is trust in God and hard work." [37]

In his later reflection on his ministry, he still esteemed this trait as essential for faithful preaching. "No man will ever be the Lord's prophet, however eloquent or learned he may be, unless he knows what it is to sit silent before God and in the silence to hear the still, small, most mighty Voice that penetrates the soul." [38]

Maclaren was not simply an advocate for personal holiness; he was the embodiment of it. In the pulpit, "His sermons show how his heart and mind were anchored on essential Christian truth." [39] Maclaren explained his convictions regarding a preacher's personal devotion to Scripture and its impact on his preaching: "The preacher who has steeped himself in the Bible will have a clearness of outlook which will illuminate many dark things, and a firmness of touch which will breed confidence in him among his hearers. He will have the secret of perpetual freshness, for he cannot exhaust the Bible. . . . Our sufficiency is in God, and God's sufficiency will be ours in the measure in which we steadfastly follow out the purpose of making our preaching truly biblical." [40]

Not only did his personal holiness draw him close to his beloved Savior and position him as a useful instrument in the hand of God, it also solidified his personal reputation and credibility as a preacher. His character was widely regarded as one of "singular purity, depth, simplicity, and humility." [41] This enhanced his pulpit ministry as God used his personal life as a testimony to corroborate the truth of the Scriptures and the power of the gospel. As Dargan observed, "Of course, he had his faults, but these were not such as to damage the effect of his public work. His beautiful home life, his delightful friendship, his fidelity in his charge, all supported his public ministry." [42] As a result of his devotion to personal holiness and the ensuing credibility as God's messenger, Maclaren's preaching continued to grow in prominence and influence.

---

37. Larsen, *Company of the Preachers*, 580.
38. Fant and Pinson, *20 Centuries of Great Preaching*, 5:10. Maclaren originally stated this as part of an address to Baptist and Congregational Unions in London in 1901. Fant and Pinson cite it from *The Baptist Handbook of 1902.*
39. Dargan, *History of Preaching*, 576.
40. Fant and Pinson, *20 Centuries of Great Preaching*, 5:7.
41. Dargan, *History of Preaching*, 575.
42. Ibid., 575–76.

Ultimately, his conviction regarding the consecration of the preacher, his commitment to Scripture as divine revelation, and his faith in the transforming power of the gospel combined to establish the theological core of Maclaren's preaching.

METHODOLOGY FOR PREACHING

Maclaren's proficiency as an expositor and his skilled application of the Scriptures emerged from his unwavering doctrinal convictions. But the most daunting part of the interpretive task is determining an application of the sacred text that is both appropriate to the world of the listener and yet accurate to the original meaning of the passage. Maclaren consistently demonstrated an ability to preserve this hermeneutical balance. His fidelity to the biblical text *and* commitment to contemporary relevance provide contemporary preachers with the opportunity to develop a model for textual application through careful analysis of his expositions. By examining portions of Maclaren's sermons in each of the four primary biblical genres (Hebrew narrative, prophecy, gospel, and epistle),[43] the influence of his theological convictions on his methodology for applying various biblical texts can be observed. More important, his approach can serve as a foundational model for contemporary preachers.

Hebrew Narrative

According to Maclaren, the narrative genre deserves special attention from the expositor for interpretation and application because of the Divine Author's choice to use narrative as one of his primary means of self-disclosure throughout his Word. The prominence and nature of the narrative genre, particularly Hebrew narrative, provides greater opportunity for errors in textual application. Maclaren's approach to applying Hebrew narrative demonstrates possible ways some pitfalls in applying narratives can be avoided and provides some helpful examples for the proper application of Hebrew narrative texts.

His exposition of the creation account in Genesis 1:26–2:3 is one such example. Here, Maclaren clearly considers the intention of the original author for the historical audience in his early definition of the purpose of the text. He stated, "We are not to look to Genesis for a scientific cosmogony. . . . Its purpose

---

43. The four biblical genres evaluated here are the same four genres that Sidney Greidanus considers in his recognized preaching work *The Modern Preacher and the Ancient Text* (Downers Grove, IL: InterVarsity, 1988). Primarily, these were chosen because of the universality of their recognition as biblical genres and their corresponding frequent treatment by biblical scholars. Also, they represent some of the broadest extremes in terms of their distinction as literary genres from one another. Finally, by no means is this a comprehensive description or analysis of Maclaren's application from the various genres, but they serve the purpose of illustrating the differences in interpreting and applying various genres.

is quite another, and far more important; namely, to imprint deep and ineffaceable the conviction that the one God created all things. Nor must it be forgotten that this vision of creation was given to people ignorant of natural science."[44] For Maclaren, the identification of the original purpose of the text always provided the initial boundaries for the contemporary applications that can be drawn.

One example that aptly demonstrates Maclaren's approach to narrative texts is found in his treatment of Achan's sin in Joshua 7:1–12. A notable strength of Maclaren's method in preaching narrative texts was the way he maintained the original format of the text by telling the story. Maclaren allowed the power of the narrative drama to impact his listeners in the way it would have affected the original recipients of the text. Maclaren then proceeded to identify "general lessons" that could be derived from the salient points of the narrative.

The transition to application is obvious in Maclaren's exposition through the rhetorical question, "What lessons are taught here?" Yet Maclaren did not make application through contemporary metaphor, allegory, or character association like many preachers do today. Largely, the applications of the text are derived from the theological truths that were the primary intention of the original author. Maclaren cleverly used language that associates the historical text with the contemporary hearer, but clearly focused on the character and activity of God as the basis for application. He challenged, "God's soldiers must be pure. . . . It is true today, and will always be true, that the victories of the Church are won by its holiness far more than any gifts or powers of the mind, culture, wealth, eloquence, or the like." He continued, "If Christian effort seems ever fruitless, the first thing to do is to look for the 'Babylonish garment' and the glittering shekels hidden in our tents. . . . Our success depends on God's presence, and God's presence depends on our keeping his dwelling-place holy."[45]

For the most part, the theological nature of Maclaren's application of narrative texts was admittedly general in relation to the details of people's lives. However, when Maclaren made specific application through the identification of particular sins and situations, it is important to note the fidelity to the text that he maintained. For example, in consideration of the current exposition on Achan's sin, Maclaren identified the sin as covetousness and addressed its contemporary manifestations within the church.[46] This further demonstrates Maclaren's unwavering commitment to honor the original author's intentions in the modern-day application of the text.

---

44. Alexander Maclaren, *Expositions of Holy Scripture: Volume 1, Genesis to 1 Samuel* (Grand Rapids: Eerdmans, 1959), 1.

45. Ibid., 150.

46. Ibid., 152.

Ultimately, Maclaren consistently applied Hebrew narratives by maintaining the structure of the story, making specific applications that corresponded to the details of the text, and avoiding the common pitfalls of principlization by making application theologically oriented and Christ-centered. Maclaren's model of handling narrative texts provides some guidelines for contemporary preachers. When determining application for the genre of Hebrew narrative, the expositor must locate the application in the author's intended relevance for the original audience in order to accurately apply the textual truths. Specifically related to Hebrew narrative, the preacher must guard against ignoring the literary form and the corresponding implications of revelation through narrative, recognizing the theocentric purpose of narrative accounts.[47] Additionally, expositors of Hebrew narrative must guard against anthropocentric application and must explain and apply the textual truth through a christocentric understanding.

Prophecy

In approaching prophetic texts, preachers must recognize that the fundamental nature of prophecy is not the prediction of future events, but, rather, it is the declaration of God's message to God's people. Some preachers struggle with applying prophecy based on flawed assumptions. As Osborne observes, "Since Old Testament prophecy was given to a culture long passed from the scene, many assume that it no longer speaks to our day. Nothing could be further from the truth."[48] Instead, as Greidanus notes, "Prophetic literature openly declares its immediate relevance by presenting itself as preaching."[49]

Maclaren recognized the immediate relevance of prophetic texts and provides some helpful examples for applicational guidelines. One example is Amos 5:4–15. Here, Amos communicated a message from the sovereign Lord to Israel. Maclaren established the relationship between the recipients of the original message and the contemporary listeners by providing a brief description of the historical context in which Amos ministered and by drawing a contemporary comparison. Maclaren stated, "If one fancies a godly Scottish Highlander sent to the West end of London, or a Bible-reading New England farmer's man sent to New York's 'upper-ten,' one will have some notion of this prophet, the impressions made, and the task laid on him. He has a message to our state of society which, in many particulars, resembles that which he had to rebuke."[50]

---

47. Greidanus, *Modern Preacher*, 216.
48. Grant Osborne, *The Hermeneutical Spiral* (Downer's Grove, IL: InterVarsity Press, 1991), 219.
49. Greidanus, *Modern Preacher*, 228.
50. Maclaren, *Expositions of Holy Scripture*, 4:157.

In drawing the parallel between Amos's historical context and his own contemporary setting, Maclaren established the bridge for the contemporary relevance of Amos's message. This fundamental truth is not dependent on the cultural specifics, such as "a tax on their grain" and "pleasant vineyards," but can be directly transferred to the present-day audience. However, Maclaren did not rest on this contextual parallel as a determining factor for application, since it cannot always be drawn. Instead, Maclaren focused much of his attention on the theological truths that transcend culture and time, while he identified the specific historical and contemporary relevance.

Perhaps the best example of this prudent practice is his comments on Amos's charge to seek the Lord. Maclaren explained the historical significance and the contemporary implications, stating:

> Amos's first call to Israel is but the echo of God's to men, always and everywhere. All circumstances, all inward experiences, joy and sorrow, prosperity and disaster, our longings and our fears, they all cry aloud to us to seek his face. That loving invitation is ever sounding in our ears. And the promise which Amos gave, though it may have meant on his lips the continuance of national life only, yet had, even on his lips, a deeper meaning, which we now cannot but hear in it. For, just as to 'seek the Lord' means more to us than it did Israel, so the consequent life has greatened, widened, deepened into life eternal. But Amos's narrower, more external promise is true still, and there is no surer way of promoting true well-being than seeking God. . . . The fundamental principle of Amos's teaching is an eternal truth, that to seek God is to find Him, and to find Him is life.[51]

The important aspects of this quote summarize the necessary elements of textual application from prophetic texts. Maclaren considered the immediate context of Amos and did not alter the original meaning in the slightest. In fact, he demonstrated the contemporary relevance of Amos's message as it is.

However, Maclaren also identified a deeper understanding of Amos's words that can now be applied as a result of further revelation. This type of interpretation does not seek to change the original meaning, but sheds more light on the transcendent truths through additional revelation that is grounded in Scripture and Christ himself. Beyond the faithfulness to Amos's original intention, Maclaren's emphasis on a christocentric understanding for the contemporary audience is also vital for faithful interpretation and application.

---

51. Ibid., 158.

One final characteristic of Maclaren's application of a prophetic text that pronounces the Word of the Lord is the nature of the specific applications he identifies. Maclaren did not limit himself to general theological propositions, but in fact named specific areas of life in which the text applied. He made additional application comments on the text, stating, "The second part gives a vivid picture of the vices characteristic of a prosperous state of society which is godless, and therefore selfishly luxurious. First, civil justice is corrupted, turned into bitterness, and prostrated to the ground. Then bold denouncers of national sins are violently hated. Do we not know that phase of an ungodly and rich society?"[52]

Notice that the essence of the application is not generically found in the similarity of the social context as it may first appear. Amos's message is transferable because the specific sins he addresses still existed among Maclaren's contemporary listeners, not because they lived in generally similar societies. Furthermore, Maclaren limited his identification of the points of application to that which Amos named specifically.

Maclaren demonstrated an effective approach to applying prophetic texts that can also provide the foundations of a model for application. As contemporary preachers attempt to determine the practical relevance of prophetic texts, the guiding principles specifically related to this genre include the intentional form of the message, the common audience of God's covenant people—Israel and the church—and the theocentric nature of prophecy. And perhaps most significant in Maclaren's application of prophetic texts is that his christological interpretation of the individual passage not only provides the contemporary bridge for the church, but allows for a more comprehensive understanding of the original author's intent. With proper understanding of these, and through the effective example of Maclaren, appropriate contemporary application can be identified from prophetic passages.

Gospel

Interpreting the gospel genre presents many unique challenges because it contains a number of other genres.[53] However, the expositor must recognize the existence of subgenres and that their proper interpretation requires their governance by the overall literary genre. The difficulty of a precise understanding of the multidimensional nature of the gospel genre poses significant hurdles. Since Christ's parables and teachings within the Gospels often state their teaching purpose, considering the narrative genre within the Gospels can help us identify Maclaren's approach to applying passages in the Gospels.

---

52. Ibid., 160.
53. Greidanus, *Modern Preacher,* 264.

Maclaren demonstrated some similarities to his handling of Hebrew narratives when handling narrative texts within the gospel genre. One such trait is the emphasis on the power of story to communicate a message. As part of the sermon, Maclaren vividly and accurately described the historical events to effectively identify the original author's purpose. Of course, this precision required consideration of the historical and literary contexts, which Maclaren also included as part of the message. Maclaren also made theological applications in both the gospel and Hebrew narratives. Both of these traits combined with some other unique principles to guide application for the contemporary hearer.

Maclaren's exposition of the gradual healing of the blind man in Mark 8:22–25 provides an example of his application of narratives within the gospel. Although the similarity with Hebrew narratives of story and context help Maclaren to identify the original author's intent, there is another trait that is unique to the gospel narrative accounts that serves as the final determiner of meaning. Maclaren's method demonstrates that the expositor must consider Jesus's intent and purpose of the miracle to ultimately determine the contemporary applications.

Commenting on this unique miracle of Jesus, Maclaren posed the rhetorical question, "What is the meaning, and what the reason, and what the lessons of this unique and anomalous form of miraculous working?"[54] This question created intrigue in the heart of the listener and the answer gave further insight into his method of application. He continued, "For I think that the answer will open up to us some very precious things in regard to that great Lord, the revelation of whose heart and character is the inmost and the loftiest meaning of both his words and his works."[55]

Obviously, Maclaren's application of gospel narratives centered on the character of Christ, from which contemporary relevance can be drawn for the believer in any age. Some of the implications are the result of a Christian's responsibility to emulate Christ. In commenting on Jesus's isolation of the blind man prior to healing him, Maclaren noted, "Is there not in it . . . a lesson for all you good-hearted Christian men and women, in all your work? If you want to do anything for your afflicted brethren, there is only one way to do it—to come down to their level and get hold of their hands, and then there is some chance of doing them good. We must be content to take the hands of beggars if we are to make the blind see."[56]

But the emulation of Christ is not the only practical implication Maclaren draws from the miracle. Maclaren also made application for the hearer that

---

54. Maclaren, *Expositions of Holy Scripture*, 5:318–19.
55. Ibid., 319.
56. Ibid., 322.

associated them with the object of Jesus's affection. It is important to observe that Maclaren did not spiritualize the nature of the miracle for the sake of application. Maclaren honored the historical text by allowing the physical act to be a physical healing, and at the same time was able to draw appropriate and faithful implications from the character Jesus demonstrates.

Therefore, for narrative texts within the gospel genre, Maclaren adopted his characteristic principles for Old Testament narrative texts, including the consideration of historical and literary contexts, form, and theological significance. Yet the distinctive nature of the Gospels as historical accounts of the life of Jesus that communicate his character and person through his work result in unique principles. Consequently, the heart of Jesus that is demonstrated through his life events and miracles is the ultimate determiner of application for the contemporary hearer. This allows direct transfer and relevance of the gospel narratives through the character of Christ that is "the same yesterday and today and forever" (Heb 13:8), and thus is applicable in the life of the believer in any stage of history.

Maclaren's interpretation and application of the gospel genre continue to demonstrate an effective approach to determining contemporary relevance while maintaining fidelity to the biblical text. Furthermore, his clear method provides a helpful model for contemporary preachers to identify and implement his expositional approach with practical application. Obviously, listeners must be challenged with direct responses to Christ's teaching. But, in addition, the gospel accounts display the heart and character of Christ as the ideal for all believers to emulate. Contemporary scholars recognize this same principle. As Greidanus asserts, "The relevance of a sermon on the Gospels is given already in the fact . . . that the Gospels relate the story of the Founder and Lord of the church. That relevance is enhanced by the fact that the Gospels as a whole as well as in their parts are open-ended and include Christians today."[57] He goes on to summarize this approach in opposition to common mistakes that should be avoided: "When one sees the real relevance of the Gospels, one will no longer need to establish it by questionable means such as enjoining the listeners to imitate or shun the behavior of the minor characters, or by moralizing, psychologizing, or spiritualizing. The relevance of the Gospels is given in the revelation of Jesus Christ, our Savior and Lord."[58]

These aspects of sermon application from the gospel genre are embodied by Maclaren's examples and can be employed by the contemporary expositor.

---

57. Greidanus, *Modern Preacher,* 308.
58. Ibid.

Epistle

While narrative is the most extensively used genre in the Bible, the most prominent in the New Testament is unquestionably the epistle genre. The genre of epistle includes twenty-one of the twenty-seven books in the New Testament, which makes the principles for preaching and applying the Epistles crucial for the contemporary expositor. An advantage of the epistle genre over some of the others is its single historical horizon of the letter's author addressing the early church.[59]

This benefit of a more direct transference from the historical setting to the contemporary setting is reflected in Maclaren's expositions. Throughout his expositions of the Epistles, the first person plural pronoun is ubiquitous. This is a result of Maclaren's association of the contemporary church with the early churches to which the letters were originally addressed. Maclaren also noted the similarities between the present-day cultures and the historical context of the letters, their authors, and their recipients. But other application principles are observable in his expositions. For example, in Maclaren's exposition of Philippians 3:8–9, he does not focus as much on the similarities of the historical and contemporary cultural contexts as much as the common nature of contemporary and historical believers.

Initially, Maclaren affirmed the theological truths of the text and explained them in full. As in all of his expositions, his comments are informed by the surrounding literary context. The contextual understanding elucidates the meaning of the preaching passage he chose. His explanation of the theological truths of the text was clear and concise. For example, in commenting on verse nine, Maclaren explained, "To seek after a righteousness which is 'my own,' is to seek what we shall never find, and what, if found, would crumble beneath us. To seek the righteousness which is from God, is to seek what He is waiting to bestow, and what the blessed receivers blessedly know is more than they dreamed of."[60]

It is important to recognize that even in the explanation of the text, Maclaren used first person plural pronouns that automatically associated his audience with the original author and audience of the text. This direct association enabled him to then identify specific application that the theological truth of the text required, exhorting, "There must be the constant abandonment of self, and the constant utilising of the grace given."[61]

One other point of interest in Maclaren's application of epistle texts is the nature of his text selection. Maclaren frequently chose one verse or even a portion of a verse to expound. This was particularly important to the issue of application as it presented the danger of misinterpretation and, consequently, misapplication.

---

59. Ibid., 311.
60. Maclaren, *Expositions of Holy Scripture*, 9:333.
61. Ibid., 9:333–34.

Maclaren effectively guarded against this danger by maintaining a constant awareness of the literary context of the verse. Most important to his text selection, Maclaren often focused on expounding the application of a verse. Since Maclaren included verses in the surrounding context in the explanatory portions of the sermon, the passage's relevance was never accomplished at the expense of context.

The epistle genre is perhaps the simplest of the genres to determine application as a result of the single horizon of the audience of the church. However, its simplicity should neither be mistaken for ease nor the absence of potential error. The application must be derived from the text and is not open-ended in terms of possibilities, but is limited by the purpose of the original author and is most effective when it aligns with the identical application of the original audience. Even though Maclaren identified specific applications that derive from the text, he also recognized that an attempt to be too specific could lead to possible infidelity. Ultimately, the relevance as it relates to the epistle must focus on the continuity of a faithful covenant God, the purpose of the passage, analogies between then and now, principle and practice, and the address of the whole person.[62]

CONTRIBUTIONS TO PREACHING

The life and ministry of Alexander Maclaren left an indelible mark on his generation. The beautiful blend of textual exposition and contemporary relevance is perhaps the most significant contribution Maclaren made to the field of preaching. Contemporary relevance was not an option for Maclaren, as it permeated every aspect of his preaching. In addition, Maclaren always determined the practical relevance of a text in light of theological truth. He avoided anthropocentric application that focused on people's efforts or attempts. Instead, he let the propositional nature of Scripture govern people's response. More specifically, and finally, Maclaren applied the various biblical genres through a christological understanding of humanity, sin, grace, and the church.

Today's preachers can learn from faithful expositors of history such as Alexander Maclaren. The recognition of Maclaren's expositional skill combined with the relevant preaching acclaimed by the people of his day endorse Maclaren as an excellent example of how contemporary application may be made without violating the text's meaning. Through his masterful blend of hermeneutics and homiletics, his preaching continues to impact generations of preachers. Through his example, may we all grow in our ability to be faithful to the biblical text by proclaiming its timeless truths with relevant application.

---

62. Ibid., 9:336–39.

Sermon Excerpt

Light at Eventide (2 Timothy 4:1–5)[63]

The master's eye makes diligent servants; the tremendous issues for speaker and hearer suspended on the preaching of the gospel, if they were ever burning before our inward vision, would make superfluous all opportunity and power. How we should preach and teach and live if the great white throne and He who will sit on it were ever shining before us! Would not that sight burn up slothfulness, cowardice, perfunctory discharge of duty, mechanical repetition of scarcely felt words, and all other selfishnesses and worldlinesses which sap our earnestness in our work? . . . But the general work of "preaching the word" is to be accompanied with special care over the life of believers, which is to be active in three closely connected forms. Timothy is, where needful, to "convict" of sin; for so the word rendered "reprove" means, as applied to the mission of the Comforter in John xvi.8. "Rebuke" naturally follows conviction, and exhortation, or, rather, consolation or encouragement, as naturally follows rebuke. If the faithful teacher has sometimes to use the lancet, he must have the balm and the bandage at hand. And this triple ministry is to be "with all longsuffering" and "teaching." . . . Healthful teaching is distasteful. Men's ears itch, and want to be tickled. The desire of the multitude is to have teachers who will reflect their own opinions and prejudices, who will not go against the grain or rub them the wrong way, who will flatter the mob which calls itself the people, and will keep "conviction" and "rebuke" well in the background. That is no reason for any Christian teacher's being cast down, but is a reason for his buckling to his work, and not shunning to declare the whole counsel of God. The true way to front and conquer these evil tendencies is by the display of an unmistakable self-sacrifice in the life, by sobriety in all things and willing endurance of hardship where needful, and by redoubled earnestness in proclaiming the gospel, which men need whether they want it or not, and by filling to the full the sphere of our work, and discharging all its obligations. ◆

---

63. Maclaren, *Expositions of Holy Scripture*, 10:96–98.

BIBLIOGRAPHY

Atkins, Gaius G., ed. *The Best of Alexander Maclaren*. Manchester: Ayer Composition, 2002.

Cotterell, Peter and Max Turner. *Linguistics and Biblical Interpretation*. Downers Grove, IL: InterVarsity Press, 1989.

Dargan, Edwin Charles. *A History of Preaching*. 2 vols. Grand Rapids: Baker, 1968.

Estes, Daniel J. "Audience Analysis and Validity in Application." *Bibliotheca Sacra* (1993): 219–29.

Fant, Clyde E., Jr., and William M. Pinson Jr. *20 Centuries of Great Preaching: Volume 5, 1826–1912*. Waco, TX: Word, 1971.

Greidanus, Sidney. *The Modern Preacher and the Ancient Text*. Downers Grove, IL: InterVarsity Press, 1988.

Keylock, Leslie R. "Alexander Maclaren: In Christ, in Peace, in Hope." *Fundamentalist Journal* 8, no. 1 (January 1989): 56–58.

Larsen, David L. *The Company of the Preachers*. Grand Rapids: Kregel, 1998.

Maclaren, Alexander. *A Year's Ministry: First Series*. New York: Funk & Wagnalls, 1902.

_____. *Counsels for the Study and Life*. Louisville: The Review & Expositor, 1925.

_____. *Expositions of Holy Scripture*. Edited by W. Robertson Nicoll. 11 vols. Grand Rapids: Eerdmans, 1959.

Maclaren, Elizabeth T. *Dr. Maclaren of Manchester: A Sketch*. London: Hodder & Stoughton, 1911.

Osborne, Grant R. *The Hermeneutical Spiral*. Downers Grove, IL: InterVarsity Press, 1991.

Pattison, T. Harwood. *The History of Christian Preaching*. Philadelphia: American Baptist, 1903.

Pitts, John. "Alexander Maclaren: Monarch of the Pulpit." *Christianity Today* 8 (5 June 1964): 7–9.

Vines, Jerry and David Allen. "Hermeneutics, Exegesis, and Proclamation." *Criswell Theological Review* (1987): 309–34.

Catherine Booth
Preacher of Holiness

ROGER J. GREEN

In 1829, Catherine Mumford (1829–1890) was born into a Christian family whose theological allegiance was to the teachings of John Wesley. Catherine reflected the biblical and Wesleyan vision of the Christian life and married William Booth who, in 1858, was ordained by the Methodist New Connexion Church. Catherine began her preaching in 1860 while William was still a Methodist minister. She was not ordained but believed that her authority to preach came from God through the Scriptures, as witnessed, for example, by several women in ministry in the New Testament and by the promise of Pentecost that "your sons and daughters will prophesy" (Acts 2:17). She was certain that she had been called by the Holy Spirit to preach. Her ministry of preaching lasted thirty years—through the founding of The Christian Mission in 1865 in London that evolved into The Salvation Army in 1878. Her preaching was matched by her administrative abilities, and she was known as the "Army Mother." Catherine Booth was an example to thousands of women who found their voices in preaching because she had the courage to following God's leading in her own life.

HISTORICAL BACKGROUND

Catherine Mumford, born on January 17, 1829, in Ashbourne, Derbyshire, England, was the daughter of Sarah and John Mumford.[1] She had only one sibling, John, and after his move to America, the family appeared to lose any meaningful contact with him. Catherine's Methodist mother was suspicious

---

1. There are several biographies of Catherine Booth. An older biography written by her son-in-law is Frederick de Latour Booth-Tucker, *The Life of Catherine Booth: The Mother of The Salvation Army*, 2 vols. (New York: Revell, 1892; London: The Salvation Army, 1892) and the abridged version, *The Short Life of Catherine Booth* (London: The Salvation Army, 1893; 1912). For a recent biography of Catherine Booth see Roger J. Green, *Catherine Booth: A Biography of the Cofounder of The Salvation Army* (Grand Rapids: Baker, 1996). See also Andrew M. Eason and Roger J. Green, *Settled Views: The Shorter Writings of Catherine Booth* (Lanham, MD: Lexington, 2017).

of education outside the home, and so Catherine received her early educational training within the home, concentrating on the Bible and Christian history.[2] Catherine read the entire Bible eight times by her twelfth birthday, and was therefore well acquainted with the biblical stories, the language of the Bible, and basic biblical doctrines as learned through Methodist theology.

The Mumford family eventually moved to London and there, in 1852, Catherine met a Methodist lay preacher by the name of William Booth. He had been reared in poverty in Nottingham. William's father died when he was thirteen, and he became the sole supporter of his mother and three sisters. He moved to London at the age of nineteen to find work and to preach. A mutual friend introduced William and Catherine. They were engaged in 1852 and married on June 16, 1855. This was the beginning of one of the great love stories of Victorian England.

It was in William's second Methodist New Connexion appointment, Gateshead, that Catherine had commenced her own preaching ministry in 1860. William had just finished his sermon on Pentecost Sunday and was prepared to pronounce the benediction. Catherine rose to her feet from the first row of pews and moved toward the pulpit. Catherine recounted the following incident:

> He stepped down to ask me, "What is the matter, my dear." I said, "I want to say a word." He was so taken by surprise, he could only say, "My dear wife wants to say a word," and sat down. He had been trying to persuade me to do it for ten years. I felt as if I were clinging to some human arm— and yet it was a Divine arm—to hold me. I just got up and told the people how it came about. I confessed, as, I think, everybody should, when they have been in the wrong and misrepresented the religion of Jesus Christ. I said, "I dare say many of you have been looking upon me as a very devoted woman, and one who has been living faithfully to God, but I have come to know that I have been living in disobedience, and to that extent I have brought darkness and leanness into my soul, but I promised the Lord three or four months ago, and I dare not disobey. I have come to tell you this, and to promise the Lord that I will be obedient to the heavenly vision."[3]

In retrospect, Catherine confessed that she did not at the time realize the results of that first step: "I never imagined the life of publicity and trial that it

---

2. See chapter 4, "Methodist and Holiness: Catherine Booth, William Cooke, and the Scriptures" in Timothy Larsen, *A People of One Book: The Bible and the Victorians* (Oxford: Oxford University Press, 2011).

3. "Our Army Mother's First Sermon," *All The World* (June 1897): 245. See also "Our Army Mother's First Sermon," *Harbor Light* (July 1899): 233; Booth-Tucker, *The Life of Catherine Booth*, 1:360–62; Green, *Catherine Booth: A Biography*, 135.

would lead me to, for I was never allowed to have another quiet Sabbath when I was well enough to stand and speak. All I did was to take the first step. I could not see in advance. But the Lord, as He always does when His people are honest with Him and obedient, opened the windows of heaven and poured out such a blessing that there was not room to contain it."[4]

John Larsson wrote that "Catherine never did things by halves. When within weeks of her giving her first sermon William Booth was taken ill, she fulfilled not only her own preaching engagements but also all of William's."[5]

And so began Catherine Booth's preaching ministry; a ministry that would last for nearly thirty years until her promotion to glory on October 4, 1890. Her last sermon was preached at the request of the renowned Dr. Joseph Parker, at the City Temple of London. Her authority for preaching came from the prompting of the Holy Spirit in her life. And the thousands who heard her preach recognized that authority.

As Catherine's reputation as a preacher grew, she was able to accept invitations to preach in churches of various denominations. Providentially, the most important invitation came in 1865 in London. During this time, Catherine moved to London and stayed with her parents, while William continued his preaching in the north. When William came to London again in 1865 to join Catherine, he found his way to the notorious section of London known as East London and joined a group of street evangelists who were conducting tent meetings in an unused Quaker burial ground. There William Booth found his destiny and he and Catherine began a ministry to the poor of East London that eventually was named The Christian Mission. That mission evolved into The Salvation Army in 1878.[6]

The Booths had three boys and five girls. One of the girls was physically challenged and so had to remain in the Booth home. However, the other girls were encouraged by both mother and father to use all the gifts God had bestowed upon them—including preaching—and those four women all had international preaching ministries with The Salvation Army in places as diverse as France, India, Canada, and the United States. The three daughters-in-law also became preachers. Their preaching ministries, along with various administrative gifts, placed the Booth women in the public sphere. One of the daughters, Evangeline Booth, followed her father and her brother Bramwell to become the General and international leader of The Salvation Army.

---

4. Booth-Tucker, *The Life of Catherine Booth,* 1:362.

5. John Larsson, *Those Incredible Booths* (London: Salvation Books, 2015), 22.

6. An excellent one-volume history is Frederick Coutts, *No Discharge in This War* (New York: The Salvation Army, 1974).

By the time of Catherine's death in 1890, The Salvation Army had opened work throughout Britain, Australia, New Zealand, India, Canada, the United States, and several European countries. Catherine, while she had no official officer rank and had never been ordained by any denomination, was recognized by her followers as the "Army Mother," and her authority came through her gifts of preaching, teaching, writing, and administration.

THEOLOGY OF PREACHING

Catherine was reared in the Methodist tradition that declared the authority of the Bible. Both The Christian Mission and The Salvation Army borrowed from Methodist doctrines as they constructed their own theological framework. A work entitled *Salvation Story* clearly states the following: "While their (Salvation Army Articles of Faith) origin is nowhere stated, their roots are clearly in the Wesleyan tradition. The articles bear a striking similarity in words and content to Methodist New Connexion doctrines, which can be traced back to at least 1838. William Booth was an ordained minister of the New Connexion, whose founders claimed their doctrine to be 'those of Methodism as taught by Mr. Wesley.'"[7]

Authority of Scripture as the Authority for Women Preaching

In contrast to a growing criticism in the nineteenth century that questioned biblical authority, the first doctrine of The Christian Mission and The Salvation Army stated, "We believe that the Scriptures of the Old and New Testaments were given by inspiration of God and that they only constitute the Divine rule of Christian faith and practice."[8] The theological framework for Catherine Booth's preaching was clearly from her commitment to the authority of the Scriptures. She was a serious student of the Bible all her life and was attentive to the teachings of the Bible in her own life. "The result, not unexpectedly, was that Catherine routinely thought, spoke, and wrote in biblical language and patterns of thought."[9] Her sermons were scripturally based and frequently elaborated biblical doctrines.

While some questioned the legitimacy of a woman preaching the gospel, Catherine Booth would not be silenced. For her, women in ministry

---

7. *Salvation Story: Salvationist Handbook of Doctrine* (London: The Salvation Army International Headquarters, 1998), 130–31. See also Roger J. Green, "Doctrines: History" in John G. Merritt, ed., *Historical Dictionary of The Salvation Army* (Oxford: Scarecrow, 2006), 138–41.

8. *Salvation Story*, ix.

9. Larsen, *A People of One Book*, 90.

was a biblical principle, and the Bible gave her and other women the authority to preach. Her own authority to preach came from the Spirit of the Lord and not from some earthly source. She defended the right of women to preach even before she herself had begun preaching. In 1859, Phoebe Palmer, an American Methodist holiness teacher, was teaching in Britain near Gateshead where William Booth was ministering. A local preacher, Arthur Augustus Rees, publicly denounced women speaking in public. Catherine Booth wrote a pamphlet challenging Rees's opposition and there spelled out the biblical authority for women in ministry.[10]

Catherine was inspired by women who prophesied in the Old Testament, but found the height of women in ministry in the New Testament, with examples such as Mary Magdalene, the daughters preaching on the Day of Pentecost, and the several women mentioned in the New Testament who had various ministries, including preaching. And she was convinced that such passages as Galatians 3:28 provided biblical and theological justification for women in ministry. She wrote, "If this passage does not teach that in the privileges, duties, and responsibilities of Christ's Kingdom, all differences of nation, caste, and sex are abolished, we should like to know what it does teach, and wherefore it was written."[11] Catherine Booth saw this passage as dealing not only with the promise of salvation for all people, but also what life in Christ looks like as those who are saved labor for the kingdom. She outlined this in her pamphlet in 1859 and applied it to her own life and ministry when she began preaching in 1860. As Andrew Eason noted, "Catherine's scriptural arguments in this area were not unique, but they were framed in such a manner to give the practice a sound theological foundation. Furthermore, her contention that women had a *right* to preach the gospel was significant for her age, going beyond the rationale of other defenders of female ministry. Importantly, this language of rights found its way into The Christian Mission, which became The Salvation Army in 1878."[12]

Reared in the Wesleyan tradition, Catherine Booth surely had heard of women in ministry and now, secure in the knowledge that the Holy Spirit

---

10. This pamphlet, thirty-two pages in length, was first published in 1859 as *Female Teaching; or the Rev. A. A. Rees versus Mrs. Palmer, Being a Reply to a Pamphlet by the Above Named Gentleman on the Sunderland Revival* and was republished in London in 1861 by C. J. Stevenson. For the third edition, the title was changed to *Female Ministry; or Women's Right to Preach the Gospel* (London: Morgan & Chase, 1870), a title that reflected that this edition broadened Catherine's theology of ministry beyond the original controversy to the ministry of the growing Christian Mission. It was this edition that was reprinted in several of Catherine's writings and by The Salvation Army in the twentieth century.

11. Catherine Booth, *Female Ministry*, 19. Her arguments from the Galatians passage in this third edition are more cogently presented than in the original pamphlet entitled *Female Teaching*.

12. Andrew Mark Eason, *Women in God's Army: Gender and Equality in the Early Salvation Army* (Waterloo, ON: Wilfrid Laurier University Press, 2003), 153–54.

empowers both men and women in ministry, Catherine Booth became a preacher.[13] She might not have done so had she developed a more reserved personality, but Catherine Booth had settled views on many matters and fearlessly argued those views. The phrase "settled views" became common in Catherine's writing and preaching. For example, writing to William Booth before their marriage, while defending the equality of women with men, she admonished William: "Let me advise *you*, my Love, to get settled views on this subject and be able to render a *reason* to every caviller [sic], and *then* fearlessly incite *all* whom you believe the *Lord* has *fitted* to help you in your Master's work, male or female, Christ has given them no *single talent* to be hid in a napkin, and yet oh what thousands are wrapped up and buried, which used and improved would yield 'some thirty, some sixty, yea and some an *hundred* fold.'"[14]

No settled views were more important than women in ministry, and Catherine rose to the challenge and defended the biblical authority for her own preaching as well as the preaching of any woman who felt called by God. [15]

Christian Holiness

Catherine's theological emphasis in her preaching focused on holiness more than any other doctrine. She believed this was central to the gospel message. Her learning of the message of holiness came from her upbringing in a Wesleyan home and was confirmed as she heard the preaching and teaching of American Methodists such as James Caughey and Phoebe Palmer as well as the like-minded holiness preacher Charles Grandison Finney. Catherine's preaching on holiness often began with an exposition of the sin that has dominated the human heart since the fall of humanity, and the need for believers to have the assurance that they are delivered from sin at the time of their conversion. However, that is only the beginning of the Christian pilgrimage, and sanctification by faith moves beyond justification and saves the believer from continual and deadly sin.

John Wesley, in the previous century, had been reared in the Anglican tradition, was trained at Oxford University, and was an ordained priest in the Church of England.[16] He realized many Christians had an understanding of justification by faith, but he found that those same people had little awareness

---

13. See Paul Wesley Chilcote, *John Wesley and the Women Preachers of Early Methodism* (Metuchen, NJ: Scarecrow, 1991).

14. Booth Papers. Mss. 64802, The British Library. Andrew Eason and I recently published a book on Catherine Booth's writings and titled the book *Settled Views: The Shorter Writings of Catherine Booth*.

15. See Roger J. Green, "Settled Views: Catherine Booth and Female Ministry." *Methodist History* 31, no. 3 (April 1993): 131–47.

16. The most complete contemporary biography of John Wesley is Henry D. Rack, *Reasonable Enthusiast: John Wesley and the Rise of Methodism* (Philadelphia: Trinity Press International, 1989).

of growing in that faith, conforming to the image of Christ, and embracing the biblical doctrine of sanctification. For Wesley, this doctrine was central to his theology and was clearly communicated by Christ in Matthew 22:37–40, "'Love the Lord your God with all your heart and with all your soul and with all your mind.' This is the first and greatest commandment. And the second is like it: 'Love your neighbor as yourself.' All the Law and the Prophets hang on these two commandments."

This agape-centric understanding of sanctification was foundational for Wesley and was replicated in the life and theology of his disciples. Wesley often used the term *perfect love* to communicate his views on this topic. Wesleyan theologian Kenneth J. Collins has defined Wesley's doctrine of perfect love saying, "Entire sanctification or Christian perfection describes . . . the characteristics of holy love reigning in the human heart, a love that not only embraces the love of God and neighbor, but that also excludes all sin."[17] This is language with which Catherine Booth was not only familiar, but comfortable.[18]

As the Christian progresses and moves toward the restoration of the image of Christ in his or her life, there is the developing awareness that deliverance from sinning is a possibility, and that loving God and loving the neighbor becomes the hallmark of the believer. At the same time, however, Catherine understood that the freedom granted to humanity before the fall but lost after the fall was again restored through prevenient grace. Because every human being possesses such freedom, even the person filled with holy love can still turn against God and neighbor in sinning. However, she assured her listeners in the words of 1 John 1:9, "If we confess our sins, he is faithful and just and will forgive us our sins and purify us from all unrighteousness."

In a sermon appropriately entitled "The Perfect Heart," Catherine assured her readers that Christian perfection is possible—as perfection in loyalty to

---

17. Kenneth J. Collins, *The Theology of John Wesley: Holy Love and the Shape of Grace* (Nashville: Abingdon, 2007), 298.

18. Catherine Booth never contended for only one phrase that described holiness. She wrote, "It has been called, 'The second conversion,' 'The higher life,' 'The full assurance of faith,' 'Christian perfection'—to distinguish it from Adamic and angelic perfection—'Perfect love,' 'Inner sanctification,' 'The rest of faith.' We do not contend for names. The main point is this, that *the experience* designated by most of these terms amounts practically to the same thing, which is BEING SAVED FROM SIN. We care not what you call it so that you understand the blessing to mean that. I prefer to use God's terms in everything, and so I select His designations. I think the Holy Ghost understood best the ideas He wished to convey, and therefore I like the terms He has used such as sanctification, holiness, perfect love. However, we simply take what we like best and do not contend about them." Catherine Booth, *Holiness: Being an Address Delivered in St. James's Hall, Piccadilly, London* (London: International Headquarters, 1881), 7. For an analysis of the holiness theology of Catherine in the context of the early Salvation Army see R. David Rightmire, "'And the Holy Spirit fell upon them....' Transitions in Salvation Army Holiness Theology: A Historical Assessment" in Denis Metrustery, ed., *Saved. Sanctified and Serving: Perspectives on Salvation Army Theology and Practice* (Milton Keynes: Paternoster, 2016), 73–88.

God, perfection in obedience to God, and perfection in trusting God. She preached the following about such trusting: "Perhaps, that ought to have come first, for it is the very root of it all. Oh, how beautiful Abraham was in the eyes of God; how God glories over him. How do I know that Abraham had a perfect heart toward God? Because he trusted Him. No other proof—no less proof—would have been of any use. I dare say he was compassed with infirmities, had many erroneous views, manward and earthward, but his heart was perfect towards God."[19]

After Catherine convinced her listeners of sin, showed the way of redemption, and demonstrated the promises of God following salvation, she would press her message home and call her listeners to the higher life of holy love: "Oh! I have the most awful realization that you will be eternally better or worse for these services, and so I want you to come up higher. I don't want you to go back, and get cold and indifferent to these things, because here is the hope of the world, if there is any hope for it, in people getting filled with the Spirit, people getting so woke up to God and His glory, and the interests of His Kingdom, that they should be just as anxious for souls as other people are for sovereigns."[20]

METHODOLOGY FOR PREACHING

Harold Begbie was chosen by the Booth family to be the official biographer of William Booth. In the biography, he related an interesting story that captured the preaching style of Catherine Booth. Dr. Randall Davidson, who at the time was the chaplain to the archbishop of Canterbury and later himself the archbishop of Canterbury, often heard Catherine preach. He had "a very warm admiration for Catherine Booth, describing her as one of the most remarkable women he ever met."[21] On one occasion he went to Exeter Hall in London to hear Catherine preach and took his father with him. After the sermon, the elder Davidson turned to his son and said, "If ever I am charged with a crime, don't bother to engage any of the great lawyers to defend me; get that woman."[22]

Generally, Catherine Booth preached for about an hour and addressed the people like a lawyer. One of her spiritual mentors was Charles Grandison Finney, himself a trained lawyer. He used his skills as a lawyer when he preached, and Catherine Booth apparently preached in a similar style, as the comments

19. Catherine Booth, "The Perfect Heart" in *Godliness: Being Reports of a Series of Addresses Delivered at James's Hall, London, During 1881* (Boston: McDonald & Gill, 1883), 106–7.

20. Catherine Booth, "Filled with the Spirit" in *Aggressive Christianity: Practical Sermons by Mrs. Catherine Booth* (Boston: McDonald & Gill, 1883), 146–47.

21. Harold Begbie, *The Life of General William Booth* (New York: Macmillan, 1920), 2:26.

22. Ibid.

of Davidson demonstrate. For Catherine, the Scriptures contain nonnegotiable truths. On this she was settled and convinced that people should then agree, based on the authority of Scripture. This was confirmed by those who heard Catherine Booth preach. Soon after Catherine began her preaching ministry and while preaching in St. Ives in 1862, one eyewitness wrote that "the sermon was one of the most closely reasoned and logical discourses we have heard for a long time, and accustomed as we have been for many years to hard and close thinking, it was to us a refreshing and sanctifying discourse."[23] Elijah Cadman, an early leader in The Salvation Army, stated that "she was very sedate in speaking, but mightily convincing."[24] Daniel Steele, a leader in the American Methodist Holiness Movement who published many of Catherine Booth's sermons in America, related this story in his introduction to *Aggressive Christianity:* "My first knowledge of Mrs. Booth was obtained in 1880, from a letter of a straight-laced Presbyterian doctor of divinity, published in one of the organs of that denomination in New York. He had listened to all the celebrities in London, not excepting Spurgeon and Parker, but had heard no speaker who had moved him so deeply as a woman preaching in a hall in the West End of London. The woman was Mrs. Booth."[25]

While Catherine was preaching at Chatham in 1873, the *Chatham News* provided one of the few descriptions we have of Catherine's preaching: "Mrs. Booth possesses remarkable powers as a preacher. With a pleasing voice, distinct in all its tones, now colloquial, now persuasive, she can rise to the height of a great argument with an impassioned force and fervor that thrills her hearers. Quiet in her demeanor, her looks, her words, her actions are peculiarly emphatic. She can indeed 'suit the action to the word, the word to the action.' And yet there is no ranting—nothing to offend the most fastidious taste—but much to enchain the attention. 'The matter is full, the manner excellent.'"[26]

This was in keeping with Catherine's own definition of preaching. "What *is* preaching? Paul says it is 'Speaking to edification, exhortation, and comfort,' *not* mind, speaking to one's own satisfaction, with fluency, eloquence and demonstration!"[27]

As her preaching matured throughout nearly thirty years of ministry, her listeners would comment on her remarkable preaching power and her ability to present a very solemn argument. However, it was often noted that this was not

23. *The Revival*, no. 152 (19 June 1862): 231.
24. Catherine Bramwell-Booth, *Bramwell Booth* (London: Rich & Cowan, 1933), 194.
25. Daniel Steele, introduction to *Aggressive Christianity, by Catherine Booth* (Boston: McDonald & Gill, 1883), 8.
26. Quoted in Booth-Tucker, *The Life of Catherine Booth*, 2:65.
27. Bramwell-Booth, *Bramwell Booth*, 72.

merely a rhetorical device. Even the Unitarian Frances Power Cobbe wrote, "She has an immense store of sound sense and practical experience, combined with a genuinely high ideal of life and duty. After listening to her many times for hours together, I have found myself bringing away more fresh and sound ideas, and less 'padding,' than from any series of discourses it has been my fate to hear for many a day."[28]

That "high ideal of life and duty" is what attracted people to Catherine's preaching, as well as to her personally. People of every station in life sensed a sincerity in her preaching, and in this she conformed to Wesley's sense of sincerity as the foundation to all preaching. In his sermon entitled "On Corrupting the Word of God," Wesley said,

> Many have observed that nothing conduces more to a preacher's success with those that hear him than a generally good opinion of his sincerity. Nothing gives him a greater force of persuasion than this; nothing creates either greater attention in the hearers or a greater disposition to improve. When they really believe he has no end in speaking but what he fairly carries in view, and that he is willing they should see all the steps he takes for the attainment of that end, it must give them a strong presumption, both that what he seeks is good, and the method in which he seeks it.[29]

Catherine's advice to her eldest son, William Bramwell, signified this observation by Wesley. Writing to him on his nineteenth birthday she said, "I believe that if you were to *embrace* the vocation, and set yourself to live for it, preaching would become easy and natural to you."[30]

Catherine had the advantage of preaching both to the wealthy of the West End and to the poor who entered the doors of The Christian Mission in East London. Her message to all her listeners, however, was that of redemption in Christ. All have sinned, and the path of redemption has been provided by God through Christ. She encouraged the poor, reminding them that the favor of God reaches to them. And like Wesley before her, she "did not demur when preaching to the wealthy but condemned them for the sins attendant with their wealth—greed, selfishness, pride, or lack of concern for the poor and dispossessed of the world."[31]

---

28. Frances Power Cobbe, "The Last Revival," *The Contemporary Review* (August 1882): 185.

29. John Wesley, "On Corrupting the Word of God," in *The Works of John Wesley, Sermons*, ed. Albert C. Outler, 4 vols. (Nashville: Abingdon, 1987), 4:245.

30. Bramwell-Booth, *Bramwell Booth*, 67.

31. Green, *Catherine Booth: A Biography*, 273.

Catherine was not without her settled views on preaching, and her advice about preaching reflected her own theological commitments as well as her style of preaching. Catherine said, "We need men and women who are trained for the fight, not only people who have experienced a change of heart, but who are drilled in knowing how to use the weapons of the Spirit—knowing how to handle God's truth. . . . You must preach God's justice and vengeance against sin as well as His love for the sinner. You must preach hell as well as heaven."[32]

She was concerned about the method of preaching used by her Salvationists. She often gave this kind of advice: "One great qualification for successful labour is power to get the truth home to the heart. Not to *deliver* it. I wish the word had never been coined in connexion with Christian work. 'Deliver' it, indeed—*that* is not in the Bible. No, no; not to deliver it; but drive it home—send it in—make it *felt*. That is your work."[33]

Catherine followed her own advice; her sermons often began with a biblical text and a challenging title. A good example is her sermon entitled "Popular Christianity: Sham Compassion and the Dying Love of Christ." In that sermon, she confronted popular theological notions, demonstrating their flaws, and then moved on to biblical Christianity and the ideas that can be supported by biblical texts. Her sermons always ended with a challenge to the listeners to follow Christ in the ways outlined in the sermon. Her arguments were clear, her settled views were precisely stated, and her calls to commitment to Christ were compelling.

CONTRIBUTIONS TO PREACHING

Catherine Booth's contributions to the field of preaching were many, but two will be mentioned here. First, as has been stressed, throughout Catherine's nearly thirty-year ministry of preaching and writing, she provided justification for and an example of a woman who faithfully preached the gospel. Early in her preaching ministry, Catherine wrote in a letter to her parents, "I have every reason to think that the people receive me gladly everywhere, and that prejudice against female ministry melts away before me like snow in the sun."[34] Catherine's preaching ministry opened the door for women to serve in The Christian Mission and The Salvation Army—women in teaching ministries, administrative ministries, and missionary ministries. Because of Catherine's ministry, literally

---

32. "Mrs. Booth's Last Public Address (continued)," *The War Cry* (25 October 1890), 9. See also "Mrs. Booth at the City Temple," *The War Cry* (30 June 1888): 9.

33. Booth-Tucker, *The Life of Catherine Booth*, 2:546.

34. Booth Papers, The British Library, Mss. 64806, letter dated 1 April 1863.

thousands of women are using their gifts for the sake of Christ and his kingdom. This includes the women preachers in The Salvation Army and other denominations who have been encouraged by her example. The Army, although a relatively small denomination, ministers in 127 countries. And women in various ministries, including the preaching of the gospel, are prominent.

The second contribution to the field of preaching was her emphasis on the biblical and Wesleyan doctrine of holiness. Those had always been at the center of attention for both Catherine and William and their preachers and teachers in both The Christian Mission and The Salvation Army. But these two emphases—women in ministry and holiness of heart and life—are inextricably linked to each other. No scholar has done more admirable work in developing that relationship than Andrew Mark Eason in his book entitled *Women in God's Army: Gender and Equality in the Early Salvation Army*. The author carefully notes the nuances in the thinking of Catherine Booth, but gives credit to her for moving ahead in these two areas of influence. Eason writes the following:

> There has been no shortage of studies on the relationship between nineteenth-century evangelical women and the doctrine of holiness, and various historians have drawn attention to how an appreciation for the work of the Holy Spirit could lead to an expansion of women's roles in religious groups from Methodism to Pentecostalism. . . . This kind of empowerment could be seen in some degree in The Salvation Army as well. Catherine Booth, for instance, not only explained her own call to preach within the context of holiness, but also stressed the role of the Spirit in the public lives of the Army's Hallelujah Lasses. She believed that the power of the Holy Spirit helped to explain the success of these women, many of whom came from humble backgrounds.[35]

And so Catherine Booth, though promoted to glory, still speaks through the women who have followed her example to preach the gospel. Their authority to do so comes first from their understanding of the ministry of the Holy Spirit in their lives, providing the holy intention to fulfill their vocation. And secondly, such authority comes from the power of God to fulfill Jesus's commandment to love God and neighbor, and thereby the witness of their own lives of holiness of heart and life is what ultimately gives power to their preaching of the timeless gospel.

---

35. Eason, *Women in God's Army,* 87.

Sermon Excerpt

Addresses on Holiness in Exeter Hall, 1881[36]

I think it must be self-evident that it is the most important question that can possibly occupy the mind of man—how much like God we can be—how near to God we can come on earth preparatory to being perfectly like Him, and living, as it were, in His very heart for ever and ever in Heaven. Anyone who has any measure of the Spirit of God must perceive that this is the most important question on which we can concentrate our thoughts; and the mystery of mysteries to me is how anyone, with any measure of the Spirit of God, can help looking at this blessing of holiness and saying, "Well, even if it does seem too great for attainment on earth, it is very beautiful and very blessed. I wish I could attain it." That, it seems to me, must be the attitude of every person who has the Spirit of God—that he should hunger and thirst after it, and feel that he shall never be satisfied till he wakes up in the lovely likeness of his Saviour. And yet, alas! We do not find it so. In a great many instances the very first thing professing Christians do is to resist and reject this doctrine of holiness as if it were the most foul thing on earth.

I heard a gentleman saying a few days ago—a leader in one circle of religion—that for anybody to talk about being holy showed that they knew nothing of themselves and nothing of Jesus Christ. I said, "Oh, my God! It has come to something if holiness and Jesus Christ are at the antipodes of each other. I thought he was the centre and fountain of holiness. I thought it was in Him only we could get any holiness, and through Him that holiness could be wrought in us." But this poor man thought this idea to be absurd.

May God speak for Himself! Ever since I heard that sentiment I have been crying from the depths of my soul, "Lord, speak for Thyself; powerfully work in the hearts of Thy people and awake them. Take the veil from their eyes, and show them what Thy purpose in Christ Jesus concerning them is. Do not let them be bewildered and miss the mark; do not leave them, but Lord reveal it in their hearts." There is no other way by which it can be revealed, and, if you will let Him, He will reveal it in your heart. ♦

---

36. Booth, *Godliness*, 133–34.

BIBLIOGRAPHY

Primary Sources

Booth, Catherine. *Female Ministry; or Women's Right to Preach the Gospel.* London: Morgan & Chase, 1870.
_____. *Female Teaching: Or, the Rev. A. A. Rees versus Mrs. Palmer, Being a Reply to a Pamphlet by the Above Gentleman on the Sunderland Revival.* 2nd ed. London: Stevenson, 1861.
_____. *Holiness: Being An Address Delivered in St. James's Hall, Piccadilly, London.* London: International Headquarters, 1881.
_____. *Aggressive Christianity.* Boston: McDonald & Gill, 1883.
_____. *Godliness: Being Reports of a Series of Addresses Delivered at James's Hall, London, During 1881.* Boston: McDonald & Gill, 1883.
_____. *Popular Christianity.* Boston, MA: McDonald & Gill, 1887.
_____. *Practical Religion.* London: International Headquarters, 1891.
_____. *The Highway of Our God: Selections from the Army Mother's Writings.* London: Salvationist Publishing & Supplies, 1955.
_____. *Life and Death.* London: Salvationist Publishing & Supplies, n.d.

Secondary Sources

Booth-Tucker, Frederick. *The Life of Catherine Booth: The Mother of The Salvation Army.* 2 vols. London: International Headquarters of The Salvation Army, 1892.
Chilcote, Paul Wesley. *John Wesley and the Women Preachers of Early Methodism.* Metuchen, NJ: Scarecrow, 1991.
Eason, Andrew Mark. *Women in God's Army: Gender and Equality in the Early Salvation Army.* Waterloo, ON: Wilfrid Laurier University Press, 2003.
Eason, Andrew M. and Roger J. Green. *Settled Views: The Shorter Writings of Catherine Booth.* Lanham, MD: Lexington, 2017.
Green, Roger J. "Settled Views: Catherine Booth and Female Ministry." *Methodist History* 31, no. 3 (April 1993): 131–47.
_____. *Catherine Booth: A Biography of the Cofounder of The Salvation Army.* Grand Rapids: Baker, 1996.
_____. "Booth, Catherine Mumford (1829–1890)," Pages 30–31 in *Historical Dictionary of The Salvation Army.* Edited by John G. Merritt. Lanham, MD: Scarecrow, 2006.
Larsen, Timothy. *A People of One Book: The Bible and the Victorians* (Oxford: Oxford University Press, 2011).
Rightmire, R. David. "'And the Holy Spirit fell upon them. . . .' Transitions in Salvation Army Holiness Theology: A Historical Assessment." Pages 73–88 in *Saved, Sanctified and Serving: Perspectives on Salvation Army Theology and Practice.* Edited by Denis Metrustery. Milton Keynes: Paternoster, 2016.

Charles Haddon Spurgeon
The Prince of Preachers

THOMAS J. NETTLES

Remembered as the Prince of Preachers, Charles Spurgeon (1834–1892) ministered in Victorian England and had an impact reaching to the Americas and throughout Europe. In 1857, the editor of Spurgeon's works introduced him, saying, "The preaching of Mr. Spurgeon in London is one of the most remarkable phenomena of the present times. The loftiest and humblest minds, the rich and the poor, the titled and the lowly, in uncounted crowds, through the courts where he ministers, listen with rapture to his glowing words; hundreds are pricked to the heart, and God is honored in the conversion of sinners and the joy of his people."[1] Thirty-five years later, the final volume of his works claimed, "Church history will have to reckon Mr. Spurgeon as one of the greatest preachers of all times and of all climes. Such is his indefeasible heritage of fame as a preacher."[2]

HISTORICAL BACKGROUND

Charles Haddon Spurgeon was born in Kelvedon, Essex, on June 19, 1834. He was the first of seventeen children, eight of whom survived infancy.[3] Soon after Charles's birth, his parents, John and Eliza Spurgeon, moved to Colchester where John became clerk of a coal merchant and served as pastor of a Congregational church in Tollesbury, nine miles away. Each week John Spurgeon traveled there by horse and carriage to serve the congregation, and when Charles was fourteen months old and the birth of a second child was at hand, he was sent to live with his grandparents in Stambourne. His grandfather, James Spurgeon, served as

---

1. W. C. Wilkinson, introduction to volume 1 of *Sermons of Rev. C. H. Spurgeon*, 20 vols. (New York: Funk & Wagnalls, 1857–1892), 1:v. Volume 1 of this series was published in 1857. The series was distributed evenly through the years until Spurgeon's death.

2. The final volume consists of a biography: G. Holden Pike, *Charles Haddon Spurgeon: Preacher, Author, Philanthropist, with anecdotal reminiscences.* Hereinafter this will be referenced as *SS* followed by volume number and page. *SS*, 20:iv.

3. Portions of this chapter have been used with permission from my publication on Charles Spurgeon. Tom J. Nettles, *Living by Revealed Truth: The Life and Pastoral Theology of Charles Haddon Spurgeon* (Fearn, Scotland: Mentor, 2013).

pastor of the independent congregation in town. Ann, his seventeen-year-old aunt, also lived there at the time.

Charles stayed in Stambourne for four-and-a-half years, returning home to live with his parents in 1840, though he often returned to Stambourne for summer visits or vacations. One of the last books Spurgeon wrote was entitled *Memories of Stambourne*,[4] and it was written to show how small events often bear large fruit in one's life. In the book, Spurgeon reminisced about his impressions of life in the company of his grandparents, beginning what he later referred to as "the ingatherings of continual observation."[5] The book is filled with vivid, detailed memories. Spurgeon speaks about a rocking horse so steady that even a member of Parliament might retain his seat—the only horse Spurgeon ever enjoyed riding. He recalls his amazement at the number of windows darkened and closed off to avoid the penalties of a law that taxed each house according to its number of windows, leading him to wonder if Parliament owned the light. He remembered his grandmother and aunt putting cookies on the bottom shelf for "the child," a lesson that would later encourage him to make sweet doctrines just as accessible to his hearers.

Spurgeon was fascinated by the library that belonged to the manse—a room filled with Puritan volumes bound in "sheepskins and goat skins," including Foxe's *Book of Martyrs*. His reading of that book contributed to a lifelong impression that Roman Catholicism was oppressive. In the library, he also found Bunyan's *Pilgrim's Progress*, a book he read more than one hundred times and whose characters wander in and out of his sermons and writings. The existence of such a library at the manse impressed Spurgeon with the usefulness—even the necessity—of ministers having a good library. In a later lecture to his students, Spurgeon recalled his grandfather's library, writing, "A good library should be looked upon as an indispensable part of church furniture; and the deacons, whose business it is 'to serve tables,' will be wise if, without neglecting the table of the Lord, or of the poor, and without diminishing the supplies of the minister's dinner-table, they give an eye to his study-table, and keep it supplied with new works and standard books in fair abundance."[6]

---

4. Charles Spurgeon and Benjamin Beddow, *Memories of Stambourne* (London: Passmore & Alabaster, 1891). The material mentioned below is scattered throughout this work as well as Charles H. Spurgeon, *Autobiography*, 2 vols. (Edinburgh: Banner of Truth Trust, 1976), 1:3–31.

5. Charles Spurgeon, *Feathers for Arrows* (London: Passmore & Alabaster, 1870), vi.

6. Charles Spurgeon, *Lectures to My Students* (London: Passmore & Alabaster, 1881), 192. This was in Lecture XIII "To Workers with Slender Apparatus." Another volume of *Lectures* was published in 1881. *The Art of Illustration* was published in 1894, having been an unfinished manuscript at Spurgeon's death. *Commenting and Commentaries* was published in 1876 and by the publication of 1893 had reached fourteen thousand in circulation. All four of these volumes were printed as *Lectures to My Students* by Pilgrim Publications of Pasadena, Texas, in 1990. This will be cited as *Lectures* and volume number in order of the Pilgrim edition.

From an early age, young Charles showed a propensity for pastoral exhortation. Charles recalls hearing his grandfather fretting about Tom Roades, a church member who whiled away his time at the pub, so one afternoon the young Spurgeon took it upon himself to go to the pub and exhort Roades to stop hurting his pastor by his behavior. Charles returned to the house and announced, "I have killed old Roades." The quizzical James Spurgeon soon found a repentant Roades knocking at his door.

As a child, Charles's grandfather promised him a penny for each rat he would kill; his grandmother promised him the same reward for each hymn he would memorize. While killing rats was more immediately profitable, the memorization of hymns had significant long-term benefits. A scan of Spurgeon's sermons will reveal his pertinent use of the poetry and theological insight of many hymns. Among his often-used phrases you will find Cowper's "E'er since by faith I saw the stream Thy flowing wounds supply, redeeming love has been my theme and shall be till I die."[7] Toplady contributed "Nothing in my hand I bring, simply to Thy cross I cling"[8] as well as "Payment God cannot twice demand, first at my bleeding Surety's hand, and then again at mine."[9] John Newton provided useful application with "'Tis a point I long to know, Oft it causes anxious thought, 'Do I love the Lord, or no; am I His or am I not?'"[10]

At one point Charles was granted permission to observe his grandfather in sermon preparation, which came with instructions that he not be a distraction, as eternity might ride on his ability to be quiet. Charles also joined the Monday morning fellowship between his grandfather and a local Anglican vicar, an experience that was foundational to Spurgeon's love of spiritual, doctrinally-sound Catholic Anglicans as well as his hatred of the artificiality of status created by a state church.

While in Stambourne on a visit to his grandparents, young Charles met Richard Knill, an agent for the London Missionary Society. In 1844, this genial and transparent Christian witness took notice of ten-year-old Charles and for three days woke him at 6:00 a.m. Each morning, they went to a garden where Knill conversed and prayed with Charles. By the conclusion of their time together, Knill was predicting Charles would be called to ministry, would preach in Rowland Hill's chapel, and would sing "God Moves in a Mysterious Way." He extracted a promise from Charles to memorize the hymn.[11]

---

7. William Cowper, "There Is a Fountain."
8. Augustus Toplady, "Rock of Ages."
9. Augustus Toplady, "From Whence This Fear and Unbelief?"
10. John Newton, "'Tis a Point I Long to Know."
11. Spurgeon, *Autobiography*, 1:27–31.

Soon after the Knill encounter and for the next five years, Charles came under increasingly severe conviction for his sin. He described God's law as "flogging me with its ten-thronged whip, and then rubbing me with brine afterwards, so that I did shake and quiver with pain and anguish, and my soul chose strangling rather than life, for I was exceeding sorrowful." Spurgeon also found that his conscience bore constant witness against him. "Our heavenly Father does not usually cause us to seek the Saviour till He has whipped us clean out of all our confidence," he noted.[12] The poignant prayer of his mother stuck like hooks in his mind: "Now, Lord, if my children go on in their sins, it will not be from ignorance that they perish, and my soul must bear witness against them at the day of judgment if they lay not hold of Christ." Those words, so Spurgeon testified, "pierced my conscience, and stirred my heart."[13]

Spurgeon's attempt to escape this looming cloud of divine wrath led him to consider naturalism and produced a solipsistic frame of mind, a pathway to complete nihilism and skepticism. "I went to the very bottom of the sea of infidelity," he remembered, and found food for ministry in surmising, "Now, whenever I hear the sceptic's stale attacks upon the Word of God, I smile within myself, and think, 'Why, you simpleton! How can you urge such trifling objections? I have felt, in the contentions of my own unbelief, ten times greater difficulties.'"[14] A year of school at Maidstone under the tutelage of an Anglican vicar led him to conclude that he was a Baptist. As the vicar sought to convince him to receive baptism at the hands of an Anglican priest, Spurgeon responded, "Oh no! I have been baptized once, before I ought; I will wait next time till I am fit for it." In later reflections Spurgeon wryly reported, "It is due to the Church of England catechism that I am a Baptist."[15]

In 1849, Spurgeon attended school at Newmarket in Cambridge. There he met one of the maids, Mary King, who was "a staunch Calvinist, logical, clear-headed, and had a wonderful knowledge of the Bible."[16] He often spoke with her of the doctrines of grace both before and after his conversion and testified, "I do believe that I learnt more from her than I should have learned from any six doctors of divinity of the sort we have nowadays."[17] All these doctrinal and experiential reflections came to fruition on January 6, 1850. Spurgeon was fifteen years old, and a snowstorm had hindered him from hearing his father preach during

---

12. Ibid., 1:58.
13. Ibid., 1:44.
14. Ibid., 1:67.
15. Ibid., 1:35, 38.
16. G. Holden Pike, *The Life and Work of Charles Haddon Spurgeon*, 6 vols. (London: Cassell & Company, n.d.), 1:40.
17. Spurgeon, *Autobiography*, 1:39.

a winter dismissal from school. As an alternative, Spurgeon wandered into the Artillery Street Primitive Methodist Church in Colchester. In the absence of the minister, an anonymous layman preached briefly but powerfully from Isaiah 45:22 (KJV): "Look unto me and be ye saved, all the ends of the earth: for I am God, and there is none else." From Spurgeon's several recollections we can reconstruct the vital elements of the sermon. To whom must one look for salvation? Not to the Father for election, nor to the Spirit for calling, but to the Son. This does not demand lifting your finger, nor lifting your foot, nor rising to walk, but just look—anyone can look! "Look unto me; I am sweating great drops of blood for you; look unto me, I am scourged and spit upon; I am nailed to the cross, I die, I am buried, I rise and ascend, I am pleading before the Father's throne, and all this for you."[18] The preacher located Spurgeon in the congregation and pointed to him, saying, "Young Man, obey my text—You look miserable and miserable you will remain if you do not obey the words of my text."[19]

Spurgeon said that all at once "I could have leapt for joy of heart; I felt that I understood that text, 'The mountains and hills shall break forth before you into singing, and all the trees of the field shall clap their hands.'"[20] Later Spurgeon would often refer to this moment of spiritual clarity and power as a particular manifestation of sovereign electing love. Three months after his conversion he told his father, "This faith is far more than any of us deserve; all beyond hell is mercy, but this is a mighty one. Were it not all of sovereign, electing, almighty grace, I, for one, could never hope to be saved. God says, 'You shall,' and not all the devils in hell, let loose upon a real Christian, can stop the workings of God's sovereign grace, for in due time the Christian cries, 'I will.'"[21]

Spurgeon was baptized on May 3, 1850 by Mr. Cantlow at Isleham Ferry on the River Lark. Prior to his baptism, he urgently sought permission from his father, assuring him that "conscience has convinced me that it is a duty to be buried with Christ in baptism, although I am sure it constitutes no part of salvation."[22] John Spurgeon delayed in giving an answer but finally relented. Having received permission,[23] Spurgeon was baptized and gave notice, "My timidity was washed away; it floated down the river into the sea, and must have been devoured by the fishes, for I have never felt anything of the kind since. Baptism also loosed

---

18. MTP, 1861:224.

19. Spurgeon, *Autobiography*, 1:88. See also *SS*, 1:1, 2; 318–19.

20. *SS*, 4:69.

21. Iain Murray, *Letters of Charles Haddon Spurgeon* (Edinburgh: The Banner of Truth Trust, 1992), 24. This will be referred to as Murray, *Letters*.

22. Ibid., 22.

23. Charles Spurgeon, *Letters of C. H. Spurgeon,* collected and collated by his son Charles Spurgeon, 1923. These were accessed online at http://www.romans45.org/spurgeon/misc/letters.htm. This will be referred to hereinafter as Spurgeon, *Letters*. This letter was received on April 20, 1850.

my tongue, and from that day it has never been quiet. I lost a thousand fears in that River Lark, and found that 'in keeping his commandments there is great reward.'"[24] To his mother's lamentation that in praying for his conversion, she had not mentioned his being a Baptist, he responded, "Ah, mother! The Lord has answered your prayer with His usual bounty, and given you exceeding abundantly above what you asked or thought."[25]

Spurgeon became a member of St. Andrew's Street Baptist Church and began to teach Sunday school. Soon he was instructing the other teachers, quipping that he would rather be a SST (Sunday School Teacher) than a DD (Doctor of Divinity). He also joined the Lay Preachers' Association and, in the fall of 1850, was sent to Teversham, three miles from Cambridge, where under the ruse of an ingeniously worded invitation, he preached his first sermon based on 1 Peter 2:7, "To you who believe, this stone is precious."

Spurgeon's preaching soon gained widespread attention, and he received a six-month invitation to preach at Waterbeach in October 1851. At that time, the church had twelve members, but within two years there were over four hundred people attending, and Spurgeon had preached over six hundred sermons.[26] His father and others urged him to consider collegiate theological training, yet due to an unusual miscommunication, he missed his interview with Joseph Angus, the principal at Stepney. As Spurgeon contemplated the peculiar providence that led to this mistake, a verse of Scripture came strongly to his mind: "Seekest thou great things for thyself, seek them not!" (Jer 45:5 KJV). He never again pursued further formal education.

In November 1853, at the age of nineteen, Spurgeon received an invitation to New Park Street in London, and after a three-month trial, he accepted the enthusiastic call of the congregation. Soon crowds began to gather to hear the new young preacher. The chapel had to be expanded, but it was still far too small. Spurgeon noted, "When I first became a Pastor in London, my success appalled me, and the thought of the career which it seemed to open up, so far from elating me, cast me into the lowest depth, out of which I uttered my *Miserere* and found no room for a *Gloria in excelsis*."[27] Efforts to accommodate the growing crowds led him to off-site preaching at Exeter Hall and the Surrey Garden Music Hall. While Spurgeon was preaching at Exeter Hall, the papers had a field day, referring to his preaching style as a "prostitution of the pulpit" and

---

24. Spurgeon, *Autobiography*, 1:149–50.
25. Ibid., 1:45.
26. For a discussion of the outlines and manuscripts of these sermons, see *The Lost Sermons of C. H. Spurgeon: His Earliest Outlines and Sermons between 1851 and 1854*, ed. Christian T. George (Nashville: Broadman & Holman, 2016).
27. Spurgeon, *Autobiography*, 1:263.

"pulpit buffoonery." Critics said his rhetoric oozed with "oratorical tricks, daring utterances . . . coarse sentiments," all tied up with "a clap-trap style," handling the mysteries of Christianity "rudely, roughly, and impiously." His demeanor reflected "insolence so unblushing, intellect so feeble, flippancy so ostentatious," that its impact amounted to "blasphemy from a parson."[28]

On January 8, 1856, Spurgeon married Susannah Thompson, who gave birth to twin boys on September 20. A month later, on October 19, 1856, at the opening service at the Surrey Music Hall, either pranksters or Spurgeon's enemies cried "fire" just as the crowd was finally settling in. The panic that ensued resulted in seven deaths and over twenty injuries. Spurgeon was devastated, and he admitted carrying the emotional imprint of that event throughout his ministry.

On August 15, 1859, the cornerstone was laid for the Metropolitan Tabernacle, and over two years later the congregation entered the building in January 1861, with a series of special services. Eventually the Tabernacle became the home base for sixty-six benevolence ministries, the most prominent of which were the Pastors' College, the orphanages, the Almshouses, the evangelists' society, the colportage society, and Mrs. Spurgeon's book fund.

Spurgeon's collected sermons were bound for publication and widely distributed every year from 1855 until 1917, and he edited a newsletter entitled *The Sword and the Trowel* every month from 1865 until his death in 1892, contributing articles and as many as twenty-five book reviews per issue. Among the 140 books Spurgeon wrote is a massive commentary on the Psalms, entitled *Treasury of David*, designed to help ministers preach the Psalms.

Spurgeon affirmed that "we are not to go about the world searching out heresies."[29] Nevertheless, many people with questions and concerns sought him out for advice, and involvement in various controversies punctuated Spurgeon's ministry. He issued ongoing warnings against the anti-Christian impact of Roman Catholicism, its hierarchy having been reestablished in England in 1850. Spurgeon also steadily criticized the state-church status of Anglicanism and took issue with evangelicals in that church over the issue of infant baptism. The most devastating controversy, however, occurred when Spurgeon sought to reveal the theological decline among pastors in the Baptist Union. Known as the "Downgrade Controversy," it led to Spurgeon's resignation from the Baptist Union in October 1887. The fallout from this included ongoing relational tensions and the loss of close friends, as well as criticism from his former students. All this exacerbated Spurgeon's physical weakness caused by years of struggle with gout

---

28. Ibid., 1:316–25.
29. Spurgeon, *Lectures*, 2:32.

and nephritis. These enemies united their debilitating forces, strengthened even further by a case of influenza, to bring about his death in Menton, France, on January 31, 1892.

THEOLOGY OF PREACHING

Charles Spurgeon's theology of preaching started with the fitness and calling of the preacher. Spurgeon believed that no one should undertake the task of preaching who is not called to it and gifted for it: "The ministry is a high and honorable calling when a man is really fitted for it; but without the necessary qualifications it must be little better than sheer slavery with a fine name to it."[30] Though he rejected the division in the church between clergy and laity, he knew, nevertheless, that God had set aside some individuals as "successors of those who, in olden times, were moved of God to declare his word, to testify against transgression, and to plead his cause."[31] So vital and necessary was this call that Spurgeon renounced any attempt to fulfill such a ministry without it. He warned, "Take heed that ye touch not God's holy ark, with unholy fingers. You may all preach if you can, but take care that you do not set yourselves up in the ministry, without having a solemn conviction that the Spirit from on high has set you apart; for, if you do, the blood of souls will be found in your skirts."[32]

So how did one discern a call to ministry? First, they must have a saving experience of the gospel. This should seem self-evident, but Spurgeon often made this a key point: "Ah! It will be well for some if they shall be able to wash their hands of the blood of souls, for verily in the cells of eternal condemnation there are heard no yells of horror more appalling than the shrieks of damned ministers."[33] He stated plainly, "It should be one of our first cares that we ourselves be saved men." A person ignorant of the truth to which they call others makes misery for oneself and puts oneself under "perpetual slavery." Such a person must hate the sight of a pulpit as a "galley slave hates the oar."[34] The unconverted person is unserviceable to others for they have never traveled the road along which they seek to be a guide. Even worse, these kinds of preachers bring great mischief to

---

30. Charles Spurgeon, *The Sword and the Trowel* (London: Passmore & Alabaster, 1865–1892), 1883:109. This monthly publication of Spurgeon's will be listed as *ST* with year and page numbers.

31. Spurgeon, *Lectures*, 2:3.

32. Charles Spurgeon, *Spurgeon's Expository Encyclopedia*, 15 vols. (Grand Rapids: Baker, 1977), 5:465. Hereinafter this will be noted as *SEE*, along with volume and page numbers.

33. Charles Spurgeon, *The Saint and His Saviour* (Tain, Ross-shire, Scotland: Christian Focus, 1989), 143–44.

34. Spurgeon, *Lectures*, 1:5. This is in a lecture entitled "The Minister's Self-Watch."

the church, highlighting formalism as worship, fashionable manners as holiness, and cultured concerts and rhetoric as reverence, and often set forth human philosophy and historical heresy as the content of their proclamation. "Take heed to yourselves," Spurgeon warned, "lest you perish while you call upon others to take heed of perishing."[35]

A call to preach also necessitates an esteem for the superior worthiness and power of the gospel. Spurgeon believed the gospel is worthy because of the person in whom its effectuality consists—Jesus Christ. It is worthy in that its final purpose is to glorify God and effect conversion, forgiveness, and the transformation of rebels. Those who glory in the ministry must have mental and spiritual knowledge of the doctrines of grace, the foundation for all effective, God-glorifying ministry.[36]

A call to preach means one is unable to give oneself fully to anything *other than* gospel ministry. Spurgeon viewed the first sign of a call as an "intense, all-absorbing desire for the work," and he called this an "irresistible, overwhelming, craving and raging thirst for telling others what God has done to our own souls."[37] By his own admission, this impulse stayed with Spurgeon till the end of his life, and though preaching physically exhausted him, its prospect energized his spirit with an intrinsic earnestness that marked all his preaching. "In many instances," Spurgeon noted, likely reflecting on his own experience, "success is traceable almost entirely to an intense zeal, a consuming passion for souls, and an eager enthusiasm in the cause of God." Such earnestness must be evident "when actually engaged in preaching."[38]

Yet while earnestness is necessary, it cannot suffice for every aspect of a call to preach. If one is to enter the ministry, Spurgeon felt it was best for that person to have the natural endowments for the task. Mental endowments are essential to setting forth the exposition in a way that is understandable. Spurgeon frequently interviewed men for the Pastors' College "who are distinguished by enormous vehemence and zeal, and a conspicuous lack of brains."[39] He believed such men would do as well without education as with it, so he turned them down. Spurgeon said that feebleness of mind leads to a lack of resolution regarding doctrine and inclines some to oscillate between strange doctrines and orthodoxy. He believed physical endowments were necessary to make oneself understood, and that a person with a sunken chest (indicating a lack of lung capacity) should not

---

35. Ibid., 1:7.
36. Ibid., 1:23; *ST* 1877:129, 211.
37. Spurgeon, *Lectures*, 1:23.
38. Ibid., 2:145, 146.
39. Ibid., 1:34

aspire to ministry. He said that if parents wanted their children to be preachers, they must take care of their teeth, because bad teeth make for poor articulation.

There must also be an evident indication that God's blessings rest on a person's efforts: "There must be some measure of conversion-work in your irregular labours before you can believe that preaching is to be your life-work." And since the call to ministry in a formal sense comes from the prayerful judgment of the church, some evidence must exist that one's preaching is "acceptable to the people of God."[40]

Although Spurgeon solemnly resisted admitting a "untested, unlearned, doctrinally vacuous novice, who scarcely [knew] the alphabet of the gospel," he did not want to ignore the transcendent power involved in qualifying a person for the call to preach. In 1856, as a twenty-two-year-old young man, Spurgeon heard a barrage of "opprobrious titles that worldlings" cast on him. Yet harlots were saved, drunkards reclaimed, and "abandoned characters" changed. In light of that experience, Spurgeon was driven to say, "The only endowment necessary for success in the ministry is the endowment of the Holy Ghost." Apart from worldly approval, Spurgeon affirmed, "If you have a solemn conviction in your souls that God has really ordained you to the work of the ministry, and if you have obtained a seal to your commission in the conversion of even one soul, let not death or hell stop you; go straight on, and never think you must have certain endowments to make a successful preacher."[41]

By this, Spurgeon did not mean that a person completely devoid of natural, cognitive, and moral standards could meet the biblical qualifications. What he meant was that Scripture and the Spirit, not the world, governed God's church. Some people might have diminished endowments but nevertheless possess an unction for preaching such that God would grant them effectiveness in a place fit for their gifts.

THEOLOGY FOR PREACHING

The Authority of Scripture in Preaching

Fundamental to Spurgeon's theology for preaching was a commitment to the sole authority and infallible truthfulness of the Bible as the book of revealed truth. Preaching on the Bible during his first year at New Park Street, Spurgeon soared into an apostrophe: "O Bible! It cannot be said of any other book, that it is perfect and pure; but of thee we can declare all wisdom is gathered up in thee,

---

40. Ibid., 1:28, 29.
41. *SEE* 5:465.

without a particle of folly. . . . This is the book untainted by any error; but is pure, unalloyed, perfect truth. Why? Because God wrote it. Ah! Charge God with error if ye please; tell him his book is not what it ought to be."[42]

In 1874, four years after the first Vatican Council and the proclamation of the doctrine of papal infallibility, Spurgeon preached a sermon entitled "Infallibility." He did not wonder that people sought infallibility somewhere but was astonished that they would canonize the pope of Rome. "It is so monstrous that men should believe in papal infallibility, that did they not themselves avow it we should think it most insulting to accuse them of it." For Spurgeon, one of the mysteries of rational personhood is "how any mind can by any possible contortion twist itself into a posture in which it will be capable of accepting such a belief." Spurgeon dismissed other sources of authority, and, looking to the rock of Scripture, asserted, "We have a more sure word of testimony, a rock of truth upon which we rest, for our infallible standard lies in, 'It is written.' The Bible, the whole Bible, and nothing but the Bible, is our religion." The Bible is "pure, unerring truth," and in it one finds "infallibility and nowhere else."[43]

The Necessity of Exposition in Preaching

A faithful preacher must also be committed to the exposition of Scripture. "Homilies should flow out of texts, should consist of a clear explanation, and an earnest enforcement of the truths which the texts teach." Spurgeon looked on expository preaching as "the great need of the day, its best protection against rising errors, and its surest means of spiritual edification."[44] "What are sermons but commentaries?" Spurgeon asked. "At least they ought to be." He urged ministers to utilize the best commentaries along with original study of the text.[45] The goal of preaching in this way is a thorough understanding of the Bible through mastering the text one book at a time: "The close, critical, exhaustive investigation of one part best qualifies for a similar examination of another."[46]

Spurgeon preached both divine sovereignty and human responsibility, identifying the whole counsel of God as saying "what that text means honestly and uprightly." He spoke about how a preacher gets a text and then "kills it" by

---

42. *SS* 1:31.

43. Charles Spurgeon, *Metropolitan Tabernacle Pulpit*, 63 vols. (Pasadena, TX: Pilgrim, 1970–2006), 1874:697–99. This will be noted hereinafter as *MTP* with year and page numbers. Volumes 1–6 are entitled *New Park Street Pulpit* and will be identified *NPS* with volume number and page number.

44. Spurgeon, *Lectures*, 4:iii. This is from the preface of Spurgeon's *Commenting and Commentaries*.

45. Spurgeon kept abreast of the growing corpus of commentaries in the last half of the nineteenth century, as indicated by his frequent reviews of them in *The Sword and the Trowel*. In his personal library he had hundreds of commentaries by the Puritans, and he had developed a keen sense of the strengths of each Puritan writer and would refer to the most fitting commentary for the text on which he was working.

46. *ST* 1866:94.

wringing its neck and stuffing it "with some empty notions" to set on the table "for an unthinking people to feed upon." No one preaches "the whole counsel of God who does not let God's Word speak for itself in its own pure, simple language."[47] Preaching "texts of Scripture out of their connection, twisted and perverted, are not 'It is written,'" Spurgeon insisted. "The plain meaning of the word should be known and understood. Oh, read the word, and pray for the anointing of the Holy Spirit, that you may know its meaning, for so will you contend against the foe."[48]

Spurgeon believed knowledge of Scripture in its etymological and canonical context was necessary because we no longer receive special revelation today. No one would know the truth of God if they looked for it apart from a disciplined study of the Word of God. "Mark!" Spurgeon exhorted, "The Holy Spirit does not now reveal fresh truth, beyond what is already in the Word of God." The Spirit has in writing pronounced a curse "upon any who shall add to this book; and you may rest assured that the Holy Spirit will not so transgress in a matter which he has peremptorily forbidden all his children to commit." Spurgeon knew of some who claimed to utter prophecies or have special visions. "Their proper destination is Bethlehem Hospital [a London psychiatric hospital]," he surmised, "and we begin directly to shun them and their books." Spurgeon was clear "that the Holy Spirit makes no such fresh revelations to men now, but teaches us what Christ taught, bringing all these things to our remembrance." The Spirit's work is to make clear "what Christ has taught and only that."[49]

The Holy Spirit's Operation in Preaching

With rare exceptions, Spurgeon had a cessationist view of the miraculous gifts, yet he taught Spirit-conviction as one of the qualifying elements of a call to ministry and maintained an immovable submission to the Spirit's blessing alone as the source of true effectiveness and power in ministry. Connected to this was his firm belief in the unity of Spirit and truth; one cannot expect true blessing from the Spirit if one has adopted beliefs that bypass biblical truth and the sole sufficiency of Christ. In his last address to his Pastors' College Evangelical Conference, and with the conflict of the Downgrade still reverberating in his soul, Spurgeon preached, "Do you think, dear friend, that you can be wiser than the Holy Spirit? And if his choice must be a wise one, will yours be a wise one if you begin to take of the things of something or somebody else?"[50] Only the things of

---

47. *NPS*, 6:27.
48. *MTP*, 1874:707.
49. *SEE* 9:52.
50. *SEE* 9:83.

Christ bring the Spirit to empower one's ministry. A theology excogitated "out of your own vast brain" will never bring the Spirit as a cowitness to a sermon.

In a lecture to his students on this theme, Spurgeon testified: "To us the presence and work of the Holy Spirit are the ground of our confidence as to the wisdom and hopefulness of our life work." He embraced the biblical idea expressed by Jonathan Edwards as a "new sense of things," a heart-evidence and verification of the unopposable reality of divine things. Spurgeon contended, "By the sensitiveness of our spirit we are as much made conscious of the presence of the Spirit of God as we are made cognizant of the existence of the souls of our fellow-men by their action upon our souls, or as we are certified of the existence of matter by its actions upon our senses."[51]

Spurgeon even used Edwards's analogy of the infallible sensibility of the taste of honey to demonstrate this point: "There was a time when our palates were so depraved that we preferred bitter things," but now the Holy Spirit has impressed the sweetness of the gospel on our spiritual palates, and we have "honey in the mouth, and the taste that enjoys it."[52] In applying this idea, Spurgeon asked, "Have you and I felt the Holy Spirit at work with us, endearing doctrine, and making it more precious to us?"[53] If not, if we do not seek the Holy Spirit as a true teacher, we will be blown about with every wind of doctrine. Spurgeon would have none of it: "I am open to conviction, but I shall never see the man that can convince me out of my hope, my all. Before I could quit my faith in the substitutionary work of the Lord Jesus Christ, and my confidence in the everlasting covenant ordered in all things and sure, I should have to be ground to powder, and every separate atom transformed."[54]

He made this application to all Christians, observing that "every Christian knows experimentally that he never does learn the truth fully, and hold it tenaciously, except by the teaching and sustaining grace of God the Holy Spirit. . . . We must have everything we truly learn burnt into us by the Holy Ghost."[55]

An Exposition and a Sermon

Spurgeon believed preaching should be nothing less than exposition. He viewed sermons as commentaries, and while the sermon might include more, it could not omit expository comments and still be considered preaching.[56] While Spurgeon had no objection to discreet, Bible-tethered spiritualizing—and even

51. Spurgeon, *Lectures*, 2:2.
52. *SEE* 9:82.
53. Ibid., 9:54.
54. *SS* 19:53.
55. *SEE* 9:51
56. *ST* 1866:94.

criticized homileticians who condemned it—he warned against any violation of the historical grammatical sense of the text.[57] Spurgeon arranged every service to include an exposition of a long text and then a sermon, or discourse. Sometimes these occurred together, while at other times they were two distinct and unique parts of his homily. If some of his sermons were thematic, doctrinal, topical, or only tangentially related to the text, they were used to supplement a featured exposition of Scripture reading punctuated with brief expository remarks. Spurgeon found that "brief comments upon Scripture" in the ordinary service were both instructive and a source of "real delight" to his people. He insisted: "Earnestly do I advocate commenting," and believed the extra study would provide expanding and long-term benefits. "As a rule," Spurgeon claimed, "I spend much more time over the exposition than over the discourse."[58] He made short pithy comments on several verses. Sometimes these comments had a devotional nature; others focused on the particular use of a word. Often, they had a brief theological point with interspersed reminders of the context, or he made a very practical point from a theologically-loaded text.

An exposition on John 16 provides an example of how he used this "commenting" during a service. Spurgeon read verses 5 and 6 and commented, "But now I go my way to him that sent me; and none of you asketh me, Whither goest thou? But because I have said these things unto you, sorrow hath filled your heart." Spurgeon's commenting captures the flow of Jesus's narrative by giving existential relevance to the sorrow of the disciples while also pointing the hearer to the solution they must bear in mind. "We sometimes endure a needless sorrow, for the asking of a single question might remove it. Our Lord says to his disciples, 'If you knew where I was going, and understood my motive in going, your sorrow at my departure would be assuaged.'" Spurgeon continued with substantial comments on several verses of this extended text.[59]

Following the exposition of John 16:1–33, Spurgeon preached on John 16:14: "The Spirit's Office Towards Disciples." His aim was to preach an expansive doctrinal message on how the Spirit glorifies Christ in the lives of disciples, and he included a short exposition of Christ as prophet, priest, and king. He also made it clear that the Spirit gives an ever-renewed sense of the love of Christ to the believer: "No joy can be compared with that of the love of Christ shed abroad in your hearts. When the Spirit has thus filled your thoughts and hearts, he will be sure to occupy your tongues." In yet another of his points, Spurgeon gave voice to a compelling presentation of the eternal covenantal love for his people

57. Spurgeon, *Lectures*, 1:102–16.
58. Spurgeon, *Lectures*, 4:22, 24.
59. *SEE* 9:67.

and finished with these words: "If there is one doctrine, however, more sweet and yet more deep than another, it is the divine doctrine of that eternal union which exists between Christ and his people. It is the Spirit's work to take the golden key, and let us into this secret cabinet."[60]

Preaching Saturated with Doctrine

Having a separate time of exposition allowed Spurgeon to preach doctrine in its fullness. He was able to connect the particular text with the entire canon and synthesize doctrinal truths within the span of his text. He would inform his listeners that they could "know whether thou be a child of light, or a child of darkness" by asking "are the doctrines of grace essential verities with thee?" The true Christian is ready to accept all that God "has revealed concerning himself, his Son, his Holy Spirit, the cross, life, death, hell, and the eternal future." This kind of reception of truth is "to walk in the light. All other teaching is darkness."[61]

In 1865, Spurgeon noted, "There are some doctrines which are not often preached in certain pulpits; they are supposed to be rather dangerous." He firmly believed that doctrine is derived from a full understanding of Scripture and that we must not be afraid of the deep things of God. At one point he shared with a minister his dislike for a certain hymn book, for he "could never find a hymn that sang of the covenant of grace or the doctrine of election." The minister replied, "That is no disadvantage to me, for I never say anything about those doctrines." Spurgeon replied that certain truths will yield their fruit of delight only to those "who have passed through the rudiments, and have done with the grammar-school, and can enter into the university." He believed that Christ is glorified in preaching when "the Spirit makes us understand the eternal love of Christ to his people, and his covenant engagements for them."[62]

In an 1884 sermon on "How to Meet the Doctrine of Election," Spurgeon cautioned thought and prudence in discussing the doctrine of election—not caution in avoiding it, but caution in failing to discuss it. Spurgeon thought it was wise for ministers to "introduce them [congregants] to the deeper truths of our theology." These had best be heard from "loving, tender-hearted Christians." He considered it bad policy to conceal truth from people, for "the more light the better." If we do not believe it, then we should revise our creed; but "in the name of common honesty let us hide nothing that we believe." Having known

---

60. Ibid., 9:69–77.
61. *MTP* 1887:558.
62. *SEE* 9:75.

the doctrinal system of grace from his youth, he testified, "It commands the enthusiasm of my whole being."[63]

By 1891, Spurgeon had closed the parenthesis around his ministry. He taught that knowing the fundamentals and the saving content of the gospel provides security, but these are preparatory for grasping "the glorious mysteries of the everlasting covenant, of the sovereignty of God, of his eternal love and distinguishing grace." Spurgeon believed these doctrines should not weary us but should invite us to venture in: "I would have every Christian wish to know all that he can know of revealed truth."[64]

Preaching Focused on Christ

Spurgeon preached doctrine to point to Jesus Christ as Lord and Savior. If he spoke about election, he would say, "Election is a good thing; to be chosen of God, and precious; but we are elect in Christ Jesus." On the blessing of adoption, he would say, "Adoption is a good thing; . . . ay, but we are adopted in Christ Jesus and made joint-heirs with him." So too, "Pardon is a good thing—who will not say so?—ay, but we are pardoned through the precious blood of Jesus." And as to the matchless grace of justification, we know that it is "a noble thing, to be robed about with a perfect righteousness, but this too finds its center and sub-stance in Christ." Our preservation and future perfection in heaven also comes from being in Christ, being raised with him, and being finally conformed to his image: "He is all the best things in one." The Father has invested all of this in his beloved Son and "the Holy Spirit shall glorify Christ by making us see that these things of Christ are, indeed, of Christ, and completely of Christ—and still are in connection with Christ—and we only enjoy them because we are in connection with Christ."[65]

Preaching to Pierce the Heart

Spurgeon knew that the preaching of doctrine and the preaching of Christ had as its goal the experiential application of truth, and this would take form in the increased holiness and assurance of the believer and in the salvation of the unbeliever. Revelation was verbal and plenary, yet that revelation came through the deeply felt experience of the writers. This implied that those preaching revealed truth should seek to duplicate the writers' sense of urgency in those who hear (Gal 4:19–20). Spurgeon would say on many occasions: "It is not for me to be amusing you with some deep things that may instruct your intellect but

---

63. Ibid., 7:35.
64. *MTP* 1891:317–18.
65. *NPS* 5:141.

do not enter your hearts; it is for me to fit the arrow to the string and send it home—to unsheathe the sword—be the scabbard never so glittering, to cast it aside, and let the majesty of naked truth smite at your hearts."[66]

Spurgeon's applications flowed naturally from his own experience of the truth and power of doctrine. He worked tirelessly to properly apply and insinuate truth into the experience of all who heard him preach. Spurgeon was clear and artful in using terse verbal barbs designed to help "fellow-archers" sink convicting barbs into hearts, barbs that would be difficult to remove.[67] In the end, however, Spurgeon knew that only the Spirit could "fit the arrow to the string," as only he created the "new sense of things" necessary for the irreversible grasp of truths holy and saving. "The act of faith is an indication that the new birth has taken place."[68]

Preaching the Invitation of Christ through the Spirit

Spurgeon believed there is no doctrine of Scripture that discourages a sinner from coming to Christ and there is no doctrine that excuses a sinner from faith in Christ and love to him. Spurgeon was masterful in fitting the content of his message to an evangelistic appeal, urging sinners to make a decision for Christ. In a sermon at Exeter Hall in 1861 based on Jeremiah 2:18, Spurgeon focused on the words, "And now what hast thou to do in the way of Egypt, to drink the waters of Sihor?" He closed the sermon:

> If it is a prudent thing to damn your soul eternally for the sake of a few hours of mirth—say so—go and do it like an honest man! But if it is unwise to forget forever and only think of today; if it is the strongest madness to lose your life to gain the mere apparel with which the body is to be covered; if it is madness to fling away jewels, and hoard up dust as you are doing, then I pray you, I beseech you, answer the question—"What have you to do in the way of Egypt, to drink the waters of Sihor?" . . . "Let the wicked forsake his way and the unrighteous man his thoughts: and let him return unto the Lord, and He will have mercy upon him. And to our God, for He will abundantly pardon." Lo, the cross is lifted up before you! Jesus bleeds! His wounds are streaming with His life-blood! Yes and with yours, too! Believe, sinner! Trust Him—with your whole heart trust Him! Come to Him, come to Him! With weeping and supplication I pray you come!

---

66. *SS* 4:198.

67. Spurgeon, *Feathers for Arrows*. Charles Spurgeon, *Barbed Arrows*, comp. by Charles Spurgeon Jr. (Chicago: Revell, 1896).

68. *SEE* 7:492.

Knowing the terrors of the Lord, I beseech you! As one who pleads for his own life, I plead with you! By heaven, by hell, by time flying so swiftly, by eternity approaching so silently, by death, by judgment, by the awful soul-reading eyes, by the rocks whose stony bowels shall refuse your prayer to fall upon you, by the trumpet, and the thunders of the resurrection morning, by the pit of hell and by the flame—I pray you think, and believe in Him who is the Lamb of God which takes away the sins of the world! God bless my words to you through His Spirit's energy, and He shall have the praise forever and ever! Amen.[69]

METHODOLOGY FOR PREACHING

Spurgeon sought to preach for no more than forty-five minutes, and he believed a preacher should not try the patience of his people or go beyond the limits of their physical endurance. He believed long-winded sermons would not lead an audience to learn more, but less. Preachers who gave false indications of finality followed by extra points gave the impression that they were undisciplined, unorganized, and untrustworthy. Spurgeon's preaching methodology is not clearly delineated or easily replicated, but he did leave several points of observation that are instructive for preachers who want their own words to be like "an arrow fitted to the string."

Vocally Edifying

Spurgeon believed excellent content that was jumbled and mangled by a bumbling delivery shrouded a message, so he taught several things regarding the vocal delivery of a sermon. One descriptor noted: "He used [his voice] without any apparent effort, and it answered every purpose of his will," and the person hearing "never heard from it one note that grated harshly on the ear." It was an "instrument of speech that either needed no management, or was so perfectly managed that it seemed to need none."[70]

Spurgeon gave plenty of advice to his fellow preachers. He urged the preacher to take care of his teeth, for poor teeth make for poor articulation. He endorsed the conscious vocal habit of enunciating words to the end of a sentence so that the last words would not fall into oblivion. He taught that preachers should stop using rhythms of speech that had become predictable and distracting. Spurgeon spoke out against "servant girlified dawdling in speech" as well as bawling and

---

69. *MTP* 1861:64.
70. *SS* 20:vii, viii.

roaring. Idiosyncrasies should be corrected whenever possible. Even though he often defended a natural style and disliked affectation, Spurgeon was relentless and merciless in hunting down unpleasant sounds and criticizing others. Some men's throats seem to him to be "furred up, like long-used teakettles," and in others, they rang like brass music, with a vicious metallic sound. Others had a "sharp discordant squeak, like a rusty pair of scissors." One talks without using his lips, ventriloquizing most horribly, while another speaks as if he had a hot dumpling in his mouth.[71]

Physically Engaging

Spurgeon read books about the use of gestures in delivery, and he formed his own opinions on their use in the pulpit. "Do not be completely unanimated," he advised, "as if your message should have no interest to yourself or anyone else." At the same time, he advised that preachers should not be wild and jerky but under control and not distracting. A failure to move around has some pitfalls, but too much activity can make a clown of the preacher. Face and arms should animate the message and help give it proper emphasis, but they should not degenerate into a pantomime that substitutes movement for message: "Wave your hands a little less, smite the Bible somewhat more mercifully, and in general take matters rather more calmly." As might be expected, Spurgeon had artistic illustrations detailing the foibles and fitness of certain gestures.[72]

Illustratively Clarifying

Spurgeon is well-known for employing striking images and illustrations as servants of the text. But he was careful to avoid turning them into amusements that navigated away from the text. Fit, pungent illustrations gave clarity and attractiveness to a message, and his were often no more than half a sentence or at most two or three lines. Spurgeon frequently used similes and metaphors to create a rapid succession of pictures that would fill the mind of the listener. His artful use of images was the result of a lifelong practice of keenly observing both nature and people. Sometimes a fitting anecdote would take longer to share, but many illustrations were simple phrases that brought to mind an immediately instructive image, such as "Chubb's patent locks" (a reference to secrets of the covenant reserved only to the elect), "lofty trees laden with fruit" (an image of union with Christ providing all the spiritual blessings), "like partridges upon the mountain" (the apparent helplessness of Christians being pursued by hostile

---

71. Spurgeon, *Lectures*, 1:117–24. This is "Lecture VIII. On the Voice."
72. Ibid., 2:96–143.

authorities), and "dead men unwinding their own sheets" (speaking of the necessity of regeneration prior to any activity toward God). Apart from the help of the Spirit, Spurgeon believed a preacher's words "glide like oil over a slab of marble." He warned against the abuse of illustrations or using them as substitutes for more important content. He noted that older and more mature preachers typically use fewer illustration and anecdotes, for their content is as clear as it is profound.

CONTRIBUTIONS TO PREACHING

Charles Spurgeon continued the legacy of doctrinal Puritan preaching, adding to it the evangelistic thrust of the Great Awakening. He became the most well-known preacher during the golden era of nineteenth-century preaching, and his dynamic delivery and mastery of language appealed to the masses. Spurgeon's work of equipping future pastors and passing on his insights through his publications has anchored him a place in Christian history. He challenges the church in each generation to maintain a clear and consistent vision centered around at least four commitments.

First, preachers must have a constant focus on the inviolable truth of Scripture as the sole source of sermonic content. Second, there must be a conscious and transparent dependence on the Holy Spirit, both for a call to preach and for the successful execution of that call. Third, in both the study and the pulpit there must be a commitment to a corporate worship experience that includes careful verse-by-verse exploration of an extended text and a thematic or doctrinal expansion of a more succinct selected text. And finally, Spurgeon taught that a person's conscience cannot afford to choose friends at the expense of one's faith. One cannot pursue popularity at the expense of principle.

Sermon Excerpt

Compel Them to Come In[73]

Well, brother, I have told you the message. What sayest thou unto it? Do you turn away? You tell me it is nothing to you? You cannot listen to it . . . but you will go your way this day and attend to your farm and merchandize. Stop, brother, I was not told merely to tell you and then go about my business! No, I am told to compel you to come in!. . .

73. *NPS* 5:19–24 (selected portions). This sermon was preached in Exeter Hall on December 5, 1858.

I am in earnest with you in my desire that you should comply with this command of God! You may despise your own salvation, but I do not despise it. You may go away and forget what you shall hear, but you will please to remember that the things I now say cost me many a groan ere I came here to utter them! My inmost soul is speaking out to you, my poor brother, when I beseech you by Him who lives and was dead and is alive for evermore! Consider my Master's message which He bids me now address to you. But do you spurn it?. . . Then I must change my tone a minute. I will not merely tell you the message and invite you as I do with all earnestness and sincere affection—I will go further! Sinner, in God's name I command you to repent and believe! Do you ask me from where is my authority? I am an ambassador of heaven!. . . Now, does anything else remain to the minister besides weeping and prayer? Yes, there is one thing else. God has given to His servants not the power of regeneration, but He has given them something akin to it. It is impossible for any man to regenerate his neighbor. . . . What can we do, then? We can now appeal to the Spirit! I know I have preached the gospel—that I have preached it earnestly. I challenge my Master to honor His own promise! . . . I cannot compel you, but You, O Spirit of God, who has the key of the heart, You can compel! Did you ever notice in that Chapter of the Revelation, where it says, "Behold I stand at the door and knock," . . . the same person is described as He who hath the key of David. So that if knocking will not avail, He has the key and can and will come in! Now, if the knocking of an earnest minister prevail not with you this morning, there remains still that secret opening of the heart by the Spirit, so that you shall be compelled! . . . Now, I throw it into my Master's hands. It cannot be His will that we should travail in birth and yet not bring forth spiritual children! It is with Him. He is master of the heart and the day shall declare it—that some of you compelled by sovereign grace have become the willing captives of the all-conquering Jesus, and have bowed your hearts to Him through the sermon of this morning!

BIBLIOGRAPHY

Murray, Iain. *Letters of Charles Haddon Spurgeon*. Edinburgh: The Banner of Truth Trust, 1992.

Pike, G. Holden. *The Life and Work of Charles Haddon Spurgeon*. 6 vols. London: Cassell & Company, n.d.

Spurgeon, Charles. *Autobiography*. 2 vols. Edinburgh: The Banner of Truth Trust, 1962.

_____. *Feathers for Arrows*. London: Passmore & Alabaster, 1870.

_____. *Lectures to My Students*. (4 volumes in one). Pasadena, TX: Pilgrim, 1990.

_____. *Letters of C. H. Spurgeon,* collected and collated by his son Charles Spurgeon, 1923. Accessed online at http://www.romans45.org/spurgeon/misc/letters.htm.

_____, and Benjamin Beddow. *Memories of Stambourne.* London: Passmore & Alabaster, 1891.

_____. *Metropolitan Tabernacle Pulpit.* 63 vols. Pasadena, TX: Pilgrim, 1970–2006.

_____. *The Saint and His Saviour.* Tain, Ross-shire, Scotland: Christian Focus, 1989.

_____. *Sermons of Rev. C. H. Spurgeon.* 20 vols. New York: Funk & Wagnalls, 1857–1892.

_____. *Spurgeon's Expository Encyclopedia.* 15 vols. Grand Rapids: Baker, 1977.

_____. *The Sword and the Trowel.* London: Passmore & Alabaster, 1865–1892.

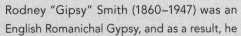

Rodney "Gipsy" Smith

Forgotten Evangelist

BILL CURTIS

Rodney "Gipsy" Smith (1860–1947) was an English Romanichal Gypsy, and as a result, he was raised in a culture of primary orality. Despite his limited educational opportunities, he rose from obscurity to global prominence as an evangelist. His evangelistic ministry spanned seventy years, from his early days with The Salvation Army until his death in 1947. During those years, he led some of the most significant revival meetings in the world, including in England, Europe, South Africa, Australia, and America, where he made forty trips during his ministry. Despite the longevity and global scope of his ministry, and the accolades he received from men like Alexander Maclaren, F. B. Meyer, G. Campbell Morgan, John Henry Jowett, Joseph Parker, Thomas Spurgeon, and S. Parkes Cadman, his legacy as a famous evangelist has diminished over time.

HISTORICAL BACKGROUND

Rodney "Gipsy" Smith[1] was born to Cornelius Smith and Mary (Pollie) Welch on March 31, 1860, near Epping Forest, in Essex, England.[2] In 1865, Gipsy was travelling[3] with his family through the county of Hertfordshire, near the town of Baldock, when two of his siblings contracted smallpox. And despite the precautions taken by his father to quarantine the children from the rest of the family, his pregnant mother contracted the disease as well. Pollie Welch Smith delivered

---

1. The *American Heritage Dictionary* uses "Gypsy" as its primary spelling. It includes "Gipsy" as an alternate spelling. William Morris, ed., *American Heritage Dictionary*, New College Edition (Boston: Houghton Mifflin, 1979), 589. Gypsy scholars are divided on their usage of the word. Rodney Smith used the alternate spelling, Gipsy. Consequently, the alternate spelling will be used when referring to Smith in this chapter. All other references will utilize the primary spelling. All uses of the primary or secondary spelling in quotes have been left as the original authors intended.

2. Gipsy Smith, *Gipsy Smith: His Life and Work* (New York: Revell, 1901; Ambassador Productions Ltd., 1996), 17.

3. This spelling, in its various forms and contexts, is used to denote both Travellers and their journeys. Donald Kenrick, *Historical Dictionary of the Gypsies (Romanies)* (London: Scarecrow, 1998), 170.

her sixth child, Louise, shortly before dying. Louise succumbed to the disease two weeks later.

Four years later, in the spring of 1869, Cornelius set off in search of salvation with his brothers, Woodlock and Bartholomew. Their journey brought them to London, where they established lodging at Shepherd's Bush. While there, Cornelius and Bartholomew were converted to Christianity at the mission hall in Latimer Road. Woodlock was converted shortly thereafter.[4]

Following his father's conversion, Gipsy struggled with his own spiritual needs. When he was sixteen, his family travelled to the town of Bedford. Remembering that his father had been influenced spiritually by hearing someone read *Pilgrim's Progress*, he sought out John Bunyan's monument in the city and stood before it. While there, he made the decision to become a Christian. Smith made his decision public on November 17, 1876, at the Primitive Methodist Chapel in Cambridge, where his family were members during that time. He would later write of that night: "How much that meant to me and mine and *thousands more!* . . . It will take *eternity* to reveal what has grown out of that Gipsy boy's decision for Christ."[5]

Smith's conversion became the source of his desire to become literate. After all, he had been raised in a culture of primary orality, a descendent of the British Romanichal Gypsies. With the aid of the Bible, an English dictionary, and a Bible dictionary, Smith began the process of self-education. He felt a desire to preach soon after his conversion. He ventured into ministry by singing hymns for the people to whom he sold his family's wares. In time, he came to be known as "the singing gipsy boy."[6] When he was alone, Smith practiced his preaching in the fields and on his journeys. He wrote, "One Sunday I entered a turnip-field and preached most eloquently to the turnips. I had a very large and most attentive congregation. Not one of them made an attempt to move away."[7] Although it was unknown to him at this early age, he was preparing for a global preaching ministry.

In the spring of 1877, Smith participated in a meeting led by William Booth at the headquarters of The Christian Mission in London. During the meeting, Booth suddenly introduced him to the assembled audience as the "Gipsy boy" and allowed him to sing and share a brief testimony. Following the meeting, Booth invited him to become an evangelist with The Christian Mission. At that moment, Smith "officially" surrendered his life to the preaching ministry.

---

4. David Lazell, *Gypsy from the Forest: A New Biography of the International Evangelist Gypsy Smith (1860–1947)* (Bridgend, South Wales: Bryntirion, 1997), 30–32. q.v. Smith, *Life and Work*, 57–66.

5. Gipsy Smith, *My Life Story* (New York: Scott, 1892), 39.

6. Ibid., 87.

7. Ibid., 85–86.

He began his work with The Christian Mission as their thirty-sixth missioner on June 25, 1877.[8]

Smith's initial work with The Christian Mission in London (later called The Salvation Army) was inauspicious at best. With little experience, and almost no education, he was at a distinct disadvantage in his ministry. Nevertheless, he continued to work on his reading, and he began to learn the methods of The Christian Mission. He assisted with visitation and open-air meetings. During this time, much was made of his Gypsy heritage. He was often announced as "Rodney Smith, the converted Gipsy boy."[9] In time, Smith ventured out from London to speak in neighboring towns, occasionally speaking to crowds that numbered well over a thousand.

Following six months of preparation in London, Smith was assigned to the town of Whitby, North Yorkshire. Although his stay lasted only three months, they were significant ones. While there, he met his future wife, Annie Pennock. When William Booth learned of the blossoming relationship between them, he quickly assigned Smith to another location. Nevertheless, on December 17, 1879, Rodney Smith married Annie Pennock.

Smith's final station as a missioner of The Salvation Army was in Hanley, Staffordshire. He arrived in Hanley on December 31, 1881, and, as he smelled the sulfur and saw the smoke rising from the potteries, he felt he had arrived near the "bottomless pit."[10] His ministry began with little support, poor lodgings, inadequate accommodations for public meetings, and hostility from the local people.

Undaunted, Smith repaired the meeting hall, involved local dignitaries in special meetings, and built relationships with the people. His efforts resulted in tremendous success. A great revival began in the city, and soon it was affecting every Nonconformist church within twenty miles. Smith wrote, "I preached every Sunday to crowds of from seven thousand to eight thousand people, and every night in the week we had the place crowded for an evangelistic service."[11] By his own admission, Smith's ministry in Hanley produced perhaps the greatest single mission station in the history of The Salvation Army to that time. Amazingly, he accomplished this feat in only six months.

At the end of six months, General Booth requested that Smith move to another sphere of ministry. Prior to leaving Hanley, a group of men were commissioned by area churches to recognize him for his faithful labors in their

---

8. Smith, *My Life Story*, 41–42; q.v., Gipsy Smith, *Forty Years an Evangelist* (New York: Doran, 1923), 85–86; Smith, *Life and Work*, 96, 101.

9. Smith, *Life and Work*, 102.

10. Ibid., 125.

11. Ibid., 130.

community. At a special meeting, these men presented him with a gold watch. When the Booths discovered that he had received this gift, they dismissed him from The Salvation Army for a violation of policy. He said later, "I knew in my heart that I was not a Salvationist after their sort. I felt thoroughly at home in The Christian Mission, but rather uncomfortable and out of place in The Salvation Army."[12] Smith's dismissal served as the impetus for the expansion of his evangelistic ministry.

Smith remained in Hanley for four more years. His work there motivated him to continue his self-education. Preaching to the same audience week after week made him aware of his need for additional sermon material. He wrote, "My first reading outside my Bible consisted of *Matthew Henry's Commentaries*, the lives of some early Methodists, the Rev. Charles Finney's *Lectures on Revival Sermons to Professing Christians*, and *The Way to Salvation*, and the books of Dr. Parker, Dr. McLaren, Robertson of Brighton, something of Spurgeon and of John Wesley."[13] He stated, "I read for two things—ideas, and a better grip of the English language. As I toiled through these pages—for my reading was still toiling—I lived in a new world."[14] As he read, he began to encounter theology. By his own admission, however, this area was not a significant point of emphasis in his ministry.[15] Over time, he began to sense the call of God to a wider field of evangelistic ministry. As a result, he resigned his pastorate of the unaffiliated Congregational Church at Hanley in 1886.[16] From 1886 to 1889, Smith expanded his evangelistic ministry throughout England, Scotland, and Wales. From 1891 to 1897, Smith's ministry expanded throughout England and the world. During these years, Smith also made his first five visits to America. Gipsy Smith had become a global evangelist without really trying.

Following Smith's return to England from America in 1896, S. F. Collier used his influence with the National Council of Evangelical Free Churches (NCEFC) to suggest that Gipsy Smith become their first full-time evangelist. After two interviews with Thomas Law, the General Secretary of the National Council, Smith agreed to become their evangelist. He began his ministry on September 1, 1897. Although the NCEFC would later add two more staff evangelists, Gipsy Smith would be known as their "evangelist-in-chief" during his fifteen years of service. It was during these years that he became one of the most famous evangelists in the history of the church.

---

12. Ibid. q.v., Smith, *Life and Work*, 134–35.

13. Smith, *Life and Work*, 149.

14. Ibid., 150.

15. Gipsy Smith, *The Beauty of Jesus: Memories and Reflections* (London: Epworth, 1932), 27–28.

16. Smith, *My Life Story*, 51. q.v. "The Story of Gipsy Smith's Career: His First Visit to America," *Free Church Chronicle* (March 1899); Smith, *Life and Work*, 157–58.

Gipsy Smith held many meetings during his early years with the NCEFC (1897–1901).[17] However, one meeting that will serve as an example from these years occurred in England in 1900. During that year, Thomas Law led the NCEFC to begin the new century with a series of simultaneous revivals throughout England, and many of the finest preachers in England participated.[18] During this emphasis, Smith led a revival for Thomas Spurgeon at the famed Metropolitan Tabernacle in London. Over twelve hundred people passed through the inquiry rooms during the campaign. Spurgeon wrote of the meeting: "From the outset Gipsy Smith secured the ear of the people, and soon he had the joy of winning their hearts for Christ. . . . He preached a full and free salvation, and illustrated all with thrilling incidents culled largely from his own wonderful experience."[19]

Smith remained active during his middle years with the NCEFC (1902–1905). One of his key meetings during this time occurred in South Africa in 1904. From 1899 to 1902, the British were engaged in a battle against the Boers in the Second Boer War. It was in the aftermath of this conflict that Thomas Law received a request for Gipsy Smith to hold a series of meetings in South Africa. After Law agreed to send him, churches in both countries began to pray earnestly that there would be a tremendous movement of God during this campaign. Smith conducted nine meetings in South Africa from April 11, 1904, to September 21, 1904. Smith's South African mission was very successful. He wrote, "The number of people who attended the mission in the aggregate would be considerably over 300,000. . . . Those who were personally dealt with amounted to 16,000 or 20,000; but these figures do not tabulate all the results."[20]

Smith continued to hold meetings around the world during his final NCEFC years (1906–1912). His Boston, Massachusetts, meeting, held during his sixth American campaign from 1906 to 1907, will serve as an example from these years. Early in 1906, Smith was retained by the Evangelical Alliance of Boston to conduct a citywide meeting. Five thousand, one hundred people made salvation decisions.[21] George Mehaffey wrote, "The Evangelistic campaign in

---

17. It would be difficult to record all of Smith's meetings during these years, but N. J. E. Appleton identified many of these meetings in his thesis entitled, "Gipsy Smith: The Free Church Years—1897–1912" (MA thesis, Cambridge University, 1970). Appleton identified 82 meetings conducted by Smith in England and Scotland during the years 1897–1901. Smith made no trips to America during this period.

18. "The Simultaneous Mission, 1901: With Portraits of Some of the Missioners," *Free Church Chronicle* 3, no. 26 (1901): 32–51. The list of preachers who participated in the simultaneous revival included John Clifford, Hugh Price Hughes, F. B. Meyer, G. Campbell Morgan, and Joseph Parker.

19. Smith, *Life and Work*, 322.

20. Gipsy Smith, *A Mission of Peace: Evangelistic Triumphs in South Africa, 1904* (London: National Council of Evangelical Free Churches, 1904), 186–87.

21. James Alexander, "Opinions and Appreciations," in *The Gipsy Smith Missions in America: A Volume Commemorative of His Sixth Evangelistic Campaign in the United States 1906–1907*, ed. Edward E. Bayliss (Boston: Interdenominational Publishing Company, 1907), 124.

Boston, under the leadership of Gipsy Smith, has surpassed any similar effort here since the great revival conducted by Dwight L. Moody."[22] This meeting is indicative of the kind of success Smith experienced in his campaigns during these years.[23]

Despite the fact that he had pledged his lifetime allegiance to the NCEFC as recently as 1909, Gipsy Smith resigned in 1912. The sheer numbers of people in America may have influenced his desire to spend more time there. While he continued to hold meetings in England, Scotland, and Australia in the years ahead, America became the primary focus of his future ministry.[24] Despite his departure from the NCEFC, Smith maintained his affiliation with the Wesleyan Methodist church. He stated in 1923, "I am a loyal member of the Wesleyan Methodist Church. It is the church I love."[25]

As Britain battled Germany in World War I, Smith felt called to serve his country as a chaplain. The Young Men's Christian Association (YMCA) was the only organization willing to accept his services, however. He stated of his chaplaincy, "I had the entree to the whole British line. I was made a sort of travelling bishop, and I had the biggest field that any man had during the war."[26] Smith spent over three years ministering to the Allied soldiers in France. He wrote, "I saw thousands of boys, thousands and thousands, turn their hearts to God during those three and a half years. During the days of the war . . . half a million British boys signed decision cards in Y.M.C.A. huts and other centres and gave themselves to Christ."[27] This tremendous harvest of souls was one of the positive outcomes of the war.

While much is known of Smith's itinerary throughout the early years of his ministry, his later years are more difficult to assess. Although he still worked with the Home Mission Department of the Wesleyan Methodist Church, he was on his own and did not keep detailed records of his meetings. As a result, his works provided only a small glimpse into his evangelistic campaigns during this time.

---

22. George W. Mehaffey, "An Appreciative Word," in *Gipsy Smith Missions in America*, 80; "Gipsy Smith in America: Wonderful Boston Campaign," *Free Church Chronicle* 9, no. 97 (1907): 12.

23. As research and the records of the *Free Church Chronicle* (1897–1912) indicated, Smith's focus of ministry appeared to shift from 1906 to 1912. The Pacific Coast campaign of 1911–1912, one of Smith's last with the NCEFC, was one of his greatest to date. During this campaign he visited seven major cities, preached over four hundred times to audiences numbering 1.25 million people in total, and had between thirty to forty thousand people pass through the inquiry rooms. "Gipsy Smith Home Again," *Free Church Chronicle* 14, no. 162 (1912): 115.

24. Smith, *Forty Years*, 169. For example, by 1923, Smith had already taken eleven additional trips to America, bringing his total to twenty at that time.

25. Ibid., 101.

26. Ibid., 137.

27. Ibid., 156.

Smith mentioned several significant campaigns during these years, including the Sheffield campaign of 1922–1923. It was during this campaign that he spoke on the radio for the first time to a potential audience of over one million people.[28] He mentioned another meeting held in Glasgow in 1923. While there, he was compared once again to Moody. Hubert Simpson said, "For about thirty years I have been looking for the man who was in the real succession to Moody and Drummond, and I think I have at last found one who is worthy to wear the mantle."[29]

During that same year, he returned to Hanley, the town where so much had happened during the early years of his ministry. Smith wrote of the campaign: "I addressed nearly 300 meetings, and probably spoke to 500,000 people, though it would be difficult to give any reliable figure, several open-air crowds and overflow meetings having to be added, while the number to whom I preached twice when broadcasting no one could estimate."[30]

Smith's love for America continued until the end of his life. By 1923, he stated that he had made twenty trips to America, and by 1932, he claimed the number was thirty. Harold Murray, his biographer and friend, claimed that he made his fortieth trip to America near the end of his life.[31] Smith identified several key American meetings from this period of his life. In 1929, for instance, he led a successful mission in Winston-Salem, North Carolina, where he claimed that 27,500 decision cards were signed.[32]

Throughout the years, Annie Pennock Smith was one of Smith's most loyal supporters. She stayed faithfully by his side, from their early days in The Salvation Army to their many journeys around the world in evangelistic meetings. Theirs was a genuine relationship of love and service, and the limited references to their personal lives suggest a good relationship. Sadly, Annie died on March 4, 1937, while Smith was preaching in America. As a result, he was unable to be present at her burial. As you might imagine, his family and friends were injured by his decision to remain in the States, yet the state of intercontinental travel made those situations nearly impossible. Rodney and Annie had been married for fifty-eight years.

Perhaps the most perplexing decision that Smith made during his life, and the most damaging to his ministry, was his decision to marry Mary Alice Shaw following the death of his first wife. Little has been written about this event. Smith first met Mary Alice Shaw when she was a child. Somehow, he maintained

---

28. Smith, *Forty Years*, 110.
29. Ibid., 117.
30. Ibid., 121.
31. Harold Murray, *Gipsy Smith: An Intimate Memoir* (Sheffield, UK: Cliff College, 1947), 29.
32. Smith, *Beauty of Jesus*, 127, 132–33.

contact with her throughout the following years. In a move that surprised and saddened many of his family members and friends, Smith married her a little more than a year after Annie died. Harold Murray felt positive about the relationship and believed that Gipsy Smith married Mary Alice because he was lonely, longed for companionship, and needed her help in his ministry. [33] Murray's positive view of Smith's remarriage was not the majority opinion, however. Smith suffered from the consequences of this decision for the rest of his life. His remarriage was looked upon with disdain for several reasons. First, in the eyes of his family members it took place "before Annie's body was cold."[34] Second, Mary Alice was fifty years his junior. Third, there were rumors that Mary Alice married Smith for his money.[35]

The final years of Smith's ministry were spent primarily in America, where he continued to conduct meetings. When World War II began, he chose to remain in the United States. During this time, little information concerning his ministry made its way back to England, and that which did was often unflattering. When he did return to England following the war, his health was failing.

Through it all, however, Smith remained in good spirits. Murray wrote, "Thinking of all the active past made it painful to see him in his weakness just before he sailed for Heaven. Yet he was quiet, content, hopeful, grateful, anxious to talk about all the work he was able to do before he was compelled to retire from the field. . . . He did not wail and whine about decline. He said, 'If I never preach again, I've had a good innings.'"[36]

Believing that the weather in Florida would help him recover from his ailments, he sailed for America on the first peacetime voyage of the *Queen Mary* following World War II. He died on August 4, 1947, as the *Queen Mary* entered New York Harbor. His ashes were returned to England and buried in Epworth Forest, the ancient grounds where his Gypsy ancestors had camped and where he had been born.

As can be imagined, Gipsy Smith's decision to marry Mary Alice was a scandalous thing to the churches in 1937. As a result, many of the churches that had hosted him in the past refused to do so following this decision. However, this decision is slightly easier to understand when considering his ethnic and cultural heritage as a Gypsy. It was not uncommon in that day for older men to marry

---

33. Murray wrote, "Surely the fact is that he married in order that he might have a fit companion who would forward that work; and Mary Alice married because she not only admired him but meant to further the work, to hold up his hands as in his declining years he proclaimed her Saviour." Murray, *An Intimate Memoir*, 27–28.

34. Mrs. Romany Watt, interview by William J. Curtis, April 1999, interview 1 transcript, Author's Personal Collection, Florence, SC.

35. Murray disputed this claim by stating that Mary Alice steadfastly refused to be included in Smith's financial affairs. Murray, *An Intimate Memoir*, 27–28.

36. Ibid.

younger women; he would have seen this occur on numerous occasions through-out his life. For Smith, it may have seemed completely rational. Yet, given his ministry context, it was a fateful decision.

Fant and Pinson noted, "It is strange indeed that so many great preachers could have spoken so highly of the preaching of Gipsy Smith without more atten-tion being devoted to his work. Among the great evangelists, even Moody did not receive commendation from such ecclesiastical extremes as Smith did; only Billy Graham has been endorsed by as many differing ministers and denomi-nations." His decision to marry Mary Alice did more than hurt his ability to schedule revival meetings near the end of his life. It also did great damage to his legacy as an evangelist. Unfortunately, history often remembers the end more than the beginning. It appears that Gipsy Smith's decision so colored the way that preaching historians viewed him, that he was systematically relegated to a place of lesser importance in the chronicles of preaching history. Today, he is the forgotten evangelist.[37] Yet, this is unfair both to "The Gypsy" and to the history of preaching. After all, this global evangelist preached for seventy years. As a result, at the time of his death he may have preached to more people than any evangelist or pastor who had ever lived. Only Billy Graham, with the benefits of modern technology, has likely preached to more.[38]

THEOLOGY OF PREACHING

Smith never received any formal seminary training in either theology or hom-iletics. As noted, he was familiar with several books that may have influenced his preaching, and he spent time with renowned preachers who may have influ-enced his preaching as well. He gave the following example of an encounter with Henry Ward Beecher: "When I was preaching in Exeter, he was passing through, and happening to notice my name he came out of his way to see me. In the most fatherly way he gave me some good advice as to my studies and as to sermon-making."[39] What this advice was, however, remains a mystery. Consequently, Smith left little to instruct us as to his theology of preaching.

The pastors of Smith's day had different opinions about his preaching. Monro Gibson wrote, "He is more expository than any other evangelist whom

---

37. See my new critical biography about Gypsy Smith for an exhaustive study of his life. It includes a complete biography, an overview of his Gypsy culture and the impact of primary orality on his life, a complete analysis of his evangelistic, preaching, and delivery methodology, as well as an analysis of the influence of primary orality on his preaching style, using Walter Ong's psychodynamics of orality. *Gypsy Smith: The Forgotten Evangelist* (Timmonsville, SC: Seed Publishing Group, 2017).

38. Ibid.

39. Smith, *Forty Years*, 67.

I have heard, and neither his exegesis nor his theology, so far as appeared, would do discredit to a graduate of our theological schools."[40] The great Alexander Maclaren held a different opinion about Gipsy Smith. He wrote, "[Smith] is not an orator, nor a scholar, nor a theologian. He is not a genius. But, notwithstanding these deficiencies in his equipment, he can reach men's hearts, and turn them from darkness to light in a degree which many of us ministers cannot do."[41] This unique ability to turn people's hearts "from darkness to light," resulted from the combination of his preaching methodology and his delivery style.

Smith devoted himself to one central theological theme in his preaching: the gospel of Jesus Christ. He stated, "The Gospel is not entertainment, an essay, a lecture, something to tickle the ears and stimulate the brain. It is the good news of salvation."[42] John Clifford said of him, "The message of the evangelist goes straight to the heart of the gospel."[43] Smith believed that gospel preaching would always have an audience.

While Smith was intent on communicating the gospel, he refused to involve himself in the theological discussions of his day. Whether he understood the issues under discussion or simply chose to ignore them is unclear. Nevertheless, he did his best to avoid them.[44] Harold Murray wrote, "He was not a man who liked debate or controversy . . . and did not go out of his way to talk about Fundamentalism or Modernism, Christian Science, Spiritism, or the Second Coming of Christ."[45]

Smith described his theology by saying, "No modernism has altered my appeals. I don't insult people by assuming they don't believe the truths. I preach to them. . . . I am not trying, I assure you, to correct the world's theology: I am a fisher of men."[46] Instead, he urged Christians to focus on the message of the gospel. "In season and out of season I shall urge those who are building up a reputation for mere eloquence and oratory to put aside their brilliant theological, philosophical, historical or poetical essays, and just as Ian MacLaren put it, 'say a guid [sic] word for Jesus.'"[47] Those who heard him preach acknowledged this tendency in his preaching. One reporter said, "There is no theology and no dogmatism in Gipsy Smith's sermons. He simply talks to his hearers

40. Monro Gibson, "A Tribute to Gipsy Smith," *Free Church Chronicle* (December 1899): 414.
41. Smith, *Life and Work*, 10–11.
42. Smith, *Forty Years*, 82.
43. Smith, *Life and Work*, 325.
44. Simeon Gilbert, "Gipsy Smith: A Chicago Estimate," *The Free Church Chronicle* 9, no. 101 (1907): 129.
45. Murray, *An Intimate Memoir*, 19.
46. Smith, *Beauty of Jesus*, 27.
47. Smith, *Forty Years*, 82.

from the word of God and from his heart, pouring out the great yet simple truths the Bible teaches, and giving to them the light that has been thrown on them by a life devoted to living them."[48] This helps explain, also, why he never even attempted to flesh out a theology of preaching; his intent was praxis, not theory.

Since the theme of Smith's preaching was the gospel of Christ, it is no surprise that his sermons focused on the key elements of the gospel message: the cross, sin, repentance, faith, and the illuminating work of the Holy Spirit. Smith emphasized the cross in his preaching. While he rarely mentioned the theological implications of Christ's atonement, he discussed the cross itself often in his preaching. He stated, "When he [God] had to save the one world that had got overboard it meant death—it meant Christ's death."[49] He said elsewhere, "If it is salvation you want, this is the way: Christ, and Christ crucified."[50]

Smith's preaching was renowned also for its declamation of sin. He said, "There will be no peace of God, no rest of God in the soul until sin is put away. It is religious cant and humbug to talk about rest when you know sin has not been driven out of the soul. It will never be ours until sin is put beneath the feet forever, or nailed to His cross."[51] He understood that this knowledge of sin was essential for repentance to occur in the lives of his listeners. Smith wrote, "We try . . . to make them understand distinctly what true repentance is, and that the first step towards the Kingdom is repentance. And then the next step is faith."[52] In his sermon entitled "Bible Repentance," he said, "If the repentance is not genuine, everything is false. . . . In Bible language, it is turning, turning from sin to God."[53]

Even as Smith pointed people to the cross, preached against sin, and urged people to turn to Christ in repentance and faith, he understood the necessity of the Holy Spirit's work in conversion. He wrote, "Your religious paraphernalia will not be sufficient to get sinners converted without the Holy Ghost. . . . You will never convert them until you convict them of sin, and you will never do that without the power of the Holy Ghost."[54] He knew his message would be ineffective unless "the Holy Spirit searched the heart and awakened the conscience and illuminated the judgment" of his listeners.[55]

---

48. "Gipsy Smith's Work Impressed Brooklyn," *The Brooklyn Daily Eagle*, 18 March 1907, 5.
49. "The Night Service in Dr. Cadman's Church," *Gypsy Smith in Brooklyn: An Account of the Meetings in March, 1907, as Reported Daily in The Brooklyn Daily Eagle* (Brooklyn: Brooklyn Daily Eagle, 1907), 56.
50. "Young Men Turn Out to Hear Gipsy Smith," *Gipsy Smith in Brooklyn*, 21.
51. "Gipsy Smith Ends First Week's Campaign," *Gipsy Smith in Brooklyn*, 27.
52. *The Quiver* (London: Cassell & Company, 1901), 275–76.
53. "Gipsy Smith Preaches Doctrine of Repentance," *Gipsy Smith in Brooklyn*, 14.
54. Smith, *Beauty of Jesus*, 173.
55. Smith, *Mission of Peace*, 67.

METHODOLOGY FOR PREACHING

What remains for us to do is reconstruct his preaching methodology. While Smith provided little insight into the actual process he followed in sermon preparation, he did provide some clues. Smith had a tremendous aversion to sermon manuscripts. It appears that Smith rarely, if ever, preached with notes. Biographer David Lazell wrote that he "could talk for well over an hour without any notes and still hold his congregation."[56] His willingness to preach without notes was a significant element of his preaching. Not only did he reject the notion of using a manuscript, he claimed that he had never even written a sermon.[57]

The fact that Smith did not prepare formal manuscripts does not mean his sermons were impromptu, however. He often thought about his sermons well in advance of delivering them.[58] However, as the years went by and he completed his stock of sermons, he became more spontaneous in his sermon preparation. Later in life he wrote, "Very often I do not decide what the text or the sermon will be until half-way through the service. . . . The sight of a face, the line of a hymn, some little interruption, may change the whole trend of my thought."[59] This practice of audience analysis helped Smith discern the condition of his audience before he preached.

Smith rejected the use of certain developmental elements in his sermon preparation. For instance, he rejected the traditional practice of enumeration. Instead, he based his sermons on the length of time available. Murray wrote, "There is no 'firstly,' 'secondly,' 'thirdly,' or 'finally,' in Gipsy's sermons. He finishes when he looks at the watch on his wrist and knows the time at which he promised to conclude is near."[60] As a result, the length of Smith's sermons appears to have varied considerably. Several sources said he preached for at least an hour, while another said his most famous sermon, "From Gipsy Tent to Pulpit," lasted for more than two hours.[61]

Similarly, Smith did not utilize traditional homiletical forms. P. S. Henson noted, "The thing that strikes you most, perhaps, is his utter disregard of method.

---

56. David Lazell, *From the Forest I Came* (London: Concordia, 1970. Repr., Chicago: Moody, 1973), 20.

57. Smith, *Beauty of Jesus*, 48. q.v., Smith, *Forty Years*, 138–39. Smith's personal papers at Southeastern Seminary, Wake Forest, contain hand-written notes, which although difficult to read, appear to be simple outlines of sermons. Apparently, he is referring to the writing of a complete sermon manuscript.

58. *The Quiver*, 275–76. One description of his sermon preparation stated, "He pays great attention to the preparation of his sermons, sometimes thinking over a text for a fortnight before speaking upon it."

59. Smith, *Beauty of Jesus*, 48. q.v., Murray, *Sixty Years*, 122, 128.

60. Murray, *Sixty Years*, 127.

61. "Gipsy Smith in America: Wonderful Boston Campaign," 12–13. q.v., "Gipsy Smith in America: Portland and Manchester Missions," *Free Church Chronicle* 9, no. 98 (1907): 45; Lazell, *From the Forest I Came*, 25.

We cannot conceive of him as taking a little excerpt of Scripture and elaborating a discourse upon it after the regular homiletical fashion. He does not deal with the Scriptures as he would with dead lumber, to be sawed and planed and then nailed or dovetailed into those often empty forms that are labeled 'sermons.' He makes you realize rather the truth of that saying of the Prince of preachers, 'The words that I speak unto you, they are spirit and they are life.'"[62]

Smith incorporated certain developmental elements into his sermons, however. Perhaps the most effective element in Smith's preaching was his use of illustrations; his sermons were filled with them. One writer noted, "His power of apt telling phrase is remarkable, and his wonderful gift of vivid imagery has been used at times with irresistible effect."[63] He did not find his illustrations in books, but took them rather from his own "experience and imagination."[64] Indeed, it was his use of illustrations that often led his listeners to respond to his message. He wrote, "In my missions I have thanked God many a time when I have seen men and women melted by some simple narrative."[65] While Smith rejected sensationalism, he embraced the use of emotion to communicate the gospel, and his emotion often found its expression through his illustrations.

Smith also used illustrations and analogies to incorporate the element of argumentation in his sermons. He wanted to reach his listeners intellectually, but he placed a limitation on his ability to do so. He wrote, "I have appealed to their intellect, *as well as I know how*. My job, however, is not to tell them what I don't know; it is to tell them that Jesus saved me, and that He will save them."[66]

Several people wrote brief descriptions of Smith's use of argument. John Clifford said, "He moves the heart of his audience to its utmost depths. But he never forgets that man has an intellect, and thinks and reasons."[67] Other writers applauded his use of argument by equating the "sanity of his reasoning" with the power of his emotive skills[68] or by stating that "his argument always moved along with the music of falling tears."[69] Smith's argumentation via illustration reached the heart of both the educated and the uneducated alike.[70]

---

62. P. S. Henson, "Gipsy Smith as a Preacher," in *The Gipsy Smith Missions in America: A Volume Commemorative of His Sixth Evangelistic Campaign in the United States 1906–1907*, ed. Edward E. Bayliss, (Boston: Interdenominational Publishing Company, 1907), 35.

63. "Our Missioners," *Free Church Chronicle* 3, no. 34 (1901): 256.

64. "Gipsy Smith: A Brilliant Sketch from a Welsh Paper," *Free Church Chronicle* 5, no. 43 (1902): 174.

65. Smith, *Beauty of Jesus*, 15.

66. Ibid., emphasis added.

67. Smith, *Life and Work*, 325.

68. "Our Missioners," 256.

69. Frank W. Gunsaulus, "An Estimate of the Chicago Mission," *The Free Church Chronicle* 9, no. 99 (1907): 78.

70. Smith, *Life and Work*, 328.

The need to rely on written accounts of Smith's preaching makes describing his delivery style a challenging endeavor. As one writer lamented, "No adequate idea of the sermons of Mr. Smith can be conveyed by literal reports of his words, which are apt in forcefulness, illustration, and analogy, for he preaches with greater force and effectiveness by gesture, manners, and intonation of voice."[71]

While few knew how to describe the source of his preaching ability or the proper way to describe his style, many attributed his gifts to his Gypsy heritage. One writer noted, "Gipsy Smith has been very completely made and equipped for this work. He owes a great deal to his gipsy ancestry and his gipsy life."[72] Simeon Gilbert said that Smith never lost touch with the Gypsy boy inside him, and as a result, he was able to "put his whole soul" into his preaching.[73] Whether Smith's style was attributable to his Gypsy background, his natural talent, or a combination of both, it was unique and powerful.

Smith's use of emotion affected his sermon delivery as well.[74] His preaching had a "wooing note," and "the pathos of his heart's message" was powerful.[75] His pathos was further enhanced by his earnestness.[76] A journalist said, "One thing more than another has power to impress the hearts and minds of men—earnestness. Let a man be what he will, if he would succeed he must be able to convince his fellows that he believes in his own mission, that he himself is inspired with a sense of its reality—in a word, that he is in earnest."[77]

One of the most intriguing aspects of Smith's delivery was the way in which he incorporated humor into his preaching. In an age where the use of humor in worship was often discouraged, Smith felt comfortable both allowing and encouraging it. He wrote, "I like freedom in the pulpit. I cannot understand the good folk who are shocked by spontaneous demonstrations in church. I can never see why it should be a sin to laugh with a pure happy laughter in the Father's house."[78]

Smith's gestures were another aspect of his sermon delivery skills and appear to have been as natural as his communication. A journalist wrote, "The grace of manner and perfection of gesture are wholly natural."[79] Elsewhere, his gestures

---

71. "Gipsy Smith at Colchester," *Free Church Chronicle* 3, no. 29 (1901): 120. q.v., Smith, *Life and Work*, 268.

72. "Gipsy Smith at Rotherham," *Free Church Chronicle* 3, no. 25 (1901): 11.

73. Gilbert, "Gipsy Smith: A Chicago Estimate," 127. q.v., Lazell, *From the Forest I Came*, 21.

74. Smith, *My Life Story*, 60. q.v., "Gipsy Smith at Denbigh," *Free Church Chronicle* 8, no. 91 (1906): 196; Cadman, "Gipsy Smith in America: The Brooklyn Mission," 126.

75. S. Parkes Cadman, "Gipsy Smith in America: The Brooklyn Mission," *Free Church Chronicle* 9, no. 101 (1907): 126–27.

76. "Gipsy Smith's London Campaign: At St. James's Hall," *Free Church Chronicle* 5, no. 47 (1902): 288. q.v., Cadman, "Gipsy Smith in America: The Brooklyn Mission," 126.

77. "Gipsy Smith: A Brilliant Sketch," 173.

78. Smith, *Beauty of Jesus*, 56.

79. "Gipsy Smith's Autobiography," *The Free Church Chronicle* 3, no. 36 (1901): 324.

were described as "picturesque."[80] During his 1907 campaign in Brooklyn, New York, *The Brooklyn Daily Eagle (The Eagle)* published some drawings depicting his many gestures. The images suggest that Smith used a wide variety of gestures, some large and dramatic, others peaceful and reposed.[81]

Smith utilized movement as part of his delivery style also. Unlike some in his day, he moved about the platform while preaching. He made reference to this by describing an event that occurred in Louisville, Kentucky, in 1920. During that meeting, someone put a pulpit on the stage for him, which he promptly pushed to the side. He explained his action by saying, "I appreciated the thought, but have always preferred to speak from an unfurnished platform."[82] Photographs of Smith's later meetings reveal him preaching without a pulpit.[83] He enjoyed the freedom to do as he pleased in his meetings, and that included the freedom to move about the platform while preaching.[84]

CONTRIBUTIONS TO PREACHING

Gipsy Smith's background in the world of primary orality shaped his preaching style and influenced those who heard him. Like Moody and Sunday, he brought the language of everyday people into the pulpits of the world. Smith's use of simple words and sentence structures made the gospel message available to all, not just the educated elite. Indeed, this may be the greatest contribution to preaching by all of the evangelists from this era.

Similarly, Smith demonstrated the amazing ability to communicate the gospel in the most descriptive of terms. His sermons were littered with beautiful pictures of the world around him. His was the language of poetry and pathos, capable of evoking memory and moving emotion in the hearts of his listeners. Gone were the cold, sterile manuscripts of the educated pastors. In their place, Smith brought warmth, life, and passion. He brought the Scriptures and the gospel to life for all who were willing to listen.

Smith also incorporated the language of narrative. He had been raised in the world of stories; stories that helped develop and retain the memories of his family and people. As a result, his sermons were not artfully constructed expositions, filled with points and subpoints. Rather, they were filled with stories, which were based on the stories of the Bible. He might read the biblical story, but

80. "Gipsy Smith: A Brilliant Sketch," 174.
81. "Gipsy Smith, Evangelist, Stirs Big Audiences," *The Brooklyn Daily Eagle*, 5 March 1907.
82. Smith, *Forty Years*, 169.
83. "Gipsy Smith Revival Highlights," *The Boston Herald*, 5 November 1935.
84. Smith, *Beauty of Jesus*, 56.

more often than not he would retell it in his own creative way. Then he would add stories from his life and ministry that would connect the individual stories of his listeners with that of the text. In other words, Smith was doing narrative preaching before the term had ever been coined, and in doing so, he brought his listeners into the amazing world of the biblical text.

Further, Smith modeled extemporaneous preaching for the ministers of his day. Without the encumbrance of a manuscript, Smith was able to use all of his physical and emotional energy on the delivery of the message. He was able to stay in tune with the changing atmosphere of his audience as he taught, tailoring the message to their particular background and response.

CONCLUSION

Smith's life and ministry were both unique and remarkable. From humble beginnings, he became one of the premier evangelists of his day. He preached on five continents during his seventy years of ministry and was used by God to reach hundreds of thousands with the gospel. In an age where sermon manuscripts and deductive logic prevailed, Smith's extemporaneous preaching and inductive approach, birthed in a culture of primary orality, were compelling and influential in his effectiveness and longevity.

Sermon Excerpt

Repent Ye[85]

What is repentance? It is not sorrow for sin. You can be sorry, you can weep without repenting—something more than a tear is needed. Do not think because you can weep over a sermon that you are not far from God, or because the pastor made an appeal to heart and conscience that you are a subject of grace. Such weeping may be like that you experience when you are at a funeral, or are reading a sentimental novel. Your tears sometimes are an insult to God. "Woe to them who cover my altars with tears, or bring a vain oblation, I am weary of them. To obey is better than sacrifice, and to hearken than the fat of rams."

Repentance is not promising to do better. You promised that you

---

85. "Repent Ye," Mark 1:14, Chicago 1909Clarify/ complete note? Is this a published sermon? Add publishing information if available.

would be better last watch-night. Many and many a time have you said after a drunken spree, "What a fool I am." After bringing on yourself guilt and shame you have said, "I have played the fool, I will climb up out of this slough of despond. I will be a better man, a better woman." Are you now further in the mire? Have you not more entanglements today than ever? You have made promises enough to reach the skies and the angels, who have beheld the breaking of those promises and have shuddered to the tips of their wings.

Repentance is turning—turning—from sin to God. It is a long journey. Do not insult God by talking about church membership and communion until you have turned from sin to God. Have you repented after that fashion? In other words, it is putting your hand on your heart and getting hold of the curse of your life. For I have discovered that there may be a dozen sins in a man's life, but there are not a dozen that predominate. There is one over-mastering, enslaving habit, and if that is surrendered all your sins will slip away as whipped curs. You must get that sin by the hair and its roots and lay it at the feet of Jesus and say, "This is my sin, I will die before I commit it again." Repentance is turning from darkness to light, from sin to God. I cannot make it easier; the Bible does not; Jesus does not. There must be the surrender, and nothing less than that will satisfy your conscience, nothing less will be acceptable to God, and nothing less will bring you peace. ◆

BIBLIOGRAPHY

Books Cited

Alexander, James. "Opinions and Appreciations." Pages 119–20 in *The Gipsy Smith Missions in America: A Volume Commemorative of His Sixth Evangelistic Campaign in the United States 1906–1907*. Edited by Edward E. Bayliss. Boston: Interdenominational Publishing Company, 1907.

Curtis, William J. *Gypsy Smith: The Forgotten Evangelist*. Timmonsville, SC: Seed Publishing Group, 2017.

Fant, Clyde E., Jr., and William M. Pinson Jr. *20 Centuries of Great Preaching: Volume 7, Watson [Maclaren] to Rufus Jones, 1850–1950*. Dallas: Word, 1971.

Gipsy Smith in Brooklyn: An Account of the Meetings in March, 1907, as Reported Daily in The Brooklyn Daily Eagle. Brooklyn: Brooklyn Daily Eagle, 1907.

Henson, P. S. "Gipsy Smith as a Preacher." Pages 34–36 in *The Gipsy Smith Missions in America: A Volume Commemorative of His Sixth Evangelistic Campaign in the United States 1906–1907*. Edited by Edward E. Bayliss. Boston: Interdenominational Publishing Company, 1907.

Lazell, David. *From the Forest I Came*. London: Concordia, 1970. Repr., Chicago: Moody, 1973.

_____. *Gypsy from the Forest: A New Biography of the International Evangelist Gypsy Smith (1860–1947)*. Bridgend, South Wales: Bryntirion, 1997.

Mehaffey, George W. "An Appreciative Word." Pages 80–81 in *The Gipsy Smith Missions in America: A Volume Commemorative of His Sixth Evangelistic Campaign in the United States 1906–1907*. Edited by Edward E. Bayliss. Boston: Interdenominational Publishing, 1907.

Morris, William, ed. *American Heritage Dictionary, New College Edition*. Boston: Houghton Mifflin, 1979.
Murray, Harold. *Gipsy Smith: An Intimate Memoir*. Sheffield, UK: Cliff College, 1947.
_____. *Sixty Years an Evangelist*. London: Marshall, Morgan & Scott, 1937.
"Our Missioners," *The Free Church Chronicle* 3, no. 34 (1901): 256–57.
The Quiver: An Illustrated Magazine. London: Cassell & Company, 1901.
Smith, Gipsy. *The Beauty of Jesus: Memories and Reflections*. London: Epworth, 1932.
_____. *Forty Years an Evangelist*. New York: Doran, 1923.
_____. *Gipsy Smith: His Life and Work*. New York: Revell, 1901; repr., Greenville, SC: Ambassador Productions Ltd., 1996.
_____. *A Mission of Peace: Evangelistic Triumphs in South Africa, 1904*. London: National Council of Evangelical Free Churches, 1904.
_____. *My Life Story*. New York: Scott, 1892.

Articles Cited

Cadman, S. Parkes, "Gipsy Smith in America: The Brooklyn Mission," *Free Church Chronicle* 9, no. 101 (1907): 126–27.
Gibson, Monro. "A Tribute to Gipsy Smith." *The Free Church Yearbook* (1899): 414.
Gilbert, Simeon. "Gipsy Smith: A Chicago Estimate." *The Free Church Chronicle* 9, no. 101 (1907): 127.
"Gipsy Smith at Colchester." *The Free Church Chronicle* 3, no. 29 (1901): 120.
"Gipsy Smith at Rotherham." *The Free Church Chronicle* 3, no. 25 (1901): 11–12.
"Gipsy Smith: A Brilliant Sketch from a Welsh Paper." *The Free Church Chronicle* 5, no. 43 (1902): 173–74.
"Gipsy Smith in America." *The Free Church Chronicle* 9, no 97 (1907): 12–14.
"Gipsy Smith Home Again." *The Free Church Chronicle* 14, no. 162 (1912): 115–16.
"Gipsy Smith's Autobiography." *The Free Church Chronicle* 3, no. 36 (1901): 323–25.
"Gipsy Smith's London Campaign." *The Free Church Chronicle* 5, no. 47 (1902): 288–89.
"Gipsy Smith Revival Highlights," *The Boston Herald* (5 November 1935).
Gunsaulus, Frank W. "Gipsy Smith in America." *The Free Church Chronicle* 9, no. 99 (1907): 78–79.
"The Simultaneous Mission, 1901." *The Free Church Chronicle* 3, no. 26 (1901): 32–51.

Miscellaneous Gipsy Smith Materials Cited

"Cornelius Smith Family Tree", AD, April 1993, personal papers of Mrs. Romany Watt, Oxford, England.
Watt, Mrs. Romany. Interview by William J. Curtis, April 1999. Interview 1, transcript. Author's Personal Collection, Florence, SC.

Miscellaneous Gipsy Smith Materials Consulted

Appleton, N. J. W. "Gipsy Smith: The Free Church Years—1897 to 1912." MA thesis, Cambridge University, 1970.

PART Two

Nineteenth-Century North American Preaching

The nineteenth century was one of great upheaval and change across the Western world. Following the American and French Revolutions, culture experienced a new revolution—an industrial one. As new inventions, innovations, and technology began to sweep through Europe and America, so did fresh views about humanity's treatment of each other. The abolition of slavery in England, and later in America, produced new opportunities for all people. During this time people began migrating from rural to urban settings, and the result was the development of large centers of industry in massive cities. This was the age of modernity.

Not only was Western culture freeing itself from the old ways of life, it was also freeing itself from the old ways of thinking. Philosophers began to reimagine many of the classic, historical worldviews, and they had an influence in every area of life. Politically, Carl Marx was writing his *Communist Manifesto*, which imagined government without a monarchy. Scientifically, Charles Darwin was writing *On the Origin of Species*, which imagined a world created by chance. Psychologically, Sigmund Freud was writing *The Interpretation of Dreams*, which imagined a world of sexual freedom. Theologically, Freidrich Schleiermacher was writing *Der christliche Glaube nach den Grundsätzen der evangelischen Kirche* (The Christian faith according to the principles of the Protestant church), which imagined hermeneutics as the interpretation of a biblical author's psychological understanding rather than the interpretation of the author's writings. Philosophically, everything was subject to debate.

Preachers in nineteenth-century America required the unique ability to navigate through the headwinds of modernity, while remaining faithful to the gospel claims of a centuries-old faith. Following the Civil War, black preachers were free to begin using their gifts in wider arenas. Two such preachers were **George Liele** (1750–1829) and **John Jasper** (1812–1901). Liele was an outstanding pastor, but was best known as a church planter. Two churches in Savannah, Georgia, and two churches in Kingston, Jamaica, claim Liele as their founding pastor. John Jasper was a famed pastor and communicator. Massive crowds would gather whenever he was announced as the preacher, and his famous sermon "The Sun Do Move" remains a classic in the history of preaching. These men, and countless others like them, made famous the beautiful, gospelcentric narrative that is black preaching.

The Industrial Revolution created an environment for a revolution of methods within the church as well. As the population began to shift from rural to urban settings, circuit-riding preachers of the seventeenth to eighteenth centuries were replaced with revivalist preachers. The Second Great Awakening produced a new generation of revival preachers, beginning with **Charles Finney** (1792–1875). It was Finney who also introduced many new methods of evangelistic preaching, including the use of the "anxious bench." **D. L. Moody** (1837–1899) got his start in the booming urban center of Chicago, and preached effectively in both the US and England. **Billy Sunday** (1862–1935), the former professional baseball player who challenged people to run down the "sawdust trail," used his platform as a means for preaching against social evils, primarily alcohol abuse. These revivalists, and many others, preached topical sermons that revolved around the gospel as the cure for sin and social ills.

Along with black preaching and revivalist preaching, the academic preachers of the nineteenth century wrestled with the challenge of interpreting Scripture for a changing culture. Some maintained a confidence in the infallibility of Scripture; others chose a different path. The first great Baptist homiletician was **John A. Broadus** (1827–1895). Broadus was one of the original professors for the Southern Baptist Theological Seminary, and later served for a brief time as its president. His book *On the Preparation and Delivery of Sermons* was the first Baptist textbook on expository preaching, and it influenced Baptist preaching for nearly a hundred years. **B. H. Carroll** (1843–1914), the famed pastor of the First Baptist Church of Waco, Texas, was fully committed to the divine authority of the Scriptures and the task of biblical preaching. He became the first president of Southwestern Baptist Theological Seminary prior to his death.

Henry Ward Beecher and Phillips Brooks stand in contrast to Broadus and Carroll. **Henry Ward Beecher** (1813–1887) became one of the most famous preachers in America from his pulpit in New York City. Beecher rejected the Calvinism of his father and embraced a modernist understanding of biblical interpretation and preaching. He became best known for developing a preaching methodology that viewed the gospel as the means for political and social change. **Phillips Brooks** (1835–1893) was an internationally renowned preacher from Boston, who had the unique gifts of mind and speech that seldom attach themselves to one person. His famous definition of preaching, "truth through personality," revealed his belief that interaction with the Scriptures should be less about doctrine and more about experience.

The conviction, range, and focus of the preachers and preaching in nineteenth-century America is wide and varied, but there are lessons to learn. Some are lessons to follow and some are lessons to leave behind.

George Liele
Former Slave and First American Baptist Missionary

TERRIEL BYRD

George Liele (1750–1829) was the first American Baptist missionary that traveled abroad as a church planter. Shortly before the ministry of Adoniram Judson, Liele—a former slave—traveled from his Georgia roots to Jamaica to plant indigenous churches among slaves and freedmen and to shepherd Christ's sheep. Liele was one of America's truly inspirational, gifted, and innovative missionary pastors/preachers, and his evangelistic and church-planting endeavors provide a historical and foundational study for missions, church planting, and the importance of persevering in pastoral duties in spite of difficult cultural challenges.

HISTORICAL BACKGROUND

George Liele was born in Virginia to a slave couple named Liele and Nancy. In 1764, George, along with nine other slaves,[1] became the property of Henry Sharp of Savannah, Georgia.[2] In his classic work *The History of the Negro Church: Pioneer Negro Preachers,* Carter G. Woodson shares that George's conversion was the result of hearing the preaching of his slavemaster's minister: "George Liele was born in Virginia about the year 1750, but soon moved with his master, Henry Sharpe, to Burke County, Georgia, a few years before the Revolutionary War. As his master was a deacon of the Baptist church of which Matthew Moore was pastor, George, upon hearing this minister preach from time to time when accompanying his owner, became converted and soon thereafter was baptized by this clergyman."[3]

Several years after George was converted by the preaching of Matthew Moore, a white Baptist minister, he moved with his master to the area of Silver

---

1. David T. Shannon, ed., *George Liele's Life and Legacy: An Unsung Hero* (Macon, GA: Mercer University Press, 2012), 42.

2. Carter G. Woodson, *The History of the Negro Church* (Washington, DC: The Associated Publishers, 1921), 37. Henry H. Mitchell, *Black Church Beginnings: The Long-Hidden Realities of the First Years* (Grand Rapids: Eerdmans, 2004), 53.

3. Woodson, *History of the Negro Church*, 37.

Bluff, Georgia, where George himself began preaching.[4] Liele recalls his own salvation experience in a letter dated December 18, 1791. In vivid detail, he recounts the experience and provides us a glimpse of his emerging theological understanding, an understanding that laid the foundation for his evangelistic ministry and his calling into the pastoral ministry:

"I always had a natural fear of God from my youth, and was often checked in conscience with thoughts of death, which barred me from many sins and bad company. I knew no other way at that time to hope for salvation but only in the performance of my good works. About two years before the late war, the Rev. Mr. Matthew Moore, one Sabbath afternoon, as I stood with curiosity to hear him, he unfolded all my dark views, opened my best behavior and good works to me which I thought I was to be saved by, and I was convinced that I was not in the way of heaven, but in the way to hell. This state I labored under for the space of five or six months. The more I heard or read, the more I saw that I was condemned as a sinner before God; till at length I was brought to perceive that my life hung by a slender thread, and if it was the will of God to cut me off at that time, I was sure I should be found in hell, as sure as God was in Heaven. I saw my condemnation in my own heart, and I found no way wherein I could escape the damnation of hell, only through the merits of my dying Lord and Saviour Jesus Christ; which caused me to make intercession with Christ, for the salvation of my poor immortal soul; and I full well recollect, I requested of my Lord and Master to give me a work, I did not care how mean it was, only to try and see how good I would do it." When he became acquainted with the method of salvation by our Lord Jesus Christ, he soon found relief, particularly at a time when he was earnestly engaged in prayer; yea he says, "I felt such love and joy as my tongue was not able to express. After this I declared before the congregation of believers the work which God had done for my soul, and the same minister, the Rev. Matthew Moore, baptized me, and I continued in this church about four years, till the vacuation" of Savannah by the British.[5]

Today, there remain four churches that lay claim to George Liele as their founder. These include two churches in Savannah, Georgia: First African

---

4. Albert J. Raboteau, *Slave Religion: The "Invisible Institution" in the Antebellum South* (New York: Oxford University Press, 2004), 140.

5. Milton C. Sernett, ed., *Afro-American Religious History: A Documentary Witness* (Durham, NC: Duke University Press, 1985), 44–45.

Baptist Church and the First Bryan Baptist Church (named after its cofounder Andrew Bryan). Also, there are two church plants in Kingston, Jamaica, that claim Liele as their founder: East Queen Street (Baptist) Church and Hanover Street Baptist Church.[6] The latter were planted during the years of the American Revolution, after Liele and his master fled to Jamaica with the escaping British army. During his time in Jamaica, Liele organized the first black Baptist congregation of the Caribbean, which he named Ethiopian Baptist.[7]

Little is known of Liele's educational background, but according to Steven A. Cook, a member of the Jamaica Assembly, "He was not a well-educated man, but he found time to read some good literature."[8] The culture of that time did not encourage the education of slaves, often forbidding them from learning to read: "In Georgia, where Liele lived, slave literacy was a controversial matter."[9] In an essay in *George Liele's Life and Legacy: An Unsung Hero,* Julia Frazier notes: "The methods used by blacks to get an education during slavery were circuitous and often folklorists, among others, traced the perils and possibilities of black literacy through the paths of households, hush harbors, slave narratives, white and black churches, established and informal schools, antislavery and abolitionist organizations, southern plantations, northern cities, early American print culture, colonial experiments, antebellum reforms, and postbellum promises."[10]

Even though there are no records of how Liele learned to read and write, we do know that at some point he did acquire these skills. We know this from the many letters he exchanged with others, referencing his love for reading.[11] In one of these letters, Liele writes: "I have a few books, some good old authors and sermons, and one large Bible that was given to me by a gentleman; a good many of our members can read, and are all desirous to learn; they will be very thankful for a few books to read on Sundays and other days."[12]

One possible explanation for Liele's ability to read and write is the work of the Charles-Town Negro School. This was the most sustained effort in early America for the promotion of slave literacy and was backed by the Society for the Propagation of the Gospel in Foreign Parts (SPG), the missionary arm of the Church of England.[13] It was also promoted by Dr. John Rippon, a supporter of missions who gave large amounts of money to foreign Baptist

---

6. Shannon, *George Liele's Life and Legacy,* 6.
7. Ibid., 77.
8. Woodson, *History of the Negro Church,* 40.
9. Shannon, *George Liele's Life and Legacy,* 84.
10. Ibid., 85.
11. Ibid., 89.
12. Ibid., 47.
13. Shannon, *George Liele's Life and Legacy,* 85.

missionary societies.[14] We know that Liele was acquainted with Dr. Rippon, as they exchanged letters. In addition, many of the missionary efforts to educate slaves dovetailed with the Great Awakening of the late 1700s. This expansion of Christianity throughout the American colonies ran parallel with the expansion of the evangelical Christian movement after the Anti-Slavery Ordinance of 1787 was passed. The antislavery clause of the Northwest Ordinance allowed Quakers and other antislavery advocates to bring with them freed blacks from Virginia and North Carolina to Ohio.[15]

During the late eighteenth and early nineteenth centuries, evangelicalism began to take hold among enslaved Africans and their descendants, some of whom were free, although most remained slaves.[16] These missionary endeavors also led to the rise of several all-black church congregations, though, as Henry H. Mitchell notes, "a spirited debate still goes on as to which was the first independent black church in the United States."[17]

MINISTRY BACKGROUND AND SOCIAL CONTEXT

As noted earlier, Liele was converted and baptized by the Reverend Matthew Moore while residing in Savannah, Georgia. Reverend Moore's preaching inspired and convicted Liele to accept the free gift of salvation, and Liele continued under the tutelage of Reverend Moore for four more years. Liele writes of his call to the ministry: "Desiring to prove the sense I had of my obligation to God, I endeavored to instruct the people of my own color in the word of God; the white brethren seeing my endeavors, and that the word of the Lord seemed to be blessed, gave me a call at a quarterly meeting to preach before the congregation."[18] Noting Liele's preaching ability, it was not long before Reverend Moore had him licensed as a probationer, and Liele began preaching at several different plantations for the next three years (he preached at Brunton Land and Yamacraw, about half a mile from Savannah).[19] Until that point, it was most common for blacks to hear the message of evangelical Christianity from whites, but the conversion of Liele led to the emergence of several other black slave preachers, both licensed and unlicensed. These preachers began working toward the con-

14. Ibid., 89.

15. Terriel R. Byrd, *History of the First African Methodist Episcopal Church and the First Colored Baptist Church of Oxford, Ohio: 1865–1985* (The Oxford Press: Oxford, Ohio, Archived at Lane Public Library Historical Society, 1985).

16. Timothy E. Fulop and Albert J. Raboteau, *African-American Religion: Interpretive Essays in History and Culture* (New York: Routledge, 1997), 92.

17. Mitchell, *Black Church Beginnings*, 53.

18. Ibid., 45.

19. Ibid.

version of their own people.[20] At that time Liele was still a slave of Mr. Henry Sharpe, who was a deacon of the church pastored by Moore. According to Baptist letters, a few years before his British master, Henry Sharpe, died, he gave Liele his freedom.[21]

> Mr. Sharpe in the time of the war was an officer, and was at last killed in the king's service, by a ball which shot off his hand. The author of this account handled the bloody glove, which he wore when he received the fatal wound. Some persons were at this time dissatisfied with George's liberation, and threw him into prison, but by producing the proper papers he was released; his particular friend in this business was Colonel Kirkland. At the vacuation of the country I was partly obliged to come to Jamaica, as an indented [*sic*] servant, for money I owed him, he promising to be my friend in this country. I was landed at Kingston, and by the colonel's recommendation to General Campbell, the governor of the Island, I was employed by him two years, and on leaving the island, he gave me a written certificate from under his own hand of my good behavior. As soon as I had settled Col. Kirkland's demands on me, I had a certificate of my freedom from the vestry and governor, according to the act of this Island, both for myself and family.[22]

Before Liele sailed to Jamaica in 1782, his evangelistic efforts led to the conversion of a slave named Andrew Bryan, to whom he preached from John 3:7 (KJV), "Ye must be born again." Not long after Liele's departure to Jamaica, Bryan began to preach to both blacks and whites.[23]

We should note the legacy of Liele's international ministry as well. He was directly connected to the founding of black congregations in at least three countries: America, Africa, and Jamaica. And through his influence with other black preachers, Liele was indirectly responsible for several other international church plants. When the British evacuated the American colonies, David George, one of Liele's protégés, was carried to Nova Scotia where he gathered a church in 1784. This group would go on to plant a congregation in West Africa as well: "David George led a group of freed slaves to Sierra Leone in West Africa in 1792. There they organized the first Baptist Church in Africa."[24] But Liele's own missionary

---

20. Fulop and Raboteau, *African-American Religion*, 92.
21. Ibid., 45
22. Ibid., 45
23. Raboteau, *Slave Religion*, 141
24. Marvin A. McMickle, *An Encyclopedia of African American Christian Heritage* (Pennsylvania: Judson, 2002), 30.

efforts were most noticeable on the Caribbean island of Jamaica. Upon his arrival to Jamaica, he began faithfully preaching and teaching, organizing the church around a Baptist polity.[25] Those who had been converted under his leadership continued to advance the cause of Christian evangelism and church planting.

While Liele did not affirm the institution of slavery, he was wise, prudent, and respectful of his overseers, and the system in which he found himself: "One of the masters, speaking of the wholesome influence of Liele's preaching, said that he did not need to employ an assistant nor to make use of the whip whether he was at home or elsewhere, as his slaves were industrious and obedient, and lived together in unity, brother love, and peace."[26] Following the admonition of the apostle Paul, he tried to live by this verse: "For I have learned to be content whatever the circumstances" (Phil 4:11). To avoid re-enslavement, Liele remained in Jamaica following the start of the American Revolution, eventually settling there. Yet, rather than complaining about his dislocation, he faithfully carried on his work of spreading the gospel as Christ's ambassador.

A letter written September 16, 1790, by Reverend Joseph Cook of South Carolina describes the success of Liele's church-planting efforts: "A poor negro, commonly called, among his own friends, Brother George, has been so highly favored of God, as to plant the first Baptist Church in Savannah, and another in Jamaica."[27] In later years, describing Liele's preaching to Jamaican slaves, it was said: "Among the Jamaican slaves the most successful Christian denomination were the Baptist."[28] Much of this was the result of Brother George Liele. Liele may have decided to change the name of the church from First Baptist Church to Ethiopian Baptist Church in an effort to win over the former African slaves. He was a unique and influential figure in Jamaica at that time: "It must have been a curious sight for enslaved people in Jamaica to see a person of African ancestry preaching Christianity in 1783."[29] Carter G. Woodson records the growth of the church in Jamaica: "Within a few years, he had a following of about 500 communicants, and with the help of a number of inspired deacons and elders extended the work far into the rural districts. In addition to his ministerial work, he administered the affairs of these various groups, taught a free school, and conducted a business at which he earned his living."[30]

One of the marks that set Liele apart from other churches was his embrace of business as a means of funding the work of ministry. He was an early adopter

25. Winthrop S. Hudson, *Religion in America*, 4th ed. (New York: Macmillan, 1987), 28.
26. Woodson, *History of the Negro Church*, 40.
27. Sernett, *Afro-American Religious History*, 44.
28. Raboteau, *Slave Religion*, 28.
29. Ibid., 129.
30. Woodson, *History of the Negro Church*, 38–39.

of merging Christian ministry with what he referred to as "free enterprise." His will indicates that he was a responsible Christian businessman interested in providing for the economic, physical, and religious well-being of those in his care.[31] Liele also exhibited outstanding administrative and inspirational acumen for ministry, particularly in his work with the Jamaica Assembly:

> At first, this work was largely inspirational, stirring up the people here and there; and many thought that it would be a movement of short duration; but becoming convinced that this was the real way of salvation and life, persons adhering to this new creed contributed sufficiently to its support to give it a standing in the community. Within a few years we hear of the purchase for a sum of nearly 155 pounds of about three acres of land at the east end of Kingston, on which they built a church. When success had crowned Liele's first efforts there, he took steps toward the establishment of an edifice at Spanish Town, which was completed a few years later. The records show, too, that he interested in his cause some men of influence like Mr. Steven A. Cook, a member of the Jamaica Assembly, who solicited funds for him in England. Of him Mr. Cook bears this testimony: "He is a very industrious man, decent, humble in his manners, and I think, a good man."[32]

Today, historians recognize that Liele laid "the foundation for Baptist witness in Savannah and Kingston and in that sense is a pioneer of the Baptist missionary enterprise and Baptist global relationships."[33] The Baptist way of worship and practice of church was a good fit for newly freed slaves. "Like their white Methodist and white Baptist counterparts, many blacks desired a freer, less formal worship style."[34] Not surprisingly, during the early Great Awakenings, the Baptist and Methodists were more successful in converting slaves than were their Presbyterian brethren.

THEOLOGY OF PREACHING

Liele was deeply rooted in the evangelical Christianity of his time, yet he remains uniquely tied to the African American preaching tradition as a pioneering figure. Shannon notes two ways in which Liele was a pioneer among black preachers:

---

31. Shannon, *George Liele's Life and Legacy*, 146.
32. Woodson, *History of the Negro Church*, 40.
33. Ibid., 8.
34. Terriel R. Byrd, *I Shall Not Be Moved: Racial Separation in Christian Worship* (Latham, MD: University Press of America, 2000), 27.

"The first is in the understanding of himself and his Christian faith in relation to Africa, and the second concerns the positive stance of the Baptist churches to all aspects of the life of the community in which they are set."[35] The Bible was the means by which freed black slaves acquired a new theology: "It was from the Bible that the slaves learned of the god [sic] of the white man and of his ways with the world and with men. The slaves were taught that the God with whom they became acquainted in the Bible was the ruler of the universe and superior to all other gods."[36]

Liele himself was the spiritual grandchild of the ministry of George White-field, and in this sense an indirect product of the Great Awakening. This revival of the 1700s, spawned by the ministry and preaching of Edwards, Wesley, and Whitefield, gave birth to "an enormous increase of African public commitment to the Christian faith."[37] Traces of cultural idioms are frequently borrowed from one culture to another, and we find evidence of this among early African American converts as they adapted the preaching and worship styles of these Great Awakening revivalists. Mitchell explains the connection:

> We can see a trail of cultural compatibility beginning with two 1745 conversions under Whitefield, in Connecticut, a trail running to the white church in Kiokee, Georgia, where, George Liele, the founder of the Silver Bluff church, was converted. The trail is well marked. Shubal Stearns (1706–1771) and his sister's husband, Daniel Marshall (1706–1784), were the Whitefield converts. In 1751, they decided to become Baptists and soon felt the call to head south, where the First Great Awakening was in bloom. After fruitful labors in revivals and church starts in Virginia and North Carolina, Daniel Marshall launched several Baptist congregations around Kiokee, Georgia, near Augusta. George Liele, a slave born in Virginia in 1750, was converted in 1772, in Buckhead Creek Baptist Church, where his master was a member.[38]

Many of the white Christians in Liele's life saw gifts and potential in him. Henry Sharpe, Liele's former slave master, recognized in George "an aptitude for Bible study plus communication skills as a preacher, and gave him permission to utilize his talents."[39] Pastor Moore, who was influential in his conversion,

---

35. Shannon, *George Liele's Life and Legacy*, 9.
36. E. Franklin Frazier and C. Eric Lincoln, *The Negro Church in America: The Black Church Since Frazier* (New York: Schocken Books, 1974), 18–19.
37. Mitchell, *Black Church Beginnings*, 37.
38. Ibid., 38–39.
39. Ibid., 47.

observed how well Liele received his Baptist theological orientation and named him a "studious disciple." In a letter addressed to John Rippon, Liele wrote that he accepted "election, redemption, the Fall of Adam, regeneration and perseverance, knowing the promise of all that endure in Grace, Faith and Good Works to the end will be saved."[40] Liele critically engaged with theological concepts, demonstrating the breadth and depth of his theological acumen. His grasp of theology also included a sound knowledge of church polity, and Liele often spoke of his Jamaican church organizational achievements. In a letter to the editor of the English Baptist Annual Register, he wrote: "I have deacons and elders, a few teachers of small congregations in the town and country, where convenience suits them to come together; and I am pastor. I preach twice on the Lord's Day, in the forenoon and afternoon, and twice in the week, and have not been absent six Sabbath days since I formed the church in this country. I receive nothing for my services; I preach, baptize, administer the Supper, and travel from one place to another to publish the gospel and to settle church affairs, all freely."[41]

Benjamin Baker suggests that "the black pastor's model is formulated by historical roots, congregational expectations, community expectations, and personal identity."[42] And as Warren H. Stewart Sr. notes: "The genius of black preaching is grounded in its almost 'intuitive' ability to fulfill effectively and accurately the primary purpose of hermeneutics in biblical interpretation, 'who correctly handles the word of truth' (2 Tim 2:15)."[43] The seriousness with which Liele embraced his conversion experience and his later call to the preaching ministry is indicative of his awareness and appreciation for the sovereignty of God. All his efforts were done in light of that overarching theological reality.

As a Baptist minister, "Liele's understanding of the Baptist Church and her place in society can be inferred from the Church Covenant he drew up for the church he established in Kingston which was to inform Baptist witness island-wide."[44] One major tenet of the covenant was its defense of law and order. As Shannon points out: "The covenant might be read from two points of view, depending on whether it was being read by the enslaved or the slaveholder."[45] Rather than going behind the backs of the slave masters, Liele sought to accommodate their concerns by requiring all of his church members to first gain permission from the slave masters prior to joining his congregation, "unlike so many

40. Ibid. 9.

41. Raboteau, *Slave Religion*, 140.

42. Benjamin Baker, *Shepherding the Sheep: Pastoral Care in the Black Tradition* (Nashville: Broadman, 1983), 16.

43. Warren H. Stewart, Jr., *Interpreting God's Word in Black Preaching* (Pennsylvania: Judson, 1984), 13.

44. Shannon, *George Liele's Life and Legacy*, 9.

45. Ibid., 10.

Baptist and Methodist Missionaries who came forward preaching freedom of body and mind and soul to all men and thereby stirring up the slaves in certain parts."[46] George refused to accept a slave without the permission of his or her master: "No enslaved person were allowed to join the church without the slave-holders' permission, with 1 Peter 2:13–16 and 1 Thessalonians 3:13 cited as justification."[47] This accommodation guaranteed a peaceful relationship between slave, slaveholder, and the church. In some cases, slave preachers were used by their masters as an instrument of control, a means of preventing potential uprisings or insurrections. While this can be seen as an unjust form of manipulation, it also demonstrates the enormous impact of the slave preacher, whose influence among his fellow slaves could be used to unify or to incite protest and rebellion. In Liele's case, his motivation for demanding permission from slaveholders seems to be his own choice, related to his theological embrace of the Baptist Covenant. Interestingly, this practice was not followed by his friend Andrew Bryan, whose church in 1790 numbered 225 full communicants and about 350 converts, "many of whom" did not have their masters' permission to be baptized.[48]

METHODOLOGY FOR PREACHING

George Liele's preaching followed the common style of "black preaching," encompassing a wide range of diverse patterns, structures, and styles. The roots of this style can be traced back to Africa, with the emerging African American church culture of the black slaves evolving into something distinct from both African preaching and evangelical white preaching. The preaching of black slaves remained authentically African but was transformed under the influence of the new Christian revivals.[49]

Liele first encountered Christian preaching from white preachers, but over time he developed his own bicultural preaching model, and "in turn [he] passed this African-resonant model on to David George, Jesse Peter, and the succeeding preachers at these first African American churches."[50] His preaching made use of powerful exhortation mixed with tonality—the "holy whine" characteristic of early Baptist styles in the American South.[51] Evans E. Crawford writes in his book *The Hum: Call and Response in African American Preaching*: "Instead of the more common homiletical concepts—outline, development, exposition,

---

46. Woodson, *History of the Negro Church*, 40.
47. Ibid., 10.
48. Raboteau, *Slave Religion*, 141.
49. Mitchell, *Black Church Beginnings*, 38.
50. Ibid., 59.
51. Ibid., 39.

structure, and so forth—[African America preaching reveals] a musical understanding of the way sermons are heard and the oral response they awaken in listeners, who in turn are heard by the preacher and one another."[52] Unfortunately,
we do not have any records of the preaching of George Liele today. As a consequence, what we know of his preaching must be inferred from other sources to
learn what he might have said in the content of his sermons.[53] His preaching
style was likely quite similar to that of other black preachers who sought to bring
the Bible to life in the lives of their congregants. One example of Baptist slave
preaching that was likely similar to the preaching of Liele is found in the slave
preacher John Jasper. Here is an example of Jasper preaching on the devil's temptation of Adam and Eve: "Adam worn't wid her; doan know whar he wuz,—gorn
bogn' orf sumwhars. He better bin at home tendin' ter his family. Dat ain' de
only time, by a long shot, dat dar bin de debbul ter pay at home wen de man hev
gorn gaddin' eroun', instid uv stayin' at home an' lookin' arter his family."[54]

James Weldon Johnson further illustrates this style of black slave preaching
in his book *God's Trombones: Seven Negro Sermons in Verse*. Johnson shows that
the structure, style, and content of colonial slave preaching had a poetic, almost
musical quality to it.

Scholars of African American preaching have identified at least four common characteristics of African American preaching. First, it has strong biblical
content: "Some have maintained that what sets the African American sermon
apart is its strong Biblical content, a product of high regard African Americans
continue to have for the scriptures."[55] In addition, the preacher makes creative
use of language: "The traditional black church expects and appreciates rhetorical
flair and highly poetic language in the preaching of the gospel."[56] Third, there is
always an appeal to the emotions. This is a holistic approach to preaching, one
that encompasses not only the mind but the body and spirit as well: "Many black
preachers, contemplating the audible participation of those in the pew, intentionally slow their cadences, time their pauses, and chant or semi-chant their
phrases in a most adept and deliberate manner."[57] Fourth, there is an embrace
of ministerial authority. This authority is often granted to the black preacher
by the love and admiration the congregation has for their leader: "Typically,

52. Evans E. Crawford, *The Hum: Call and Response in African American Preaching* (Nashville: Abingdon, 1995), 16.

53. Shannon, *George Liele's Life and Legacy*, 73.

54. Mechal Sobel, *Trabelin' On: The Slave Journey to an Afro-Baptist Faith* (Westport, CT: Greenwood, 1979), 54.

55. Cleophus J. LaRue, *The Heart of Black Preaching* (Louisville: Westminster John Knox, 2000), 9.

56. Ibid., 10

57. Ibid., 11.

African American congregations view their preachers as special representatives of God, or, even more, as manifestations of the divine presence and thus worthy of great reverence and admiration."[58] Liele's preaching was likely guided by several of these qualities and commitments, as well as his understanding of the Baptist Covenant. Again, Shannon highlights the influence of the Covenant on Liele's life:

> From America, George Liele took with him a covenant that he used in churches he organized. The covenant was entitled, "The Covenant of the Anabaptist church, begun in America, December 1777, and in Jamaica, December 1783." The first section of the covenant states, "We are of the Anabaptist persuasion because we believe [in the authority of the Bible]." What Liele advanced in his covenant was a church of purity and simplicity—authority of the Scriptures, consisting only of people who are baptized by total immersion (non-baptism of infants but pastoral blessings); autonomy of the local church; a believer's church; religious liberty; democracy in voting on issues of the church; separation of church and state (no participation in government and no holding of public office); and nonviolence, including no participation in war. Liele emphasized faith and mission as the primary focus of the church and the church as a source of renewal. He also espoused that "faith" came from an inner conviction and not from an external compunction.[59]

As an evangelical Christian, Liele was clearly committed to the mission of preaching the gospel of Jesus Christ as the means of God's eternal salvation for the human soul.

Throughout his life as a Christian believer and preacher, Liele's Baptist identity remained constant. He was steadfast in his embrace of core Anabaptist doctrinal beliefs. Hudson writes, "Of all the Reformation groups none had been subjected to more bitter persecution than the Anabaptist. They were earnest people, deeply devout, who rejected infant baptism and sought to practice full obedience to the commands of Christ, refusing among other things to take oaths, hold public office, or bear arms."[60] In letters and historical records, constant reference is made to Liele's adherence to the Covenant, including his refusal to "take oaths, hold public office, or bear arms." This reflects conformity

---

58. Ibid., 12.
59. Shannon, *George Liele's Life and Legacy*, 11
60. Hudson, *Religion in America*, 54.

with well-established practices of the Baptists of his day.[61] George Liele would likely have been considered what Lewis Baldwin characterizes as a progressive accommodationist—one who sought to work within the system in order to enact change: "Progressive accommodationists have historically emphasized cooperating with the sociopolitical and economic order with the intention of creating a just and peaceful society for everyone. This stream of thought dates at least as far back as Jupiter Hammon (1702–1786), the black preacher/poet who counseled his people to adjust to their enslavement while awaiting gradual emancipation. It found its fullest expression with Booker T. Washington in the late nineteenth century, and has been advanced most recently by nationally-known black preachers such as Joseph H. Jackson and E. V. Hill."[62]

Carter G. Woodson echoes this sentiment concerning Liele when he says, "The unusual tact of George Liele was the key to his success. He seemed to know how to handle men diplomatically, but some of his policies may be subject to criticism."[63]

CONTRIBUTION TO PREACHING

How do we assess George Liele's contribution to the history of preaching? There are three important aspects we should consider. One of Liele's most significant and well-documented contributions relates to the role of the black preacher/pastor and his unique leadership style. As Benjamin Baker writes, "The black pastor is called upon to be all things to all his people at all times. There are even times when it seems that he is to be more and do more than even the Good Shepherd."[64] Liele was a pioneer of this traditional model of leadership among black preachers in America. As a pioneer African American missionary preacher, both before and after the American Revolution, his attention was divided between two distinct persecuted people groups in America and Jamaica. In Jamaica, Liele established a school, which had two important benefits: "Firstly, it provided instruction in Christian faith within the Baptist tradition, and secondly, it gave the educational tools to the learners to negotiate for themselves alternatives within their society."[65]

In addition to his leadership style, Liele illustrates the importance of the preacher as a mentor and spiritual father. Liele's friend David George was converted under Liele's preaching: "David was older than George Liele and had

---

61. Ibid.
62. Lewis Baldwin, *To Make the Wounded Whole* (Minneapolis: Fortress, 1990), 9.
63. Woodson, *History of the Negro Church*, 40.
64. Baker, *Shepherding the Sheep*, 16.
65. Ibid., 147.

known him since Liele was a boy . . . [but] David George did not let this stop him from believing what Liele preached. The sermon was, 'Come unto me all ye that labor and are heavy laden, and I will give you rest.' When the sermon ended, David went to Liele and told him, 'I am so.'"[66] Following his conversion, David became a close companion of Liele and sought to be mentored by him. He went on to become the first black pastor of Silver Bluff Baptist Church in 1775.[67] As mentioned earlier, Liele also led Andrew Bryan to Christ, who later went on to pastor First African Baptist Church of Savannah.[68] Through his investment in other men and his work in discipling and equipping them as preachers, he demonstrated the role of a black preacher as a spiritual father. Liele invested his life in training and developing other ministers, pouring into them and teaching them how to do ministry. In this, he was following the model given by the apostle Paul, who instructed Timothy: "You then, my son, be strong in the grace that is in Christ Jesus. And the things you have heard me say in the presence of many witnesses entrust to reliable people who will also be qualified to teach others. Join with me in suffering, like a good soldier of Christ Jesus" (2 Tim 2:1–3).

In *George Liele's Life and Legacy*, David Shannon draws out this comparison to the apostle Paul even further. Shannon identifies several similarities between the two men, pointing out that the apostle Paul and George Liele shared a dual lineage (Jewish/Roman and African/American) and noting that both men had radical conversion experiences and a strong commitment to evangelization, spreading the gospel across the sea. Both men also had dual vocations. Paul was a tent maker, and Liele was a businessman and church builder, and they both solicited funds for the spread of the gospel. Finally, Shannon notes that both men made great use of letter writing to encourage converts and fellow workers to continue the spread of the gospel.[69]

Liele's final contribution was his advancement of evangelism among oppressed people in the harsh context of slavery. "George Liele introduced Afro-centric lenses. Perhaps because it was within the context of slavery and radical oppression that two forms of spirituality emerged: Native Baptist and the Revival Church. Both demonstrated a hermeneutic that sought to liberate the preacher from any obstacles that would keep him from clearly seeing the context in which he must speak. When this is done, the liberating process of God as made known through His Word can begin."[70]

---

66. Shannon, *George Liele's Life and legacy*, 49–50.
67. Ibid., 51–52.
68. Raboteau, *Slave Religion*, 141.
69. Shannon, *George Liele's Life and Legacy*, 80.
70. Stewart, *Interpreting God's Word*, 24.

George Liele was able to adapt his preaching to meet the needs of oppressed people without compromising the gospel. He demonstrated that there is no cultural context where the gospel of Jesus Christ cannot penetrate the hearts of humanity. This practice continued among the Jamaican churches that he founded: "It was not long, however, before independent churches under the direction of Jamaican leaders started to reinterpret Christian doctrine. By the middle of the nineteenth century, African and Baptist beliefs had begun to fuse in the Native Baptist movement, the precursor of present-day Revivalist groups in Jamaica."[71]

There is much we can learn from the life and ministry of this great man of God. The Reverend George Liele—Baptist preacher, pastor, missionary, and skilled leader—died in 1826, but his legacy continues to speak of his commitment to God and his passion for preaching the truth among oppressed peoples.[72]

BIBLIOGRAPHY

Baker, Benjamin. *Shepherding the Sheep: Pastoral Care in the Black Tradition* (Nashville: Broadman, 1983).

Byrd, Terriel R. *I Shall Not Be Moved: Racial Separation in Christian Worship* (Latham, MD: University Press of America, 2000).

Crawford, Evans E. *The Hum: Call and Response in African American Preaching* (Nashville: Abingdon, 1995).

Frazier, E. Franklin, and C. Eric Lincoln. *The Negro Church in America: The Black Church Since Frazier* (New York: Schocken, 1974).

Fulop, Timothy E., and Albert J. Raboteau, eds. *African-American Religion: Interpretive Essays in History and Culture* (New York: Routledge, 1997).

Genovese, Eugene D. *Roll Jordan Roll: The World the Slaves Made* (New York: Vintage Books, 1976).

Hudson, Winthrop S. *Religion in America*, 4th ed. (New York: Macmillan, 1987).

LaRue, Cleophus J. *The Heart of Black Preaching* (Louisville: Westminster John Knox , 2000).

McManners, John, ed. *The Oxford Illustrated History of Christianity* (New York, Oxford University Press, 1990).

Mitchell, Henry H. *Black Church Beginnings: The Long-Hidden Realities of the First Years* (Grand Rapids: Eerdmans, 2004).

Raboteau, Albert J. *Slave Religion: The "Invisible Institution" in the Antebellum South* (New York: Oxford University Press, 2004).

Sernett, Milton C., ed. *Afro-American Religious History: A Documentary Witness* (Durham, NC: Duke University Press, 1985).

Shannon, David T., ed. *George Liele's Life and Legacy: An Unsung Hero* (Macon, GA: Mercer University Press, 2012).

Stewart, Warren H., Jr. *Interpreting God's Word in Black Preaching* (Pennsylvania: Judson, 1984).

Woodson, Carter G. *The History of the Negro Church*. Washington, DC: The Associated Publishers, 1921.

---

71. Raboteau, *Slave Religion*, 28.
72. Shannon, *George Liele's Life and Legacy*, 55.

Charles Finney
Persuading Sinners to Submit Immediately to Christ

ROBERT W. CALDWELL III

Charles Finney (1792–1875) was one of the most important American revivalists in the nineteenth century. Trained as a lawyer and raised in the New England theological tradition, his evangelistic preaching aimed at securing immediate conversions by discarding doctrines associated with the lengthier conversions of an earlier generation. He emphasized the freedom of the will, the sinner's natural and moral ability to comply with the gospel, and the obligation of every sinner to submit immediately to Christ.

HISTORICAL BACKGROUND

Charles Grandison Finney was born in Warren, Connecticut, in 1792 and spent the majority of his childhood as a farm boy in central New York State.[1] He later related that his family was never significantly religious, though they did periodically attend local Presbyterian and Baptist churches. Finney grew up in the formative decades of the new nation where democratic, populist, and experimental impulses were prevalent. These features molded America's religious landscape, which fueled the growth of popular denominations (Methodist and Baptist), the emergence of new movements such as restorationism, and the appearance of new religions altogether, like Mormonism. American revivals also felt these shifts. The Second Great Awakening (1790–1835), which was well underway during Finney's youth, was, on the whole, more experientially intense, less theologically exact, and less Calvinistic when compared with the First Great Awakening. In short, American religious life was undergoing a dramatic transformation throughout Finney's youth.

---

1. For two excellent biographies on Finney, see Keith J. Hardman, *Charles Grandison Finney, 1792–1875: Revivalist and Reformer* (Syracuse: Syracuse University Press, 1987; repr., Grand Rapids: Baker, 1990), and Charles E. Hambrick-Stowe, *Charles G. Finney and the Spirit of American Evangelicalism*, Library of Religious Biography (Grand Rapids: Eerdmans, 1996).

Theologically, the most important background to Finney's ministry was the New England Theology promoted by the Congregationalists of the northeast.[2] New England Theology was a unique school of Calvinism which originated in the writings of Jonathan Edwards (1703–1758) before it was repackaged by his disciples Joseph Bellamy and Samuel Hopkins.[3] It gained a sizable following in both Congregational and Presbyterian pulpits throughout the northeast by the turn of the nineteenth century and was a primary factor in the New England phase of the Second Great Awakening.[4] New England Theology was an intensely theological and revivalistic version of Calvinism that heralded two seemingly contradictory lines of thought. First, it maintained central features of traditional Calvinist preaching, such as the sovereignty of God in salvation and the fact of human *moral* inability (human beings reject Christ because they lack the moral inclination to choose him as their greatest happiness). Second, it underscored God's benevolent regard to all of creation (God is lovingly disposed to the entire system of being) as well as a human being's *natural* ability to comply with the terms of the gospel (individuals theoretically could choose Christ because there is no defect in their createdness; they *can* choose Christ if only they *would* do so).[5] As we shall see below, Finney had a love-hate relationship with the New England Theology, adopting some of its central features while sharply rejecting others.

Finney spent the majority of his twenties (1810s) as a restless, unconverted young man trying to figure out what to do with his life. After abandoning an attempt to go to Yale and then spending several years teaching secondary school in New Jersey, he finally moved close to home in Adams, New York, where he began preparations to become a lawyer. There, Finney became increasingly drawn to spiritual things: he regularly attended the local Presbyterian church, zealously studied the Scriptures, and vigorously sought salvation in Christ. His search came to a point of crisis in October 1821, when under deep conviction

---

2. For an overview of this tradition, see the introduction to Douglas A. Sweeney and Allen C. Guelzo, eds., *The New England Theology: From Jonathan Edwards to Edwards Amasa Park* (Grand Rapids: Baker Academic, 2006), 13–24.

3. This group has had several names throughout its history in America, including the "New Divinity" movement and "Hopkinsianism."

4. For an excellent study on this phase of the Second Great Awakening, see David W. Kling, *A Field of Divine Wonders: The New Divinity and Village Revivals in Northwestern Connecticut, 1792–1822* (University Park, PA: Pennsylvania State University Press, 1993).

5. The North American origin of this distinction between the will's natural ability and moral inability is found in Paul Ramsay, ed. *Works of Jonathan Edwards, Volume 1: Freedom of the Will* (New Haven: Yale University Press, 1957), 156–62. For sources that describe God's benevolent regard to creation, see Joseph Bellamy, *True Religion Delineated* in *The Works of Joseph Bellamy, D.D.* (Boston: Doctrinal Tract and Book Society, 1853; repr. of the original 1750 publication), 1:124–25, and Samuel Hopkins, *An Inquiry into the Nature of True Holiness* in *The Works of Samuel Hopkins, D.D.* (Boston: Doctrinal Tract and Book Socieity, 1852; repr. of the original 1773 publication), 3:40–41.

of sin and a sense of God's wrath, he resolved to lay hold of God's promises.[6] "I seized hold of them, appropriated them, and fastened upon them with the grasp of a drowning man," he noted in his *Memoirs*.[7] By the end of the day, Finney had experienced a powerful conversion: "[I]t seemed as if I met the Lord Jesus Christ *face to face*. . . . I received *a mighty baptism of the Holy Ghost*." "The Spirit," he continued, "descended upon me in a manner that seemed *to go through me*, body and soul . . . *like a wave of electricity*, going through and through me . . . in *waves*, and *waves of liquid love*."[8] Finney's dramatic conversion was soon followed by his call to become an evangelist, and for the remainder of his life he marshaled his energies toward this end.[9]

Finney's ministry can be divided into three phases. First, he was a full-time itinerant revivalist from 1824–1832. During these years, he was constantly on the move as he conducted powerful revivals in the smaller venues of central New York State (Rome, Utica, Troy) before later tackling the larger urban centers of Philadelphia, New York, Rochester, and Boston. His nine-month campaign in Rochester (1830–1831) was arguably his greatest, as thousands professed saving faith in Christ. Throughout these years, Finney perfected his "new measures" revival techniques—long protracted meetings and the "anxious bench"—which were designed to attract sinners' attention and focus their minds on the gospel.[10] As we shall see below, his new measures contributed both to his renown as an effective revivalist as well as his reputation as a dangerous heretic.

His immense success as a revivalist drew the attention of the wealthy Tappan brothers, who encouraged Finney to transition to the second phase of his career, that of a full-time pastor in New York City.[11] During this five-year period (1832–1837), Finney served two churches, transitioned from Presbyterianism to Congregationalism, and became a bestselling author with the publication of his popular *Lectures on Revivals of Religion* (1835).[12]

In 1837, Finney entered the third phase of his career by joining the faculty of the fledgling Oberlin College near Cleveland, Ohio. There he taught pastoral and systematic theology, pastored Oberlin's First Congregational Church,

---

6. For the full details of Finney's conversion, see Garth M. Rosell and Richard A. G. Dupuis, eds., *The Memoirs of Charles G. Finney: The Complete Restored Text* (Grand Rapids: Zondervan, 1989), 16–26. Finney also mentions a few details of his conversion in his sermon "Conditions of Being Saved," in Charles G. Finney, *Sermons on Gospel Themes* (New York: Revell, 1876), 171–72.

7. Finney, *Memoirs*, 21.

8. Ibid., 23. See also Finney, *Sermons on Gospel Themes*, 171–72.

9. For details of his life between his conversion and his early ministry, see Hardman, *Charles Grandison Finney*, 48–58.

10. Hambrick-Stowe, *Finney and the Spirit of American Evangelicalism*, 108–09, 114.

11. For details, see Ibid., 131–64.

12. Charles G. Finney, *Lectures on Revivals of Religion* (New York: Leavitt, Lord, 1835).

and periodically led evangelistic campaigns throughout North America and beyond.[13] As professor and later president of Oberlin (1851–1866), he led the school to champion numerous moral crusades that many evangelicals were spearheading at the time, such as the abolition of slavery, women's rights, temperance, and Sabbatarianism.[14] In addition to *Lectures on Revivals,* his most important writings are his massive two-volume *Lectures on Systematic Theology* (1846–1847) and his *Memoirs* (published posthumously in 1876).[15] His death in 1875 saw the passing of one of the most influential American revivalists of the nineteenth century.

THEOLOGY OF PREACHING

At his core, Charles Finney was an evangelistic preacher; everything about him tended toward the grand purpose of communicating the gospel to fallen human beings. This point must be understood as we turn our attention to Finney's theology. We look in vain if we attempt to find there a theology of massive erudition and systematic coherence which tied up every loose end. Finney's system was designed for the evangelist's pulpit, not the professor's lectern. Thus, in order to appreciate his theology of preaching, we must discern the outlines of Finney's entire theology because the whole system was designed to motivate and inspire evangelistic action.

We see this evangelistic accent in Finney's doctrine of God. According to Finney, God is to be understood as the benevolent and disinterested moral governor of the universe. As a *moral* governor, he presides over the moral world (the world of angels and human beings) in such a way that he moves creatures' minds by means of moral suasion (the inducements of rewards and punishment) rather than directly by means of "physical" transformation.[16] "God converts the soul by motives," he preached.[17] "Motives are the grand instrument of moving mind[s]."[18] As a *disinterested* and *benevolent* governor, Finney held that God does all things from a disposition that seeks the maximum happiness of the entire system of being in general.[19] Thus, in his work of human redemption, God "works upon a

---

13. Finney conducted two evangelistic tours of England in 1849–1850 and in 1859–1860.

14. For details, see Hambrick-Stowe, *Finney and the Spirit of American Evangelicalism*, 171–79.

15. Charles G. Finney, *Lectures on Systematic Theology*, 2 vols. (Oberlin, OH: Fitch, 1846, 1847).

16. Finney, *Systematic Theology*, 1:16–17.

17. Charles Finney, "Sinners Bound to Change Their Hearts," in *Sermons on Important Subjects* (New York: Leavitt, Lord, 1835), 40.

18. Finney, "Traditions of the Elders," in *Sermons on Important Subjects*, 57.

19. According to Finney, benevolence (both in God and in humankind) is the loving disposition to manifest goodness to universal existence. Disinterestedness is the quality of showing regard to the object of one's affection not out of selfish concerns but purely out of concern for the intrinsic worth of that object

vast and comprehensive scale. He has no partialities for individuals, but moves forward in the administration of his government with his eye upon the general good, designing to convert the greatest number and produce the greatest amount of happiness within his kingdom."[20] This understanding of God's relationship with the moral world, drawn from the New England theological tradition,[21] was designed in part to bolster evangelistic activism: God does not reserve his goodness for a chosen few but has a positive stance toward all creatures. As part of his providential plan, he sends ministers to preach the gospel, and he also sends his Holy Spirit, who powerfully pours motives into the minds of sinners, urging them to repent of sin and embrace the Savior. When hearing the gospel presented in this light, sinners are not immediately confronted with the realities of their personal inability or spiritual helplessness. Rather, Finney believed they are emboldened by a more optimistic message that motivates action.

Finney's theological anthropology (i.e., his doctrine of humanity and the effects of sin) was also designed to bolster evangelistic preaching. This is a vast topic in Finney's theology, so we must confine ourselves to two key points. First, Finney zealously maintained the freedom of the human will in choosing or refusing the gospel call. In fact, he did not feel the need to defend the position because he noted that it is a self-evident truth, a "first truth" of human reason.[22] Biblically, Finney argued that the very fact that God delivers hundreds of commands throughout Scripture presupposes human ability to comply. "It is a dictate of reason, of conscience, of common sense, and of our natural sense of justice, that if God require of us the performance of any duty or act, he is bound in justice to give us power to obey; i.e., he must give us the faculties and strength to perform the act."[23] As he fleshed out the implications of this doctrine, Finney came to reject one of the key features of New England Theology: its emphasis on the sinner's moral inability to comply with the gospel. This doctrine, he maintained, is a "metaphysico-theological FICTION."[24] By contrast, he basically affirmed that unconverted human beings possess *both* natural and moral ability to comply with the gospel.[25]

(i.e. one is *dis*interested in one's own good and wholly interested in the intrinsic worth and good of the beloved object). These themes are often implied throughout Finney's writings, but a good place where he covers the nature of benevolence and disinterestedness can be found in *Systematic Theology*, 1:209–16.

20. Finney, "Doctrine of Election," in *Sermons on Important Subjects*, 216.

21. For the New England backgrounds to Finney's theology see Hambrick-Stowe, *Finney and the Spirit of American Evangelicalism*, 29–43, and Allen C. Guelzo, "An Heir or a Rebel? Charles Grandison Finney and the New England Theology," *Journal of the Early Republic* 17 (Spring 1997): 61–94.

22. Finney, *Systematic Theology*, 2:17–19, 44.

23. Finney, "Sinners Bound to Change Their Hearts," in *Sermons on Important Subjects*, 25.

24. Finney, *Systematic Theology*, 2:14.

25. Traditional Calvinists sharply criticized Finney's theology as resurrecting Pelagianism. For example, see Charles Hodge, "On Revivals of Religion," in *Essays, Theological and Miscellaneous Reprinted from the Princeton Review*, second series (New York: Wiley & Putnam, 1847), 94.

A second important feature of Finney's theological anthropology concerns his analysis of the nature of moral action. According to Finney, human action is praiseworthy or blameworthy only if that action is *voluntary*; *"voluntariness,"* he noted, "is indispensable to moral character."[26] His point was that God holds individuals morally responsible only for actions they have actually committed; he does not hold them responsible for aspects of their existence that lie outside of their will, like possessing a nature that is sinful and which "lies behind" one's choices, causing an individual to sin. Natures are not sinful, Finney argued; people who make selfish choices are.[27]

These points exerted a powerful effect on Finney's sermons. Evangelistic preaching must take aim at sinners' wills by exposing their radical selfishness and persuading them to change the supreme preference of their minds toward God's benevolent purposes.[28] This focus arose directly out of his theology: God is benevolently disposed to all moral creatures and directs the moral world toward their highest happiness; he has created individuals with free will to govern their lives and has provided them with directions (the moral law) to follow, which they can follow if they choose; and he holds them responsible only for actual choices they have made. Emerging from these points is a path to salvation that is crystal clear: I must repent of sin, forsake my private interests, place my faith in Christ the Savior, and embrace God's benevolent pursuit of the world's happiness by denying myself and calling others to faith.

Finney's seemingly rosy portrait of the sinner's natural, volitional capabilities must not lead us to conclude that he believed sin to be a minor hindrance in the way of salvation, or that the Holy Spirit is unnecessary to the process. As a matter of fact, Finney's words on the wickedness of sin are reminiscent of the Puritan tradition. The unconverted truly hate God for who he is; "If you are an impenitent sinner, you have never, in a single instance, obeyed your Maker.... When God has fanned your heaving lungs, you have breathed out your poisonous breath in rebellion against the eternal God.... Ought not God then to hate you with all his heart?"[29]

Ministers should not coddle the unconverted by calling them "poor sinners," nor should they speak as if they are truly seeking Jesus. This concept he believed was a "LIE. No sinner ever sought Jesus with all his heart three days, or three minutes."[30] These harsh comments emerged directly out of his affirma-

---

26. Finney, "How to Change Your Heart," in *Sermons on Important Subjects*, 32b (N.B. there are two pages labeled 32 in the original).

27. Finney, "Total Depravity," in *Sermons on Important Subjects*, 136–37.

28. See Finney, "Why Sinners Hate God," in *Sermons on Important Subjects*, 155, and Finney, *Systematic Theology*, 1:518.

29. Finney, "How to Change Your Heart," in *Sermons on Important Subjects*, 47.

30. Finney, *Lectures on Revivals*, 327–28.

tion that sin is essentially selfishness, which is a limited principle of self-regard that directly contrasts (and thus hates) God's universal benevolence.[31] Indeed, so powerful is the stronghold of this selfish principle in the heart, that Finney repeatedly affirmed the necessity of the Holy Spirit's agency in salvation. "[The] truth by itself will never produce the effect [of salvation], without the Spirit of God."[32] Elsewhere, he wrote that "unless God interpose the influence of his Spirit, not a man on earth will ever obey the commands of God."[33]

How does this language of necessity cohere with Finney's robust concept of the natural will's ability to comply with the gospel? Finney does not give a nuanced, sophisticated theological answer to this question. Rather, he offered an illustration which he believed captured the biblical portrait of how the diverse agents of salvation converge. He asks his readers to imagine themselves watching a man deep in thought walking towards the precipice of Niagara Falls, unaware of his great danger. At the moment he lifts his foot to take the final step "you lift your warning voice above the roar of the foaming waters, and cry out, *Stop*. The voice pierces his ear, and breaks the charm that binds him; he turns instantly upon his heel, all pale and aghast he retires, quivering, from the verge of death."[34] When we ask "Who saved this man's life?" several valid answers come to mind: the man who yelled stop, the message itself ("Stop!"), the man himself who ceased walking into the falls, and God who providentially oversaw the entire event. Finney's basic point is that this illustration is a parable of the three main agents in the process of salvation: the man yelling "Stop!" is like the *preacher* heralding the message of life and death; the *Holy Spirit* impresses the gospel message deeply on the mind of the one in danger of destruction, inducing the individual to turn from his or her fatal path; and the man who heard the message and changed course is like the *individual* who hears the gospel and repents and believes.

Admittedly, all the theological loose ends are not neatly tied up here. Finney was not a trained systematic theologian, as is well-known. While this point does not get him off the hook for the theological positions he promoted (some of which were extremely problematic), it does enable us to see how he utilized theology for evangelistic purposes. Hence, if we step back and survey the trajectories of his thought, the following summary emerges. Human beings live in a world where God is a benevolent moral governor who disinterestedly seeks the world's greatest happiness. All moral agents possess free will, and though they

---

31. Finney, "Sinners Bound to Change Their Own Hearts," in *Sermons on Important Subjects*, 33.
32. Finney, *Lectures on Revivals*, 45.
33. Ibid., 9.
34. Finney, "Sinners Bound to Change Their Own Hearts," in *Sermons on Important Subjects*, 20–21; see also Finney, *Lectures on Revivals*, 181–83 for another instance of the same illustration.

sin freely, they are equipped with all the resources needed to return to God if they so choose. In spite of this, the Holy Spirit's agency is necessary for salvation, since only he can apply the truths of the gospel to sinners' specific situations and powerfully induce them to embrace it. In a way, Finney's entire theology is a prolegomena to preaching, for it establishes the conditions necessary for successful evangelistic proclamation. How Finney actually carried out this task will be the subject of the next section.

METHODOLOGY FOR PREACHING

It is somewhat difficult to study Charles Finney's preaching because he was an extemporaneous preacher. His published sermons were largely recorded by stenographers who had Finney review them before they were sent to press. In spite of this, we can get a clear picture of his method by examining these sermons, looking at his own statements about his preaching, and sampling eyewitness accounts of his work in the pulpit.[35]

Throughout his life, Finney was an outspoken advocate and apologist for the extemporaneous method of preaching. Not only did he believe it honored the sovereignty of the Holy Spirit, but he argued that it was uniquely suited for evangelism for at least two reasons. First, he noted that extemporaneous preaching enables the preacher to connect better with his audience because such preaching mimics the tone of a conversation. Preaching from a written manuscript, Finney noted, does not enable such a direct encounter with the audience because it reproduces the reflections of some past meditation rather than presently confronting people with the gospel. "The very style of communicating thought, in what is commonly called a good style of writing, is not calculated to leave a deep impression on the mind, or to communicate thought in a clear and impressive manner. It is not laconic, direct, pertinent. It is not the language of nature."[36] Preaching by its very nature must be direct and to the point, targeted to the specific situations of the hearers so that the gospel may impact their lives. Thus, many observers noted the conversational nature of Finney's preaching, as if it were more like the minister *talking* directly to the audience rather than preaching. "His sermons are almost all extemporaneous," David Bartlett observed, "and therefore he changes rapidly from one point or thought to another, yet never loses sight of the main thread of discourse. Much of his address has a personal

---

35. For two studies that examine Finney's preaching, see David B. Chesebrough, *Charles G. Finney: Revivalistic Rhetoric*, vol. 31 of *Great American Orators* (Westport, CT: Greenwood, 2002) and Roy Alan Cheesebro, "The Preaching of Charles G. Finney" (PhD diss., Yale University, 1948).

36. Finney, *Lectures on Revivals*, 202.

manner which, though perhaps more powerful when spoken, does not appear as smoothly when written."[37] In his *Memoirs,* Finney noted that many "have said [about my preaching]: 'Why it don't seem like preaching; but it seems as if Mr. Finney had taken me alone, and was conversing with me face to face.'"[38]

A second reason he emphasized extemporaneous preaching is because it freed him to engage in extensive pastoral visitation before public evangelism. Finney came to believe that one of the secrets to effective evangelism lay in acquiring a thorough knowledge of the spiritual condition of the people in a region before preaching began. "Preachers ought to know the religious opinions of every single sinner in his congregation," he noted. Without such knowledge, "How otherwise can he preach to them? How can he know how to bring forth things new and old, and adapt truth to their case? How can he hunt them out unless he knows where they hide themselves? He may ring changes on a few fundamental doctrines, Repentance and Faith, and Faith and Repentance, till the day of judgment, and never make any impression on many minds."[39]

By gaining a thorough knowledge of the particular struggles that community members faced, Finney could use the pulpit to pinpoint specific concerns that actual people were experiencing and directly apply the gospel to their situations. His commitment to extemporaneous preaching afforded him the time to acquire this in-depth knowledge he used in his evangelistic sermons.

Structurally, Finney's sermons followed a simple, predictable outline that derived from the tripartite Puritan plain style of preaching (text, doctrine, application) that was common in his day. He began with a reading from a short biblical passage and would immediately identify a concept (e.g., faith) related to the text that would serve as the main subject of his sermon. He would then proceed to the main body of the sermon where he explored the various facets of that concept. Subsequently, he concluded with a series of "remarks," where he would apply the text to the people in his audience. Generally, his sermons lasted well over an hour, sometimes two hours.[40] It was within this simple framework that Finney would unleash the full arsenal of his rhetorical skills. While an extensive analysis of Finney's preaching technique is beyond the scope of this study, we can explore four strategic tools found in his homiletical toolbox to catch a glimpse of his sermonic style.

First, Finney held that sermons need to aim primarily at informing the intellect with the content of the gospel while at the same time making sure that the

---

37. David W. Bartlett, *Modern Agitators* (New York: Miller, Orton, & Mulligan, 1855), 169, as quoted in Chesebrough, *Charles G. Finney*, 108.

38. Finney, *Memoirs,* 91.

39. Finney, *Lectures on Revivals,* 185.

40. Cheesebro, "The Preaching of Charles G. Finney," 154.

soul's emotions are excited within reasonable limits. Finney has often been car-
icatured as a preacher who pushed the limits of religious excitement during his
revivals in an effort to secure dramatic conversions. This charge sharply counters
his own statements concerning the dangers of untamed religious emotionalism
during revivals. Finney maintained that if the flames of religious excitement are
fanned too extensively during a revival, then the human intellect and will can be
overwhelmed, leading to a "dangerous" and "fanatical" situation. "I have often
seen persons in so much excitement that the intelligence seemed to be almost
stultified, and anything but reason seemed to have the control of the will. This is
not religion, but enthusiasm."[41] By contrast, Finney held that God has structured
the human soul in such a way that its will is to be primarily guided by the intellect
and secondarily by the soul's emotions, which he termed the "sensibility."[42] Thus,
for Finney, evangelistic activity has the primary goal of informing the mind with
the content and obligations of the gospel so that the will might be induced to
submit to Christ.[43] "Religion," he wrote, "consists in the heart's obedience to the
law of the intelligence, as distinguished from its being influenced by emotion
or fear."[44] Must we conclude from this that religious feeling is superfluous to
evangelistic preaching? No, Finney answered, because religious excitement has a
crucial role to play in heralding the gospel; namely, it attracts sinners' attention.
Once that attention is secured, however, the preacher should focus on pouring
truth into the mind rather than continually stirring religious excitement: "We
should present to their minds the character of God, his government, Christ, the
Holy Spirit, the plan of salvation, any such thing that is calculated to charm the
sinner away from his sins, and from pursuing his own interests, and that is calculated to excite him to exercise disinterested and universal love."[45] Thus, religious
excitement, while important to revivals of religion, must be maintained within
proper limits and never be allowed to overshadow one's rational apprehension of
the gospel message. "The more calm the soul can be kept while it gazes on those
truths [of the gospel], the more free is the will left to comply with obligation as it
lies revealed in the intelligence."[46]

Finney's second strategic tool was to excite religious concern through the
message of immediacy. By powerfully impressing on his listeners the message

---

41. Charles G. Finney, *Reflections on Revival*, ed. Donald W. Dayton (Minneapolis: Bethany Fellowship Inc., 1979), 39.

42. Finney, *Systematic Theology*, 2:53, 65–67.

43. Finney, *Lectures on Revivals*, 169. For Finney's understanding on the natural order of the soul's faculties, see "How to Change Your Heart," in *Sermons on Important Subjects*, 32b.

44. Finney, *Reflections on Revival*, 38.

45. Ibid., 40.

46. Ibid., 41.

that "now is the day of salvation!" Finney sought to expose sinners to the existential weight of their present obligation to submit to Christ. Sin, Satan, and theological error, Finney believed, had blunted the sheer gravity of this immediacy by leading many to conclude that they must wait for some set of conditions to obtain before embracing the gospel. "Some wait to become more dead to the world. Some to get a broken heart. Some to get their doubts cleared up, before they come to Christ."[47] Others concoct innumerable excuses designed to put off the choice of faith and repentance. These include the excuses of inability ("I have no ability to come to Christ"), of possessing a sinful nature ("I have a sinful nature and cannot turn to Christ"), of believing that Christ will not accept my repentance ("Christ won't receive me"), of waiting to feel greater conviction of sin ("I don't feel convicted enough"), or of lacking a sense of the Christian graces ("I don't feel a love for God").[48] Not only do these excuses delay salvation, but they also involve the sinner in condemning God, because lurking in the midst of each excuse is the charge that God somehow has not granted the sinner the resources to come to Christ. To Finney, this "waiting system" was worse than complete nonsense; it was actually a "soul killing poison" that has landed countless multitudes in hell.[49] He powerfully strove to counter the waiting system with the message of immediate repentance. God, Finney repeatedly thundered, has granted every sinner all the resources to find salvation in Christ *now*: he has provided the Savior for you, he has sent a preacher to call you to Christ, he has sent his Holy Spirit to strive with your souls, and by nature he has given you the natural and moral ability to comply with the terms of the gospel. What set of conditions are there left to fulfill, other than the consent of your stubborn, selfish wills? "The requirement of the gospel is, repent *now*, and believe that your soul may live. It gives not the sinner a moment's time to wait; it presses upon him with all the weight of Jehovah's authority, instantly to ground his weapons, and submit to God."[50]

Third, Finney often stoked the religious imagination by painting vivid scenes of the afterlife to communicate theological truths. We see this in his many imaginings of heaven and hell. Finney noted that the biblical representations of "the final doom of the wicked are exceedingly striking."[51] First, there is the image of the "bottomless pit" throughout the book of Revelation. "A deathless soul is

---

47. Charles G. Finney, "Way of Salvation," in *Lectures to Professing Christians* (New York: Taylor, 1837), 294.

48. See Finney, "The Excuses of Sinners Condemn God," in *Sermons on Gospel Themes*, 73–97 for his entire list of excuses.

49. Finney, "Traditions of the Elders," in *Sermons on Important Subjects*, 75.

50. Ibid., 74.

51. Finney, "The Wages of Sin," in *Sermons on Gospel Themes*, 51.

cast therein; it sinks and sinks and sinks, going down [to] that awful pit which knows no bottom, weeping and wailing as it descends, and you hear its groans as they echo and re-echo from the sides of that dread[ed] cavern of woe!"[52] He treats the image of the lake of fire and brimstone (Rev 19:20, 20:10, 21:8 KJV) in a similar manner: "You see lost sinners thrown into its waves of rolling fire; and they lash its burning shore and gnaw their tongues for pain."[53] In an effort to convey the eternal nature of the sinner's destruction in hell, he invokes another image that hits closer to home, the scene of a loved one in the midst of agony on the death bed.

> Did you ever see [someone] die? . . . How long was he dying? . . . When my wife died, her death struggles were long and heart-rending. If you had been there, you would have cried mightily to God—"Cut it short! O, cut it short and relieve this dreadful agony!" But suppose it had continued, on and on, by day and by night—day after day, through its slow moving hours, and night after night—*long* nights, as if there could be no morning. The figure of our text supposes an eternal dying. Let us conceive such a case. . . . A poor man cannot die! He lingers in the death-agony a month, a year, five years, ten years—till all his friends are broken down, and fall into their graves under the insupportable horror of the scene: but still the poor man cannot die! . . . What would you think of such a scene? It would be an illustration—that is all—a feeble illustration of the awful *"second death!"*[54]

By piling image upon image of the horrors of hell, Finney endeavored to confront sinners with their final end in an effort to convince them of their dire plight, and hopefully move them to repentance.

Finney also employed this strategy with regard to heaven, not only to portray the glorious setting of the saints there, but sometimes to demonstrate the error of heretical views. For example, in one 1831 sermon, Finney took aim at the heresy of "restorationist" universalists who believed that the temporary fires of hell could restore the damned to the blessedness of heaven. In countering their views, Finney took an unusual strategy. He first draws attention to the focus of the saints' heavenly praise, which emphasizes the worthiness of the Lamb's sacrifice on behalf of the redeemed (Rev 5:12). He then asks his listeners to imagine a scene where these heavenly worshipers are rudely interrupted by a group of trespassers who have just arrived in heaven giving thanks to the hellfire that purged

---

52. Ibid., 52.
53. Ibid.
54. Ibid., 52–53. Finney was twice a widower and married three times.

them from their remaining sins. Edwards Amasa Park, a young seminary student at Andover Seminary at the time, recorded the scene of Finney's sermon:

> No sooner had he uttered the word "blessing" [from Rev 5:12, KJV] than he started back, turned his face from the mass of the audience before him, fixed his glaring eyes upon the gallery at his right hand, and gave all the signs of a man who was frightened by a sudden interruption of divine worship. With a stentorian voice he cried out: "What is that I see? What means that rabble-rout of men coming up here? Hark! Hear them shout! Hear their words: 'Thanks to *hell-fire!* We have served out our time. Thanks! *Thanks!* WE HAVE SERVED OUT OUR TIME. THANKS TO HELL-FIRE!'" Then the preacher turned his face from the side gallery, looked again upon the mass of the audience, and after a lengthened pause, during which a fearful stillness pervaded the house, he said in gentle tones: "Is this the spirit of the saints? Is this the music of the upper world?"[55]

With those rhetorical questions, Finney placed his finger on the fundamental error of these "restorationists": heaven's worshipers do not praise God because they have finished paying for their sins by hellfire. Rather, they resound with praises to the Lamb, who alone has ransomed them from death by his death and resurrection. Finney's imaginary narrative exposed the folly of the restorationists' erroneous views.

The effect of Finney's sermon was electrifying. Park noted how he could feel the trembling excitement of the men who sat with him on the pew when Finney preached these words. What is even more remarkable is that Park could remember the specific details of this sermon almost six decades later: "The power of the whole sermon was compressed into that vehement utterance. It is more than fifty-eight years since I listened to that discourse. I remember it well. I can recall the impression of it as distinctly as I could a half-century ago; but if every word of it were on the printed page, it would not be the identical sermon of the living preacher."[56]

Fourth, and finally, Finney employed "new measures" techniques in tandem with his preaching to tailor the gospel to people in specific circumstances. Finney was famous for devising what became known as the system of "new measures" revivalism—revival practices which were designed to apply the gospel to

---

55. Park's comments are found in G. Frederick Wright, *Charles Grandison Finney* (Boston: Houghton Mifflin, 1893), 73–74.

56. Ibid., 74. Park (1808–1900) was a well-known Congregationalist minister and Edwardsean theologian who taught at Andover Seminary from 1847–1881.

sinners with radical specificity. The most well-known of these measures were the anxious meetings, where convicted sinners came to a meeting to receive counsel about the state of their souls from a trained minister; the protracted meeting, lengthy services devoted to sustained attention on the gospel; and the anxious bench, a place (like a seat, pew, or area) near the front of the congregation where convicted sinners could go during a revival service to receive specific prayer and counsel about the state of their souls. Finney employed these measures to provide settings where sinners could be directly confronted with their specific duties related to the gospel.[57] Critics charged that these techniques were innovative but unbiblical and manipulative. The anxious bench, for instance, was often criticized as a setting where sinners are hard-pressed to accept the gospel prematurely. It is true that Finney trained his anxious bench counselors to guide sinners to choose Christ; what else would one expect from a man who vigorously taught the doctrines of spiritual ability and immediate repentance? Yet it is equally true that he never encouraged an easy-believism. Indeed, the type of spirituality that Finney heralded—one that emphasized disinterested benevolence, self-denial, and a hatred for all sin—rendered any such idea an impossibility. "It is naturally impossible that you should be saved," he preached, "until you are so well pleased with Christ in all respects as to find your pleasure in doing His."[58] New measures, then, are to be understood as a practical extension of his theology of immediacy and his conviction that sinners must be particularly and individually confronted with the obligations of the gospel. Ultimately, they served as parahomiletical aids to his evangelistic preaching since they created a context for sinners to reflect deeply upon the gospel and receive pointed counsel on how it specifically applied to their situation.

CONTRIBUTIONS TO PREACHING

Finney's impact on evangelistic preaching was immense. In what remains, we can identify three significant contributions he made to evangelical homiletics in nineteenth-century America. First, Finney unhinged the proclamation of the gospel from doctrines which were viewed as impeding *immediate* evangelistic action. As noted, Finney strongly opposed theological positions which he

---

57. Finney was deeply concerned with applying the gospel specifically to individuals through these measures. The anxious meeting is "appointed for the purpose of holding personal conversation with anxious sinners, and to adapt instruction to the cases of individuals, so as to lead them immediately to Christ." Likewise, the purpose of the anxious bench is "where the anxious may come and be addressed particularly, and be made subjects of prayer, and sometimes conversed with individually." Finney, *Lectures on Revivals*, 242 and 247 respectively.

58. Finney, "Conditions of Being Saved," in *Sermons on Gospel Themes*, 182.

believed delayed a sinner's immediate submission to Christ, such as moral inability, a Calvinistic version of total depravity, and the expectation that one must experience a lengthy period of conviction prior to receiving a new heart. He was convinced this "waiting system" had led multitudes to hell. By dismissing these doctrines, Finney emboldened generations of revivalists and ministers to follow suit in their preaching.

Second, Finney's theology of immediacy—that is his advocacy of the doctrines of spiritual ability, the freedom of the will, and immediate repentance—combined with his new measures techniques, focused the goal of evangelistic preaching exclusively on the sinner's choice for Christ. The moment of salvation was no longer marked by the discovery of a new heart, that is, a heart replete with new affections for Christ and the fruits of the Spirit. Such discoveries often took time to discern. Rather, in the wake of Finney's spectacular revivals, salvation was identified with one's volitional submission to Christ because Finney came to identify the "new heart" with that moment of submission. Consequently, after Finney, more American revivalists increasingly came to view the goal of evangelistic preaching as securing a sinner's decision for Christ.

Lastly, Finney's dual emphasis on the theology of immediacy and new measures revivalism helped render American evangelistic preaching more pragmatic. Earlier revival preaching was heavily preoccupied with the deeper structures associated with theological anthropology, including the unbeliever's sinful nature, the new heart, and one's religious affections. It also underscored soteriological doctrines related to human nature, such as original sin, the soul's abilities and inabilities, the terrors of the law, and the nature and experience of justifying faith. While a rich Protestant theology animated this earlier preaching, Finney feared that it was overly preoccupied with murky depths of the human psyche, and was out of touch with people's real lives. By contrast, Finney's soteriology focused predominantly on the tangible fruits of human choice, a focus he believed provided a much more reliable barometer of authentic spirituality. Finney's spectacular revivals encouraged other evangelists to embrace a similar pragmatism in their preaching. It is thus no surprise to find that D. L. Moody, the next major American revivalist, was known not for his rich theological preaching, but for sermons that highlighted simple stories of people who found salvation and redemption through faith in Jesus Christ.

Finney was not the sole cause of this pragmatic turn in American religion. At the time of his ordination, he was stepping into a river of American revivalism which was increasingly charting a course toward more practical approaches to ministry. Consequently, it is better to understand Finney as a great mirror of the age, one who reflected the transformation occurring in American revivalism with crystal clarity. His major innovations—the anxious bench, quantifying techniques that reliably yielded revivals, and identifying immediate repentance and faith in Christ as the moment of a sinner's salvation—concentrated these pragmatic impulses that were already developing in American revivalism. As such, he left a deep and long-lasting imprint on the subsequent history of evangelical preaching in North America and beyond.

Sermon Excerpt
Tradition of the Elders[59]

Hence when they have been called upon to repent, and believe the gospel, they have replied that they were willing and waiting God's time. The inference from their premises was irresistible, that they must wait, and consequently a compromise ensued; instead of calling upon him, and insisting upon his immediate repentance; instead of urging him to make to him a new heart and a new spirit, on pain of eternal death, he has been told to pray, to use the means, to call upon God for the influences of his spirit and wait for sovereign grace to change his heart. Thus when the sinner has felt straitened, and shut up to the faith, and ready to break down under the pressure of the requirements to repent and believe the gospel; his conscience has been relieved; the pressure of obligation mitigated, and the agonizing obligation to instant submission deferred. The sinner has found his pains removed, his obligation to present duty postponed; he has turned away, in the use of means, quenched the Spirit, prayed himself to sleep, and sunk to the depths of hell. And no wonder; for the requirements of God are set aside, and another rule of duty substituted in their place. The requirement of the gospel is, repent now, and believe that your soul may live. It gives not the sinner a moment's time to wait; it presses upon him with all the weight of Jehovah's authority, instantly to ground his weapons, and submit to God. He feels hedged in, as with a wall of fire; he pants, and struggles, and is driven to extremity; he prays, but still the gospel cries repent and believe; . . . But here comes in the charming, soothing opiate of inability. He meets some one, who tells him to use the means; that God is sovereign, that he cannot repent

---

59. Note: Finney here contrasts two forms of evangelism, the "waiting system" and his own approach of immediate repentance. Finney, "Tradition of the Elders," in *Sermons on Important Subjects*, 74–75.

himself; that he must not think to take the work out of the hands of God; that if he prays, and waits, at the gospel pool, he has no reason to be discouraged; that by and by, he has every reason to hope that God will change his heart. . . . Thus another requirement being substituted for that of God, the power of the gospel is broken; and the commandment that was about to crush the sinner in the dust, that had hedged him in, and gave him no gleam of hope, but in instant submission, is rendered of no effect by this tradition. The sinner breathes easier, feels relieved from the pressure of present obligation, drinks the lethean draught of the soul-killing poison, and goes down to hell. ◆

BIBLIOGRAPHY

Selected Writings by Charles Finney

Finney, Charles G. *Lectures on Revivals of Religion.* New York: Leavitt, Lord, 1835.
_____. *Lectures on Systematic Theology.* 2 vols. Oberlin, OH: Fitch, 1846, 1847.
_____. *Lectures to Professing Christians.* New York: Taylor, 1837.
_____. *Reflections on Revival.* Compiled by Donald W. Dayton. Minneapolis: Bethany Fellowship Inc., 1979.
_____. *Sermons on Gospel Themes.* New York: Revell, 1876.
_____. *Sermons on Important Subjects.* New York: Leavitt, Lord, 1835.
Rosell, Garth M., and Richard A. G. Dupuis, eds. *The Memoirs of Charles G. Finney: The Complete Restored Text.* Grand Rapids: Zondervan, 1989.

Selected Studies on Charles Finney

Cheesebro, Roy Alan. "The Preaching of Charles G. Finney." PhD diss., Yale University, 1948.
Chesebrough, David B. *Charles G. Finney: Revivalistic Rhetoric.* Great American Orators, No. 31. Westport, CT: Greenwood, 2002.
Guelzo, Allen C. "An Heir or A Rebel? Charles Grandison Finney and the New England Theology." *Journal of the Early Republic* 17 (1997): 61–94.
Hambrick-Stowe, Charles E. *Charles G. Finney and the Spirit of American Evangelicalism.* Library of Religious Biography. Grand Rapids: Eerdmans, 1996.
Hardman, Keith J. *Charles Grandison Finney, 1792–1875: Revivalist and Reformer.* Syracuse: Syracuse University Press, 1987; repr., Grand Rapids: Baker, 1990.
Rosell, Garth M. "Charles G. Finney: His Place in the Stream of American Evangelicalism." Pages 131–47 In *The Evangelical Tradition in America.* Edited by Leonard I. Sweet. Macon, GA: Mercer University Press, 1984.
Sweet, Leonard I. "The View of Man Inherent in New Measures Revivalism." *Church History* 45 (1976): 206–21.
Wright, G. Frederick. *Charles Grandison Finney.* Boston: Houghton Mifflin, 1893.

John Jasper
Preaching for Social and Eschatological Freedom

ALFONZA W. FULLWOOD
ROBERT SMITH JR.

By all accounts, John Jasper (1812–1901) was destined to be a preacher of the gospel. How else does one explain his incredible preaching genius and prominence during a period in America when there were few advantages or opportunities for free African Americans, let alone for enslaved African Americans? Moreover, how else does one account for his prominence during a period when African American lives were a constant symbol of degradation and dehumanization? He had no pedigree, formal education, credentials, or resume. Yet and still, Jasper possessed a rare gift and passion for preaching the gospel, and led thousands to yield to the power of the cross. Beyond leading thousands to Christ, his preaching and remarkable eloquence attracted and puzzled the intellectual elite, the politically powerful, the sophisticated aristocracy, the religious magisterial and ecclesiastic, and the ordinary citizenry. And once Jasper gained his freedom, his preaching and impact became even more extraordinary.

HISTORICAL BACKGROUND

On July 4, 1812, John Jasper was born into slavery on the Peachy pantation of Fluvanna County, Virginia.[1] He was the last of twenty-four children born to Phillip and Nina Jasper, and his father died just two months before his birth. Little information exists on his father; nonetheless, the little that is known indicates he had an inclination to preach and tendencies toward alcohol consumption.[2] There is, however, enough information on his mother to conclude that she held some influence around the plantation community. Most notably, she had

---

1. The Peachy family enjoyed substantial holdings to include slave properties, making them one of the largest in Fluvanna County. They owned three large farms and the great plantation in Fluvanna County, which required large numbers of slaves to maintain such an operation. See Richard Ellsworth Day, *Rhapsody in Black: The Life Story of John Jasper* (Pennsylvania: Judson, 1953), 34.

2. Phillip was a Baptist preacher only in the strict sense and limitations permitted as a slave. His father was African-born and transported to the New World, resulting from the Atlantic slave trade. And, therefore,

a godly heart and a strong prayer life. Her piety should not be separated from Jasper's passion and zeal to preach the gospel. She constantly prayed, "Lord if this chile you's sendin me is a boy, doan' let him do nothin' else but sing de praises of Jesus."[3] She favored the biblical story concerning John the Baptist, the forerunner of Christ. At the birth of Jasper, her family and friends suggested naming him after his father. She pushed back saying, "No, sir! His name is John."[4] All of this shows that Nina was a Christian woman whose prayers were answered concerning her son—he became a man who proclaimed the praises of Christ through his preaching ministry.

Growing up as a slave boy, Jasper's tasks began at an early age. When he was eight years old, he worked as a cart boy, holding the oxen while other workers loaded and unloaded the cart. When he was ten years old, he waited on tables, and two years later his duties increased to assistant gardener.[5] Perhaps from a slave's point of view he had a privileged role on the plantation. He was assigned to the "big house" as a house servant like his mother. Jasper benefited from such a position because he was exposed to the "manners of Virginia aristocracy" in ways field hands did not experience. Unlike field workers, his mannerism appeared "like the courtly, dignified, royal people in the Great Houses."[6] He "received an [informal] aristocratic education, and he never lost it."[7] Still, Jasper worked as a field hand on several plantations as a consequence of the declining economic situations of his owners. On many occasions, his masters hired him out to other plantations.[8] In 1834, Jasper became the property of John Blair Peachy of Williamsburg, Virginia. There he met and married Elvy Weaden from another plantation.[9] The twenty-two-year-old Jasper had a very short-lived marriage, which was common for many slaves. He faced charges of running away because his owner rejected his getting married as a legitimate explanation for his absence. As a punishment, his owner did not allow him to see his wife. For this reason, his marriage for all practical purposes ended. Elvy requested a release from the union, and she remarried the following year. As a result, Jasper harbored deep bitterness, sending him into a downward spiral of moral failure.[10]

---

it is reasonable to conclude that the "cultural memories" of Africa had a strong influence in the Phillip Jasper family, one generation removed from the motherland, Africa. Ibid., 39–40.

3. Ibid.

4. Ibid., 41.

5. Day, *Rhapsody in Black,* 45.

6. Ibid.

7. Ibid.

8. Ibid., 46. In 1825, John was hired out to Peter McHenry in Richmond. He was then hired out to Dr. James Woldridge in 1826, and worked in the coal pits of Chesterfield County. Finally, he was brought back to Richmond in 1827, hired out to Samuel Hardgrove as a stemmer in the tobacco factory.

9. Ibid., 46–47.

10. Day, *Rhapsody in Black,* 47.

Jasper married on three other occasions, including a second marriage to Candace Jordon. They had six children, but the marriage ended in divorce. Later, Jasper married his third wife, Mary Anne Cole, who was a widow with one child. They did not have any additional children together, and she died in 1874. In 1876, Jasper married his fourth wife, Martha. They also had no children.[11]

After the death of John Blair Peachy, Samuel Hardgrove (who had previously hired Jasper for several years) purchased him from the Peachy family. Hardgrove enjoyed a distinguished reputation as a successful businessman. He was one of the leading citizens in Richmond, Virginia, and he served as a deacon at the First Baptist Church of Richmond. Arguably, Jasper experienced a more favorable climate in his relationship with Hardgrove. It appears that this relationship marked the beginning of a path that led to an eventual spiritual awakening for Jasper. Hardgrove developed warm and earnest affections for Jasper and for his spiritual life.[12] Not accustomed to such caring consideration, he became more malleable to the gospel of Christ than before. In addition to the Christian influence of Hardgrove, the prayers of Jasper's mother were supremely impactful. Her faith should not be discounted in view of Jasper's path to conversion. At age twenty-seven, he had a dramatic experience that precipitated a life-changing journey. He describes his experience in 1839 this way:

> I was down in Capitol Square in Richmond. Folks were swarming around and laughing and hurrahing when all of a sudden God's arrow of conviction went into my proud heart and brought me low. I left there badly crippled. . . . No one in that factory could beat me at that work. But that morning the stems wouldn't come out to save me, and I tore up the tobacco by the pound and flung it under the table. Fact is the darkness of death was in my soul that morning. Of all sinners, I was the worst. I thought I was going to die right then, and when I suppose it was my last breath, I flung up a cry, "Oh, Jesus, have mercy on me." Before I knowed it, a light broke in my heart, I was as light as a feather. I felt like I would just knock the factory roof off with my shouts.[13]

---

11. It is important to remember that slave marriages were not legal and in many instances not honored by the slave masters (as seen in Jasper's first marriage to Elvy) as unions and families were often shattered and torn apart in an inhumane way by the auction block. The slave trade in America for the most part did not consider preservation of family. See Albert J. Raboteau, *Slave Religion: The "Invisible Institution" in Antebellum South* (New York: Oxford University Press, 1978), 4.

12. Samuel Hardgrove had profound influence in Jasper's life as "all records agree that Hardgrove's piety and deep religious convictions, the world owes much of the subsequent career of the genius, Jasper." See Day, *Rhapsody in Black*, 52.

13. Ibid., 55–59.

Jasper's conversion experience filled the air with uncontrollable emotional shouts and animated dances.[14] Hearing about Jasper's conversion, Hardgrove rejoiced and embraced him with tears, saying, "Your Savior is mine and therefore we are brothers."[15] For Jasper, this experience represented not only a conversion but also a call to preach the gospel of Jesus Christ. Years later, Jasper explained: "Oh that happy day! Can I ever forget it? That was my conversion morning, and that day the Lord sent me out with the good news of the kingdom. For more than forty years I've been telling the story. My step is getting rather slow, my voice breaks down, and sometimes I am awful tired, but still I'm telling it. My lips shall proclaim the dying love of the lamb with my last expiring breath."[16]

Not surprising but important to keep in mind is that until 1839, Jasper was illiterate. Illiteracy was not uncommon among slaves; most were not permitted to learn to read or write. In spite of these limitations and controls, Jasper gained assistance in learning to read from William Johnson, a slave preacher. In spite of the plantocracy's strict rule against the education of slaves, Johnson taught Jasper to read the Bible. Being eager to learn, Jasper was reading and writing in just seven months. It would be safe to say that such desire to learn was infused by his calling to proclaim the gospel. With unrelenting effort, he read and studied the Bible intently at every opportunity. This success of his informal education was inextricably linked to the development of his preaching practice. To this end, he seized every opportunity to observe the preaching methods of others. Beyond learning through observation, he also engaged in conversations with those who supported his preaching ministry.[17]

Jasper sought out other believers and was embraced by the congregation of the Old African Baptist Church. The officers of the church baptized him, but they were a little leery about his claim of conversion since up until recently his lifestyle had been in moral bankruptcy because of the forced separation from his first wife.[18] Yet and still, the church licensed Jasper one month later.

Jasper took advantage of every occasion to preach the gospel.[19] Interestingly enough, funerals were a pathway that led to occasions to preach. While slaves

---

14. See Albert J. Raboteau, *Canaan Land: A Religious History of African Americans* (New York: Oxford University Press, 1999), 47–48. Such an emotional experience dramatized in shouts and dances was common among slave conversions. These types of religious expressions represented traces of African religious practices played out in singing, dancing, and spirit possession. It is usually referred to as a "ring shout," where Christian slaves gathered in a circle, clapping, bodies swaying, and feet stomping in rhythmic fashion. Even today such a tradition continues to influence the African American worship experience.

15. Day, *Rhapsody in Black*, 55–59.

16. Ibid., 59.

17. Ibid., 63–64.

18. Ibid., 63.

19. Ibid.

were allowed to hold funerals for their dead, white preachers generally preached the eulogy.[20] On one such occassion, Jasper gained an opportunity to address an audience at the funeral of another slave. As was customary, a white minister preached the funeral but allowed Jasper to give the dismissal prayer following the sermon.[21] Jasper prayed, and it was reported that "in ten minutes he just hoisted them all up to glory while he was praying. Then when he got through with that prayer, the white people said, 'From now on we want to hear John Jasper.'"[22] Remarkably for that period, Jasper continued to preach and pray on the platform with other white ministers. He also continued to distinguish himself in preaching compared to the others.[23] Hence, his reputation quickly spread as a preeminent funeral preacher.[24]

For the slave communities in Richmond and surrounding areas, their preference was clear. They elevated Jasper to their first option when preaching the funerals of their dead. On such occasions, he preached in a manner that "his vivid and spectacular eloquence resulted in an uproar of groans, shouts, fainting women, and people who were swept to the ground to lie in a trance-like state sometimes for hours."[25] Admittedly, it was extraordinary for a slave preacher to hold such eloquence and preaching genius. It was even more remarkable considering his deprived legal slave status that prohibited education.

Still, Jasper's extraordinary preaching popularity meant that several churches wanted to utilize his preaching gift. Hardgrove granted Jasper time off to accommodate the demand for his preaching, so he served as supply preacher to several African American churches in Petersburg, Virginia. Among these

---

20. Ibid. Also see E. Franklin Frazier, *The Negro Church in America* (New York: Schocken), 11. Frazier reported that slaves preferred their own (slave preacher) to preach their service and bury their dead. Also, slave funerals were great social events for the slave community, almost rising to the level of a celebration, not of the life they endured as a slave but an occasion to provide the dignity, honor, and respect that were denied them. Such events held deep eschatological meaning and hope, believing their loved ones were going to a better "plantation" under God's rule, where there were no more tears, sorrow, pain, and degradation. This explains the strong other-world focus prominent in the African American preaching tradition.

21. Ibid. Slaves lived under tough restrictions and were forbidden to hold any assembly of three to five individuals without the expressed consent of the master. And even so, when the master granted permission for such a gathering, it occurred under the watchful eyes of the overseer or presence of a white man. Further impediments had to do with the legal limitations that prohibited African American preachers' ordination. See Day, *Rhapsody in Black*, 64.

22. William E. Hatcher, *The Unmatched Negro Philosopher and Preacher* (New York: Revell, 1908), 42–43.

23. See Day, *Rhapsody in Black*, 65–66.

24. Hatcher, *Unmatched*, 88. Hatcher writes, "It came to pass that Jasper was the stock funeral fixture in Amelia County. Anything short of the Jasper standard was no funeral at all. There must be an uproar, fainting, shouting men, pictures of triumphant deathbeds, victors in white, rejoicing around Jesus' throne: Jesus so exalted that everybody was ready, right then and there, to start crowning Him Lord of all! Before the torrent of Jasper's vaulting eloquence, people were swept to the ground, and, sometimes for hours, many were in trances, not a few lying as they were dead!" (p. 38). Also see Day, *Rhapsody in Black*, 65–68.

25. William H. Pipes, *Say Amen, Brother!: Old-Time Negro Preaching: A Study in American Frustration* (Detroit: Wayne State University Press, 1992), 65.

churches were the Third Baptist Church, Gilfield Street Baptist Church, and Harrison Street Baptist Church. With his mule and cart, Jasper rode over twenty miles, which took a half-day of travel.[26] Beyond this, he also served the First Baptist Church of Weldon, North Carolina.[27] It is important to bear in mind that these churches were not prominent. But nonetheless, they provided opportunities for Jasper's preaching prominence to grow. Because of his growing popularity, Jasper "depopulated the other negro churches and drew crowds that could not be accommodated."[28]

It is important to note that the anomaly of Jasper's preaching was symbolized in his enormous appeal to whites. This appeal included the aristocracy and the common citizens. Among them were legislators, governors, lawyers, journalists, and academicians who were enamored with Jasper's preaching. It is equally important to understand the impetus behind the literally thousands of whites drawn to his preaching. In historical context, they were drawn mostly out of curiosity, eager to see this slave preacher display his much-publicized preaching gift.[29] In this sense, his preaching was not just monocultural. During this period in America, especially in the South, it was uncommonly multicultural.[30] Considering such an appeal, it is still surprising that many whites called for Jasper to preach in preference to white preachers.[31]

All indications reveal that Jasper took the gospel seriously when preaching. But the gospel also tempered his life in such a way that he showed no harboring of resentment or hatred against whites. Again, before his conversion he harbored much bitterness exacerbated by the situation with his first wife. On the other

---

26. Day, *Rhapsody in Black*, 72.

27. Day, *Rhapsody in Black*, 77. Ironically, this author had the occasion to preach at the First Baptist Church of Weldon.

28. Hatcher, *Unmatched*, 45.

29. William Eldridge Hatcher reports going often to hear Jasper preach on Sunday afternoon. Two of his members, a professor at Richmond College, and a successful lawyer in the city, expressed grave concerns about his loyalty to Jasper and his frequenting Jasper's church. Hatcher asked them to accompany him to hear Jasper preach, and if their feeling persisted after hearing Jasper then he would give their complaint consideration. After they heard Jasper preach, the lawyer said to Hatcher, "Hear that, and let me say to you that in a life time I have heard nothing like it, and you ought to hear that man whenever you can." See Hatcher, *Unmatched*, 70–71.

30. This is important, particularly in light of the legal and cultural restrictions placed on African Americans preaching to whites, let alone their own people. But it appears that rules, customs, and laws were suspended as Jasper was an exception to such prohibitions, which confirms his extraordinary preaching ability and the respect and admiration whites had for him.

31. Day, *Rhapsody in Black*, 72–74. It was reported that Dr. Benjamin Kean, pastor of a large Petersburg white church, noticed a decline in attendance. When he inquired concerning their absence, their reply was, "Down the road in the old Third Church, listening to Rev. John Jasper." Responding, Kean says, . . . "He can't be a minister. God never ordains Negroes." He took three of his deacons to Jasper's church on a Sunday afternoon, finding many of his missing members. After hearing Jasper preach, he said to his congregation during the evening service, "I attended services at John Jasper's church this afternoon. . . . Jasper's great! He is the only colored man ever ordained to preach the Gospel!!"

hand, Jasper held certain affections toward whites as a result of his conversion.[32] Such affections were evidenced in his reaching out to wounded Confederate soldiers during the Civil War. More specifically, he preached and gave comfort and aid at the Richmond hospital.[33] Surprisingly, even the pro-slavery Southern soldiers grew to respect and accept him.

Jasper revealed another example of Christian leadership. At a crucial period on the heels of the Emancipation, he functioned as a moral leader for newly freed slaves. Also, his preaching served as a moral compass in the city of Richmond. During the fall of Richmond to the Union army, Jasper witnessed mobs of angry and vengeful African Americans looting the premises of whites. In sum, he confronted them on one occasion with these words, "Richmond has fallen! We are free! But in the Name of God, let us act like men!"[34] Here, in perspective, the significance of Jasper's role is seen in a watershed moment in America. Specifically, in a broader perspective, this important moment held far-reaching implications, especially social control for freed slave communities.

At this point in his life, Jasper had been a slave for fifty years, and for twenty-five of those years he was a slave preacher. After his own emancipation following the American Civil War, freedom was not without cost. It presented enormous challenges for Jasper as well as for other freed slaves. At the very outset, they had to adjust to supporting themselves in their new social and economic independence. There were no "forty acres and a mule"; Jasper supported himself finding odd jobs in war-torn Richmond. His first employment opportunity as a free man (for compensation) was cleaning bricks from ruins of the city.[35] Still, he continued to serve several churches in the Richmond area, leading to an enduring legacy.

Jasper founded the Sixth Mount Zion Baptist Church in Richmond in 1867. His preaching drew large numbers, and the congregation quickly outgrew the buildings. On one occasion, Jasper baptized three hundred people in two hours on a Sunday morning in 1870.[36] For this reason, Jasper erected a much larger building in 1872 that was "respectable in almost any part of Richmond and a model Negro church in the post war period in the South."[37] The landmark

---

32. Hatcher, *Unmatched,* 34–35.

33. Day, *Rhapsody in Black,* 78.

34. Ibid., 79.

35. Ibid., 83. When the end of the war brought freedom to Jasper, he had only eighty-seven cents and a rent bill due for forty-two dollars. He secured a job cleaning bricks for fifty cents per thousand.

The "forty acres and a mule" concept was a promise made, subsequent to the Civil War, by the United States government promising that freed slaves would receive forty acres and a mule so they could have their own home and farm to make a life for themselves.

36. Ibid.

37. Day, *Rhapsody in Black,* 81–85. "Jasper's final edifice had side-wall galleries. About a thousand seats on the main floor . . . lighted by gas . . . sixteen floor-to-ceiling windows (passing behind the galleries) . . . baptistry under the pulpit . . . spacious pulpit platform, 'so Jasper can cavort' . . . [and a] large bell tower."

structure remains in Richmond today for historical significance, which will be discussed later. The Sixth Mount Zion Baptist Church became a constant home to enormous crowds, growing to 2,500 members by 1887.

As indicated earlier, Jasper experienced popularity among white people. But in light of such a time in history, a very strange twist of circumstances occurred within the auditorium: there was a "Jim Crow section for white people."[38] Nevertheless, Jasper still experienced some rejection from other leaders in his community. Educated African American ministers had little admiration for him and criticized Jasper publicly. In the Richmond newspapers, these ministers wrote concerning Jasper's famous sermon, "The Sun Do Move": "We enter our solemn protest against all such base fabrications. The idea of the sun running around the earth and the earth standing still! That sermon is out of time and place. Much harm will come. Many will try to get into Sixth Mt. Zion and get hurt. No gospel in such sermons! Let him preach Christ and Him crucified!"[39]

Richard Day maintained that these ministers were driven by jealousy on account of Jasper's preaching prominence. More specifically, they saw a decline in attendance in their worship because of Jasper's preaching. In the end, these ministers failed in their attempt to discredit Jasper and his preaching ministry.

It's important to understand that the training of these ministers produced a type of African American preacher much different than Jasper. In many ways, Jasper was a folk preacher, and for twenty-five years an antebellum slave preacher. Still, his church became a "shrine" and a "Richmond institution."[40] In fact, the Virginia State Legislature as a body visited Sixth Mount Zion to hear him preach.[41] During Jasper's life, the Richmond newspapers carried feature stories concerning his legendary preaching ministry and, more specifically, his legendary sermons.

Unlike many leading African American preaching figures of his era and thereafter, Jasper did not devote himself to improving the life of the community through politics. Nor did he rely on other institutions and organizations dedicated to improving the conditions of freed slaves. Rather, he stayed within the limits of his pulpit at a very crucial period, lifting the hopes of an entire city. In particular, he used his gift of eloquence and oratory to infuse the religious and social life of African Americans. His influence was felt not only in Richmond, but in many counties in Virginia. In this way, his church served as a religious and social center, creating a social and religious vision for Richmond and its vicinity.

---

38. Ibid., 84–86. When the local paper of Richmond publicized about Jasper preaching, crowds both white and African American gathered at Jasper's church three hours early in order to get a seat (p. 91–92).

39. Day, *Rhapsody in Black*, 92.

40. Ibid., 86.

41. Ibid., 116.

As black church historian Carter G. Woodson reported, Jasper "established for himself throughout Virginia and adjacent States a reputation for piety and sincerity, which, without political influence, made him a power in the country."[42] As Woodson and other historians have suggested, Jasper's popularity was not limited to Richmond and the state of Virginia. He was indeed a national religious figure who attracted interest and appeal far beyond his local church.

Though Jasper received national attention, it is important not to attribute his prominence only to his colorful and aesthetic style of preaching. More than just vivid oratory, storytelling, imagery, or imaginative language, Jasper's views were as astonishing as they were controversial. No greater example is seen than in his most famous sermon, "The Sun Do Move." In this sermon, Jasper expressed his literal interpretation of the Bible and his unwavering belief in God. This sermon revealed what is known as the "Jasperian theory," presenting "imagery of a flat earth around which the sun rotates."[43] It was this sermon that elevated him to national prominence, particularly in the eastern United States. And it was this sermon that became a national attraction, evidenced by Jasper receiving over two hundred and fifty requests to preach it. E. A. Randolph reported Jasper's lecture tour:

> He lectured in the cities of Washington, Baltimore, Philadelphia, and some of the New Jersey cities. He lectured in Lincoln Hall, Washington, to a crowded house. Many congressmen and other distinguished men were present to hear him on his famous subject, "the sun." He had good houses wherever he lectured, and was received kindly by all. When asked by someone about his lecturing in the North after his return, he replied by saying, "I regard my tour North a very successful one." He has often lectured upon the subject in Richmond to crowded houses, both white and colored. It might be, as a great many claimed, they only went to Jasper's lectures to hear what he had to say and how he said it, not that they believed in his theory, or that they could learn anything from him by hearing him preach. The fact is, however, they did go. He lectured in the Mozart Hall to as fine and intelligent an audience as ever went to hear any of the great literary lecturers of the country. He was invited to deliver his lecture before the Virginia Legislature.[44]

---

42. Carter G. Woodson, *The History of the Negro Church* (Washington, DC: The Associated Publishers, 1921), 216.

43. The Jasperian theory was based on the Zetetic school of thought that held that the earth was flat based on gravity of the planet. Jasper used various selected passages of Scripture to support such an astronomical argument. At a minimum, this shows that Jasper, although a self-made man, read profusely other sources beyond the Bible.

44. E. A. Randolph, *The Life of Rev. John Jasper, Pastor of Sixth Mt. Zion Baptist Church: From His Birth to the Present Time, with His Theory on the Rotation of the Sun* (Richmond, VA: Hill, 1884), 36.

At the very least, Jasper's demand across the country demonstrated his remarkable preaching ability and prominence.

On the second Sunday in March 1901, Jasper preached his final sermon, entitled "Ye Must Be Born Again." On March 28, 1901, at the age of eighty-nine, Jasper whispered, "I have finished my work. I am waiting at the river, looking across for further orders." He died in his sleep. His death mirrored the old Negro spiritual, "I Looked over Jordon An' what did I see / Comin' for to carry me home! / A band of angels Comin' After me / Comin for to carry me home!"[45] Jasper received honor in death as he did in life, as evidenced in an article the *Richmond Dispatch* ran about his life and legacy: "John Jasper became famous by accident, but he was a most interesting man apart from his solar theory. He was a man of deep conviction, a man with a purpose in life, a man who earnestly desired to save souls for heaven. He followed his divine calling with faithfulness, with determination, as far as he could, to make the ways of God known to men, his saving help among all nations. And the Lord poured upon his servant, the 'continual dew of his blessings.'"[46]

On April 7, 1901, the city of Richmond had a memorial service for Jasper. Grace Street Baptist Church, which had the largest auditorium in the city, hosted the funeral, and Pastor William Hatcher gave the memorial address in honor of Jasper's life.[47] Additionally, the city of Richmond, Virginia, established the John Jasper Monument as a symbol of his legacy and prominence. His fame holds such importance in the annals of history that, in the 1950s, the Virginia Department of Transportation rerouted an interstate highway in an effort to preserve the structure of his church. What is more, the state established a second monument in Jasper's honor in 2002.

Currently, Sixth Mount Zion Baptist Church holds an annual Founder's Day celebration of Jasper's life and legacy. As part of the observance, the church selects and recognizes "Jasper Trailblazer Honorees."[48] Indeed, Richmond has had no citizen held in higher esteem than Jasper. In order to further assess his preaching legacy, it will be important to consider the factors that informed and shaped his preaching.

---

45. Day, *Rhapsody in Black*, 142.

46. Hatcher, *Unmatched*, 14.

47. Ibid., 22. Even at the burial site in Richmond, Jasper's headstone towers over all the other monuments, including world-famous tennis player Arthur Ashe.

48. These honorees are selected based on their distinguished service in the community. The church opened its John Jasper Memorial Room & Museum in 1926, which houses nineteenth-century artifacts associated with Jasper's life and pastorate. The museum remains open to the public and continues to be a large attraction throughout the year. The original structure still stands. Benjamin Ross, church historian, supplied this information via phone interview.

THEOLOGY OF PREACHING

Jasper's preaching ministry emerged in the colonial period. To a certain extent, his preaching "came under the influence of the colonial preacher."[49] Keep in mind, preaching occupied a central place in two colonies in the seventeenth century, including New England and Virginia. (As pointed out above, Jasper was a slave in Virginia and after his freedom remained there until his death.) A larger concentration of slaves was situated in the Virginia colony. It seems that the preaching of this colony focused more on personal responsibility. They gave no interest or concern to politics. Their priority emphasized the role of "leaders of men and communities."[50] Later, the eighteenth century ushered in a more emotional style of preaching, consisting of "fervent, powerful, evangelistic preaching."[51] These periods provide a window into Jasper's theology of preaching. They also offer a path to understanding assumptions that shaped his preaching practice. In view of this period, Jasper showed strong fundamentalist, or evangelical, views concerning the authority of Scripture. Such strong views should not come as a surprise, for valid reasons. The Great Awakening cast a large shadow in the eighteenth century that "crystallized Negro old-fashion preaching."[52] And Jasper, more than any other slave preacher, represented the best of "Negro old-fashion preaching."[53]

Four factors primarily shaped Jasper's preaching assumptions and ultimately his practice. First, and perhaps the most dominant factor that informed Jasper's preaching assumptions and practices, was his African religious influence. Several features of African religious heritage gave impetus to his style, including shouting and speaking in an expressive manner for the purpose of persuasion. Another feature consisted of emotion and imaginative insight, which explains the reason his sermons were largely a product of his imagination. Yet another feature bordered on performance speech intended to impress and persuade for the purpose of strong delivery.[54]

The second factor to shape Jasper's preaching was that the colonial pulpit influenced the assumptions and practices of his preaching, both in style and substance.

Third, and closely related to the second, is the influence of preaching during the Great Awakening led by George Whitefield. It was emotional and loud,

---

49. Pipes, *Say Amen*, 60.
50. Ibid.
51. Ibid.
52. Ibid.
53. Ibid., 64.
54. Pipes, *Say Amen*, 59.

with excitement and enthusiasm aimed to impress and move the soul.[55] This style of preaching was easily transferable and adaptable because of its semblance to African religious practices.

Fourth, the bondage and inhumane treatment of slaves influenced the way Jasper did his preaching. His purpose was to move the people into the presence of the Lord. For him, this style was used to create a psychological "escape mechanism" from the harsh realities they faced.[56] These four factors shaped Jasper's preaching assumptions and practice.

METHODOLOGY FOR PREACHING

In the African American preaching tradition, the narrative approach—shaped by African indigenous factors—was the dominant method used, and Jasper used such a method. Admirers and observers widely viewed Jasper as one of the most skillful storytellers in the African American preaching tradition. Black church historian Henry Mitchell noted, "The most famous of all storytellers was John Jasper."[57] From Jasper's preaching practice, one can see how methodological preference in some instances informed his text selection. Jasper selected biblical stories to dramatize the plight of his congregation. He possessed a powerful and colorful imagination that lifted his audience. Using this skill, he vividly painted in concrete and precise details the events of the preaching text. In typical fashion, Jasper evoked his listeners' imaginations by "stringing together picture after picture" concerning the biblical story.[58] And in many ways, the biblical story became his listeners' story. Weaving the stories into the life experience of his marginalized congregation marked his preaching practice. It bears repeating that the African American preaching tradition favored a narrative or story form influenced by African cultural practices.[59]

Jasper used the storytelling method as a vehicle to accomplish his desired outcome. He infused the lives of his congregation and community with the bright light of hope in the sovereignty of God as liberator. Further, he advanced an entertaining and sensational storytelling style of preaching to persuade or bring about certain results. These stories were told in concrete images that came alive in the sermon. This style deeply affected Jasper's audience, particularly his slave constituency.

---

55. Ibid., 74.
56. Ibid., 67–68.
57. Henry H. Mitchell, *Black Preaching: The Recovery of a Powerful Art* (Nashville: Abingdon, 1990), 70.
58. Ibid., 65.
59. See Ibid. Mitchell argues, "The key to understanding the different styles of preaching is in the word culture: Preaching is carried out in the idiom, imagery, style and worldview of a particular people" (p. 11).

It is important to note that folk preaching did not draw on traditional rhetorical methods based on the classical arguments of Aristotle. Jasper sought to persuade his listeners through the sensational narration of a biblical story.[60] As stated earlier, Jasper aimed to "persuade and instruct his hearers [slaves and postwar congregation members] along the road to an escape from this world by having them look forward to a future life." [61] Such a strong eschatological style of preaching represented the bedrock of slave preaching in the Deep South. Nowhere was this more evident than funerals where intentional appeals to emotion were common. At the least, the mourners and crowds expected Jasper to stir their emotions into "screams, shouts" and "getting happy."[62] In many ways, they were persuaded that their loved ones had moved to a place of peace, and happiness where the "Marse" (Master) was kinder, gentler, and caring. Typical of most slave preaching in the South, Jasper's purpose of preaching focused on getting the Spirit to move his listeners.[63] In this way, he articulated a strong eschatological vision for his listeners.

CONTRIBUTIONS TO PREACHING

History has cemented Jasper's legacy as a remarkable preacher. Even so, the importance of his legacy in the history of Christian preaching goes beyond technical homiletical questions.

During the period in which Jasper lived, his contribution included the influence of his preaching on a bound and marginalized community in Richmond and the surrounding areas. To an impoverished community, he functioned as a priest attending to their wounds with the gospel of Christ during a period of enormous turmoil in America's history. At that time, slaves were seen as chattel, sold or hired out to serve economic interests of slave owners. Essentially, this human trafficking meant families were torn apart—along with countless other atrocities—and became the only life slaves knew.[64] Jasper's preaching lifted their burdens while bound and provided the oppressed

---

60. Ibid., 70–72. See Pipes, *Say Amen*, 64–67. Charles W. Koller sees narration as a "rhetorical process." See Charles W. Koller, *Expository Preaching without Notes Plus Sermons Preached without Notes* (Grand Rapids: Baker, 1962).

61. Pipes, *Say Amen*, 74. Such an emotional and escapist homiletic, common in the African American preaching tradition, explains why sermons are other-worldliness focused and eschatological in scope, still pervasive today in most African American pulpits, a point previously made. Jasper's style in terms of form, method, and content typified the eighteenth and nineteenth centuries' untrained African American preacher, such as George Liele, Andrew Bryan, and Black Harry. For additional figures see Woodson, *The History of the Negro Church*.

62. Pipes, *Say Amen*, 74.

63. Ibid.

64. See Raboteau, *Slave Religion*, 4–42.

community strength to cope. He also acted in the capacity of a prophet in the service of the gospel to the oppressed, reminding them that "trouble don't last always." His sermons engendered hope that enabled them to believe in a better day for their future.

Another important factor to consider when examining Jasper's legacy is that he avoided issues of civil rights because of his antebellum thinking. But his pastoral vision provided a ministry important in casting a social and moral vision for thousands who found themselves free. Specifically, he was instrumental in "establishing family life and essential moral qualities among the newly freed" in Richmond and other surrounding counties.[65] As pointed out earlier, he showed an example of such influence as a moral leader when he spoke out against the behavior of some freed slaves. They harbored much anger and revenge and began to loot the property of white people when Richmond fell. Jasper became the moral voice against any revengeful act of thievery and violence.[66] Simply put, Jasper's pastoral and preaching ministry was existentially relevant to the harsh realities of slaves and freed African Americans in the South. The vision he cast enabled them to sing in a strange land, "I'm so glad trouble don't last always / Oh my Lord, what shall I do?" Again, it is important to reiterate that Jasper's most significant contribution was in sustaining bound and oppressed people during their worst times in the history of America with the hope of the gospel of Christ.

Jasper remained an antebellum and folk preacher throughout his preaching ministry. His ministry covered several crucial periods of change, including slavery, Civil War, post-Civil War, the Reconstruction era, and the turn of the twentieth century. Above all else, his unyielding trust in Scripture never changed.[67] He raised the aspirations of an entire city of African Americans and many whites. The masses of freed slaves had to rebuild their lives with meager means. Jasper's extraordinary preaching ability inspired them, giving them not only an eschatological hope, but a faith in God who addresses issues of a marginalized community. [68] Such genres of a "better day" continue to shape the African American sermon today. One can only imagine the magnitude of Jasper's contribution under different conditions and circumstances in history. Yet, he was the most famous and celebrated preacher of his culture and, arguably, of his time.

---

65. Mitchell, *Black Preaching*, 70.
66. See footnote 38.
67. Mitchell, *Black Preaching*, 67.
68. See Cleophus J. LaRue, *The Heart of Black Preaching* (Louisville: Westminster John Knox, 2000), 36.

Sermon Excerpt

Where Sin Come From? (Genesis 3)[69]

But where was the wrong? Where, indeed? It was in Eve's believin' the devil and not believin' God. It was doin' what the devil said and not doin' what God said. And you come here and ask me where sin come from! You see now, doan you? It come out of the pit of hell where it was hatched 'mong the angels that was flung out of heaven 'cause they disobeyed God. It come from that land where the name of our God is hated. It was brought by that ole serpent, the father of lies, and he bring it that he might fool the woman, and in that way set up on the earth the works of the devil. Sin is the black child of the pit, it is. It come from the ole serpent at first, but it's here now, right in poor Jasper's heart and in your heart; wherever there is a man or a woman in this dark world in tears there is sin—sin that insults God, tears down His law, and brings woes to everybody.

And you, stung by the serpent, with God's wrath on you and your feet in the path of death, askin' where sin come from? You better fly the wrath of the judgment day.

But this is enough. I just took time to tell where sin come from. But my tongue can't refuse to stop to tell you that the blood of the Lamb slain from the foundation of the world is greater than sin and mightier than hell. It can wash away our sins, make us whiter than the drivin' snow, dress us in redemption robes, bring us with shouts and hallelujahs back to that fellowship with our Father, that can never be broken long as eternity rolls! ◆

BIBLIOGRAPHY

Charles W. Koller, *Expository Preaching without Notes Plus Sermons Preached without Notes.* Grand Rapids: Baker, 1962.

Day, Richard E. *Rhapsody in Black: The Life Story of John Jasper.* Pennsylvania: Judson, 1953.

Edwards, O. C., Jr. *A History of Preaching.* 2 vols. Nashville: Abingdon, 2004.

Fant, Clyde E., Jr., and William M. Pinson Jr. *20 Centuries of Great Preaching: An Encyclopedia of Preaching.* 13 Vols. Waco, TX: Word, 1971.

Harris, James H. *Preaching Liberation.* Fortress: Minneapolis, 1995.

Hatcher, William E. *John Jasper: The Unmatched Negro Philosopher and Preacher.* New York: Revell, 1908.

Hicks, H. Beecher., Jr. *Images of the Black Preacher: The Man Nobody Knows.* Pennsylvania: Judson, 1977.

---

69. Sermon taken from Clyde E. Fant Jr. and William M. Pinson Jr., *20 Centuries of Great Preaching: An Encyclopedia of Great Preaching,* 13 vols. (Waco, TX: Word, 1971), 239–42.

LaRue, Cleophus J. *The Heart of Black Preaching.* Louisville: Westminster John Knox, 2000.

Lincoln, C. Eric., and Lawrence H. Mamiya. *The Black Church in the African American Experience.* Durham: Duke University Press, 1999.

Mitchell, Henry H. *Black Preaching: The Recovery of a Powerful Art.* Nashville: Abingdon, 1990.

Moyd, Olin P. *Sacred Art: Preaching and Theology in the African American Tradition.* Pennsylvania: Judson, 1995.

Pipes, Williams H. *Say Amen, Brother!: Old-Time Negro Preaching: A Study in African Frustration.* Detroit: Wayne State University Press, 1992.

Raboteau, Albert, J. *Canaan Land: A Religious History of African Americans.* New York: Oxford University Press, 1999.

_____. *Slave Religion: The "Invisible Institution" in Antebellum South.* New York: Oxford University Press, 1978.

Smith, Robert, Jr. *Doctrine That Dances: Bringing Doctrinal Preaching and Teaching to Life.* Nashville: Broadman & Holman, 2008.

Thomas, Frank A. *They Like to Not Quit Praisin' God: The Role of Celebration in Preaching.* Cleveland: United Church Press, 1997.

Troeger, Thomas, H. *Imaging a Sermon.* Nashville: Abingdon, 1990.

Woodson, Carter G. *The History of the Negro Church.* Washington, DC: The Associated Publishers, 1921.

Young, Henry J. *Major Black Religious Leaders: 1755–1940.* Nashville: Abingdon, 1977.

Henry Ward Beecher

Preaching Action Over Theology

MICHAEL DUDUIT

Today when many Americans would be hard-pressed to name any prominent preacher, it is difficult to visualize the way in which a single preacher captured and held the imagination of the American people just a century-and-a-half ago. Among his contemporaries, it was not uncommon to hear Henry Ward Beecher (1813–1887) referred to as the most popular and influential preacher of his day—a day when a number of pulpiteers held large national audiences of their own. Beecher went beyond the traditional bounds of the Protestant preacher and created a national pulpit from which he sought to apply the Christian message to a variety of issues in the political and social arena. Beecher turned his pulpit into a rhetorical vehicle for achieving political and social change. In so doing, he not only influenced the political structures of his own day, but left a lasting impression on the American religious scene.

HISTORICAL BACKGROUND

Henry Beecher's father, Lyman Beecher (1775–1863), was among New England's more illustrious divines. A graduate of Yale, where he studied under both Ezra Stiles and Timothy Dwight, he soon developed a reputation as a revivalist, moral reformer, and staunch defender of Calvinist orthodoxy, especially in his struggle with the Unitarians. Like others in the New Divinity tradition, Lyman Beecher was a major reinterpreter of Calvinist doctrine, seeking to make Calvinism more palatable to the new American mentality. He argued that a person was a sinner by choice, not by nature, and that each person was held individually responsible for their own actions as a free moral agent. He modified the language of the Westminster Assembly's Shorter Catechism for his children's instruction, revising it to say that people were unwilling to obey God, not unable to do so.[1]

---

1. Marie Caskey, *Chariot of Fire: Religion and the Beecher Family* (New Haven: Yale University Press, 1978), 50.

In 1810, Lyman Beecher was called to the First Church in Litchfield, Connecticut, where Henry Ward was born on June 24, 1813. The family moved to Boston in 1826, where Lyman filled the pulpit of Hanover Church and campaigned against the Unitarian heresy in its own stronghold. In Boston, Beecher "brought the tactics of revivalism to the service of conservatism against the liberals and Unitarians."[2]

In a family noted for intellectual achievement, Henry seemed out of place. He was moved from one unsuccessful educational experience to another. Eventually, young Beecher began dreaming of a life at sea; his father, still determined that each of his sons was eventually destined for the ministry, suggested further study so that he might set sail as an officer. He was soon enrolled at Mount Pleasant School in Amherst, Massachusetts, where his educational adventure took a positive turn and eventually led to study at Amherst College. While at Mount Pleasant, Beecher underwent some type of religious experience during a time of revival, and he joined his father's church in Boston. Dreams of a nautical career gave way to ministerial ambitions, much to Lyman's delight.[3]

Amherst College was founded in 1821 as an orthodox alternative to Harvard Unitarianism,[4] and here some of the characteristic elements of Beecher's career took shape. Of particular significance was his involvement in the Athenian Society (the college's debating organization), wherein he gained practical experience in public speaking and studied a variety of social and political topics, including slavery. When a group of students created an antislavery society at Amherst in July 1833, Beecher was a charter member; the faculty soon dissolved the group lest it become a divisive force among the students.[5]

Upon graduation in 1834, Beecher joined his father in Cincinnati, where he had gone two years earlier to accept the presidency of Lane Theological Seminary and the pastorate of the Second Presbyterian Church. Lyman saw the West as a challenging target for the orthodox, who needed to train ministers to win the territory and preserve it from the forces of Roman Catholicism.

Though he loved and respected his father and shared his concern for the West, the younger Beecher had already begun to move away from his father to a considerable extent. Never satisfied with Lyman's intellectual approach to faith,

2. Sydney E. Ahlstrom, *A Religious History of the American People*, 2nd ed. (New Haven: Yale University Press, 2004), 422.

3. Lyman Abbott and S. B. Halliday, *Henry Ward Beecher: A Sketch of His Career* (Hartford: American, 1887), 31–32.

4. William C. Beecher and Rev. Samuel Scoville, *A Biography of Rev. Henry Ward Beecher* (New York: Cosimo, 2006), 112.

5. Clifford E. Clark Jr., *Henry Ward Beecher: Spokesman for a Middle-Class America* (Urbana: University of Illinois Press, 1978), 17, 23–24.

Henry substituted an emotional, intuitive approach. Where the father stressed God's power and justice, the son came to emphasize God's love and mercy.

While at Amherst, Beecher had become severely troubled over doubts about Calvinist doctrine. He was baffled by the question of how individuals were converted. His revolt against Calvinist orthodoxy continued, though quietly, even after he joined his father at Lane Seminary for theological study. A significant event in this spiritual pilgrimage was the attempt by Presbyterian heresy hunters to oust Lyman because of his theological modifications. Despite these concerns, Beecher graduated from Lane in 1837, was examined by the Cincinnati Presbytery, and became licensed to preach. On June 15, he received a call from the First Presbyterian Church in Lawrenceburgh, Indiana, a thriving river town.

Organized in 1829 with fourteen charter members, the church drew primarily poorer women and a small number of men. The Methodist church in Lawrenceburgh was the socially prominent one.[6] Beecher recalled his first congregation with something less than pleasure: "I remember that the flock which I first gathered in the wilderness consisted of twenty persons. Nineteen of them were women, and the other was nothing."[7] Later that summer he returned east to marry his fiancée of seven years, Eunice Bullard.

A new encounter with Calvinist orthodoxy confronted Beecher in connection with his ordination. The battle lines within Presbyterianism had already been drawn between Old School (conservatives) and New School (those willing to modify Calvinist doctrine, such as Lyman Beecher). The young Beecher was examined by an Old School presbytery and, to everyone's surprise, he was approved unanimously. His experience in theological debate—learned at his father's knee—had served him well. However, the presbytery passed a new resolution requiring anyone being licensed or ordained to identify himself with the Old School faction. Beecher refused, and proceeded to lead his small church out of the presbytery and into a New School body, which ordained him.[8]

After two years in Lawrenceburgh, Beecher was plagued by debt, lived a primitive lifestyle, and had been unable to spark a revival, so in May 1839, he accepted a call to the Second Presbyterian Church of Indianapolis, a church with thirty-two members.[9] It was some improvement over Lawrenceburgh, but not much. As one commentator observed, Indianapolis in 1839 "had less than

6. Clark, *Henry Ward Beecher: Spokesman*, 43–44.

7. Jane Schaffer Elsmere, *Henry Ward Beecher: The Indiana Years, 1837–1847* (Indianapolis: Indiana Historical Society, 1973), 8–9.

8. Abbot and Halliday, *Henry Ward Beecher: A Sketch*, 42.

9. Elsmere, *Henry Ward Beecher: The Indiana Years*, 78–80, 86–87, 95.

four thousand inhabitants, and it may be said that its chief attractions were mud and malaria."[10]

As a pastor in Lawrenceburgh and then Indianapolis, Beecher was less concerned with orthodox theology than with responding to the needs of the common people in the West; his preaching reflected this increasing concern to target his appeal to the average person, especially after his move to Indianapolis. Yet he was still strongly influenced by Calvinist thought. His first book, *Lectures to Young Men* (1844), for example, had as its underlying foundation the total depravity of humankind and the necessity of a miraculous conversion by a sovereign God. The lectures dealt with idleness, gambling, intemperance, cheating, and various aspects of personal morality, with an emphasis on conversion to Christian living.[11]

Though the Calvinist influence was obviously still a factor in his thought, Beecher soon shed the theology of his father with which he had struggled since his youth. The definitive step was his acceptance of a call from Plymouth Church in Brooklyn. In 1847, Brooklyn was a relatively new suburb of New York that was on the verge of explosive growth. In just two decades, the population would grow from 30,000 to 295,000, making it the third-largest city in the nation.[12] The city contained thirty-nine churches, only one of them Congregational.[13]

A group of Brooklyn businessmen had plans to start a new Congregational church in the city. In order to bring Beecher to New York for some friendly persuasion, arrangements were made to have him invited to address the American Home Missionary Society in May 1847. While there, he delivered the first sermon at the new Plymouth Church on May 16.[14]

Beecher had considered a return to the East because of fears for his family's health, especially that of his wife, Eunice. The primitive conditions of a frontier town like Indianapolis had drained her physically and emotionally. During his trip that summer, Beecher also preached at the prestigious Park Street Church in Boston, and that congregation sought him as associate pastor.[15] After his return to Indiana, Beecher found himself courted at great length by the founders of Plymouth Church, and he finally accepted their call as pastor in August, citing his wife's health as the reason for the move in his letter of resignation to his Indianapolis congregation.[16]

---

10. John Henry Barrows, *Henry Ward Beecher: The Shakespeare of the Pulpit* (New York: Funk & Wagnalls, 1893), 84.

11. Henry Ward Beecher, *Seven Lectures to Young Men on Various Important Subjects* (Indianapolis: Moore, 1844).

12. Clark, *Henry Ward Beecher: Spokesman*, 76.

13. Noyes L. Thompson, *The History of Plymouth Church* (New York: Carleton, 1873), 25.

14. Ibid., 28.

15. Elsmere, *Henry Ward Beecher: The Indiana Years*, 287.

16. W. C. Griswold, *The Life of Henry Ward Beecher* (New York: Hurst, 1887), 24.

Located in the fashionable Brooklyn Heights area, the church drew heavily from the new middle class that was moving to the suburb. The church was started with twenty-one members in 1847, but by the end of Beecher's first decade as pastor, the church boasted 1,241, not including 346 names which had been dropped during that period, for a grand total of 1,586 people.[17] It had become the city's largest church and, according to one source, the nation's largest as well.[18]

Membership alone did not tell the whole story. In January 1850, the church moved into a new sanctuary with seating for 2,100 people—a size virtually unprecedented for American churches of the day. By 1857, however, the sanctuary proved inadequate, and extra seats were attached to the pews, able to be folded up to clear the aisle when not in use; these seated about eight hundred more. Approximately three hundred additional people were allowed to stand around the back and sides.[19] Even this was insufficient by 1867, when as many as 3,500 people would seek admission to a service. Ten to twelve ushers and six police officers handled the crowds and turned away hundreds every Sunday.[20]

Not only was the congregation larger than those he had led in the West, the people were more advanced educationally, socially, and financially. Like Beecher, many of them were uncomfortable with the coldness and sterility of their fathers' faith. They were achieving success and experiencing the self-esteem that accompanied it; thus, they sought a more positive worldview and self-image than they had received from their New England heritage. Beecher shared that desire and, much like Ralph Waldon Emerson, he became part of a romantic revolt against the austere intellectual faith of his heritage. His sermons and writings reflect his emphasis on the heart rather than the head, and over the years this orientation grew stronger.

Through his sermons, books, lectures, and periodicals, Henry Ward Beecher reached a huge national audience in the mid-nineteenth century and wielded an enormous influence over the public mind. As with most public figures, he was both admired and despised, but for forty years as pastor of Brooklyn's Plymouth Church, Beecher was rarely ignored. As William McLoughlin has indicated, "Beecher was the high priest of American religion. His pulpit was the nation's spiritual center—at least for that vast body of solid, middle-class Protestant citizens who were the heart of the nation."[21] In a contemporary study of twenty-one

17. Thompson, *The History of Plymouth Church*, 96.

18. Henry Fowler, *The American Pulpit* (New York: Fairchild, 1856), 197.

19. Beecher and Scoville, *A Biography of Rev. Henry Ward Beecher*, 223–24.

20. James Parton, "Henry Ward Beecher and His Church, 1867," in *The Church and the City: 1865–1910*, ed. Robert D. Cross (Indianapolis: Bobbs-Merrill, 1967), 135.

21. William G. McLoughlin, *The Meaning of Henry Ward Beecher: An Essay on the Shifting Values of mid-Victorian America* (New York: Knopf, 1970), 252.

American preachers, some 70 out of 515 pages were devoted to Beecher, more than twice the space given to any other subject.[22] Another biographer, writing in 1893, called Beecher, "The most brilliant and fertile pulpit-genius of the nineteenth century, and the most widely-influential American of his time."[23] Phillips Brooks, who is himself counted among the princes of the American pulpit, considered Beecher "the greatest preacher of America and of our century,"[24] and just before his own death cited him as "the greatest preacher Protestantism has ever produced."[25]

THEOLOGICAL DEVELOPMENT

Beecher became increasingly aware of his shift away from Calvinist orthodoxy, as he expressed in a letter to Eunice when he was twenty, studying theology at Lane, and facing examination to receive his license to preach. "There are some points which I must not, will not, subscribe to."[26]

Theologically, Beecher proceeded to abandon more and more orthodox Calvinist doctrine. He had always tried to avoid eternal damnation as a sermon topic; he soon abandoned it entirely. He once remarked of Edwards's sermon "Sinners in the Hands of an Angry God" that "a person of moral sensibility alone at midnight, reading that awful discourse, would well nigh go crazy."[27] In two 1849 articles on conversion, Beecher further departed from orthodoxy by stressing that this radical religious change was accomplished in accordance with natural law. God produces results through the natural functioning of the human mind, not in spite of human capability.[28] Beecher came to believe that people must make a free choice for or against God—no notion of election or predestination—and a person is left with "the same faculties, intellectual, moral, social, and animal, before conversion as after."[29] Beecher had an optimistic view of human nature, even in connection with a theology of conversion, gradually adopting a belief in human perfectibility, in contrast to the Calvinist doctrine of total depravity.[30]

---

22. Fowler, *The American Pulpit.*
23. Barrows, *Henry Ward Beecher: The Shakespeare,* vii.
24. *Proceeding of a Council in Plymouth Church* (Brooklyn: Plymouth Church, 1890), 51.
25. Newell Dwight Hillis, "Henry Ward Beecher: A Sermon Preached in Plymouth Church, Sunday, January 4, 1903" (Brooklyn: Eagle, 1903), 7.
26. Mrs. Henry Ward Beecher, "Mr. Beecher As I Knew Him," *Ladies Home Journal* 8, no. 12 (November 1891): 9.
27. Caskey, *Chariot of Fire,* 227.
28. Henry Ward Beecher, "A Correspondence," *The Independent* 1, no. 56 (27 December 1849): 222.
29. Henry Ward Beecher, "Is Conversion Instantaneous," *The Independent* 1, no. 56 (27 December 1849): 222.
30. McLoughlin, *The Meaning of Henry Ward Beecher,* 17.

In rejecting total depravity, Beecher did not deny human sinfulness. In an 1869 sermon, "The God of Comfort," he explained, "No man can be a charitable man who does not believe that his fellow-men are depraved. I will not say totally; for I do not believe in the doctrine of total depravity. They are depraved, and that is enough."[31]

Beecher broke most significantly with Calvinist theology in relation to the nature of God. Even in his father's modified (or as Henry called it, "alleviated") Calvinism, there was a concept of a sovereign God of wrath, justice, and authority. It was a notion Beecher found harsh and comfortless. In an 1869 sermon, "Human Ideas of God," Beecher explained at length his dispute with Calvinistic ideas of the divine nature and activity. At the heart of his argument is a claim for moral unity; one cannot claim one standard of morality for humanity and another for God, yet that is exactly the dilemma that Calvinism had adopted, Beecher believed: "When, therefore, men . . . have taught us that God lives for his own glory, how many hearts have turned away! Not even the fear of being lost could compel them to worship a Supreme Being who sat seeking that which he utterly forbids us to seek—his own selfish glory. To teach that God has a right to do as he pleases—unless he pleases to do benevolently—is to teach a view of God which cannot but offend the moral understanding."[32]

God does not have a right to rule simply because he is powerful, Beecher argued, for such a position authenticates "moral despotism." Rather, God rules because of his moral quality, which cannot be less than humanity's own. Who could worship a God who would demand that people perform certain actions to live, then withholds the power to do them and punishes them for their failure?

As William McLoughlin has shown, Beecher was both a reflection of and leader in the mid-nineteenth century reconstruction of Calvinism taking place in American thought. His rejection of Lyman Beecher's theology was characteristic of "the rebellion of a whole generation of Americans against the teachings of their fathers," and his personal contributions helped greatly in relieving the religious anxiety that followed such a significant ideological shift.[33]

Yet it would be incorrect to see Beecher's connection with Calvinism as total abandonment. To the contrary, in one important area Beecher absorbed this heritage and allowed it to shape much of his career: the desire for social reform.

---

31. Henry Ward Beecher, "The God of Comfort," *The Sermons of Henry Ward Beecher*, First Series (New York: Ford, 1869), 21.

32. Henry Ward Beecher, "Human Ideas of God," *The Sermons of Henry Ward Beecher*, Second Series (New York: Ford, 1869), 113.

33. McLoughlin, *The Meaning of Henry Ward Beecher*, 38, 85, 250.

Henry Ward Beecher inherited his father's interest in reform but moved beyond Lyman in both methodology and subjects for reform. Beecher saw the necessity of the church taking a stand on moral issues, but unlike his father he did not believe Christians should be limited to "moral suasion," which is an appeal to morality in order to influence change, and voluntary societies to achieve their goals. Lyman thought ministers should keep a healthy distance from the dirty business of politics, once saying, "I have never witnessed a clergyman active in the collision of party politics without feeling and perceiving that others felt that the man was out of his place and religion disgraced."[34]

Henry followed his father's method of moral suasion in some areas, such as temperance,[35] but increasingly realized that the reformer had to move into the political realm to achieve significant results. As he pointed out in an 1846 sermon, "The general connection of each man with public affairs is such that no moral reformation can well be set afoot without in some way being connected with politics."[36] In fact, the church in the United States was uniquely obligated to lend its influence to the movements for social reform. This involvement, at least in some areas of reform, would have to be through political action rather than moral appeals. Though he had earlier accepted his father's belief that revivalism and voluntary societies could so shape the public consciousness that reform would be inevitable, Beecher's involvement in antislavery efforts and the debate over the extension of slavery into the territories convinced him that moral suasion alone was insufficient.[37]

As a result, Beecher adopted a new attitude toward political and social reform in which he would use his pulpit and pen as weapons in seeking change. Unlike his father, he would actively support candidates and seek legislation to further his desired objectives. And while Lyman directed his reforming efforts to such areas of personal morality as temperance and Sabbath-breaking, Beecher broadened the national perspective on the prerogatives of the pulpit, actively addressing such topics as slavery, women's rights, and economic issues such as trade and labor unions. Ultimately, such an expansion of the pulpit's role in the political arena laid one portion of a foundation for the activists who came to be identified with the term "Social Gospel" in the late nineteenth and early twentieth centuries. A large part of Beecher's political significance lay in his extension and refinement of clerical influence in the political sphere.

---

34. Paxton Hibben, *Henry Ward Beecher: An American Portrait* (New York: Doran, 1927), 308.

35. Clark, *Henry Ward Beecher: Spokesman*, 104.

36. Henry Ward Beecher, Sermon, July, 1846, Beecher-Scoville Collection, Yale University Archives, hereafter cited as Yale MSS.

37. Clark, *Henry Ward Beecher: Spokesman*, 127.

The disestablishment of the state churches had been one major element in changing the once-intimate relationship between the minister and the political world. The rise of revivalism, seen most clearly in the Second Great Awakening and its residue, also helped to emphasize in the American mind the notion of religious faith as residing primarily in the individual rather than within the community. Whereas in the colonial past, the minister was the acknowledged leader of the community in matters of the mind and soul, now the individual was the master of his or her own religious destiny.

Henry Ward Beecher eventually moved beyond both his father and other contemporaries in advocating for direct political involvement from the pulpit. Indeed, he would come to be the ultimate personification of the "political pulpit" for the entire century. It is no wonder, then, that Beecher came to be seen by many of his contemporaries as "the chief champion in the New World of the pulpit's duty to apply Christianity to all the great ethical concerns of business and society."[38]

METHODOLOGY FOR PREACHING

For some forty years at Plymouth Church, Beecher preached twice on Sunday and gave a weekly Friday evening lecture-room talk (with a normal attendance of seven hundred to eight hundred).[39] During these years he refined and polished his homiletical skills and developed his own perspective on the meaning and methodology of preaching.

To Beecher, preaching was action centered, not theologically oriented. Its purpose was to change people's lives, not their minds. The "aim and design of preaching," explained the Brooklyn orator in one sermon, is to "gain, hold, mold and fashion the hearts of men to the noblest dispositions and best conduct."[40] True preachers are not those who are most pleasing to the audience, but those who are most effective in bringing into human life "the most effectual work of God."[41] In this effort the personal magnetism and power of the preacher are vital elements. "Your living power must be brought in personal contact with men; you must catch them and compel them to come with you," Beecher proclaimed in his 1870 Princeton lecture entitled "Successful Preaching."[42] Beecher's definition of oratory as "the art of influencing conduct with the truth set home by all the

---

38. Barrows, *Henry Ward Beecher: The Shakespeare*, 168.
39. Ibid., 133.
40. Henry Ward Beecher, Sermon (undated), Yale MSS.
41. Henry Ward Beecher, Sermon (undated, but probably 1849–1855, since manuscript is on a blue paper that is most commonly found in Beecher's sermons of this period), Yale MSS.
42. Lionel Crocker, *Henry Ward Beecher's Speaking Art* (New York: Revell, 1937), 93.

resources of the living man" is yet another reflection of this view of the nature of preaching.[43]

When Plymouth Church burned down in 1849, the new structure was rebuilt to accord with Beecher's concept of preaching. The pulpit (actually a simple speaker's rostrum which left Beecher's body visible) was placed at the front and center of the congregation, close to the audience to allow the preacher's "social and personal magnetism" to work more effectively.[44] Beecher enjoyed a large frame and a powerful, well-modulated voice that could be heard throughout the sanctuary. He used few gestures and normally spoke slowly and deliberately, though he would at times "indulge in passionate outbursts."[45]

Beecher used notes containing a rough outline of his message, but as the sermon continued, he paid less and less attention to his notes. The material was fresh, since he did not prepare his notes for Sunday morning until early that day, and his notes for Sunday evening during the afternoon. He explained his method of sermon preparation:

> I read a book for information and inspiration. If, while reading, a thought comes to me which is worth expanding, I write down the title of the book, the passage which suggested the thought, the hour of the day, or the night, the local surroundings, in fact anything which will enable me to reproduce my exact mood-then I write till I have nothing to say on that topic. I fold my manuscript, write the name of the topic on its back, and lay it away. On Sunday morning I begin my sermon. I know what my congregation is thinking about, and my subject is generally in the line of their thought. . . . I hunt among my manuscripts, find the one I want, and have a sermon at hand which with a little alteration and addition serves my purpose. I try to get back into the mood in which I was when I wrote the manuscript. Then I go into the pulpit and let my mind swing.[46]

His notations would begin after breakfast and continue until the final bell rang at the church. Since his residence was nearby, he was able to allow a minimum lapse of time between preparation and delivery. Even so, he would occasionally pull a bit of paper from his vest, jot a few lines during the congregational

---

43. Henry Ward Beecher, *Oratory* (Philadelphia: National School of Oratory, 1886), 20. This is the text of an address presented at the school on May 29, 1876.

44. Beecher, *Lectures on Preaching*, 62, in which the words came like a torrent," according to one contemporary observer.

45. J. N. Ruffin, *Lives of Famous Orators* (London: Taylor & Francis, 1922), 152–53. Ruffin is quoting from *Oratory and Orators* (1879) by William Matthews.

46. Ruffin, *Lives of Famous Orators*, 149–50.

singing, and deliver an entirely different sermon than the one previously prepared, based on the inspiration of the moment.[47] Beecher's style of "extempore
preaching," he claimed, allowed him greater liberty in the pulpit and helped to
avoid the stale delivery he feared from a full manuscript.[48]

Beecher's sermon ideas came from his observation of people. He delighted
in haunting the small shops of Brooklyn to watch and converse with craftsmen
at work. From his weekly expeditions, he would gather information and ideas
that provided the foundations of many of his sermons.[49] This use of observation
of people as a source for sermonic material illustrates one of the key elements
in Beecher's conception of preaching: that is it must be targeted to the audience
being reached. This idea is seen again and again in the Lyman Beecher Lectureship on Preaching, which Beecher delivered in 1872 (he also occupied the
lectureship the next two years, the only individual to present these prestigious
lectures three times). As Beecher observed in his second lecture, "Sympathy with
your people, insight of their condition, a study of the moral remedies, this will
give endless diversity and fertility to your subjects for sermons. The wants of your
people must set back into the sermon, and give it depth, direction, and current."[50]

Because the preacher often must appeal to different educational, social, and
economic levels within the same congregation, Beecher stressed the need to vary
the style of sermons. Since a specific appeal may reach some listeners and not
others, the form of the appeal must not be limited to a single type. For those
requiring intellectual preaching, offer sermons of that type; likewise, seek
to satisfy those who can be reached through the emotion or the imagination.
"Take men as it has pleased God to make them; and let your preaching, so far as
concerns the election of material, and the mode and method by which you are
presenting the truth, follow the wants of the persons themselves, and not simply
the measure of your own minds."[51]

As rhetorical scholar Lionel Crocker observed, Beecher was Aristotelian in
the sense that he approached the rhetorical task with an audience-centered perspective.[52] The key to his homiletical method was his analysis of the audience to be
reached. As a result, the characteristic elements of his sermons tended to be based
on his observation and analysis of the needs and attitudes of his congregation.

---

47. Mrs. Henry Ward Beecher, "Mr. Beecher As I Knew Him," *Ladies' Home Journal* 9, no. 6 (May
1892): 5.

48. Beecher, *Lectures on Preaching*, 168.

49. Beecher, "Mr. Beecher," 5.

50. Beecher, *Lectures on Preaching*, 36.

51. Ibid., 50.

52. Lionel Crocker, "The Rhetorical Influence of Henry Ward Beecher," *Quarterly Journal of Speech*
18 (February 1932): 87.

Beecher believed strongly that most people could be best reached through an appeal to their emotions. In the Yale lectures, he suggested that six would be touched by such an appeal for every one that was motivated by reason.[53] Crocker observed that Beecher would have agreed with Cicero's observation in *De oratore* that humankind make far more determinations through hatred, or love, or desire, or anger, or grief, or joy, or hope, or fear, or error, or some other affection of mind, than from regard to truth, or any settled maxim, or principle of right, or judicial form or adherence to laws.[54]

However, Beecher did not avoid the use of reason or factual material in his sermons. As his associate Lyman Abbott pointed out, he would use facts to support a truth, then lay them aside as he used an emotional appeal to press home the truth with his audience.[55] An example is seen in the sermon "Victory of Hope in Sorrow." Using a series of biblical texts, Beecher argues that suffering is a part of the Christian life that must be accepted and that feelings of sorrow are not wrong. He then offers a limitation: sorrow should not become an orgy of self-recrimination and misery. This sparks a passage in which the emotional appeals are obvious: "And yet, how many are there that lose friends, how many mothers are there out of whose arms has gone their darling child, who are fond of going back in memory to pain themselves. How they think of every spasm, of every sigh and groan, of the fair departed one! How do they mourn to think there was so much pain and suffering! Oh! That he might have gone with a sweeter and kinder release. So all that is harrowing is brought back again, gathered, and worn, as it were."[56]

A glance at some of Beecher's sermon titles further illustrates this dependence on emotional appeal. Typical titles include: "Heart House," "The Love of God," "The Value of Deep Feelings," "Summer in the Soul," "Christian Joyfulness," "The Primacy of Love," and "The Era of Joy." Beecher's occasionally excessive emotionalism and love of sensual beauty led Thoreau to call him a "magnificent pagan."[57]

This strong emotional element in Beecher's sermons explains, in part, the importance of illustration for him. He devoted an entire Yale lecture to illustrations as means of persuasion, and used them freely in his own sermons. Beecher believed they helped people understand abstract ideas more clearly, were an aid to memory, stimulated the imagination, provided a mental release for the

---

53. Beecher, *Lectures on Preaching*, 47.
54. Lionel Crocker, *Henry Ward Beecher's Art of Preaching* (Chicago: The University of Chicago Press, 1934. Quoted from *De Oratore*, Book II, chapter xlii.
55. Lyman Abbott, "Henry Ward Beecher," *Atlantic Monthly* 92, no. 552 (October 1903): 543.
56. Henry Ward Beecher, *Sermons*, First Series (London: Dickinson, 1870), 499–500.
57. Vernon L. Parrington, *The Beginnings of Critical Realism* (New York: Harcourt, Brace, 1930), 76.

audience, helped to communicate a single truth to a varied audience, and enabled the minister to subtly introduce controversial topics.[58]

Newell Dwight Hillis, who followed Beecher and Abbott as pastors of Plymouth Church, studied Beecher's written manuscripts and noted the way in which he would often elaborate a proposition in his text, then, apparently as an afterthought, would strike through the discussion and replace it with a striking illustration.[59] Beecher's concern was never carefully wrought theology, but communication with the common people. In one lecture-room talk he noted, "I have never been accustomed to preach according to the class of subjects belonging to a system of theology. I have preached very much as a mother feeds her children, giving them the thing which their health requires. That which I am continually watching is the spiritual vitality which is produced."[60]

Beecher believed preaching was, at its heart, an instrument aimed at raising people's lives to a higher moral and ethical level. This concept of preaching grew out of his view of the nature of Christianity as a "system of influence" through which God seeks to educate and develop the human race to its highest capacity.[61]

It is worthwhile to note that with such a view of the Christian faith, social and political action become integral elements of human participation in the divine process. According to Beecher, the one constant feature that characterized the teachings of Christ was their focus on individual conduct and character.[62] The business of the church, therefore, was not primarily to prepare people for an afterlife, but to "build up men in the qualities of Jesus Christ," and it was toward that goal that preachers should aim.[63] The truth of a person's faith is not what they are on Sunday, Beecher insisted, but what they are during the week in the midst of their everyday life.[64]

The purpose of preaching, then, is not to provide insights into theological concepts, but to guide people to a more ethical, Christlike lifestyle, Beecher argued. He believed the pulpit was losing its influence because preachers were bound by the idea that their sermons must consist of doctrinal and theological truisms. Beecher believed cold, abstract preaching—which was out of contact

---

58. Beecher, *Lectures on Preaching*, 127–35.

59. Henry Ward Beecher, *A Treasury of Illustration* (New York: Revell, 1904), x.

60. Henry Ward Beecher, "A Look at the Past Year," *Christian Union* 1, no. 1 (1 January 1870): 3. Text of Lecture-Room Talk of December 10, 1869.

61. Henry Ward Beecher, "The Era of Joy," *The Christian Union* 3, no. 1 (4 January 1871): 5. Text of Beecher's Christmas sermon of December 5, 1870. Beecher's published sermons and Lecture-Room talks were recorded by a stenographer.

62. Henry Ward Beecher, sermon, August 27, 1843, Yale MSS.

63. J. B. Pond, *A Summer in England With Henry Ward Beecher* (New York: Fords, Howard & Hulbert, 1887): 158.

64. Henry Ward Beecher, *Notes from Plymouth Pulpit* (New York: Derby & Jackson, 1858), 250.

with the daily existence of average people—was the primary cause of neglect of churches in his day. "Dry bones never will feed the souls of men," he asserted. "Living truths, in living form, applied to living events, will interest and profit."[65]

CONTRIBUTIONS TO PREACHING

Henry Ward Beecher represents a transitional figure in the history of American preaching. Theologically, his preaching offers a vivid example of the shift from the Calvinist theology of his father to a more liberal, romantic theological perspective that reflected the philosophical currents of his era.

He also represented an attempt to apply preaching to emerging social issues of his day, such as women's suffrage and the labor movement. In terms of preaching to political and social issues, he was best known for his antislavery preaching and activities, which helped make him the most widely known American preacher of his day.

Sermon Excerpt

The Essence of Religion[66]

What is the true church? That is the true church which produces and is adapted to produce the largest harvest of love. You cannot test a church by its history; you cannot test a church by its logic, nor by its concatenations of argument. That is the true church that is most nearly allied to the mind and spirit of Jesus Christ, and the mind and spirit of Jesus Christ is that God so loved the world that He gave His Son to die for it. Greater love hath no man than that He laid down His life for His friends; that is the interpretation. That, then, is the true Church; not that which is largest, or the most numerous, or the most decorated, or the most acerb in its theology, or the most historic in its claims; but that which continually brings forth the sweet fruits of righteousness in the form of love.

God be thanked, there are grand, true churches in the communion of the catholic church; there are holy men among them, and there are churches under their administrations where I see unfolded the sweetest and choicest flowers in the garden of the Lord. Humble they are; so is

---

65. Henry Ward Beecher, sermon, n.d., Yale MSS.

66. From "The Essence of Religion" contained in *Sermons by Henry Ward Beecher, Plymouth Church, Brooklyn*, Vol. 1 (New York: Harper & Brothers, 1869).

the violet. Unpretentious they are, not widely grown; neither is the vine. But we know that they are gardens of the Lord. Churches there are round about whose boundaries tower the hollyhock and the pretentious sunflower, and nothing besides. Churches that bring forth righteousness, and are adapted to bring forth in their ruling ideas all the sweet fruits of the Spirit of God, they have the note that they are of the Church of Jesus Christ. Now, what is conversion? We hear a great deal about it. Conversion is the kindling in a soul of the light of love. No man is illuminated at conversion entirely: it is the rising light that shines brighter and brighter unto the perfect day. Before every part of the vast chamber of the human soul shall receive its light, time and suffering and experience must be passed through; but the beginning of the life of love—that, and only that, is conversion. Some men think that they are converted because they had a horrible conviction, and because they said they were brought out of the miry clay and had their feet set upon the rock. They look back to that experience, and they say, "I was converted at four o'clock in the afternoon on the 10th of June, eighteen hundred and so and so." Your clock may be right, but the thing itself is not perhaps worthy of a revelation; for I have not been able to perceive that you are a particle less proud; I think on some grounds you have been more avaricious; I think you have traded on your reputation for piety; I think you have taken on airs by reason of your supposed now superiority. There are a thousand reasons why I do not think many conversions are good because they do not bring forth the fruit of love. ♦

BIBLIOGRAPHY

Abbott, Lyman. "Henry Ward Beecher," *Atlantic Monthly* 92, no. 552 (October 1903).

Abbott, Lyman and S. B. Halliday. *Henry Ward Beecher: A Sketch of His Career*. Hartford: American, 1887.

Ahlstrom, Sydney E. *A Religious History of the American People*. 2nd ed. New Haven: Yale University Press, 2004.

Barrows, John Henry. *Henry Ward Beecher: The Shakespeare of the Pulpit*. New York: Funk & Wagnalls, 1893.

Beecher, Henry Ward. "A Correspondence," *The Independent* 1, no. 56 (December 1849).

_____. "Is Conversion Instantaneous," *The Independent* 1, no. 56 (December 1849).

_____. *Seven Lectures to Young Men on Various Important Subjects*. Indianapolis: Moore, 1844.

_____. "The God of Comfort." In *The Sermons of Henry Ward Beecher*, First Series. New York: Ford, 1869.

_____. "Human Ideas of God," in *The Sermons of Henry Ward Beecher*, Second Series. New York: Ford, 1869.

_____. *Oratory*. Philadelphia: National School of Oratory, 1886.

_____. *Lectures on Preaching*. New York: Ford, 1872.

_____. *Sermons*, First Series. London: Dickinson, 1870.

_____. *A Treasury of Illustration*. New York: Revell, 1904.

_____. "A Look at the Past Year." *Christian Union* 1, no. 1 (1 January 1870).

_____. "The Era of Joy." *The Christian Union* 3, no. 1 (4 January 1871).

_____. *Notes from Plymouth Pulpit*. New York: Derby & Jackson, 1858.

_____. "The Essence of Religion" in *Sermons by Henry Ward Beecher, Plymouth Church, Brooklyn*. Vol. 1. New York: Harper & Brothers, 1869.

Beecher, William C. and Rev. Samuel Scoville. *A Biography of Rev. Henry Ward Beecher*. New York: Cosimo, 2006.

Beecher, Mrs. Henry Ward. "Mr. Beecher As I Knew Him," *Ladies' Home Journal* 9, no. 6 (May 1892).

_____. "Mr. Beecher As I Knew Him." *Ladies' Home Journal* 8, no. 12 (November 1891).

Caskey, Marie. *Chariot of Fire: Religion and the Beecher Family*. New Haven: Yale University Press, 1978.

Clark Jr., Clifford E. *Henry Ward Beecher: Spokesman for a Middle-Class America*. Urbana: University of Illinois Press, 1978.

Crocker, Lionel. *Henry Ward Beecher's Speaking Art*. New York: Revell, 1937.

_____. "The Rhetorical Influence of Henry Ward Beecher." *Quarterly Journal of Speech* 18 (February 1932).

_____. *Henry Ward Beecher's Art of Preaching*. Chicago: The University of Chicago Press, 1934. Quoted in *De Oratore*, Book II, chapter xlii.

Elsmere, Jane Schaffer. *Henry Ward Beecher: The Indiana Years, 1837–1847*. Indianapolis: Indiana Historical Society, 1973.

Fowler, Henry. *The American Pulpit*. New York: Fairchild, 1856.

Griswold, W. C. *The Life of Henry Ward Beecher*. New York: Hurst, 1887.

Hibben, Paxton. *Henry Ward Beecher: An American Portrait*. New York: Doran, 1927.

Hillis, Newell Dwight. "Henry Ward Beecher: A Sermon Preached in Plymouth Church, Sunday, January 4, 1903." Brooklyn: Eagle, 1903.

McLoughlin, William Gerald. *The Meaning of Henry Ward Beecher: An Essay on the Shifting Values of mid-Victorian America*. New York: Knopf, 1970.

Parrington, Vernon L. *The Beginnings of Critical Realism*. New York: Harcourt, Brace, 1930.

Parton, James. "Henry Ward Beecher and His Church, 1867." In *The Church and The City: 1865–1910*. Edited by Robert D. Cross. Indianapolis: The Bobbs-Merrill Company, Inc., 1967.

Pond, J. B. *A Summer in England With Henry Ward Beecher*. New York: Fords, Howard & Hulbert, 1887.

Ruffin, J.N. *Lives of Famous Orators*. London: Taylor & Francis, 1922.

Thompson, Noyes L. *The History of Plymouth Church*. New York: Carleton, 1873.

John Albert Broadus

Carefully Expositing the Authoritative Scriptures

HERSHAEL W. YORK

Though known today primarily as a professor, seminary president, and author, his contemporaries recognized John Albert Broadus (1827–1895) as among the greatest preachers of the nineteenth century. He is the most accomplished and recognized homiletician that Baptists have produced; no other figure casts so large a shadow on homiletics in three successive centuries. One of four founding members of the faculty of The Southern Baptist Theological Seminary and its second president, Broadus is remembered more because of his magnum opus, *A Treatise on the Preparation and Delivery of Sermons*, than for his preaching itself. Yet in his day and across a broad theological spectrum, Broadus was regarded as one of the most skillful and effective preachers in the world.

HISTORICAL BACKGROUND

John A. Broadus was born in 1827 to a Virginia farming family that was "Baptist to the core."[1] The youngest son of Major Edmund Broadus and Nancy Sims Broadus far surpassed his classmates in academic abilities. His father spent much time "explaining farming and political matters to him, encouraging him to read, asking him questions and encouraging him to express his opinions."[2] His intellect, coupled with a rigorous work ethic, distinguished and commended him throughout his life.

While still a teenager himself, Broadus opened his own school—as was common then—and became a schoolmaster with the purpose of saving the money necessary to attend university, where he planned to study medicine.[3] Many of

---

1. Archibald Thomas Robertson, *Life and Letters of John Albert Broadus* (Philadelphia: American Baptist, 1910), 3.
2. Tom Nettles, "John Broadus," in *The Baptists: Beginnings in America* (Fearn, Tain, Scotland: Christian Focus), 2:285.
3. Ibid., 294–95.

his friends thought that so brilliant and gifted a young scholar should move toward the ministry, but Broadus would have none of it. He "always came to the conclusion that preaching [was] not [his] office."[4]

Just before embarking on his medical studies, Broadus heard a sermon by a well-known preacher, A. M. Poindexter, on Jesus's parable of the talents. The sermon so gripped him that he committed himself to the gospel ministry. Years later, Broadus described his experience: "[Poindexter] seemed to clear up all difficulties pertaining to the subject; he swept away all the disguises of self-delusion, all the excuses of a fancied humility. . . . For the decision of that hour [I am] directly indebted, under God, to A. M. Poindexter; and amid a thousand imperfections and short-comings, that work of the ministry has been the joy of [my] life."[5]

Broadus matriculated at the University of Virginia with a determination to acquire as much knowledge as possible, through diligent, disciplined study. As Broadus's admiring son-in-law, the venerable Greek scholar A. T. Robertson, noted, "With what relish this brilliant student absorbed everything in the University! . . . He was drinking deep at this pure spring. No man ever quaffed here who drew more refreshment and inspiration."[6]

Significantly, the young preacher availed himself of every opportunity to improve as a speaker. He joined the prestigious Jefferson Society, where he soon became the top debater and honed his powers of elocution, persuasion, and rhetoric. According to Robertson's biography, one of Broadus's colleagues at the university observed:

> He cultivated a great power of application and grew to have a great ability to work, and was not ashamed that others should know it. The wonderful result of his steady, methodical industry was that in after years he could do unheard-of things in the briefest time. His disciplined faculties were so under his will that the result, while natural, was surprising. . . . He demanded of himself the best he could do in all that he did. The resulting clearness and correctness of his thinking begat that limpid, lucid, crystalline purity of expression which marked his writing and speaking.[7]

Even after graduation, Broadus continued to cultivate his interests in theology, church history, preaching, language, geography, and "old English divines,"

---

4. Ibid., 295.
5. John A. Broadus, *Sermons and Addresses* (Richmond: Johnson, 1887), 399.
6. Robertson, *Life and Letters of John Albert Broadus*, 65.
7. Ibid., 66.

like John Owen.[8] An avowed linguaphile, he mastered Greek, Hebrew, Latin, and eventually added many other languages to his repertoire. In 1850, he married Maria Charlotte Harrison, the daughter of one of his professors and mentors at the University of Virginia, and embarked on what was, by all accounts, a very happy marriage and lifelong love.[9]

In 1851, the newlywed minister accepted a bivocational call as pastor of the Charlottesville Baptist Church and assistant professor of classics at the university. During the seven years he spent in Charlottesville, he took two years' leave of absence from the church to serve as chaplain to the university. Of this unusual circumstance, biographer Thomas McKibbens noted, "Broadus seemed during those early years of ministry to struggle over the exact nature of his calling. He was pulled in two different directions: when in the pastorate, he longed for the classroom; in the classroom, he yearned for the pulpit."[10]

His preaching ability was already becoming noteworthy for its eloquence and effectiveness. Some students matriculated at the University of Virginia simply because he was a professor there and pastored nearby.[11] During his last year of ministry in Charlottesville, a young Lottie Moon, later an iconic Baptist missionary to China, was converted under his preaching.

In 1859, Broadus was invited to join the founding faculty at the new Southern Baptist Theological Seminary in Greenville, South Carolina, along with James P. Boyce, William Williams, and Basil Manly Jr. Though at first he declined, not wanting to leave the pastoral ministry[12] or his friends and family in Charlottesville,[13] the young pastor eventually acquiesced and soon settled into a new calling[14] that became his life's work and passion. Within two years after its inception, the very existence of the fledgling seminary was threatened by the devastation of the Civil War, as well as the lack of young ministers to train because they were fighting in the terrible conflict. During the war, Broadus became a chaplain to the Army of Northern Virginia at the direct request of Stonewall Jackson.[15]

When the war ended, the seminary attempted to reopen its doors in 1865, but was in dire straits. When the four faculty members came back together to

---

8. Nettles, "John Broadus," 296.

9. Ibid.

10. Thomas R. McKibbens Jr., "John A. Broadus: Shaper of Baptist Preaching," *Baptist History and Heritage* 40, no. 2, (Spring 2005): 20.

11. Nettles, "John Broadus," 297.

12. Vernon Latrelle Stanfield, "Introduction: John Albert Broadus: Preacher Extraordinary," in *Favorite Sermons of John A. Broadus* (New York: Harper & Brothers, 1959), 4.

13. William Mueller, *A History of Southern Baptist Theological Seminary* (Nashville: Broadman, 1959), 67.

14. Robertson, *Life and Letters of John Albert Broadus*, 158.

15. David S. Dockery, "Mighty in the Scriptures" in *John A. Broadus: A Living Legacy* (Nashville: Broadman & Holman, 2008), 19.

decide whether they could feasibly reopen the school, Broadus spoke with deep resolve: "Suppose we quietly agree that the seminary may die, but we'll die first."[16] The great homiletician, who had commanded the attention of full classrooms and congregations just a few years before, found himself lecturing on homiletics to two pupils, but one dropped out and his lone remaining student was blind.[17] Southern Seminary historian William Mueller explains: "Rather than canceling the class, Broadus lectured to his lone pupil week after week, honing the content that later became the book *The Preparation and Delivery of Sermons*."[18]

The Reconstruction years challenged Broadus with extreme emotional, physical, and financial troubles. According to Greg Wills, he "fell ill in 1866 and pleaded for repayment from those who owed him anything, but he was 'utterly unable to obtain any money.' He had to beg a small loan from a friend who had nothing to spare."[19] The many invitations he received to serve as pastor of a large church or president of a university—including Vassar and the University of Chicago—were, no doubt, enticing in the midst of his poverty, "but he ever felt that his duty was to remain at Southern."[20]

After teaching homiletics at the seminary for several years, Broadus began to take more administrative duties at the seminary and so saw the need finally to reduce his classroom lectures to textbook form so that his successors could more easily and consistently teach what he had taught. He was convinced of his theology and methodology and wanted to preserve it for future generations. The result was his magnum opus, *A Treatise on the Preparation and Delivery of Sermons*,[21] originally published at his own expense for one thousand dollars. The book was so readily accepted and widely adopted, that it did not take long for him to recoup his investment.

Though he was a consummate preacher and homiletician, as evidenced by his invitation to deliver the Lyman Beecher Lecturship on Preaching at Yale in 1889, Broadus's expertise went far beyond the pulpit. His commentary on Matthew stood as a standard until well into the twentieth century. A. T. Robertson

---

16. Nettles, "John Broadus," 300.

17. Gregory Wills, *Southern Baptist Theological Seminary, 1859–2009* (New York: Oxford University Press, 2009), 65. Abbreviated hereafter as *SBTS*.

18. Mueller, *A History*, 67.

19. Wills, *SBTS*, 69.

20. Ibid., 71.

21. John A. Broadus, *A Treatise on the Preparation and Delivery of Sermons* (Louisville: The Southern Baptist Theological Seminary, 2012). Herein referred to as *Treatise* from this point on. This is the first and only reprint of Broadus's original edition. The 1898 edition was extensively edited and revised by E. C. Dargan, the 1944 edition by J. B. Weatherspoon, and the 1979 edition by Vernon Stanfield. At least fifty different editions were published, none of them exactly like the original until 2012. All quotations from the *Treatise*, therefore, are taken from this reprint of the first edition because these are Broadus's exact words.

called him "the greatest teacher of language that I have ever known."[22] Timothy George noted, "His facility with classical languages prepared him to write a major commentary on the Gospel of Matthew and to serve as an editor of the homilies of John Chrysostom in the Nicene and Post-Nicene Fathers series."[23] He wrote *A Catechism of Bible Teaching* for the instruction of children, published by the Baptist Sunday School Board in 1891. At the same time, he delivered scholarly lectures around the country on textual criticism and the historical Jesus.[24] There is hardly any facet of church, seminary, or denominational life in which Broadus did not have a significant and memorable impact.

In 1889, upon the death of his dear friend and colleague James P. Boyce, Broadus became the second president of The Southern Baptist Theological Seminary in the closing years of his ministry and just twelve years after its postwar move to Louisville. David Dockery summarized that final chapter of the great minister's life:

> The added responsibility of presidential leadership and the death of Boyce had a considerable impact on Broadus. A. T. Robertson observed that after 1889 Broadus never regained the buoyancy of life he once had. In his final years as president, Broadus' health continued to grow weaker. Yet his standing as a national Baptist leader continued to build the seminary both financially and in terms of national and international recognition. The great Baptist leader, preacher, and scholar died on March 16, 1895. On that day, the *Louisville Courier-Journal* reported, "There is no man in the United States whose passing would cause more widespread sorrow than that of Doctor Broadus."[25]

In *Modern Masters of Pulpit Discourse,* W. C. Wilkinson called Broadus a preacher "hardly second to anyone in the world."[26] E. C. Dargan, Broadus's successor as professor of preaching at Southern Seminary, as well as the first to edit and revise his *Treatise,* named him "one of the greatest of his age and country."[27] No one held him in higher regard and greater veneration than A. T. Robertson, Broadus's son-in-law and junior colleague on the faculty. Robertson

---

22. A. T. Robertson, *A Grammar of the Greek New Testament in the Light of Historical Research* (New York: Doran, 1914), 47.

23. Timothy George, "Introduction to John A. Broadus," in *John A Broadus: A Living Legacy,* eds. David Dockery and Roger Duke (Nashville: Broadman & Holman, 2008), 5.

24. Dockery, "Mighty in the Scriptures," 21.

25. Ibid., 21.

26. William Cleaver Wilkinson, *Modern Masters of Pulpit Discourse* (Pennsylvania: Judson, 1905), 344.

27. E. C. Dargan, "John Albert Broadus—Scholar and Preacher," *The Crozer Quarterly* (April 1925): 171.

related that he personally heard the preaching of Phillips Brooks, Alexander Maclaren, Joseph Parker, D. L. Moody, and Charles Spurgeon, yet he said that Broadus was "the equal of any man I have ever heard."[28] Upon Broadus's death, W. H. Whitsitt, Theodore Harris, and A. H. Newman all threw aside any fear of hyperbole and simply said, "He was the greatest man I have ever known."[29]

Warmed by a love of Christ and his Word, fueled by a commitment to thorough and accurate exegesis, kindled by a redemptive rhetoric, and set ablaze by utter dependence on the Holy Spirit, Broadus lit the path on which subsequent expositors still travel. Though Estill Jones said Broadus "was responsible for steering Southern Baptist preaching into the expository style,"[30] in truth his impact still goes far beyond Southern Baptist preaching and is found almost anywhere the Bible is faithfully exposited.

THEOLOGY OF PREACHING

When historians study the theology of most preachers, they usually have to work backward, poring over sermons and statements and inferring the underlying doctrinal presuppositions. Rarely do they enjoy the largesse of the preacher's theological commitments distilled into a single, clear document, but that is precisely their advantage in Broadus's case. The seminary's *Abstract of Principles*, written by Basil Manly Jr. and signed by each of the four founding faculty members, are the clearly defined theological principles that lay behind and supported the preaching and homiletics of John A. Broadus.

When the original charter of the The Southern Baptist Theological Seminary was adopted in 1858, it contained twenty articles of belief regarded as the "fundamental laws" that govern the institution's purpose and teaching. Rooted in the Second London Confession, itself a Baptist revision of the earlier Westminster Confession, the *Abstract of Principles* reflected doctrines that had been agreed on by Baptist associations in Philadelphia and Charleston, and had greatly influenced Baptists of both the North and the South.[31] Broadus himself was part of the meeting that hammered out the confessional statement over the course of five days. Its inception bears his monumental influence, and its document displays his actual signature. Leaving no room for redefinitions of the terms or any "private arrangement" with those who invest him for office, the

---

28. A. T. Robertson, *The Minister and His Greek New Testament* (New York: Doran, 1923), 118.
29. Nettles, "John Broadus," 293.
30. J. Estill Jones, "The New Testament and Southern," *Review & Expositor* 82, no. 1 (Winter 1985): 22.
31. R. Albert Mohler, "Don't Just Do Something, Stand There" (Preached at The Southern Baptist Theological Seminary chapel, Louisville, KY, August 31, 1993), http://www.sbts.edu/resources/articles/dont-just-do-something-stand-there/.

Abstract states, "Every professor of the institution shall be a member of a regular Baptist Church; and all persons accepting professorships in this Seminary shall be considered, by such acceptance, as engaging to teach in accordance with, and not contrary to, the *Abstract of Principles* hereinafter laid down, a departure from which principles on his part shall be grounds for his resignation or removal by the Trustees."[32] No one can doubt that any of the four founding professors held to the theology of the *Abstract*.

Dockery characterizes the doctrinal statement, saying, "The theological tradition reflected in the *Abstract* is in line with historic orthodoxy at every point. The soteriology can be called moderately Calvinistic and the ecclesiology Baptistic. Broadus' work was carried forth in a manner faithful to this tradition."[33]

Judging by his wholehearted assent to the *Abstract*, therefore, Broadus's preaching was committed to particular doctrinal positions that he regarded as of primary importance. Among these were a high view of Scripture; an orthodox belief in a Trinitarian God who controls and decrees or permits all things that come to pass and elects some people as recipients of his saving grace, who are consequently called, justified, and glorified; a human race that is completely fallen and lost apart from the atoning work of Christ; the regenerating work of the Holy Spirit that results in repentance and faith and the justification of the forgiven sinner by the imputation of the righteousness of Christ; the sanctification and final perseverance of the saved; a congregationally governed local church with two symbolic ordinances (not sacraments) of baptism and the Lord's Supper and with two offices of elders and deacons; regular observance of the Lord's Day; the liberty of conscience under the lordship of Christ; and the resurrection of the dead to judgment and either eternal life or eternal punishment.

Scripture as the Authoritative Foundation for Preaching

Within these doctrinal commitments, three specific aspects stand out. First and most significantly, Broadus preached with complete confidence in the Bible. As Mueller notes, "Broadus believed that the Bible did not merely contain but *is* the Word of God."[34] For him the authority of the Bible was "paramount and permanent" as he noted, "Wherever the Bible undertakes to teach, its teachings are true. It does not attempt to teach on all subjects. It uses popular language that must be interpreted accordingly. But whatever it intends to teach, that is

---

32. Basil Manly Jr.,"The Abstract of Principles," The Southern Baptist Theological Seminary, http://www.sbts.edu/about/abstract/.

33. Dockery, "Mighty in the Scriptures," 31.

34. Mueller, *A History*, 80.

paramount in authority."[35] Broadus traveled to Europe and was very familiar with the higher criticism that was emanating from Germany and taking hold in American seminaries and Christian institutions. He had many cordial and close relationships with higher-critical scholars who practiced what came to be known as the "new theology," but he rejected anything that called the truth and authority of the Word of God into question. Broadus's personal warmth enabled him to remain friends with many contemporary higher-critical scholars, and he "wanted to avoid rupturing his relationship with them personally and institutionally,"[36] so he distanced himself from their views while always retaining their friendship.

If Broadus would ever have been tempted to sacrifice his views on Scripture for the sake of relationship, it would have been when his brilliant former student and subsequent colleague, Crawford H. Toy, began to promote higher-critical views at Southern. So much has been written about this first major doctrinal controversy at the seminary that it need not be recounted with great specificity here, but a few salient details highlight Broadus's doctrinal commitment and intentional rejection of a destructive approach to the Bible.[37]

Toy had professed faith and been baptized in 1856 during Broadus's tenure as pastor of the Baptist church in Charlottesville and had studied with him in the university as well. He followed his pastor to the newly founded Southern Seminary in 1859, though his studies were interrupted by the war. After the war ended, he studied Semitic languages at the University of Berlin from 1866–1868, and was elected to Southern's faculty a year later to teach Hebrew, Old Testament interpretation, and special courses in Syriac and Arabic. When Toy, with whom Broadus had translated Johann Peter Lange's commentary on 1 and 2 Samuel from German, began to publicly promote a higher-critical approach, Broadus himself was troubled. In response to Toy's questioning of the traditional understanding of inspiration and the Mosaic authorship of the Pentateuch, as well as disseminating his dismissal of the Genesis account of creation, Broadus solemnly advised Boyce that Toy should tender his resignation over the matter,[38] even though he was Toy's "father in the faith and beloved mentor."[39] Though the controversy would be a defining moment in the seminary and denomination's history, it served no less to define the bedrock foundation of Broadus's preaching, which would be lashed to the inspired and infallible Scriptures.

---

35. John A. Broadus, "The Paramount and Permanent Authority of the Bible,"(Philadelphia: American Baptist, 1883), 8.

36. Wills, *SBTS,* 181.

37. See Wills, *SBTS,* 108–49.

38. Ibid., 127.

39. Ibid., 130.

Evangelism as the Soteriological Mission of Preaching

The second element of Broadus's theology was that he was evangelistic. Not only did he believe in the necessity of personal faith in Jesus Christ for salvation, but he also believed that the Holy Spirit used expository preaching as the primary means by which people could hear the gospel and be regenerated. "The great appointed means of spreading the good tidings of salvation through Christ," he wrote in his introduction to the *Treatise*, "is preaching—words spoken, whether to the individual, or to the assembly." He continued:

And this, nothing can supersede. Printing has become a mighty agency for good and for evil; and Christians should employ it, with the utmost diligence and in every possible way, for the spread of truth. But printing can never take the place of the living word. When a man who is apt in teaching, whose soul is on fire with the truth which he trusts has saved him and hopes will save others, speaks to his fellow-men, face to face, eye to eye, and electric sympathies flash to and fro between him and his hearers, till they lift each other up, higher and higher, into the intensest thought, and the most impassioned emotion—higher and yet higher, till they are borne as on chariots of fire above the world—there is a power to move men, to influence character, life, destiny, such as no printed page can ever possess. *Pastoral work* is of immense importance, and all preachers should be diligent in performing it. But it cannot take the place of preaching, nor fully compensate for the lack of power in the pulpit. The two help each other, and neither of them is able, unless supported by the other, to achieve the largest and most blessed results. . . . It follows that preaching must always be a necessity, and good preaching a mighty power.[40]

Broadus undeniably modeled a deep Calvinistic understanding of God's sovereign work in salvation that compelled him to preach and to train preachers. Going even beyond the requirements of the *Abstract*, Broadus believed in particular redemption, the view that Christ died to accomplish the salvation of some though not all, yet his view was nuanced because, to his mind, so also were certain biblical texts. Of the phrase that Christ would "give his life as a ransom for many" in Matthew 20:28, he wrote in his commentary: "Christ's atoning death made it compatible with the divine justice that all should be saved if they would accept it on that ground; and in that sense he 'gave himself a ransom for all'

---

40. Broadus, *Treatise*, 1–2.

(1 Tim. 2:6), 'tasted death for every man' (Heb. 2:9), comp. 1 John 2:2; but his death was never expected, nor divinely designed, actually to secure the salvation of all, and so in the sense of specific purpose he came '*to give his life a ransom for many.*' Comp. 26:28; Heb. 9:28; Rom. 5:15, 18; Is. 53:12. *Henry:* 'Sufficient for all, effectual for many.'"[41]

In his catechism for children, Broadus further fleshes out the harmony where many see only dissonance.[42] As Nettles notes about his catechism, "In the integration of these ideas Broadus asserts at once the particularity and certainty of redemption for an elect people and the reality of responsibility that all have to respond to God's universal overtures of mercy to a condemned world."[43] Clearly, Broadus's view of particular redemption does not prevent him from preaching the gospel to all. To the contrary, he asserts that anyone who *will* be saved *may* be saved. Any deficiency lies in the sinner's unwilling heart, not in the atonement. The preacher, therefore, should preach with earnestness and passion because they preach a message of free salvation, completely accomplished and offered by Christ, available to all who will repent and believe, and the only means by which one may be made right with God. No one could reasonably argue, therefore, that Broadus's Calvinism made him any less evangelistic. To the contrary, his robust theology fueled his passion for powerful proclamation.

Baptist Identity as the Motive of Preaching

The third major element of Broadus's theology was its undoubtedly and uncompromisingly Baptistic character. Other evangelical traditions paid lip service to the importance of preaching, but they often put their pulpits on the side of the sanctuary and the sacraments in the center. Baptists rejected that architectural convention and put the pulpit front and center, signifying even visually that preaching is the central act of Christian worship.

Though Broadus was warmly welcomed and held in high esteem by many people in diverse denominations, even among those who held the higher-critical views, he never apologized for, or retreated from, his Baptist convictions. He was

---

41. John A. Broadus, *Commentary on Matthew* (1886; repr., Grand Rapids: Kregel, 1990), 419.

42. Of particular note are these questions and answers: Q: What was Christ's chief work as Savior? A: Christ died and rose again for his people. Q: Is the atonement of Christ sufficient for all men? A: The atonement of Christ is sufficient for all, and would actually save all if they would repent and believe. Q: Does God give his renewing Spirit as he sees proper? A: Yes, God gives his renewing Spirit to those whom he always purposed to save. Q: Does faith come before the new birth? A: No, it is the new heart that truly repents and believes. Q: Is repentance necessary to a sinner's salvation? A: Those who will not turn from sin perish. Q: Has God commanded his people to proclaim salvation to all men? A: Yes, God commands his people to proclaim salvation to all men. John A. Broadus, "Catechism," in *Selected Works of John A. Broadus*, ed. A. T. Robertson (Cape Coral, FL: Founders, 2001), 3:191–222. The selection of these particular questions and responses is from Nettles, "John Broadus," 312.

43. Nettles, "John Broadus," 312.

committed to congregational government, soul competence, believer's baptism, the symbolic nature of the ordinances, and the autonomy of the local church. Though he preached in many secular institutions, denominational schools, and churches with other theological commitments, his Baptist identity was unquestioned. James Patterson summarizes, "Overall, Broadus's conservative orthodoxy encompassed a full acceptance of the inspiration and authority of Scripture, a sharp awareness of the interpretive issues in biblical studies, a seasoned historical intuition, a thorough supernaturalism, and a moderately Reformed theological perspective."[44] In an academic and theological environment that was increasingly amorphous, Broadus's distinct allegiance to biblical fidelity and Baptist distinctives makes the breadth of his influence all the more remarkable.

METHODOLOGY FOR PREACHING

Since Broadus carefully crafted his preaching methodology and, after years of distillation in the cauldron of the classroom and mellowing in the pulpit, wrote it in a book of nearly five hundred pages, providing an analysis of that methodology in a few paragraphs may seem foolhardy if not impossible. The hope of this analysis is not only that it might faithfully represent Broadus's thought and teaching, but that it will provoke an interest in the primary sources of his writing and legacy.

Broadus divided his thought into more subcategories than most people could ever comprehend, but his approach to preaching had four large and overwhelming characteristics. The first, and by far the most important, aspect was that preaching must be rooted in the biblical text. As Albert Mohler says in his introduction of the *Treatise* reprint, "Broadus was committed to the exposition of the Bible, and to a grammatical and historical method of biblical interpretation. He believed in a method of preaching that respected the text and sought to serve it. He believed in the total truthfulness and authority of the Bible as the Word of God and he sought to teach preachers to respect, love, study, and preach that Word."[45]

Broadus was even careful to define exactly what "text" he meant. The very first section of the very first chapter is "Meaning of the Term Text," and he insists that the only text worthy of preaching is "the text of Scripture, the Greek text, the sacred text, as opposed to comments, translations, and other modes of using it."[46] Broadus was a master of the Greek text and, though he would affirm that

---

44. James Patterson, "Broadus's Living Legacy," in *John A. Broadus: A Living Legacy*, eds. David Dockery and Roger Duke (Nashville: Broadman & Holman, 2008), 246.

45. Mohler, introduction to *Treatise*, iv.

46. Ibid., 21.

those who could preach only from an English text could still be faithful preachers, he would also affirm that knowledge of the original languages is preferred because it is more readily revelatory of the mind of the author.

The proper interpretation of the text was the foundation of the sermon. "To interpret and apply his text in accordance with its real meaning is one of the preacher's most sacred duties."[47] Broadus himself admits that this principle should be obvious, but laments that "it is often and grievously violated."[48] Carefully employing grammatical-historical examination of the text enabled and empowered the preacher to comprehend and communicate the author's intended meaning.

Oddly enough, Broadus never argued for a systematic series of sermons through books or large passages. This is perhaps the greatest omission and weakness of the *Treatise*. He spends a great deal of space writing about the selection of a text, but never advocates simply expounding biblical truth in the same manner that one encounters it, line upon line and precept upon precept. If anything, Broadus cautions to "guard against monotony" in the texts chosen,[49] and to have a variety of texts, being sure not to miss any of the sections of Scripture over the course of one's ministry. He is unequivocal that "preaching was originally expository"[50] and should be in every preacher's ministry, but he does not insist on a continuous exposition that gives listeners a strategic grasp of the author's overall argument.

The second hallmark of Broadus's preaching method was that it must be logical. Perhaps no homiletician in the English language has owed more to classical rhetoric than Broadus. Both in the *Treatise* and in his Yale lectures, he insisted on using the canons of rhetoric to develop a sermon. According to Roger Duke, Broadus "drew from two classical rhetorical treatises. These were *De Inventione* by Cicero and *Institutio Oratoria* by Quintilian. . . . He gleaned what met his needs."[51] Broadus modeled a great commitment to the proper arrangement of a sermon in order to move the listener to act in accordance with the truth of the text.

His Lyman Beecher Lectures on Preaching at Yale, given in January 1889, reflected Broadus's commitment to certain "canons." Among his topics were "freshness in preaching," style, and arrangement.[52] Broadus clearly saw the power of the Holy Spirit and the preacher's effort as complementary and not in any way contradictory.

---

47. Ibid., 33.
48. Ibid.
49. Ibid., 31.
50. Broadus, *Treatise*, 21.
51. Roger Duke, "John Albert Broadus," in *John A. Broadus: A Living Legacy* (Nashville: Broadman & Holman, 2008), 77–78.
52. Mark M. Overstreet, "Now I Am Found: The Recovery of the 'Lost' Yale Lectures and Broadus's Legacy of Engaging Exposition," in *John A. Broadus: A Living Legacy* (Nashville: Broadman & Holman, 2008), 156–75.

Third, Broadus contended that preaching must be applicational. He did not mince words: "The application in a sermon is not merely an appendage to the discussion, or a subordinate part of it, but is the main thing to be done."[53] With equal fervor he averred that the application should take place throughout the sermon and not merely at the end. He was even willing to criticize Jonathan Edwards because the venerable Puritan always formally announced the application instead of weaving it into the sermon more imperceptibly.[54]

He was not interested in preaching merely to convince listeners of truth or to obtain intellectual assent to a set of facts. He insisted on being biblical, but he was equally adamant that the preacher should be persuasive. "The chief part of what we commonly call application is *persuasion*. It is not enough to convince men of truth, nor enough to make them see how it applies to themselves, and how it might be practicable for them to act it out—but we must 'persuade men.'"[55] Only a persuasive preacher could truly be eloquent. "Eloquence is so speaking as not merely to convince the judgment, kindle the imagination, and move the feelings, but to give a powerful impulse to the will."[56] In other words, eloquence was not measured by the beauty of the rhetorical display, but by its ability to lead the listener to act. For Broadus, the preacher's ultimate goal lay in helping members of a congregation experience life change as a result of hearing the Word. The sermon was not a time for vague generalities, but of specific instruction. "It is exceedingly useful to add hints as to the actual doing of the particular duty, so as to make it seem a practical and a practicable thing, so as to awaken hope of doing better, and thus stimulate effort."[57]

Finally, Broadus paid more attention to delivery than any of his contemporaries and very few homileticians since. However rich its content, preaching must be engaging. He bemoaned, "Far too many preachers ignored the means through which the message of God was preached."[58] Energy, style, passion, vocal inflection—everything mattered, even the way the preacher reads the text.

According to Overstreet, in both the *Treatise* and the Yale lectures, Broadus drove the preacher to embrace extemporaneous preaching. They must learn to trust themselves, he argued. The preacher must trust their preparation and entrust themself to God by preparing a sketch of the sermon, leaving it at home, and preaching with freedom. . . . The most gifted of preachers engaged themselves, if not at first, in the practice of free delivery.[59]

---

53. Broadus, *Treatise*, 197.
54. Ibid., 197.
55. Ibid., 198.
56. Ibid., 3.
57. Ibid., 198.
58. Overstreet, "Now I Am Found," 169.
59. Ibid., 169.

CONTRIBUTIONS TO PREACHING

Broadus's name may not be as widely known, nor his book as commonly read as it was in the late nineteenth and twentieth centuries, but his impact is perhaps more pervasive now than ever before. His DNA runs deep in the veins of contemporary expositors. Nearly everything written on expository preaching is derivative of Broadus's *Treatise* to some extent, often massively so. When John R. W. Stott wrote *Between Two Worlds* in 1982, his call was not for a new form of preaching, but a recovery of biblical preaching. "I believe that nothing is better calculated to restore health and vitality to the Church or to its members into maturity in Christ" wrote Stott, "than a recovery of true, biblical, contemporary preaching."[60] No one had been more responsible for laying the foundation upon which Stott was building than Broadus.

The first edition of the *Treatise* was published in 1870 at Broadus's own expense because few publishers thought they could make any money publishing a book on preaching; however, that single volume has been published in at least fifty editions and translated into many different languages. The book has never been out of print since its original publication.[61] Twenty-eight years after its original publication, E. C. Dargan would write, "The book was a great success" and would claim that "it became the most popular and widely read text-book on homiletics in the country." He noted twenty-two printings and stated that it had been "adopted in many theological seminaries of different denominations as the text-book, and in many where no text-book is used it is highly commended for study and reference," as well as being used in Japan and China with a Portuguese edition underway.[62] When Dargan wrote those words in 1898, however, the book was just getting started.

Contemporary expositors readily admit their indebtedness to Broadus. Tom Nettles has provided an excellent survey of the continuing impact of the *Treatise* in his contribution in *John A. Broadus: A Living Legacy*. Nettles cites his own survey of Southern Baptist homileticians, as well as David Alan Smith's doctoral dissertation, "Introductory Preaching Courses in Selected Southern Baptist Seminaries in Light of John A. Broadus's Homiletical Theory,"[63] to demonstrate that Broadus's homiletical theories are still in use today, even if *Treatise* itself is

---

60. John Stott, *Between Two Worlds: The Challenge of Preaching Today* (Grand Rapids: Eerdmans, 1982), 338.

61. Mohler, introduction to *Treatise*, iv.

62. Broadus, *Treatise*, v-vi.

63. David Alan Smith, "Introductory Preaching Courses in Selected Southern Baptist Seminaries in Light of John A. Broadus's Homiletical Theory" (PhD diss., University of Michigan, 1995).

not.[64] He further highlights some debt to Broadus in the homiletical books and theories of James F. Stitzinger, Irvin A. Busenitz, John MacArthur, John Carrick, Bryan Chapell, David Larsen, and Joseph Webb.[65] Over one hundred years before I defined expository preaching as "any preaching that explains authorial intent and makes appropriate application,"[66] Broadus said it better.

Broadus's commitment to the authority and careful exposition of Scripture, the thorough and logical preparation of the sermon, and a passionate, engaging delivery by the preacher still provide a model for preaching today. In fact, Broadus's model has not only withstood the test of time but also has proven timeless. He would be as at home with modern speech-act theory as he was with Cicero. He would urge inner-city preachers to identify with their congregants as much as he did his lone blind student immediately after the Civil War. His *Treatise* has been republished and reissued and translated into multiple languages precisely because it has *worked* in training preachers how to open the sacred text and preach it to needy hearts wherever and whenever they may be found.

Sermon Extract

How the Gospel Makes Men Holy (Romans 7:24–25)[67]

"How shall I be good?" is a question that used sometimes to rise in your mind when you were a child, sometimes when nobody would imagine you were thinking of such things as that. "How shall I get to be good." And it is a question which, amid all the commotion of this runaway life of ours, comes back to us very often, comes back even to people whom you would not suppose to be thinking of such things at all. The grossly wicked men, the men who are the slaves of vice, many of them, perhaps all of them, have their moments when there is a sort of longing that rises in their souls to be good, and when the hope returns, indestructible, that somehow or other they will get to be good after all. It became a sort of jest a few years ago, I know, to speak of "the wickedest man in New York," but I wonder sometimes if the wickedest man—whoever he might

64. Tom Nettles, "The Enduring Impact and Relevance of *A Treatise*" in *John A. Broadus: A Living Legacy* (Nashville: Broadman & Holman), 198–200.

65. Nettles, "Enduring Impact," 201–11.

66. Hershael W. York and Bert Decker, *Preaching with Bold Assurance: A Solid and Enduring Approach to Engaging Exposition* (Nashville: Broadman & Holman, 2003), 33.

67. Broadus, *Sermons and Addresses*, 97–109.

happen to be, considered as God considers—does not sometimes want to be good.

For many of us it has been much more than a vague longing that comes back again and again. It has been an earnest effort, sometimes a fearful struggle, when we have been trying to be good, and we have wondered whether something would not come in the course of the varied experiences of life, that would render it easier for us to conquer in this struggle, easier to become good. As a man lives on, he cannot help thinking—it is so hard now—he cannot help thinking it will become easier to be good. And when changes occur in his outward life he hopes now to find it easier. He sets up a new home, it may be, and has a vague feeling that there he will be able to be good. He marries a pious woman, may be, and although he may not say a word about it, he has a sort of notion that perhaps that will be blessed to him, and he will become pious too. He loses a parent whom he leaned on, maybe he loses a little child that lay in his bosom, and amid the strange feelings that rise up then, and which he would not tell any one about, he thinks, "Now surely I shall become good." And so, as the experiences of life come and go, men still hope to be good. Who is there here to-day that does not hope to be good? Who is there here to-day that at this solemn moment, when we are thinking about the soul and its immortality, does not feel that to be good is the loftiest human aspiration and the best earthly attainment? O tell me, do you not feel it? ♦

BIBLIOGRAPHY

Broadus, John A. *A Treatise on the Preparation and Delivery of Sermons*. 1870. Repr., Louisville, KY: Southern Baptist Theological Seminary, 2012.

_____. *A Treatise on the Preparation and Delivery of Sermons*. Edited by E. C. Dargan. 1870. Repr., New York: Doran, 1898.

_____. *Commentary on Matthew*. 1886. Repr., Grand Rapids: Kregel, 1990.

_____. *Sermons and Addresses*. Richmond: Johnson, 1887.

_____. "The Paramount and Permanent Authority of the Bible." Philadelphia: American Baptist, 1883.

_____. *Selected Works of John A. Broadus*. Edited by A. T. Robertson. 4 vols. Cape Coral, FL: Founders, 2001.

Dargan, E. C. "John Albert Broadus-Scholar and Preacher." *The Crozer Quarterly* (April 1925): 171.

Dockery, David S. "Mighty in the Scriptures: John A. Broadus and His Influence on A. T. Robertson and Southern Baptist Life." Pages 12–44 in *John A. Broadus: A Living Legacy*. Edited by David Dockery and Roger Duke. Nashville: Broadman & Holman, 2008.

Duke, Roger D. *John Albert Broadus: Prince of the Pulpit*. Mountain Home, AR: BorderStone, 2014.

George, Timothy. "Introduction to John A. Broadus: A Living Legacy." Pages 1–11 in *John A. Broadus: A Living Legacy*. Edited by David Dockery and Roger Duke. Nashville: Broadman & Holman, 2008.

Jones, J. Estill. "The New Testament and Southern." *Review & Expositor* 82, no. 1 (Winter 1985): 21–29.

Manly Jr., Basil. "The Abstract of Principles." The Southern Baptist Theological Seminary. http://www
.sbts.edu/about/abstract/

McKibbens, Thomas R., Jr. "John A. Broadus: Shaper of Baptist Preaching." *Baptist History and Heritage*
40, no. 2 (Spring 2005): 18–24.

Mohler, R. Albert. "Don't Just Do Something, Stand There." Preached at The Southern Baptist Theological
Seminary Chapel, Louisville, KY, August 31st, 1993. http://www.sbts.edu/resources/articles/
don't-just-do-something-stand-there/.

Mueller, William A. *A History of Southern Baptist Theological Seminary.* Nashville: Broadman, 1959.

Nettles, Tom. "John Albert Broadus." Pages 285–321 in vol. 2, *The Baptists: Beginnings in America.* Fearn,
Tain, Scotland: Christian Focus, 2006.

_____. "The Enduring Impact and Relevance of 'A Treatise on the Preparation and Delivery of Sermons.'"
Pages 176–211 in *John A. Broadus: A Living Legacy.* Edited by David Dockery and Roger Duke.
Nashville: Broadman & Holman, 2008.

Overstreet, Mark M. "Now I Am Found: The Recovery of the 'Lost' Yale Lectures and Broadus's Legacy of
Engaging Exposition." Pages 156–175 in *John A. Broadus: A Living Legacy.* Edited by David Dockery
and Roger Duke. Nashville: Broadman & Holman, 2008.

Patterson, James. "Broadus's Living Legacy." Pages 239–62 in *John A. Broadus: A Living Legacy.* Edited by
David Dockery and Roger Duke. Nashville: Broadman & Holman, 2008.

Robertson, A. T. *A Grammar of the Greek New Testament in the Light of Historical Research.* New York:
Doran, 1914.

_____. *The Minister and His Greek New Testament.* New York: Doran, 1923.

_____. *Life and Letters of John Albert Broadus.* Philadelphia: American Baptist, 1910.

Smith, David Alan. "Introductory Preaching Courses in Selected Southern Baptist Seminaries in Light of
John A. Broadus's Homiletical Theory" PhD Diss., Ann Arbor, MI: UMI, 1995.

Stanfield, Vernon L. "Introduction: John Albert Broadus: Preacher Extraordinary." Pages 1–13 in *Favorite
Sermons of John A. Broadus.* New York: Harper & Brothers, 1959.

Stott, John. *Between Two Worlds: The Challenge of Preaching Today.* Grand Rapids: Eerdmans, 1982.

Wilkinson, William Cleaver. *Modern Masters of Pulpit Discourse.* Pennsylvania: Judson, 1905.

Wills, Gregory A. *Southern Baptist Theological Seminary: 1859–2009.* New York: Oxford University Press,
2009.

York, Hershael, and Bert Decker. *Preaching with Bold Assurance: A Solid and Enduring Approach to
Engaging Exposition.* Nashville: Broadman & Holman, 2003.

Phillips Brooks
Preaching the Personality of the Preacher

CHARLES W. FULLER

Phillips Brooks (1835–1893) famously defined preaching as "truth through personality" during his 1877 Lyman Beecher Lectures on Preaching at Yale University—a phrase still commonly encountered in homiletics textbooks. His preaching was very popular, especially in his pastoral tenure at Boston's Trinity Church, and his sermons were published widely. He approached the pulpit in a manner congruent with the theological shifts of the late nineteenth century, moving away from concrete doctrinal assertions to a more personal, experiential form of the faith.

HISTORICAL BACKGROUND

Born the "consummate flower" of Puritan lineage reaching back nine generations, Phillips Brooks entered the world on December 13, 1835, as the second son of William Gray Brooks and Mary Ann Phillips.[1] Mary Ann wielded powerful spiritual influence in the family—seeing four of her sons enter the ministry—continuing the legacy of her own father, John Phillips, who was a strong defender of the Puritan heritage. However, Brooks's father, William Gray, grew up with only a meager interest in religion. Indeed, William was a Unitarian, and when he married Mary Ann in 1833, they continued to attend a Unitarian congregation until she could take it no longer. In 1839, at her insistence, the family rented a pew at St. Paul's Episcopal in Boston, where Phillips would spend his formative years under the preaching of Alexander H. Vinton, a pietistic Calvinist. Brooks held Vinton in high regard, but certain aspects of Vinton's preaching irked him, especially the emphasis on emotional conversion.[2]

Brooks graduated third in his class from Harvard College in 1851. While there, he read insatiably, consuming volumes of Elizabethan poetry and con-

---

1. Lewis Brastow, *Representative Modern Preachers* (New York: Hoder & Stoughton, 1904), 195.
2. Alexander V. G. Allen, *Life and Letters of Phillips Brooks* (New York: Dutton, 1901), 1:142.

temporary romantic authors. The extent to which these works affected Brooks's religious thought at the time proves difficult to estimate, but a "scrutiny of his college essays reveals no tendency to dwell upon the subject of religion."[3] After graduating, Brooks accepted a teaching post at Boston Latin School, from which he resigned in less than six months, apparently falling prey to his own youthfulness and relatively bashful demeanor.

The failure threw Brooks into a personal crisis. James Walker, Harvard's president, steered him toward Christian ministry, and Brooks returned to Vinton to seek consent. Vinton approved, and in addition to suggesting Virginia Theological Seminary, he reminded Brooks that it was "customary to have received confirmation before becoming a candidate for orders" and that "conversion was generally regarded as prerequisite for confirmation." Brooks replied that he "did not know what conversion meant."[4] Gillis Harp, a Brooks biographer and analyst, observes, "That the son of Mary Ann Phillips and a long-time parishioner of St. Paul's claimed not to understand the meaning of conversion suggested that some sort of internal rebellion against his evangelical upbringing had occurred."[5] There is no record of any conversion experience for Brooks, at least not in the evangelical sense.

Brooks's years at Virginia Theological Seminary (1856–1859)—a low-church, conservative Episcopal school—were not easy ones, nor was he contented. His disliked the Southern culture, academic sloth, and dogmatic Calvinism taught in the classroom.[6] His dissatisfaction with his environment, though, inspired him toward a more personal course of study. His notebooks from these years indicate that an "amalgam of liberal Romantic Evangelicalism and literary Romanticism" filled his reading.[7] Like his college essays, Brooks's private writings in his seminary years yield surprisingly few references to anything resembling the faith in which he was raised.[8] As Brooks inhaled romantic influences, he began to exhale evangelical doctrine, openly rejecting traditional tenets such as total depravity, and growing impatient with the very idea of systematic doctrine.[9]

One month after graduating from Virginia Seminary in 1859, Brooks moved to Philadelphia to pastor the Church of the Advent. By 1869, though, he had returned to lead Boston's Trinity Church, where he identified with the Broad

---

3. Ibid., 1:87.
4. Ibid., 1:142.
5. Gillis J. Harp, *Brahmin Prophet: Phillips Brooks and the Path of Liberal Protestantism* (New York: Rowman & Littlefield, 2003), 22.
6. Ibid., 29–34; John F. Woolverton, *The Education of Phillips Brooks* (Chicago: University of Illinois Press, 1995), 50.
7. Harp, *Brahmin Prophet*, 28, 32–33.
8. Woolverton, *Education of Phillips Brooks*, 90.
9. Harp, *Brahmin Prophet*, 33–34; Allen, *Life and Letters*, 1:169, 1:303–4.

Church movement—a liberal wing of Episcopalians. His popularity soared in Boston, and his influence stretched beyond denominational and theological lines, mostly due to his preaching. In 1877, his growing celebrity earned him an invitation from Yale Divinity School to deliver the annual Lyman Beecher Lectureship on Preaching, in which he offered his now-famous definition of preaching. During his lecture, Brooks stated, "Preaching is the communication of truth by man to man. It has in it two essential elements, truth and personality. Neither of those can it spare and still be preaching. . . . [P]reaching is the bringing of truth through personality."[10]

Brooks's concept has been hailed as "perhaps the most famous definition of preaching found anywhere in American homiletical literature."[11] While he served as the pastor of Boston's Trinity Church and later as bishop over the Protestant Episcopal Diocese of Massachusetts, Brooks's sermons left strong—almost mesmerizing—impressions on listeners. In 1874, John Tulloch, principal of St. Mary's College in Aberdeen, visited Boston. After interacting with local elites like Henry Wadsworth Longfellow, Ralph Waldo Emerson, and Oliver Wendell Holmes, he attended a worship service to hear Brooks preach. He immediately wrote to his wife: "I have just heard the most remarkable sermon I have ever heard in my life . . . from Mr. Phillips Brooks. . . . I have never heard preaching like it, and you know how slow I am to praise preachers. So much thought and so much life combined; such a reach of mind, such a depth and insight of soul. I was electrified. I could have got up and shouted."[12]

For Brooks, the late 1870s and 1880s were filled with delivering lectures, publishing sermons, and extensive travel for speaking. Brooks's preaching not only filled Trinity Church on Sundays; throngs of Boston's businessmen and intelligentsia also packed the building to hear his lunchtime sermons on weekdays.[13] In 1889, Brooks was nominated as bishop of Massachusetts and was elected despite opposition from traditional evangelicals. The work of the episcopate, however, drained Brooks, and his health deteriorated. He died, perhaps from diphtheria, on January 23, 1893. When Brooks died, Boston came to a standstill. The day of his funeral, thousands clogged the streets around Trinity Church, and nearly all businesses—including the stock exchange—suspended activities. Memorial services were held as far away as California and England. Within a week of his death, the effort to build a statue in his likeness brought in

10. Phillips Brooks, *Lectures on Preaching* (New York: Dutton, 1877), 5.

11. Warren W. Wiersbe, "Phillips Brooks: A Preacher of Truth and Life," in Phillips Brooks, *The Joy of Preaching* (Grand Rapids: Kregel, 1989), 9.

12. Margaret Oliphant, *A Memoir of the Life of Principal Tulloch* (London: Blackwell & Sons, 1889), 292.

13. Thomas Alexander Hyde, "The Rev. Phillips Brooks," *The Arena* 1 (1890): 716–17.

so much money that other memorial projects had to be started and some dona-tions turned away.[14] Brooks's successor, William Lawrence, spoke no hyperbole in saying that the impact of Brooks "passed over all denominational boundaries. Thousands outside his own church looked to him as their religious interpreter and pastor. . . . No one church, therefore, can claim him as exclusively hers. He belonged to the Christian world of the nineteenth century."[15]

With such colossal and far-reaching influence, Brooks's lectures at Yale were, to many preachers, nothing less than the unveiling of a homiletical hero's secrets of success. When Brooks received the invitation to give the Lyman Beecher Lectureship, he began pondering "the principles" by which he had "only half-consciously been living and working for many years."[16] As the lectures came to pass, the secrets—or principles—became clear and could be summarized in one simple phrase: truth through personality. Expressed by a highly celebrated master of the pulpit, this simple yet profound definition of preaching moved quickly to the forefront of homiletics and was widely discussed throughout the opening decades of the twentieth century and beyond.[17] Even after the passing of more than a century, in the preface to a 1989 reprint of the *Lectures on Preaching*, Warren Wiersbe claimed that "everything useful written on homiletics in Amer-ica . . . is in one way or another a footnote to Phillips Brooks."[18]

PHILLIPS BROOKS IN THEOLOGICAL MILIEU

In many respects, Brooks's life reveals an embodiment of the nineteenth-century swing toward a liberal, romantic form of the Christian faith. His was a period of great ideological fluctuation, during which undercurrent shifts in philos-ophy caused sweeping changes in theology.[19] In the early part of the century, Reformed theologians effectively used major tenets of Scottish Common Sense Realism to combat deism, mostly by pointing out consistencies between moral laws derived from experience and those contained in the Bible.[20] Not long after, however, the champions of the Second Great Awakening—especially Charles G. Finney—challenged many of the premises of Calvinism, and a distinctly

14. Norman Bruce McLeod, "Levels of Relevance in Preaching: A Historical Study of the Communication of the Word to the World by a Witness, with special attention to the principles of interpretation used in the preaching of Phillips Brooks from 1859 to 1892" (ThD diss., Union Theological Seminary, 1960), 133–35.

15. William Lawrence, *Phillips Brooks: A Study* (New York: Houghton Mifflin, 1903), 41–43.

16. Brooks, *Lectures on Preaching*, 1.

17. Ozora Davis, "A Quarter-Century of American Preaching," *The Journal of Religion* 6 (1926): 137.

18. Wiersbe, "Preacher of Truth and Life," 7.

19. William G. McLoughlin, ed., *The American Evangelicals, 1800–1900* (New York: Harper & Row, 1968), 1.

20. Ibid., 2–4.

Arminian concept of God's relationship with humanity supplanted the Calvinistic approach.[21] By midcentury, the doctrinal distinctions between Calvinism and Arminianism faded to the point that denominations were divided simply as "evangelical" and "unevangelical."[22]

Arminian evangelicalism celebrated the freedom of the individual, as an increasingly romantic strain of philosophy entered the American picture, mostly as a rebellion against the naturalistic and empiricist limitations imposed by the Enlightenment. Romanticism reasserted the power of intuition and feeling, arguing that these subjective means provide access to ultimate realities that Enlightenment methodologies can never contemplate.[23] On one hand, romanticism became something of an ally to Christianity during a period in which the Enlightenment threatened to reduce all reality to the natural and observable.[24] By separating faith from the realm of reason, romanticism reopened the religious doorway that the Enlightenment had nearly closed. On the other hand, romanticism presented a danger to Christianity in that its subjective "longing for the infinite" tends to cast a monistic view between the divine and the natural that results in a hyper-elevated view of humanity. For example, David Friedrich Strauss came to consider Christ's incarnation as mythological but symbolic of the deeper truth of the unity between the human and the divine, saying, "Humanity is the union of the two natures—God become man, the infinite manifesting itself in the finite, and the finite spirit remembering its infinitude."[25] Brooks embraced this thought rather fully.

The general effect of this romanticized Christianity on evangelicalism was a move from cognitive doctrines to a religion of the heart, rendering a form of the faith that was "too amorphous to be threatened by Darwin or the higher critics."[26] Indeed, romanticism provided the very avenue through which Christianity came to terms with the new challenges presented by Darwinism and biblical criticism. Viewing the Bible as poetry or literature conveniently mitigated the threat of criticism, and the romantic view of the progress of humanity seemed

---

21. Ibid., 4–5.

22. Robert Baird, *Religion in America* (New York: Harper, 1844), 287–88.

23. Steve Wilkins and Alan G. Padgett, *Faith & Reason in the 19th Century*, vol. 2 of *Christianity & Western Thought: A History of Philosophers, Ideas & Movements* (Downers Grove, IL: InterVarsity Press, 2000), 24–25.

24. Frederick Copleston, *Modern Philosophy: Empiricism, Idealism, and Pragmatism in Britain and America*, vol. 8 of *A History of Philosophy* (New York: Doubleday, 1967), 147–48. See also John Henry Muirhead, *The Platonic Tradition in Anglo-Saxon Philosophy* (London: Macmillan, 1931).

25. David Friedrich Strauss, *Life of Jesus*, trans. George Eliot (New York: Macmillan, 1892), 780.

26. McLoughlin, "Introduction," 23. J. Gresham Machen argues that the sole root of liberalism is naturalism. He appears to overlook, however, the way that romanticism enabled the amalgamation of Christianity and modernism. J. Gresham Machen, *Christianity and Liberalism* (New York: Macmillan, 1923), 2.

sufficient to support some "vague idea" of the evolutionary process.[27] In this new, romanticized evangelicalism, the major emphases focused on the emotions, the "personality of Jesus," and conversion through transfusing "Jesus Christ into your whole life."[28]

Some rejected this romantic turn, but the influence of romanticism— together with the general optimism of the nineteenth century—was pervasive enough that it allowed the term "evangelical" to be applied quite broadly. By the closing years of the century, "evangelicalism" often included wholesale romantics and many who were actually more akin to what Lyman Beecher once called the "Liberal System."[29]

HOMILETICAL METHOD AND THEOLOGY

While "truth through personality" as a general statement fits nicely into most preaching models, Harp notes that Brooks's thoughts on preaching represent a radical departure from the textual, doctrinal preaching passed down from prior evangelical Protestants.[30] Brooks's definition came as the fruit of a homiletical shift largely facilitated by a "softening of the dogmatic structure of evangelical Protestantism to the point that the quickening of the religious sentiment was widely held to be a better aim for the preacher than the inculcation of a fixed body of doctrine."[31] In other words, Gilded Age romanticism paved an easy path away from dogmatic Christianity toward a more subjective, experiential, and doctrinally ambiguous form of the faith. The sum result for Brooks's pulpit was that "the ministry of the word became inextricably bound up in Brooks's system with the personality of the preacher. Such an approach served to augment the evangelical cult of pulpit celebrity as it shifted away from the traditional emphasis on a body of defined propositional truth to be communicated. In this way, a Romanticized Christianity switched the primary focus from an external message . . . toward the subjective character of the messenger appealing to the religious sentiment of its auditors."[32]

By mitigating external authority and maximizing personal experience, Brooks took only one component of Christian preaching and made it central—namely,

27. McLoughlin, "Introduction," 22; Barry Hankins, *American Evangelicals: A Contemporary History of a Mainstream Religious Movement* (New York: Rowman & Littlefield, 2008), 23–26.

28. McLoughlin, "Introduction," 14, 20.

29. Lyman Beecher, *The Faith Once Delivered to the Saints* (Boston: Crocker & Brewster, 1824), 5.

30. Harp, *Brahmin Prophet*, 117.

31. Lawrence Buell, "The Unitarian Movement and the Art of Preaching in 19th Century America," *American Quarterly* 24 (1972): 167, quoted in Harp, *Brahmin Prophet*, 111.

32. Harp, *Brahmin Prophet*, 117.

the personality of the preacher.[33] Brooks, in his lectures, goes as far as to maintain that the preacher's personality, fully engaged, is the key to effective preaching, and that preaching itself is a revelation of the preacher's personality. He claimed,

> The truth must come really through the person, not merely over his lips, not merely into his understanding and out through his pen. It must come through his character, his affections, his whole intellectual and moral being. It must come genuinely through him. I think that, granting equal intelligence and study, here is the great difference which we feel between two preachers of the Word. The Gospel has come over one of them and reaches us tinged and flavored with his superficial characteristics, belittled with his littleness. The Gospel has come through the other, and we receive it impressed and winged with all the earnestness and strength that there is in him. . . .
>
> [A] man's best sermon is the best utterance of his life. It embodies and declares him. If it is really his, it tells more of him than his casual inter-course with his friends, or even the revelations of his domestic life. If it is really God's message through him, it brings him out in a way that no other experience of his life has power to do.[34]

Furthermore, because God's revelation to humanity primarily concerns revelation of himself and his personality more than it is a revelation of objective facts, any discussion of truth must reach the level of personality.[35] God is personal, and the center of his personality is his will, so the truth that comes from him is directed toward the personalities and wills of people, his highest creations.[36]

Temporally speaking, one of the factors that ushered in Brooks's emphasis on personality and helped to weaken Protestant theology in general was the intellectual challenge the Enlightement—having descended from academia to the wider culture—presented to Christianity. Many parishioners, feeling as though they had no reason to remain, had exited the pews.[37] Into this situation, Brooks became a "symbol of certainty in an age of doubt," largely by embodying a broad Christianity with calm confidence, thereby making the Christian religion believable

---

33. Ibid.
34. Brooks, *Lectures on Preaching*, 8, 135.
35. Brastow, *Reresentative Modern Preachers*, 227, 229–30; Lawrence, *Phillips Brooks: A Study*, 34.
36. Brastow, *Representative Modern Preachers*, 229–30.
37. Norman Bruce McLeod, "The Preaching of Phillips Brooks: A Study of Relevance versus Eternal Truth," *Religion in Life* 34, no. 1 (Winter 1964–1965): 51.

again.[38] In one sermon, Brooks stated, "When He sees you and me trembling for fear lest such and such a theory may gather so much evidence that we cannot reject it, but will have to own it to be true, it seems to me that I can almost hear Him say, 'My children, if it be true, do you not want to believe it? I have known it all along. By coming to the truth you come to me, who have held the truth in my bosom—nay, by whom the truth is true. Do not be frightened. I cannot be taken by surprise.'"[39]

He was "a good symbol—handsome, eloquent, romantically solitary, apparently so confident and full of faith, and untroubled by, though not unaware of, winds and currents that were leaving others in doubt and uncertainty,"[40] and thus, "hundreds of people who felt themselves sinking into unbelief turned to him with the desperation of drowning men."[41]

Brooks's personable approach, while in some sense a pragmatic response to his time, was not without a theological foundation. Biographers and theologians alike consistently identify the incarnation of Christ as the very center of his doctrine and homiletic.[42] Allen asserts that the incarnation "became . . . the ground principle of his theology and of his life. . . . Over the mystery of the Incarnation Phillips Brooks was perpetually brooding, till it became to him what the doctrine of the 'Divine Sovereignty' had been to his Puritan ancestors."[43] Indeed, the incarnation was for Brooks what "knit the universe, God, and his creation into living unity,"[44] and hence gave preaching its highest paradigm. "There is no real leadership of people for a preacher," according to him, "except that which comes as the leadership of the Incarnation came."[45]

On the doctrinal level, Brooks's formulation of the incarnation was generally orthodox in that he affirmed in Nicene fashion that Christ was of the same essence as the Father, although he likely struggled with the two-nature distinction of Chalcedon.[46] Yet as the "great Christian humanist" who "bent all his energies to the task of interpreting and ennobling human existence,"[47]

---

38. Ibid., 56; see also Joseph Britton, "The Breadth of Orthodoxy: On Phillips Brooks," in *One Lord, One Faith, One Baptism: Studies in Christian Ecclesiality and Ecumenism in Honor of J. Robert Wright*, eds. Marsha L. Dutton and Patrick Terrell Gray (Grand Rapids: Eerdmans, 2006), 144–62.

39. McLeod, "Preaching of Phillips Brooks," 59.

40. Ibid., 56–57.

41. Lawrence, *Phillips Brooks: A Study*, 85.

42. Brastow, *Representative Modern Preachers*, 232; David Lewis White, "The Preaching of Phillips Brooks" (ThD diss., The Southern Baptist Theological Seminary, 1949), 70, 76; Wiersbe, "Preacher of Truth and Life," 16.

43. Allen, *Life and Letters*, 2:517–19.

44. Lawrence, *Phillips Brooks: A Study*, 13.

45. Brooks, *Lectures on Preaching*, 85.

46. Francis Gerald Ensley, "Phillips Brooks and the Incarnation," *Religion in Life* 20, no. 3 (1951): 352, 357; Allen, *Life and Letters*, 2:841.

47. Brastow, *Representative Modern Preachers,* 195–97. Brastow calls Brooks a "Christian humanist" in the sense that Brooks purported a lofty sense of humanity's worth but nonetheless maintained evangelical

Brooks applied the doctrine in a decidedly anthropocentric manner, using it in service of what was for him an even greater core truth and the very reason for preaching: the value of the human soul.[48] For Brooks, the incarnation displays a real affinity between God and humanity and proves that people are, by nature, children of God.[49] Francis Ensley captures the approach when he claims of Brooks: "[He] regarded Christ's Incarnation as a specification of a universal principle that holds in all life. What he found in Jesus Christ he generalized. If the Incarnation portrays the actual humanity of God . . . it equally proclaims the potential divinity of man. If Jesus Christ is a revelation of what God is, he is also a sign of what man may become. . . . The Incarnation is at heart a doctrine about human potentiality, a confirmation of human hopes."[50]

In Brooks's own words, "Christ was what man had felt in his soul that he might be. Christ did what man's heart had always told him that it was in his humanity to do."[51] Brooks's anthropological application of the incarnation wielded massive ramifications with respect to his soteriological views. While he did not explicitly deny the substitutionary atonement of Christ, and at times he sounded quite evangelical in his views of justification,[52] his lectures remain ambivalent on the subject.[53] On balance, he seemed to locate redemption in humanity's innate ability to follow the pattern revealed in the incarnation. Christ's incarnation was for Brooks the uniting of wills, and salvation now occurs to the extent that incarnation—the uniting of wills—recurs.[54] In this way, salvation becomes less about the imputation of righteousness and more about the actualization of righteousness already present. In a sermon titled "The Nearness of God," Brooks intimately ties the incarnation with salvation, saying,

> Christ was not a God coming out of absence. He was the ever-present God, revealing how near He always was. And so of the new life of Christ in man. It is not something strange and foreign, brought from far away. It is the deepest possibility of man, revealed and made actual. When you stand at last complete in Christ, it is not some rare adornments which He has lent

---

terminology in his anthropology. Wiersbe asserts, "In these beliefs, Brooks was certainly influenced by Horace Bushnell's *Christian Nurture*." Wiersbe, "Preacher of Truth and Life," 20.

48. Brooks, *Lectures on Preaching*, 255–56.

49. As opposed to the natural man being at enmity with God. Lawrence, *Phillips Brooks: A Study*, 38–39; Allen, *Life and Letters*, 2:521.

50. Ensley, "Phillips Brooks and the Incarnation," 352–53.

51. Phillips Brooks, *Visions and Tasks: And Other Sermons* (New York: Dutton, 1910), 282.

52. White, "Preaching of Phillips Brooks," 88–90. See also Phillips Brooks, *The Purpose and Use of Comfort: And Other Sermons* (New York: Dutton, 1910), 37–56.

53. Brooks, *Lectures on Preaching*, 32–33.

54. Brooks, *Visions and Tasks*, 291.

from His Divinity to clothe your humanity with. Those graces are the signs of your humanity. They are the flower of your human life, drawn out into luxuriance by the sunlight of the divine Love. You take them as your own, and wear them as the angels wear their wings.[55]

Although Lewis Brastow rightly notes the general vagueness of Brooks's theological expression, he aptly captures Brooks's basic soteriological thought in asserting,

> The atonement . . . must be conceived from the point of view of the incarnation. It is not, therefore, a transaction between a Christ and a God who stand outside of humanity, but who are revealed in and are identified with humanity, and the efficaciousness of the atonement is not in the sufferings of Christ, but in the obedience of His holy will. The reconciliation of God and man is not a forensic transaction dealing with ideal relations, but an actual participation of man in the righteousness of God. . . .
>
> The New Testament representation that man becomes a child of God by identification with Christ is based upon the already existing fact that he is such by nature. If he were not God's child by nature, he could never become His child by grace. Christianity does not create, but only declares, the fact, and furnishes the requisite provision for its realization. In coming to Christ, we come to ourselves, as in coming to us, Christ "came to his own." Sin on its negative side is a failure to realize one's sonship with God; on its positive side, it is refusal to accept and actualize the fact. . . . Regeneration, conversion, sanctification, are the beginning and the completion of the process by which one comes to the recognition of one's self as a child of God, and lives agreeably to the fact.[56]

For Brooks, humanity is neither irrevocably good nor hopelessly depraved. Rather, humanity is the magnificent, infinitely valuable crown jewel of God's creation, endowed with the ability to overcome the plague of sin by following the perfect example set forth in the incarnation. Consequently, the ultimate test of religion is whether or not it can "make men better men."[57] Truth, flowing from the fount of the revelation of God's personality in the incarnation and centered in his will, must be infused into the personalities of people to build character. Preaching, as a means to this end, serves to "translate speculative truth into

55. Phillips Brooks, *Seeking Life: And Other Sermons* (New York: Dutton, 1904), 56.
56. Brastow, *Representative Modern Preachers*, 232–33.
57. Phillips Brooks, *Essays and Addresses: Religious, Literary, and Social* (New York: Dutton, 1895), 545.

personal character and to relate it clearly and practically to daily life,"[58] and so must be defined fundamentally as "truth through personality."

CONTRIBUTIONS TO PREACHING

Ralph G. Turnbull contends that Phillips Brooks "gave the church the imperishable idea about preaching"[59] when he defined preaching as "truth through personality." Indeed, during the decades since Brooks coined the phrase, it has been utilized so widely that one can hardly read a homiletics text without encountering it. Undoubtedly, Christian preaching—in essence—cannot escape being "truth through personality." The axiomatic nature of the phrase, however, has led many evangelicals to endorse Phillips Brooks and cite his slogan uninhibitedly and without reflection.

Out of Brooks's romantic and incarnational theology emerged a homiletic that had as its goal the perfection of those who are already "full of the suggestion of God"—a decidedly humanistic aim.[60] Although Brooks used evangelical terminology and engaged his preaching with evangelistic fervor, he nevertheless formulated "truth through personality" in a manner inconsistent with evangelical convictions. His idea that preaching is the "continuation, out to the minutest ramifications" of Christ's incarnation presents a relationship between the preacher and God's Word that—while permissible within his romantic anthropology—borders on heresy. There is only one incarnation, and preachers are witnesses to it, not replications of it.

Sermon Excerpt

The Candle of the Lord (Proverbs 20:27)[61]

An unlighted candle is standing in the darkness and someone comes to light it. A blazing bit of paper holds the fire at first, but it is vague and fitful. It flares and wavers and at any moment may go out. But the vague, uncertain, flaring blaze touches the candle, and the candle catches fire and at once you have a steady flame. The candle is glorified

---

58. Raymond W. Albright, *Focus on Infinity: A Life of Phillips Brooks* (New York: Macmillan, 1961), 162.

59. Ralph G. Turnbull, *A History of Preaching, Volume 3: From the Close of the Nineteenth Century to the Middle of the Twentieth Century, and American Preaching during the Seventeenth, Eighteenth, and Nineteenth Centuries* (Grand Rapids: Baker, 1974), 111.

60. Brooks, *Lectures on Preaching*, 259.

61. Phillips Brooks, *The Candle of the Lord and Other Sermons* (New York: Dutton, 1881), 1–6.

by the fire and the fire is manifested by the candle. The two bear witness that they were made one another by the way in which they fulfill each other's life. . . .

Can we not see, with such a picture clear before us, what must be meant when it is said that one being is the candle of another being? There is in community a man of large, rich character, whose influence runs everywhere. You cannot talk with any man in all the city but you get, shown in that man's own way, the thought, the feeling of that central man who teaches all the community to think, to feel. . . .

I think that we are now ready to turn to Solomon and read his words again and understand them. "The spirit of man is the candle of the Lord," he says. God is the fire of this world, its vital principle, a warm pervading presence everywhere. . . . And now of this fire the spirit of man is the candle. What does that mean? If, because man is of a nature which corresponds to the nature of God, and just so far as man is obedient to God, the life of God, which is spread throughout the universe, gathers itself into utterance; and men . . . see what God is, in gazing at the man whom He has kindled,—then is not the figure plain? . . . The fire of the Lord has found the candle of the Lord, and burns clear and steady, guiding and cheering instead of bewildering and frightening us, just so soon as a man who is obedient to God has begun to catch and manifest His nature.

I hope that we shall find that this truth comes very close to our personal, separate lives. . . . Solomon says that the true separateness and superiority of and centralness of man is in that likeness of nature to God, and that capacity of spiritual obedience to Him, in virtue of which man may be the declaration and manifestation of God to all the world. So long as that truth stands, the centralness of man is sure. "The spirit of man is the candle of the Lord." ♦

BIBLIOGRAPHY

Albright, Raymond W. *Focus on Infinity: A Life of Phillips Brooks*. New York: Macmillan, 1961.
Allen, Alexander V. G. *Life and Letters of Phillips Brooks*. 3 vols. New York: Dutton, 1901.
Baird, Robert. *Religion in America*. New York: Harper, 1844.
Beecher, Lyman. *The Faith Once Delivered to the Saints*. Boston: Crocker & Brewster, 1824.
Brastow, Lewis O. *Representative Modern Preachers*. New York: Hodder & Stoughton, 1904.
Britton, Joseph. "The Breadth of Orthodoxy: On Phillips Brooks." Pages 144–62 in *One Lord, One Faith, One Baptism: Studies in Christian Ecclesiality and Ecumenism in Honor of J. Robert Wright*, Marsha L. Dutton and Patrick Terrell Gray. Grand Rapids: Eerdmans, 2006.
Brooks, Phillips. *Essays and Addresses: Religious, Literary, and Social*. New York: Dutton, 1895.

_____. *Lectures on Preaching*. New York: Dutton, 1907.

_____. *The Purpose and Use of Comfort: And Other Sermons*. New York: Dutton, 1910.

_____. *Seeking Life: And Other Sermons*. New York: Dutton, 1904.

_____. *Visions and Tasks: And Other Sermons*. New York: Dutton, 1910.

Buell, Lawrence. "The Unitarian Movement and the Art of Preaching in 19th Century America." *American Quarterly* 24 (1972): 166–90.

Copleston, Frederick. *Modern Philosophy: Empiricism, Idealism, and Pragmatism in Britain and America*. Vol 8 of *A History of Philosophy*. New York: Doubleday, 1967.

Davis, Ozora. "A Quarter-Century of American Preaching." *The Journal of Religion* 6 (1926): 135–53.

Ensley, Francis Gerald. "Phillips Brooks and the Incarnation." *Religion in Life* 20, no. 3 (1951): 350–61.

Hankins, Barry. *American Evangelicals: A Contemporary History of a Mainstream Religious Movement*. New York: Rowman & Littlefield, 2008.

Harp, Gillis J. *Brahmin Prophet: Phillips Brooks and the Path of Liberal Protestantism*. New York: Rowman & Littlefield, 2003.

Hyde, Thomas Alexander. "The Rev. Phillips Brooks." *The Arena* 1 (1890): 716–17.

Lawrence, William. *Phillips Brooks*. Boston: Houghton Mifflin, 1903.

_____. *Phillips Brooks: A Study*. New York: Houghton Mifflin, 1903.

Machen, J. Gresham. *Christianity & Liberalism*. New York: Macmillan, 1923.

McLeod, Norman Bruce. "Levels of Relevance in Preaching: A Historical Study of the Communication of the Word to the World by a Witness, with special attention to the principles of interpretation used in the preaching of Phillips Brooks from 1859 to 1892." ThD diss., Union Theological Seminary, 1960.

_____. "The Preaching of Phillips Brooks: A Study of Relevance versus Eternal Truth." *Religion in Life* 34, no. 1 (Winter 1964–1965): 50–67.

McLoughlin, William G. "Introduction." In *The American Evangelicals, 1800–1900*, 1–27. New York: Harper & Row, 1968.

Muirhead, John Henry. *The Platonic Tradition in Anglo-Saxon Philosophy*. London: Macmillan, 1931.

Oliphant, Margaret. *A Memoir of the Life of Principal Tulloch*. London: Blackwell & Sons, 1889.

Strauss, David Friedrich. *Life of Jesus*. Trans. by George Elliot. New York: Macmillan, 1892.

Turnbull, Ralph G. *A History of Preaching, Volume 3: From the Close of the Nineteenth Century to the Middle of the Twentieth Century, and American Preaching during the Seventeenth, Eighteenth, and Nineteenth Centuries*. Grand Rapids: Baker, 1974.

White, David Lewis. "The Preaching of Phillips Brooks." ThD diss., The Southern Baptist Theological Seminary, 1949.

Wiersbe, Warren W. "Phillips Brooks: A Preacher of Truth and Life." Pages 9–21 in Phillips Brooks, *The Joy of Preaching*. Grand Rapids: Kregel, 1989.

Wilkins, Steve, and Alan G. Padgett, *Faith & Reason in the 19th Century*. Vol. 2 of *Christianity & Western Thought: A History of Philosophers, Ideas & Movements*. Downers Grove, IL: InterVarsity Press, 2000.

Woolverton, John F. *The Education of Phillips Brooks*. Chicago: University of Illinois Press, 1995.

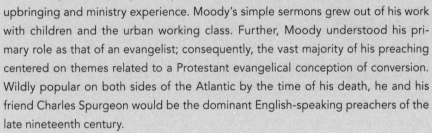

D. L. Moody
First International Evangelist

GREGG L. QUIGGLE

The preaching of Dwight Lyman Moody (1837–1899) reflects his life. Poorly educated and raised in poverty by a widowed mother, Moody was a layperson whose life experiences played a defining role in his preaching. His earnest, straightforward style of speech reflected his upbringing and ministry experience. Moody's simple sermons grew out of his work with children and the urban working class. Further, Moody understood his primary role as that of an evangelist; consequently, the vast majority of his preaching centered on themes related to a Protestant evangelical conception of conversion. Wildly popular on both sides of the Atlantic by the time of his death, he and his friend Charles Spurgeon would be the dominant English-speaking preachers of the late nineteenth century.

HISTORICAL BACKGROUND

Moody was born during a period of Protestant hegemony. However, as the century progressed, the movement was faced with four distinct threats that ultimately split the movement and weakened its domination: (1) urbanization, (2) resultant Roman Catholic immigration, (3) slavery and the Civil War, and (4) the emergence of new theologies, some from within America and others imported from Europe and Great Britain.[1] This evolving Protestantism and eventual evangelicalism would shape Dwight Moody's life and ministry.[2]

---

1. Mark Noll, *The Work We Have to Do: A History of Protestants in America,* (New York: Oxford University Press, 2000), 76–96. Certainly, other factors go into the destruction of evangelical Protestant hegemony and its ultimate splintering. However, these are the major causes. For a more nuanced and detailed study, see Martin E. Marty, *Righteous Empire: The Protestant Experience in America* (New York: Dial, 1970). See especially chapters 10–20.

2. For this article I will be using David Bebbington's definition of evangelicalism, which emphasizes four key elements in evangelicalism: conversionism, activism, biblicism, and crucicentrism. David Bebbington, *Evangelicalism in Modern Britain: A History from the 1730s to the 1980s* (London: Unwin Hyman, 1989), 1–17.

The son of Edwin Moody and Betsy Holton, Dwight was the sixth of nine children, seven boys and two girls. He was born on his mother's birthday, February 5, 1837, in the northern Massachusetts town of Northfield, on the Connecticut River close to the New Hampshire and Vermont borders.[3] Moody's father was hardworking, but by some accounts a drinker and a bit of a profligate. In 1841, Edwin died suddenly, leaving Betsy eight months pregnant with twins and seven other children under the age of thirteen. In addition, it became quickly apparent that Edwin had accrued significant debt. Faced with severe financial straits, Betsy was often forced to send the boys away during the winter months to live with other families. In Dwight's case, this was his lot for seven years after his father's death. In this situation, schooling became a luxury.[4] At best, Dwight received four years of education, attending the local school as he was able between the ages of six and ten.[5]

Edwin's death also resulted in the family's introduction to the Protestant church, in this case the local Unitarian church. Oliver Everett, the young pastor of the local Unitarian church, quickly befriended the family in this time of distress, and in response, Mrs. Moody and the family joined the church. The church's Unitarianism seems a bit dubious. In William Moody's biography, he asserts that the whole family was baptized "in the name of the Father and of the Son and of the Holy Ghost."[6] Young pastor Everett's theological convictions seem equally murky. One source describes him as "liberal in doctrine and imbued with the teaching of Christ."[7] Later in life, Moody is purported to have called him "*the* true shepherd of God."[8]

What is quite clear is that Everett's influence on Moody was not a result of his preaching. As a boy, Moody seems to have endured religion, rather than embracing it. Moody recalled that he detested Sundays. He claimed sermons bored him, and he actively tried to avoid going to church.

---

3. James Findlay, *Dwight L. Moody: American Evangelist, 1837–1899* (Chicago: University of Chicago Press, 1969), 25–42; and Lyle Dorsett, *A Passion for Souls: The Life of D. L. Moody* (Chicago: Moody, 1997), 28–30.

4. Charles F. Goss, *Echoes from the Pulpit and Platform* (Hartford: Worthington, 1900), 490–495; and Dorsett, *A Passion for Souls*, 34.

5. There is one piece of evidence that Moody did some additional schooling later in life. Dwight Moody is listed as a student in the 1853 catalog of the "Northfield Institute." In 1853, Moody would have been sixteen years old. The school's catalog indicates a curriculum consisting of English, Higher English, Latin, Greek, French, Pencil Drawing, Painting, and Piano. See *Third Annual Catalogue of the Instructors and Teachers of Northfield Institute, Northfield, Mass., for the Year Ending November 1853*. A copy is available at the Northfield Historical Society, Northfield, MA. This unedited excerpt from a letter written when he was twenty reflects the state of his education: "I think we have things sometimes come a bo(?) us to try ower faith and God likes us to cling on as the Samest sais in one place God likes to chastise them whome he loves so let us pray for each other. I have brout you befor God in my prayers & hope you have done the same." D. L. Moody, letter to brother, March 17, 1857, Moody Bible Institute Archives, Chicago, IL.

6. Quoted in Dorsett, *A Passion for Souls*, 30.

7. Powell manuscript in Northfield archives, nd., 96.

8. Ibid.

By the age of seventeen, bored and with limited employment opportunities in Northfield, Moody struck out for Boston. In Boston he secured employment with his uncle, Samuel Holton, in Holton's shoe store.[9] But the job came with a condition. Specifically, Uncle Samuel insisted that Moody attend the Mount Vernon Congregational Church in Boston. While attending Sunday school at Mount Vernon, Moody came to the attention of a middle-aged Sunday school teacher named Edwin Kimball. Under Kimball's patient tutelage, Moody embraced evangelical Christianity in 1855.[10]

Consequently, the Mount Vernon Congregational Church in Boston would be the context for Moody's first extended exposure to evangelicalism. The pastor was the Reverend Edward N. Kirk. Before coming to Mount Vernon, Kirk had earned a reputation in New England as a revivalist and pastor, having worked with Charles Finney in upstate New York.[11] Kirk's brand of revivalism was distinctive. He was sophisticated, and his preaching was fluent and articulate. Kirk eschewed crude emotionalism and manipulation, preferring to woo his audiences.[12] Kirk's preaching apparently impressed the young Moody, as he would later claim that Kirk was "one of the most eloquent men I ever heard."[13]

During these years, Moody remained a restless but driven and ambitious young man. He quickly tired of Boston and in 1856 headed west to the new booming metropolis on the Midwestern plains—Chicago. While Boston was the scene of Moody's first exposure to evangelicalism, Chicago was where his new religious sentiments matured. It is where Moody was made into a full-fledged evangelical. Chicago was significant in three ways relative to Moody's development. First, Moody was nurtured in the evangelical community in Chicago. While Moody had an initial conversion experience in Boston, it was developed and solidified in Chicago. It was in Chicago that Moody became fully immersed in the teachings, practices, and personalities of the evangelical faith. Second, Chicago exposed the problems of urbanization for Moody. In Chicago, Moody became personally and intensely involved with the poor, learning of their plight firsthand. Finally, it was in Chicago that Moody began to develop his preaching.[14]

---

9. Dorsett, *A Passion for Souls*, 43–44.

10. Ibid., 43–44, 46–47; and William R. Moody, *The Life of Dwight L. Moody* (Chicago: Revell, 1900), 39–41.

11. Edward N. Kirk, *Lectures on Revivals* (Boston: Congregational Publishing Society, 1875).

12. Richard Carwardine, *Transatlantic Revivalism: Popular Evangelicalism in Britain and America, 1790–1865* (Westport, CT: Greenwood, 1978), 22.

13. J. C. Pollock, *Moody: A Biographical Portrait of the Pacesetter in Modern Mass Evangelism* (New York: Macmillan, 1963), 12.

14. Gregg L. Quiggle, "An Analysis of Dwight Moody's Urban Social Vision" (PhD diss., 2009, The Open University), 74–75.

Troubled by the plight of urban children, Moody began an independent Sunday school in one of the worst areas of the city.[15] The school flourished and garnered quite a reputation, even beyond Chicago.[16] The school played an important part in Moody's development as a preacher and the honing of his public speaking skills. By teaching children, he learned the power of simple messages.

In 1859, one of the volunteers at the Sunday school, Emma Revell, caught Moody's eye. Emma was a refined, well-educated young woman who had immigrated to America from London with her family. She was younger than Dwight, but maintained a high degree of reserve and self-control. He, by comparison, was impulsive and bombastic, enjoying the spotlight. They were married on August 28, 1862.[17] From this point on, Emma would play an important role in Moody's ministry. She was particularly helpful in shaping his writing and public speaking.

As Moody's work with the Sunday school began to expand, he also became involved with the Chicago YMCA. By 1866, he had risen through the ranks to become its president. Under his leadership, the YMCA greatly expanded its work among Chicago's urban poor.[18] The YMCA also served as his entrance into the American Civil War. Working with the United States Christian Commission, a branch of the YMCA, Moody went to the front lines nine different times to conduct services among Union troops. Additionally, he ministered to Southern prisoners at Camp Douglas, a prisoner of war camp just south of Chicago.[19] By the end of the Civil War, Moody had an established reputation and was increasingly in demand as a speaker.

It is in this postwar period that Moody added what would become one of the signatures of his preaching campaigns—music. Despite being tone deaf, Moody had observed the power of music. Impressed with the musical talent of a US Treasury employee named Ira Sankey, Moody began aggressively recruiting the mutton-chopped singer. Finally, in 1871, Moody convinced Sankey to join him in his work in Chicago.[20]

After working together in Chicago, Moody and Sankey determined to start a tour of the United Kingdom in 1873. The duo was well received and their popularity increased.[21] They remained in the United Kingdom until 1875, preaching throughout England, Scotland, and Ireland. Their tour climaxed with

---

15. Findlay, *American Evangelist*, 110. Moody understood this and struggled to overcome the gulf between the evangelical church and the working class.

16. Dorsett, *A Passion for Souls*, 64–74.

17. Moody, *Life of Moody*, 56; and Dorsett, *A Passion for Souls*, 68–69.

18. Dorsett, *A Passion for Souls*, 77–86.

19. Moody, *Life of Moody*, 82.

20. Dorsett, *A Passion for Souls*, 163–64, 174–75.

21. Moody, *Life of Moody*, 154–60.

a four-month stay in London where approximately 2.5 million people attended the meetings.[22]

By the time they returned to the United States, the pair had attained celebrity status. Consequently, upon their return, invitations for citywide crusades poured in from all over America. Moody chose to start in Brooklyn on October 31, 1875. From Brooklyn, the meetings moved to Philadelphia, New York, and Boston.[23] Finally, Moody headed west to his second home, Chicago. The Chicago crusade started October 1, 1876, in a ten-thousand-seat tabernacle. It would run for sixteen weeks, closing on January 16, 1877.[24]

In many ways, these years were the pinnacle of Moody's work as a traveling evangelistic preacher. Most scholars agree that he would never again enjoy this degree of success.[25] Nevertheless, Moody continued working as a revivalist. Besides touring cities in the United States, he would make a second tour of the United Kingdom in the early 1880s, and lead a campaign focused on the Chicago World's Fair of 1893.[26] However, he branched out in other areas, especially in education. Moody's educational activity left him a lasting institutional legacy. From the late 1870s into the 1880s, he founded five schools, three in Northfield, one in Chicago, and one in Glasgow, Scotland.[27] He continued preaching at revivals and working to establish his schools until his death in 1899.

By the time of his death, Moody had honed his craft as an evangelistic preacher. His preaching reflected his life. The sermons struck a compassionate note, reflecting the young Oliver Everett. They reflected the simplicity and plain-spokenness of his upbringing in Northfield and his work with children. There was an earnestness and urgency born from dealing with the dying soldiers of the Civil War. Echoing what he first observed under Revered Kirk in Boston, they eschewed excessive emotion. Reflecting his own sentiments, the sermons took on a businesslike tone while reflecting the sentimentalism of the Victorian ideals of the day. The sermons show his deep affinity for the urban masses, reflecting his own struggle as a poor, fatherless boy. Finally, all of these various elements are

---

22. Dorsett, *A Passion for Souls*, 206–207; and Findlay, *American Evangelist*, 171. The 2.5 million figure is a total number of attendees, which may include people who attended more than once.

23. Findlay, *American Evangelist*, 195–205.

24. Dorsett, *A Passion for Souls*, 247–48.

25. Ibid., 267. Dorsett challenges this assertion but admits he changed his focus from solely being a revivalist.

26. Stanley N. Gundry, *Love Them In: The Life and Theology of Dwight Moody* (Grand Rapids: Baker, 1976), 52.

27. In Massachusetts the three schools were a Bible school, a school for girls, and a school for boys. The Bible school is gone but the girls' and boys' schools remained and later merged into a single school, the Northfield Mount Hermon School. Moody Bible Institute in Chicago is still functioning and the Glasgow school was renamed Scottish School of Christian Mission in 2015.

shaped by the basic theological commitments of the evangelical Protestantism of the era.

THEOLOGY OF PREACHING

Belief in the Bible was at the bedrock of Moody's preaching. As he put it, "I have one rule about books. I do not read any book, unless it will help me understand the Book."[28] His insistence that a Bible be placed in the cornerstone of his school in Northfield was a symbol of its importance. Moody read, studied, quoted, and preached the Bible. His son wrote after his death, "He knew his Bible as very few have done, and was always wearing out Bibles, covering the margins with references and notes."[29] One account of his preaching concluded, "It was said that Moody's preaching abounded with nothing so much as with the Scripture."[30] One cannot study the life of Moody and not gain an immediate sense of the central role Scripture played in his life.

Moody believed the Bible was reliable and should be preached as such. In Boston he said, "Men may go on scoffing and making light of the Bible, but you will find it out to be true by and by."[31] Writing to his son William in 1888, Moody expressed his frustration with those who called into question the reliability of the text. "I hope you will have the courage to stand up against any man who does not preach all the truth. I have little sympathy with any man who would attempt to undermine any man in the Bible."[32]

Not only was Moody committed to the reliability of the Bible, he also saw it as authoritative. For Moody, the Bible rebutted all skeptics. When asked about the authority of the Bible, he remarked, "I am not here to defend the Bible; it will take care of itself."[33] Preaching in Boston, Moody remarked, "The Bible is a match for all infidels; that is the reason so many Christians are overcome by infidels because they do not know their Bibles well enough."[34] Indeed, it was the final authority for Moody on all issues. As *The Free Church Monthly Record* put it, "An appeal to Scripture is with them [Moody and Sankey] the end to all controversy."[35]

---

28. Dwight Moody, *Glad Tidings: Comprising Sermons and Prayer Meeting Talks Delivered at the New York Hippodrome* (New York: Treat, 1876), 452.

29. Moody, *Life of Moody*, 163.

30. The Missionary Record of the United Presbyterian of February 1874, 76.

31. D. L. Moody, *To All People: Comprising Sermons, Bible Readings, Temperance Addresses, and Prayer-Meeting Talks, delivered in the Boston Tabernacle by Dwight Moody* (New York: Treat, 1877), 298.

32. D. L. Moody, Letter to William, October 20, 1888, Special Collections, Yale Divinity School Library, D. L. Moody Papers.

33. J. W. Hanson, *The Life and Works of the World's Greatest Evangelist Dwight L. Moody* (Chicago: Conkey, 1900), 165.

34. The Free Church Monthly Record of February 1874, 27. This is the Free Church in Scotland.

35. Ibid.

THEOLOGY IN HIS PREACHING

Moody was not a deeply reflective person. He was energetic, more of a doer than a thinker. His writings consist primarily of collections of his sermons and anecdotes written down by others. Moody eschewed preaching doctrinally complex sermons. He learned his craft by teaching Sunday school and preaching to soldiers. Further, Moody was primarily an evangelist. As his son William pointed out, Moody "preferred to devote his energies to evangelistic work, yielding to the denominational churches the function of indoctrinating the Christian faith."[36]

Therefore, some have opined that Moody was either indifferent to theology, did not like it, or possessed little of it.[37] However, this is simply not true. Moody did not believe that sincere faith alone was sufficient. He believed that faith must also have the correct object. This is where doctrine came into play. In fact, as early as the 1870s, Moody had preached sermons that laid out his concept of faith, which followed a traditional approach: knowledge, intellectual assent, and trust—what he referred to as "laying hold."[38]

What theology Moody did possess was more caught than taught. He loved listening to others preach and took voracious notes. He constantly sought opportunities to talk with Bible teachers and scholars, peppering them with questions. He maintained a close friendship with Spurgeon and always looked carefully at Spurgeon's outlines as he prepared his own sermons.[39]

In surveying Moody's sermons, two basic theological elements in his preaching emerge. First, Moody evidenced a profound understanding of the love of God. This was a core belief that became a kind of defining doctrine for Moody. Second, he embraced the standard evangelical conception of salvation. Specifically, Moody's basic theological construct was the "Three Rs": ruined by sin, redeemed by Christ, and regenerated by the Holy Ghost. This underscored his concept of conversion and put him in line with past evangelical revivalists.

The Love of God

The love of God was a central theme of Moody's evangelistic preaching.[40] It was arguably the central theme of his life. He believed the core attribute of

---

36. Moody, *Life of Moody*, 107.

37. Gundry, *Love Them In*. Gundry summarizes the various theories on Moody's attitude toward theology on pages 62–70.

38. Dwight Moody, *Wondrous Love* (London: Hawkins, 1875), 261–64; Moody, *Glad Tidings*, 270–73.

39. David Bebbington called Moody "one of Spurgeon's most ardent admirers in the United States." This assessment is confirmed in an 1881 letter from Moody to Spurgeon. He wrote, "I have for years thought more of you than any other man preaching on this earth." From the time of his conversion, Moody claimed to have heard of Spurgeon. He also claimed, "Everything I could get hold of in print that he ever said, I read." David Bebbington, *The Dominance of Evangelicalism: The Age of Spurgeon and Moody* (Downers Grove, IL: InterVarsity Press, 2005), 45.

40. Gundry's *Love Them In* is the definitive work on Moody's theology. As the title indicates, Gundry

the Godhead is love and that it should dominate the church. As he put it, "The sun is light, and can't help shining; God is Love, and he can't help loving."[41] Expanding on this Moody explained elsewhere, "I found a verse in I Peter, iv. 8, today. I never saw it before: 'Above all things put on love.'"[42] He went on to urge the listeners, "Think much of that one expression. Put it at the head of the list. Faith is good, but this is above it. Truth is good: but what are we if we do not have love? May the dear church get such a flood of love from on high that it will fill all our hearts."[43] Again, in a sermon published under the title "Charity," Moody argued that many ministers, despite having great preaching skills, lacked converts in their ministry because they did not have love as their motive. As he put it, "A man though he is deep in learning and theology, if he has no love in his heart, he will do no good."[44] For Dwight Moody, the God of the Bible was preeminently love, and preachers of the Bible should reflect that love in their hearts and sermons.

A Theology of Conversion

Dwight Moody was widely admired by the ecclesiastical community. His preaching was embraced by most varieties of Protestants, and it even found a following among some Roman Catholics. Certainly his emphasis on love helps explain this broad audience, but another factor was the simplicity of his message. Moody's faith was formed and nurtured in the womb of evangelicalism. Its basic teachings formed the backbone of his doctrine. These core elements of evangelicalism as Moody articulated them were the aforementioned "Three Rs."[45] As an early observer put it, these "Three Rs" not only framed his preaching but, "according to this triad of topics, he lays out all his campaigns."[46]

The first "R" was "ruined by sin." Moody defined human beings as "ruined by sin," meaning that they were both sinful and sinners, a condition traceable to Adam. As he put it in 1870, "You may say that the earth is a vast hospital. Every

sees love as the central theme in Moody's preaching. See also Darrel B. Robertson, "The Chicago Revival, 1876: A Case Study in the Social Function of a Nineteenth-Century Revival" (PhD diss., The University of Iowa, 1982), 221.

41. W. H. Daniels, *Moody: His Words, Work, and Workers* (New York: Nelson & Phillips, 1877), 262.

42. Moody, *Life of Moody*, 151.

43. Ibid.

44. Dwight Moody, *"The Gospel Awakening": Comprising the Sermons and Addresses, Prayer Meeting Talks and Bible Readings of the Great Revival Meetings Conducted by Moody and Sankey* (Chicago: Revell, 1883), 379–80.

45. In his book *Love Them In*, Gundry traces these three themes throughout most of Moody's sermons. See also George M. Marsden's book, *Fundamentalism and American Culture*, 2nd ed. (New York: Oxford University Press, 2006), 35. In addition, one of Moody's personal Bibles at the archives in Northfield Schools contains the following comment on the inner leaf: "This book teaches three things, Ruin, Redemption, Regeneration."

46. Quoted in Daniels, *Moody*, 256.

man and woman coming into it needs a physician. If you search you will find every one wounded. By nature we are sinners."[47] A little over a decade later, he restated his position, "Men are all bad by nature; the old Adam stock is bad, and we cannot bring forth good fruit until we are grafted into the one True Vine."[48] In another of his published sermons, he put it this way, "I don't care where you put man, everywhere he has tried he is a failure. He was put in Eden on trial; and some men say they wish they had Adam's chance. If you had you would go down as quickly as he did."[49] Clearly, for Moody sin is a matter of human nature, not the environment.

He believed that because we are sinners by nature, we all sin. As he put it in his sermon called "Repentance": "Is there a man here who can say honestly, 'I have not got a sin that I need ask forgiveness for, I haven't one thing to repent of'?" A man who has broken one commandment of God is as guilty as he who has broken ten. If a man don't feel this, and come to Him repentant and turn his face from sin toward God there is not a ray of hope. Nowhere can you find one ray from Genesis to Revelation. Don't go out of this Tabernacle saying, 'I have nothing to repent.'"[50]

Given the fallen state of humanity, Moody argued for the necessity of the second "R," redemption by Christ. His concept of redemption was very basic: "[B]eing bought back, we sold ourselves for naught, and Christ redeemed us and bought us back."[51] Humanity's only escape is through the work of Christ. As Moody explained it, "You ask me what my hope is; it is, that Christ died for my sins, in my stead, in my place, and therefore I can enter into life eternal."[52] Elsewhere in the same sermon, the point was reiterated: "If you ask me what you must do to share this blessing, I answer, go and deal personally with Christ about it. Take the sinner's place at the foot of the cross. Strip yourself of all your righteousness and put on Christ's."[53] Moody argued, "If the Word of God don't teach that, it don't teach anything."[54]

Moody proclaimed the power of the blood of Jesus to restore the soul, "So the soul is restored to its full beauty of color when it is washed with the blood of Jesus Christ."[55] He also believed it covered sins. He told the story of a boy in

---

47. Dwight Moody, *New Sermons, Addresses and Prayers by Dwight Lyman Moody* (New York: Goodspeed, 1877), 128.

48. D. L. Moody, *Twelve Select Sermons* (Chicago: Revell, 1881), 21.

49. Ibid., 21.

50. D. L. Moody, *Moody's Sermons, Addresses and Prayers* (St. Louis: Thompson, 1877), 259.

51. D. L. Moody, *Twelve Select Sermons*, 120.

52. Ibid., 29.

53. Ibid., 28.

54. Quoted in Gundry, *Love Them In*, 102.

55. Dwight Moody, *Heaven: Where It Is, Its Inhabitants, and How to Get There* (Chicago: Revell, 1884), 94.

Ireland who was asked by his teacher if there was "anything God cannot do; and the little fellow said, 'Yes, He cannot see my sins through the blood of Christ.' The blood covers them."[56] Moody reinforced the point in one of his illustrations: "Look at that Roman soldier as he pushed his spear into the very heart of the God-man. What a hellish deed! But what was the next thing that took place? Blood covered the spear! Oh! Thank God, the blood covers sin."[57] In fact, for Moody, teaching on the saving role of the blood of Christ was nonnegotiable. Preaching in London in 1875, he made his point clearly and forcefully: "If you are in a church, either Dissenting or Established, and the minister doesn't preach the blood, get out of it as Lot out of Sodom."[58]

Moody's final "R" was regeneration by the Holy Ghost. Moody believed while the cross is something done *for* humanity, regeneration by the Holy Spirit is something done *to* humanity. The Holy Spirit causes a necessary change in human nature. Moody considered this synonymous with conversion—the new birth or being born again. He claimed, "We must be born of the Spirit, hearts must be regenerated—born again." He believed that every conversion was a supernatural work done by God.[59]

Moody saw this as a crucial doctrine. As he put it, "This doctrine of the New Birth is therefore the foundation of all our hopes for the world to come. It is really the A B C of the Christian religion. . . . If a man is unsound on this doctrine he will be unsound on almost every other fundamental doctrine in the Bible."[60]

Moody was also quite clear about what regeneration is not. He asserted that it is not attending church, making a resolution to change one's ways, praying, partaking of the Eucharist, or being baptized.[61] For Moody, "THERE MUST BE A NEW CREATION. Regeneration is a new creation; and if it is a new creation it must be the work of God."[62] Regeneration, as Moody understood it, was an inside-out event. It was not an outside-in moral reformation. He explained it this way: "And I cannot help believing in the regeneration of man, when I see men who have been reclaimed. . . . Old things have passed away, and all things have become new. They are not reformed only, but REGENERATED—new men in Christ Jesus."[63] Conversion from the inside out was Moody's ultimate goal.

---

56. Moody, *Twelve Select Sermons,* 35.

57. Dwight Lyman Moody, *Anecdotes and Illustrations of D. L. Moody: Related by Him in His Revival Work* (Chicago: Rhodes & McClure, 1877), 183.

58. Quoted in Gundry, *Love Them In,* 172.

59. Moody, *To All People,* 199.

60. D. L. Moody, *The Way to God and How to Find It* (Chicago: Revell, 1884), 23.

61. Ibid., 25, 26.

62. Ibid., 27.

63. Ibid., 30.

Although Moody did preach on other topics, like the Holy Spirit's work to bring power to Christian service, premillennialism, and temperance, these were secondary themes. Moody was a preacher of simple, evangelistic themes. These themes—love and the "Three Rs"—represent what he sees as the salvific message of the Bible.

METHODOLOGY FOR PREACHING

Given Moody's conception of the Bible, it is hardly surprising that he is an advocate of expository preaching. Probably the best way to understand what Moody meant by expository preaching is his admiration for Spurgeon. For Moody, Spurgeon seems to be the archetype of a preacher. In William Moody's biography of his father, he notes that as Moody prepared a sermon, he always checked to see if Spurgeon had preached the text. If he had, Moody would immediately look it up in the collection of Spurgeon's sermons.[64]

Addressing young people considering ministry, Moody says, "If you take my advice, you will seek not to be a text preacher, but an expository preacher. I believe what this country needs is the Word of God."[65] Moody's frustration about the state of preaching is evident as he writes, "I am tired and sick of moral essays. It would take about a ton of them to convert a child five years old."[66] He also lamented people who use the Bible as a "text" exclaiming, "They get a text and away they go. They get up in a balloon and talk about astronomy . . . and a little geometry . . . and they wonder why people never read the Bible." He also condemns what he calls "oratory preaching."[67] He bemoaned the fact some seem to think this is the only type of preaching to which people will listen. However, he claimed such preaching is often forgotten within twenty-four hours. Instead, he implored his audience to "give people the Word of God."[68] Moody was convinced the only effective preaching reflected the teachings of the Bible.

Consequently, Moody always started with the Bible. As one might expect, Moody's approach to Bible study emphasized the practical. Moody's 1895 book entitled *Pleasure and Profit in Bible Study* provides a detailed look at how Moody studied the Bible. This short book provides a list of practical Bible study methods. These examples include a study of the characters of the Bible, using your concordance to study words and themes, study Old and New Testament books together,

---

64. Moody, *Life of Moody,* 447.
65. D. L. Moody, *Pleasure and Profit in Bible Study* (Chicago: Revell, 1895), 42.
66. Ibid.
67. Ibid.
68. Ibid.

read whole books before reading chapters, etc. Moody also suggested tools to aid study. For example, Moody encouraged the student of the Bible to acquire a concordance to guide them through various topics in the Bible.[69] He also recommended having several Bibles and always writing notes in the margins. In fact, he went so far as to provide a recommended set of symbols to mark out themes. The approaches to Bible study that he recommended reflected his own study habits. As might be expected, these studies provided the basic substance for his sermons.

Although his sermons were the product of his Bible study, they are not tightly organized exegetical studies. While Moody extolled expository preaching for pastors, he saw his role as evangelist, not pastor. His sermons reflect that fact. His sermons are very loosely outlined. This is not to say that they are chaotic, but rigorous and intricate arguments were not Moody's forte. Further, given his primary audience, they would likely have been ineffective. Moody prepared by identifying main ideas drawn from his Bible study. These served as a frame for the sermon. He would then build around this frame using sentimental illustrations, personal recollections, anecdotes, and pithy sayings he had collected. He carried around large envelopes he was constantly filling with things he heard or saw. As he prepared sermons he would selectively choose from this collection. This allowed Moody to preach multiple versions of the same sermon. The product is a sermon that is predominately narrative in nature and delivered in a straightforward and earnest manner. As might be expected, they also reflected his rather unique approach to grammar, by including phrases like, "The Spirit done it," "tain't no use," and "git right up."[70]

This was all delivered at an alarming rate of speed. As one observer put it, "Moody seemed to seize the idea that his messages were to be delivered over wires kept hot and that there was neither time nor money to be wasted in their delivery."[71] The observer continued, noting that in passages of intense excitement, the sentences possessed an explosive quality suggesting a pack of firecrackers set off by accident.[72] Another said his sermons' endings had the feel of a cavalry charge, saying one either went with it or got out of the way.[73] The speed of his delivery combined with his limited vocabulary meant he rarely used words with three or four syllables. When he dared use them, they often emerged in a tortured fashion. For example, some claimed Moody was the only man living who could say Jerusalem in two syllables.[74]

---

69. Ibid., 54.
70. Moody, *Life of Moody*, 238.
71. Goss, *Echoes from the Pulpit*, 96.
72. Ibid., 96, 97.
73. Timothy George, ed., *Mr. Moody and the Evangelical Tradition* (New York: T&T Clark, 2004), 4–5.
74. Goss, *Echoes from the Pulpit*, 97.

Moody came from hardy stock. He was a robust man filled with what seemed to be boundless energy. Moody would preach for weeks on end with little rest between meetings. Although his sermons were not particularly lengthy, they reflected an urgency that came from deep within. His preaching voice was described as being of a tenor pitch and powerful enough that he could speak to crowds in the thousands. In addition to his voice, Moody possessed what was described as a commanding eye while in the pulpit. As he spoke, he used a variety of hand gestures ranging from pointing to the heavens to pounding the pulpit.[75] Perhaps this account by one who observed him preach many times best describes Moody's earnest, urgent, straightforward preaching of the Bible's message of salvation: "I have seen him when the expenditure of power scared me. I have felt the platform shake under the movements of his body, seen the sweat start from his forehead, his eyes blaze, his muscles grow tense and rigid. I have felt as one does when a great engine puffs and pants upon a slippery track the steam escaping and the wheels revolving without gripping the track. But, he always got the track at last. He always pulled his load. These mighty struggles always carried his audience."[76]

CONTRIBUTIONS TO PREACHING

Wilbur Smith estimated that Moody developed about 260 different sermons that he preached to millions of listeners during his most active years between 1875 and 1899.[77] These would be collected in volumes that are still being sold and have been read by additional millions. The breadth of his impact is stunning, given he was never formally trained for the clergy, schooled in homiletics, or ordained for ministry. He became a towering figure, causing Martin Marty to go so far as to claim Moody "could plausibly have been called Mr. Revivalist and perhaps even Mr. Protestant."[78] Given the enormous popularity of his preaching, his approach became normative for vast segments of the English-speaking world.

One lasting impact of Moody's preaching was to simplify the sermon. This simplicity that typified Moody's preaching can probably be traced to his early days working with children in the Sunday school. His sermons, devoid of gloss and rhetorical flourish, often startled those who had never heard him preach. No one who heard Dwight Moody preach left unsure of his message. Moody's preaching stands as a powerful reminder of the need for clarity in preaching.

---

75. Ibid., 98–99.
76. Ibid., 100.
77. Wilbur M. Smith, ed., *The Best of D. L. Moody* (Chicago: Moody, 1971), 13–15.
78. Martin E. Marty, introduction to *Dwight L. Moody: American Evangelist 1837–1899*, by James F. Findlay Jr. (Chicago: The University of Chicago Press, 1969), 1.

Moody also established and legitimized preaching by laypeople. Moody was not ashamed of the fact he was a layperson and would quickly correct any who referred to him as "Reverend." As he put it, he preferred to be called "plain Dwight L. Moody, a Sabbath school worker."[79] Moody believed much of the work of the church can and must be done by lay preachers, evangelists, and teachers. This is particularly reflected in his vision for what would become Moody Bible Institute. Moody hoped the institute would provide the church with a legion of trained lay preachers and evangelists to work among the unreached masses found in the growing urban centers of the mid- to late nineteenth century. The impact of his own preaching served as justification for that effort.

Moody's commitment to the Bible and simplicity in preaching is still relevant. His commitment to evangelism and lay preaching, with a focus on urban centers, certainly speaks to our time. As we are daily faced with the reality of the fragility of human life, Moody models an earnestness and urgency that can be instructive for today's preachers of the Bible.

Sermon Excerpt
The New Birth[80]

But I can imagine someone say, "If that is to have a new birth, what am I to do? I can't create life. I certainly can't save myself." You certainly can't, and we don't preach that you can. We tell you it is utterly impossible to make a man better without Christ, and that is what men are trying to do. They are trying to patch up this old Adam's nature. There must be a new creation. Regeneration is a new creation, and if it is a new creation it must be the work of God. In the first chapter of Genesis man don't appear. There is no one there but God. Man is not there to help or take part. When God created the earth, he was alone. When God redeemed the world he was alone. "That which was born of the flesh is flesh, and that which is born of the Spirit is Spirit." . . . A man might just as well try to leap over the moon as to serve God in the flesh. Therefore, that which is born of the flesh is flesh and that which is born of the Spirit is Spirit. Now God tells us in this chapter how we are to get into his kingdom. We

---

79. Moody, *Life of Moody*, 132.
80. Moody preached various versions of this sermon at least 184 times between 1881 and 1889. Henry Drummond, *Dwight L. Moody: Impressions and Facts* (New York: McClure, Philips, 1900), 126.

are not to work our way in, not but that salvation is worth working for. We admit all that. If there were rivers and mountains in the way, it would be worth swimming those rivers and climbing those mountains. There is no doubt that salvation is worth all that, but we don't get it by our works. It is to him that worketh not, but believeth. We work because we are saved; we don't work to be saved. We work from the cross but not towards it. Now it is written, "Work out your salvation with fear and trembling." Why you must have your salvation before you can work it out. Suppose I say to my little boy, "Go and work out that garden," I must furnish him the garden before he can work it out. Suppose I say to him, "I want you to spend that $100 carefully." "Well," he says, "let me have the $100 and I will be careful how I spend it." I remember when I first left home and went to Boston, I had spent all my money, and I went to the post-office three times a day. I knew there was only one mail a day from home, but I thought by some possibility there might be a letter for me. At last I got a letter from my little sister, and I was awful glad to get it. She had heard that there were a great many pickpockets in Boston, and a large part of that letter was to have me be very careful not to let anybody pick my pocket. Now I had got to have something in my pocket in order to have it picked. So you have got to have salvation before you can work it out. ♦

BIBLIOGRAPHY

Bebbington, David. *The Dominance of Evangelicalism: The Age of Spurgeon and Moody.* Downers Grove, IL: InterVarsity Press, 2005.

_____. *Evangelicalism in Modern Britain: A History from the 1730s to the 1980s.* London: Unwin Hyman, 1989.

Carwardine, Richard. *Transatlantic Revivalism: Popular Evangelicalism in Britain and America, 1790–1865.* Westport, CT: Greenwood, 1978.

Daniels, W. H. *Moody: His Words, Work, and Workers.* New York: Nelson & Phillips, 1877.

Dorsett, Lyle. *A Passion for Souls: The Life of D. L. Moody.* Chicago: Moody, 1997.

Evensen, Bruce. *God's Man for the Gilded Age.* New York: Oxford, 2003.

Findlay, James F., Jr. *Dwight L. Moody: American Evangelist, 1837–1899.* Chicago: University of Chicago Press, 1969.

George, Timothy, ed. *Mr. Moody and the Evangelical Tradition.* New York: T&T Clark, 2004.

Goss, Charles F. *Echoes from the Pulpit and Platform.* Hartford: Worthington, 1900.

Gundry, Stanley N. *Love Them In: The Life and Theology of Dwight Moody.* Grand Rapids: Baker, 1976.

Moody, Dwight L. *Bible Characters.* Chicago: Revell, 1888.

_____. "The Gift of Power." Page 18 in *Short Talks.* Chicago: Bible Institute Colportage Association, 1900.

_____. *Glad Tidings: Comprising Sermons and Prayer Meeting Talks Delivered at the New York Hippodrome.* New York: Treat, 1876.

_____. *Golden Counsels.* Boston: United Society of Christian Endeavor, 1899.

_____. *"The Gospel Awakening": Comprising the Sermons and Addresses, Prayer Meeting Talks and Bible Readings of the Great Revival Meetings Conducted by Moody and Sankey.* Chicago: Revell, 1883.

_____. *Great Joy: Comprising Sermons and Prayer-Meeting Talks, Delivered at the Chicago Tabernacle.* New York: Treat, 1877.

_____. *Heaven: Where It Is, Its Inhabitants, and How to Get There.* Chicago: Revell, 1884.

_____. *How to Study the Bible.* Chicago: Revell, 1876.

_____. *Moody's Sermons, Addresses and Prayers.* St. Louis: Thompson, 1877.

_____. *New Sermons, Addresses and Prayers.* New York: Goodspeed, 1877.

_____. *The New Sermons of Dwight Lyman Moody.* New York: Goodspeed, 1880.

_____. *The New Sermons, Addresses and Prayers.* New York: Goodspeed, 1880.

_____. *Pleasure and Profit in Bible Study.* Chicago: Revell, 1895.

_____. *Secret Power: Or the Secret of Success in Christian Life and Work.* Chicago: Revell, 1881.

_____. *Sowing and Reaping.* New York: Revell, 1898.

_____. *To All People: Comprising Sermons, Bible Readings, Temperance Addresses, and Prayer-Meeting Talks, delivered in the Boston Tabernacle by Dwight Moody.* New York: Treat, 1877.

_____. *To the Work! To the Work!* Chicago: Revell, 1884.

_____. *Twelve Select Sermons.* Chicago: Revell, 1881.

_____. *The Way to God and How to Find It.* Chicago: Revell, 1884.

_____. *Anecdotes and Illustrations of D. L. Moody: Related by Him in His Revival Work.* Chicago: Rhodes & McClure, 1877.

Moody, William R. *The Life of Dwight L. Moody.* Chicago: Revell, 1900.

Pollock, J. C. *Moody: A Biographical Portrait of the Pacesetter in Modern Mass Evangelism.* New York: Macmillan, 1963.

_____. *Moody: The Biography.* Chicago: Moody, 1963.

_____. *Moody without Sankey.* London: Hodder & Stoughton, 1963.

Quiggle, Gregg L. "An Analysis of Dwight Moody's Urban Social Vision." PhD diss., 2009, The Open University.

Rosell, Garth, ed. *Commending the Faith: The Preaching of D. L. Moody.* Peabody, MA.: Hendrickson, 1999.

Smith, Wilbur. *An Annotated Bibliography of D. L. Moody.* Chicago: Moody, 1948.

_____, ed. *The Best of D. L. Moody.* Chicago: Moody, 1971.

B. H. Carroll

Preaching Sermons
Saturated with Scripture

ROBERT MATZ
JERRY SUTTON

Best known as the founder of Southwestern Baptist Theological Seminary, B. H. Carroll (1843–1914) rose to prominence as Texas's prince of preachers. From the pulpit of the First Baptist Church of Waco, Carroll's exacting biblical exposition propelled him to a nationwide notoriety among Baptists through denominational service, convention meetings, and Baptist newspapers. Emphasizing the divine authorship and authority of the Bible, Carroll understood that in preaching, one speaks for God by bringing a multitude of Scriptures to bear on each sermon topic.

HISTORICAL BACKGROUND

Benajah Harvey Carroll, known simply by his initials, B. H., stood as a Texas Baptist icon. Best identified as the founder and first president of Southwestern Baptist Theological Seminary in Fort Worth, Carroll lived a colorful, difficult, and highly influential life. At heart, he was and will always be known as a Texas Baptist preacher and educator.

Carroll was born near Carrollton, Mississippi, on December 27, 1843, the seventh of thirteen children. The family soon moved to Arkansas, and then in 1858, they moved to Texas. Carroll's father, also named Benajah, was a bivocational Baptist preacher. In his early teenage years, B. H. made a profession of faith and was baptized, but in his own words, it was a mere formality and simply served to ensconce him in his self-professed infidelity. [1] Explaining his "infidelity," he wrote, "But my infidelity related to the Bible and its manifest

---

1. The authors are much indebted to the work of Dr. Robert A. Baker. Many of the primary sources were assimilated by him in this historical account of Southwestern Seminary's founder, founding, and development. Gratitude is expressed as well to Robert Burgess, Director of Digital Services at Southwestern Seminary's Webb Roberts Library for assisting us to review the B. H. Carroll archives on the Fort Worth Campus. Robert A. Baker, *Tell the Generations Following: A History of Southwestern Baptist Theological Seminary, 1908–1983* (Nashville: Broadman, 1983), 57.

doctrines. I doubted that it was God's book; that it was an inspired revelation of his will to man." He further explained, "I doubted the miracles. I doubted the divinity of Jesus of Nazareth. But more than all, I doubted his vicarious expiation for the sins of men." In short, he concluded, "I doubted any real power and vitality in the Christian religion."[2]

In 1859, Carroll matriculated at Baylor University where he quickly developed the reputation as the school's best debater. A few years later, in 1861, Carroll was married, and with the outbreak of the Civil War, became a soldier from 1862–1864. While away at war, he and his wife divorced due to her alleged infidelity. Carroll's military career was cut short by a debilitating wound while fighting for the Confederacy in Louisiana. He returned to Texas a broken and bitter man. While recuperating at home in Texas, he opened a school at Yellow Prairie, which he soon relocated to Caldwell. All the while, he was disillusioned with his circumstances and with his infidelity. [3] Describing his own despondency, he wrote, "With all the earnestness of a soul . . . I brought a broken and bleeding, but honest heart to every reputed oracle of infidelity. I did not ask for life or fame or pleasure. I merely asked for light to shine on the path of right." He explained, "Once more I viewed the anti-Christian philosophies, no longer to admire them in what they destroyed, but to inquire what they had built up, what they offered to a hungry heart and a blasted life." Insightfully, he now saw things differently. "Why had I never seen it before? How could I have been so blind to it? These philosophies, one and all, were mere negations. They were destructive, but not constructive." He finally realized, "They overturned and overturned and overturned; but, as my soul lives, they built up nothing under the whole heaven in the place of what they destroyed." Finally seeing the futility of his own infidelity, he concluded, "They are all wells without water, and clouds without rain." Declaring his own disillusionment, he declared, "Here now was my case: I had turned my back on Christianity, and had nothing in infidelity; happiness was gone, and death would not come." In short, his life was a wounded and miserable mess.[4]

Carroll began reading his Bible in spite of his bitterness. In the fall of 1865, while attending a Methodist camp meeting at his mother's insistence, he was convicted of his sin and finally surrendered his life to Jesus Christ. [5] Describing his own conversion he wrote, "I did not see Jesus with my eye, but I seemed to

2. B. H. Carroll, *Sermons and Life Sketch of B. H. Carroll*, comp., J. B. Cranfill. (Philadelphia: American Baptist, 1895), 15.

3. Baker, *Tell the Generations*, 60–61.

4. Carroll, *Sermons*, 17–18.

5. Baker, *Tell the Generations*, 62.

see him standing before me, looking reproachfully and tenderly and pleadingly, seeming to rebuke me for having gone to all other sources for rest but the right one, and now inviting me to come to him." Carroll concluded the testimony by saying, "In a moment I went, once and forever, casting myself unreservedly and for all time at Christ's feet, and in a moment the rest came, indescribable and unspeakable, and it has remained from that day until now."[6]

Shortly after his conversion, Carroll was baptized by his college friend, W. W. "Spurgeon" Harris, and then affiliated with the Baptist Church in Caldwell.[7] Looking back to the night of his conversion experience, he related, "I knew then as well as I know now that I would preach; that it would be my life work; that I would have no other work." His brother J. M. Carroll [8] said about his brother's conversion, "Grace did more for Harvey Carroll than for any other man I have ever known. Never was a life more thoroughly made over."[9]

Soon after, Carroll entered into marriage a second time, wedding Ellen Bell. The president of Baylor University, Rufus Burleson, performed the ceremony on December 28, 1866. Theirs would be a long and happy marriage. Yet the postwar years in Texas were brutal; making ends meet was difficult, and then they lost an infant child. To provide for his family during this time, Carroll would preach in different churches as invited, teach during the week, and work on the side as a farmer.[10]

In 1869, Carroll was invited to become the pastor of the New Hope Baptist Church in McLennan County. The next year, at Baylor President Burleson's encouragement, he was invited to preach on alternate Sundays for the First Baptist Church in Waco. The following year, in March 1871, the church called Carroll to be their permanent pastor. Under his leadership, the church grew rapidly. His sermons would be carried first in the Baptist papers of Texas and soon to Baptists around the country through other state Baptist newspapers. He would stay at the church for twenty-eight years.[11]

As a pastor, Carroll was known for his preaching, evangelism, discipleship, leadership, teaching, administration, and fund-raising. He helped start numerous churches, and his church was known for its generosity in giving to missions and missional causes. Carroll helped organize the Baptist General Convention of Texas, and served as a trustee at The Southern Baptist Theological Seminary

---

6. Carroll, *Sermons*, 22.

7. Baker, *Tell the Generations*, 63–64.

8. Better known for his Trail of Blood theology, which B. H. never fully embraced.

9. Carroll describes his conversion in his autobiographic sermon, "My Infidelity and What Became of It." Carroll, *Sermons*, 15–23. These quotes are found on page 23.

10. Jeff Ray, *B. H. Carroll* (Nashville: The Sunday School Board, 1927), 16–17.

11. Baker, *Tell the Generations*, 66–67.

and Baylor University. He was known as a champion of Baptist orthodoxy as well as Baptist unity. Upon the death of the famed John Broadus, Carroll was often viewed as the principal leader of Southern Baptists.[12]

One of Carroll's most important roles was as a mentor for university students, especially young preachers. He was influential in the spiritual formation of young men like George W. Truett, eventual pastor of First Baptist Church in Dallas; Lee Scarborough, his successor as president of Southwestern; and Jeff D. Ray, long-term professor of homiletics at Southwestern Baptist Seminary. Robert Baker pointed out that an entire generation of Baylor students, many of them young ministers, sat under Carroll's preaching.[13] One admirer wrote, "Whatever may be said of his versatility, in my judgment his greatest influence over the students of Baylor was from the pulpit. . . . In the course of the nearly thirty years he preached in Waco, thousands of students were gripped and held in the same way." Baker concluded that "Carroll loved to preach, counting it the principal function of his pastoral work."[14]

Under Carroll's leadership, the First Baptist Church gave one-third of the funds collected in Texas to foreign, home, and state missions offerings. He was a model for young preachers on how to lead and run a Baptist church. Carroll was also known as the tip of the spear in promoting civic righteousness. He led the fight on behalf of prohibition and other issues of civic concern.

While serving as pastor, Carroll found great joy in helping to equip young people for the ministry. Someone might well write a book, "Carroll as Mentor." In 1893, Carroll was instrumental in forming Baylor's Bible Department. In fact, he was appointed to the chair of exegesis and systematic theology. In the first year of the new program's existence, seventy-five students enrolled. For years, Carroll had been teaching students on a voluntary basis. Now he would be instrumental in establishing accredited ministerial training.[15]

After the death of his second wife, and with his brother's encouragement, Carroll resigned his position as pastor of the First Baptist Church of Waco in 1899. He subsequently assumed the responsibility as head of the recently formed Texas Baptist Education Commission. His chief concern, however, was the growth and development of Baylor's Bible Department. Carroll believed that the preparation of young ministers was the key to the prosperity of Texas churches in the coming century. From his position in the Education Commission, Carroll

---

12. Alan Jeffery Lefever, "The Life and Work of Benajah Harvey Carroll" (PhD diss., Southwestern Baptist Theological Seminary, 1992), 178ff.

13. Ibid., 73–74.

14. Ray, *B. H. Carroll*, 105.

15. Baker, *Tell the Generations*, 98.

envisioned the founding of a theological seminary, although it was a matter that he kept to himself.

While serving as the head of the Education Commission, Carroll also assumed the role of dean of Baylor's Bible Department. During this time, he married his third wife, Hallie Harrison. In 1905, Carroll launched the drive to raise funds to establish Southwestern Seminary in Fort Worth. The Baylor trustees voted to establish the seminary in 1905, but the Baptist General Convention of Texas voted in 1907 to separate the seminary from Baylor and establish it as a separate entity with its own trustees, budget, administration, faculty, and facilities. The first class convened on October 3, 1910. Carroll served as its first president until his death on November 11, 1914.

THEOLOGY OF PREACHING

Carroll had a nearly eidetic memory. According to his brother J. M., he could recall both the book and the page of something he had read years before. His brother wrote, "His memory in many other things was just as striking and remarkable as his memory of books."[16] Coupled with his retentive mind was a giftedness with words both spoken and written. Besides the fact that Carroll had mastered the art of effective preaching, he was a prodigious writer. He left behind his seventeen-volume *The Interpretation of the English Bible*, eighteen volumes of sermons, five volumes of popular addresses, and numerous other influential writings.[17]

Carroll, by the testimony of the multitudes who heard him, was a brilliant communicator; he delighted in his role as a preacher. He wrote, "I thank God that He put me in this office; I thank Him that He would not let me have any other; that He shut me up to this glorious work; and when I get home among the blessed on the bank of the everlasting deliverance and look back toward time and all of its clouds and sorrows, and pains, and privations, I expect to stand up and shout for joy that down there in the fog and the mists, down there in the dust and struggle, God let me be a preacher."[18] In the words of James Spivey, "His power was in persuasive oratory."[19]

---

16. Ibid., 55.

17. Ibid., 74. Among his strongest attributes was his organizational ability. This skill was manifested in virtually everything he touched, from his pastoral responsibilities, to his organizing of the Texas Baptists, to his adeptness in raising huge sums of money for a multiplicity of evangelical causes. His organizational ability was especially beneficial in his work in the field of education. His work on behalf of Baylor University, the Southern Baptist Theological Seminary, the Texas Baptist Education Commission, and finally the founding of Southwestern Seminary was unparalleled.

18. Carroll, *Sermons,* 125.

19. James T. Spivey, "Benajah Harvey Carroll (1843–1914)" in James Leo Garrett, ed., *The Legacy of Southwestern: Writings That Shaped a Tradition* (North Richland Hills, TX: Smithfield, 2002), 4.

A. J. Barton, who followed Carroll as pastor of Waco's First Baptist Church, once remarked that "an important part of the greatness of Carroll was his total personality." He explained, "Across the years, now nearly a third of a century, I see as vividly as if it were yesterday, or even today, the towering figure, the giant intellect, the gentle heart, the beaming face, the laughing eyes, the lifting and helping hands of our Kingdom Hero, and I am forced to exclaim from a heart of deep admiration and great joy, 'There stands the greatest achievement of the life of BH Carroll.'" Barton stood in awe at the transformation of Carroll from skeptic and infidel into a sensitive and loving minister of the gospel.[20]

According to Spivey, "The two ideas controlling Carroll's life were 'an authoritative Bible and the reality of Christian experience.'"[21] Carroll embraced a traditionally conservative view of Scripture and the Christian faith. In historic categories, he believed in the Bible's infallibility. "The Bible not only contained the word of God, but also is God's very word."[22]

Carroll was a classic Trinitarian in the Baptist tradition. He embraced the New Hampshire Confession. Yet he did not embrace a Calvinist soteriology, but taught that a person is saved after they hear the gospel, repent, and believe. Then a person is regenerated. Regeneration is the result and not the cause of a person's salvation. In Carroll's teaching, salvation included four elements: "Redemption, atonement, justification, and adoption." Carroll held to the traditional Baptist understandings of the ordinances of baptism and the Lord's Supper. Although Carroll leaned toward Landmarkism in some of his beliefs, like closed Communion, he was by his own admission not a Landmarkist.[23] With respect to eschatology, Carroll, like many Baptists of his generation, held to a form of postmillennialism.

For B. H. Carroll, preaching was the great work of his life. As his sermons are studied and dissected, the focus of his messages becomes clear. If the essence of preaching is answering the "what?" (What does it say?), "so what?" (What does it mean?), and "now what?" (What do I do about it?), Carroll gave particular attention to the first two portions. He was preoccupied with helping the hearer understand the proper explanation and interpretation of the text. He was less concerned with the application of the text.

Carroll wrote this concerning the critical importance of the preaching task: "An inspired man, when he speaks, does not speak his will; when he writes, he does not write his will, but he speaks and writes for God, being moved by the Holy Spirit." In light of this conviction, Carroll asked his fellow ministers,

---

20. Baker, *Tell the Generations,* 67.
21. Spivey, "Carroll," 6–7.
22. Ibid.
23. Ibid., 7–9.

Ministers of God, have you studied these Scriptures? . . . Are any sheep of your flock hungry? . . . Have you heard any of them crying for the "sincere milk of the word," while you crammed them with solid food they were unable to digest? . . . My brother, if you would magnify your office, make the Word of God your life-study. Let down your buckets into the wells of salvation; lengthen your cords and let them down deep, and draw up the water fresh and sparkling every day, and give it out freely to your thirsty congregation.[24]

In Carroll's understanding, the preacher was God's spokesperson. They literally spoke for God and represented God on earth. Therefore, what the preacher said and did was as God's representative.

METHODOLOGY FOR PREACHING

Commenting on Carroll's homiletical method, J. B. Cranfill stated that "he can dig deeper to find God's Truth and then climb higher to reveal it than any man that ever lived."[25] George Truett, who labeled Carroll the greatest preacher Texas had ever known,[26] stated that from Carroll's preaching he "received more help in [his] study and estimate of God's Holy Word than from any other earthly source."[27] Those who heard Carroll preach or read his sermons in state Baptist newspapers realized that his preaching methodology was centered on his approach to Scripture.

Carroll's sermons were an outgrowth of his approach to the Bible. As noted above, Carroll understood the Bible to be God's inspired Word. Carroll's high view of the Bible was well-known. He frequently argued for its full inspiration, infallibility, and authority.[28]

Aside from his high view of the Bible, Carroll also found external sources of knowledge to be useless for preaching. Human philosophy "never by searching can find out God or things that relate to God and the supernatural."[29] Darwinism "has nothing to do with the supernatural."[30] Carroll "felt shame, sorrow and contempt . . . [when he] heard nice enough things from the pulpit, but nothing

---

24. Carroll, *Sermons*, 110.

25. B. H. Carroll, *River of Life*, ed. J. B. Cranfill (Nashville: Sunday School Board, 1928), 9.

26. B. H. Carroll, *Baptists and Their Doctrines*, ed. Timothy George and James Spivey (Nashville: Broadman & Holman, 1999), 4.

27. Carroll, *River of Life*, 12.

28. B. H. Carroll, *Inspiration of the Bible: A Discussion of the Origin, the Authenticity, and the Sanctity of the Oracles of God*, ed. J. B. Cranfill (New York: Revell, 1930), 15–27.

29. Ibid., 30.

30. Ibid., 31.

from the Word of God." [31] Instead of science, philosophy, or nice things, he wanted his sermons to be "literally saturated with Scripture."[32]

Thus, it is not surprising that when one comes to his sermons, one finds that they are almost always consumed with a prolonged commentary on the meaning of multiple biblical texts. Commenting on Carroll's method, Robert Robinson argues that Carroll "would rather pursue and explain the text within the context to the point of boredom than lift it out of its setting."[33] Indeed, his entire homiletical methodology is centered on his approach to the biblical text.

Carroll's primary interest in every sermon was that his listener come to a proper understanding of the biblical text in its original context. "However far, and by whatever license a minister may depart from the primary meaning of a text in its immediate connection, it is always obligatory that he should first give the primary and contextual import and then explain how the general principle contained in it may be safely applied to all his deductions from it."[34] As a result, Carroll's approach to preaching was dominated by the biblical texts. As one scholar notes of Carroll's preaching, "In the average sermon by Carroll the treatment of the text was a gigantic undertaking."[35] An examination of Carroll's introductions, sermon bodies, and conclusions reveals this to be the case.

The purpose of the sermon introduction is to introduce the audience to the sermon and the biblical text. Such has been commonly assumed to include the ideas of introducing (and often directly stating) the sermon's purpose and of commanding the audience's attention. Yet for Carroll, such concerns were secondary. Carroll's primary (almost exclusive) goal in the introduction was to introduce a right understanding of the biblical text. His introductions oriented to his chosen text's biblical context and not to the interests of the audience. This orientation to the textual context is seen in his sermon topics and titles, his sermon's purpose statements, and in opening of section of most of his sermons.

Carroll derived his topics and titles directly from the text he was examining. For example, "The Foundation of the Church of Christ" from Matthew 16:18, which states "on this rock I will build my church"; "The Glory of the Church" from Ephesians 3:10, 21, which states "to him be glory in the church"; and "God

---

31. B. H. Carroll, *The Pastoral Epistles of Paul, 1 and 2 Peter, Jude, and 1, 2, 3 and John*, vol. 16 in *An Interpretation of the English Bible*, ed. J. B. Cranfill (Grand Rapids: Baker, 1973), 157.

32. "One man, in criticizing my first book of sermons, said, 'There is too much scripture in it.' I thanked him for his criticism. I try to preach sermons that are literally saturated with scripture." Ibid., 157.

33. Robinson does note that Carroll on rare occasion ignored the meaning to the text, which is surprising given everything that has been described about Carroll, but notes that by and large his preaching was consumed with textual explanation. Robert Jackson Robinson, "The Homiletical Method of Benajah Harvey Carroll" (ThD diss., Southwestern Baptist Theological Seminary, November 1956), 68–69.

34. Carroll, *Sermons*, 105.

35. Robinson, "The Homiletical Method," 72.

Is Faithful" from 2 Thessalonians 3:3, which states "the Lord is faithful."[36] When asked to address a special gathering, Carroll selected a text to fit the occasion and titled his sermon accordingly. Once when speaking on theological education, he titled his sermon "Theological Seminaries and Wild Gourds or the Problem of Ministerial Education." His text was 2 Kings 4:40, and he examined the sons of the prophets harvesting wild gourds and their resulting statement to Elijah, "Man of God, there is death in the pot."[37] His goal in selecting the topic was "to convey the meaning of the text to his listeners. He usually plucked the central idea from his Scripture passage and used it in phrasing his topic."[38]

Carroll's textual emphasis dominated all aspects of his sermon introduction. While most preaching theory argues that the sermon should be oriented around a purpose statement early in the sermon,[39] Carroll rarely utilized such statements. Robert Robinson looked at "two hundred forty-one printed sermons of Carroll . . . [and] only seventeen times did he definitely state his proposition."[40] On the occasion when Carroll did have a purpose statement, it was normally to explain the meaning of a chosen text or texts.[41]

As Carroll's introductions progressed, he would labor over the textual context while often bringing other biblical texts to bear. The sermon "Christ's Marching Orders" exemplifies this pattern. Before turning to the meaning of the Matthean Great Commission, Carroll labored over the timing, location, and recipients of this passage in his introduction. Regarding the timing, he noted both the immediate context of the passage in Matthew as well as the larger context of the passage in relation to the other appearances of the risen Christ in the other gospels. Regarding the location, he examined not only the Matthean context, but also the Markan and Lukan contexts of the Commission. Regarding the recipients, he noted from the context and from numerous passages from throughout the rest of the New Testament that the passage was for the church.[42]

There were occasions when Carroll did not go to the text immediately. Sometimes he would begin with the doctrine which his text addressed.[43]

---

36. B. H. Carroll, *Christ and His Church*, ed. J. B. Cranfill (Nashville: Sunday School Board, 1928), 37, 83, 169. Robinson provides numerous other examples. See Robinson, "The Homiletical Method," 80–89.

37. R. Robinson brings out numerous other examples. Robinson, "The Homiletical Method," 82.

38. Ibid., 83.

39. Such has been commonly assumed from Carroll's day to the present. See John A. Broadus, *A Treatise on the Preparation and Delivery of Sermons*, 23rd ed. (New York: Armstrong, 1898),155ff; and Haddon W. Robinson, *Biblical Preaching: The Development and Delivery of Expository Messages*, 2nd ed. (Grand Rapids: Baker Academic, 2001), Chapter 2.

40. Robinson, "The Homiletical Method," 95.

41. Ibid., 96–102.

42. B. H. Carroll, *Christ's Marching Orders*, ed. J. B. Cranfill (Dallas: Helms, 1941), 37, 83, 169. Robinson provides numerous other examples. See Robinson, "The Homiletical Method," 80–89.

43. See "Confession" and "Assurance" in Carroll, *Sermons*, 221, 231.

Other times he would begin with a special occasion that had prompted the sermon.[44] In still other sermons, he would begin with a series of texts pertaining to a topic.[45] Yet in each case, he would return to the meaning of the text. In summary, Carroll's introductions were not focused on raising a need or arousing listener interest. Rather, they were almost entirely focused on the need to discover a right understanding of the biblical texts and doctrines that filled the sermon.

While much of contemporary evangelical preaching theory argues for expository preaching as the best way to safeguard divine authority,[46] a study of the body of Carroll's sermons reveals that he almost certainly would disagree. This is surprising given that Carroll's sermons were unapologetically textual and rooted in an understanding of the text in its original context. Yet they were not expository, at least according to most contemporary definitions of the term.[47] Carroll's sermons were not concerned with bringing his hearers to a right understanding and application of a singular text. Rather, his sermons bring the hearer to a full understanding of the entirety of the Bible's teaching as it related to the idea or doctrine taught within the text(s) being considered.[48] As a result, while Carroll continued to make much of the context of the text(s) under consideration, Carroll's content, structure, and development revealed that his primary aim in his sermons was to reveal the complete revelation of God on a subject matter.

As a result, the content of Carroll's sermons often lacked unity.[49] His desire to explain the mind of God on a matter took precedence over that goal. He

---

44. "The Cotton Palace and the Sunday Opening" in Carroll, *Sermons*, 406. "Our Historic War Dead" in B. H. Carroll, *Christian Education and Some Social Problems,* ed. J. B. Cranfill (Fort Worth: no publisher, 1948) 174.

45. "Twenty Prayers of Jesus" in B. H Carroll, *Messages on Prayer*, ed. J. B. Cranfill (Nashville: Broadman, 1942), 27, 47.

46. See for example R. Albert Mohler, *He Is Not Silent: Preaching in a Postmodern World* (Chicago: Moody, 2008), chapters 3–4.

47. While there is a variation in definitions of exposition, as preaching theory has progressed over the last thirty years, expository preaching has been increasingly defined as the communication of a biblical concept based on the proper study of a single Bible passage which is then applied to hearers. Carroll's preaching, while rigorously textual, normally led him to explain multiple texts. Thus, while R. Robinson argues Carroll is an expositor, contemporary definitions of the term make this descriptor inappropriate. Robinson, "The Homiletical Method," 150ff; cf. Robinson, *Biblical Preaching*, 21; Jerry Vines and Jim Shaddix, *Power in the Pulpit: How to Prepare and Deliver Expository Sermons* (Chicago: Moody, 1999), 29; Bryan Chapell, *Christ-Centered Preaching: Redeeming the Expository Sermon*, 2nd ed. (Grand Rapids: Baker Academic, 2005), 131.

48. Carroll's understanding of inspiration reveals his goal in this methodology. Carroll believed every part of the Bible is inspired. While every text expresses "ideas from God," every biblical author's understanding of these ideas is limited. The authors often "did not understand [what they wrote]. They studied their own prophecies just as we study them. They knew that God had inspired them to say these things, but they did not understand." Their limited understanding is why God's inspiration continued until the "Scriptures were completed . . . incapable of being added to." Such was necessary because while what each author wrote was "perfect according to its viewpoint, [it was] incomplete so far as the whole is concerned, all views being necessary in order to complete the view." Thus, "it takes a blended view of all to make the whole thing correct." Carroll's preaching provides this blended view. Carroll, *Inspiration of the Bible: A Discussion*, 20, 21, 23, 24.

49. Robinson, "The Homiletical Method," 131–35.

frequently employed multiple texts and propositional statements as he explored a textually derived subject matter. His sermon entitled "The Modern Social Dance" is illustrative. Carroll opened by offering a brief exposition of Job 21:7, 11, 13–15, noting that these verses were the only reference in Scripture to social dancing.[50] He also provided an overview and brief contextual explanation of all the other passages referencing dancing. Yet the bulk of his sermon was oriented around ten separate justifications Christians offer for dancing and a series of textually derived responses to these justifications. The sermon is approximately thirteen thousand words and examined more than forty passages of Scripture from more than fifteen different books of the Bible. With almost every reference, Carroll provided some of the larger surrounding context.[51] While this sermon is an extreme example, as one studies Carroll's preaching, one sees that the use of numerous biblical texts and how they pertained to a singular text was normative for him.[52]

Regarding sermon structure and development, Carroll approached both individual texts and sermons as a whole in much the same way as a lawyer might bring the full weight of their reasoning abilities to "overwhelm all mental opposition."[53] In "The Tragedy of Unbelief," Carroll called attention to Israel's unbelief in their fear of entering the promised land.[54] He built a case that God was just in condemning them:

> Look at the facts. First, the Lord had promised these people before they left Egypt that they should have this particular land. There never was a more solemn promise given, and every display of His power or manifestation of His presence was in the direction of putting them in possession of this country. No rational conclusion could be drawn, from the facts commencing with the miracles in Egypt up to this encampment at Kadesh-Barnea, but that the same Divine power would be exerted in installing them in their promised home.... [Second,] God had spied out that land. I read you His report of it from the eighth chapter of Deuteronomy.... [Third,] there is an inspired report concerning this land, God's testimony about it. Having His report of the land, let us see what His command was. I turn to the

---

50. Carroll, *Christian Education*, 76.
51. Ibid., 76–115.
52. Robinson, "The Homiletical Method," 131–36.
53. Ibid., 137.
54. Robinson notes this sermon as typical of Carroll's expository methodology. Yet such can scarcely be called such by modern definitions. His stated text was Numbers 13:30, yet Carroll's main idea came from Hebrews 3 regarding not entering God's rest. Ibid., 152; B. H. Carroll, *The Faith That Saves*, ed. J. B. Cranfill (Dallas: Helms, 1939), Chapter 4.

first chapter of Deuteronomy and nineteenth verse . . . God says, "The land is thus and so." God says, "I will give it to you." Faith walks by trust in the Divine commandment. But these people want to walk by sight, not faith.[55]

The body of a sermon normally also contains application and illustration. While such elements are found in Carroll's sermons, his use of both elements is atypical. His applications were normal, generalized, and broad.[56] His illustrations were varied, drawn from sources as divergent as Greek mythology or the life of a farmer. They were closely related to the concepts of the text he preached. He frequently drew upon Greek and English etymology to illustrate the meaning of a single word in the text. He contrasted secular forms of knowledge with the ideas of Scripture in order to show the superiority of a biblical mindset.[57] As a result, Carroll's sermons, while giving light to the text, "lacked sharp, absorbing interest."[58]

Carroll's preaching resists classification according to normal contemporary definitions of homiletics. It does not satisfy standard definitions of expository, textual, topical, or even theological preaching.[59] Perhaps Carroll's preaching could be characterized as canonical preaching, in that it attempts to bring both the context of a passage and whole of the canon's teaching on the ideas of that passage in order to provide complete understanding.

The third major movement within the sermon is the conclusion. While Carroll's introductions and sermon bodies reflected a substantive wrestling with the biblical text, Carroll's conclusions were far more succinct. His introductions were often over one thousand words, the bodies of his sermons even longer, yet his conclusions were typically brief at under one hundred words.[60] In so doing, Carroll called greater attention to the understanding of the text than to its application.

His conclusions occasionally summarized the sermon's outline or its main idea, but typically centered around a direct evangelistic appeal or invitation. While Robinson has criticized him on this point,[61] such for Carroll was the

---

55. Carroll, *The Faith That Saves*, 54–55.

56. Carroll's tendency to address his text rather than his audience contributed to this tendency. Note Robinson, "The Homiletical Method," 69.

57. For example, he contrasted secular poetry and music with the Psalms in a sermon on theological education and in a sermon in the Cotton Palace in Waco contrasted a newspaper article on that facility's amenities with biblical prohibitions against lasciviousness. Carroll, *Christian Education*, 47. Carroll, *Sermons*, 416.

58. Robinson, "The Homiletical Method," 191.

59. Carroll's insistence on exegeting each text he encountered is unique and causes his sermon form to resist such standard classification. Definitions for the forms can be found in Vines and Shaddix, *Power in the Pulpit*, 29. For more on textual preaching see Haddon W. Robinson and Craig Brian Larson, *The Art and Craft of Biblical Preaching: A Comprehensive Resource for Today's Communicators* (Grand Rapids: Zondervan, 2005), 412–17, cf. Robinson, "The Homiletical Method," 149–50.

60. Robinson, "The Homiletical Method," 112–14, 124–55, 166.

61. Ibid., 156–57.

logical outworking of his canonically focused homiletic. In a sermon on the inspiration of the Bible, Carroll argued that the primary application of the Bible to the individual was salvation. He stated, "The main point . . . is this: If you close that Book; if you tear out its pages; if you shut out its light, in all the whole universe of God there is not revealed a way by which a sinner can be saved, not one in the world."[62] Carroll understood the invitation as the proper application of the doctrine of Scripture. The individual's response to the evangelistic appeal demonstrated the hearer's proper understanding of the biblical texts which Carroll had expounded.

CONTRIBUTIONS TO PREACHING

Carroll's contributions to the field of preaching are multiple. First, there is the founding of Southwestern Seminary. The school he started has educated tens of thousands of preachers and pastors. His understanding of the preaching task as rooted in biblical authority has defined that institution's ethos throughout its history. Even today, the school's motto of "Preach the Word, Reach the World" bears Carroll's mark.

Second, Carroll's understanding of preaching shaped Baptist preaching throughout the first half of the twentieth century. One of his protégés, Jeff Ray, taught over five thousand preaching students. Ray's textbook on preaching emphasizes explaining the biblical text.[63] Ray wrote a biography of Carroll in which he notes how Carroll shaped his own understanding of expository preaching.[64] Other students included George Truett, L. R. Scarborough, and J. Frank Norris. All considered him a primary influence on their own preaching methodologies.

Third, Carroll's methodology acts as a bridge between the textual preaching more common in his own era and the expository preaching presently advocated. The textual preaching of Carroll's era was frequently characterized by sermons that took their lead from a singular text but then looked elsewhere in the text for much of their development.[65] As noted above, contemporary exposition seeks to explain a singular text. Like textual preachers, Carroll built his sermons around a single text and developed much of his sermon from other texts; yet, like expository preachers, he sought to faithfully explain the text in context, even when this meant he ended up explaining a multitude of texts in a sermon.

---

62. B. H. Carroll, *Revival Messages*, ed. J. B. Cranfill (Grand Rapids: Zondervan, 1939), 153.
63. Jeff Ray, *Expository Preaching* (Grand Rapids: Zondervan, 1940).
64. Ray, *B. H. Carroll*, foreword.
65. Stephen D. Matthewson, "What Makes Textual Preaching Unique," in *The Art and Craft of Biblical Preaching: A Comprehensive Resource for Today's Communicators*, ed. Haddon W. Robinson, trans. Craig Brian Larson (Grand Rapids: Zondervan, 2005), 413.

Fourth, in light of these historical contributions, Carroll's preaching challenges contemporary preachers to build sermons that are faithful to the meaning of both the human and divine authors of the biblical text. Arguing that God speaks in Scripture with a singular voice and thus that the voices of the human authors of Scripture are less significant, Carroll sought to bring all relevant Scriptures to bear on the various ideas of his chosen text or texts. This approach allowed Carroll to act as God's spokesman while still providing the context of each reference. Carroll's goal was "to preach sermons that are literally saturated with scripture."[66] In studying his sermons, preachers learn not just how to explain a text, but also how to explain the whole counsel of God.

Finally, Carroll models persuasive, urgent preaching. The gospel stood as the culmination of his every sermon, while the invitation to respond to the gospel was always the sermon's proper application. A study of Carroll's invitations is fruitful for any student of evangelistic preaching or for any preacher who desires greater effectiveness in evangelistic appeals.

Sermon Excerpt

Theological Seminaries and Wild Gourds, or the Problem of Ministerial Education[67]

Who Were the Sons of the Prophets?

They were companies, or schools, of young men in training for the prophetic office. They were called sons in the sense of disciples or pupils. "Sitting before him" is a phrase equivalent to "receiving instruction from him." The chief prophet before whom they sat and learned was called their father, or master, in the sense of teacher.

It is evident from the history that the object of the instruction was to qualify them for greater efficiency in the prophetic office to which it is presupposed they had received a divine call. While the history clearly implies that this training for his service had the approval of God, it does not imply that his exclusive method was to use only trained and educated men for the prophetic office. Sometimes he called into this work men who were utterly without training in the schools. And the record shows

---

66. Carroll, *The Pastoral Epistles*, 157.
67. Carroll, *Christian Education*, 40–44. Based on 2 Kings 4:38–41.

that these rough men did thorough and acceptable work. For example, Amos, who says: "I was no prophet, neither was I a son of a prophet; but I was a herdsman, and a dresser of sycamore-trees: and the Lord took me from following the flock, and the Lord said unto me, Go, prophesy unto my people Israel."

In other words, the Lord will have trained men and he will have untrained men. And mark you, there were not two orders in his ministry, one higher than the other. Amos was as high as anybody. Applying the case to our own time, the mistake would be serious to have only an educated ministry, or for churches to seek for pastors only those trained in a theological seminary. . . .

What Was Taught in These Seminaries?

Looking through the Old Testament from Samuel to Malachi, we may determine with reasonable certainty the main points in their course of study. This course at any rate included sacred music, instrumental and vocal; poetry, history and the word of God. Their training in music filled the world with the fame of the songs of Zion. Even in the captivity, when their silent harps were hanging from the willow trees, when sadness made the tongue of praise cleave to the roof of the mouth, when disuse robbed the right hand of its cunning in striking the chords of the harp, even there, the idolaters who wasted them, longed to hear one of the songs of Zion. And their poetry—it is matchless now. God was their muse and his works of creation, providence and grace was their theme. We may affect to depreciate it; we may prefer in our families and schools to teach our children the secular songs of inferior bards, but transcendently above Homer, Milton, Virgil, Horace, Dante, Bryant, Byron and Longfellow is that sublime, God-inspired word of Hebrew Poetry.

These prophets were also the historians of their times and to them as human agents we are largely indebted for the sacred chronicles of the past as well as the forecasts of the future. But mainly were they taught the Word of God. They were instructed to hold it as the supreme standard of human conduct and creeds. To look no other where for a revelation of secret things. To this instruction of the sons of the prophets Isaiah probably refers. ◆

BIBLIOGRAPHY

Baker, Robert A. *Tell the Generations Following: A History of Southwestern Baptist Theological Seminary, 1908–1983*. Nashville: Broadman, 1983.

Broadus, John A. *A Treatise on the Preparation and Delivery of Sermons*. 23rd ed. New York: Armstrong, 1898.

Carroll, B. H. *Sermons and Life Sketch of B. H. Carroll*. Compiled by J. B Cranfill. Philadelphia: American Baptist, 1895.

_____. *The Pastoral Epistles of Paul, 1 and 2 Peter, Jude, and 1, 2, 3 and John*. Vol 16 of *An Interpretation of the English Bible*. Edited by J. B. Cranfill. Grand Rapids: Baker, 1973.

_____. *Baptists and Their Doctrines*. Edited by Timothy George and James Spivey. Nashville: Broadman & Holman, 1999.

_____. *Christ and His Church*. Edited by J. B. Cranfill. Nashville: Sunday School Board, 1928.

_____. *Christ's Marching Orders*. Edited by J. B. Cranfill. Dallas: Helms, 1941.

_____. *Christian Education and Some Social Problems*. Edited by J. B. Cranfill. Fort Worth: No Publisher, 1948.

_____. *Inspiration of the Bible: A Discussion of the Origin, the Authenticity and the Sanctity of the Oracles of God*. Edited by J. B. Cranfill. New York: Revell, 1930.

_____. *Faith That Saves*. Edited by J. B. Cranfill. Dallas: Helms, 1939.

_____. *Messages on Prayer*. Edited by J. B. Cranfill. Nashville: Broadman, 1942.

_____. *Revival Messages*. Edited by J. B. Cranfill. Grand Rapids: Zondervan, 1939.

_____. *River of Life*. Edited by J. B. Cranfill. Nashville: Sunday School Board, 1928.

Chapell, Bryan. *Christ-Centered Preaching: Redeeming the Expository Sermon*. 2nd ed. Grand Rapids: Baker Academic, 2005.

Lefever, Alan Jeffery. "The Life and Work of Benajah Harvey Carroll." PhD diss., Southwestern Baptist Theological Seminary, 1992.

Matthewson, Stephen D. "What Makes Textual Preaching Unique." Pages 412–17 in *The Art and Craft of Biblical Preaching: A Comprehensive Resource for Today's Communicators*. Edited by Haddon W. Robinson and Craig Brian Larson. Grand Rapids: Zondervan, 2005.

Mohler, R. Albert. *He Is Not Silent: Preaching in a Postmodern World*. Chicago: Moody, 2008.

Ray, Jeff D. *B. H. Carroll*. Nashville: The Sunday School Board, 1927.

_____. *Expository Preaching*. Grand Rapids: Zondervan, 1940.

Robinson, Haddon W. *Biblical Preaching: The Development and Delivery of Expository Messages*. 2nd ed. Grand Rapids: Baker Academic, 2001.

Robinson, Haddon W., and Craig Brian Larson, eds. *The Art and Craft of Biblical Preaching: A Comprehensive Resource for Today's Communicators*. Grand Rapids: Zondervan, 2005.

Robinson, Robert Jackson. "The Homiletical Method of Benajah Harvey Carroll." ThD diss., Southwestern Baptist Theological Seminary, November 1956.

Spivey, James T. "Benajah Harvey Carroll (1843–1914)." In *The Legacy of Southwestern: Writings That Shaped a Tradition*. Edited by James Leo Garrett. North Richland Hills, TX: Smithfield, 2002.

Vines, Jerry, and Jim Shaddix. *Power in the Pulpit: How to Prepare and Deliver Expository Sermons*. Chicago: Moody, 1999.

Billy Sunday
Prohibitionist Preacher and Baseball Evangelist

KRISTOPHER K. BARNETT

Billy Sunday (1862–1935) left a professional baseball career to become one of the greatest American evangelists of the twentieth century and reportedly addressed one hundred million people without the aid of public address systems, radio, or television. It is estimated that at least one million people walked through the "sawdust" to shake the hand of the evangelist. The context of his ministry was an America where people found themselves in a changing environment. The population was shifting from rural to urban areas, and the shift in population coincided with a shift in culture, values, and religious beliefs. Billy Sunday, a product and member of this shifting culture, spoke in his own unique and powerful manner to individuals facing a new world.

HISTORICAL BACKGROUND

In November 1862, the Civil War threatened to destroy the United States of America. William Ashley Sunday entered the world at this turbulent juncture in American history.[1] The hardship of war directly impacted the Sunday home.

---

1. An array of biographical material on Billy Sunday exists. Several volumes were produced as Sunday's ministerial career began to climb: Theodore Thomas Frankenberg, *The Spectacular Career of Rev. Billy Sunday: Famous Baseball Evangelist* (Columbus, OH: McLelland, 1913); Theodore Thomas Frankenberg, *Billy Sunday, His Tabernacles and Sawdust Trails* (Columbus, OH: Heer, 1917). The second volume essentially provides a reprint of the first with a few updated details. Although highly favorable to the evangelist, Frankenberg's volumes were not authorized by Sunday; Elijah P. Brown, *The Real Billy Sunday: The Life and Works of Rev. William Ashley Sunday, D. D., the Baseball Evangelist* (New York: Revell, 1914.) Brown's work was authorized by Sunday and was later sold in the tabernacle meetings; William T. Ellis, *Billy Sunday: The Man and His Message* (Philadelphia: Myers, 1914). Ellis's work was also authorized by Sunday; Lee Thomas, *The Billy Sunday Story* (Grand Rapids: Zondervan, 1961). After the evangelist's death, the family authorized Lee Thomas to tell Sunday's story. William McLoughlin, *Billy Sunday Was His Real Name* (Chicago: University of Chicago Press, 1955). McLoughlin offers a more critical evaluation of Sunday's finances during the periods of greatest success. He also points out reasons for the decline of Sunday's ministry; Lyle Dorsett, *Billy Sunday and the Redemption of Urban America* (Grand Rapids: Eerdmans, 1991). Despite his chronological distance from the subject, Dorsett's work offers unique insight due to the availability of The Sunday Papers. These papers were compiled from files located in the Sunday home. The Sunday Papers are located on twenty-nine reels of

Sunday's father died of disease in the Union army before Sunday was two months old.[2] The death of Sunday's father cast a shadow of difficulty on the family that shaped the future evangelist's formative years.

The financial burden of raising a family alone proved difficult for Mary Jane Sunday. She remarried, but that relationship ended in divorce. The single mother moved in with her parents, but the financial difficulties continued. Eventually, Mary Jane Sunday sent young Billy and his older brother Ed to a home for soldiers' orphans in Glenwood, Iowa.[3] Billy later described the parting: "One of the saddest memories of my life is the recollection of the grief I felt when leaving the old farm to go to Ames to take the train to Glenwood."[4] Although not ideal, the orphanage offered Sunday a Christian environment in which to grow. The children memorized Scripture and offered prayers nightly.[5] While in the orphanage, Sunday flourished. Young Billy noticed that he had exceptional athleticism, specifically foot speed.[6] This discovery would impact Sunday's initial career choice and pave the way for future ministry.

Billy Sunday left the orphanage at the age of fifteen. After a brief and unsuccessful return to the family farm, the young man struck out on his own, landing in Nevada, Iowa.[7] Influenced by a kind family who looked out for him, Sunday enrolled in high school where he excelled in oratory and athletics.[8] After high school, Billy Sunday moved to Marshalltown, Iowa. In Marshalltown, he worked for a furniture company and played baseball for the local team. One of the local ladies who enjoyed baseball happened to be the aunt of "Cap" Anson, the captain-manager of the Chicago White Sox. She encouraged Anson to give Billy an opportunity to try out for the team.[9]

In 1883, as "Cap" Anson prepared for the upcoming season, he noticed that

---

microfilm and include correspondences, sermon outlines, revival plans, and a variety of other materials. The Papers provide previously unavailable insight into Billy and Helen Sunday's lives. Their use makes Dorsett's work notable. Robert F. Martin, *Hero of the Heartland: Billy Sunday and the Transformation of American Society* (Bloomington: Indiana University Press, 2002). In *Hero of the Heartland*, Martin attempts to provide analysis of the evangelist's emotional and psychological makeup. Although occasionally overreaching, this work does provide fresh insight. Homer Rodeheaver, *Twenty Years with Billy Sunday* (Nashville: Cokesbury, 1936). The musician who worked with Sunday from 1909 until the evangelist's death provides insightful contributions about Sunday's life.

    2. Frankenberg, *The Spectacular Career*, 28. Sunday's name came from his father, who wrote to his pregnant wife from the battlefields of the Civil War encouraging her to name the baby William Ashley if it were a boy. Ellis, *The Man and His Message*, 448.

    3. Frankenberg, *The Spectacular Career*, 31.

    4. Ellis, *The Man and His Message*, 458.

    5. Thomas, *The Billy Sunday Story*, 25.

    6. Dorsett, *Redemption of Urban America*, 13.

    7. After an angry outburst from his grandfather, Billy left the farm. In Sunday's words, "He swore at us and it cut me to the heart." Ellis, *The Man and His Message*, 467–68.

    8. Martin, *Hero of the Heartland*, 7; Roger A. Bruns, *Preacher: Billy Sunday and Big-Time American Evangelism* (New York: Norton, 1992), 29–30.

    9. Ellis, *The Man and His Message*, 476–77.

his team needed speed. He remembered his aunt's description of the fellow in Marshalltown, so he sent a telegram to Billy Sunday offering a tryout.[10] This tryout would open the door to a new world for Billy Sunday. Sunday quit his job, bought a suit, borrowed some money for the trip, and traveled to Chicago, leaving Iowa for the first time.[11]

When Billy Sunday met the team, Anson proposed a race between Sunday and the fastest player on the team. Sunday accepted the proposal and won the race. Anson hired the Iowa farm boy on the spot.[12] Elijah Brown quotes Anson's assessment of Sunday's skills: "Sunday was, in my opinion, the strongest man in the profession on his feet, and could run the bases like a frightened deer. His greatest lack as a ball player was his inability to bat as well as some of the hard-hitting outfielders. He was a fast and brilliant fielder, a fine thrower, and once on first base he could steal more bases than any of his team mates [sic]."[13]

Billy Sunday played professional baseball from 1883 to 1890. He played for Anson in Chicago until 1888 when he was traded to the Pittsburgh Alleghenies. He played in Pittsburgh until the 1890 season when he was again traded, this time to Philadelphia. After the trade to Philadelphia, Sunday asked to be released from his contract. Billy was not tired of the sport, and his skills were increasing not diminishing.[14] But an event that had occurred while Sunday was playing for the White Stockings eventually led him to leave the game he loved.

In 1886, while Billy Sunday was playing for Chicago, he and his teammates went out to visit a local saloon.[15] After drinking, the ball players sat outside listening to the music coming from the Pacific Garden Mission. A former gambler and counterfeiter, Harry Monroe, invited the group to come and join the meeting. Although no other players expressed an interest, Sunday turned to his friends and exclaimed, "Boys, I bid the old life good-by."[16]

Sunday went to the meeting that night and for several more nights. Finally, one evening during Monroe's sermon, Sunday responded to the invitation and accepted Jesus Christ as his Savior. [17] Sarah Dunn Clarke, the wife of the mis-

10. Dorsett, *Redemption of Urban America*, 18.

11. Ellis, *The Man and His Message*, 478.

12. Ibid., 478–79. Anson's style and impact on the game led some to refer to the period between 1880 and 1892 as "The Age of 'Pop' Anson." Dorsett, *Redemption of Urban America*, 20.

13. Brown, *The Real Billy Sunday*, 34.

14. Martin, *Hero of the Heartland*, 37–43.

15. McLoughlin, *Sunday Was His Real Name*, 6.

16. Ellis, *The Man and His Message*, 486–87.

17. Dorsett, *Redemption of Urban America*, 27. Billy Sunday often spoke of his conversion from the pulpit, utilizing the circumstances to paint vivid word pictures for his audience. For example, in "The Devil's Boomerangs, or Hot Cakes Off the Griddle," Sunday told of his conversion and described how his buddies missed their opportunity to receive the salvation that he discovered that day. D. Bruce Lockerbie, *Billy Sunday* (Waco, TX: Word, 1965), 25–31.

sion's founder, counseled Sunday, helping him to understand the free gift of grace given by Jesus Christ.[18]

Sunday's conversion radically transformed his life. Sunday quit drinking alcohol and joined the Jefferson Park Presbyterian Church.[19] Sunday's popularity as a baseball player made his conversion important news. Soon churches and religious organizations sought Billy Sunday as a speaker. [20] These initial invitations eventually paved the way for Sunday's second career as a revivalist.

Sunday followed a gradual path to full-time ministry. After his conversion in 1886, Sunday continued to play baseball professionally while speaking and serving at the YMCA. Sunday found fulfillment in his work at the YMCA and considered leaving baseball as early as 1887.[21] However, Sunday stuck with baseball until 1891 when he received his release from the lucrative contract he had recently signed with Philadelphia.[22] Sunday turned from a position paying four hundred dollars a month to a position offering less than a hundred dollars a month as an assistant secretary at the YMCA.[23]

Billy Sunday worked diligently in his position at the YMCA for three years in the midst of a nationwide depression.[24] Then he discovered that evangelist J. Wilbur Chapman needed an advance man to prepare the way for his campaigns. Sunday accepted the position and learned from the famous Chapman for two-and-a-half years.[25] Chapman had a profound influence on Billy's ministry and later wrote the forward to one of Sunday's biographies.[26] Sunday served with Chapman until the elder evangelist decided to return to the pastorate, which left Sunday looking for a job.

At this important juncture, Billy received a call from Garner, Iowa.[27] The first call for the former baseball player to lead a revival came from Billy Sunday's home state. Sunday experienced success in Garner, which led to additional invitations.[28] Positive responses in other cities led to additional opportunities.

---

18. Brown, *The Real Billy Sunday,* 38–39.

19. His association with the Presbyterian Church was hardly theological in nature. It so happened that his sweetheart, Helen "Nell" Thompson, attended the Presbyterian Church. See Ellis, *The Man and His Message,* 487–88. Sunday is quoted as saying, "If she had been a Catholic, I would have been a Catholic—because I was hot on the trail of Nell." McLoughlin, *Sunday Was His Real Name,* 6. The couple married on September 5, 1888. Frankenberg, *The Spectacular Career,* 76. Nell would be an invaluable partner for Billy Sunday's life and ministry.

20. Dorsett, *Redemption of Urban America,* 29.

21. Martin, *Hero of the Heartland,* 41.

22. Dorsett, *Redemption of Urban America,* 40–42.

23. Martin, *Hero of the Heartland,* 42.

24. Ellis, *The Man and His Message,* 501.

25. Ibid., 502.

26. Frankenberg, *The Spectacular Career,* 7.

27. Ellis, *The Man and His Message,* 502.

28. Ibid.

Sunday was invited to stay longer at several places, but he declined because he didn't have any more sermons to preach.[29] From 1896 to 1907, Sunday preached sixty-six documented revivals. Sunday spoke in tents that he tied off himself.[30] Despite less than favorable conditions in these early meetings, Sunday experienced success.[31] One author refers to this formative period in Sunday's career as the "Kerosene Circuit."[32]

As Sunday's name spread, so did the attendance at his revivals. Increased attendance brought an increase in finances, which allowed Sunday to expand the ministry and hire assistants.[33] As the ministry grew, the campaigns began to change. After a snowstorm destroyed Sunday's tent in 1906, he started requiring that cities build a tabernacle to house the campaigns. The semi-permanent wooden tabernacles provided shelter from weather and ample space for crowds.[34]

Although not the first to use a tabernacle for a campaign, Sunday did it consistently. The use of the tabernacle revealed the level of popularity that Sunday's crusades attained.[35] The building of each tabernacle also created an opportunity for fellowship and interaction with Sunday's team and, in early years, Sunday himself worked with volunteers to build the structure. After completion of the building, the volunteers typically enjoyed a game of baseball to celebrate.[36] The dedication of the tabernacle served as a high point for publicity.[37]

The tabernacle led to two phrases commonly associated with Sunday's revivals: the "sawdust trail" and the "trail hitter." The sawdust trail described the aisles of the tabernacles. They were coated with sawdust to settle the dirt floors of the tabernacle. The phrase "sawdust trail" developed out of Sunday's 1910 campaign in Bellingham, Washington. When entering the woods, lumberjacks would carry bags of sawdust on their shoulders. The lumberjacks would leave a trail of sawdust behind to help them find their way out of the virgin forests. This provided an appropriate analogy for those who accepted Christ. Those who responded to Sunday's invitation were called "trail hitters."[38]

Billy Sunday's later urban crusades produced an incredible amount of trail hitters. The New York City crusade of 1917 produced 98,269 trail hitters.[39] Not

---

29. Ibid., 502–3.
30. Ibid., 503.
31. McLoughlin, *Sunday Was His Real Name*, 15–16.
32. Dorsett, *Redemption of Urban America*, 61.
33. McLoughlin, *Sunday Was His Real Name*, 16.
34. Dorsett, *Redemption of Urban America*, 64.
35. Ibid., 65.
36. The construction of the tabernacle often resembled a barn raising, with the entire community contributing. Ibid., 67.
37. McLoughlin, *Sunday Was His Real Name*, 71.
38. Dorsett, *Redemption of Urban America*, 91–92.
39. Ibid., 92. Additional statistics from Sunday's crusades in this era:

surprisingly, Billy Sunday was a household name in America. By 1914, Sunday was recognized in a poll by *American Magazine* as the eighth-greatest man in America.[40] Like Billy Graham was to contemporary Americans, Sunday was perceived as popular and influential. In January 1915, he made his first visit to Washington, DC, where he interacted with President Woodrow Wilson and Secretary of State William Jennings Bryan.[41] Sunday dined with mayors and congressmen, and John D. Rockefeller became a special friend.[42]

Billy Sunday capitalized on his popularity to build interest in his campaigns. Sunday accepted free publicity available from newspapers. The newspapers often printed copies of Sunday's sermons, thus spreading the evangelist's message and stirring interest in his campaigns. He never turned down an interview and maintained a cooperative relationship with the journalists assigned to cover his campaigns. Sunday never hesitated to pose for pictures. He even climbed to the top of hotel buildings to pose for pictures on the roof to ensure the best possible lighting.[43]

Following the New York campaign of 1917 and the Chicago campaign of 1918, Sunday's revivals began to slowly decrease in size.[44] This does not imply that Sunday's career suddenly dropped into oblivion. Quite the contrary, cities continued to call for Billy Sunday.[45] However, the prominence and attendance of the revivals continued to ebb.

Much of the decline of Billy Sunday's ministry following World War I can be attributed to a loss in credibility. President Hoover, whom Sunday backed strongly, proved unsuccessful in his efforts in the White House.[46] In addition, the close of World War I left many Americans disillusioned. The victory was bittersweet, and many felt unsatisfied with the terms of peace.[47] Sunday had

City	Year	Trail Hitters
Philadelphia	1915	41,724
Syracuse	1915	21,155
Kansas City	1916	25,646
Detroit	1916	27,109
Boston	1917	64,484
Buffalo	1917	38,853

Some, like McLoughlin, question the credibility of these figures and of the long-term effects on those who walked the trail. McLoughlin, *Sunday Was His Real Name*, 197–222. However, the sheer volume of individuals making decisions reveals Sunday's popularity.

40. McLoughlin, *Sunday Was His Real Name*, 49.

41. Ibid., 57.

42. Dorsett, *Redemption of Urban America*, 93–94.

43. Rodeheaver, *Twenty Years,* 102–3.

44. Dorsett, *Redemption of Urban America*, 128.

45. Ellis, *The Man and His Message*, 502.

46. Dorsett, *Redemption of Urban America*, 149–50.

47. David T. Morgan, "The revivalist as patriot: Billy Sunday and World War I," *Journal of Presbyterian History* 51 (1973): 215.

strongly backed the war effort and promised positive results that did not come to fruition.

Problems in the evangelist's home also impacted public perception.[48] His sons chose rebellious paths, and the actions of his children damaged Sunday's credibility.[49] As the shifting culture continued to change, Billy Sunday's value system lost credibility. Sunday had benefited from a broad acceptance of a Midwestern mentality. As Americans embraced modernity, the appeal of Sunday's "old-time religion" diminished. Those who had once seen Sunday as a welcome connection to their rural roots began to perceive Sunday as an unnecessary reminder of their past.[50]

After World War I, Sunday lost his most bitter enemy. Sunday had risen in popularity while preaching against alcohol, but Prohibition removed Sunday's favorite sparring partner.[51] After Prohibition passed, Sunday changed the aim of his ire to immigrants, bootleggers, communism, and modernity.[52] Unfortunately for Sunday, his new sparring partners attracted less public interest.

The shifting culture also offered competition to Sunday's brand of revivalism. Other forms of entertainment such as radio, television, and organized sports offered people new diversions.[53] The rise in prominence of the national pastime had given Billy Sunday a start. Ironically, the sport's continued rise coincided with the evangelist's decline.

Billy Sunday continued to preach until his death in 1935. Sunday's funeral service was held in Chicago at Moody Memorial Church. The four-thousand-seat sanctuary was full, with many standing.[54] The service harkened back to the old tabernacle days. The people sang and celebrated the life of Billy Sunday as numerous members of the Sunday party spoke with great affection about the "boss." In a manner that would have pleased the baseball evangelist, the congregation received an appeal to accept Christ as their Savior.[55] In his book, Rodeheaver reported, "I believe Mr. Sunday was the greatest evangelist since the Apostle Paul, and he could utter the same words: 'I spend and am spent.'"[56]

---

48. Martin, *Hero of the Heartland*, 122–23.
49. Dorsett, *Redemption of Urban America*, 126. In 1921, George left his wife and family for another woman. Billy Jr., who was serving as a pianist in the revival meetings, was caught in a compromising situation with a female companion.
50. Martin, *Hero of the Heartland*, 131.
51. McLoughlin, *Sunday Was His Real Name*, 260.
52. Ibid., 148, 276; Martin, *Hero of the Heartland*, 133.
53. McLoughlin, *Sunday Was His Real Name*, 260.
54. Lockerbie, *Billy Sunday*, 61.
55. Thomas, *The Billy Sunday Story*, 210.
56. Rodeheaver, *Twenty Years*, 145.

THEOLOGY OF PREACHING

An analysis of Billy Sunday's theology for preaching must begin by acknowledging the baseball evangelist's seeming disinterest in theology. Sunday often quipped, "I don't know any more about theology than a jack-rabbit does about ping-pong, but I'm on the way to glory."[57] He also asserted, "I have never seen a minister who preached doctrines and creeds and evolution and all such things who had any real concern for the souls of his people."[58] Similarly, Sunday predicted, "When some of the preachers stop preaching about the New Jerusalem and start preaching against the whisky crowd and the red-light district in these cities something is going to happen."[59]

Sunday's apparent aversion to theology requires explanation and contextualization. First, Sunday's move from baseball player to evangelist left little room for formal, theological education. A lack of education would immediately create natural limitations on theological awareness and interest. Second, the evangelist's popularity coincided with theological liberalism. Therefore, his disdain for theology was specifically an aversion to liberal, academic theology. Sunday preferred practical theology grounded in common sense. "Religion needs a baptism of horse sense. That is just pure horse sense."[60] He used horse sense arguments to undercut the spread of liberal views:

> I have read a great deal—not everything, mind you, for a man would go crazy if he tried to read everything—but I have read a great deal that has been written against the atonement from the infidel standpoint-Voltaire, Huxley, Spencer, Diderot, Bradlaugh, Paine, on down to Bob Ingersoll— and I have never found an argument that would stand the test of common sense and common reasoning. And if anyone tells me he has tossed on the scrap heap the plan of atonement by blood, I say, "What have you to offer that is better?" and until he can show me something that is better I'll nail my hopes to the cross.[61]

Christological Focus

As the previous quote implies, Billy Sunday centered his theology in Christ's atoning work on the cross.

---

57. Billy Sunday, "Old Time Religion," https://www.biblebelievers.com/billy_sunday/sun8.html.
58. Billy Sunday, "Gethsemane," https://www.biblebelievers.com/billy_sunday/sun16.html.
59. Billy Sunday, "The Devil's Boomerang," https://www.biblebelievers.com/billy_sunday/sun18.html.
60. Billy Sunday, "The Need for Revivals," https://www.biblebelievers.com/billy_sunday/sun2.html.
61. Billy Sunday, "Atonement Through the Blood of Jesus," https://www.biblebelievers.com/billy_sunday/sun4.html.

When someone tells you that your religion is a bloody religion and the Bible is a bloody book, tell them yes, Christianity is a bloody religion; the gospel is a bloody gospel; the Bible is a bloody book; the plan of redemption is bloody. It is. You take the blood of Jesus Christ out of Christianity and that book isn't worth the paper it is written on. It would be worth no more than your body with the blood taken out. Take the blood of Jesus Christ out and it would be a meaningless jargon and jumble of words.[62]

The evangelist warned that vague preaching that omitted Christ's redemptive actions would yield no results. "Why these meager results? Why the expenditure of so much energy and time and money? It is because there is not a definite effort put forth to persuade a definite person to accept a definite Saviour at a definite time—and that time is NOW."[63] Sunday preached with certainty that everyone needed Christ. "It's Jesus Christ or nothing for every sinner on God's earth."[64] The evangelist believed the simple gospel trumped liberal theology and even his own revival practices. "Nobody is kept out of heaven because he does not understand theology. It isn't theology that saves, but Christ; it is not the sawdust trail that saves, but Christ in the motive that makes you hit the trail."[65] Some critics asserted that this approach oversimplified the faith. For example, when Sunday encouraged unemployed workers to simply get saved and get jobs, critics asserted that this wasn't enough; they needed more help.[66] Despite criticisms and cultural movement toward a social gospel, Sunday remained committed to a conservative, biblical faith rooted in a strong Christology.[67] Billy Sunday believed that faith in Christ was the answer to everything. He challenged the lost to be saved and the converted to live out their faith.[68]

Moralistic Tendencies

Sunday believed that Christ saved sinners, but he also believed that converted sinners had a responsibility to confront sin. The fiery evangelist committed himself to battle sin. He noted: "I'm against sin. I'll kick it as long as I've got a foot, and I'll fight it as long as I've got a fist. I'll butt it as long as I've got a head. I'll bite it as long as I've got a tooth. And when I'm old and fistless and

---

62. Ibid.
63. Billy Sunday, "He that Winneth Souls is Wise," https://www.biblebelievers.com/billy_sunday/sun3.html.
64. Sunday, "Atonement Through the Blood of Jesus."
65. Sunday, "Old Time Religion."
66. McLoughlin, *Sunday Was His Real Name*, 135, 138.
67. Dorsett, *Redemption of Urban America*, 57, 76.
68. Ibid., 70–71.

footless and toothless, I'll gum it till I go home to Glory and it goes home to perdition!"[69]

He expected his listeners to join that battle as well. Sunday attacked those who hid behind human nature as an excuse to continue in their sinful ways. Backsliders often drew harsh rebukes from Billy Sunday.[70]

In his fight against sin, Sunday favored one opponent above all the rest. Ellis asserts that Billy was "happiest and most successful" when attacking the liquor industry.[71] The evangelist demanded that his audiences join his crusade against the liquor industry. "When the Church of God stops voting for the saloon, the saloon will go to hell. When the members stop having cards in their homes, there won't be so many black-legged gamblers in the world. This is the truth. You can't sit around and fold your arms and let God run this business; you have been doing that too long here."[72] Billy campaigned consistently for Prohibition, living to see Prohibition enacted and later repealed.[73]

The strong emphasis on sin often gave the evangelist's preaching a moralistic tone. The evangelist claimed a high view of Scripture. "I believe the Bible is the word of God from cover to cover. I believe that the man who magnifies the word of God in his preaching is the man whom God will honor."[74] However, at times the moralistic emphasis of Sunday's preaching overshadowed the biblical under-pinnings. For example, by 1905, his Prohibition sermon, "Get on the Water Wagon," replaced his sermon "Inspiration of the Bible" as his primary message.[75]

Sunday's tendency toward moralism also threatened to overshadow the christological focus by implying that right living could merit salvation. For example, Sunday asserts, "Keep the devil out of the boys and girls and he will get out of the world. The old sinners will die off if we keep the young ones clean."[76] Perhaps more disconcerting, Sunday also declares, "If every man lived right today, no boy would go to hell tomorrow."[77] The implied effectiveness of right living is undeniable in that statement. Fortunately, Sunday's statements and sermons typically occurred in the context of a multi-night revival. Therefore, listeners likely received clear christological assertions as a framework for poten-tially moralizing messages.

69. Lockerbie, *Billy Sunday,* 63.

70. Billy Sunday, "Backsliding," https://www.biblebelievers.com/billy_sunday/sun5.html.

71. Ellis, *The Man and His Message,* 80.

72. Sunday, "The Need for Revivals."

73. Ellis, *The Man and His Message,* 81. Sunday's revivals often resulted in saloon closings.

74. Sunday, "Old Time Religion."

75. McLoughlin, *Sunday Was His Real Name,* 31.

76. Billy Sunday, "Motherhood," https://www.biblebelievers.com/billy_sunday/sun17.html.

77. Billy Sunday, "Show Thyself a Man," https://www.biblebelievers.com/billy_sunday/sun15.html.

METHODOLOGY FOR PREACHING

Billy Sunday's unique and creative style of preaching contributed greatly to the evangelist's success. His mentor, Wilbur Chapman, helped Sunday develop a preaching style. Sunday learned from his mentor but wisely developed his own style to fit his temperament and skills.[78] Although he did not receive a high school diploma, the education level Sunday received likely exceeded that of the average American.[79] Billy Sunday possessed a strong work ethic that translated into positive study skills. Before his career as an evangelist, Sunday's baseball teammates reported that he often spent the entire trip buried in his Bible. He would mouth the words of Scripture that he read and occasionally take notes in a notebook.[80] Sunday continued this study habit as he traveled from town to town for his revivals.[81] Rodeheaver pointed out that Sunday possessed an "unreserved consecration to the task of preaching."[82] He asserted, "As long as I knew him he gave to the work of preaching the Gospel every ounce of physical, mental, and spiritual energy."[83] This "unreserved consecration" applied to sermon delivery as well as sermon development.

Audiences marveled at the evangelist's energetic sermon delivery. He ran and jumped across the platform. He pounded the pulpit or occasionally even stood on it. The chair on the platform received similar vicious treatment.[84] Sunday's constant motion caused the evangelist to perspire. As his temperature rose, and to heighten the effect of his sermon, Sunday would often pull off the outer layers of his clothing.[85] Sunday's "acrobatics" often receive attention when discussing the evangelist's preaching style. However, Billy Sunday's effectiveness in preaching exceeded his unconventional delivery. The baseball evangelist possessed the mysterious quality often labeled "charisma." Rodeheaver described it this way: "He possessed an enormous voltage of that curious, mysterious power which is difficult to name. Sometimes it is called magnetism, sometimes personality. At any rate, he could project it at will, and it seemed to color and brighten and vivify anything he had to say. Even though one may have heard a sermon again and again, there was never lacking that peculiar thrill as you listened to his preaching."[86]

---

78. Dorsett, *Redemption of Urban America*, 54.
79. Ibid., 14.
80. Bruns, *Preacher: Billy Sunday*, 54.
81. Dorsett, *Redemption of Urban America*, 62.
82. Ibid., 10.
83. Rodeheaver, *Twenty Years*, 11.
84. McLoughlin, *Sunday Was His Real Name*, 159–60.
85. Ibid., 161.
86. Rodeheaver, *Twenty Years*, 18.

Sunday established rapport with his audience by making them feel as though he were speaking directly to them.[87] Similar life experiences and expectations enabled Sunday to communicate with sincerity, which Rodeheaver ranked as Sunday's strongest appeal.[88] The evangelist's word selection also accentuated his sincerity. Sunday's sermons contained slang expressions. He rationalized his use of slang by noting that he employed the tactics necessary to reach the lost. By his estimate, many of the lost spoke only in obscenity, profanity, and slang. Sunday concluded that it was better for him to use slang than the other two.[89] By using the contemporary jargon, Sunday spoke words that ninety-nine percent of the congregation understood.[90]

Another aspect of Sunday's charisma appeared in his sermon structure. His sermons progressed in a logical fashion. Next to sincerity, Rodeheaver saw Sunday's reasonableness as his greatest asset. His sermons rested on "sound, homely reason."[91] The message made sense in the mind of the hearer. In order to accentuate his logic, Sunday often used statistics. Culturally, people appreciated these appeals to expertise.[92] Although his sermons typically lasted an hour, he kept the audience's attention by alternating between serious and lighter subjects.[93] Lighter subjects typically included humor. Rodeheaver described Sunday's humor as infectious.[94] He would employ witty one-liners to get laughs from his audience and gain access to their hearts and minds.[95]

If logic, statistics, and humor did not convince the congregation, Sunday would eagerly resort to stories.[96] Sunday masterfully utilized stories as illustrations. For example, Rodeheaver admired Sunday's ability to bring the story of David and Goliath to life. "For twenty years, he made me hear anew the whistle of that pebble and the impact."[97] Sunday would also use contemporary illustrations to complete his arguments and emphasize his points.[98] For example, at the conclusion of a sermon on alcohol, Billy told the heart-wrenching story of some children whose drunken father murdered their mother. The evangelist pulled on

87. McLoughlin, *Sunday Was His Real Name*, 155. Sunday's ability to connect with people might have developed from his formative years growing up in the orphanage. Also, traveling with the baseball team allowed him to see a variety of people in multiple places. Frankenberg, *The Spectacular Career*, 42–44.

88. Rodeheaver, *Twenty Years*, 22.

89. McLoughlin, *Sunday Was His Real Name*, 164.

90. Rodeheaver, *Twenty Years*, 22.

91. Ibid., 18.

92. Martin, *Hero of the Heartland*, 113.

93. Rodeheaver, *Twenty Years*, 20.

94. Ibid.

95. Frankenberg, *The Spectacular Career*, 33.

96. Ibid.

97. Rodeheaver, *Twenty Years*, 24.

98. Ibid., 47.

the heartstrings of his listeners as he told of the children kissing their father after he had hung himself.[99]

CONTRIBUTIONS TO PREACHING

Billy Sunday, the baseball evangelist, impacted millions of trail hitters through his evangelistic crusades of the early twentieth century. His spectacular ministry also impacted the field of preaching in general and future preachers specifically. Among Sunday's many contributions, this section will highlight the most important: Sunday's place in the chain of revivalists, Sunday's individualized delivery style, and the impact of cultural context on the preacher's ministry.

Billy Sunday's historical contributions appear in light of the tradition of revivalism in America. Some might categorize Sunday as just another evangelist. While this dismissive statement has a degree of accuracy, it overlooks Sunday's value as a bridge and innovative contributor to this field. Billy Sunday faithfully played his part as a connection between the evangelists of the nineteenth century and those of the twentieth century. Sunday followed in the footsteps of notable evangelists like D. L. Moody and J. Wilbur Chapman. His ministry also offered a tangible link to future evangelists like Mordecai Ham and Billy Graham. He learned from his predecessors and added his own unique contributions to evangelistic crusades. Sunday offered a model of efficiency in staffing and structure that future revivalists would imitate. He increased the scope and scale of evangelistic crusades with the use of tabernacles and the monumental number of trail hitters in his urban crusades. The community-wide efforts of the Sunday party sound strikingly familiar to the later efforts of the Billy Graham Evangelistic Association. Billy Sunday contributed to the field of preaching by carrying on an existing tradition while simultaneously advancing that tradition through unique innovations.

Sunday's unique, acrobatic style might lead to erroneous conclusions about the evangelist's impact on preaching. Even casual students of preaching recall Billy Sunday's unique style. This style drew criticism from some contemporaries, who called him a "religious huckster" and a "side-show spectacle."[100] Contemporary analysis of Sunday might conclude that Sunday opened the proverbial floodgates to questionable pulpit antics. While this line of thought might have some validity, a closer look reveals the true value in this component of Sunday's preaching, which must be analyzed in the appropriate context. Sunday's unique, animated preaching style contributes to the field of preaching, not by opening a

99. Lockerbie, *Billy Sunday*, 40.
100. Lockerbie, *Billy Sunday*, 1.

Pandora's box of all sorts of reckless antics in the pulpit. Rather, Sunday's unique pulpit persona reminds preachers of the value in finding and utilizing personal pulpit strengths. All preachers must find and cultivate their own pulpit style and that style should serve the important cause of emphasizing and clarifying the biblical message at all costs.

The theatrics of Sunday's preaching served to capture the imagination of audiences across the country. Sunday gained an audience at a time when many refused to listen. Obviously, pragmatic evaluation can yield deceptive results. However, it is important to consider why this style worked for the evangelist. It worked for Sunday because the theatrics seemed natural to the baseball player turned evangelist. The charismatic, larger-than-life persona fit the evangelist's character. Sunday did not possess formal theological training, so passion was the evangelist's primary asset. Running the bases, sliding into home, and pounding the pulpit helped the evangelist communicate his natural passion for the gospel, and it conformed to his personality and past experience. Sunday's delivery style would not work for all preachers. For many, if not most preachers, this approach would distract from the substance of the message. However, Sunday employed these methods as a means of accentuating his personal pulpit strengths.

Cultural context played an enormous role in Sunday's success. Many who lived in urban America at the turn of the century had recently transplanted from the country. The nation was shifting from an agrarian society to a more industrial society. The farmers' children who came to the city discovered that jobs in an office or a factory did not always provide personal satisfaction.[101] As some faced the disappointment of this cultural shift, they developed a nostalgic longing for the past. As one biographer states, "Sunday offered Americans of the twentieth century the ideology of the nineteenth century."[102]

Americans at the turn of the century appreciated and enjoyed a success story. They liked to hear of those who had scaled the ladder of success. Billy Sunday fit the bill. From humble beginnings at an orphanage in Iowa, Sunday gained nationwide acclaim.[103] In fact, Sunday had already realized the American dream once in his baseball career. His success as an evangelist marked Sunday's second climb up the ladder.[104] Sunday's diverse success captivated the imagination and drew attention.

The American church in the early twentieth century needed a jolt. The changing culture had negatively impacted the church in general, specifically the

---

101. McLoughlin, *Sunday Was His Real Name*, 120.
102. Ibid., 35.
103. Martin, *Hero of the Heartland*, 49.
104. Lockerbie, *Billy Sunday*, 2.

urban church. The impact of the previous evangelists, Chapman and Moody, was waning.[105] By 1917, less than one third of the population claimed church membership.[106] Protestant churches in the cities struggled with low attendance.[107] Urban pastors looked for a new evangelistic leader to stir their sleepy congregations.[108] They discovered him in Billy Sunday.

Billy Sunday's success and later decline point to the impact of cultural context on effective preaching ministry. Sunday's ministry coincided with the American shift from rural to urban values. Sunday's personal experiences placed him in a position to speak into the shifting culture. The evangelist understood his audience and connected with them through his words and actions. Sunday's astute cultural awareness enabled the evangelist to speak with passion on the cultural issues of the day: politics, prohibition, and morality. Of course, as noted above, this cultural connection also played a part in Sunday's later decline when his political positions failed to bring about the results he had predicted.

The impact of culture on Sunday's ministry offers a mixed note of encouragement and warning. Preachers must understand the cultural climate in which they preach, and they must carefully exegete Scripture in light of the surrounding climate. Preachers should help their congregations understand politics in light of the Bible. However, as seen in the example from Sunday's ministry, preachers must be cautious when preaching on political issues that they do not wed their preaching ministry to political parties or platforms to the extent that political positions outshine the good news of the gospel. For example, Sunday concentrated a great deal of attention on the dangers of alcohol, pushing passionately for Prohibition. Sunday provides a positive example by addressing an important social issue. However, at times it seems that Sunday's attack on alcohol overshadowed the evangelist's emphasis on the gospel. Like Sunday, contemporary pastors address a culture with declining moral values. This can easily lead pastors to focus on the immorality that they oppose at the exclusion of the gospel they propose. Thoughtful pastors should strive to be known more for what they are for (the gospel), than for what they are against (immorality).

CONCLUSION

The transition from the nineteenth to the twentieth century was bumpy in America. The times produced several larger-than-life characters. Among the

---

105. McLoughlin, *Sunday Was His Real Name*, 193.
106. Ibid., 151.
107. Dorsett, *Redemption of Urban America*, 112.
108. McLoughlin, *Sunday Was His Real Name*, 47.

greats like Teddy Roosevelt, John D. Rockefeller, and P. T. Barnum, emerged an Iowa farm boy named Billy Sunday.

Billy Sunday emerged from one world to enter another. Sunday moved from the country to the city just as an entire nation attempted to make the same journey. The path of Billy Sunday collided with the path of the nation and the two walked together. Sunday stood as the guide along the journey, warning people of the dangers along the way. The nation listened for a period of time. Billy Sunday led the nation down the path, but then the two parted ways. The nation became comfortable with the values of the city, but Billy Sunday never did. Sunday chose instead to live his life as he encouraged others to do: "Live the Christian life; men will admire you, women will respect you, little children will love you, and God will crown your life with success. And when the twilight of your life mingles with the purpling dawn of eternity, men will speak your name with honor and baptize your grave with tears when God attunes for you the evening chimes of life."[109]

Sermon Excerpt
Atonement through the Blood of Jesus[110]

Jesus gave his life on the cross for any who will believe. We're not redeemed by silver or gold. Jesus paid for it with his blood (1 Peter 1:18). When some one tells you that your religion is a bloody religion and the Bible is a bloody book, tell them yes, Christianity is a bloody religion; the gospel is a bloody gospel; the Bible is a bloody book; the plan of redemption is bloody. It is. You take the blood of Jesus Christ out of Christianity and that book isn't worth the paper it is written on. It would be worth no more than your body with the blood taken out. Take the blood of Jesus Christ out and it would be a meaningless jargon and jumble of words.

If it weren't for the atoning blood you might as well rip the roofs off the churches and burn them down. They aren't worth anything. But as long as the blood is on the mercy seat (Lev. 16:14), the sinner can return, and by no other way. There is nothing else. It stands for the redemption. You are not redeemed by silver or gold, but by the blood of Jesus Christ.

---

109. Ellis, *The Man and His Message*, 515.
110. Sunday, "Atonement through the Blood of Jesus."

Though a man says to read good books, do good deeds, live a good life and you'll be saved, you'll be damned. That's what you will. All the books in the world won't keep you out of hell without the atoning blood of Jesus Christ. It's Jesus Christ or nothing for every sinner on God's earth.

Without it not a sinner will ever be saved. Jesus has paid for your sins with his blood. The doctrine of universal salvation is a lie. I wish every one would be saved, but they won't. You will never be saved if you reject the blood.

I remember when I was in the Y.M.C.A. in Chicago I was going down Madison Street and had just crossed Dearborn Street when I saw a newsboy with a young sparrow in his hand. I said: "Let that little bird go."

He said, "Aw, g'wan with you, you big mutt."

I said, "I'll give you a penny for it," and he answered, "Not on your tintype."

"I'll give you a nickel for it," and he answered, "Boss, I'm from Missouri; come across with the dough."

I offered it to him, but he said, "Give it to that guy there," and I gave it to the boy he indicated and took the sparrow.

I held it for a moment and then it fluttered and struggled and finally reached the window ledge in a second story across the street. And other birds fluttered around over my head and seemed to say in bird language, "Thank you, Bill."

The kid looked at me in wonder and said: "Say, boss, why didn't you chuck that nickel in the sewer?"

I told him that he was just like that bird. He was in the grip of the devil, and the devil was too strong for him just as he was too strong for the sparrow, and just as I could do with the sparrow what I wanted to, after I had paid for it, because it was mine. God paid a price for him far greater than I had for the sparrow, for he had paid it with the blood of his Son, and he wanted to set him free. ♦

BIBLIOGRAPHY

Bruns, Roger A. *Preacher: Billy Sunday and Big-Time American Evangelism.* New York: Norton, 1992.
Brown, Elijah P. *The Real Billy Sunday: The Life and Works of Rev. William Ashley Sunday, D.D. The Baseball Evangelist.* New York: Revell, 1914.
Dorsett, Lyle W. *Billy Sunday and the Redemption of Urban America.* Grand Rapids: Eerdmans, 1991.
Ellis, William T. *Billy Sunday: The Man and His Message.* Philadelphia: Myers, 1914.
Frankenberg, Theodore Thomas. *The Spectacular Career of Rev. Billy Sunday: Famous Baseball Evangelist.* Columbus, OH: McLelland, 1913.

_____. *Billy Sunday, His Tabernacles and Sawdust Trails.* Columbus, OH: Heer, 1917.

Graham, Billy. *Just As I Am: The Autobiography of Billy Graham.* San Francisco: Harper, 1997.

Lockerbie, D. Bruce. *Billy Sunday.* Waco, TX: Word, 1965.

Martin, Robert F. *Hero of the Heartland: Billy Sunday and the Transformation of American Society.* Bloomington: Indiana University Press, 2002.

McLoughlin, William. *Billy Sunday Was His Real Name.* Chicago: University of Chicago Press, 1955.

Morgan, David T. "The revivalist as patriot: Billy Sunday and World War I." *Journal of Presbyterian History* 51 (1973): 199–215.

Rodeheaver, Homer. *Twenty Years with Billy Sunday.* Nashville: Cokesbury, 1936.

Sunday, Billy. "Atonement Through the Blood of Jesus." https://www.biblebelievers.com/billy_sunday/sun4.html.

_____. "Backsliding." https://www.biblebelievers.com/billy_sunday/sun5.html.

_____. "The Devil's Boomerang." https://www.biblebelievers.com/billy_sunday/sun18.html.

_____. "Gethsemane." https://www.biblebelievers.com/billy_sunday/sun16.html.

_____. "He That Winneth Souls Is Wise." https://www.biblebelievers.com/billy_sunday/sun3.html.

_____. "Motherhood." https://www.biblebelievers.com/billy_sunday/sun17.html.

_____. "The Need for Revivals." https://www.biblebelievers.com/billy_sunday/sun2.html.

_____. "Old Time Religion." https://www.biblebelievers.com/billy_sunday/sun8.html.

_____. "Show Thyself a Man" https://www.biblebelievers.com/billy_sunday/sun15.html.

_____. "Why Delay Your Real Conversion?" https://www.biblebelievers.com/billy_sunday/sun6.html.

Thomas, Lee. *The Billy Sunday Story.* Grand Rapids: Zondervan, 1961.

PART Three

Twentieth-Century European Preaching

While the nineteenth century ended with increasing modernization and secularization, the twentieth century sought full implementation of what had been started. The technological advances of the century changed the world in ways that, in the previous century, would have been unimaginable. The continued secularization of the continent proffered a world that would be free of the superstitions and traditions that had engulfed previous generations in political and religious strife. What had begun with such promise for continental peace was soon shattered by World War I. Even as that war was billed "The War to End All Wars," the very seeds of the World War II were embedded in the conditions of the Peace Treaty of Versailles. Ideologies such as fascism, Nazism, communism, and nationalism offered preferred interpretations of social ordering that proved incompatible and ultimately destructive of promised utopias.

The speed of change in this century was no less unsettling than the intellectual changes. The chief claim of modernity was the certainty and discoverability of absolutes. A shift began to take shape philosophically that had been in the making for some time. Intellectual elites denied the possibility of objective truth due to their historical localization. Instead of Truth, there are truths. Each truth is culturally conditioned and dependent on a variety of factors that are dependent on the individual or group.

As has always been the case, Christianity was challenged to respond to the situation. Christians in Europe saw the rise and the demise of a dizzying array of theological interpretations (i.e., neoorthodoxy, demythologization, eschatological theology, theology of hope, and existential theology) that claimed to be faithful to the tradition and at the same time more applicable to the contemporary situation. There were several voices that aimed to bring clarity.

One such voice is **Karl Barth** (1886–1968). Without question, Barth stands as one of the most influential theologians of the twentieth century. Barth's theology, specifically his *Church Dogmatics*, was produced under the shadow of the pulpit. While there are differing opinions regarding Barth's theology, Barth as a preacher offers us a robust view of God and his Word. Standing on the homiletical shoulders of Barth, the preacher can abandon their timid proclamations of and about God. **Dietrich Bonhoeffer** (1906–1945) is another voice that many will know from his book *The Cost of Discipleship*, his role in the assassination attempt on Hitler, and his subsequent execution. Maybe not as well-known are his contributions to the field of preaching. Bonhoeffer had a very developed Christology in his preaching that resisted a quiet and placid faith. Rather, his preaching demanded an active commitment and vibrant faith response to the Word.

D. Martyn Lloyd-Jones (1899–1981) stands as a monumental figure in the history of expositional preaching. His book *Preaching and Preachers* is a must-read for anyone who takes seriously the practice of preaching. His preaching focused on sinners and their need for salvation. The need of sinners for salvation was one of great urgency and this stress became a central component of Lloyd-Jones's preaching. It also stands as a lasting reminder that preaching meets the most urgent need of the church. **John Stott** (1921–2011), in his book *Between Two Worlds*, writes that preaching is not mastering certain techniques, but rather the preacher being mastered by certain convictions. Chief among those convictions of the preacher, in Stott's view, is when the preacher speaks, Christ speaks. Here Stott echoes Charles Simeon, who was a major influence on Stott. The preacher is the ambassador of Christ, and as ambassadors represent their governments and speak for the government, so the speech of the preacher is the speech of Christ.

Karl Barth
Preaching Christ

WILLIAM H. WILLIMON

The enduring value of Karl Barth (1886–1968) for preachers is that he was a theologian. Barth never took his eyes off the central subject of truly Christian preaching—the one God who meets us as Father, Son, and Holy Spirit; God who elects to be God for us and elects us to be for God. Through a lifetime of preaching, theological reflection, and writing, Barth consistently allowed the triune God who is revealed in Scripture to govern his thought. Reading Barth's sermons reminds contemporary preachers of the joy of talking about this God rather than speaking of ourselves, our assorted idols, or our congregations. Shortly before his death, Karl Barth said in a radio broadcast: "My whole theology, you see, is fundamentally a theology for parsons. It grew out of my own situation when I had to teach and preach and counsel a little."[1]

HISTORICAL BACKGROUND

Though he lived a full, engaged life, Barth would be quick to add that his life was not as interesting as what God revealed to Karl Barth about God. Like John the Baptist in Matthis Grünewald's *Crucifixion* (his favorite painting), Barth kept pointing, in all his sermons, to the relentlessly self-revealing God who speaks to us in Jesus Christ, through the power of the Holy Spirit.[2] Barth said the preacher is John the Baptist as he is depicted in the *Crucifixion*; Baptist's long, bony finger is the sermon pointing to God on a cross.

After a brilliant run as a seminary student, Barth was an assistant at Calvin's old pulpit in Basel; then he was called to the dreary Swiss village of Safenwil (population 1,625) in the Aargau in 1911, arriving two years before electricity.[3]

---

1. Karl Barth, *Letzte Zeugnisse* (Zurich: EVZ-Verlag, 1969), 19.
2. This chapter is a distillation of William H. Willimon, *Conversations with Barth on Preaching*, (Nashville: Abingdon, 2006).
3. The history of Barth as a young preacher, along with a number of his early sermons, can be found in William H. Willimon, *The Early Preaching of Karl Barth: Fourteen Sermons with Commentary*, trans. John E. Wilson (Louisville: Westminster John Knox, 2009).

Preaching made the young pastor miserable. Though he was the son of a pietist pastor, he had few opportunities to preach. Now he trudged to church every Sunday "with a sermon in [his] head, good or bad . . . behind the dung-cart."[4]

THEOLOGY OF PREACHING

His inaugural sermon was on John 14:24, in which he told his church, "I am not speaking to you of God because I am a pastor. I am a pastor because I *must* speak of God, if I am to remain true to myself."[5] That sermon began a decade of Safenwil sermons. Barth found preaching to be intellectually demanding work. Every sermon was written "painstakingly and down to the last detail,"[6] sometimes as if with "terrible birth-pangs." One sermon was begun and ended five times before it was finally written. Though he always produced a manuscript, he did not read his sermons but delivered them in his lively, energetic, highly modulated style. Though he experienced preaching as "a limitless problem," "impossible from the start," Barth said later that his grand theological achievement, his massive *Church Dogmatics,* came out of the crucible of Sunday-after-Sunday sermons hammered on the hard, demanding, anvil of the pulpit.[7]

Throughout his theological career, he spoke of preaching as an impossible possibility. There are too many reasons having to do with the nature of human sinfulness (particularly our propensity toward idolatry), and also with the nature of a crucified, resurrected God, that preclude a human being from standing up and saying anything for God. And yet, by the grace of God, it is possible to preach because God in Christ is relentlessly revealing, communicative, and determined to be in relationship with his creatures.

As for the Safenwil congregation's reception of these sermons, Barth admitted that he demanded great intellectual effort from his listeners. His sermons tended be long, even for his day. He always took a biblical text, focusing almost exclusively on that text, often only a verse or two. When his congregation resisted the forced diet of enthusiastic Socialism and incipient existentialism that permeated these early sermons, Barth bluntly snapped, "If I wanted to be liked, I would keep quiet."[8]

On the first day of August 1914, World War I erupted. Barth read a newspaper manifesto, signed by ninety-three German intellectuals, including "all [his]

---

4. Ibid., x.
5. Ibid.
6. Ibid., xi.
7. Eberhard Busch, *Karl Barth: His Life from Letters and Autobiographical Texts,* trans. John Bowden (Grand Rapids: Eerdmans, 1975), 75–77.
8. Ibid., xii.

German teachers," praising the war and urging everyone to rally behind the kaiser. Jolted, Barth said that "the teaching of all [his] theological masters in Germany"[9] was suspect. The failure of their theology to give them the resources to withstand the ideology of German nationalism and the evil of war led the young pastor to question all the "exegesis, ethics, dogmatics, and preaching that [he] had hitherto held to be essentially trustworthy."[10]

He raged against the war in his sermons but gradually realized, through careful, attentive reading of Scripture, that the conflict between a loving God and the idolatrous modern world may be more radical even than Socialism or the war.[11] Barth and a couple of pastor friends began, "more reflectively than ever before . . . reading and expounding the writings of the Old and New Testaments. And behold, they began to speak to us—very different than we had supposed we were obliged to hear them speak in . . . 'modern theology.'"[12] Of this maturation Barth said, "It . . . came down on me like a ton of bricks round about 1915" that the admission of the impossibility of speaking about God with modern philosophical tools could be used by God as the beginning of an ability to speak of God; to confess misunderstanding is to move toward comprehension.[13]

In October 1917, Barth asked his church for a four-week study leave. In August 1919, after a painstaking, verse-by-verse study of Paul's letter to the Romans, the village pastor and brash young scholar burst on the European theological scene with his commentary on Romans. Nothing like *The Epistle to the Romans* had been seen in the German-speaking theological world. Here was an unabashed *theological* reading of Scripture. To pompous, self-important historical critics, Barth said in the preface, "I entirely fail to see why parallels drawn from the ancient world . . . should be of more value for an understanding of the Epistle than the situation in which we ourselves actually are."[14] He then went on to ridicule or ignore much that his professors believed to be necessary for saying anything about Scripture from the pulpit.

Barth conducted his exposition of Romans without any effort to contextualize either Paul or the reader, without speculation about historical antecedents or attempt to reconstruct any prior theological development for what Paul had to say. After the resurrection, what matters is our present and future with God,

9. Ibid., xi.

10. Ibid.

11. Barth's announcement of his fresh, life-changing encounter with Scripture is his lecture, "The Strange New World within the Bible" (1916) in Karl Barth, *The Word of God and the Word of Man,* trans. Douglas Horton (New York: Harper & Brothers, 1957).

12. Willimon, *The Early Preaching of Karl Barth,* xii.

13. Busch, *Karl Barth: His Life,* 66.

14. "Preface to the Second Edition," Karl Barth, *The Epistle to the Romans,* trans. Edwyn C. Hoskyns, 6th ed. (London: Oxford University Press, 1933).

not the history of the text. Barth simply began with what Paul said and worked from there, verse-by-verse, humbly, continually surprised and delighted by Paul. Few German scholars took the Word of God that seriously, or approached the text in that sort of way.

Against those critics who came to the biblical text with a sense of scarcity, telling preachers that they lacked the historical background or sophisticated linguistic skill to hear the text speak—Barth began with an assumption of miraculous abundance. The style of *Romans* has been called "expressionistic"—brash, assertive, energetic prose. Dismissing Luther's *deus absconditus*,[15] or the hidden God, Barth boldly asserted that God speaks, reveals, attacks, and that theology is, of necessity, a process of prayerful submission to the God who comes to us here, now. In Jesus Christ, there is a decisive and irrefutable, constant and ever-present event of unveiling.

Barth handles Scripture by letting it handle him. God says too much to us, more than we can assimilate; a surplus of meaning remains. The text throbs with personal revelation, as if there is a surfeit of divine knowledge; God billows over us with wave after wave of dramatic, stunning self-disclosure, though disclosing a surprising, uncontainable God we had not expected.

In *Romans* we first encounter a number of themes that reappear throughout Barth's later work; insights that have nurtured preachers over the years. First, his condemnation of "religion," defined in *Romans* as "a vigorous and extensive attempt to humanize the divine . . . to make it a practical 'something,' for the benefit of those who cannot live with the Living God, and yet cannot live without God."[16] God is self-disclosing, yet, paradoxically, seemingly more distant and odd the closer God comes to us. The more we know of God, the more we realize how corrupted, accommodated, and tame are our notions of him. In Jesus Christ—God with us—we encounter the reality of Kierkegaard's "infinite qualitative distinction" between us and God.[17]

Faith is that which comes to us as an external address, not as an expression from our interiority. Theology is about the objective self-revelation of God, not an exploration or expression of our subjectivity. The message of the church need not bow to the intellectual rules of this age; this murderous, intellectually timid, and evasive age must bow to the truth who is Jesus Christ.

All the necessary work of reconciliation has been accomplished in the life and work of Jesus Christ; nothing awaits our contribution. The trouble between us and God has been solved by God. The gospel is a call to live joyfully in the

---

15. Cf. Barth, *Romans*, 42.
16. Barth, *Romans*, 332.
17. Willimon, *Conversations with Barth on Preaching*, 77.

light of Jesus's work, not an uphill struggle to justify ourselves to God through our pitiful human efforts. From all eternity, God has elected to be our God and has elected us to be for God.[18] When asked what we know of God, Barth repeatedly referred to 2 Corinthians 5:19, "God was reconciling the world to himself in Christ."[19] Period. The Christian is not an especially virtuous, intelligent, or pious person; Christians are simply those who have heard the news and have learned what it is to be loved by God.

THE DOGMATIC THEOLOGIAN

In 1921, while working on a revision of *Romans* (in which Barth would even more decisively break with his received theology), Barth was invited to assume a professorate in Göttingen. He began work as a dogmatic theologian, but always with homiletical intent. His *Göttingen Dogmatics* is obviously written for preachers. There Barth said that theology begins not with scholarly rumination on abstractions, but with "the concrete situation of preachers mounting the pulpit steps."[20]

Göttingen Dogmatics reads like the ruminations of a preacher, and he explains the role of the preacher, saying: "Christian preachers dare to talk about God. Even on the presupposition of the mediation of revelation by holy scripture this venture would always be impossible without the third presupposition that God acknowledges it and will himself speak as we speak, just as he spoke to the prophets and apostles and still speaks through them. . . . It is pure doctrine if the word of the preacher gives free play to God's own Word."[21]

From a brilliant run in Göttingen, where he had taught Calvin and Reformed theology, Barth was elevated to the University of Münster and then to Bonn, where he began his massive *Church Dogmatics*. Dogmatic theology renders service to the church and its messengers by rigorously testing the church's speech. The "first axiom of theology" is the first commandment, "You shall have no other gods before me" (Exod 20:3).[22]

Church Dogmatics could be read as a vast biblical commentary. Every theological assertion is rigorously tested by the specifics of the biblical text. Scripture keeps dogmatics theological because Scripture speaks primarily about God and only secondarily or derivatively about us.

---

18. I work Barth's doctrine of election and its significance for preachers in William H. Willimon, *How Odd of God: Chosen for the Curious Vocation of Preaching* (Louisville: Westminster John Knox, 2015).

19. Ibid., 32.

20. Karl Barth, *Göttingen Dogmatics: Instruction in the Christian Religion, Volume 1*, ed. Hannelotte Reiffen, trans. Geoffrey W. Bromiley (Grand Rapids: Eerdmans, 1991), 85.

21. Barth, *Göttingen Dogmatics*, 265.

22. Willimon, *Conversations with Barth on Preaching*, 162, 245.

Because of his interest in preaching, Barth begins *Church Dogmatics* with the longest exposition of the Trinity in many centuries.[23] If we do not have a God who speaks here and now in the processions and revelation of the Father, Son, and Holy Spirit, then we really have nothing to say about God. Christ is the Word. Christ preaches before we preach. Everything is set in motion with the primal Genesis claim, "And God said. . . ."

> The promise of the Word of God is not as such an empty pledge which always stands, as it were, confronting a person. It is the transposing of a person into the wholly new state of one who has accepted and appropriated the promise, so that irrespective of his attitude to it he no longer lives without this promise but with it. The claim of the Word of God is not as such a wish or command which remains outside the hearer without impinging on his existence. . . . Whatever may be his attitude to God's claim, the person who hears the Word now finds himself in the sphere of the divine claim; he is claimed by God.[24]

Throughout the many volumes of *Dogmatics,* Barth manages always to be addressed by the biblical text, retaining the same almost childlike wonder before Scripture that characterized *Romans.* Even as an experienced hermeneut, Barth is continually stunned and delighted by the sheer otherness of the biblical text.[25] For preachers searching for something to say, Barth declares, "The message which Scripture has to give us, even in its apparently most debatable and least assimilatable parts, is in all circumstances truer and more important than the best and the most necessary things that we ourselves have said or can say."[26]

With revelation, there is no possessing and controlling. Theologians (including preachers) must come to God empty-handed, without presuppositions. Revelation is an event, a bolt of lightning that obliterates our cherished propositions and certitudes and theological systems. All of our Bible study must be training in the art of humbly receiving the Word of God as it is given to us—fresh, surprising, and demanding.

---

23. Karl Barth, *Church Dogmatics*, trans. G. W. Bromiley; eds. G. W. Bromiley and T. F. Torrance, vol. 1 (Peabody, MA: Hendrickson, 2010).

24. Barth, *Church Dogmatics*, 1.2:152.

25. Barth's editors and translators, G. W. Bromiley and T. F. Torrance, compiled a wonderful resource for preachers, *Church Dogmatics Index, with Aids for the Preacher* (Edinburgh: T&T Clark, 1977), that not only gives us a complete index of Scripture and subjects in the *Dogmatics* but also a rich selection of exegetical and expository texts from the *Dogmatics* that are keyed to the assigned Scripture texts in the German Lutheran lectionary. *Karl Barth: Preaching Through the Christian Year,* eds. John McTavish and Harold Wells (Grand Rapids: Eerdmans, 1978) contains a judicious selection of passages from the *Church Dogmatics* that are keyed to the seasons of the liturgical year for use by preachers in the preparation of sermons.

26. Barth, *Church Dogmatics*, 1.2:152.

Barth not only spoke of revelation as an "event" but also called the church that is engendered by the Word as an "event." The church is not an institution, a formal structure, a container and dispenser of salvation, or a continuing, established community. The church is created afresh in each generation through daring conversation with the fecund, generative Word:

> As the church that is founded on the apostolic word, the church is never a given factor. It has to be repeatedly founded anew by an apostolic word. It can exist only in the event of the speaking and hearing of this apostolic word as God's Word. Thus the church is an institution only as an invitation, as a waiting for the church. In the church we are always on the way to the event of the church. Thus the ministry as the stepping forth of individuals is an act which must repeatedly become a reality by the calling of God. Ordination is a canonical act, but its significance is as a pointer to God's calling to the extent that in ordination the ordained come to hear the Word of God, which, however, they must constantly hear afresh. [27]

Christ is not so much the one who dies on the cross to save us from our sins; Barth tends to stress the incarnational, God-man miracle of Bethlehem more than the atoning work on Golgotha. Stressing a thoroughgoing Chalcedonian Christology, Barth stresses that God's work of atonement does not begin at the cross but rather is eternal, before creation, in the eternal identity of the triune God who is for us even before we were created. God's identity is to be God for us, and he has created us—and daily works in us—to be for God. When he speaks of the atonement, Barth characterizes Christ as the Prodigal Son who journeys out into the far country of our sin and death in order to bring us back to the Father's house. Christ is the Prodigal Son; we are Judas, who, though we have no claim or right to be with the Father, are chosen by the Son to be at his table in the power of the Holy Spirit.

While the theology of Barth's *Dogmatics* is far too rich and multifaceted to allow generalization, our greatest American interpreter of Barth, George Hunsinger, devised a set of recurring motifs in *Dogmatics:* [28]

1. Actualism

A human being exists as a divine act. Revelation is God's continual condescending to humanity. This event is miraculous, ever new. All knowledge of God

---

27. Barth, *Church Dogmatics*, 4.3:76.
28. George Hunsinger, *How to Read Karl Barth: The Shape of His Theology* (New York: Oxford University Press, 1997), 31.

is a gift of God. There is no "having," in our relationship with God, only God's continual acts of giving and our constant receiving.

2. Particularism

Only God can speak of God. And God's particular way of speaking is the event called Jesus Christ. Christians, through thought and speech, must always discipline themselves to stay close to this particular revelation, the eternal Word, and be suspicious of all abstraction and generalization as potential ways of escaping the particular Word made flesh. Jesus Christ is the unique source for all thinking, and the peculiar test for validity of our God statements.

3. Objectivism

Revelation and salvation are mediated through ordinary creaturely objects. Divine self-giving, self-enactment is "objective"—real, valid, and effective—whether acknowledged and received by creatures or not. Barth therefore rejects so much of modern theology's subjective, inward experience as an inadequate means of talking about God. The incarnation is a fact that requires only our acknowledgment. Barth emphasizes that revelation is objective; it has a self-existence and an over-againstness in relationship to us. Thus, God must move toward us, for we have no way of moving toward God.

4. Personalism

God comes to us as a personal address—not in abstract or general concepts. Knowledge of God is fellowship with God. Truth is personal (i.e., Jesus the Christ). Justification and sanctification are aspects of vocation, God's personal address to us. Jesus Christ is the objective fact of revelation; the Holy Spirit works that fact in us as a subjective reality. In Barth, "subjective" is always a reference not to our personal experience, but to the work of the Holy Spirit in us, to God's subjectivity offered to us, made an "object" to us so that we might commune with God. Truth is encounter and communion, and salvation is always an address, a vocation.

5. Realism

Theological language, by the grace of God, miraculously refers to God. By the grace of God, our talk about God is no mere projection of our subjectivities but a realistic dealing with reality. Theological language is analogical and actually refers to reality. Barth can thus speak of theology as a "science" in which theology remains tied to a real object of investigation—the self-revealing God.

6. Rationalism

Theological language is rational, cognitive. Controlled by its object (God in Jesus Christ), theology is a "science" that follows rational procedures that are congruent with the object of its investigation. Theology need not retreat into the subjective recesses of human feelings. Theology is rational in that it is guided by certain rules of thought dictated by its subject matter (God in Jesus Christ). Salvation is noetic, a fact that is rationally acknowledged as a true fact.

These are characterizations, themes, and motifs, not the substance of Barth's theology. There is no subject of theology, no substance other than Jesus Christ.

BARTH AS PREACHER

With the rise of the Nazis in the 1930s, Barth became a leader in the Confessing Church, eventually authoring the Barmen Declaration, a bold confession of faith declaring the freedom of preaching from the dictates of the state.[29] It is illuminating that Barth believed that the most effective Christian response to Hitler was preaching. "Jesus Christ is the one word of God to whom we must listen in life and in death," thundered forth the Barmen. Behind the declaration is Barth's conviction that the nineteenth century theological error was to suppose that divine revelation is problematic, not sufficiently given in Christ, and therefore must be derived from the depths of human self-consciousness or human moral experience where God is somehow waiting to be progressively discovered. The condition for the possibility of encountering God was thus found in the interior depths of the self. Yet when our personal encounter with God was understood in these terms—the terms set by human nature—it was inevitable, Barth argued, that two things would and did eventually happen. First, Jesus Christ would cease to be understood unequivocally as the Lord; and second, we ourselves would consequently come to usurp the center which rightfully belongs to him. Rather than understanding ourselves from him, we would come to understand him from ourselves. Rather than take him on his own terms as the Lord—that is, as God's unique, final, and binding revelation—we would take him on our own terms as a postulate of our experience—"as an ideal case or an idea of our possibility and our reality."[30] In other words, we would refuse to give God glory (Rom 1:21), devising some means of getting to God through our own glorious selves.

---

29. The Barmen Declaration is a kind of extended exposition of the doctrine of justification and its relevance not only for preaching but also, by implication, for the relationship of Christian preaching to the state. See Karl Barth, *Community, State, and the Church*, trans. G. Ronald Howe (Garden City, NY: Anchor, 1960).

30. Barth, *Church Dogmatics*, 2.1:150.

Barth infuriated the University of Bonn's aging, sympathetic-to-the-Nazis professor of preaching by informing him that he would give a series of lectures on preaching. Those lectures were eventually published as his great homiletical tour de force, *Homiletics*.[31] It is unjustified to regard *Homiletics* as a full-orbed Barthian homiletic. These lectures were given under the gathering storm clouds of Nazism, though there is no mention of Nazis or Hitler. Barth says that we must preach "as if nothing had happened." The "nothing" is Hitler, whom Barth refused to mention in his lectures (though Nazis attended some of Barth's preaching lectures and reported back to their superiors). The lectures are rightly viewed as an "emergency homiletic,"[32] preaching for a church that is fighting for its life. Preaching in a pressured time of crisis is preaching that must be strictly submissive to the biblical text, disregarding congregational approval or disapproval, shunning cultural affirmation, and adhering only to close exposition of the text: "Preachers must not be boring. To a large extent the pastor and boredom are synonymous concepts. Listeners often think that they have heard already what is being said in the pulpit. They have long since known it themselves. The fault certainly does not lie with them alone. Against boredom the only defense is again being biblical. If a sermon is biblical, it will not be boring. Holy scripture is in fact so interesting and has so much that is new and exciting to tell us that listeners cannot even think about dropping off to sleep."[33]

The biblical text assaults the congregation, invades like a meteor, and strides into the middle of a congregation and its worldly preoccupations and worries. The very form and structure of the sermon is itself a kind of theological claim, as the preacher moves from direct encounter with the specifics of the text, saying no more or less than the text says. The preacher begins, as it were, in midconversation, holding up the jewel of the text before the congregation, admiring every facet of its brilliance. The job of the preacher is not to make the text relevant to the congregation but rather to allow God to make the congregation relevant to the biblical text. The preacher is more fascinated by the ancient text than by the contemporary congregational context.

Matters became so dangerous for the German church that preachers dared not take their eyes off a God who saves, who judges, who teaches, who kills, and who makes alive. Though Barth makes a studied effort not to refer, in his homiletic lectures, to the current political situation in Germany, listeners easily

---

31. Karl Barth, *Homiletics,* trans. Geoffrey W. Bromiley and Donald E. Daniels (Louisville: Westminster John Knox, 1991).

32. Angela Dienhart Hancock, *Karl Barth's Emergency Homiletic, 1932–1933: A Summons to Prophetic Witness at the Dawn of the Third Reich* (Grand Rapids: Eerdmanns, 2013).

33. Barth, *Homiletics,* 80.

surmise that the way to counteract paganism in the form of national socialism is by close, obedient attentiveness to another God than Caesar. God will speak in the night, in the storm, if we will dare to listen. And the word God speaks is a life-giving, victorious word.

In *Homiletics*, Barth famously rails against sermon introductions, illustrations, endings, and beginnings. He says that the sermon begins without introduction or any attempt to lure the congregation into the text. The great misunderstanding, especially in modern times, Barth believed, was to suppose that a personal encounter with God was somehow given in the structure of human nature itself. The preacher need only uncover that point of contact within the listener's self and build a bridge to that innate point of contact.[34] Barth's denial of that point of contact was due not to his great pessimism about human nature, but rather to his great optimism about the self-revelatory capacity of the Trinity. According to Barth, preaching that thinks it has uncovered some human yearning for the Word has deceived itself, offering the world nothing more than a false god. As for the true God, the Word made flesh, the Word "completes its work in the world in spite of the world."[35]

On December 10, 1933, Barth preached in the university chapel in Bonn, only one year into Hitler's Reich. Taking Romans 15:5–13 as his text, Barth preached on the gentile Christians' continuing indebtedness to Israel since Christ has received us and has grafted we outsiders onto the promises of God to Israel. Some of the congregation walked out in the middle of the sermon. A little while later, Barth was ejected from his professorship in Bonn. A number of his students gathered at the station to bid Barth a tearful farewell as he returned to his native Switzerland. They asked him for a few words of encouragement as the storm clouds gathered in Germany. "Exegesis, exegesis, exegesis," he urged as he departed for Basel.

CONTRIBUTIONS TO PREACHING

Barth's robust view of an active, surprising, living God puts Barth at some distance from lots of the sermons that I hear and many that I preach. God too often enters the sermon as some sort of vague mystery about whom little is to be said. We presume to know more about our cultural context or the subjectivity of our

---

34. Reginald Fuller says that preachers "are concerned with two poles—the text and the contemporary situation. It is their task to build a bridge between these poles." Reginald Fuller, *The Use of the Bible in Preaching,* (Philadelphia: Fortress, 1981), 41. This is the sort of nineteenth century text-to-sermon move that Barth deplores.

35. Karl Barth, *Witness to the Word: A Commentary on John I,* trans. Geoffrey W. Bromiley, ed. Walther Fürst (Grand Rapids: Eerdmans, 1986), 66.

listeners than we know of God. Barth thought it exactly the opposite: Because of Jesus Christ, we know more of God than we will ever know of the subjectivities of our listeners.

Our pastoral inclinations lead us to quickly abandon the text and improvise, offering exclusively human advice derived from limited human experience. There is a modern sort of modesty that refuses to claim too much for God. Presuming intellectual integrity, this reticence to do theology is in most cases the simple fear that to speak decisively about who God is and who God isn't would endanger our godlike aspirations to run the world as we please. Meanwhile, thin descriptions of God are killing our sermons.

No wonder Barth wrote such long books, and so many of them; the voice of God is so gloriously fecund that talk about God is never done. When we're working with such a self-revealing God, there is always something else for a preacher to say next Sunday.

Barth believed that we've got more gospel than we can possibly bring to speech. God has said so much, and spoken in such a fertile, thick, multivalent manner, that we've got more than enough to say right now, right here. Barth claimed that theology was a form of prayer—openhanded reception of the lavish gifts that God gives. And preparation for preaching is prayer too.

By so robustly focusing on the activity and presence of a living God, Karl Barth can restore in modern preachers our sense of nerve and our conviction that what the world needs most is a clear, direct, enthusiastic sermon that presents the true and living God. We have been, says Barth, far too deferential to the modern world in our preaching, too intimidated by current culture and its idols, and too subservient to the whims of our congregations. As Barth said in a number of contexts, at our Holy Spirit–induced best, "Preachers dare."[36] Barth tells us poor preachers that we can find continual rejuvenation, confident that despite our poor preaching and our people's poor listening, the Word of God is forever triumphant:

> People with their various (but by nature unanimously hostile) attitudes towards the Word of God come and go. Their political and spiritual systems (all of which to some extent have an anti-Christian character) stand and fall. The Church itself (in which somewhere the crucifixion of Christ is always being repeated) is to-day faithful and to-morrow unfaithful, to-day strong and to-morrow weak. But although Scripture may be rejected by its enemies and disowned and betrayed by its friends, it does not cease . . .

---

36. Willimon, *Conversations with Barth on Preaching*, 266.

to present the message that God so loved the world that He gave his only-begotten Son. If its voice is drowned to-day, it becomes audible again to-morrow. If it is misunderstood and distorted here, it again bears witness to its true meaning there. If it seems to lose its position, hearers and form in this locality or period, it acquires them afresh elsewhere. The promise is true, and it is fulfilled in the existence of the biblical prophets and apostles in virtue of what is said to them and what they have to say. The maintaining of the Word of God against the attacks to which it is exposed cannot be our concern and therefore we do not need to worry about it. Watchmen are appointed and they wait in their office. The maintaining of the Word of God takes place as a self-affirmation which we can never do more than acknowledge to our own comfort and disquiet. We can be most seriously concerned about Christianity and Christians, about the future of the Church and theology, about the establishment in the world of the Christian outlook and Christian ethic. But there is nothing about whose solidity we need be less troubled than the testimonies of God in Holy Scripture. For a power which can annul these testimonies is quite unthinkable.[37]

This is the witness of Karl Barth for us preachers.

Sermon Excerpt
Deliverance to the Captives[38]

During the last decades of his life, Barth regularly preached to the prisoners in the Basel jail. Those sermons, *Deliverance to the Captives,* are the best introduction to Barth as a preacher and a less intimidating encounter with Barth's theology than the *Dogmatics.* The sermons in this collection are simple, straightforward, upbeat, and pastoral. Here is the mature Barth, caring for an unusual congregation by preaching good news:

'They crucified him with the criminals.' Which is more amazing, to find Jesus in such bad company, or to find the criminals in such good company? . . . Like Jesus, these two criminals had been arrested . . . , locked up and sentenced. . . . And now they hang on

---

37. Barth, *Church Dogmatics*, 1.2:680–81.
38. Karl Barth, *Deliverance to the Captives,* trans. Marguerite Wieser (New York: Harper, 1961).

their crosses with him and find themselves in solidarity and fellowship with him. They are linked in a common bondage never again
to be broken . . . a point of no return for them as for him. There
remained only the shameful, pain stricken present and the future of
their approaching death. . . .

'They crucified him with the criminals.' . . . This was the first
Christian fellowship. . . . To live by this promise is to be a Christian community. The two criminals were the first certain Christian
community.[39]

In a Christmas sermon Barth characterizes the incarnation as a matter of rescue because,

"He stands by you:" A drowning man cannot pull himself out of
the water by his own hair. Neither can you do it. Someone else must
rescue you. This is the good news of Christmas. He who stands by
you and helps you is alive and present! It is he who was born that
Christmas Day! Open your eyes, open your ears, open your heart!
You may truly see, hear and experience that he is here, and stands
by you as no one else can do! He stands by you, really by you, now
and for evermore![40]

Repeatedly he assures the prisoners that in Jesus Christ, they are
loved and actively embraced by God. Barth tells them, in more than
one sermon, that their prison captivity is in no way significant in their
relationship with God. Repeatedly he tells them that their imprisonment
is no more noteworthy than the sad captivity of the citizens of Basel who
don't know how chained they are in their bogus assertions of individual
freedom and autonomy.

Again, we see Barth preaching to the jailhouse congregation on the
gratuitous nature of God's salvation in Christ:

'By grace you have been saved!' How strange to have this message addressed to us! Who are we, anyway? Let me tell you quite

---

39. Barth, *Deliverance to the Captives*, 38.
40. Ibid., 138.

frankly: We are all together great sinners. Please understand me: I include myself. I stand ready to confess being the greatest sinner among you all; yet you may then not exclude yourself from the group! Sinners are people who in the judgment of God, and perhaps of their own consciences, missed and lost their way, who are not just a little, but totally guilty, hopelessly indebted and lost not only in time, but in eternity. We are such sinners. And we are prisoners.

Believe me, there is a captivity much worse than the captivity in this house. There are walls much thicker and doors much heavier than those closed upon you. All of us, the people without and you within, are prisoners of our own obstinacy, of our many greeds, of our various anxieties, of our mistrust and in the last analysis of our unbelief. We are all sufferers. Most of all we suffer from ourselves. We each make life difficult for ourselves and in so doing for our fellowmen. We suffer from life's lack of meaning. We suffer in the shadow of death and of eternal judgment toward which we are moving. We spend our life in the midst of a whole world of sin and captivity and suffering. But now listen. Into the depth of our predicament the word is spoken from on high: By grace you have been saved![41] ◆

BIBLIOGRAPHY

Barth, Karl. *Church Dogmatics.* Trans. by G. W. Bromiley. Edited by G. W. Bromily and T. F. Torrance. 14 vols. Peabody: Hendrickson Publishers, 2010.

_____. *The Epistle to the Romans.* Trans. by Edwin C. Hoskyns. 6th ed. London: Oxford University Press, 1933.

_____. *Göttingen Dogmatics: Instruction in the Christian Religion.* Edited by Hannelotte Reiffen. Trans. by Geoffrey W. Bromily. Grand Rapids: Eerdmans, 1991.

_____. *Homiletics.* Trans. by Geoffrey W. Bromily and Donald E. Daniels. Louisville: Westminster John Knox, 1991.

_____. *Witness to the Word: A Commentary on John I.* Trans. by Geoffrey W. Bromily. Edited by Walther Fürst. Grand Rapids: Eerdmans, 1986.

Busch, Eberhard. *Karl Barth: His Life from Letters and Autobiographical Texts.* Trans. by John Bowden. Grand Rapids: Eerdmans, 1975.

Hancock, Angela Dienhart. *Karl Barth's Emergency Homiletic, 1932–1933: A Summons to Prophetic Witness at the Dawn of the Third Reich.* Grand Rapids: Eerdmans, 2013.

Hunsinger, George. *How to Read Karl Barth: The Shape of His Theology.* New York: Oxford University Press, 1997.

Willimon, William H. *Conversations with Barth on Preaching.* Nashville: Abingdon, 2006.

_____. *The Early Preaching of Karl Barth: Fourteen Sermons with Commentary.* Trans. by John E. Wilson. Louisville: Westminster John Knox, 2009.

---

41. Ibid., 37.

Dietrich Bonhoeffer
Costly Preaching

KEITH W. CLEMENTS

Dietrich Bonhoeffer (1906–1945) is best known as a radical theologian, an outspoken advocate of the Confessing Church in Nazi Germany, an activist in the ecumenical peace movement, and a courageous participant in the political resistance to Hitler. It was this commitment that ultimately cost him his life. As a preacher, from his student days to the end of his life, he took preaching seriously as one entrusted with a cross-bearing ministry.

HISTORICAL BACKGROUND

Bonhoeffer's preaching cannot be separated from his life, and his life cannot be separated from the turmoil of its context.[1] He was born into a comfortable, upper-middle-class family in the last years of imperial Germany, and while still a child, he experienced the devastating impact of the First World War, in which one of his brothers died. Growing up, he knew firsthand the social and political unrest that followed Germany's defeat. Deciding while still a young teenager to be a theologian and pastor in the Lutheran Church, he acknowledged the challenge the church would face in reestablishing its credibility in a Germany very different from 1914. His theological studies in Tübingen, Rome, and Berlin led him to focus his interest on the nature of the church, together with an enthusiasm (though never wholly uncritical) for Karl Barth's theology of the Word of God. He completed his doctoral thesis, *"Sanctorum Communio,"* at the age

---

1. Extensive use is made in this chapter of the Dietrich Bonhoeffer Works English Edition (DBWE) published by Fortress. The volumes are referenced in the notes as DBWE, followed by the respective volume number, title (on first citation, with publication year, etc.) and the page numbers of cited passages. For Bonhoeffer's life, see the definitive biography by Eberhard Bethge, *Dietrich Bonhoeffer: A Biography*, rev. ed. (Minneapolis: Fortress, 2000); also Ferdinand Schlingensiepen, *Dietrich Bonhoeffer 1906–1945: Martyr, Thinker, Man of Resistance* (London: T&T Clark, 2010).

of twenty-one in 1927. Destined for academic brilliance, he became a lecturer in the University of Berlin, but not before extending his experience by a year as student pastor to the German congregation in Barcelona, Spain, and then a year of further study at Union Theological Seminary, New York, from 1930 to 1931. He was ordained as a pastor in November 1931, by which time he had become an ecumenical peace activist as an honorary youth secretary for the World Alliance for International Friendship through the Churches.

Adolf Hitler came to power at the end of January 1933, and soon the "church struggle" began in earnest, with the attempt led by the so-called German Christian Movement to make the Protestant church a "truly German" church. This attempt to make the church conform to the Nazi ethos focused on debarring so-called non-Aryans (people of Jewish descent) from pastoral office. Bonhoeffer was in the forefront, along with Karl Barth and Martin Niemöller, in the opposition movement, which led to the formation of the Confessing Church. This movement was founded on the famous Barmen Theological Declaration of May 1934. At this time, Bonhoeffer was serving as pastor of two German congregations in London from October 1933 to April 1935. From there, he returned to take charge of an illegal, underground seminary of the Confessing Church at Finkenwalde on the Baltic coast. Over one hundred students passed through Finkenwalde before the seminary was closed by the Gestapo in 1937. The work continued in a more clandestine fashion in Confessing Church parishes in a remote area of Farther Pomerania.

Fearing conscription into Hitler's army, Bonhoeffer accepted an invitation to go to the USA in 1939 to serve indefinitely as a lecturer. Not wanting to abdicate his responsibility to the Confessing Church in Germany, he decided to return just before the outbreak of war, despite all the dangers awaiting him at home. Now forbidden to speak or preach in public, his theological work largely took the form of writing his major work, *Ethics*. In late 1940, he was recruited by his brother-in-law, Hans von Dohnanyi, into the *Abwehr* (military intelligence) political resistance and a plot to overthrow Hitler. His task was to visit ecumenical contacts in neutral countries with information about the resistance in order to solicit support from Allied governments. He was arrested in April 1943. His eighteen months in Tegel Military Prison, Berlin, were occupied with writing. This included a secret correspondence with his close friend (and later biographer) Eberhard Bethge, which included an exploration of a "religionless Christianity" in a "world come of age." Following the failed assassination attempt on Hitler on July 20, 1944, he was transferred to the Gestapo prison in central Berlin, then to Buchenwald concentration camp in early 1945. While being transported south with a party of other prisoners whom the Nazis hoped to keep beyond the reach of the Allied armies' advance, he was seized by the Gestapo and hanged at Flossenbürg execution camp on April 9, 1945, barely a month before the German surrender.

Bonhoeffer lived in especially challenging times for Christian preaching. With the widespread collapse of assumptions about "Christian civilization" following the First World War, preachers had to decide whether the gospel was a message *of* the culture and religion of the Western world or, as with Karl Barth, a message of judgment and grace *to* that world. Second, following Hitler's revolution, the question was whether the gospel was to be fashioned to conform to the Nazi ethos of nationalism, racism, militarism, and the pseudo-Christianity of the "German Christians," or to be proclaimed as the way of costly grace and obedient discipleship.[2] Would Christians rather form a church that enjoyed the powers and privileges bestowed by Caesar? Or a church of the cross? Further, Bonhoeffer was himself a complex personality. His preaching manifests a passionate, unequivocal commitment where his soul is laid on the line. As Eberhard Bethge says of Bonhoeffer's time as a student and newly ordained pastor in Berlin from 1931–1932, "Only as a preacher was he fully present; here he devoted himself without any reservations or qualifications. Preaching was the great event for him. . . . For Bonhoeffer nothing in his calling competed in importance with preaching."[3] At every stage of his career, he labored with immense care over every sermon, and as seminary director, he enjoined his students to do likewise.

Over seventy of Bonhoeffer's sermons have survived for inclusion in his published collected works (together with a number of biblical studies and meditations).[4] The particular contexts for nearly all of these are known: the Barcelona congregation, 1928–1929; various churches in Berlin where he was guest preacher during 1931–1933; his two London congregations (the United Church, Sydenham, and St. Paul's Reformed Church, Aldgate), 1933–1935, where he had the most continuous pulpit ministry of his career; the Finkenwalde seminary, 1935–1937; and thereafter the collective pastorates when some of the sermons were also circulated in letters to current and former students. The homiletics lectures and exercises he gave to his students at Finkenwalde are of supreme importance for our understanding of his preaching.[5]

---

2. Bonhoeffer would explore these themes in his famous book *Discipleship*, DBWE 4 (Minneapolis: Fortress, 2001), first published in German as *Nachfolge*, 1937. The first English edition was titled *The Cost of Discipleship*.

3. Bethge, *Dietrich Bonhoeffer*, 234.

4. A very useful anthology of thirty-one of the sermons, with introduction and commentary, is Isabel Best, ed., *The Collected Sermons of Dietrich Bonhoeffer* (Minneapolis: Fortress, 2012).

5. See DBWE 14, *Theological Education at Finkenwalde: 1935–1937* (Minneapolis: Fortress, 2013), for "Lecture on Homiletics," 487–536; "Homiletical Exercise," 632–53 and 753–81.

THEOLOGY OF PREACHING

Dietrich Bonhoeffer's core belief about preaching is most cogently expressed in what he said in an actual sermon—the first one he preached to his congregation at Sydenham, London, in October 1933:

> This is what makes a sermon something unique in all the world, so completely different from any other kind of speech. When a preacher opens his Bible and interprets the Word of God, a mystery takes place, a miracle: the grace of God, who comes down from heaven into our midst and speaks to us, knocks on our door, asks questions, warns us, puts pressure on us, alarms us, threatens us, and makes us joyful again and free and sure. When the Holy Scriptures are brought to life in a church, the Holy Spirit comes down from the eternal throne, into our hearts, while the busy world outside sees nothing and knows nothing about it—that God could actually be found here.[6]

A sermon is not, therefore, a discourse *about* God, but is God's own self in Christ, immediately present, addressing the hearers and calling for faith. Bonhoeffer complained the church had become trivialized: "We prefer quiet and edification to the holy restlessness of the powerful Lord God, because we keep thinking we have God in our power instead of allowing God to have power over us . . . because in the end we ourselves do not want to believe that God is really here among us, right now, demanding that we hand ourselves over, in life and death, in heart and soul and body."[7] Finally, it is because "we pastors keep talking too much about passing things . . . instead of knowing that we are no more than messengers of the great truth of the eternal Christ."[8] This quote from a sermon on 2 Corinthians 5:20: "We are therefore Christ's ambassadors," expresses Bonhoeffer's high, almost sacramental, view of preaching. The preacher is the one through whom God issues his call that we must be reconciled to him. Beneath this understanding of preaching lies a very Lutheran, incarnational Christology. In his homiletics lectures to his Finkenwalde students, Bonhoeffer states: *"The sermon derives from the incarnation of Jesus Christ and is determined by the incarnation of Jesus Christ.* It does not derive from some universal truth or emotional experience. The word of the sermon is the incarnate Christ. The incarnate

---

6. DBWE 13, *London, 1933–1935* (Minneapolis: Fortress, 2007), 323.
7. Ibid., 324f.
8. DBWE 13, 324.

Christ is God. Hence the sermon is actually Christ. God *as* human being. Christ *as* the word. As the Word, Christ walks through the church-community."[9]

The preached words do not point beyond themselves to the "real" Word; they are themselves, in all their humanness, the Word made human, who embraces and bears the humanity, sin, and suffering of the hearers. A sermon therefore does not need to "make concrete" the gospel or "apply" it to the lives of the hearers. The incarnate Jesus Christ himself, present and speaking, judging and forgiving, is all the concreteness that is required.

Just two weeks before Hitler's accession to power, Bonhoeffer gave a sermon on "Overcoming Fear" from Matthew 8:23–27. He declared, "But be comforted; I have overcome the world! Christ is in the boat! And this place . . . is the pulpit of the church. From this pulpit the living Christ himself wants to speak, so that wherever he reaches somebody, that person will feel the fear sinking away, will feel Christ overcoming his or her fear."[10] Bonhoeffer was passionate about preaching the living Christ. In a sermon on the story of the rich man and Lazarus, preached in Berlin in May 1932, he begins: "One cannot understand and preach the gospel concretely enough. A real evangelical sermon must be like holding a pretty red apple in front of a child or a glass of cool water in front of a thirsty person and then asking: do you want it?"[11]

The "tangibility" of which Bonhoeffer speaks is the touching of the human heart and will by Christ, who calls for faith and obedience. His sermons are not piously edifying discourses about religion in general or Christianity in particular. Nor are they emotionally manipulative exercises in spiritual uplift. They are calls for a decision to place one's whole life in trust and obedience to the God of Jesus Christ. There is a tautness and austerity about them, yet they point to the apprehension of true *joy*. Even as the "church struggle" deepened in grim earnest, on Ascension Day 1933, he could say: "Joy in the sermon—how hard that is for us people of today. That's because we are listening to the preacher and not to Christ. . . . But heavenly joy Christ can give us, even through his frail church, and we should look for it only from him, not from the preacher. In the sermon it is Christ who wants to visit us and wants himself to be our heavenly joy." [12]

This theology of the incarnate, living Christ addressing the congregation through the sermon has a direct consequence for how Bonhoeffer seeks to open the hearts and minds of his hearers to Christ. He is always aware that in his congregation there will be a whole range of preoccupations, anxieties, fears, hopes,

9. DBWE 14, 509f.
10. DBWE 12 *Berlin: 1932–1933* (Minneapolis: Fortress, 2009), 457.
11. DBWE 11, *Ecumenical, Academic and Pastoral Work: 1931–1932* (Minneapolis: Fortress, 2012), 443.
12. DBWE 12, 469f.

doubts, questions, and aspirations. For example, in his first London sermon, he acknowledged that the arrival of a new and unknown pastor prompted all sorts of emotions in the congregation, as the members "look forward toward the future with some reservations and somewhat worriedly, somewhat fearfully. . . . So a moment like this is brimming and loaded with feelings of the most personal sort: pain, joy, worry, confidence."[13] Bonhoeffer simply acknowledged these feelings. He did not evaluate them critically. He permits them. They are the feelings of human beings, and the living Christ will come to meet them with his appeal to be reconciled and his offer of a "new heart."

Often in Bonhoeffer's preaching we find an acknowledgment of the world's concerns represented in his audience in all their unvarnished actuality, and then the opening of the door for Christ to speak directly to them. His sermon for Remembrance Sunday[14] 1933 voices the question "Where have our dead gone?" and describes with unremitting clarity the desolation of the bereaved who continually ask of the departed, "Where are you?" The memory of his family's grief at the loss of his brother Walter in 1918 was surely speaking here. He offers no anodynes to take away the pain; in fact, he allows the pain of the unanswerable question "Where?" to rise to the point where it is truly seen to be without answer, other than "at peace," because the dead are with God. Then he speaks of the resurrection and the life.[15] Another example is taken from a sermon preached in London on the July 8, 1934, just after Hitler's brutal massacre of some two hundred suspected rivals of the Nazi Party, the so-called *Röhm Putsch*. Bonhoeffer does not deal directly with this atrocity, but rather with the different attitudes people take to any grim event—especially that of seeking someone to blame: "In the face of terrible human catastrophes, Christians are not to assume the arrogant, know-all attitude of looking on and judging, but rather are to recognize: this is my world in which this has happened. This is the world in which I live, in which I sin by sowing hate and lovelessness day by day."[16] The phrase, *"This is my world"* is a regular motif in Bonhoeffer's preaching: a clear-eyed view of the world as it actually is. This is the world that the incarnate Christ takes on himself, even to the cross. In this sense, Bonhoeffer's preaching is always a "worldly" interpretation of the gospel.

Bonhoeffer's theology of preaching has three further consequences. First, contemporary readers of his sermons, especially those preached in the Nazi

13. DBWE 13, 321.

14. The German *Totensonntag*, observed in November each year, is a religious holiday commemorating the dead, not to be confused with commemoration of those who died in war. Sermon in DBWE 13, 331–36.

15. Cf. what Bonhoeffer writes from prison ten years later at Advent 1943: "Only when one loves life and the earth so much that with it everything seems to be lost and at its end may one believe in the resurrection of the dead and a new world." DBWE 8, *Letters and Papers from Prison* (Minneapolis: Fortress, 2010), 192.

16. DBWE 13, 369.

period, may well be surprised at how little direct reference there seems to be to the social and political context. We do not find explicit denunciations of Hitler, anti-Semitism, or Germany's preparations for war. But this was not a sign of timidity on his part.[17] Rather, as a preacher, his primary concern was to his audience and their specific responsibility to believe and obey in light of their difficult context. As he tells his Finkenwalde students: *"The true concrete situation* is never the apparent historical situation but rather that of human beings, *of sinners before God,* in their attempts to secure themselves against God. That the crucified Christ lives today is proof that the concrete situation of human beings is merely the situation to which Christ is the answer."[18] Thus, Bonhoeffer believed the preacher's primary task is to seek obedience from their listeners.

A dramatic example of this occurred at the ecumenical conference on Fanø Island, Denmark, in August 1934. Bonhoeffer preached from Psalm 85:8: "I will listen to what God the LORD says: he promises peace to his people, his faithful servants." Again, his comments on the world scene were used as a call for ecumenical fellowship. He appealed to the universal church to take action in the face of a world re-arming for war: "The hour is late. The world is choked with weapons, and dreadful is the mistrust which looks out of all men's eyes. The trumpets of war may blow tomorrow. For what are we waiting? . . . We want to give the world a whole word—a courageous word, a Christian word. . . . Who knows if we shall see each other again another year?"[19] Bonhoeffer does not leave his hearers in doubt that he understands what is about to take place and appeals to their obedience and faith in Christ. In Berlin, on February 26, 1933, he preached for the first time after Hitler took power. It was when the Nazi revolution was riding high on popular acclaim. Crude triumphalism was reigning, and the "German Christians" were calling for their "truly German church," which, riding on the back of the new political order, would be a church guaranteed of success and power in the land. From the book of Judges, Bonhoeffer took the story of Gideon, the young Israelite called by God to deliver his people from the Midianites. With small numbers, God wins the victory through him, and at the end of the day, Gideon resists calls for him to be made ruler: "I will not rule over you, nor will my son rule over you. The LORD will rule over you" (Judg 8:23).[20] Bonhoeffer comments: "Gideon conquers, the church conquers,

---

17. Note should be taken, for example, of the radio talk Bonhoeffer gave on February 1, 1933, immediately after Hitler's coming to power. It was called "The Younger Generation's Altered View of the Concept of *Führer,*" and warned against an idolization of power in the guise of respect for "authority." The broadcast was interrupted before he finished speaking. See Bethge, *Dietrich Bonhoeffer,* 259f; DBWE 12, 266–68.

18. DBWE 14, 494.

19. DBWE 13, 309f.

20. DBWE 12, 467.

we conquer, because faith alone conquers. But the victory belongs not to Gideon, the church, or ourselves, but to God. And God's victory means our defeat, our humiliation: it means God's derision and wrath at all human pretensions of might, at humans puffing themselves up and thinking that they are somebodies themselves. It means the world and its shouting is silenced, that all our ideas and plans are frustrated; it means the cross."[21]

Could there be any more powerful criticism of Nazi triumphalism, or any clearer warning to those who wanted the church to win apparent "strength" through fusion with that form of power? Could there be any more cogent appeal for faith to say no to such blandishments, and yes to the way of Jesus Christ and his cross? In sermon after sermon, before and during the Nazi period, Bonhoeffer repeatedly points his hearers to the one ground, the hope, the rock, on which their decisions of trust and obedience are to be based, in distinction from the false gods of worldly power and religious bravado.

A second feature in Bonhoeffer's sermons is a restrained and disciplined use of "illustrations." He does not totally eschew them. For example, he uses the game of chess as a picture of life, its chances and the eventual master-move of death.[22] He tells of the poet Petrarch momentarily feeling guilty at being enraptured by the beauty of the world.[23] He alludes to Gandhi as an example.[24] But compared with many preachers, there is a lack of anecdotes about the famous, the heroic, and the extraordinarily saintly figures of past and present. Such stories may well uplift, of course, but they can also simply amuse or distract. More dangerously, they can subtly demoralize and devalue the hearers who are led to feel that they are being presented with a level of Christianity beyond the reach of ordinary folk, or at least so far detached from their own life situation as to be unreal. Bonhoeffer, by contrast, is concerned with allowing the living Christ, the Word, in all his concreteness, to confront his hearers with his comfort and challenge. He believed Christ would work his transformative power in *their* lives and the life of their church so as to render any other dramas superfluous. They are to be the actors in the drama of faith, played out on their stage of everyday life. There is no need for stories from elsewhere. Through the gift of faith, people's own stories will supply the drama.

Third, Bonhoeffer's preaching did not lapse into moralism. The moralising preacher tends to elevate themselves above challenging sin. We find Bonhoeffer attacking pride, vanity, hypocrisy, injustice, and indifference; he recognizes

21. Ibid.
22. DBWE 13, 309.
23. DBWE 13, 354.
24. DBWE 13, 370.

sin and is willing to call people to repentance. Characteristically, when talking about the human condition, he speaks in the first-person plural, saying "we" rather than "they" or "you." This was consistent with his observation to a Swiss friend, "We are the ones to be converted, not Hitler."[25]

METHODOLOGY FOR PREACHING

Bonhoeffer's sermons are structured with remarkable consistency. He begins with a citation of the biblical passage or verse in mind, followed immediately by pithy opening remarks either on what is striking (or puzzling) about this Scripture or what is likely to be in the minds of the congregation. Then comes an argument in which the text is contemporized to address the hearers' situation, which is questioned in a challenging and arresting way. He then concludes with an exhortation toward faith and obedience, often with a brief prayer or the verse of a hymn. He tends to speak in the present tense when narrating a biblical story, which heightens the contemporizing effect. Because of his directness, his preaching often conveyed the impression of being spontaneous utterances. Behind each one, however, lay painstaking preparation. During his London ministry, he and his friend Julius Rieger, another pastor in London, would often call each other to share thoughts on their forthcoming Sunday sermons. Bonhoeffer's sermons were either written or typed into full manuscripts. They were often subject to amendment or major revision up to the point of delivery. He would regularly observe the major Christian holidays in his preaching. As noted earlier, he would avoid preaching about specific political or social current events. On occasion, he would preach a series on a developing theme, as in his four sermons on 1 Corinthians 13, delivered in London in October 1934.[26] This series culminated on Reformation Sunday, deliberately reasserting the apostle Paul's emphasis on the primacy of love in face of a diluted Lutheran view of "faith alone." This prefigured his attack on "cheap grace" in his book *Discipleship*.

For a fuller understanding of Bonhoeffer's methodology, we should turn again to the homiletics lectures he gave in the Finkenwalde seminary. These are reconstructed from several of his students' notes.[27] Bonhoeffer states that the preacher is commissioned by Jesus Christ. This commission is given to *the church* as a distinct community of discipleship and it provides the basic orientation of the sermon. Bonhoeffer disagreed with the "German Christian" claim that it is solidarity with "the people" (*Volk*) that meets the need of the hour. The source

---

25. Letter to Erwin Sutz, September 11, 1934, DBWE 13, 218.
26. DBWE 13, 375–96.
27. See DBWE 14 for "Lecture on Homiletics," 487–536; "Homiletical Exercise," 632–53 and 753–781.

of preaching is the Bible: "It pleased God to speak to us in the word of the Bible alone."[28] A sermon is an exposition of the Bible which is concrete and does not need any application. Any text is appropriate to the situation of the "church-community."[29] The God of the cross is speaking throughout the Bible, "Appropriate textual exposition, not application, and existing obediently in the present situation as a Christian. Not conscious contact with the situation of the *Volk* but rather standing as a whole in word and existence, that is what makes it present."[30] The text of Scripture can be trusted to be concrete. A sermon comes about first through prayer for the Holy Spirit's presence, then meditation on how one will convey the text to the congregation. This is followed by questions put to the text and examining of one's own motives for perhaps bending or weakening the text for one's own sake. Then repeated reading of the text until its center comes into view. Bonhoeffer said, "Then the sermon unfolds on its own, without being forced."[31] Following, he provides some practical advice:

> You should write the sermon down if at all possible during the day, not at night. Otherwise you will be excited in the evening and then sober up the next morning. You should not write the sermon all at once. Stay with the chosen text! . . . If possible do not read any other sermons on this text until your own draft is finished. Although it is good to read commentaries, it is not absolutely necessary. Clear conceptual disposition, otherwise difficult to learn and also not good. Begin at latest on Tuesday, have it finished at latest on Friday! You must work on it at least twelve hours. A *written* sermon that is finished is *not* yet a *finished* sermon! Memorize not words but connected lines of thought. . . . A sermon is born twice, once in the pastor's own study and once *in the pulpit*, the latter representing the real origin. An ill-prepared preacher will be insecure and will have to distract listeners from that insecurity through all sorts of devices deriving from his own vanity: noise, pathos, appeal to teary emotions. . . . [There should be] prayer in the sacristy before the sermon . . . [and] after the sermon, prayer for the fruit of God's word through the Spirit.[32]

According to Bonhoeffer, the whole point of the sermon is that God's Word come alive of its own power in addressing the congregation. He desired a limited

---

28. DBWE 14, 492.
29. "Church-community" is the preferred translation in DBWE of the German *Gemeinde* (which in common usage can variously denote "community," "congregation," or "parish") to stress that Bonhoeffer in this context is usually referring to the specific character of a Christian community gathered under the Word of God.
30. DBWE 14, 493.
31. DBWE 14, 496.
32. Ibid.

introduction, "Proceed as quickly as possible to the matter at hand, and do not be overly anxious about doing so. An overly general, dull introduction ruins the entire listening experience, and people will quickly fall asleep. *Get in people's face with the text itself.* The best disposition derives from the text itself."[33] The shape and content of the sermon is determined by the text. So, too, is the kind of language used, which should be as natural as possible, eschewing a consciously cultivated "preaching style." He states, "The language should not be that of the populist speaker who is trying to persuade or educate listeners. Avoid superlatives, exclamations, appeals! This constitutes a false identity with the word, as if we ourselves were the subject of that word. The word of God is itself the exclamation point that we do not need to add."[34]

Pious and poetic language is to be avoided. Dogmatism and "street language" is to be avoided. Bonhoeffer warns against post-sermon exhaustion. This occurs when the preacher confuses themselves with the Word. A pastor who feels utterly depleted after preaching has made himself the subject rather than a laborer who should remain in the background. "*God depletes himself,* not the pastor." Accordingly, there is the "terrible danger" of the pastor who is satisfied with his sermons.[35] Bonhoeffer believes, "A sermon is a witness to Jesus Christ and not a human endeavour."[36] For that reason, the preacher is the one in need of pastoral care after the sermon, and the greatest benefit is to be able to conduct the sacrament of Holy Communion. Bonhoeffer always sees the sermon in the context of the worship service as a whole, the preparation of which he took with great seriousness. Choosing the hymns well beforehand, for example, can itself aid in the sermon preparation. The whole sequence of preparation, delivery, and post-preaching reflection must be borne by prayer.

Bonhoeffer's homiletics lectures largely presuppose a ministry to congregations of regular attenders. But what of evangelization? Bonhoeffer was acutely aware of the importance of this, but pointed out that the situation in Germany was particularly challenging. The national church could be judged to be not only godless, but in a state of apostasy. Still, millions of Germans knew nothing of Christ personally and were baptized. He said, "It is they whom we should and indeed want to serve with evangelization."[37] But, he argues, the work of evangelization should be brought not by an individual but a church-community (*Gemeinde*), "as a brotherhood living together under the word," a kind of core

---

33. DBWE 14, 498.
34. DBWE 14, 506.
35. DBWE 14, 509.
36. DBWE 14, 515.
37. DBWE 14, 521.

congregation. He points to the ways in which the apostolic ministry in the New Testament was often one of partnership as exemplified in the relationship between Paul and Timothy.[38] Later, in prison, he would take up the issue of communicating the gospel in a "nonreligious" world in a more far-reaching way.

CONTRIBUTIONS TO PREACHING

As preacher, Bonhoeffer stands apart from many of the accepted notions of preaching in the modern era. In the English-speaking Protestant world, the first half of the twentieth century saw a variety of forms of preaching: apologetic, psychological, expository, devotional, and man-centered (i.e., Brooks's 'truth through personality'). There were two approaches that vied for dominance in most pulpits: topical and expository sermons. In the former, the preacher starts with some problematic contemporary aspect of the world and human experience and seeks to shed light on it from the Christian faith. In the latter approach, the preacher begins with an exposition of Scripture or an explication of a Christian doctrine, then seeks to "apply" it to the ethical issues or personal problems faced by people or to some current social concern or a situation in the church. During his year of study (1930–1931) at Union Theological Seminary in New York, Bonhoeffer was exposed to the unique approach of Harry Emerson Fosdick, renowned preacher at the Riverside Church.[39] Fosdick's "problem-solving" method of preaching was hardly congenial to Bonhoeffer. It is one thing to address people in all their human need. It is quite another to mold that humanness into a problem to be solved by a bit of spiritual insight. For Bonhoeffer, that is to trivialize both the human person and the gospel. To allow a human need or problem to be diagnosed without any reference to the Word of revelation is to prejudge whether such a "need" is really the most important matter to be "solved" by faith.[40] The most important needs are exposed by the Word of God, which is not to be confused with purely human insight. Indeed, the danger was of human wishes trying to determine and control the Word of God itself. In June 1939, while in New York and agonizing over whether he should stay in the USA or return to Germany, Bonhoeffer records in his travel diary how he went to Riverside Church for the Sunday morning service and met American

---

38. There is one recorded occasion when Bonhoeffer certainly preached in evangelistic fashion: at Bruay-en-Artois in northern France in September 1934, where his friend Jean Lasserre was pastor and invited Bonhoeffer and the other participants in the small conference that he was hosting in his parish to join him in open-air preaching. Lasserre recalled later that Bonhoeffer seemed to have an aptitude for this: "He gave me the feeling that he was quite at ease in such a work to which he probably was not accustomed ... He really spoke the Gospel to the people in the street." See Bethge, *Dietrich Bonhoeffer*, 392.

39. Bethge, *Dietrich Bonhoeffer*, 157.

40. See e.g. DBWE 6, *Ethics* (Minneapolis: Fortress, 2005), 354f.

pragmatism still in full flow: "Worship at Riverside Church. Simply unbearable. Text: a statement from Jane James (!) about "accepting a horizon," namely God as the necessary horizon for humankind. Preacher Lucco, Professor of Yale; the whole thing a discreet, opulent, self-indulgent, self-satisfied celebration of religion. With such an idolization of religion, the flesh, which was accustomed to being held in check by the word of God, revives. Such preaching renders people libertine, egoistic, indifferent. Do the people really not know that one can do as well or better, without "religion"—if only it weren't for God himself and his word?"[41]

Neither, as we have seen from his teaching at Finkenwalde, did Bonhoeffer simply opt for the alternative "expository" approach of first biblical exegesis and then "application" to the concrete situation. This would be to assume a separation between the present situation and the Word, which could then be bridged by intellectual effort. This approach to application ignores the incarnate Christ who is already crossing the divide into our midst and into the world we recognize as our own. Therefore, Bonhoeffer's understanding of preaching will not find universal favor, but it makes for an important contribution to the history of preaching.

Regardless of whether his approach is accepted or not, it provokes a healthy question to every preacher: Are you taking *God in Christ* seriously enough? Just how effective was Bonhoeffer in the pulpit? Did his hearers really hear what he wished them to hear? In one of his London congregations, some found his sermons too challenging—more existentially than intellectually challenging. If Bonhoeffer had survived, what would his preaching be like after the Great War? He believed he was witnessing the end of an age when people could be told who Christ is "with words—whether with theological or pious words."[42] So how do you preach and "what does a church, a congregation, a sermon, a liturgy, a Christian life, mean in a religionless world?"[43] Such questions have given rise to much speculation in the more than seventy years since Bonhoeffer's death. As you trace his life and preaching ministry from his student years to his time in prison, there are certain themes he builds upon. Perhaps his story is the case of the theologian starting to catch up with the preacher.[44]

---

41. DBWE 15, *Theological Education Underground: 1937–1940* (Minneapolis: Fortress, 2012), 224. The "Jane James" referred to is probably the pragmatist philosopher William James.

42. DBWE 8, *Letters and Papers from Prison* (Minneapolis: Fortress, 2010), 362.

43. DBWE 8, 364.

44. For example, the sermon preached in Barcelona on April 15, 1928 (DBWE 10, *Barcelona, Berlin, New York: 1928–1931* [Minneapolis: Fortress, 2008], 492) emphasizes the "worldliness" of the resurrection faith: "God lives, lives for the world. . . . We are together with God, walk down the street with God, encounter God in the foreigner on the road, the beggar at the door. The world is God's world; wherever we go, we encounter God, and Jesus, the Resurrected, is with us." The Trinity Sunday sermon of May 27, 1934 (DBWE 13, 360–63) speaks of the greatest "mysteries" being not of what is beyond us, but closest to us. The 1934 sermon on 2 Corinthians 12:9 (DBWE 13, 401–04) emphasizes the suffering God.

Finally, it is poignant to note the evidence we have of his very last sermon preached—at their request—to his fellow prisoners being transported south from Buchenwald concentration camp as the American forces drew near from the west. On Low Sunday, 1945, they were assembled in a schoolroom in Schönberg, Bavaria, a group of diverse nationalities, of various confessions (Protestant and Catholic), or of no belief, and of contrasting political outlooks, and all of them caught between hopes and fears for their immediate future. The recollections of the two British prisoners in the party have the ring of authenticity, and testify that the intentionality of Bonhoeffer's preaching, of letting the living Christ speak directly to the actual human situation, was maintained to the very end: "Pastor Bonhoeffer held a little service and spoke to us in a manner which reached the hearts of all, finding just the right words to express the spirit of our imprisonment and the thoughts and resolutions which it had brought."[45] And "the text of the sermon, I remember, was, 'By his sufferings are we healed.' And the main theme he drew from this was not that we could in any way rely on God to answer prayers for our specific release and return to our families, but rather for the assurance of salvation."[46]

This happened as the Gestapo were mounting the stairs to the schoolroom to take him away to Flossenbürg and to his death. Still, Bonhoeffer was able both to deliver the scriptural word and enable people to say, "This is my, our, world." Then he could say in his final message to one of his English friends, "This is the end, for me the beginning of life."[47]

Sermon Excerpt

The Magnificat (Luke 1:46–55)[48]

The judgment and redemption of the world—that is what is happening here. . . . What does this mean? Is it not just a figure of speech, the way pastors exaggerate a beautiful, pious legend? What does it mean to say such things about the Christ child? If you want to see it as just a way of speaking, well, then go ahead and celebrate Christmas and Advent in the same pagan way you always have, as an onlooker. For us it is not just a figure of speech. It is what we have said: that it is God, the Lord and

---

45. Payne Best, *The Venlo Incident* (London: Hutchinson, 1950), 200.

46. Hugh Falconer, reminiscence recorded in a British Broadcasting Corporation radio interview, cited in Keith Clements, *Bonhoeffer and Britain* (London: CCBI, 2006), 131.

47. Best, *The Venlo Incident*, 200; see also Bethge, *Dietrich Bonhoeffer*, 927.

48. DBWE 13, 345f.

Creator of all things, who becomes so small here, comes to us in a little corner of the world, unremarkable and hidden away, and wants to meet us and be among us as a helpless, defenceless child—not as a game or to charm us, because we find this so touching, but to show us where and who God really is, and from this standpoint to judge all human desire for greatness, to devalue it and pull it down from its throne.

The throne of God in the world is set not on the thrones of human-kind but in humanity's deepest abyss, in the manger. There are no flattering courtiers standing around his throne, just some rather dark, unknown, dubious-looking figures, who cannot get enough of looking at this miracle and are quite prepared to live entirely on the mercy of God.

For those who are great and powerful in this world, there are two places where their courage fails them, which terrify them to the very depths of their souls, and which they dearly avoid. These are the manger and the cross of Jesus Christ. No one who holds power dares to come near the manger; King Herod also did not dare. For here thrones begin to sway; the powerful fall down, and those who are high are brought low, because God is here with the lowly. Here the rich come to naught, because God is here with the poor and those who hunger. God gives there the hungry plenty to eat, but sends the rich and well-satisfied away empty. Before the maidservant Mary, before Christ's manger, before God among the lowly, the strong find themselves falling; here they have no rights, no hope, but instead find judgment. ✦

BIBLIOGRAPHY

Best, Isabel, ed. *The Collected Sermons of Dietrich Bonhoeffer*. Minneapolis: Fortress, 2012.
Best, Payne. *The Venlo Incident*. London: Hutchinson, 1950.
Bethge, Eberhard. *Dietrich Bonhoeffer: A Biography*. Rev. ed. Minneapolis: Fortress, 2000.
Bonhoeffer, Dietrich. *Discipleship*. DBWE 4. Minneapolis: Fortress, 2001.
_____. *Ethics*. DBWE 6. Minneapolis: Fortress, 2005.
_____. *Barcelona, Berlin, New York 1928–1931*. DBWE 10. Minneapolis: Fortress, 2008.
_____. *Letters and Papers from Prison*. DBWE 8. Minneapolis: Fortress, 2010.
_____. *Ecumenical, Academic and Pastoral Work: 1931–1932*. DBWE 11. Minneapolis: Fortress, 2012.
_____. *Berlin: 1932–1933*. DBWE 12. Minneapolis: Fortress, 2009.
_____. *London, 1933–1935*. DBWE 13. Minneapolis: Fortress, 2007
_____. *Theological Education at Finkenwalde: 1935–1937*. DBWE 14. Minneapolis: Fortress, 2013.
_____. *Theological Education Underground: 1937–1940*. DBWE 15. Minneapolis: Fortress, 2012.
Clements, Keith. *Bonhoeffer and Britain*. London: CCBI, 2006.
Schlingensiepen, Ferdinand. *Dietrich Bonhoeffer 1906–1945: Martyr, Thinker, Man of Resistance*. London: T&T Clark, 2010.

D. Martyn Lloyd-Jones

Preaching *of* the Word and Preacher *for* the Word

CARL TRUEMAN

Any history of preaching in the Christian church would be incomplete if it failed to give significant attention to the ministry of Dr. D. Martyn Lloyd-Jones (1899–1981). Not only was he an important figure in the development of numerous evangelical organizations in Britain in the twentieth century, but he was also a pivotal figure in the revival of expository preaching as the central act of the gathered church. His preaching changed the lives of many of those who sat under it and provided a fundamental paradigm for later generations of preachers. Lloyd-Jones not only exemplified what could be done in the pulpit, but also managed to project a vision of the romance of preaching—of the power of the preacher and the preached Word—to those who looked to him for leadership and example. His legacy includes both a massive body of published sermonic material and a definite theology of preaching.

HISTORICAL BACKGROUND

D. Martyn Lloyd-Jones was born in in Cardiff, Wales, on December 20, 1899. After the family moved to London, Lloyd-Jones attended a grammar school and then studied at St. Bartholomew's Hospital. Beginning in 1921, he worked as the assistant of Sir Thomas Horder, the royal physician. Lloyd-Jones had felt a certain calling to ministry even before he was himself converted.[1] But in 1927, having become an evangelical Christian, he abandoned what had promised to be a most successful medical career and took a call to be minister at a small church, Sandfields, in Aberavon, South Wales, where he remained until 1939. His time at Sandfields was marked by a radical focus on the preached Word and

---

1. Iain H. Murray, *D. Martyn Lloyd-Jones: The First Forty Years 1899–1939* (Edinburgh: Banner of Truth, 1982), 81.

the redirecting of the church away from the politics of the era toward a more heavenly-minded spiritual gospel. This set the tone for Lloyd-Jones's subsequent ministry: the task of the preacher was the exposition of the Word as a means of pointing toward heavenly realities, rather than contemporary political and social concerns.[2]

In 1939, Lloyd-Jones accepted the call to become assistant to G. Campbell Morgan (1863–1945) at Westminster Chapel in London.[3] At this time he also became president of the InterVarsity Fellowship of Students, a group founded some decades earlier as a breakaway from the liberally-inclined Student Christian Movement.[4] Lloyd-Jones was thus becoming a figure of national prominence in the rising British evangelical movement. When Campbell Morgan retired, Lloyd-Jones became the sole pastor at Westminster Chapel, the place where he was to minister until his retirement in 1968. During that time, he preached the various sermons on which his reputation and influence rest, most notably those on the Sermon on the Mount, Romans, and Ephesians.[5] His practice was to preach twice on a Sunday but also to conduct Friday night Bible studies. The latter, however, were not Bible studies in the conventional sense, but were simply additional sermons. This meant that many in London who attended other churches on Sunday were still able to sit under his ministry, and thus his influence extended well beyond the bounds of nonconformity to Anglicans, including James I. Packer and others.

The 1960s, with the growing power of the ecumenical movement, raised many questions about church cooperation in an acute form. Lloyd-Jones's concern over the problematic nature of cooperation with nonevangelicals had been evident since his refusal to give public to support Billy Graham's mission to England in 1954.[6] Matters came to a head in 1966 when he made a speech at the National Assembly of Evangelicals calling for evangelical ministers to withdraw from mixed denominations and come together in a pan-evangelical alliance. John Stott famously used his position as chairman to respond immediately and expressed his disagreement. In the following year, the National Evangelical Anglican Congress at Keele committed Anglican evangelicals to working within the ecclesiastical structure of the Church of England.[7] The final blow came

---

2. Murray, *The First Forty Years*, 143.

3. Murray, *The First Forty Years*, 353.

4. Iain H. Murray, *D. Martyn Lloyd-Jones: The Fight of Faith 1939–1981* (Edinburgh: Banner of Truth, 1990), 6–7.

5. He also preached sermons on revival, including his teaching on the sealing of the Spirit and on supernatural gifts, which were to become controversial after his death when they were posthumously printed in the midst of rise of the charismatic movement in the 1980s.

6. Murray, *The Fight of Faith*, 301–5.

7. On the fateful year of 1966; see the account in Murray, *The Fight of Faith*, 513–32.

in 1970, when Packer coauthored a volume with another evangelical and two Anglo-Catholics, an act which led Lloyd-Jones to break decisively with him.[8]

The clash with Stott and the split with Packer were decisive for Lloyd-Jones's post–Westminster Chapel years. He was more isolated from mainstream, Anglican-led British evangelicalism. He also became somewhat more anti-intellectual, or at least antiacademic, in his overall approach to theology. Thus, he was involved in the founding of London Theological Seminary in 1977, where it was made a point of principle that there should be no formal link to any secular educational institution for degree-awarding purposes, as Lloyd-Jones was convinced that such a link represented a desire for intellectual respectability and had proved fatal at a place like London Bible College, which had by that time drifted somewhat leftward in its theological commitments.[9]

Lloyd-Jones continued to preach until late in 1980, when illness and old age forced him to retire from public life. He died on March 1, 1981. Appropriately for a patriotic Welshman, it was St. David's Day.

Practical Influences for Preaching

Today, we live in an era dominated by media and the concomitant sound-bite culture it encourages. Yet it is not so long ago that public speaking was a powerful and valued art form. So it is perhaps worth noting that some of Lloyd-Jones's earliest exposure to the art of rhetoric came from his experience of the British Parliament. Iain Murray notes that the proximity of the Houses of Parliament to his childhood home in London meant that Martyn and his brother Harold were frequent visitors to the Strangers' Gallery in Westminster. While we can only speculate about the impact this would have had, it seems reasonable to assume that witnessing orators of the caliber of David Lloyd George in action on the floor of the Commons must have had an impact.[10]

Far more significant than his witnessing of the oratory of the great politicians of the era, however, was the medical training Lloyd-Jones received under Sir Thomas Horder.[11] Horder taught that the key to medicine was diagnosis,

---

8. Colin Buchanan, G. D. Leonard, E. L. Mascall, and J. I. Packer, *Growing into Union: Proposals for Forming a United Church of England* (London: SPCK, 1970); Murray, *The Fight of Faith*, 656–57. On the break between Lloyd-Jones and Packer, see Carl R. Trueman, "J. I. Packer: An English Nonconformist Perspective," in Timothy George, ed., *J. I. Packer and the Evangelical Future: The Impact of His Life and Thought* (Grand Rapids: Baker, 2009), 115–29.

9. Murray, *The Fight of Faith*, 712.

10. Murray, *The First Forty Years*, 38–39. The Strangers' Gallery is the public area in the House of Commons from which debates can be watched.

11. I am indebted in this section to the research of Benjamin Randolph Bailie, "The Doctor of Ministry: The Impact of Martyn Lloyd-Jones' Medical Training on His Homilectical Methodology," PhD diss. (Southern Baptist Theological Seminary, 2014).

and diagnosis was as much an art form as a science, a gift rather than something that could be taught.[12] Further, two things needed to be considered: the current condition of any patient and the condition of full health to which any treatment was to be tailored. These two poles determined the treatment to be applied and also brought to the fore the need for the clinician to be familiar with the general principles of healthy physiology and the facts of the patient's condition.[13]

These basic principles informed Lloyd-Jones's own approach to preaching. In an anecdote he recounts in *Preaching and Preachers*, he tells of a sermon he delivered at an Oxford college chapel. After he had finished, he was approached by the wife of the principal: "[She] came rushing up to me and said, 'Do you know, this is the most remarkable thing I have known in this chapel.' I said, 'What do you mean?' 'Well,' she said, 'do you know that you are literally the first man I have ever heard in this chapel who has preached to us as if we were sinners.' She added, 'All the preachers who come here, because it is a college chapel in Oxford, have obviously been taking exceptional pains to prepare learned, intellectual sermons, thinking we are all great intellects.'"[14]

Of course, Lloyd-Jones was being thoroughly consistent with his method of first principles. The congregation in this Oxford chapel was comprised of sinners who needed salvation. Christ was the way of salvation, and so he preached to them as sinners, pointing them to Christ. Whatever relevance their intellects may have had that day, this first principle caused Lloyd-Jones to alter his basic approach, because their intellects did not have an impact either on the problem or on the solution.[15]

THEOLOGICAL INFLUENCES FOR PREACHING

When we come to specifically Christian/theological influences on Lloyd-Jones, two are of particular note: Peter Taylor Forsyth and the eighteenth-century revival leaders.

Forsyth (1848–1921) was a Scottish Congregationalist theologian who had studied under Albrecht Ritschl (1822–1889), the German liberal theologian.

---

12. Ibid., 43–44.
13. Ibid., 48–49.
14. D. Martin Lloyd-Jones, *Preaching and Preachers: 40th Anniversary Edition* (Grand Rapids: Zondervan, 2012), 137–38.
15. The principal's wife ended her speech thus: "They do not seem to understand that though we live in Oxford we are nevertheless sinners." Lloyd-Jones then declares this "a statement of fact." Lloyd-Jones, *Preaching and Preachers*, 138. This also exemplifies why Lloyd-Jones thought evangelistic preaching should be especially theological because "you cannot deal properly with repentance without dealing with the doctrine of man, the doctrine of the Fall, the doctrine of sin and the wrath of God against sin. Then when you call men to come to Christ and to give themselves to Him, how can you do so without knowing who He is, and on what grounds you invite them to come to Him, and so on." Ibid., 76.

Through a personal moral crisis, he came to focus on the cross of Christ as central to the Christian message. Forsyth was far from a conservative evangelical, holding both to higher-critical views of the Bible and to typical nineteenth-century criticism of Chalcedonian Christology. Nevertheless, his short book *The Cruciality of the Cross* (1910) played a vital role in maturing Lloyd-Jones as a preacher. Here is how Lloyd-Jones expressed the issue, recollecting a moment when a friend challenged him on the emphases of his sermons: "I was like Whitefield in my early preaching. First I preached regeneration, that all man's own efforts in morality and education are useless, and that we need power from outside ourselves. I assumed the atonement but did not distinctly preach it or justification by faith. This man set me thinking and I began to read more fully in theology."[16]

It was reading Forsyth that brought the cross to the center of his preaching.[17] This is an important point for any preacher to consider. The declaration of the imperatives of the faith, the need to repent and to believe—and that of the great indicatives—the work that God in Christ has done, must always be coordinated in such a way that legalism is avoided while at the same time the existential urgency of the individual's situation is pressed home. By focusing on the cross, an appropriate relationship between the two can be achieved.

The previous reference to Whitefield points to another, and stronger, influence on Lloyd-Jones's preaching: the great revivalists of the eighteenth century, particularly George Whitefield (1714–1770) and Jonathan Edwards (1702–1758). Revival, while very hard to define either theologically or sociologically, gripped Lloyd-Jones's imagination throughout his ministry, and Whitefield and Edwards were thus archetypal preachers for him. In fact, in speaking of the great theologians of the past, Lloyd-Jones went so far as to make the eighteenth century men the prism through which earlier theology should be refracted: "I myself am an eighteenth-century man, not seventeenth-century; but I believe in using the seventeenth-century men as the eighteenth-century men used them."[18] What he meant by this was that the seventeenth-century Puritans preached doctrine, but the eighteenth-century revivalists—Whitefield, Wesley, Howell Harris, Daniel Rowland, etc.—preached the powerful, experiential love of God; doctrine was a means to understanding this great love, but not an end in itself.

Such a view of Puritan preaching is a caricature, but it is a caricature that reveals much about Lloyd-Jones's own understanding of the purpose of theology

---

16. Quoted in Murray, *The First Forty Years*, 191.

17. Murray notes, however, that Forsyth's doctrinal deficiencies prevented him from having an extensive influence on Lloyd-Jones. The doctrinal note in his sermons was generally enhanced by his reading of the works of the Princeton theologian B. B. Warfield (1851–1921). Murray, *The First Forty Years*, 286.

18. Lloyd-Jones, *Preaching and Preachers*, 131.

and the purpose of the preached Word.[19] This connects to the notion of unction, with which we shall deal below, but it is worth noting at this juncture that what Lloyd-Jones was concerned about was the existential impact of preaching. Conversion was vital, as was the transformation of the individual through the presence of God mediated via the proclaimed Word in the power of the Spirit. As the revivalists were validated for Lloyd-Jones by the fact that their preaching was accompanied with dramatic results, so he desired to see the same.

We might also note that this served somewhat to undermine a robust ecclesiology. Lloyd-Jones himself exhibited an increasingly skeptical attitude to traditional, formal theological training, fearing that it blunted zeal. This finds a corollary in his emphasis on the revivalists. Men such as Whitefield and Wesley operated with a profoundly ambiguous relationship to formal church structures and authority. Lloyd-Jones's congregationalism and his general disregard for careful ecclesiology are in step with this revivalist trait. One might hesitate to say he was a pragmatist, but he certainly subordinated many traditional ecclesiological concerns to the need for evangelism and revival.[20]

'Unction' and Preaching

Perhaps the strangest aspect of Lloyd-Jones's theology of preaching is his notion of unction, the role of the Holy Spirit in preaching. As such, this is not an isolated doctrine but a specific application to the act of preaching of his more general understanding of the sealing of the Holy Spirit. Lloyd-Jones saw this as a post-conversion matter, involving direct and intense assurance of faith and often accompanied with obvious powerful phenomena.[21] This is surely the most problematic aspect of his approach to the pulpit but, ironically, possibly the one that was closest to his own heart. Indeed, this is the subject which he treats last in *Preaching and Preachers*, and that precisely because it is, in his words, "the greatest essential" in the act of preaching.[22] In the chapter "Demonstration of the Spirit and of Power," Lloyd-Jones traces the power of the Spirit from the proclamation of the Word from Elijah on Mount Carmel through the ministry

---

19. See the similar comment about him by his grandson Christopher Catherwood, quoted in Ian M. Randall, "Lloyd-Jones and Revival," in Andrew Atherstone and David Ceri Jones, eds, *Engaging with Martyn Lloyd-Jones: The Life and Legacy of 'the Doctor.'* (Downers Grove, IL: InterVarsity Press, 2011), 91.

20. A good source for understanding Lloyd-Jones's emphasis on the eighteenth-century men is D. M. Lloyd-Jones, *The Puritans: Their Origins and Successors* (Edinburgh: Banner of Truth, 1987).

21. For his teaching on this, see the sermons on Ephesians 1:13 in D. Martyn Lloyd-Jones, *God's Ultimate Purpose: An Exposition of Ephesians 1:1 to 23* (Edinburgh: Banner of Truth, 1978); also D. Martyn Lloyd-Jones, *Joy Unspeakable: Power and Renewal in the Holy Spirit* (Wheaton, IL: Shaw, 1985). For a sympathetic discussion, see Tony Sargent, *The Sacred Anointing: The Preaching of Dr. Martyn Lloyd-Jones* (London: Hodder & Stoughton, 1994).

22. Lloyd-Jones, *Preaching and Preachers*, 321–22.

of Christ, the apostles in Acts, the Reformation, the Pilgrim Fathers, White-field, Wesley, and the Welsh revivalists. In each case, he points to the dramatic results that came from the Word proclaimed.

While generally sympathetic with Lloyd-Jones's emphasis on preaching and on his commitment to the idea that God works primarily through this means, many may find themselves dissenting profoundly on this point. The theological issues are immense. First, there is no biblical basis for the teaching. The key verse from which the chapter takes its title, 1 Corinthians 2:4, is not rooted in an elaborate theology of the special advent of the Holy Spirit at particular moments, but is rather part of a more general polemic which pits Paul's approach against that of the Corinthians, absorbed as they are in more worldly models of power. A second verse which might also be deployed to justify special moments of unction is 1 Thessalonians 1:4–5, but there Paul's point is about the proof of election of the Thessalonian Christians being the fact that they received the Word with assurance. The tenor of scriptural teaching is that the Bible is to be faithfully preached; the results of that preaching—loosing or binding—lie in the work of the Spirit on those who hear and not on the one who is proclaiming the Word. Lloyd-Jones's exegesis of this verse, in which he sees the assurance being referred to as that of Paul, not of those responding to the Word, involves a contrived and incorrect reading of the text whereby it is made to conform precisely with what Lloyd-Jones wants it to say. This is not good exegesis nor sound theology.[23]

Second, the notion of unction, closely connected as it is to revival, overrides his theological instincts. Indeed, fascination with revival and with moments of unusual spiritual experiences clearly acts as something of an interpretive grid for his reading of history. Thus, Lloyd-Jones views Wesley as a hero because he preached a revival, even though his theology would have been regarded as remarkably defective on a host of points, from election to sinless perfection. Third, Lloyd-Jones applies the whole idea in a subjective manner. In *Preaching and Preachers*, he applies his exegesis of 1 Thessalonians 1:4–5 as follows:

> It gives clarity of thought, clarity of speech, ease of utterance, a great sense of authority and confidence as you are preaching, an awareness of a power not your own thrilling through the whole of your being, and an indescribable sense of joy. You are a man possessed,' you are taken hold of, and taken up. I like to put it like this—and I know of nothing on earth that is comparable to this feeling—that when this happens you have a feeling that you are not actually doing the preaching, you are looking on. You are

---

23. Ibid., 339.

looking on at yourself in amazement as this is happening. It is not your effort; you are just the instrument, the channel, the vehicle: and the Spirit is using you, and you are looking on in great enjoyment and astonishment. There is nothing that is in any way comparable to this. That is what the preacher himself is aware of.[24]

There are numerous problems with this passage. While it is no doubt inspiring and certainly instills in the reader something of the mysterious romance of preaching, it is ultimately a species of subjective mysticism. That preaching in the Spirit is somehow analogous to an out-of-body experience is nowhere taught in the Bible. Further, building on his incorrect understanding of 1 Thessalonians 1:4–5, it makes the subjective experience of the preacher a key factor in the effective nature of that which is preached. This is both theologically without warrant and experientially inaccurate. It places a subjective category at the very heart of Lloyd-Jones's understanding of preaching.

Most preachers know that their own experience of their own sermons is not typically a good guide to how they have been received by the congregation. A preacher will often preach a sermon which they consider to fall dead from the pulpit and then find that members of the congregation have been greatly helped by it. At other times, they may preach one that they regard as powerful and moving, only to find the congregation largely indifferent. The truth is, preachers are poor judges of their own production. Lloyd-Jones continues, applying the teaching to the congregation: "What about the people? They sense it at once; they can tell the difference immediately. They are gripped, they become serious, they are convicted, they are moved, they are humbled. Some are convicted of sin, others are lifted up to the heavens, anything may happen to any one of them. They know at once that something quite unusual and exceptional is happening."[25]

Here, the subjective experience of the Holy Spirit by the preacher has an impact on the congregation. Now, such a thing might happen; but to make this a normative category for preaching, or (even worse) the aspirational goal, is simply wrong. Does Scripture imply that Noah's preaching was in some sense spiritually inadequate because it failed to transform any but the members of his own family? Not at all.

And this is where the unfortunate practical implications of this teaching must be acknowledged. The notion of unction, and indeed the notion of revival

---

24. Ibid., 339–40.
25. Ibid., 340.

itself, tend to point the preacher away from the ordinary routines of pastoral ministry. Yes, Lloyd-Jones is right that the preacher should pray for the Spirit to accompany the proclamation of the Word. But the preacher should also be confident that every time the Word is faithfully proclaimed, the Spirit is present and uses that proclaimed Word to accomplish God's purposes. That is the Reformation Protestant position, over against which Lloyd-Jones's view seems both innovative and misguided. For the Reformers, God's promise, and thus God's power, is attached to the proclamation of the Word; the subjective experience of the Spirit by the preacher is neither here nor there with regard to its efficacy.[26]

Yet we might still acknowledge that the intention is good and that what Lloyd-Jones is pointing toward is admirable. Indeed, there is no doubt that Lloyd-Jones's overall intention in his development of the idea of unction was a good one: to emphasize both the existential urgency of preaching and to underscore the fact that the preacher should desire and indeed expect his sermons to have an impact. This is Paul's point in 2 Corinthians 5 where his language reflects the immediate importance of the task: Paul persuades (v. 11), God makes his "appeal" through him, and he "implores" them to be reconciled to God (v. 20). This is language which indicates the importance of the task and the desire of Paul to see results in transformed lives. Lloyd-Jones expresses the same urgency:

> Do you expect anything to happen when you get up to preach in a pulpit? Or do you just say to yourself, "Well, I have prepared my address, I am going to give them this address; some of them will appreciate it and some will not"? Are you expecting it to be the turning point in someone's life? Are you expecting anyone to have a climactic experience? That is what preaching is meant to do. That is what you find in the Bible and in the subsequent history of the Church. Seek this power, expect this power, yearn for this power; and when the power comes, yield to Him.[27]

The desire is a good one, and one that preachers need to take to heart. It is disappointing that Lloyd-Jones came to express it through such a nuance in his theology. Passion and conviction should mark all preaching, but this aspect of Lloyd-Jones's distinctive theology of the Holy Spirit is not necessary to undergird that point.

---

26. For an example of the Reformation position, see the Second Helvetic Confession (1566) I.4, which declares that "when this Word of God is today proclaimed in the Church by lawfully-called preachers, we believe that the very Word of God is proclaimed and received by the faithful" (my translation).

27. Lloyd-Jones, *Preaching and Preachers*, 340.

METHODOLOGICAL INFLUENCES FOR PREACHING

Lloyd-Jones's most famous definition of preaching was "logic on fire," echoing Lyman Beecher's definition of eloquence.[28] This neatly captures a number of his concerns. Preaching is to be structured, to have coherent theological content, and to set forth an argument.[29] It is not to be a debate or a conversation, but rather a confrontation between the truth of God and the hearts of fallen human beings.[30] It is to be rooted in biblical exposition which, for Lloyd-Jones, meant either a short passage or a single verse.[31] It is not to be merely entertaining, but it is also not to be dull. Rather, it is to grip the mind of the preacher (and to do so in a manner obvious to his listeners) such that he is not preaching about the gospel but is preaching the gospel—something which involves him, confronts him, and to which he himself stands in a certain urgent, existential relation.[32]

A sermon is not, therefore, a lecture, and preaching is not simply a display of public oratory. It has a purpose beyond itself and that purpose is "to give men and women a sense of God and His presence."[33] Indeed, Lloyd-Jones made a distinction between the sermon and the act of preaching. To an extent, this distinction connected to the problematic notion of unction, but it can perhaps be given a legitimate form if we make a careful distinction between the technicalities of construction and delivery on one hand, and the sermon's impact on the other. With regards to the former, the preacher is the agent; with regards to the latter, God is the agent. This points toward the twofold concern of the preacher: one must prepare carefully, because what one says must be true, and one must look to God to use the sermon to bring about the desired effect on the congregation.[34] Therefore, the sermon should end on a high note: "You must end on a climax, and everything should lead up to it in such a way that the great truth stands out dominating everything that has been said and the listeners go away with this in their minds."[35] The drama of preaching is clear. The sermon is not a lecture; it is not a theatrical performance. It is an action designed to confront people with the glory of God and his gospel, and so it must be filled with the content of the Bible and structured by the drama of that gospel. Neither a boring sermon, an unstructured sermon, nor a sermon delivered with indifference can be considered a true sermon.

---

28. Ibid., 110.
29. Lloyd-Jones, *Preachers and Preaching*, 69–71, 76–77, 84–85.
30. Ibid., 56–60.
31. Ibid., 85.
32. Ibid., 78–79.
33. Ibid., 110.
34. Lloyd-Jones, *Preachers and Preaching*, 108–09.
35. Ibid., 88.

Preaching and Theological Education

Anyone involved in training individuals for ministry must, at some point, confront the question of whether or not students can be trained to preach and, if so, how. Opinion varies on the matter, but Lloyd-Jones was emphatic in his own belief that preaching cannot be taught. It is a gift and a calling, not a technique that can be acquired by training. Commenting on W. E. Sangster's book *The Craft of Sermon Construction*, he declares that any such attempt will ultimately be "prostitution." He chose the word carefully, because it carries connotations of doing something merely to entice or give pleasure to another. That is not the point of preaching.[36] In fact, he used the word to demonstrate the underlying philosophy that lay behind much modern preaching: the desire to entertain or to make the congregation (perhaps better, "audience") feel good about themselves. This ran contrary to Lloyd-Jones's own philosophy of preaching, which was based on his foundational principles of diagnosing the sinful human condition and presenting Christ as the only answer. It also shaped his concern regarding the use of illustrations or personal anecdotes in sermons, as these can end up in drawing attention away from the central biblical message and toward the preacher instead. Illustrations and anecdotes, too, could become a form of prostitution. The preacher's task is not to be an entertainer.[37]

Dismissing technical books on how to preach, he then proceeded with characteristic confidence, saying: "What about the art of preaching of which I have spoken? There is only one thing to say about this; it cannot be taught. That is impossible. Preachers are born, not made. This is an absolute."[38] This does not mean, of course, that he regards it as impossible for a preacher to improve or that a young preacher is simply able to preach as if it were some innate skill. *Preaching and Preachers* is, after all, a book designed to help preachers to preach better. Rather, he recommends that the young preacher learns best by observing older preachers, both for their strengths and their weaknesses.[39]

This antipathy to the idea that preaching could be taught in a formal manner connects to Lloyd-Jones's own views of theological education. Again, bearing in mind the influence of the Welsh Calvinistic Methodists on him, it is not surprising that he was suspicious—and increasingly so from the 1950s onward—of a tendency he perceived in theological institutions toward either intellectual

---

36. See Ben Bailie's discussion of the language of prostitution in his article "Lloyd-Jones and the Demise of Preaching," in Atherstone and Jones, *Engaging with Martyn Lloyd-Jones*, 156–75, 165–67.

37. Lloyd-Jones, *Preaching and Preachers*, 243–45.

38. Ibid., 130. He also declares in the same passage that the use of video recordings to help preachers improve is "reprehensible in the extreme" and "prostitution."

39. Ibid., 131.

respectability, dry, intellectualist preaching, or both.[40] The preacher is one of spiritual authority (not technical or academic) and preaching as an act is to have an unvarnished, spontaneous power about it which formal training might easily blunt. Indeed, his criticism of Westminster Theological Seminary was that, while its stand against liberalism was heroic, its intellectualism had blunted the preaching of the gospel.[41] Even the biblical languages are to be studied merely to gain a more accurate grasp of what the Bible says.[42] Good preaching arises not from intellectual ability or scholarly knowledge but from the existential connection of the preacher to their message and of the work of the Holy Spirit in their life: "The chief thing is the love of God, the love of souls, a knowledge of the Truth, and the Holy Spirit within you. These are the things that make the preacher. If he has the love of God in his heart, and if he has a love for God; if he has a love for the souls of men, and a concern about them; if he knows the truth of the Scriptures; and has the Spirit of God within him, that man will preach."[43]

One obvious implication of this would seem to be that the unconverted person cannot preach, at least not in the true sense. That would seem to go beyond what Scripture and church history indicate. It is not the heart of the preacher, but the power of the Word which builds the church. But the basic point is indisputable: ideally, preaching should arise from an urgency which only the true Christian preacher can feel.[44]

This is one reason why Lloyd-Jones's major text on preaching, *Preaching and Preachers*, is not in any sense a technical manual. First delivered as lectures at Westminster Theological Seminary in Philadelphia, the book is more of a paean to the glories of preaching and a polemic against attempts to turn it into a question of technique or a mere exercise in effective communication. It is not to be read as a manual on how to preach, and it contains very little in terms of such advice. It should be read in order for the reader to be inspired by the romantic vision of the power of the pulpit, a spiritual force which Lloyd-Jones saw as being at the center of the drama of salvation as it plays out in the present. Those who want to be excited by the task before them are those who benefit most from

---

40. See Philip H. Eveson, "Lloyd-Jones and Ministerial Education," in Atherstone and Jones, *Engaging with Martyn Lloyd-Jones*, 176–96.

41. Ibid., 186–87.

42. Lloyd-Jones, *Preaching and Preachers*, 119. Lloyd-Jones himself had no formal theological education and was not trained in the original biblical languages. This demonstrates that one can be a great preacher without such technical knowledge, but it must be borne in mind that he was an exceptional individual, as his meteoric medical career indicates.

43. Ibid., 131.

44. As a corollary to this, Lloyd-Jones regarded a feeling of inadequacy, and thus dependence on God was a sign of a genuine call to preach: "A man who feels that he is competent, and that he can do this easily, and so rushes to preach without any sense of fear or trembling, or any hesitation whatsoever, is a man who is proclaiming that he has never been 'called' to be a preacher." Lloyd-Jones, *Preaching and Preachers*, 119.

the book. Lloyd-Jones's passion for his work as described therein is palpable and infectious.

CONTRIBUTIONS TO PREACHING

Perhaps Lloyd-Jones's greatest contribution to the field of preaching is the way in which he brought back the idea that preaching is the most urgent and important need of the church and, thus, of the world. This is a point which is clear from the outset of his ministry. His earliest public statement on the matter was the address he gave in 1925, before his call to the ministry, to the Literary and Debating Society. The lecture was entitled "The Tragedy of Modern Wales" and contained an analysis of what he considered to be wrong with contemporary Welsh life and culture. At its heart lay a plea for preaching: "The business of preaching is to give us a new prejudice, in fact the only prejudice that counts—the Christian prejudice."[45] He added,

> A nation given wholly to worldly success cannot possibly produce a great pulpit. Preaching today—again please note the glorious exceptions—has become a profession which is often taken up because of the glut in the other professions. I have already referred to the method adopted in the choice of ministers and we are reaping what we have sown. It is not at all surprising that many of our chapels are half-empty, for it is almost impossible to determine what some of our preachers believe. Another great abomination is the advent of the preacher-politician, that moral-mule who is so much in evidence these days. The harm done to Welsh public life by these monstrosities is incalculable. . . . The great cardinal principles of our belief are scarcely ever mentioned, indeed there is a movement on foot to amend them so as to bring them up-to-date. How on earth can you talk of bringing these eternal truths up to date? They are not only up-to-date, they are and will be ahead of the times to all eternity.[46]

Key elements of Lloyd-Jones's view of preaching are already obviously present (in addition to his wonderful predilection for using the word "abomination" to refer to the type of preaching and ministers he disdained): a fear of professionalism and social ambition supplanting a true evangelical call, opposition to any confusion of politics and ministry (leading inevitably, in Lloyd-Jones's opinion,

---

45. Quoted in Murray, *The First Forty Years*, 67.
46. Quoted in Murray, *The First Forty Years*, 70–71.

to some form of moralism), and a disdain for any thought of modernizing or updating the Christian message.[47] Above all, we might note that he saw the lack of good preaching as lying at the heart of the "tragedy" of his homeland. Clearly, he considered pulpit ministry to be that important. In fact, we might characterize his view of the preacher not so much as a teacher but as one standing in the line of the Old Testament prophets.[48]

Lloyd-Jones saw this view of the central importance of preaching as supported both by Scripture and by church history. On the former, his discussion in *On Preachers and Preaching* focuses on the New Testament, which is perhaps a little reductive, as the tradition of Old Testament prophets could also have been deployed to make the point. But his emphasis on the preaching of Christ, on the means by which the church grew in the book of Acts, and on Paul's theology in his letters all bear out the point. Then he makes the claim that periods in church history that witnessed the most significant decline and corruption of the church always coincided with a decline in preaching. That he casts this point as a rhetorical question indicates that he considers this to be virtually undeniable.[49] This is consistent with his understanding of revival as a powerful movement of the Spirit evidenced in preaching that leads to many dramatic conversions. This was something he prayed for daily.[50]

The reason for the importance of preaching was ultimately theological. We noted earlier how Lloyd-Jones's medical training shaped his approach to the basic priorities and content of preaching (identifying the problem and presenting the right solution). The same applied to the importance of the act of preaching itself: "The moment you consider man's real need, and also the nature of the salvation announced and proclaimed in the Scriptures, you are driven to the conclusion that the primary task of the Church is to preach and to proclaim this, to show man's real need, and to show the only remedy, the only cure for it."[51]

---

47. This latter concern he shared with P. T. Forsyth, who while adopting higher-critical views of the Bible's text, yet eschewed all notions of adapting the content of preaching to suit modern tastes. See P. T. Forsyth, *Positive Preaching and Modern Mind* (London: Independent Press, 1907).

48. Cf. Forsyth, *Positive Preaching*, 3: "Preaching . . . is the most distinctive institution in Christianity. It is quite different from oratory. The pulpit is another place, and another kind of place, from the platform. Many succeed in the one, and yet are failures on the other. The Christian preacher is not the successor of the Greek orator, but of the Hebrew prophet. The orator comes with but an inspiration, the prophet comes with a revelation."

49. Lloyd-Jones, *Preaching and Preachers*, 26–31. Cf. the opening comment of P. T. Forsyth in *Positive Preaching and Modern Mind*, 3: "It is, perhaps, an overbold beginning, but I will venture to say that with its preaching Christianity stands or falls. This is surely so, at least in those sections of Christendom which rest less upon the Church than upon the Bible. Wherever the Bible has the primacy which is given it in Protestantism, there preaching is the most distinctive feature of worship."

50. See Randall, "Lloyd-Jones and Revival," 92, where he refers to Lloyd-Jones as stating this in a letter to Philip Edgcumbe Hughes.

51. Lloyd-Jones, *Preaching and Preachers*, 37.

That was Lloyd-Jones's great contribution: the theological centrality of preaching, something for which he argued both by precept and his own outstanding example.

CONCLUSION

There is little doubt that Martyn Lloyd-Jones was one of the greatest preachers of the twentieth century, though he himself would no doubt have regarded such a description as an "abomination," given his conviction that God, not the preacher, is the true agent in the act of preaching. His sermons have provided an endless source of edification from the time he first preached them. They have also provided models for subsequent preachers (many of whom never met him or heard him live), both in terms of homiletic approach and as inspirational examples of what can be done from the pulpit.

Most significantly, in his work *Preaching and Preachers*, he offers the most important thing: a theology of preaching. If God is the real agent in preaching, then preaching is a theological act. As with any task, the better the one performing it understands what it is, the better one will do it. So it is with preaching. Lloyd-Jones did not simply inspire through his example, he also inspired through his understanding of the essence of preaching. To read *Preaching and Preachers* is to be given a vision for the power of preaching rooted in a theology of preaching. That many will find the theology flawed at points is unfortunate, but the flaws are incidental to the major point: When the preacher preaches the Word, God speaks to people and transforms them. Every preacher should keep that in mind as they enter the pulpit week by week.

Sermon Excerpt

A Miraculous Gospel (Acts 7:17–20)[52]

Look at our Lord's birth. This was a miracle, something supernatural. A young woman called Mary had a visitation by an archangel. She was just doing her work as usual, living her ordinary life, when suddenly this archangel appeared before her and said, "Hail, thou that art highly favoured." Then he proceeded to tell her that she was going to give birth

---

52. Martyn Lloyd-Jones, *Glorious Christianity*, vol. 4 of *Studies in the Book of Acts* (Wheaton, IL: Crossway, 2004), 211–12.

to a son and that He would be very wonderful. The angel said, "He shall be great, and shall be called the Son of the Highest: and the Lord God shall give unto him the throne of his father David: And he shall reign over the house of Jacob for ever; and of his kingdom there shall be no end."

Then Mary, we are told, said, "How shall this be, seeing I know not a man?" Mary looked at this archangel and said in effect, "What are you talking about? You don't seem to realize that I'm a virgin. I'm not a married woman. I have never known a man. It's impossible. I cannot have a child."

Then the angel said, "The Holy Ghost shall come upon thee, and the power of the Highest shall overshadow thee: therefore also that holy thing which shall be born of thee shall be called the Son of God. . . . For with God nothing shall be impossible" (Luke 1:28–37).

The birth of the Son of God was a miracle, a supernatural action. Oh, I know about the learned authorities; they do not understand it. "It's impossible!" they say. And they try to explain it, and they try to reproduce it; but they have been trying a long time, and it all comes to nothing. And it will always come to nothing. This was God. This was not just an ordinary child—this was God in the flesh. There is only one thing to say about that babe. It is what the apostle Paul once said: "Great is the mystery of godliness" (1 Tim. 3:16). Human capacities are inadequate to understand the birth of the Son of God. It is impertinent and wrong even to try. This was God acting immediately, directly, miraculously. ◆

BIBLIOGRAPHY

Atherstone, Andrew and David Ceri Jones, eds. *Engaging with Martyn Lloyd-Jones: The Life and Legacy of 'the Doctor.'* Downers Grove, IL: InterVarsity Press, 2011.

Bailie, Benjamin Randolph. "The Doctor of Ministry: The Impact of Martyn Lloyd-Jones' Medical Training on his Homilectical Methodology." PhD diss. Southern Baptist Theological Seminary, 2014.

Forsyth, P. T. *Positive Preaching and Modern Mind*. London: Independent Press, 1907.

Lloyd-Jones, D. Martyn. *Preaching and Preachers: 40th Anniversary Edition*. Grand Rapids: Zondervan, 2012.

_____. *God's Ultimate Purpose: An Exposition of Ephesians 1:1 to 23*. Edinburgh: Banner of Truth, 1978.

_____. *Joy Unspeakable: Power and Renewal in the Holy Spirit*. Wheaton, IL: Shaw, 1985.

_____. *Glorious Christianity*. Vol. 4 of *Studies in the Book of Acts*. Wheaton, IL: Crossway, 2004.

Murray, Iain H. *D. Martyn Lloyd-Jones: The First Forty Years 1899–1939*. Edinburgh: Banner of Truth, 1982.

_____. *D. Martyn Lloyd-Jones: The Fight of Faith 1939–1981*. Edinburgh: Banner of Truth, 1990.

John Stott

Preaching That Listens to the Word *and* the World

GREG R. SCHARF

Photo by Corey Widmer

At heart, John Stott (1921–2011) was an evangelist who wanted to see people live to the glory of God in the contemporary world. All his ministries—evangelism, pastoring, preaching, writing, and leadership—were expressions of the ministry of the Word of God. Because the Scriptures shaped his life and doctrine, and therefore his preaching and writing, he was granted unusual influence in the twentieth century and beyond.

HISTORICAL BACKGROUND

John Stott was born on April 27, 1921, the youngest child and only son of Sir Arnold and Lily Stott. John grew up on Harley Street, where some of London's most distinguished physicians practiced their medical specialties. His father was a highly regarded and exacting cardiologist and teacher of medical students, and his mother fostered a happy home environment. Although she grew up Lutheran, Lily took the children to their local Anglican parish church, All Souls Church, Langham Place. At the age of eight, like many youngsters of his day and class, John went to boarding school at Oakley Hall in Gloucestershire. There, young Stott did well academically and was appointed "head prefect," a designation bestowed upon the top student leader. In 1935, he began his studies at the fabled Rugby School in Warwickshire, where he grew not only intellectually, but also in other ways: faithfully practicing his cello, cultivating dramatic gifts, and showing an increasingly sensitive social conscience. He attended compulsory chapel and even spent time there alone in an unsuccessful search for God.

In February 1938, John Bridger, a student athlete who was a year older than John, asked him to the school's informal gathering of Christians to hear a Scripture Union worker named Eric Nash (usually called "Bash"). Bash challenged his listeners with Pontius Pilate's question, "What shall I do, then, with Jesus who is called the Messiah?" (Matt 27:22). After the meeting, Stott asked questions, and Bash answered them. He did not insist on an immediate response from Stott, however. That night, John Stott knelt by his bed and, in response to the promise of Revelation 3:20, opened the door of his life to Jesus.

As World War II loomed, Arnold Stott, a World War I veteran and physician to the royal household, was called back into military service at the rank of colonel (he was later promoted to major general). John, by contrast, was, to use his later description, "an instinctive pacifist." As someone intending to be ordained in the Anglican Church, he did not have to defend his pacifist beliefs. His stance was highly disappointing to his father, however, who did not want his son to proceed with his plans for ordination until he had read more widely in theology at Trinity College, Cambridge. John's insistence that his call to ordained ministry was genuine and nonnegotiable seriously strained what had previously been a warm relationship. Only reluctantly did the elder Stott pay his son's university expenses. John was a disciplined student with legendary concentration, yet he was also deeply involved in ministry on campus and as secretary of the so-called "Bash camps" for boys who attended elite schools. Stott finished his BA in June 1943 and, after some graduate courses, proceeded to Ridley Hall in 1944 for a final year of training in preparation for ordination.

Harold Earnshaw-Smith, rector of All Souls Church, Langham Place, where Stott attended as a boy, invited him to become a curate. He did so and was ordained in St. Paul's Cathedral on December 21, 1945. When Earnshaw-Smith died suddenly in 1950, the Parochial Church Council of All Souls successfully presented their case that the twenty-nine-year-old John Stott should succeed him as rector. He served in that role until 1975 when he became rector emeritus. In 1970, Michael Baughen assumed leadership at All Souls, first as vicar and then from 1975 on as rector. This leadership transition freed Stott to write and pursue a global ministry that was already well underway. Indeed, what John Stott described as his three renunciations—of an academic career, of ministry as a bishop, and of marriage—had already aided his expansive list of ministry pursuits. He preached at All Souls and throughout the UK, led over fifty university missions, and in the fall of 1972, he taught preaching for one term at Trinity Evangelical Divinity School. He offered Bible expositions six times at Urbana, the triennial missions gathering hosted by InterVarsity Christian Fellowship. He spearheaded influential conferences and started, revived, or lent his weight to many institutions and ministries. Among these, the London Institute for Contemporary Christianity, founded in 1983, embodied his commitment to struggle with and preach about contemporary issues. Stott offered preaching seminars in many places around the world. He finished his public ministry in 2007 at Keswick and died July 21, 2011.

Ministry Context

The ministry context in which John Stott lived, thought, and preached played a significant role in his spiritual, theological, and ministerial formation. Although it would be virtually impossible to accurately and succinctly describe all the factors which shaped any life that spanned from the Great Depression to the twenty-first century, it may be even more challenging to pinpoint what events and ideas that may have shaped John Stott's thinking and practice. Alister Chapman depicts Stott as very much the product of his environmental influences, including his upper-middle-class family, elite schools, a prestigious university, and the encouragement of Eric Nash.[1] Doubtless these and many others played a part, several of which Stott himself acknowledged, but in my judgment, these were eclipsed in his life by the internal work of the Word of God applied by the Holy Spirit. Having said that, some historical events of this period loom large in his formation. World War II broke out just as Stott, still a young Christian, went from Rugby School to Cambridge. By the nature of the case, that war required a response. Moreover, neither Cambridge University, where Stott studied theology, nor even the nominally evangelical Ridley College, where he prepared for ordination, were nurturing places for evangelicals. His interactions with both lecturers and literature became not so much a source of his theology as they were an anvil on which Stott hammered out his convictions. And he had to do so without the aid of thoughtful books that he would later write.

Ministry at All Souls was a unique challenge because the parish was so diverse. There were prominent physicians, poorer people, and on weekdays, those who worked on Oxford Street with its large retail stores. International students and business people were always present at All Souls as well. This diversity required that his pastoral ministry include strategic thinking about all facets of the pastorate, including preaching. Moreover, from the earliest days of his ministry, international travel—made easier by burgeoning airline travel—brought Stott into contact with Christians from the Majority World to whom he ministered and from whom he learned. The resistance to authority associated with the 1960s and 70s called into question cherished convictions and values. John Stott took those challenges seriously. What Stott called the "cybernetic revolution," especially the growing influence of television, shaped the expectations and capacities of parishioners. Stott wrestled with how these and other cultural dynamics should shape preaching. Moreover, a wholesale erosion of confidence in the gospel characterized the spiritual environment in which he ministered,

---

1. Alister Chapman, *Godly Ambition: John Stott and the Evangelical Movement* (Oxford: Oxford University Press, 2012), 4, 6–7, 9, 157.

and because of this, Stott was highly intentional about how he used his pulpit to engage culture for gospel ministry.

THEOLOGY OF PREACHING

Any fair analysis of Stott's theological framework as it influenced his preaching should hear his own direct and indirect testimony concerning what shaped that framework. Before undertaking that task, we should note in passing that John Stott practiced and advocated *"thinking Christianly,"* a phrase from Harry Blamires's influential 1963 book, *The Christian Mind*. Blamires wrote, "To think secularly is to think within the frame of reference bounded by the limits of our life on earth: it is to keep one's calculations rooted in this-worldly criteria. To think Christianly is to accept all things with the mind as related, directly or indirectly, to man's eternal destiny as the redeemed and chosen child of God."[2] No analysis of Stott's homiletic would be possible or indeed necessary were he himself not a *thinker* who wanted others to think wisely about all things Christian, including Christian preaching.

John Stott's theological framework for preaching was explicitly spelled out in *Between Two Worlds*. In answering objections to preaching—specifically to the contemporary revolt against authority—Stott offered not a cultural response, but one that was fundamentally theological as dictated by a straightforward reading of Scripture. First, he articulated a biblical anthropology, then described the Christian doctrine of revelation. Next, he defined Scripture as the preacher's locus of authority, and made a case for the relevance of the gospel. Finally, he underscored the dialogical character of preaching. It is in chapter three that Stott formally offered his theological foundations for preaching. The first sentence of that chapter captures the essence of Stott's homiletic: "In a world which seems either unwilling or unable to listen, how can we be persuaded to go on preaching and learn to do so effectively? The essential secret is not mastering certain techniques but being mastered by certain convictions. In other words, theology is more important that methodology. . . . If our theology is right, then we have all the basic insights we need into what we ought to be doing, and all the incentives we need to induce us to do it faithfully."[3]

What, then, is that right theology and what are those convictions? Stott marshaled and supported five arguments. First, concerning God, Stott argued that God is light, namely that he is truth and delights to make himself known.

---

2. Harry Blamires, *The Christian Mind: How Should a Christian Think?* (London: SPCK, 1963; repr., Ann Arbor, MI: Servant, 1978), 44.

3. John Stott, *Between Two Worlds: The Challenge of Preaching Today* (Grand Rapids: Eerdmans, 1982), 92.

Moreover, God has acted, taking the initiative in creation and redemption. Also, God has spoken, communicating with his people to explain his actions. Second, Stott laid out some convictions about Scripture. It is God's Word written, and no less so because the words are human words. Furthermore, God still speaks through what he has spoken, and God's Word is powerful. Third, Stott affirmed his convictions about the church, that on the one hand it is the creation of God by his Word, and on the other hand it is dependent on his Word. As such, when the pulpit is weak, the church is inevitably correspondingly weak. Fourth, Stott affirmed convictions about the pastorate, namely that shepherds care for their sheep by feeding, guiding, guarding, and healing them, and these are all aspects of the ministry of the Word. Fifth and finally, Stott affirmed his convictions about preaching. Prominent among these is that all true preaching is expository, not in the sense of the style or strategy of the sermon, but in the broader sense referring to the content of the sermon. "To expound Scripture is to bring out of the text what is there and expose it to view. . . . The opposite of exposition is 'imposition,' which is to impose on the text what is not there."[4] Exposition, thus defined, has four benefits that Stott went on to articulate: it sets limits, restricting what we say; it demands integrity, forcing us to look for "the plain, natural, obvious meaning of each text";[5] it identifies the pitfalls we must avoid, including forgetfulness of our text and disloyalty to it; and it gives us confidence to preach, the boldness of those who humbly speak for God.

Stott's explicitly stated theological framework does not exhaust the subject because a good deal more of his theological underpinning is readily apparent in his homiletical method. For instance, Stott repeatedly emphasized the importance of the preacher's character. Beneath this conviction is the doctrine of the incarnation, and the belief that the preacher is to be a visual aid to the congregation of the truth he proclaims.[6] Or, to take another example, Stott's emphasis on study is rooted at least partly in his view of Scripture. "The higher our view of the Bible, the more painstaking and conscientious our study of it should be."[7] To these biblical and theological studies, Stott wrote that we must add what he calls "contemporary studies" (i.e., the study of the world). This study will fuel our compassion for others and help equip us to speak to them with accuracy and credibility. Humility, an admission that we do not know all we should know to preach faithfully and effectively, should support both types of study—of Scripture and society. Similarly, Stott's methodology reveals his theology through his

---

4. Ibid., 125–26.
5. Ibid., 127.
6. Ibid., 78.
7. Ibid., 182.

insistence on clarity. Sermons should be clear because Scripture is clear. Every word should be carefully chosen because God breathed every word of Scripture.

We who value theology often resort to labels such as "evangelical" or "Calvinist" as shorthand for whole theological systems. Charles Simeon was reluctant to do this, and so was John Stott, who quotes him approvingly: "The author [Stott himself writes] is no friend of systematizers in Theology. He has endeavored to derive from the Scriptures alone *his* views of religion; and to them it is his wish to adhere, with scrupulous fidelity; never wresting any portion of the Word of God to favour a particular opinion, but giving to every part of it that sense which it seems to him to have been designed by its great Author to convey."[8]

This is significant because it underscores Stott's commitment not to allow any system, however valuable it might be, to filter the message of the Bible itself. Indeed, as Dockery concludes, "The text controls the structure and theme of the sermon. The text provides the authority and impetus for the sermon. Stott undoubtedly believes in the centrality of the Scriptures in preaching."[9] That is the main thing we must say about Stott's theological framework: it was biblical.[10] That is not to say that his theology of preaching consisted of selecting proof texts. He was acutely aware that he had cultural blind spots and defenses. "[We] come to our reading of the Bible with our own agenda, bias, questions, preoccupations, concerns and convictions, and, unless we are extremely careful, we impose these on the biblical text."[11] He also understood that the preacher needs to engage in cultural transposition in order to hear and apply Scripture faithfully.

Stott's primary calling as a pastor, and therefore a preacher, meant that week by week he was studying the Bible to expound it for the congregation he served. For this reason, his theology arose from his own knowledgeable submission to the Bible as opposed to being independent of it, foreign to it, or manipulative of it. Just as he opposed what he called "impository" preaching, so he was against impository theological systems. Instead, he let Scripture correct his theology. Andrew Le Peau cites an example of Stott's submissive openness to fresh light breaking forth from Scripture.[12] Stott, in 1963, at age of forty-two, was con-

---

8. Charles Simeon, *Horae Homileticae, or Discourses (in the Form of Skeletons) upon the Whole Scriptures* (London: Richard Watts, 1819–1828), 1:4–5, quoted in Stott, *Between Two Worlds*, 129. Cited here from the Zondervan 1956 edition titled *Expository Outlines on the Whole Bible*, xxiii.

9. Daniel L. Dockery, "The Theology of Scripture as a Decisive Factor in Homiletical Theory and Methodology: A Comparative Analysis of David G. Buttrick and John R. W. Stott" (PhD diss., Southeastern Baptist Theological Seminary, 2010), 180–81.

10. This is why the critical response to his tentative opinions about the nature of eternal punishment was so painful for him. He was merely endeavoring to submit his ideas to fresh biblical scrutiny.

11. John R. W. Stott, *The Contemporary Christian: Applying God's Word to Today's World* (Downers Grove, IL: InterVarsity Press, 1992), 190.

12. Andrew Le Peau, 2012 annual meeting of the Evangelical Theological Society.

fronted by Proverbs 29:7, "The righteous care about justice for the poor, but the wicked have no such concern." That verse went to work on Stott's theology, and later he publicly affirmed his commitment to concern for the poor in his 1975 *Christian Mission in the Modern World.*[13]

It should also be said that Stott's theological framework was not merely a way of codifying biblical convictions that supported and legitimized or otherwise undergirded his approach to preaching; it was also a motive and incentive and aim for preaching. He conceived of preaching as *purposeful*, and expressed its purpose ultimately in terms of the glory of God. For him it was simultaneously for the good of the church corporately and those individuals who by faith are members of it—in the New Testament sense of members of the body of Christ. It was also purposeful for those in the world whom he prayed would become such members by the preaching of the Word and the witness of the church. That is why, as early as 1999, he wrote a memorandum that captured what was expanded slightly to become the "Langham logic," the foundational concepts motivating the threefold ministry of the Langham Partnership International. It expresses in theological terms his vision for the Langham Partnership. He wrote: "We believe (1) that God wants his redeemed people to grow into maturity in Christ; (2) that it is principally the Word of God ('the sword of the Spirit') which matures the people of God; and (3) that he intends his Word to come to them specially through preaching."[14]

Ten years after the publication of *Between Two Worlds*, in *The Contemporary Christian* (1992), Stott began his case for preaching with this definition: "To preach is to open up the inspired text with such faithfulness and sensitivity that God's voice is heard and God's people obey him."[15] He expounded his own definition by advancing its two convictions about the biblical text. First, the Bible is inspired, and second, it is partially closed, meaning that its parts are not equally plain and therefore need explanation by teachers.[16] Stott then elaborates on his definition's two obligations—faithfulness to the text and sensitivity to the contemporary world. Finally, he completes his explanation of the definition by articulating its two expectations, namely that God's voice will be heard and that his people will obey him.

By 2007, in *The Living Church: Convictions of a Lifelong Pastor,* Stott was prepared to suggest five indispensable characteristics of preaching, each worded as a couplet, each indicative of an important, yet unresolved paradox. Preaching,

---

13. John R. W. Stott, *Christian Mission in the Modern World* (Downers Grove, IL: InterVarsity Press, 1975).

14. Timothy Dudley-Smith, *John Stott, A Global Ministry: A Biography; The Later Years* (Downers Grove, IL: InterVarsity Press, 2001), 421.

15. Stott, *The Contemporary Christian*, 208.

16. Stott cites 2 Pet 3:16, Eph 4:11, and Acts 8:26–39.

he wrote, is to be biblical and contemporary, authoritative and tentative, prophetic and pastoral, gifted and studied, thoughtful and passionate.[17] All of these statements concerning preaching reflect the balance, precision, and conciseness that characterized Stott's preaching. Indeed, one could argue that a degree of nuance was sacrificed to editorial precision.

We have argued that Stott's high view of Scripture and uncomplicated hermeneutic dictated a homiletic that was equally straightforward in that it was theologically alert but not smothered by a theological system. Having said that, the doctrine of incarnation looms large in Stott's theology of preaching, with emphasis not merely on Christ the incarnate one, but on God as the "primary bridge builder."[18] Preachers enter the worlds of their listeners because God entered ours in Christ. This is not to say that we compromise the message to make it palatable to our listeners, any more than Christ falsified his deity in completely assuming our humanity. We do not listen to the world in the same way we listen to the Word. Stott's biblical anthropology engendered realistic respect for listeners as those made in God's image and those for whom Christ died.[19]

METHODOLOGY FOR PREACHING

Stott's method of preparing to preach reflects the prominent place of the Bible in his homiletic and his grasp of the spiritual dynamic of preaching. In *Between Two Worlds*, he developed six steps: (1) choose your text, (2) meditate on it, (3) isolate the dominant thought, (4) arrange your material to serve the dominant thought, (5) add the introduction and conclusion, and (6) write down and pray over your message.[20] As stated, these steps do not explicitly address audience analysis, although they do presuppose insights concerning how listeners receive oral communication. That was covered in his chapter, "Preaching as Bridge-Building." Double listening became increasingly important as part of Stott's recommended methodology. In *Between Two Worlds*, he was eager to convey that preaching is something more than the interpretation of biblical documents. By developing six biblical images of the preacher (herald, sower, ambassador, steward, shepherd, and workman),[21] he emphasized the "givenness" of the message, asserting that

---

17. John R. W. Stott, *The Living Church: Convictions of a Lifelong Pastor* (Downers Grove, IL: InterVarsity Press, 2007), 98–110.

18. Mark D. Becton, "An Analysis of John Stott's Preaching as 'Bridge-Building' as Compared to the Preaching of David Martyn Lloyd-Jones." (PhD diss., Southwestern Baptist Theological Seminary, 1995), 213.

19. Ibid., 218.

20. Stott, *Between Two Worlds*, 211–59.

21. These descriptions built upon the 1961 Payton Lectures at Fuller published by Eerdmans that year as *The Preacher's Portrait: Some New Testament Word Studies*.

"preachers are not to invent it—it has been entrusted to them."[22] Yet for Stott, these biblical images did not help much in *contextualizing* the message. Using the bridge metaphor, which he conceded is not explicitly scriptural, Stott painted a picture of a chasm between the Bible and the contemporary world that must be spanned. Theological conservatives who live on the Bible side of the chasm tend to isolate themselves; liberal or radical preachers whose sermons are earthed in the real world have allowed the biblical revelation, in Stott's words, to "slip through their fingers."[23] Seeing this state of affairs as one of the greatest tragedies of our time, Stott lamented, "On the one hand, conservatives are biblical but not contemporary, while on the other hand liberals and radicals are contemporary but not biblical."[24] Aware that for many in our day the problem is not truth, but relevance, Stott qualified his metaphor in two ways. First, he acknowledged that he is not the first to undertake this bridge-building exercise; and second, he recognized the danger of so emphasizing the listener that the preacher is preoccupied with answering listeners' questions. It is not until the second part of chapter five ("The Call to Study") that Stott urged his readers to supplement biblical and theological studies with what he called "contemporary studies." These studies should begin with people, not books, but should include wide personal reading and listening to others by means of reading and resource groups.

Ten years after the publication of *Between Two Worlds*, the concept of contemporary studies took clearer shape in Stott's *The Contemporary Christian*, subtitled in the American InterVarsity Press edition as *Applying God's Word to Today's World*, but in the British edition as *A Plea for Double Listening*.[25] In this volume, Stott expanded the concerns set forth a decade earlier:

> So today, we are resolved to struggle to present the gospel in such a way as to speak to modern dilemmas, fears and frustrations . . . equally determined not to compromise the biblical gospel in order to do so. Some stumbling-blocks are intrinsic to the original gospel and cannot be eliminated, or even soft-pedalled in order to render it more palatable to contemporary taste. The gospel contains some features so alien to modern thought that it will always appear "folly" to intellectuals, however hard we strive (and rightly) to show that it is "true and reasonable" [Acts 26:25]. . . .[26]

---

22. Stott, *Between Two Worlds*, 136.
23. Ibid., 143.
24. Ibid., 144.
25. Stott, *The Contemporary Christian*, 13. That the British edition took precedence in Stott's thinking is clear from these words in the preface of the American edition: "In particular, as indicated in this book's subtitle, I believe we are called to the difficult and even painful task of 'double listening'."
26. Ibid., 26.

I am not suggesting that we should listen to God and to our fellow human beings in the same way or with the same degree of deference. We listen to the Word with humble reverence, anxious to understand it, and resolved to believe and obey what we come to understand. We listen to the world with critical alertness, anxious to understand it too, and resolved not necessarily to believe and obey it, but to sympathize with it and to seek grace to discover how the gospel relates to it.[27]

Moreover, Stott considered this discipline of double listening to be "indispensable to Christian discipleship and Christian mission."[28] This represents a clarification and expansion of his earlier definition of preaching. In 1982, Stott robustly affirmed that "the essential secret [of preaching] is not mastering certain techniques but being mastered by certain convictions. In other words, theology is more important than methodology."[29] By 1992, "methodology" which included double listening, although still less important than theology, was now *indispensable*; it was part of his definition of preaching.

Listening to the Word

Stott's own practice of the methodology that he advocated can therefore be divided into two parts: listening to the Word and listening to the world. Stott was often asked how he prepared to preach on a typical week. The answer he gave in 1982 reflected a very busy parish life in addition to involvement with other ministries that pushed sermon preparation to Saturday mornings.[30] Perhaps for this reason, he came to rely on a twofold strategy: grabbing every available moment for study throughout the week and taking longer periods of advanced reading and study that he ruthlessly guarded from intrusion or interruption. Stott's preaching was evidently the overflow of a life of study *and* of preaching. The careful exposition of any portion of Scripture stocked his storehouse with complementary and balancing truths that he could then bring to bear on any other portion on which he preached. John Stott's own life in the Word of God and his prayerful desire to be shaped and transformed by it was the soil where his sermons grew. Then, often, what Stott preached at All Souls—his consecutive expositions of biblical books or parts of books, such as the Sermon on the Mount—became popular commentaries in the *Bible Speaks Today* series of which he was the New Testament editor. Other sermons were adapted and

---

27. Ibid., 28.
28. Ibid., 29.
29. Stott, *Between Two Worlds*, 92.
30. Ibid., 202.

repreached elsewhere in the world. This practice doubtless refined Stott's ability to recontextualize biblical expositions. That leads to the second sort of listening Stott practiced: listening to the world.

Listening to the World

As was often his habit, Stott instituted practices that included others in the pursuit of his aims. This not only enabled him to practice what he preached with respect to listening to the world, but also equipped and incentivized others who joined him in that practice. One such group was "Christian Debate" which met three or four times a year, and for thirty-five years "was part of the long-term preparation for preaching."[31] Another was a reading group that met as often as once a month to reflect on a contemporary book or less frequently a play or a movie. The membership of these groups varied, but, at least when I was part of such a group in the mid-1970s, everyone in attendance had read the requisite book and came prepared to be interrogated by the rector! Other groups explored certain topics, and experts were invited to help the participants get the facts. John Stott read quite widely but in a disciplined way. His study assistants and others helped him discern which of the many tomes were truly seminal and significant and therefore worthy of his time. In this respect, Stott's preparation for preaching was communal; he brought others along in his quest to listen to and learn of the world in which he preached. Moreover, his methodology was not limited to what he did *before* preaching and his evident reliance on the power of God *during* preaching. He also prayed over the planted seed of the Word *after* preaching. Also, he was eager to receive constructive feedback, which he actively sought from discerning and observant listeners.

CONTRIBUTIONS TO PREACHING

Stott's contribution to preaching was significant largely because his life, his preaching, his writing, his institutional initiatives, and his leadership all cohered, emerging as they did from a common source—the biblical gospel of Christ crucified—and were undertaken for a single aim—the glory of God. Stott's impact was global because he was a gifted and humble preacher whose example both instructed and inspired listeners, whose writing captured and left a record of the clarity of his preaching, and whose sacrificial and wise institutional leadership fostered contexts where others could hear and obey God's Word.

---

31. Timothy Dudley-Smith, *John Stott, The Making of a Leader: A Biography; The Early Years* (Downers Grove, IL: InterVarsity Press, 1999), 258.

In the foreword to *When God's Voice Is Heard: The Power of Preaching*, a 1995 Festschrift honoring Dick Lucas upon his seventieth birthday, Stott writes, "I thank God that Dick Lucas, whose only ambition is to see expository preaching enthroned in the world's pulpits, is consistently self-effacing in style, unswerving in purpose, and uncompromising in content."[32] The traits Stott honored in Lucas are, many would say, true also of John Stott the preacher.

Stott not only preached at All Souls, he also intentionally equipped a succession of curates as biblical expositors.[33] The "Eclectic Society," which was a pastors' fraternal group that Charles Simeon attended in the 1800s and which Stott revived, also fostered the vision of biblical preaching, because every meeting included a Bible exposition.[34] Stott's global ministry was epitomized by his biblical expositions at Urbana, where hundreds of student leaders gained a vision of what could happen when the Scriptures were allowed to speak for themselves. Stott fulfilled the palpable hunger for an authentic example of a humble yet authoritative preacher. He grasped that if this example were to be replicated, institutional structures would be needed and print would need to supplement audio recordings. The Langham Partnership addressed these needs by devising ways to equip seminary and university professors, ways to create and supply books, and ways to equip preachers at the grassroots level.[35] The enduring influence of John Stott on preaching is further attested by the fact that between 1982 and 2012 there are no less than 330 citations of Stott from some 180 homiletical textbooks.[36]

What, specifically, was Stott's enduring contribution to preaching? Stott demonstrated that even in the twentieth century, when preaching was under fire and often unappreciated, it could be and should be faithful to Scripture, clear, and relevant. Stott modeled and taught these three qualities all over the

---

32. John R. W. Stott, Christopher Green, and David Jackman, *When God's Voice Is Heard: The Power of Preaching* (Leicester: Inter-Varsity Press, 2003), 10.

33. Dudley-Smith, *John Stott, The Making of a Leader*, 266.

34. Ibid., 305, 307.

35. Ibid., 311.

36. Those who want to study John Stott, his preaching, and his impact on preaching will find plenty of primary and secondary sources to assist them. When it comes to primary sources, many of his sermons preached at All Souls, Langham Place, in London may be heard online. John Stott, *John Stott at Keswick: A Lifetime of Preaching* (Colorado Springs, CO: Authentic Media, 2008) collects all his Keswick talks from 1965 to 2000. Timothy Dudley-Smith's 1995 anthology, *Authentic Christianity: From the Writings of John Stott* (Downers Grove, IL: InterVarsity Press, 1995)—especially section 50, "Ministers and Ministry"—provides a useful handle on the data. Dudley-Smith's 156-page *John Stott: A Comprehensive Bibliography* (Downers Grove, IL: InterVarsity Press, 1995) is the most comprehensive list of primary sources of all sorts.

When it comes to secondary sources, the most complete are the authorized two-volume biography by Timothy Dudley-Smith (1999, 2001), the smaller, more recent, *Basic Christian* by Roger Steer (2009), and the more critical *Godly Ambition* by Alister Chapman (2012), who had access to Dudley-Smith's source documents and others. Doctoral dissertations by Daniel L. Dockery and Mark D. Becton have confirmed the insights presented.

world. By doing so, he set a standard that became aspirational for generations of preachers who wanted to think and preach as Stott did. He valued faithfulness because he had a high view of Scripture and ministered under its authority. Consequently, he waited patiently on the Word to disclose its message instead of preaching whatever came to mind. He achieved clarity by prayerfully discerning the dominant thought of each preaching portion and then letting each part of the sermon serve that thought. He also worked hard to choose just the right words to convey the text's burden. When Stott preached, listeners did not ask, "Where did he get that?" They always said, "Why didn't I see that?" He achieved relevance by affirming that the Bible still speaks today and by understanding the contemporary world into which that Word speaks. He did not let the present dictate the agenda of his preaching, but he did work hard to demonstrate how the gospel is still good news today.

Sermon Excerpt
Good News of Reconciliation[37]

Of the four main New Testament models or metaphors of the atonement (propitiation, redemption, justification and reconciliation), reconciliation is arguably the most popular, because it is the most personal. And of the four main New Testament passages about reconciliation, this one in 2 Corinthians 5 is the fullest and most striking. It depicts three actors in the drama.

Firstly, God is the author of the reconciliation. "All this is from God" (v. 18). There are eight main verbs in this paragraph, all of which have God as their subject. The whole initiative was his. So no account of the atonement is biblical that takes the initiative away from God and gives it to Christ or, indeed, to us.

Secondly, Christ is the agent of reconciliation. "God the author, Christ the agent" is a satisfactory summary. Both verse 18 and verse 19 speak of God reconciling in or through Christ. As P. T. Forsyth put it, "'God was

---

37. In 2006, John Stott wrote *Through the Bible Through the Year*. Each daily reading cites a single verse but invites further reading in the context. These daily reflections display the sort of succinct, faithful handling of Scripture that characterized his preaching. This is a reflection entitled "Good News of Reconciliation" from 2 Corinthians 5:18, which says, "All this is from God, who reconciled us to himself through Christ and gave us the ministry of reconciliation." The larger context of this reflection commended to the reader is 2 Corinthians 5:11–21. See John Stott, *Through the Bible Through the Year: Daily Reflections from Genesis to Revelation* (Grand Rapids: Baker, 2006), 367.

in Christ reconciling,' actually reconciling, finishing the work. It was not a tentative preliminary affair. . . . Reconciliation was finished in Christ's death." How did this happen? Negatively, God refused to count our sins against us (v. 19); positively, he made the sinless Christ to be sin instead (v. 21) in order that in Christ we might become the righteousness of God. As Richard Hooker expressed it, "let it be counted folly or frenzy or whatsoever. It is our wisdom and our comfort; we care for no knowledge in the world but this, that man has sinned and God has suffered; that God has made himself the sin of men and that men are made the righteousness of God."

Thirdly, we are the ambassadors of the reconciliation. Both the ministry and the message of reconciliation have now been committed to us. In consequence, as we implore people to be reconciled to God, it is God himself who is making his appeal through us. Our task is first to expound what God has done at the cross and then to issue the appeal. It is a safe rule that there must be no appeal without an exposition and no exposition without an appeal. ◆

BIBLIOGRAPHY

Becton, Mark D. "An Analysis of John Stott's Preaching as 'Bridge-Building' as Compared to the Preaching of David Martyn Lloyd-Jones." PhD diss., Southwestern Baptist Theological Seminary, 1995.

Blamires, Harry. *The Christian Mind: How Should a Christian Think?* London: SPCK, 1963. Repr., Ann Arbor, MI: Servant, 1978.

Cameron, Julia. *The Humble Leader: John Stott.* Fearn, Scotland: Christian Focus, 2012.

Chapman, Alister. *Godly Ambition: John Stott and the Evangelical Movement.* Oxford: Oxford University Press, 2012.

Dockery, Daniel L. "The Theology of Scripture as a Decisive Factor in Homiletical Theory and Methodology: A Comparative Analysis of David G. Buttrick and John R. W. Stott." PhD diss., Southeastern Baptist Theological Seminary, 2010.

Dudley-Smith, Timothy. *John Stott: A Comprehensive Bibliography.* Downers Grove, IL: InterVarsity Press, 1995.

———. *John Stott, A Global Ministry: A Biography; The Later Years.* Downers Grove, IL: InterVarsity Press, 2001.

———. *John Stott, The Making of a Leader: A Biography; The Early Years.* Downers Grove, IL: InterVarsity Press, 1999.

Eddison, John. *A Study in Spiritual Power: An Appreciation of EJH Nash (Bash).* Chorley, UK: 10Publishing, 1982.

Edwards, David L, and John R. W Stott. *Evangelical Essentials: A Liberal-Evangelical Dialogue.* Downers Grove, IL: InterVarsity Press, 1989.

Steer, Roger. *Basic Christian: The Inside Story of John Stott.* Downers Grove, IL: InterVarsity Press, 2009.

Stott, John R. W. *The Authentic Jesus: The Certainty of Christ in a Skeptical World.* Downers Grove, IL: InterVarsity Press, 1985.

———. *Basic Christian Leadership: Biblical Models of Church, Gospel, and Ministry.* Downers Grove, IL: InterVarsity Press, 2002.

———. *Between Two Worlds: The Challenge of Preaching Today.* Grand Rapids: Eerdmans, 1982.

_____. *The Challenge of Preaching*. Abr. and rev. by Greg R. Scharf. Grand Rapids: Eerdmans, 2015.

_____. *Christ the Controversialist: A Study in Some Essentials of Evangelical Religion*. Downers Grove, IL: InterVarsity Press, 1970.

_____. *Christian Mission in the Modern World*. Downers Grove, IL: InterVarsity Press, 1975.

_____. *The Contemporary Christian: Applying God's Word to Today's World*. Downers Grove, IL: InterVarsity Press, 1992.

_____. *Evangelical Truth: A Personal Plea for Unity, Integrity, and Faithfulness*. Downers Grove, IL: InterVarsity Press, 1999.

_____. *Favorite Psalms: Selected and Expounded*. Chicago: Moody, 1988.

_____. *Focus on Christ*. Cleveland: Collins, 1979.

_____. *God's Book for God's People*. Downers Grove, IL: InterVarsity Press, 1982.

_____. *Human Rights & Human Wrongs: Major Issues for a New Century*. Grand Rapids: Baker, 1999.

_____. *I Believe in Preaching*. London: Hodder & Stoughton, 1982.

_____. *John Stott at Keswick: A Lifetime of Preaching*. Colorado Springs, CO: Authentic Media, 2008.

_____. *Last Word: Reflections on a Lifetime of Preaching*. Milton Keynes, UK: Authentic Media, 2008.

_____. *The Living Church: Convictions of a Lifelong Pastor*. Downers Grove, IL: InterVarsity Press, 2007.

_____. *Our Social and Sexual Revolution: Major Issues for a New Century*. Grand Rapids: Baker, 1999.

_____. *The Preacher's Portrait: Some New Testament Word Studies*. Grand Rapids: Eerdmans, 1961.

_____. *The Story of the New Testament: Men with a Message*. Rev. by Stephen Motyer. Grand Rapids: Baker, 2001.

_____. *Stott on Stewardship: Ten Principles of Christian Giving*. Chattanooga, TN: Generous Giving, Inc., 2003.

_____. *Through the Bible Through the Year: Daily Reflections from Genesis to Revelation*. Grand Rapids: Baker, 2006.

_____. *Understanding the Bible*. Grand Rapids: Baker, 2001.

Stott, John R. W., and Timothy Dudley-Smith. *Authentic Christianity: From the Writings of John Stott*. Downers Grove, IL: InterVarsity Press, 1995.

Stott, John R. W., Christopher Green, and David Jackman. *When God's Voice Is Heard: The Power of Preaching*. Leicester: Inter-Varsity Press, 2003.

Wright, Chris, ed. *John Stott: A Portrait by His Friends*. Nottingham: Inter-Varsity Press, 2011.

PART *Four*

Twentieth-Century North American Preaching

The twentieth century witnessed the collapse of modernity. Following World War I and World War II, the happy dreams of an industrialized utopia were replaced with tragic nightmares of an increasingly secular, disillusioned society. The deconstruction of historic worldviews was complete, and a postmodern philosophy based on evolution and self-actualization had begun. Of course, technology continued to advance at a staggering pace, altering life in countless ways—both enlarging the understanding of the cosmos and shrinking the size of the world.

Like all of culture, the church in the twentieth century struggled to find its place in a postmodern milieu. A variety of movements clamored for the church's attention, including fundamentalism, liberalism, dispensationalism, social gospel/justice, evangelicalism, and the charismatic movement. Each of these movements had their heroes and advocates who argued that their approach to Christianity best reflected life in a postmodern world. Further, the growth and development of homiletics in the twentieth century gave rise to several schools of preaching, including topical preaching, expository preaching, and the growth of narrative preaching as defined by proponents of the New Homiletic.

Because there is so much overlap between many of the movements, it is difficult to use simple categories. For instance, the twentieth century saw the rise of the most famous black preacher in American history: **Martin Luther King Jr** (1929–1968). King possessed the beautiful union of a brilliant mind and exquisite oration. His preaching, which was often focused on social justice, moved an entire nation to consider anew what it meant to be American. It also paved the way for the rise of other black pastors to levels of national prominence.

One was **E. V. Hill** (1933–2003), who was the famed pastor of Mount Zion Baptist Church in the Watts community in Los Angeles, California. Like King, Hill focused on social justice and was equally popular with both black and white audiences. Another was **Gardner C. Taylor** (1918–2015). Taylor stands firmly in the tradition of Martin Luther King Jr., as an outstanding pastor and orator. Like King and Hill, Taylor used his pulpit to address issues of social justice, but unlike them, he also theorized about the challenges and responsibility of the preaching process. His Lyman Beecher Lectures were outstanding. Upon his death in 2015, people across all ethnicities and theological circles mourned the loss of a great homiletician.

The twentieth century also saw the rise of one of America's most famous liberal preachers: **Harry Emerson Fosdick** (1878–1969). Fosdick was the first to embrace psychology as the true goal of preaching, and he taught a whole generation of religionists the value of personal "wholeness" and "self-regard." A topical preacher, he is perhaps best known for his ongoing battle against the fundamentalists and for one of his most famous sermons—"Shall the Fundamentalists Win?" The fundamentalist movement, with all of its flaws, produced a whole generation of preachers who rejected Fosdick's liberal theology in favor of conservative evangelicalism, which placed an emphasis on the inerrancy of Scripture and the necessity of personal conversion through the gospel of Jesus Christ.

Several men were leaders in this resurgence of evangelicalism. The first was **R. G. Lee** (1886–1978). Lee was the famed pastor at Bellevue Baptist Church in Memphis, Tennessee, where he served for thirty-three years. A famous orator and topical preacher, his most famous sermon is "Pay Day Someday," which he preached more than one thousand times. Lee's successor at Bellevue Baptist Church was **Adrian Rogers** (1931–2005). Rogers is perhaps the most famous Southern Baptist preacher of the twentieth century, by virtue of his thirty-three years of expository preaching ministry at Bellevue, his global media ministry, and his famous, baritone voice. Also, his leadership as three-time president of the Southern Baptist Convention helped produce the "conservative resurgence" of the SBC. Another famous Baptist preacher was **W. A. Criswell** (1909–2002). Criswell pastored the historic First Baptist Church of Dallas, Texas, for more than fifty years. A gifted orator, Criswell was one of the first truly expository preachers in the Southern Baptist Convention, and he helped train generations of preachers. Finally, **Jerry Falwell** (1933–2007) planted the famed Thomas Road Baptist Church in Lynchburg, Virginia, and created the world's largest Christian college—Liberty University. Falwell, a topical preacher, is best known for founding the Moral Majority and for using his ministry to engage culture for social change.

At the same time, the twentieth century saw the rise of the first significant female charismatic pastor—**Aimee Semple McPherson** (1890–1944). McPherson founded the International Church of the Foursquare Gospel. A Pentecostal denomination, her church emphasized charismatic sign gifts. A topical preacher, she is best known for her willingness to use new forms of media technology to produce her church services and for exposing them to churches throughout the world. Also, the twentieth century gave rise to the first truly global evangelist: **Billy Graham** (1918–2018). Graham, a Southern Baptist, was the first evangelist to have full access to radio and television, which allowed him to preach to millions of people worldwide. In the tradition of men like D. L. Moody and Rodney "Gipsy" Smith, he was adept at working across denominational lines for the purpose of hosting evangelistic campaigns, and his topical sermons were grounded in the message of the gospel. Finally, the twentieth century witnessed the rise of some great evangelical theologians and thinkers, including **J. I. Packer** (1926–). Packer influenced countless evangelical pastors and preachers through his unique ability to tackle complex societal issues from a biblical perspective. His primary work, *Knowing God*, has been listed as one of the most significant contributions to Christianity in the twentieth century.

Harry Emerson Fosdick

Prophet of Modernity

DWAYNE MILIONI

Harry Emerson Fosdick (1878–1969) was a preacher, professor, national radio spokesman, and writer with a wide influence on American religious culture. Considered the Henry Ward Beecher of his day, he championed a liberal Protestant theology. Fosdick lived in New York City and his preaching ministry spanned the decades from the 1920s through the 1940s. Fosdick revolted against the conservative Protestant orthodoxy of his day, choosing a modern view of Scripture and its interpretation through the lens of modernity. Because of his popularity and eloquence, he was the perfect spokesman for the liberal side of the fundamentalist controversy.

HISTORICAL BACKGROUND

Harry Emerson Fosdickwas born May 24, 1878, in Buffalo, New York.[1] He died ninety-one years later in Bronxville, New York.[2] He was born to a family that possessed a spirit of individualism and nonconformity. His great-grandfather was removed from his pulpit for refusing to believe in a literal hell.[3] His grandfather campaigned against alcohol intemperance and used his home as the last station on the Underground Railroad. His father, Frank Sheldon Fosdick, was a school principal.[4] Harry was raised in a liberal Baptist home.[5] The family was poor, and as a child Harry witnessed his mother suffer from a nervous breakdown.[6]

---

1. Much of this chapter has been adapted from my dissertation. See Dwayne Milioni, "The Concept of Self in the Preaching of Harry Emerson Fosdick" (PhD diss., Southeastern Baptist Theological Seminary, 2011).

2. Robert Moats Miller, *Harry Emerson Fosdick: Preacher, Pastor, Prophet* (New York: Oxford University Press, 1985), 3. For an autobiography, see Harry Emerson Fosdick, *The Living of These Days: An Autobiography* (New York: Harper, 1956).

3. Clyde E. Fant Jr. and William M. Pinson Jr., *20 Centuries of Great Preaching, Volume 9: 1878–* (Waco, TX: Word, 1971), 4.

4. Ibid.

5. Taken from Lionel Crocker, ed., *Harry Emerson Fosdick's Art of Preaching* (Springfield, IL: Thomas, 1971), 129. This volume consists of articles and statements Fosdick made about preaching, as well as articles from others in the field about Fosdick's preaching.

6. Fant and Pinson, *20 Centuries of Great Preaching*, 9:18.

At age seven, Harry was "moved" by a sermon preached by Reverend Albert Tennant on the call to missions, and he stepped forward to be baptized into church membership.[7] Miller suggests that Fosdick's decision that day was precipitated by his mother's breakdown, the death of his sister, and a fear of dying and going to hell.[8]

Harry developed a fondness for public speaking in school.[9] He also developed a love for poetry.[10] He attended church regularly, though he would later speak unfavorably about it, noting the legalism that often prevailed.[11] He joined the cadet corps while in high school, though he would later become an outspoken pacifist.[12] He excelled in his studies and graduated valedictorian of his high school class.[13]

He attended Colgate University in upstate New York, enjoying courses in public speaking, logic, and debate. He often won speaking contests and enjoyed writing for the school newspaper.[14] While in college, Fosdick struggled to reconcile modern science with the Christian faith. After studying the writings of Charles Darwin, he became a firm believer in the theory of evolution.[15]

After Harry's father suffered a nervous breakdown, he returned home to help with the financial needs.[16] He continued to explore his changing views of religion and decided not to believe anything in the Bible simply because it was contained in it. He would later say, "The Fundamentalists have hated me plentifully, but I started as one of them."[17] He returned to college saying, "I gave up all belief in God at one stage of my college career and had to fight my way back, forever unwilling to accept into my religion anything that could not appear at the bar of reason and defend itself."[18]

It was under the influence of men like Walter Rauschenbusch and Rufus Jones that Fosdick found a religion that was comfortable for him.[19] William

---

7. Ibid., 22. See also Miller, *Harry Emerson Fosdick*, 4.

8. See Miller, *Harry Emerson Fosdick*, 4. In his autobiography, it appears Fosdick is unsure when these fears began, concluding, "It was in Lancaster, so far as I now recall, the thought of God became a horror to me." See Fosdick, *The Living of These Days*, 34.

9. Ibid.

10. Crocker, *Fosdick's Art of Preaching*, 131.

11. Ibid.

12. Fosdick, *The Living of These Days*, 40.

13. Ibid., 68.

14. Miller, *Harry Emerson Fosdick*, 33.

15. Crocker, *Fosdick's Art of Preaching*, 132.

16. Miller, *Harry Emerson Fosdick*, 50.

17. Ibid., 51.

18. See Harry Emerson Fosdick, "Beyond Reason" TMs, p.6 (sermon preached at the Park Avenue Baptist Church on March 11, 1928), from the Harry Emerson Fosdick Collection, The Burke Library Archives, Union Theological Seminary, New York.

19. Fosdick, *The Living of These Days*, 55.

Newton Clarke became his spiritual mentor and made the greatest contribution to Fosdick's evolving faith.[20] Clarke helped Fosdick to distinguish between religious experience and the theological forms that people used to express them. Clarke taught Fosdick that although the stars have always existed, the science and knowledge of astronomy is constantly changing. Fosdick would coin a phrase that guided his ministry, "We must distinguish between abiding experiences and changing categories."[21] He graduated from Colgate *summa cum laude*.[22] In 1900, Fosdick entered Colgate Divinity School but soon after received a scholarship to attend Union Theological Seminary in Manhattan. Before moving, he asked Florence Whitney to marry him.[23]

Fosdick began courses both at Union and at nearby Columbia University. He also began working with the poor and homeless at a mission in the Bowery district.[24] It was more than he could mentally and physically handle, and Harry (like his mother and father) suffered a nervous breakdown.[25] For weeks he struggled with suicidal thoughts and ended up in a sanitarium for several months to treat his depression.[26] This experience led him to change the direction of his future ministry from teaching to preaching. He also became an intern at Madison Avenue Baptist Church during his senior year.[27] Due to his family and personal history of mental illness, he reluctantly agreed to be ordained in 1903. Fortunately his mother was able to attend the service, though she died from pneumonia shortly after.[28] Despite all his personal and family struggles while in seminary, he graduated *summa cum laude* in 1904.[29]

The First Baptist Church in Montclair, New Jersey, called Fosdick as pastor, and he quickly became a notable preacher.[30] A regular pulpit ministry was difficult for Fosdick to enjoy because he wanted his congregation to "catch fire" every time he preached.[31] Growing churches became one of Fosdick's greatest satisfactions.[32] But even though the church experienced dramatic growth, his liberal views made him feel as though he were skating on thin ice.

Fosdick studied sociology and economics at Columbia University, receiving

---

20. Miller, *Harry Emerson Fosdick*, 40.
21. Fosdick, *The Living of These Days*, 65. See also Miller, *Harry Emerson Fosdick*, 41.
22. Miller, *Harry Emerson Fosdick*, 34.
23. Fosdick, *The Living of These Days*, 69.
24. Ibid., 70.
25. Ibid., 73.
26. Miller, *Harry Emerson Fosdick*, 44.
27. Ibid., 54.
28. Fosdick, *The Living of These Days*, 79.
29. Ibid., 80.
30. Miller, *Harry Emerson Fosdick*, 56.
31. Fosdick, *The Living of These Days*, 84.
32. Ibid., 86.

an MA in 1908.[33] His thesis was on the organized labor movement. He believed social liberalism was essentially Christian, and admired Walter Rauschenbusch and Rufus Jones who promoted it. Rufus Jones was a Quaker, and Fosdick would eventually adopt many of the Quakers' values.[34]

As his popularity as a preacher brought national notoriety, he received international fame from his books.[35] His trilogy—*The Meaning of Prayer, The Meaning of Faith,* and *The Meaning of Service*—sold millions of copies on both sides of the Atlantic.[36]

In addition to preaching, Fosdick taught for thirty-eight years at Union Theological Seminary, the first Baptist to be hired at the nondenominational institution.[37] He taught alongside notable professors such as Reinhold Niebuhr and Paul Tillich.[38] In 1911, he became instructor of homiletics and in 1915, the Morris K. Jesup Professor of Practical Theology. He sought to apply modern concepts and higher-critical methods to the text of Scripture. He expounded these views in 1924 when he gave the Lyman Beecher Lectures on Preaching at Yale.[39]

Fosdick was initially in favor of the United States entering World War I. His lectures at Leland Stanford University resulted in his book *The Challenge of the Present Crisis.* He would later say that this was the only book he wished he had not written.[40] In 1918, he spent several months traveling through Britain, France, and Belgium, speaking to congregations, military troops, and other groups.[41] The raw brutality of World War I greatly affected him. He would eventually say, "I abhor war and I never expect to bless another one."[42] He would later become an undivided pacifist and would align his views on war with that of the Quakers.[43]

In 1918, three Midtown Manhattan Presbyterian churches decided to combine their congregations. They asked Fosdick to become their guest preacher

---

33. Ibid., 102.

34. Ibid., 111. Fosdick's growing acceptance of Quaker beliefs was more evident later in his ministry at Riverside Church. See also, Harry Emerson Fosdick, *Rufus Jones Speaks to Our Time, An Anthology* (New York: Macmillan, 1951), 1.

35. Ibid., 91.

36. Ibid., 68.

37. Miller, *Harry Emerson Fosdick*, 319.

38. Ibid., 331. Miller notes that Fosdick had a friendly relationship with Niebuhr despite some of their public disagreements. Fosdick and Tillich did not enjoy much of a social relationship.

39. Ibid., 118. These lectures would be published soon afterward. See Harry Emerson Fosdick, *The Modern Use of the Bible* (New York: Macmillan, 1924), 5.

40. Fosdick, *The Living of These Days,* 121. See Harry Emerson Fosdick, *The Challenge of the Present Crisis* (Philadelphia: American Baptist, 1917), 1. See also Miller, *Harry Emerson Fosdick,* 80. Miller notes that Fosdick ordered that the book be withdrawn from circulation, stating that although he was sincere when he wrote it, he was sincerely wrong.

41. Ibid., 124.

42. From the newspaper titled, *The World* (New York City), 2 March 1925.

43. Miller, *Harry Emerson Fosdick,* 292–95.

while retaining the services of George Alexander as their official minister.[44] Their hope was that Fosdick would eventually become a Presbyterian.[45] Fosdick enjoyed this pulpit ministry. Each Sunday lines of people extended several city blocks hoping to find a seat at Old First Presbyterian Church. Hearing Fosdick preach was compared to attending Carnegie Hall or watching Babe Ruth play baseball.[46] Fosdick's preaching began to focus less on apologetics and more on personal and social ethics.[47]

Fosdick maintained an active traveling, speaking, and writing schedule. He published *Christianity and Progress* in 1922 and *Twelve Tests of Character* in 1923. He wrote numerous articles for magazines such as *Harper's Magazine* and *Ladies' Home Journal*. He also received honorary degrees from Brown, Yale, the University of Michigan, Ohio University, and others.[48]

In 1922, Fosdick preached his famous sermon, "Shall the Fundamentalists Win?"[49] Though a plea for tolerance and charity amongst Christians, this sermon became a lightning rod that spurred a growing debate between liberal and fundamentalist Christian leaders.[50] The main matters of dispute centered on the inerrancy of Scripture, the supernatural aspects of Jesus's life, and the second coming of Christ. The sermon was printed and mailed across the country, paid for by John D. Rockefeller, a personal friend of Fosdick.[51] Fosdick would later admit, "If ever a sermon failed to achieve its object, mine did. It was a plea for good will, but what came of it was an explosion of ill will."[52]

Conservative Presbyterians, led by Princeton theologian J. Gresham Machen, joined forces with a group of dispensationalists to engage in an ecclesiastical war against their liberal and modernist counterparts.[53] Fosdick found himself at the

---

44. Fosdick, *The Living of These Days*, 133. Fosdick was offered the position of permanent pastor, but he declined because he could not subscribe to the Westminster Confession. See also Miller, *Harry Emerson Fosdick*, 94.

45. Miller, *Harry Emerson Fosdick*, 95.

46. Ibid., 95, 97.

47. Fosdick, *The Living of These Days*, 134.

48. Miller, *Harry Emerson Fosdick*, 104.

49. Harry Emerson Fosdick, "Shall The Fundamentalists Win?" TMs, p.1 (Sermon preached at the First Presbyterian Church, New York City on 21 May 1922, from the Harry Emerson Fosdick Collection, The Burke Library Archives, Union Theological Seminary, New York.

50. Fosdick, *The Living of These Days*, 144. See also Miller, *Harry Emerson Fosdick*, 115. Miller notes that this sermon had been unannounced and taken from Acts 5:38–39.

51. Miller, *Harry Emerson Fosdick*, 117. Rockefeller suggested a less offensive sermon title, "The New Knowledge and the Christian Faith," which was approved for mass distribution. Also, the elders of First Presbyterian Church approved of the content of the sermon but felt the title of the sermon was ill-chosen and provocative. See *The Observer* (New York City), 26 January 1924, from the Harry Emerson Fosdick Collection, The Burke Library Archives, Union Theological Seminary, New York.

52. Fosdick, *The Living of These Days*, 145. See also Miller, *Harry Emerson Fosdick*, 117, where he quoted Fosdick as saying, "I am profoundly sorry that it has caused a disturbance; but I cannot honestly be sorry that I preached the sermon. When I get to heaven I expect it to be one of the stars in my crown."

53. Miller, *Harry Emerson Fosdick*, 114.

center of this controversy. He was a liberal desiring inclusive fellowship, while the fundamentalists desired to remove from their denominations the churches that refused to affirm essential doctrines.[54] Fosdick became the object of attack by many in the General Assembly of the Presbyterian Church, such as Philadelphia minister Clarence Edward McCartney, statesman William Jennings Bryan, and a number of fundamentalist Baptist leaders, such as John Roach Straton.[55]

Fosdick was a liberal Baptist who caused conflict amongst Presbyterians and attempted to resign from his church, but was encouraged to remain as the national spokesman for liberal Christianity. He was dubbed "Modernism's Moses."[56] Certain fundamentalist Baptists sarcastically called him the "Baptist Bootlegger" and the "Jesse James" of the theological world.[57] Fosdick declared that mainline denominations would divide if modernism was not accepted.[58] During this time he delivered his Yale lectures on "The Modern Use of the Bible," stating his position that the Scriptures "contain the Word of God, but are not the Word of God."[59]

Eventually the General Assembly forced Fosdick's hand, and he reluctantly resigned from Old First Presbyterian Church.[60] In his final sermon, he identified himself with the apostle Paul, saying, "The real Paul was a determined heretic.... They call me a heretic. I am proud of it. I wouldn't live in a generation like this and be anything but a heretic."[61]

Fosdick was recruited by John D. Rockefeller Jr. and James C. Colgate to become pastor at Park Avenue Baptist Church in New York City.[62] He accepted the position with the following conditions: the church would remove the requirement of baptism by immersion and all sectarian restrictions from membership, and the church would agree to build a larger facility in a less affluent

---

54. Fosdick, *The Living of These Days*, 145.

55. Straton responded to "Shall the Fundamentalists Win?" with a sermon he titled, "Shall the Funnymonkeyists Win?" Calvary Baptist Church, New York City, in September of 1922. He conceded that Fosdick's motives were pure in his sermon, but compared his actions to Paul prior to his conversion, when he was persecuting Christians while thinking he was doing God's will. Then he attacks Fosdick's liberal position on inerrancy and denial of miracles such as the virgin birth of Jesus. Straton stated, "It is too much to believe! The miracles of unbelief are infinitely more difficult than the miracles of faith." See John Roach Straton, "Shall the Funnymonkeyists Win?" *The Religious Searchlight* 1, no.7 (October 1922): 1, 4.

56. Fosdick, *The Living of These Days*, 149.

57. Ibid., 153.

58. The quote was published by the *Philadelphia Inquirer*, 17 April 1925. In this brief article, Fosdick was called the "storm center of church controversy."

59. Fosdick, *The Living of These Days*, 169. In his Yale lectures, Fosdick stated, "We used to think of inspiration as a procedure which produced a book guaranteed in all its parts against error, and containing from beginning to end a unanimous system of truth. No well-instructed mind, I think, can hold that now." See Fosdick, *The Modern Use of the Bible*, 30.

60. Ibid., 175.

61. Ibid., 15. He would later add, "How respectable heretics do grow in the retrospect of history." See "Dr. Fosdick's Hail and Farewell," *The Literary Digest* 84, no. 12 (March 1925): 31.

62. Ibid., 159.

area of Manhattan that could be customized for community service programs.[63] The result was Riverside Church in the Upper West Side of Manhattan, near Columbia University and across the street from Union Theological Seminary.[64] In 1930, Riverside Church held its first service, and Fosdick's famous hymn "God of Grace and God of Glory" was sung at the dedication ceremony.[65]

Riverside Church was a numerical success.[66] The new sanctuary filled up quickly, averaging 2,300 people. Most attendees were visitors, but church members were given admission cards to guarantee their seating.[67] As Riverside Church became an architectural landmark in Manhattan, its preeminence spanned the globe, and in 1951 it was said, "There is probably no better known Protestant church in this country."[68]

As a pastor, Fosdick worked for social change.[69] He was active in the early years of Planned Parenthood, working with Margaret Sanger to limit population growth, and he also helped to establish the Euthanasia Society of America.[70] He joined forces with Alcoholics Anonymous, though he opposed Prohibition.[71] He also fought against racial and sexual discrimination.[72]

In 1935, Fosdick preached a decisive message titled, "The Church Must Go beyond Modernism." This sermon was shaped by the economic depression in the United States as well as the growing threat of another world war in Europe.[73] His concern was that modernism was overemphasizing intellectualism and that its unrealistic optimism did not align with the reality of moral decay in society. He acknowledged that Christianity needed modernism to free itself from fundamentalism, but modernism alone could not help Christianity handle the moral and ethical issues it faced.[74]

---

63. Ibid., 178. See also Miller, *Harry Emerson Fosdick*, 162. Miller lists five conditions that Fosdick set forth, including a free opening of membership to all disciples of Jesus Christ, accepting anyone who sees Christ as the ideal man, that staff ministers would not be chosen based on denominational background, and no denominational name shall be given to the church.

64. Ibid., 201.

65. Ibid., 193. See also Miller, *Harry Emerson Fosdick*, 209.

66. Ibid., 196.

67. Ibid., 233.

68. See Richard Shaull, "New York's Riverside," *The Christian Century* (28 November 1951): 1369.

69. Fosdick, *The Living of These Days*, 279.

70. Ibid., 280.

71. Ibid., 288.

72. Ibid., 289.

73. See the introduction in Harry Emerson Fosdick, *On Being a Real Person* (New York: Harper, 1943). See also, Miller, *Harry Emerson Fosdick,* 389.

74. See Harry Emerson Fosdick, "The Church Must Go beyond Modernism" TMs (sermon preached at the Riverside Church, New York City on October 3, 1935), from the Harry Emerson Fosdick Collection, The Burke Library Archives, Union Theological Seminary, New York. Fosdick states, "Fundamentalism is still with us but mostly in the backwaters. The future of the churches, if we will have it so, is in the hands of modernism." See also, Harry Emerson Fosdick, "If Jesus Were a Modernist" TMs (sermon preached at the Park Avenue Baptist Church, New York City on March 3, 1929), from the Harry Emerson Fosdick Collection, The Burke Library Archives, Union Theological Seminary, New York.

As Fosdick's ministry broadened, so did his interest in psychology and counseling. Around the time of his retirement from preaching, he wrote his most popular book, *On Being a Real Person*, which became an immediate success. It was not written for professional counselors, but for ministers and individuals who were seeking counsel for themselves.[75]

In 1946, after twenty years at Riverside Church, Fosdick handed his pulpit to Robert James McCracken.[76] His postretirement works include: *On Being Fit to Live With: Sermons on Post-War Christianity* (1946), *The Man from Nazareth* (1949), *A Faith for Tough Times* (1952), *Great Voices of the Reformation: An Anthology* (1952), *What Is Vital In Religion* (1955), *Riverside Sermons* (1958), and *Dear Mr. Brown: Letters to a Person Perplexed about Religion* (1961).[77]

Harry remained homebound until his ninetieth year.[78] In a brief tribute, "Fosdick at 90," Graham R. Hodges called Fosdick the da Vinci of twentieth-century Protestantism.[79] In October of 1969, Harry Emerson Fosdick died and his body was cremated.[80]

THEOLOGY OF PREACHING

Harry Emerson Fosdick was a liberal Protestant leader and spokesman throughout his life, opposing fundamentalism early and resisting neoorthodoxy later. He did not claim to be a Wesleyan and called the God of Calvin his devil. He opposed creedal sectarianism, insisting on individual liberty and responsibility.[81]

He believed "religion at its fountainhead is an individual, psychological experience."[82] He was more concerned with establishing a justification for faith than defending the Protestant view of justification by faith.[83] He saw doctrine as evolving rather than being static, and considered Christianity to be a dynamic force rather than a form of religious dogma. In his preaching, he stressed the

---

75. Miller, *Harry Emerson Fosdick*, 275.

76. Fosdick, *The Living of These Days*, 228. That same year he stepped down as a faculty professor at Union Theological Seminary. See also Shaull, "New York's Riverside," 1371, which describes McCracken's preaching.

77. See Eugene Exman, "Fosdick as Author," *The Christian Century* 75 (21 May 1958): 617. See also Miller, *Harry Emerson Fosdick*, 558.

78. Ibid., 568.

79. Graham A. Hodges, "Fosdick at 90: Tribute to a Man for All Seasons," *The Christian Century* 85 (22 May 1968): 684. Here Hodges states, "Setting out to comment adequately on the significance of this man's life and work . . . is as presumptuous and as impossible as trying to describe the Grand Canyon. This man for all seasons is a man hard to measure!"

80. Miller, *Harry Emerson Fosdick*, 570.

81. William Benjamin Lawrence, "Sundays in New York: Directions in Pulpit Theology, 1930–1955." (PhD diss., Drew University, 1984), 9.

82. Harry Emerson Fosdick, "What Is Religion?" *Harper's Magazine* 158 (March 1929): 425.

83. Lawrence, "Sundays in New York," 151.

need for Christianity to become a dynamic reality in a person's life.[84] As a preacher, Fosdick sought to reduce the tension between religion and science by formulating a liberal, Christian anthropology.[85]

Fosdick was not concerned with directing a Christian's faith toward a specific definition of God, rather, he wanted them to see faith as a necessary function of the human soul that must be expressed and experienced. Although he would not divorce faith from works, he would consent that "saving power" lies more in good works, or living out Christ's way of life, than by faith alone in Christ.[86] He did not emphasize placing faith in God's sovereignty or in a substitutionary atonement.[87] He held that the road to redemption was paved with moral law and human effort.[88] Faith, for Fosdick, was not to be defined by way of an orthodox system of theology, but as an individual, psychological experience.[89]

God, for Fosdick, is "the Creative Power in this universe, whose character was revealed in Christ and who reveals himself in every form of goodness, truth and beauty which life anywhere contains."[90] He denied the orthodox definition of the Trinity. Instead, he held there to be a "Trinity of experience" with God, similar to Paul's experience of the Spirit's love, joy, and peace. He encouraged Christians to take part in the experience of God.[91] He believed the best way to understand God was to perceive him as a personality, which could be seen in great human souls like Jesus, Socrates, Buddha, Confucius, and Gandhi.[92] God could also be seen by looking to the creative and redemptive activity taking place in the world.[93] He said, "I believe we come close to God wherever there is beauty, love, integrity, and truth. So often if you ask people where God is, their thoughts go shooting off among the stars, but it is deep down within human life that we find God."[94]

---

84. See Harry Emerson Fosdick, "Christianity Not a Form but a Force" TMs, p.9 (sermon preached at the Riverside Church, New York City on October 31, 1943), from the Harry Emerson Fosdick Collection, The Burke Library Archives, Union Theological Seminary, New York.

85. Larry A. Moody, "The Anthropology of Harry Emerson Fosdick: Becoming a Real Person." (PhD diss., Aquinas Institute of Theology, 1980), 60.

86. Ibid., 176.

87. Lawrence, "Sundays in New York," 343.

88. See Hardy Clemons, "The Key Theological Ideas of Harry Emerson Fosdick" (ThD diss. Southwestern Baptist Theological Seminary, 1966), 347.

89. Fosdick, "What Is Religion?," 425.

90. Harry Emerson Fosdick, *Christianity and Progress* (New York: Revell, 1922), 245.

91. Harry Emerson Fosdick, *Dear Mr. Brown: Letters to a Person Perplexed about Religion* (New York: Harper, 1961), 124. See also Miller, *Harry Emerson Fosdick*, 403, where Miller suggests Fosdick's understanding of the Trinity was like the ancient Roman actor who would wear different masks. He believed what was most important to Fosdick is that people have a "trinitarian" experience with God, who reveals himself in different "personae."

92. Miller, *Harry Emerson Fosdick*, 399.

93. Clemons, "Key Theological Ideas of Fosdick," 3.

94. Harry Emerson Fosdick, "Whose God Is Dead?" *The Reader's Digest* 89 (October 1966): 69. He also wrote, "I for one cannot escape the conviction that there is at the heart of this universe a 'Powerful Goodness' deserving our supreme loyalty."

He promoted a progressive revelation of the Scriptures that did not necessitate harmonizing the teaching of the Old Testament with those of the New Testament.[95] When interpreting the Scriptures, Fosdick utilized his concept of finding the "abiding experiences set in changing categories."[96] The Scriptures are not to be understood as revelation from God, but revelation about God, while at times—the very Word of God.[97] Rather than the Scriptures being inspired, he believed them to be "inspiring" and illuminating to the reader.[98]

Though he affirmed the humanity of Jesus, he denied his deity along with the incarnation and virgin birth.[99] He did not believe in a bodily resurrection and doubted whether Jesus ever thought of himself as the Messiah.[100] Rather than speaking about the miraculous events surrounding Jesus, Fosdick focused on the life and work of Jesus that continues to influence daily living.[101] He believed Jesus to be a lofty conception of God.[102] He held that every Christian contains an aspect of divinity, but maybe not to the same degree as Jesus.[103] He saw in Jesus the essence of the individual human personality unleashed and achieving its full potential.[104] For Fosdick, personality was the most valuable attribute in the universe because it reveals the true nature of God and gives ultimate meaning to creation.[105] He believed that Jesus championed personality by overcoming life's obstacles. He said, "Jesus in his day became a revolutionary, not in the least because he was a social agitator but because he had lighted on this simple and yet tremendous matter. He cared for nothing upon the earth except personality wherever he could find it."[106]

95. Ibid., 24. On page 29 he states, "The new approach to the Bible once more integrates the Scriptures, saves us from our piecemeal treatment of them, and restores to us the whole book seen as a unified development from early and simple beginnings to a great conclusion."

96. Ibid., 96. To explain this concept, Fosdick states on page 98, "I believe in the persistence of personality through death (*abiding stars*), but I do not believe in the resurrection of the flesh (*changing categories*)" [emphasis mine].

97. Miller, *Harry Emerson Fosdick*, 402.

98. Fosdick, *Dear Mr. Brown*, 59.

99. See Miller, *Harry Emerson Fosdick*, 409. Miller notes Fosdick would prefer to render John 1:1 as reading, "In the beginning was the Mind, and the Mind was with God, and the Mind was God. . . . And the Mind became flesh." In the same fashion that God was in Christ he would say there was an element of divinity in all of humanity.

100. Moody, "The Anthropology of Fosdick," 89.

101. Ibid., 82.

102. Clemons, "Key Theological Ideas of Fosdick," 3.

103. Moody, "The Anthropology of Fosdick," 89.

104. Clemons, "Key Theological Ideas of Fosdick," 309.

105. See Harry Emerson Fosdick, *As I See Religion* (New York: Harper, 1932), 44. See also Harry Emerson Fosdick, "Christ, Champion of Personality" TMs, p.1 (sermon preached at the Park Avenue Baptist Church, New York City on 28 April 1928), from the Harry Emerson Fosdick Collection, The Burke Library Archives, Union Theological Seminary, New York. See also Charles Stelzle, ed. *If I Had Only One Sermon to Preach* (New York: Harper, 1927), 119, where Fosdick stated that Jesus "enthroned personality at the heart of the universe." See also, Fosdick, "What Is Christianity?," 554.

106. See Harry Emerson Fosdick, "The Importance of the Individual" TMs, p.5 (sermon preached at the Park Avenue Baptist Church, New York City on December 19, 1926), from the Harry Emerson Fosdick Collection, The Burke Library Archives, Union Theological Seminary, New York.

Fosdick was optimistic about human nature and saw each person as having worth and meaning. He held that each person contained a psychological duality. One part of a person's personality is inherited, holding the capacity to work and progress. The other part is unique and creative and should be explored to reach its optimum potential.[107] He believed every personality to be dynamic and progressive, more like a flowing river than a motionless building. What is important about people is not who they are, but who they may become.[108] As a person progresses, they become integrated, or made whole.[109]

Fosdick's concept of sin was shaped by two world wars.[110] Though he affirmed humanity's ambitious free will, he recognized the will had its limitations and the potential of being severely corrupted.[111] He used terms like "forgiveness," and "receiving a second chance" in his preaching. He believed that God could provide redemption for humankind individually and socially.[112] For Fosdick, sin is the difference between what a person lacks and who they are capable of becoming. Sin was more of a psychological experience than a spiritual reality.[113]

Selfishness and moral failure were two of his favorite subjects to preach against. He said, "Moral failure is sin; it will be inexorably punished; one should be ashamed of it and turn from it, and by God's grace he may be forgiven for it."[114] Sin results in a type of psychological bondage, resulting in fear and despair. This bondage can be broken by understanding and imitating the life of Jesus. For Fosdick, sin is what damages personality and keeps a person from being integrated, or being made whole.[115]

Fosdick understood salvation in terms of becoming an integrated or whole personality.[116] He did not look to the cross as the place where salvation was found, nor did he focus on humanity's total depravity, but insisted Jesus's personality is to be modeled. He stated, "Christ's death is a part of his life; they both are of one piece, based on dedicated self-sacrifice for the good of others. He died

---

107. Ibid., 310.
108. Ibid., 317.
109. Ibid., 323.
110. Lawrence, "Sundays in New York," 215.
111. Ibid., 212. Fosdick would preach against any type of predetermination of humankind. See also Harry Emerson Fosdick, "Christianity and Freedom" TMs (sermon preached at the Park Avenue Baptist Church, New York City on January 20, 1929), from the Harry Emerson Fosdick Collection, The Burke Library Archives, Union Theological Seminary, New York.
112. Clemons, "Key Theological Ideas of Fosdick," 342.
113. Moody, "The Anthropology of Fosdick," 73.
114. See Harry Emerson Fosdick, "A Kind of Penitence That Does Some Good" TMs, p. 8 (Sermon preached at the Riverside Church, New York City on 11 October 1942), from the Harry Emerson Fosdick Collection, The Burke Library Archives, Union Theological Seminary, New York.
115. Clemons, "Key Theological Ideas of Fosdick," 315.
116. Ibid., 5.

as he lived, a savior."[117] He also said, "The fact is that conversion of life is not a theological but a profoundly human experience which takes place outside of religion as well as within it."[118] As such, Fosdick's tendency was to focus on the social implications of the gospel, exhorting his listeners to help those in need. In a 1935 sermon, he said "One might almost say that is what the Christian gospel is all about—the regeneration and elevation of man's interior motives."[119]

There were several key concepts Fosdick used to convey his understanding of the human self, or personality. These concepts are wholeness, progress, experience, self-regard, and realness. The development of these concepts occurred over time, but can be seen by looking at three of his major works which were written over the three main decades of his preaching ministry: *Christianity and Progress* (1922), *As I See Religion* (1932), and *On Being a Real Person* (1943).

Wholeness implies a person has an integrated and well-organized life. A whole personality displays unity—it is not disorganized or divided in its passions and desires. Progress is understood as a life that is continually in the process of becoming. The goal of life is for each personality to pursue and achieve its full potential and possibilities. Experience is the essence of life. It is where faith becomes real. Self-regard means a person has accepted themselves and attained an appropriate level of self-love and self-esteem. To have self-regard is not to be selfish or self-centered, but rather self-regard and self-love should result in a denying of oneself and loving others. Finally, realness describes an awareness of the person's actual self in relation to their ideal self. To become a real person, there must be self-realization, which includes an honest recognition of one's strengths, weaknesses, abilities, and inabilities. Realness helps a person avoid being overly simplistic or optimistic. It allows a person to face their sin so that they might strive to overcome these sins and become a real person. All of these terms are also seen in Jesus, who is the ultimate model of a person who idealized personality.[120]

---

117. Fosdick, *Dear Mr. Brown*, 134. See also Harry Emerson Fosdick, "Contemporary Meanings in an Old Word—Salvation" TMs (Sermon preached at the Riverside Church, New York City on 5 December 1937), from the Harry Emerson Fosdick Collection, The Burke Library Archives, Union Theological Seminary, New York.

118. Fosdick said, "When we talk about conversion of life, therefore, we are dealing with a colossal human fact which overruns all our small man-made boundaries of creed and convention." See Harry Emerson Fosdick, "Good News about Human Nature" TMs, p. 3 (Sermon preached at the Riverside Church, New York City on 31 January 1932), from the Harry Emerson Fosdick Collection, The Burke Library Archives, Union Theological Seminary, New York.

119. See Harry Emerson Fosdick, "The Mainsprings of Human Motive" TMs, p. 8 (Sermon preached at the Riverside Church, New York City on 17 February 1935), from the Harry Emerson Fosdick Collection, The Burke Library Archives, Union Theological Seminary, New York.

120. For a complete explanation of these concepts, see my dissertation, "The Concept of Self in the Preaching of Harry Emerson Fosdick." Southeastern Baptist Theological Seminary, 2011.

METHODOLOGY FOR PREACHING

Fosdick considered the sermon as the center of Protestant worship and believed the call to be a minister as primarily a call to preach.[121] He believed the pulpit had the ability to advance civilizations, and the preacher, armed with effective sermons, was to lead the advance.[122] He believed that the task of the preacher was to place premium value on humanity, and to instill faith and hope in the lives of the audience.[123]

Fosdick had been taught to speak in a way that gained a listener's verdict, and he maintained this goal as a preacher. Though he regularly preached to thousands, he entered the pulpit with the mental image of just one person in the congregation needing to be changed. He said in a sermon, "I want something to happen about this now in some individual lives here."[124] He would repeat his appeal for a person to change throughout the sermon.[125] He could masterfully conjure up the emotions of his entire audience. He said in a sermon, "That miracle of a changed life could happen here now . . . Christ can change persons. No one is so bad, so defeated, so discouraged as to be beyond reach of this truth."[126]

In his homiletics classes, Fosdick would share principles he adopted in his preaching style. Some included: "Don't raise more rabbits than you can run down"; "A sermon must end like a spear and not a broom"; "Take care lest all your sermons seem like just another slice off the same loaf of bread"; and "Preach first of all to yourself, if it hits you it will usually hit somebody else."[127]

Preaching should be a cooperative dialogue between the audience and the preacher. The sermon is meant to handle the congregation's issues, questions, and objections.[128] Fosdick said, "We need more sermons that try to face people's real problems with them, meet their difficulties, answer their questions, confirm their noblest faiths and interpret their experiences in sympathetic, wise and

121. Miller, *Harry Emerson Fosdick*, 59.

122. Ibid., 68.

123. See Norvle Alex Rodgers Jr. "A Pastoral Motif: Integrating the Preaching Style of Harry Emerson Fosdick and the Counseling Style of Wayne Edward Oates." (DMin project, Louisville Presbyterian Theological Seminary, 1982), 18.

124. Fosdick, "A Kind of Penitence That Does Some Good," 10.

125. See Harry Emerson Fosdick, "Humanizing Religion" TMs, p. 9 (Sermon preached at Temple Beth-El, New York City on 9 February 1930), from the Harry Emerson Fosdick Collection, The Burke Library Archives, Union Theological Seminary, New York. In this sermon, he concludes each paragraph repeating this appeal, "You must humanize your religion."

126. See Harry Emerson Fosdick, "The Miracle of Changed Lives" TMs, p.12 (Sermon preached at the Riverside Church, New York City on 4 October 1936), from the Harry Emerson Fosdick Collection, The Burke Library Archives, Union Theological Seminary, New York.

127. See William H. Hudnut Jr. "Fosdick as Teacher" *The Christian Century* 75 (21 May 1958): 615. Hudnut was a former homiletics student at Union.

128. Fosdick, *The Living of These Days*, 97.

understanding co-operation."[129] The sermon was to suggest and not command, explain but not exhort, and to discuss rather than dictate.[130] In evaluating Fosdick's preaching method, Landry outlines his approach:

1. Its main business is solving a vital, important problem.
2. It develops into a co-operative enterprise between the preacher and his congregation.
3. The sermon becomes a two-way conversation between the pulpit and pew. It becomes personal counseling on a group scale.
4. The sermon moves beyond talk to motivation—it creatively produces in the congregation that which is discussed in the pulpit.[131]

Therefore, the sermon is not to be a dogmatic monologue, but a creative, cooperative dialogue that actually brings to pass within the congregation what it communicates.[132]

It is estimated that Fosdick spent an hour of sermon preparation on each minute or two of sermon delivery, and his sermons typically lasted upward of thirty-five minutes.[133] He carefully guarded his morning study time throughout his ministry.[134] He did not invest much time in the study of biblical Hebrew or Greek, preferring to use a variety of English texts and a number of study tools instead.[135] He did not keep up with current biblical scholarship, preferring to read biography and philosophy, both past and present. Emerson and James were his favorite American thinkers.[136] When writing down each sermon, he imagined talking to a specific individual.[137] His weekly sermon preparation started on Monday or Tuesday morning and would last four to five hours a day until Friday. He began with "a free association of ideas," writing down whatever came to mind. Then he would read the Bible and other literature and sketch out his sermon until every sentence was complete. By writing his entire sermon beforehand, Fosdick felt he could weigh each word and then critique each phrase.[138]

---

129. Ibid., 98.
130. Edmund Holt Linn, *Preaching as Counseling: The Unique Method of Harry Emerson Fosdick* (Pennsylvania: Judson, 1966), 25.
131. Fabaus Landry, "The Preaching of Harry Emerson Fosdick: An Analysis of its Intent, Style, and Language" (DD diss., Milligan College, 1972), 30.
132. Ibid.
133. Lawrence, "Sundays in New York," 68.
134. Miller, *Harry Emerson Fosdick*, 356.
135. Ibid., 359. Miller notes that books by notable scholars such as Bultmann, Dibelius, Lightfoot, and Schlatter were absent from Fosdick's library.
136. Ibid., 361. Miller found over twenty pages of personal notes that Fosdick took from James's writings.
137. Linn, *Preaching as Counseling*, 147.
138. Ibid.

In determining a subject, he said, "I, for one, cannot start a sermon until I clearly see what I propose to get done on Sunday morning."[139] Once the topic was selected, he would consider anything that he had read or encountered in his personal counseling sessions that would shed light on this theme. Then he would consider biblical passages and his own personal experiences that might deal directly with the chosen subject.[140] A typical Fosdick sermon might contain around a dozen references to the Scriptures.[141]

Fosdick used several designs for crafting sermons. It may be a straight line of main points, such as "Six Ways in Which Modern Man Can Pray."[142] Or he might state the main points inductively, like the branches of a tree. He also utilized a narrative style, which Fosdick called a "river sermon."[143] He would usually provide a transitional sentence at the end of the introduction, the beginning of each main point, and the start of the conclusion.[144] Typically, he leaned toward deduction while crafting his sermons. He began with a central idea or a "big truth" and then moved toward the main and minor points.[145]

When writing his introduction, he would usually state the personal problem he was addressing, in order to involve the listener as soon as possible.[146] He would usually conclude with a call to action, though he would rarely invite people to join his church.[147] He would often challenge the audience to live socially responsible lives, to practice virtue and moral excellence, and to avoid the misuse of power and influence.[148] His use of illustrations have been described as being psychological rather than theological, drawing extensively from human experience.[149] Boyer contends that Fosdick used the Bible more for its illustrations than for exegetical reasons.[150] He was a gifted storyteller and often employed personal illustrations and human-interest stories from the past and present.[151] He was an artist with words, each sermon adding to his gallery of aptly drawn comparisons, personifications, allusions, and illustrations.[152]

---

139. Crocker, *Fosdick's Art of Preaching*, 42.
140. Ibid.
141. Ibid., 55.
142. Crocker, *Fosdick's Art of Preaching*, 199.
143. Linn, *Preaching as Counseling*, 75.
144. Crocker, *Fosdick's Art of Preaching*, 196.
145. See Edmund H. Linn's chapter titled, "Harry Emerson Fosdick and the Techniques of Organization" in Crocker, *Fosdick's Art of Preaching*, 198.
146. Ibid., 77.
147. Ibid., 85.
148. Ibid., 100.
149. Crocker, *Fosdick's Art of Preaching*, 168.
150. Ralph A. Boyer III. "Interrelatedness of Pastoral Counseling and Preaching With Special Emphasis Upon the Ministries of the Rev. Dr. Harry Emerson Fosdick and the Rev. Dr. Leslie Dixon Weatherhead" (ST diss., Temple University, 1960), 110.
151. See several examples for each category in Linn, *Preaching as Counseling*, 90.
152. Landry, The Preaching of Harry Emerson Fosdick," 78.

For a brief period early in his ministry, Fosdick would preach without the use of any notes, delivering his written manuscript entirely from memory. He eventually found this to be too laborious and time consuming.[153] Later, he would carry an outline into the pulpit. He enjoyed using an extemporaneous method of sermon delivery for most of his career. Eventually, he would bring a full manuscript into the pulpit, always trying to keep the listener in his mind.[154] There was nothing flamboyant about Fosdick's pulpit demeanor; his gestures were few and restrained. He usually gripped his robe and occasionally held up one hand. He would attempt to make direct eye contact with his audience as much as possible. Fosdick believed effective delivery equated to an "animated conversation" with an audience over some vital problem of life.[155] He felt that the delivery of a sermon should begin in conversational style, lead to an impassioned discourse, and then return to the conversation. He opposed the use of any manner of pulpit tricks simply to get a rise out of the congregation.[156]

Much of Fosdick's preaching success has been accredited to his ability as a wordsmith. He spent a great deal of time honing his delivery skills while in college.[157] Miller notes: "He was a consummate craftsman. The sermons are characterized by a perfectly ordered structure. They immediately arrest the attention of the listener, proceed with pace to the elaboration of a clearly stated purpose, and conclude with a ringing affirmation. Vigor, vividness, drama, power, warmth, concreteness, earnestness, beauty are all there. He favored strong, hearty Anglo-Saxon words and disfavored technical ones. Gritty colloquialisms, epigrammatic flashes, gnomic flavoring kept the listener on the alert."[158]

He rarely employed exotic or uncommon terms, preferring "strong and lusty ones."[159] In a tribute, Robert D. Clark summarized Fosdick's vocal ability: "He spoke sharply and critically, and yet hopefully, and the recurring upward inflection in his voice, the persistent suggestions of a ministerial tone served only to temper the occasional asperity of his criticism and the imperative challenge in his voice."[160] Fosdick's distinctive voice had an element of harshness; some considered it "raspy or throaty." His pronunciation and articulation were always clear and coherent, varying in pitch, emphasis, and rate.[161]

---

153. Linn, *Preaching as Counseling*, 148.
154. Miller, *Harry Emerson Fosdick*, 370.
155. Crocker, *Fosdick's Art of Preaching*, 47.
156. Ibid., 48.
157. Ibid., 376.
158. Ibid., 377.
159. Crocker, *Fosdick's Art of Preaching*, 109.
160. See Hochmuth, History and Criticism of American Public Address, 6. See also Linn, *Preaching as Counseling*, 129.
161. Miller, *Harry Emerson Fosdick*, 371.

Although he was asked on numerous occasions to write a book on preaching, Fosdick declined.[162] Still, he is famous for an article he wrote for *Harper's Magazine* in 1928 titled, "What Is the Matter with Preaching?"[163] In this article, Fosdick took issue with the preaching of his day for not connecting with the contemporary audience. He felt many sermons were mediocre and uninteresting. He then suggested an alternative approach.[164] Fosdick believed that every sermon should be about the business of solving "a vital, important problem, puzzling minds, burdening consciences, distracting lives—and any sermon which thus does tackle a real problem, throw even a little light on it, and help some individuals practically to find their way through it cannot be altogether uninteresting."[165] He believed that even if the preacher's delivery skills were less than adequate, the problem-solving method would keep the congregation coming back.[166]

Fosdick was opposed to both expository and topical methods of preaching. He found expository preaching archaic and irrelevant to the needs of the contemporary congregation. He concluded that the expository-type preacher is alone in believing the idea "that folk come to church desperately anxious to discover what happened to the Jebusites."[167] He also stated, "Preachers who seek out texts from the Bible and then proceed to give their historic settings, their logical meaning in the context, their place in the theology of the writer, with a few practical reflections appended, are grossly misusing the Bible."[168] He believed the expository method led to dullness and futility in preaching. The Bible was to be used as a searchlight—not to be glared at, but rather to cast light upon a current shadowed spot in a person's life.[169] He later admitted that an expository sermon might be acceptable if the text of Scripture was used to describe some aspect of the "abiding human experience."[170]

He also rejected topical preaching, believing it turned the pulpit into a platform and a sermon into a lecture.[171] He observed that topical preachers would typically inspect newspapers for a current story or issue and then share their ideas on the subject. He saw this method causing preachers to struggle week after week, attempting to produce independent and valuable judgments on a vast array

---

162. Fosdick, *The Living of These Days*, 96.
163. See Harry Emerson Fosdick, "What Is the Matter with Preaching?" *Harper's Magazine* 157 (July 1928): 133. See also Lawrence, "Sundays in New York," 342.
164. Fosdick, "What Is the Matter with Preaching?," 134.
165. Ibid.
166. Ibid.
167. Ibid.
168. Fosdick, "What Is the Matter with Preaching?," 135.
169. Ibid.
170. Crocker, *Fosdick's Art of Preaching*, 49.
171. Fosdick, *The Living of These Days*, 93.

of contemporary issues.[172] He stated, "If people do not come to church anxious about what happened to the Jebusites, neither do they come yearning to hear a lecturer express his personal opinion on themes which editors, columnists, and radio commentators have been dealing with throughout the week."[173] He personally felt that his own preaching floundered until personal counseling led him to an approach that made preaching an exciting adventure.

The purpose of a sermon is to tackle a personal problem and meet a human need.[174] This was Fosdick's conclusion after many hours in personal counseling sessions. He believed everyone comes to church with specific problems. This led him to believe that every sermon should focus on at least one problem that "puzzled the mind, burdened the conscience, or caused distraction in living."[175] The sermon should be designed to meet needs, or as Fosdick put it, "It should be personal counseling on a group scale, and the main thrust of the sermon should deal with a problem head-on to help the listener gain victory over it."[176]

He called his method of preaching the "project method." It has also been called, "the counseling sermon," and he saw a close relationship between his pulpit ministry and his individual counseling sessions.[177] Fosdick describes his method in simple terms: "Briefly put: start with a live issue, a real problem, personal or social, perplexing to the mind or disturbing to the conscience of the people; face that problem fairly, deal with it honestly, and throw such light on it from the Spirit of Christ that the people will go out able to think more clearly and live more nobly because of that sermon's illumination. That is real preaching, and not only has such preaching not been outgrown, but there are few things that modern folk are hungrier for than that."[178]

He considered his new method "the basis of all good modern teaching and that by beginning with the interests of people, it promoted a good psychology."[179]

The Bible was still useful in that it provided numerous examples of human experience, and Fosdick believed that his project method maintained the importance of the Bible and the best of what topical preaching had to offer. He said of the preacher, "Let him start with the people confronting him in the pews and speak as wisely and Christianly as he could to their 'business and bosoms,' and he might help at least one individual that Sunday."[180]

---

172. Fosdick, "What Is the Matter with Preaching?" 136.

173. Fosdick, *The Living of These Days*, 93.

174. Linn, *Preaching as Counseling*, 13.

175. Miller, *Harry Emerson Fosdick*, 59.

176. Fosdick, *The Living of These Days*, 94.

177. Linn, *Preaching as Counseling*, 15.

178. See Fosdick's brief introduction in Samuel McComb, *Preaching in Theory and Practice* (New York: Oxford University Press, 1926), xii.

179. Fosdick, "What Is the Matter with Preaching?," 136.

180. Fosdick, *The Living of These Days*, 96.

It is the preacher's task to create within the congregation the very thing that was spoken about. The purpose of preaching, then, was to bring the gospel to bear on the individual's life. He would often measure the success of his sermons by the number of listeners who, after his preaching, would write him or ask to meet with him for individual counseling.[181]

CONTRIBUTIONS TO PREACHING

Though he would consider personal counseling central to his ministry, history has deemed Fosdick famous as a preacher. In fact, he is acclaimed as the preeminent American preacher of his era and is said to have had the greatest religious influence on his generation.[182] He was dubbed by *Time* magazine as the best-known and most influential Protestant in the 1920s and 1930s. The *Atlanta Constitution* considered him the greatest preacher in America in the past one hundred years.[183] It was not until 1976 that a university study concluded that Billy Graham had replaced Harry Emerson Fosdick as the best-known American preacher. Though the two had never met, this is ironic in that Fosdick found Graham's theology to be "incredibly fundamentalist and dreadful, lacking any serious theological trend that was not here already present."[184]

Sermon Excerpt

The Church Must Go beyond Modernism[185]

We modernists had better talk to ourselves like this. So had the fundamentalists—but that is not our affair. We have already largely won the battle we started out to win; we have adjusted the Christian faith to the best intelligence of our day and have won the strongest minds and

---

181. See Boyer, "Interrelatedness of Pastoral Counseling and Preaching," 71. Also see Linn, *Preaching as Counseling*, 26. Linn measured Fosdick's preaching to be successful according to several criteria: those who gave immediate feedback; those who requested a private interview afterwards; those who read the sermon manuscript afterwards; the technical excellence of style, content, and composition; prophetic insight of what will correctly happen in the future; church growth; and the lasting influence of society.

182. Harold A. Bosley, "Fosdick as Preacher," *The Christian Century* 75 (21 May 1958): 611.

183. Fosdick appeared on the cover of *Time* on September 21, 1925 and October 6, 1930. See Miller, *Harry Emerson Fosdick*, 335.

184. Miller, *Harry Emerson Fosdick*, 561.

185. See Harry Emerson Fosdick, "The Church Must Go beyond Modernism" TMs (Sermon preached at the Riverside Church on 3 October 1935), from the Harry Emerson Fosdick Collection, The Burke Library Archives, Union Theological Seminary, New York.

the best abilities of the churches to our side. Fundamentalism is still with us but mostly in the backwaters. The future of the churches, if we will have it so, is in the hands of modernism. Therefore let all modernists lift a new battle cry, "We must go beyond modernism!" And in that new enterprise the watchword will be not, "Accommodate yourself to the prevailing culture!" But, "Stand out from it and challenge it!" For this unescapable fact, which again and again in Christian history has called modernism to its senses, we face: we cannot harmonize Christ himself with modern culture. What Christ does to modern culture is to challenge it. ◆

BIBLIOGRAPHY

Bosley, Harold A. "Fosdick as Preacher." *The Christian Century* 75 (21 May 1958): 611–14.

Boyer, Ralph A., III. "Interrelatedness of Pastoral Counseling and Preaching with Special Emphasis Upon the Ministries of the Rev. Dr. Harry Emerson Fosdick and the Rev. Dr. Leslie Dixon Weatherhead." ST diss., Temple University, 1960.

Clemons, Hardy. "The Key Theological Ideas of Harry Emerson Fosdick." ThD diss., Southwestern Baptist Theological Seminary, 1966.

Crocker, Lionel, ed. *Harry Emerson Fosdick's Art of Preaching: An Anthology*. Springfield, IL: Thomas, 1971.

Exman, Eugene. "Fosdick as Author." *The Christian Century* 75 (21 May 1958): 617–19.

Fant, Clyde E., Jr., and William M. Pinson Jr. *20 Centuries of Great Preaching, Volume 9: 1878–*. Waco, TX: Word, 1971.

Fosdick, Harry Emerson. *As I See Religion*. New York: Harper, 1932.

————. "Being a Christian Citizen of the World." TMs (Sermon preached at the Temple Beth-El, New York City on 9 March 1930), from the Harry Emerson Fosdick Collection, The Burke Library Archives, Union Theological Seminary, New York.

————. "Beyond Modernism." *The Christian Century* 52 (December 1935): 1549–52.

————. "Beyond Reason." TMs (Sermon preached at the Park Avenue Baptist Church on 11 March 1928), from the Harry Emerson Fosdick Collection, The Burke Library Archives, Union Theological Seminary, New York.

————. *The Challenge of the Present Crisis*. Philadelphia: American Baptist, 1917.

————. "Christ, Champion of Personality." TMs (Sermon preached at the Park Avenue Baptist Church, New York City on 28 April 1928), from the Harry Emerson Fosdick Collection, The Burke Library Archives, Union Theological Seminary, New York.

————. "Christianity and Freedom." TMs (Sermon preached at the Park Avenue Baptist Church, New York City on 20 January 1929), from the Harry Emerson Fosdick Collection, The Burke Library Archives, Union Theological Seminary, New York.

————. *Christianity and Progress*. New York: Revell, 1922.

————. "Christianity Not a Form But a Force." TMs (Sermon preached at the Riverside Church, New York City on 31 October 1943), from the Harry Emerson Fosdick Collection, The Burke Library Archives, Union Theological Seminary, New York.

————. "The Church Must Go Beyond Modernism" TMs (Sermon preached at the Riverside Church, New York City on 3 October 1935), from the Harry Emerson Fosdick Collection, The Burke Library Archives, Union Theological Seminary, New York.

————. *Dear Mr. Brown: Letters to a Person Perplexed about Religion*. New York: Harper, 1961.

————. *A Faith for Tough Times*. New York: Harper, 1952.

————. "Good News about Human Nature." TMs (Sermon preached at the Riverside Church, New York City on 31 January 1932), from the Harry Emerson Fosdick Collection, The Burke Library Archives, Union Theological Seminary, New York.

————. *Great Voices of the Reformation: An Anthology*. New York: Random House, 1952.

_____. *A Guide to Understanding the Bible: The Development of Ideas within the Old and New Testaments.* New York: Harper, 1938.

_____. "How I Prepare My Sermons: A Symposium." *The Quarterly Journal of Speech* 40 (February 1954): 50–54.

_____. "Humanizing Religion." TMs (Sermon preached at the Temple Beth-El, New York City on 9 February 1930), from the Harry Emerson Fosdick Collection, The Burke Library Archives, Union Theological Seminary, New York.

_____. "If Jesus Were A Modernist." TMs (Sermon preached at the Park Avenue Baptist Church, New York City on 3 March 1929), from the Harry Emerson Fosdick Collection, The Burke Library Archives, Union Theological Seminary, New York.

_____. "The Importance of the Individual." TMs (Sermon preached at the Park Avenue Baptist Church, New York City on 19 December 1926), from the Harry Emerson Fosdick Collection, The Burke Library Archives, Union Theological Seminary, New York.

_____. "A Kind of Penitence That Does Some Good." TMs (Sermon preached at the Riverside Church, New York City on 11 October 1942), from the Harry Emerson Fosdick Collection, The Burke Library Archives, Union Theological Seminary, New York.

_____. "A Letter by Dr. Fosdick to the Presbytery of New York." *The Churchman* 130 (18 October 1924): 13.

_____. *The Living of These Days: An Autobiography.* New York: Harper, 1956.

_____. "The Mainsprings of Human Motive" TM (Sermon preached at the Riverside Church, New York City on 17 February 1935), from the Harry Emerson Fosdick Collection, The Burke Library Archives, Union Theological Seminary, New York.

_____. *The Man From Nazareth as His Contemporaries Saw Him.* New York: Harper, 1949.

_____. *The Manhood of the Master.* New York: Association Press, 1943.

_____. "The Miracle of Changed Lives." TMs (Sermon preached at the Riverside Church, New York City on 4 October 1936), from the Harry Emerson Fosdick Collection, The Burke Library Archives, Union Theological Seminary, New York.

_____. "A Modern Preacher's Problem in His Use of the Scriptures." *Union Theological Seminary* (1915): 16–34.

_____. *The Modern Use of the Bible.* New York: The Macmillan Company, 1924.

_____. "Morals Secede From the Union." *Harper's Magazine* 164 (May 1932): 682–92.

_____. *On Being a Real Person.* New York: Harper, 1943.

_____. *On Being Fit to Live With: Sermons on Post-War Christianity.* New York: Harper, 1946.

_____. "Personal Counseling and Preaching." *Pastoral Psychology* 3 (March 1952): 15.

_____. "A Plea for Genuine Individualism." TMs (Sermon preached at the Riverside Church, New York City on 3 November 1940), from the Harry Emerson Fosdick Collection, The Burke Library Archives, Union Theological Seminary, New York.

_____. Introduction to *Preaching in Theory and Practice*, by Samuel McComb. New York: Oxford University Press, 1926.

_____. *Riverside Sermons.* New York: Harper, 1958.

_____. *Rufus Jones Speaks to Our Time, An Anthology.* New York: Macmillan, 1951.

_____. "Shall The Fundamentalists Win?" TMs (Sermon preached at the First Presbyterian Church, New York City on 21 May 1922), from the Harry Emerson Fosdick Collection, The Burke Library Archives, Union Theological Seminary, New York.

_____. *The Three Meanings: Prayer, Faith, Service.* New York: Association Press, 1934.

_____. "The Trades-Unionism of a Suburban Town." Unpublished MA thesis, Columbia University, 1908.

_____. *Twelve Tests of Character.* New York: Association Press, 1923.

_____. "The Validity of Abiding Experiences." TMs (Sermon preached at the Riverside Church, New York City on 14 November 1937), from the Harry Emerson Fosdick Collection, The Burke Library Archives, Union Theological Seminary, New York.

_____. "What Is Christianity?" *Harper's Magazine* 158 (April 1929): 551–61.

_____. "What Is Religion?" *Harper's Magazine* 158 (March 1929): 424–34.

_____. "What Is the Matter with Preaching?" *Harper's Magazine* 157 (July 1928): 133–41.

_____. *What Is Vital in Religion: Sermons on Contemporary Christian Problems.* New York: Harper, 1955.

_____. "Whose God Is Dead?" *Readers Digest* 89 (October 1966): 67–71.

Graves, Mike. ed. *What's the Matter with Preaching Today?* Louisville: John Knox, 2004.

Hodges, Graham A. "Fosdick at 90: Tribute to a Man for All Seasons." *The Christian Century* 85 (22 May 1968): 684.

Hudnut, William H., Jr. "Fosdick as Teacher." *The Christian Century* 75 (21 May 1958):

Landry, Fabaus. "The Preaching of Harry Emerson Fosdick: An Analysis of Its Intent, Style, and Language." DD diss., Milligan College, 1972.

Lawrence, William Benjamin. "Sundays in New York: Directions in Pulpit Theology, 1930–1955." PhD diss., Drew University, 1984.

Linn, Edmund Holt. "The Rhetorical Theory and Practice of Harry Emerson Fosdick." PhD diss., State University of Iowa, 1952.

_____. *Preaching as Counseling: The Unique Method of Harry Emerson Fosdick*. Pennsylvania: Judson, 1966.

Marsden, George M. *Fundamentalism and American Culture*. 2nd ed. New York: Oxford University Press, 2006.

Milioni, Dwayne. "The Concept of Self in the Preaching of Harry Emerson Fosdick." PhD diss., Southeastern Baptist Theological Seminary, 2011.

Miller, Robert Moates. *Harry Emerson Fosdick: Preacher, Pastor, Prophet*. New York: Oxford University Press, 1985.

Moody, Larry A. "The Anthropology of Harry Emerson Fosdick: Becoming a Real Person." PhD diss., Aquinas Institute of Theology, 1980.

Newton, Joseph Fort., ed. *If I Had Only One Sermon to Prepare*. New York: Harper, 1932.

Niebuhr, Reinhold. "Fosdick: Theologian and Preacher." *The Christian Century* 50 (3 June 1953): 657–58.

Shaull, Richard. "New York's Riverside," *The Christian Century* (28 November 1951): 1369.

Stelzle, Charles. ed. *If I Had Only One Sermon to Preach*. New York: Harper, 1927.

Straton, John Roach. "Shall the Funnymonkeyists Win?" *The Religious Searchlight* 1, no. 7 (October 1922): 1–7.

Vitz, Paul C. *Psychology as Religion: The Cult of Self-worship*. Grand Rapids: Eerdmans, 1977.

R. G. Lee

Rhetorical Artistry in the Pulpit

CHARLES A. FOWLER

Two generations ago, Robert G. Lee (1886–1978) made his mark in the preaching world. Best known as the pastor of Bellevue Baptist Church in Memphis, Tennessee, from 1927 to 1960, Lee stood tall among the preachers and orators of his day. Lee's life and ministry demonstrated the power of God through a man, who as a young boy gave his life to Christ and yearned to glorify that name for the rest of his days and to the ends of the earth.

HISTORICAL BACKGROUND

On November 11, 1886—in a three-room log cabin in York County, South Carolina—there erupted a jubilant, down-home Southern prophecy: "Praise God! Glory be! The good Lawd has done sent a preacher to 'dis here house!"[1] The beloved midwife of sharecroppers David Ayers and Sarah Bennett Lee had introduced baby Robert Lee to the world. This woman's celebration would eventually ring true in the fullest sense. From a young age, Robert Lee received initiation into the blessings and burdens of family life in the poor rural South. He and his siblings would rise early to the command of their firm and faithful father.

Robert enjoyed a strong relationship with his mother. Sarah Bennett loved her son with the love of Christ and instilled in him a love and trust for God's Word. Lee noted in his memoirs, "With sober emphasis, my mother said: 'Always believe the Bible—all of it—no matter who doesn't believe it.'"[2] Lee's mom prayed earnestly for her son's salvation. Her prayers were answered when Robert sensed the sinner's conviction after one of the many sermons he heard growing up. One biographer narrates the conversion:

---

1. John E. Huss, *Robert G. Lee: The Authorized Biography* (Grand Rapids: Zondervan, 1967), 16.
2. Robert G. Lee, *Payday Everyday* (Nashville: Broadman, 1974), 19.

[Lee] went out to the field to plow. He made his way between the plow handles behind a white mule, named Barney. Oppressed by a feeling that he needed the help of God, he drove to the end of a row by an old rail fence. There he stopped the mule and left the plow. The old mule stared solemnly at a strange sight. A young boy got down on his knees, took off his straw hat, and started talking to God. "Oh Lord," he prayed, "if You will save me, I'll do anything You want me to do, I'll even preach, or anything."[3]

From this moment on, Robert Lee fixed his gaze beyond the fields of cotton in South Carolina to the fields of harvest filled with souls needing to hear the good news of Jesus. At twelve years old, a born-again Robert Lee began plowing a new kind of row; he never turned back.

With the familiar faithfulness he would show over the decades, Robert fulfilled his promise to his dad to work on the farm until he was twenty-one.[4] With this debt paid, however, he immediately ventured on the long road to pulpit ministry. In order to raise the money for school, Robert spent a year working the Panama Canal. In 1909, he entered Furman University, where he thrived.[5] He graduated in 1913, not only with a diploma but also with "numerous oratorical medals and scholastic honors."[6]

In the early stages of his vocational ministry, Lee served as part-time pastor and youth pastor of twelve various churches. He then went on to pastor Edgefield First Baptist Church in South Carolina (1918–1921), First Baptist Church of Chester, South Carolina (1921–1922), and First Baptist Church in New Orleans, Louisiana (1922–1927). At the first opportunity, J. E. Dilworth—chairman of the Bellevue Baptist Church Pulpit Committee—expressed interest in calling Lee as their new pastor, but Lee respectfully declined.[7] He soon regretted his decision, and admitted to his secretary, "I made a mistake about Bellevue. I ought to have gone there."[8] To his pleasure, Bellevue agreed! "On Sunday, October 16, 1927, Bellevue extended a call for Lee to become their pastor."[9] Lee's pastorate at Bellevue lasted thirty-two years, enduring the opportunities and challenges of leading this proud congregation through the decades that included the Great Depression, World War II, and the Korean War.[10]

---

3. Huss, *Robert G. Lee*, 29.
4. Ibid., 55.
5. Ibid., 72.
6. Ibid., 80.
7. E. Schuyler English, *Robert G. Lee: A Chosen Vessel* (Grand Rapids: Zondervan, 1949), 188.
8. Ibid., 193.
9. Huss, *Robert G. Lee*, 127.
10. Ibid., 133.

From 1927 to 1960, Bellevue grew from a congregation of 1,430 to 9,421 members.[11] Woven into these figures are 24,071 individuals who joined the church along the way. For the first twenty years, Bellevue averaged over twelve new members per week![12] More importantly, 7,649 people came forward for believer's baptism. And the church gave over $2.5 million to missions.[13] In addition, on January 5, 1958, Bellevue became the first church to televise its worship services.[14]

Lee's pastoral ministry at Bellevue is legendary for his tireless shepherding. By the time of his thirtieth anniversary with the church, Lee had officiated 1,344 weddings and 891 funerals. He had written thirty books and hundreds of magazine articles. He had also ordained thirty-five younger ministers.[15] Lee was famous for making numerous ministry calls to his members during the week while also carrying out a demanding preaching schedule.[16]

Lee's commitment to the ministry of the Word will prove even more inspiring after an examination of his sermons. Preparing two or three messages a week will challenge anyone, but the obvious attention to detail and preparation shows that Lee poured his life into his preaching every bit as much as he did into his people. This one man who packed virtually every sentence he ever preached with the most vivid imagery also managed to memorize every name on his church roll.[17]

In addition to pastoring Bellevue, Lee served three terms as president of the Southern Baptist Convention (1948–1951).[18] He would eventually resign his pastorate at Bellevue on December 13, 1959.[19] From there, he embarked on a relentless preaching ministry throughout the country and the world. Huss marvels, "His record since leaving Bellevue is amazing. In 1962, he preached somewhere every day except for seventeen days; every day except twenty in 1963; every day but thirty in 1964, and every day except forty in 1965. Due to illness, he was not able to sustain such a pace in 1966, but even so had engagements for 121 days."[20]

Robert G. Lee truly had a remarkable pastoral and prophetic ministry. From

---

11. Ibid., 224.

12. English, *Robert G. Lee*, 370.

13. Huss, *Robert G. Lee*, 224.

14. Ibid., 219.

15. Ibid., 219.

16. Ibid., 231. Note also Warren W. Wiersbe and Lloyd M. Perry, *The Wycliffe Handbook of Preaching and Preachers* (Chicago: Moody, 1984), 93. Wiersbe and Perry claim that Lee made three hundred ministerial visits per year. One gets the sense, though, that this would be a very conservative estimate.

17. Lee, *Payday Everyday*, 8.

18. Huss, *Robert G. Lee*, 181.

19. Ibid., 220.

20. Ibid., 227.

this admittedly brief summary of his life and career, focus will now turn to the philosophy and particularities of Lee's ministry and preaching.

THEOLOGY FOR THE PASTORATE

As one might guess about a man who served three terms as president of the Southern Baptist Convention, R. G. Lee fully endorsed Baptist tenets. He charged his listeners to cherish and defend these convictions: "As Baptists we believe, as did our fathers, in the rights of the individual, not ecclesiastical rights; in personal faith, not proxy faith; in the priesthood of all believers, not the priesthood of a class; in free grace, not sacramental grace; in the direct approach to God, not the indirect; in believer's baptism, not infant baptism; in the voluntary principle in religion, not coercion. And we must, without apology, without fear, without ceasing, preach and practice our beliefs, carrying them out to the point of suffering."[21]

These convictions Lee held based on his interpretation of the Holy Scriptures, which he believed to be the true, unified, and sufficient Word of God. Lee entrenched his preaching and pastoring on these theological principles.[22] Lee's passion for preaching derived from his love of Scripture. If nothing else, he was a man of the Bible. He was crystal clear regarding his biblical beliefs:

> In the Bible God reveals His will and truth unto men through men, controlling the speakers and writers He selects, breathing His Spirit into them, subordinating them to His pleasure and wisdom, directing their minds and hearts and hands in such manner that they infallibly express just what He wishes to say, so that if they write history He preserves them from making the slightest mistake, so that if they predict future events, He tells them clearly and distinctly what will occur, so that if they announce doctrinal truth, it is strictly according to His breathing in every particular.[23]

So strong was Lee's stance on the Bible that he called it "The Nation's Greatest Asset." He gave six reasons for this claim. First, it was the primary factor in maintaining spiritual progress among people. Second, it was the one foundation

---

21. Robert G. Lee, "The Constraint," in *Bed of Pearls*, vol. 4 of *Robert G. Lee Sermonic Library* (Nashville: Broadman, 1936; repr., Orlando: Christ for the World, 1981), 70. For a list of eighteen beliefs Lee developed for his church, see English, *Robert G. Lee*, 266–67.

22. For a helpful interview discussing Lee's beliefs, see Huss, *Robert G. Lee*, 235–43.

23. Robert G. Lee, "The Bible, The Nation's Greatest Asset," in *The Top 10 of Robert G. Lee* (Grand Rapids: Baker, 1971; repr., Grand Rapids: Baker, 1974), 38.

adequate for a superstructure. Third, it transforms lives. Fourth, it is the enemy of all wickedness and maintains standards which prevent moral and societal decay. Fifth, in spite of its many enemies, the Bible is a book that lives on more triumphantly than any other. Sixth, Jesus is the supreme wonder of the Bible.

Here Lee exhibits his Christ-centered interpretation of Scripture. He proclaimed that "Christ is its fullness, its center, its supreme fascination. The Old Testament and the New Testament alike tell of Jesus, the great Fact of history, the great Force of history, the great Future of history."[24] With sparkle, Lee argued, "Take Jesus out of the Bible and it would be like taking calcium out of lime, carbon out of diamonds, truth out of history, invention out of fiction, matter out of physics, mind out of metaphysics, numbers out of mathematics. For Jesus alone is the secret of its unity, its strength, its beauty."[25]

With his Christ-centered hermeneutic, Lee preached a reconciliation with God through justification by faith. He explained, "In justification our death penalty has been revoked. . . . The sins of Adam were imputed to us. . . . Then on Calvary our sins were imputed to Christ. . . . Then the righteousness of Christ has been imputed to us."[26] This is the message of the gospel according to Scripture, and this was the incessant call to sinners from Lee's pulpit.

METHODOLOGY FOR PREACHING

In a letter addressed to Lee on December 28, 1970, Billy Graham exclaimed: "No man has ever served God with greater faithfulness than you. No man has ever preached the Gospel with greater eloquence than you."[27] Lee's sermons left two things without doubt: he was filled to the brim with biblical conviction and he overflowed with elegant rhetoric. His sermonic adornment merits further admiration. Several characteristics stand out.

Imagery in Preaching

When one studies Lee's sermons, one will immediately encounter a prolific use of imagery. Sights, sounds, and smells fill his paragraphs. The country boy who grew up soaking in the details of his outside world formed keen senses of observation and description. He added to these natural skills his broad education and reading accomplishments, and he became a superb speaker.

In the opening to "Offering Strange Fire," a message on the wickedness of

---

24. Ibid., 49.
25. Ibid., 50.
26. Lee, *The Top 10 of Robert G. Lee*, 29.
27. This letter was framed in the former R. G. Lee Library at Union University in Jackson, Tennesee.

Nadab and Abihu (Lev 10:1–2), Lee marveled at the richness of God's Word from the very beginning:

> In the book of Genesis, Moses, with a lightning-swift stroke of his potent pen, sets forth a veritable eternity—guided as he was in all that he wrote by the Holy Spirit. What a stretch of time—like a river so long no one can find the source of the mouth thereof—is covered by the words "In the beginning." Daringly, Moses told the story of creation in a single chapter. In the words used here, we find a continent of truth compressed into a corner of language. We find an ocean of revelation in a cup of words—all organs in one diapason as he put it all into a single line: "In the beginning God created the heavens and the earth."[28]

Ironically, while Lee celebrated Moses's ability to pack so much into such brevity, he did so himself. In one paragraph, he invites his listeners to ponder the flash of a lightning bolt, the endurance of a river, the canvas of a continent against the cramp of a corner, the vastness of an ocean against the splash of a cup, and the organs of the world against one tuning fork.

Yet another instance of Lee's imagery occurs in "And Calvary,"[29] where he celebrated the grandeur of the most significant of all mountains. First, Lee honored Mount Sinai: "Great is Sinai, sublime in solitude, robed in clouds, shrouded in smoke, illuminated with fire, where, with heaven's earthquake thunders rumbling amid the crags and gorges—where, with the lightnings blazing in zigzag paths across the dark clouds, the law was given—commandments which are not the ghostly whispers of a dead century, but commandments as authoritative today as when their proclamation broke the age-long silence of the desert."[30]

Sinai did not compare, though, with Calvary—and Lee made sure he communicated this with piercing description:

> But above and beyond all mountains as a sky-scraper is above a dugout in height, as a tree is beyond a twig in fruit bearing, as a cannon is beyond a popgun in far-reaching power, is Calvary.
>
> For there, God in bloody garments dressed, courted our love. . . .

---

28. Robert G. Lee, "Offering Strange Fire," in *Bible Fires,* vol. 16 of *Robert G. Lee Sermonic Library* (Grand Rapids: Zondervan, 1956; repr., Orlando: Christ for the World, 1981) 113.

29. It seems probable that this sermon is also known as "The Place Called Calvary," which is identified as one of Lee's personal favorite sermons he ever preached, according to Huss, *Robert G. Lee*, 144.

30. Lee, "And Calvary," in *Bed of Pearls*, 44.

There, with power to smite his enemies with a thunderbolt, he elected to die on a cross.

There, God's eternal attributes emptied their vials of burning wrath upon the sinless Sacrifice in agony enough to make the earth shudder, the sun in darkness hide, the spheres go wailing along their eternal circuits.

There God, the father of the clouds (Job 38:28), permitted him to thirst who came to remove the moral thirst of mankind.

There God, who clothes the valleys with corn (Psalm 65:13), and feeds the young ravens when they cry, left him baked under the darkening sky and answered not his cry.

No wonder the heavens went black and the sun withdrew its light and the earth reeled in its steady course, as an astonishment that love so sweet, so vast, should meet a doom so fearful. . . .

Earth has no darker sin, history no blacker page, humanity no fouler spot, than that of the Saviour's crucifixion.[31]

A reader of Lee's sermons sits in awe at the avalanche of metaphors, similes, and descriptions that plummets down his sermons. One can only imagine how his listeners felt as they, week after week, overrun by the current of so rich an imagination. It is stupefying that one man who was so busy in his pastoral ministry could find the time and make the effort to saturate his sermons with so much artistry.

Alliteration in Preaching

Alliteration is another astounding aspect of Lee's preaching. This literary device seemed to be one of his favorites in sermon development. In what was once a stand-alone sermon, Lee developed a series called *Bed of Pearls*, which consists of eight messages, most of which focus on 1 Corinthians 15:3–4.[32] These sermons (each of which would have been a main point in the original sermon) are sequentially titled: "The Curse," "The Christ," "And Calvary," "The Constraint," "The Complement," "The Contemporary," "The Consummation," and "The Confirmation."

In "Treasures of the Snow," a message that springs from Job 38:22, Lee preached five main points.[33] Each of these points represents a self-contained unit of alliteration. In his first point, Lee discussed "The Might of the Multiplicity of

---

31. Ibid., 45–46.
32. Lee, *Bed of Pearls*, vol. 4 of *Robert G. Lee Sermonic Library* (Nashville: Broadman, 1936; repr., Orlando: Christ for the World Publishers, 1981).
33. Lee, *The Top Ten of Robert G. Lee*, 72–89.

Mites." Here he encouraged Christians to resemble snowflakes, which although tiny individually can accomplish great things in force. Next, Lee proclaimed, "The Excellency of Emphasis on Things Essential." Here he argued that just like the cold snow causes people to emphasize the essentials for warmth, so too must believers emphasize the essentials of faith. Next, Lee addressed "Folks Far from Flakes Familiar." With this, Lee pointed out that just like many people in the world have never seen snow, so too many have never come to know Jesus. Fourth, Lee celebrated "The Grace of God That Glorifies." In his words, "As it reaches far and wide, the snow emphasizes the fact of God's wide-flung wondrous grace, which cleanses black hearts, making them white as snow; that clothes with the raiment of Christ's righteousness the distorted, deformed, diseased, scarred, blighted, saddened, broken, blasted, ruined, doomed lives of men and women."[34]

Finally, Lee anticipated "The Purity of Place Prepared." Here he celebrated the imagery of purity in the book of Revelation.

Two other sermons are notable examples of Lee's persistent use of alliteration. In "The Face of Jesus Christ," which finds its starting point in 2 Corinthians 4:6, Lee covered eight descriptions of Jesus's face throughout the Bible.[35] He identifies Jesus's face as: a Sad Face, a Shining Face, a Stained Face, a Smitten Face, a Set Face, a Scorching Face, a Shrouded Face, and a Seen Face. In "Comments Concerning Christ," Lee honored Christ with nine descriptions.[36] He is the Creative Christ, the Cradled Christ, the Curative Christ, the Communicating Christ, the Criticized Christ, the Crucified Christ, the Coffined Christ, the Conquering Christ, and the Coming Christ.

For many hearers, Lee's use of alliteration would verge on overbearing. One even finds it humorous at times to see how Lee can spin a phrase with a certain pet letter to make it fit the other points. This style does, however, show Lee's effort at organization. Also, his alliteration highlights his vast imagination and creativity. For this and many other reasons, Lee was a vivid preacher who captured his listeners' attention.

Picturizing in Preaching

When Lee prepared his sermons, he carried out a rather unique exercise that he coined "picturizing." Lee elaborated on this procedure: "I hardly know how to explain what I mean by 'picturizing' my sermons. In a sense, it is a sort of memorizing, and yet not really memorizing. I write out my sermons. When I

---

34. Ibid., 84. Even within this quoted sentence one can detect an intentional use of alliteration when Lee describes men and women as "distorted, deformed, diseased, scarred, blighted, saddened, broken, blasted."
35. Ibid., 90–109.
36. Ibid., 110–30.

have them typed I read them over a few times, sometimes as many as six times, and as I do, I form pictures of what I have written."[37]

This seems to be a peculiar sort of photographic memory, one which Lee employed through his intense imagination. He gave a lengthy example:

> For example, when I talk of the Cross casting its shadow and light from Calvary's hill to Pilate's court, and from Pilate's court to the meeting of the Sanhedrin with Caiaphas, and from there to Gethsemane, and from Gethsemane to the Upper Room, and from the Upper Room in Jerusalem to the Jordan River where He was baptized, and from the Jordan to Nazareth where he was brought up to Bethlehem, and from Bethlehem across the three dumb centuries, and from the three centuries, when no prophet's voice was lifted, to the Temple on Mt. Moriah, and from there to the Tabernacle in the wilderness, and from there to the bloody doorposts of the Passover night, and from there to Eden, where Despair had pitched his black pavilions on man's sterile and blasted estate—I turn what I have written into Calvary's hill on one end and the Cross on the other, with its head on Calvary's hill and its foot in Eden. Underneath this horizontal Cross I picture Pilate, and then the Jewish Sanhedrin with Caiaphas presiding, and then the Upper Room with the full moon above, in the house in the city of Jerusalem; next the garden of Gethsemane, and then the Jordan River, and John baptizing Jesus; then Bethlehem with all the folks related to our Lord. Then I picture a long bridge, three hundred miles long, across a chasm marked at the bottom with the word "s-i-l-e-n-c-e." From one end of this bridge a long finger points to the glorious Temple on Mt. Moriah. Then from Mt. Moriah an angel flies with a bucket of blood and puts it on the lintels and posts of one hundred doors. From the Passover doorposts there is a winding road with a finger pointing "to Eden," and this road ends where black tents are pitched in a desert.[38]

Lee came just short of acknowledging how unexplainable this may seem. He tried to make more sense of it for his listeners: "As I preach, pictures I have created as I read over my sermons, roll in upon me. Sometimes I have had to create two thousand different pictures for one sermon. I turn my language into pictures, and preach through pictures, which roll in upon me, and by me, and around me, by the hundreds as I preach. This is the best I can describe

---

37. English, *Robert G. Lee*, 320.
38. Ibid., 320–21.

'picturizing.' I never have a memorized typed page in my mind as I preach, but always pictures, always."[39]

In an attempt to better explain this phenomenon, one might imagine that Lee pictured images in his head much like one would use bar graphs and pie graphs to visualize data. In Lee's case, the data consists of the content of his messages—its words, sentences, paragraphs, and pages. Lee mentally visualized this data as a graphic image, filled with details that reminded him of the intricacies of his sermon. To preachers who read from manuscripts or reference thorough bullet-point outlines, this might seem overwhelming. To others who have a more visual bent, this could be a fruitful area of expertise to develop. As with most things in life, however, one might be wise to avoid mimicking Lee's exact approach, while finding ways to customize some of its benefits. Clearly this practice worked wonders for Lee. His sermons stand out as some of the most aesthetic and cultivated in history.

Sermon Delivery

When one listens to Lee's sermons, one hears a first-rate orator. Lee's passion, conviction, voice, and vocabulary blended to make every message a spellbinding gospel cry. Michael Mantalbano hits the mark when he claims, "Lee became one of the greatest orators and masters of the English language of his day."[40] By merely reading Lee's sermons, one gets a suspicion that his messages were aural marvels. And his audio recordings do not disappoint. Lee was as powerful and polished a preacher as any around.

At the pulpit, Lee rarely used notes, having thoroughly prepared through his process of "picturizing."[41] He seems to have begun most of his sermons with a very intentional pace, indicating to his listeners that they were definitely going somewhere together. With an unmistakable southern drawl, and a rather high-pitched nasal tone, Lee surged into his sermon. His volume would often rise and fall, and his rate would eventually ebb and flow. Inevitably, his conviction and urgency took over, and Lee's listeners were blasted with that day's gospel refrain.[42] Several times in each message, Lee managed to nearly scream at the top of his lungs.

Lee was a gloriously long-winded preacher. "Lee spoke an average of 5,500 words per sermon, and since he spoke about 110 words per minute, he averaged

---

39. Ibid., 321.

40. Michael P. Mantalbano, "A Critical Comparison of the Preaching of Robert G. Lee, Ramsay Pollard, and Adrian Rogers" (PhD diss., Mid-America Baptist Theological Seminary, 1993), 14.

41. Ibid., 127.

42. Even in his day and age, Lee was often invited to preach at African American gatherings. His aggressive and spirited delivery would have been a natural draw in that sermonic culture.

preaching fifty minutes per sermon."[43] By the time the message was over, one could imagine how fatigued Lee may have felt. Likewise, his listeners would probably be ready for a reprieve. They no doubt eagerly welcomed the familiar gospel invitation with which Lee would end.

CONTRIBUTIONS TO PREACHING

For the student of homiletics, Lee's sermons demonstrate and encourage the use of imagery in preaching. Deservedly, much focus during sermon preparation lands on faithful exegesis and thorough outlining. After that leg work has been accomplished, however, one would do well to consider ways to add flavor and texture to the message through imagery. Lee did not simply talk about his texts; he explored them with his hearers. While few people would succeed in using the same proportion of imagery as Lee did, many would improve their preaching by inserting a few colorful moments.

Lee also contributes a worthwhile study in sermon delivery. His pace and voice have already been observed above. In general, today's preachers can watch and listen to Lee and witness a master of pulpit energy. The few remaining video and audio recordings of Lee's sermons will benefit any who experience them.

Finally, Lee's phenomenon of "picturizing" could open a field of research and practice for many of today's preachers. As already noted, trying to emulate Lee may not work well for every preacher. Nevertheless, at the very least, bits and pieces should be gleaned from this very creative approach to sermon preparation and organization. One suspects that some of the more pictorial minds in today's pulpits could study Lee's methods and refine them with tremendous results.

Lee's influence on generations of believers and preachers is both inspiring and humbling. The lasting contributions of his life and ministry are abundant. With his published sermons and recorded messages, he can still proclaim the gospel and encourage and equip today's preachers. Also, with convictions yoked to Scripture, he helped plow the conservative ground of the Southern Baptist Convention. Today's Southern Baptist churches and institutions have benefited from Lee's influence and example of one who held high biblical truth in a time when the arms of many were growing weary. Most of all, Lee's life and ministry showcase the glory and grace of God, who mightily works in and through anyone who will diligently and compassionately sow biblical seed in the hearts of all who will listen.

---

43. Paul Gericke, *The Preaching of Robert G. Lee*, vol. 8 of *Robert G. Lee Sermonic Library* (Orlando: Christ for the World, 1981), 128.

Sermon Excerpt

Calvary[44]

Christ died! Christ died for our sins! So saith the Scriptures. Christ! And Calvary!

And Crucifixion on Calvary!

For that reason, greatly above and beyond all mountains stands Calvary.

Great is Sinai, sublime in solitude, robed in clouds, shrouded in smoke, illuminated with fire, where, with heaven's earthquake thunders rumbling amid the crags and gorges—where, with the lightnings blazing in zigzag paths across the dark clouds, the law was given—commandments which are not the ghostly whispers of a dead century, but commandments as authoritative today as when their proclamation broke the age-long silence of the desert.

Grand is old Horeb where the bush, aflame with the glory of descendent Deity, defied the laws of conflagration (Exodus 3:3).

And Hor, where, his spirit ready to wing its flight to realms of day, Aaron transferred his priestly robes to his son, and died (Numbers 33:38–39).

And Pisgah, from whose lofty height Moses saw the land which God "Sware unto Abraham" (Deuteronomy 34:4 [KJV]).

And Ebal and Gerizim, from who neighboring sides the blessings and the curses were pronounced (Deuteronomy 11:26).

And Carmel where God answered Elijah's prayer with fire from heaven (1 Kings 18:38).

And Tabor in whose shadow and on whose slopes the starts in their courses fought with Barak and his ten thousand men to overthrown Sisera and his hosts (Judges 5:20).

And Moriah where, under the leadership of Solomon, one hundred and sixty thousand men toiled seven and one-half years to build the holy and beautiful Temple.

And triple-peak Hermon where Jesus was transfigured, his countenance brighter than the sun, his garments whiter than snow.

And, Olivet of sweet farewell memories, where, with the clouds as his chariot and the wind as his steeds, he went back to God.

But above and beyond all mountains as a skyscraper is above a

---

44. Robert G. Lee, "Calvary" in *The Top Ten of Robert G. Lee* (Grand Rapids: Baker, 1971), 7–9.

dugout in height, as a tree is beyond a twig in fruit bearing, as a cannon is beyond a popgun in far-reaching power, is Calvary.

For there, God in crimson garments dressed, courted our love.

There at the interlocking of the ages, Christ put away sin by the sacrifice of Himself, redeeming man from death unto life, canceling man's debt of judicial obligation by an equivalent which afforded legal satisfaction—voluntarily passing under death's dreadful shadow, though owing the law no debt.

There, with power to smite his enemies with a thunder-bolt, he elected to die on a cross.

There, God's eternal attributes emptied their vials of burning wrath upon the sinless Sacrifice in agony enough to make the earth shudder, the sun in darkness hide, the spheres go wailing along their eternal circuits.

There God, the father of the clouds (Job 38:28), permitted Him to thirst who came to remove the moral thirst of mankind.

There God, who clothes the valleys with corn (Psalm 65:13), and feeds the young ravens when they cry, left Him naked under the darkening sky and answered not his cry.

No wonder the heavens went black and the sun withdrew its light and the earth reeled in its steady course, as in astonishment that love so sweet, so vast, should meet a doom so fearful.

No wonder that all the people came together to that sight, beholding the things that were done—beholding Love incarnate rejected, crucified, tortured—beholding the way in which men treat the embodied perfection of virtue, and then and there smote their breast and returned sorrowing (Luke 23:48).

No wonder the rocks rent—the rocks less hard than men's hearts that day—as though shattered that so great a love could find so ungrateful a return.

Earth has no darker sin, history no blacker page, humanity no fouler spot, than that of the Saviour's crucifixion.

> Irreproachable Christ's life.
> Matchless Christ's teaching.
> Astonishing Christ's miracles.
> Marvelous Christ's example.

But all of these would have availed nothing for our salvation had they not found consummation in the Cross. ♦

BIBLIOGRAPHY

English, E. Schuyler. *Robert G. Lee: A Chosen Vessel*. Grand Rapids: Zondervan, 1949.

Faulls, Gregory Stephen. "The Pastoral Evangelism of Robert Greene Lee." PhD diss., Southwestern Baptist Theological Seminary, 1997.

Huss, John E. *Robert G. Lee: The Authorized Biography*. Grand Rapids: Zondervan, 1967.

George, Timothy, and Denise George, eds. *Payday Someday and other Sermons by Robert Greene Lee*. Nashville: Broadman & Holman, 1995.

Gericke, Paul. *The Preaching of Robert G. Lee*. Vol. 8 of *Robert G. Lee Sermonic Library*. Orlando: Christ for the World, 1981.

Lee, Robert G. *A Grand-Canyon of Resurrection Realities*. Grand Rapids: Eerdmans, 1935.

_____. *Bed of Pearls*, vol. 4 of *Robert G. Lee Sermonic Library*. Nashville: Broadman, 1936; Repr., Orlando: Christ for the World, 1981).

_____. *Robert G. Lee Sermonic Library*. Orlando: Christ for the World, 1981.

_____. *The Top Ten of Robert G. Lee*. Grand Rapids: Baker, 1971. Repr., Grand Rapids: Baker, 1974.

_____. "Old Age Folks." *Baptist and Reflector*. February 25, 1971.

_____. *Payday Everyday*. Nashville: Broadman, 1974.

_____. "Payday Someday." https://www.youtube.com/watch?v=_BZepT-czgU.

_____. *The Name Above Every Name*. Taken from Dr. Lee's sermon notes, Archives, R. G. Lee Memorial Library, Union University, Jackson, Tennessee.

Mantalbano, Michael P. "A Critical Comparison of the Preaching of Robert G. Lee, Ramsay Pollard, and Adrian Rogers." PhD diss., Mid-America Baptist Theological Seminary, 1993.

Wiersbe, Warren W., and Lloyd M. Perry. *The Wycliffe Handbook of Preaching and Preachers*. Chicago: Moody, 1984.

Aimee Semple McPherson

Preaching to Capture the Imagination

AARON FRIESEN

Aimee Semple McPherson (1890–1944) is an important figure in the history of Christian preaching for a number of reasons. Few female preachers have risen to the level of fame that she garnered. Yet her preaching legacy goes far beyond the fact that she was a female. Her sermons were carefully crafted in order to connect the imagination and emotions of middle-class people to the stories and experiences of people recorded in the Bible. She pioneered new ways of communicating, designing elaborate stage sets, prop materials, and music to accompany the preached Word. She also utilized the latest technologies to deliver her sermons and teachings, becoming one of the first female preachers on the radio. A forerunner of the evangelical megachurch pastor, McPherson built and administrated Angelus Temple in Los Angeles, one of the largest church buildings on the West Coast at the time of its construction, and founded the International Church of the Foursquare Gospel, a denomination that remains one of the larger Pentecostal bodies globally.

HISTORICAL BACKGROUND

Aimee Elizabeth Kennedy was born in October 1890, and was raised on a small farm in southwest Ontario, Canada. Her father was a lifelong Methodist and her mother—thirty-five years younger than her father—was an officer in The Salvation Army. As a child, Aimee accompanied her mother to many Salvation Army services and activities each week, and her early experiences of the Army shaped her perception of how the gospel message could be effectively communicated from the pulpit.[1] It was not uncommon for Army officers to preach with the accompaniment of "noisy, attention-getting pageantry and entertainment," and it seems probable that Aimee's early experiences of that style inspired her

---

1. Edith L. Blumhofer, *Aimee Semple McPherson: Everybody's Sister* (Grand Rapids: Eerdmans, 1993), 46.

to incorporate such elements in her own preaching.[2] In fact, Aimee's famously illustrated sermons were likely patterned after a form invented by The Salvation Army preacher Evangeline Booth, daughter of William and Catherine Booth.[3]

The Salvation Army was an environment mostly supportive of women in the pulpit. Female preachers were common in The Salvation Army organization, including in the area of Canada where Aimee grew up. The Army's founding couple, William and Catherine Booth, were pioneer supporters of women serving in all areas of Christian ministry. A chapter in Catherine Booth's book *Practical Religion* entitled "A Woman's Right to Preach the Gospel" argues against the view that preaching by women is unnatural, unscriptural, or unnecessary.[4] Such strong voices in support of female preachers provided a context in which her own calling to preach could be validated. In an early conversation between Aimee and her parents about her hopes to someday become a preacher, Evangeline Booth served as a tangible example of a successful female preacher to whom she could look for encouragement and inspiration.[5]

Aimee linked her calling and success as a preacher with her having received the Pentecostal baptism in the Holy Spirit.[6] She first heard the Pentecostal teaching on Spirit baptism when an evangelist named Robert Semple began holding meetings in her hometown of Ingersoll in late 1907. Aimee attended the meetings, accepted the teaching, and began seeking her own experience of Spirit baptism and the accompanying sign of speaking in tongues. She personally received this experience in February 1908. Six months later, she married Robert, and the couple soon moved to Chicago, Illinois, where they began working alongside William H. Durham, a well-known Pentecostal minister who had founded the North Avenue Mission. In early 1909, both Robert and Aimee were ordained as ministers under Durham's mission. They were mentored in Pentecostal ministry by Durham throughout the following year and sent out as faith missionaries to China in 1910.[7]

In China, Aimee's dreams of a life colaboring alongside her husband for the work of the gospel in a foreign land came to a tragic halt. Robert contracted

---

2. Ibid., 34.

3. Ibid., 50.

4. Catherine Booth, *Papers on Practical Religion* (London: International Headquarters, 1891), 133–67.

5. Aimee Semple McPherson, *Aimee Semple McPherson: The Story of My Life* (Waco, TX: Word, 1973), 25–26.

6. McPherson recounted that immediately upon being baptized in the Holy Spirit she had a sense in her heart that she had been called to preach the gospel. Aimee Semple McPherson, *The Story of My Life* (Los Angeles: Echo Park Evangelistic Association, 1951), 43. She also strongly encouraged others who desired to be effective preachers to seek such an experience for themselves. Aimee Semple McPherson, "A Lesson in Homiletics," (unpublished notes, ICFG Archives), 1.

7. Blumhofer, *Everybody's Sister*, 80–90.

malaria and died within weeks of their arrival. Eight months pregnant, Aimee remained in China until after the birth of their daughter, Roberta. Upon their return to the United States, Aimee and Roberta lived in New York with Aimee's mother, Minnie, who had moved there from Canada to work with The Salvation Army. In New York, Aimee developed a romantic relationship with Harold McPherson. The couple married in May 1912, and immediately moved to Providence, Rhode Island. McPherson gave birth to their son, Rolf, in March 1913. McPherson's early life story was one she told again and again, and it became the basis for one of her most famous illustrated sermons, "From Milk Pail to Pulpit."[8] In it, she compared the post-China season of her life to Jonah's journey to Tarshish, resisting the call of God to go and preach. In 1913, McPherson became very sick, to the point that doctors feared for her life. Bedbound in a hospital, McPherson prayed that God would heal her. She recounted that only upon making a vow to God that she would go and preach did she become well again.[9]

McPherson's calling to preach was not initially well-received by her husband. As a result, she took the kids and left Harold and returned to her parents' home in Canada to begin the work of a traveling evangelist. Harold soon rejoined her there, and the couple set out on the road, holding evangelistic tent meetings up and down the east coast. Aimee led the services while Harold supported her in whatever ways he could. In 1918, Harold and Aimee parted ways (though their divorce did not become official until August 1921), and she set out on her own with her mother and two children. Between 1918 and 1923, they traveled across the United States eight times, and conducted thirty-eight revivals in major cities.[10] Despite her claims that her services were "ninety-nine percent soul-saving and one percent healing," McPherson gained widespread notoriety as a gifted healer as well as a preacher.[11] As McPherson's fame as a healing evangelist grew, she settled on Los Angeles as a home base for her revival campaigns. There she established the Echo Park Evangelist Association in 1921. Soon after, she began work on designing and fundraising for a large auditorium she called Angelus Temple. A testament to her powers of persuasion and charismatic leadership, the temple was built debt free and "dedicated unto the cause of inter-denominational and worldwide evangelism" on January 1, 1923. With a seating capacity of 5,300 (and the capacity was often exceeded by more than

---

8. Blumhofer, *Everybody's Sister*, 373. This is one of the few sermons of McPherson's for which there is a surviving audio recording.

9. McPherson, *The Story of My Life*, 80–87.

10. Chas H. Barfoot, *Aimee Semple McPherson and the Making of Modern Pentecostalism* (London: Equinox, 2011), 78.

11. Quoted in Daniel Mark Epstein, *Sister Aimee: The Life of Aimee Semple McPherson* (New York: Harcourt, 1993), 220.

two thousand), Angelus Temple was the largest Pentecostal church in North America at the time.[12]

McPherson's fame as the colorful preacher and leader of Angelus Temple spread quickly. McPherson presided at over twenty-one services per week at Angelus Temple, preaching and teaching at many of them. On Sundays, McPherson preached at three services to crowds totaling over twenty thousand people. In February 1924, she began broadcasting her message on KFSG radio, becoming one of the first female preachers on the radio. That same year, she also founded and began building a Bible training school.[13]

In the spring of 1926, Aimee was the subject of a high-profile controversy surrounding her sudden disappearance from a Los Angeles beach (she claimed she was kidnapped) and then reappearance at a Mexican bordertown five weeks later. This, coupled with her marriage to David Hutton in 1931 that ended in divorce less than two years later,[14] caused McPherson to lose some of her credibility, particularly with conservative and fundamentalist Christian leaders. Despite these troubles, McPherson was mostly able to rebuild trust with the general public, and the ministry of Angelus Temple continued to grow and flourish through the 1930s and during World War II. McPherson died of an overdose of sleeping pills during a crusade in Oakland, California, in September 1944. Her funeral was one of the largest ever held in Los Angeles.[15]

THEOLOGY OF PREACHING

McPherson's unique methods and style of preaching have been given more attention than her theology of preaching. Yet McPherson's approach to preaching was intentionally shaped by and grounded in the theology of her Pentecostal and Salvation Army background. McPherson adopted and expanded on the restorationist theology of radical holiness and early Pentecostal groups that believed God was gradually restoring the church to the primitive Christianity of New Testament times.[16] In her 1917 sermon entitled "Lost and Restored," she argued that

---

12. Kimberly Ervin Alexander, "Restoration, Accommodation, and Innovation: The Contributions of Aimee Semple McPherson," in *From Aldersgate to Azusa Street: Wesleyan, Holiness, and Pentecostal Visions of New Creation*, ed. Henry H. Knight III (Eugene, OR: Pickwick, 2010), 253.

13. The school was founded as Angelus Temple Training School and later was renamed the Lighthouse of International Foursquare Evangelism (L.I.F.E.). Through the 1930s, annual enrollment at L.I.F.E. was around one thousand students. Today, the school Aimee founded continues as Life Pacific University with a main campus in San Dimas, California. Blumhofer, *Everybody's Sister*, 256, 360.

14. Matthew Avery Sutton, *Aimee Semple McPherson and the Resurrection of Christian America* (Cambridge: Harvard University Press, 2007), 90–94.

15. Cecil M. Robeck, "Aimee Semple McPherson," in *The New International Dictionary of Pentecostal and Charismatic Movements*, ed. Stanley M. Burgess (Grand Rapids: Zondervan, 2002), 858.

16. Aaron T. Friesen, "Pentecostal Antitraditionalism and the Pursuit of Holiness: The Neglected Role

Pentecostalism represented the final stage in a gradual restoration of the "perfect church" of the apostles.[17] Her restorationist hermeneutic closed the contextual gap between the church of the first century and the church of the twentieth century, and it led her to consider the task of preaching as a primary means by which people could be drawn imaginatively into the living history of God's people. Her emphasis on dramatic sermons, elaborate stories, and illustrations in communicating the truths of Scripture were artful ways in which she attempted to help remove the historical distance between the text of Scripture and the context in which she ministered. She wanted to "[sweep] listeners up into the ultimate story—the great, cosmic *ur*-narrative of salvation history, the culmination of which she believed was near at hand."[18] Further, her belief that all people, regardless of education, gender, race, or socio-economic status, had an important part to play in God's drama led her to the conclusion that sermons should be crafted using simple, conversational language that anyone could relate to and understand.

Pentecostal scholar Amos Yong has proposed that one of the distinctive marks of a Pentecostal approach to biblical interpretation is that it observes the "this is that" character of Scripture. By this, Yong means that the reader's or hearer's "experience (this) is equivalent to the reality accomplished in the lives of the biblical characters or anticipated by them (that)."[19] Thus, rather than emphasizing Scripture as that which passes on truthful or factual knowledge of the past, Pentecostals emphasize the capacity of Scripture to "open up possibilities for contemporary readers and hearers by the power of the Spirit."[20] Yong's description represents well the theological underpinnings of McPherson's preaching methods. Her own biography, aptly titled *This Is That,* reveals her tendency to parallel her own life story to the various accounts of people recorded in Scripture.[21] Helping people to find continuity between their own narrative and the narratives of people recorded in the Scriptures became the guiding theological vision for her preaching. Such a philosophy is captured in the Scripture verse that she posted on the front of Angelus Temple: "Jesus Christ is the same yesterday and today and forever" (Heb 13:8).[22] At the end of the day, McPherson's

---

of Tradition in Pentecostal Theological Reflection," *Journal of Pentecostal Theology* 23 (2014): 202–6.

17. Aimee Semple McPherson, "Lost and Restored," *The Bridal Call* 1 (April 1918): 1–11.

18. Donna E. Ray, "Aimee Semple McPherson and her Seriously Exciting Gospel," *Journal of Pentecostal Theology* 19 (2010): 157.

19. Amos Yong, "Reading Scripture and Nature: Pentecostal Hermeneutics and Their Implications for the Contemporary Evangelical Theology and Science Conversation," *Perspectives on Science and Christian Faith* 63 (March 2011): 5.

20. Ibid.

21. Aimee Semple McPherson, *This Is That: Personal Experiences, Sermons and Writings* (Los Angeles: Bridal Call Publishing House, 1919).

22. Blumhofer, *Everybody's Sister*, 212. Today, every Foursquare church is required to display these words in their sanctuary.

goal in preaching was not that her listeners know exactly what happened in the past, but that they experience and respond to God's activity in the present. As a result, she would often preach on a short text and embellish and dramatize it for her audience—adding detail, emotion, dialogue, and narration in order to evoke particular emotional responses in her listeners.[23] Her success at doing so has led one scholar to argue, "She exploited the theological drama available to her from traditional sources just as effectively as she exploited the methods of Hollywood and the new media of the 1920s and 30s."[24]

Like many of her Pentecostal contemporaries, McPherson believed in the soon and imminent return of Christ for his bride, the church. This belief influenced much of her early writing (her periodical was named *The Bridal Call*), as well as her ministry from the pulpit.[25] As the time was short, preaching ought to be done as excellently as possible in order to convert as many souls as possible. Her sense of evangelistic urgency provided the impetus for the work entailed in crafting sermons that could be easily understood by all kinds of people and reliably lead them on to experiences of conversion and the baptism in the Holy Spirit.[26] In response to objections made by some members of Angelus Temple about the appropriateness of illustrated sermons in a church setting, McPherson replied, "What matters the trail so long as the goal is reached? If we can hold the wavering attention and reach the heart of just one sinner through the costumes, the scenery and the properties of the illustrated sermon, the gain is worth all the efforts."[27]

METHODOLOGY FOR PREACHING

Perhaps surprising to Pentecostals today, the sermon was not the "main event" in early Pentecostal worship services. In fact, the earliest Pentecostal worship gatherings often did not have much of a sermon at all, and if they did, the preacher worked hard to "keep the Holy Spirit in the foreground and themselves in the background."[28] The sermon was frequently short relative to other elements in the service, and it often functioned as a bridge or transitional element between

---

23. Kristy Maddux, "The Foursquare Gospel of Aimee Semple McPherson," *Rhetoric and Public Affairs* 14 (Summer 2011): 309.

24. Ray, "Aimee Semple McPherson," 155–56.

25. Ibid., 167–68.

26. Leah Payne, "Pentecostal Preachers in North America: 1890–1930," in *Scripting Pentecost: A Study of Pentecostals, Worship and Liturgy*, eds. Mark J. Cartledge and A. J. Swoboda (London: Routledge, 2016), 22–23.

27. Aimee Semple McPherson, "Foursquare!" *Sunset Magazine* 58 (February 1927): 80.

28. Grant Wacker, *Heaven Below: Early Pentecostals and American Culture* (Cambridge: Harvard University Press, 2001), 113.

times of congregational prayer and singing to times of seeking God at the altar. McPherson, however, broke with this trend in early Pentecostalism. She did not mind being front and center, and although Angelus Temple services included music accompanied by large choirs and professional musicians, dances, skits and other theater forms, these "were merely the warm up for the most important performance of the services—McPherson's sermon dedicated to her chosen theme."[29]

In her illustrated sermons, McPherson always assumed the star role, and these sermons were her chosen method for drawing her audience dramatically and emotionally into the common spiritual experiences of people in the Bible and throughout history. Her use of various media to communicate her messages necessitated more tightly programmed and structured services than those with which some early Pentecostals were accustomed.[30] Her illustrated sermons were comprised not just of a well-designed set and an engaging sermon, but also included elaborate stage directions, sophisticated pageantry, and music ensembles similar to a vaudeville act, all of which required practice, preparation, and planning in order to be done well.[31] She welcomed these more programmed and directed kinds of art and music into the Pentecostal worship service, where before those kinds of elements were considered to quench the free flow of the Spirit. Such practices by McPherson foreshadowed the reemergence of more structured and developed forms of music and art that would become commonplace in Pentecostal worship services after World War II, as they attempted to accommodate and incorporate the mainstream popular music styles of the day.[32]

The era of Pentecostal denominationalism saw a gradual trend toward churches holding separate tarrying meetings (for those seeking physical healing and Spirit baptism) outside their main congregational worship gathering.[33] McPherson was an early adopter of this trend, creating a separate worship space in the design of Angelus Temple, where she could host smaller gatherings of people who might desire individualized teaching and counsel on such matters while being sensitive to the schedule constraints of "seekers" who might attend a service out of curiosity but not wish to be kept at church indefinitely.[34] The Five

---

29. Leah Payne, *Gender and Pentecostal Revivalism: Making a Female Ministry in the Early Twentieth Century* (New York: Palgrave Macmillan, 2015), 109.

30. Daniel E. Albrecht, *Rites in the Spirit: A Ritual Approach to Pentecostal/Charismatic Spirituality* (Sheffield: Sheffield Academic, 1999), 54.

31. Thomas Fish, "Sister Aimee's Dutch Swan Song: A Study of the Illustrated Sermon," *Journal of Religion and Theatre* 8 (Fall 2009): 55.

32. Calvin M. Johansson, "Music in the Pentecostal Movement," in *The Future of Pentecostalism in the United States*, eds. Eric Patterson and Edmund Rybarczyk (Lanham, MD: Lexington, 2007), 59–60.

33. Aaron T. Friesen, "Classical Pentecostal Liturgy: Between Formalism and Fanaticism," in *Scripting Pentecost: A Study of Pentecostals, Worship and Liturgy*, eds. Mark J. Cartledge and A. J. Swoboda (London: Routledge, 2016), 56–57.

34. Sutton, *Aimee Semple McPherson*, 22.

Hundred Room (named after the reference to five hundred disciples to whom the resurrected Jesus appeared in 1 Cor 15:6) was a place for specific, in-depth teachings and prayers for healing.[35] The Hundred and Twenty Room (sometimes called "the Upper Room" after the gathered disciples described in Acts 1:15) was set aside specifically for prayer services, preparation of altar workers, and for individuals who wanted to tarry for the baptism in the Holy Spirit.[36] This allowed McPherson the freedom to cater her sermons in the main services to an evangelistic end without ignoring the spiritual needs of those who had already made a commitment to Jesus Christ. Such seeker-sensitive preaching strategies also aided her evangelistic efforts over the radio where she sought to reach the widest possible audience with the message of Jesus Christ.[37]

During the nineteenth century, there was an increased emphasis in many pulpits on the availability of an emotional connection with God through a "close," "intimate," and "heartfelt personal relationship" with Jesus Christ.[38] Such terminology was utilized in early Pentecostal revivalism and expanded to include charismatic expressions of love and commitment. McPherson's own preaching style followed these trends by utilizing dramatic emotional appeals and encouraging bodily expressions of faith and commitment. In addition, Aimee often adopted feminine personas in the pulpit (such as a bride, a maidservant or a nurse) that she could use to portray an intimate and personal relationship with Jesus Christ.[39] She chided academics that made the presence of God overly theoretical, saying, "How can people be made to love and respect and depend on the detached God of the theologians? People are hungry for a practical religion, one that will make them feel the closeness of Jesus Christ."[40]

To emphasize this closeness to Jesus, McPherson encouraged embodied and emotional responses to her messages, such as raised hands, clapping, shouting, singing, and dancing.[41] However, she also went to great lengths to prevent such embodied expression from turning into a raucous or chaotic gathering that would distract people unnecessarily. While McPherson's sense of evangelistic urgency caused her to embrace certain emotional appeals and hooks in her preaching,

---

35. Nathaniel M. Van Cleave, *The Vine and the Branches* (Los Angeles: International Church of the Foursquare Gospel, 1992), 18.

36. Aimee Semple McPherson, "If Angelus Temple Could Speak," *Bridal Call* 6 (February 1923): 16; Aimee Semple McPherson, "The Five Hundred Room," *Bridal Call Foursquare* 8 (October 1924): 21–22.

37. Michelle Krejci, "Give the Winds a Mighty Voice: Aimee Semple McPherson and Her Radio Voice," in *Delivering the Word: Preaching and Exegesis in the Western Christian Tradition*, eds. William John Lyons and Isabella Sandwell (London: Routledge, 2014), 216.

38. Kristy Maddux, "The Feminized Gospel: Aimee Semple McPherson and the Gendered Performance of Christianity," *Women's Studies in Communication* 35 (2012): 44–46.

39. Ibid., 50–55.

40. *Denver Post*, June 19, 1921. Quoted in Barfoot, "Aimee Semple McPherson," 269.

41. Maddux, "The Feminized Gospel," 51.

she also avoided excessive displays of emotionalism for the same reason—much to the criticism of other Pentecostal leaders.[42] McPherson's value of moderation is evident in a lesson on homiletics that she gave to students at her Bible training school. In it, she emphasized the need for every preacher to have a genuine experience of baptism in the Holy Spirit. At the same time, she spoke of the need for Pentecostal preachers to be able to address and rein in emotional excesses in their services for the sake of seekers. She believed that "salvation was first and of great importance" and questioned the value of any displays that would frighten or scare genuine seekers away.[43] For McPherson, the primary purpose of preaching (at least during Sunday services) was evangelistic—opening the hearts of people to receive Jesus Christ as their Lord and Savior. Discipleship and teaching ministry were important, but to be done primarily in other settings. Such a philosophy led McPherson to craft sermons that were at once whimsical, accessible, emotionally engaging, and compelling to nonbelievers.

In the tradition of American revivalism, early Pentecostal pastors often demonstrated their spiritual authority not just through their preaching ability, but in their skill at transitioning and bringing together the various elements of congregational worship into a cohesive whole. Making spontaneous song selections, creating space for prophetic words, facilitating prayer times, and initiating altar responses were all important ways in which Pentecostal preachers established their role as an anointed spiritual leader in the pulpit.[44] McPherson embraced this role in her leading of revival and worship services at Angelus Temple and on the road, but she infused it with the skill of a Broadway stage director and the style of a Hollywood actress. As her services gradually came to be known as "polished, seamless, well-orchestrated productions," her sermons were also carefully crafted and planned to fit into the flow and theme of the services. Unlike many Pentecostal preachers before her, McPherson did not often go off script, and what may have appeared to the audience like spontaneous and free-flowing services were actually extensively programmed beforehand.[45] Unlike many of her Holiness and Pentecostal contemporaries, McPherson embraced the use of the latest cosmetics and fashion. Her fashion sense enhanced her feminine persona in the pulpit. "Instead of seeing it as a mark of spiritual deficiency, [McPherson] used fashion as a tool in service to [her] revivalist messages."[46]

---

42. In 1922, McPherson faced harsh criticism from officials in The Assemblies of God for withholding certain charismatic expressions from a revival service in Wichita. Blumhofer, *Everybody's Sister*, 185–86.

43. McPherson, "A Lesson in Homiletics," 2.

44. Payne, "Pentecostal Preachers in North America," 22.

45. Payne, *Gender and Pentecostal Revivalism*, 118.

46. Leah Payne, "'Pants Don't Make Preachers': Fashion and Gender Construction in Late-Nineteenth and Early Twentieth Century American Revivalism," *Fashion Theory* 19, no. 1 (2015): 101.

Interestingly, many of the particular communication methods McPherson used to appeal to her audience at Angelus Temple were not applicable to the radio. Her signature white dress, bobbed hair, and props could not be seen. Although her fashion sense and cosmetic skill were mostly lost on her radio audience, her feminine persona was not. "With the radio, McPherson was not limited to modeling intimacy; she created it."[47] The radio allowed McPherson's voice to be heard in the most private contexts of life, and her skill at telling a story with figurative, imaginative language drew her listeners into the experience.[48] McPherson's voice was strong and captivating for radio listeners, as well as her live audience, as she effectively controlled the volume and pace of her words for dramatic effect—oscillating with ease from conversational tones to spirited and forceful exclamation.[49] Such a vocal presence represented the "ideal popular femininity" that audiences were getting used to hearing from Hollywood through the radio and on film.[50]

CONTRIBUTIONS TO PREACHING

McPherson was certainly not the first effective female evangelist of the late-nineteenth or early twentieth century. In fact, there were numerous women who successfully pioneered such a role before McPherson ever began holding revival services.[51] None of them, however, rose to the level of fame and notoriety that McPherson did. She was a household name across the United States by the time of her death, and although she performed many pastoral and administrative duties beyond the pulpit, it was her preaching that made her famous.[52] Her message was not feminist in content.[53] Nevertheless, her success as a female preacher whose presence, style, and methods embraced her femininity and used it to move and sway the masses was inspiring for many other women who also felt called to preach.

McPherson was a pioneer in the use of multimedia and varied art forms to communicate her messages. These forms, however, were not used primarily

---

47. Krejci, "Give the Winds a Mighty Voice," 218.

48. Maddux, "The Foursquare Gospel of Aimee Semple McPherson," 309–11.

49. Ibid., 313–14. A few live recordings of McPherson's preaching are available.

50. Payne, *Gender and Pentecostal Revivalism*, 113.

51. Priscilla Pope-Levison, *Building the Old Time Religion: Female Evangelists in the Progressive Era* (New York: New York University Press, 2014), 24–25.

52. Early in her ministry Aimee did not shy away from performing pastoral-shepherding duties, but as the ministry at Angelus Temple grew (in 1924 alone, the Temple reported 96,259 visitors to the healing rooms) she looked to other staff such as Paul Rader to fulfill much of the day-to-day pastoral care duties of the congregation (healing rooms, prayer rooms, weddings, funerals, counseling, etc.) so she could focus more of her pastoral energy on preaching, teaching, and writing. Barfoot, *Aimee Semple McPherson*, 440; Blumhofer, *Everybody's Sister*, 279.

53. Edith L. Blumhofer, "Reflections on the Voice of Aimee Semple McPherson," *Pneuma* 17 (Spring 1995): 21–22.

as a form of entertainment or curious attraction for her audiences as is often assumed. Rather, they were used to intentionally draw people imaginatively into the stories of the Bible in order to help them find parallels with their own story. Thus, one might argue that McPherson contributed an affective and narrative epistemology to the task of preaching in contrast to the didactic sermons common among evangelical rationalists of her day. James K. A. Smith says that this framework of belief affirms that "knowledge is rooted in the heart and traffics in the stuff of story. It's not that propositional truths can be 'packaged' in narrative format for 'the simple'; rather, the conviction is that story comes before proposition—imagination precedes intellection."[54] McPherson understood that preaching was a shared experience that had the power to shape people's perception of the reality of God in their midst. Thus, the use of story and emotion were not just tools for getting the attention of people but essential elements to help people imagine in their minds and hearts how their story was intimately connected to the person and work of Christ. When such preaching was done well, McPherson believed that proper doctrinal knowledge and understanding would naturally follow.

McPherson's illustrated sermons are prominent examples of Pentecostals adopting and adapting the latest trends in art and music for use in the church. On the one hand, McPherson's close proximity to Hollywood and flare for pageantry and multimedia caused her services and radio programs to be seen as something radically new, even among fellow Pentecostals. On the other hand, Pentecostal worship, in the tradition of American revivalism, had always been results-oriented, making a strong, forceful appeal to the listener's emotions by utilizing the most popular music forms.[55] What made McPherson's methods of communication unique among Pentecostals may have had less to do with the medium she chose and more to do with her belief that preparation, programming, and professionalism were not out of place in a Pentecostal worship service.[56] Thus, by example, McPherson encouraged Spirit-filled preachers not to rely solely on spontaneous inspiration from the Spirit in the pulpit in order to be effective communicators. Rather, they should devote much of their energy and attention to thinking through the details of how their message might be creatively communicated to their audience in a manner that is relevant, inspiring, and endearing. Few preachers could perform such a task quite as well as McPherson, but she helped pastors to see the importance of such an endeavor.

---

54. James K. A. Smith, *Thinking in Tongues: Pentecostal Contributions to Christian Philosophy* (Grand Rapids: Eerdmans, 2010), 43–44.

55. Johansson, "Music in the Pentecostal Movement," 53.

56. Payne, *Gender and Pentecostal Revivalism*, 118.

Sermon Excerpt

Barabbas[57]

Free? FREE? F-R-E-E??? Surely his ears could not hear aright! Surely this must be some horrible dream rising up to torment him.

"Make haste, Barabbas, come forth!"

Ah! the chains were loose at his feet. His hands were free. The biting iron that had long lacerated his flesh were gone. One trembling step— two—three, and he was almost to the door, but no restraining hand had fallen upon him, no voice had jeered,

"Ah, Barabbas, come forth and pay the price. Thy sin hath found thee out." Four—five—six he had gained and passed the door. Seven— eight—nine steps. He was groping his way along the corridor, stumbling blindly toward yon distant ray of light. True, the soldiers were marching behind him, but they were making no effort to seize him. What did it all mean? Surely they would seize upon him at the last moment. But, no, they are turning off in another direction and he is left alone, walking into the ever-growing light that pierces his unaccustomed eyes.

When at last, reaching the yawning doorway, clinging to its portals with one trembling hand, and shading his eyes with the other, what were his thoughts as he gazed once more upon the sunlight, and once more heard the singing of the birds, and the voices of children round about him? Were the golden threads of hope and new resolution already being woven into the texture, even amidst his bewilderment?

Oh these dangling threads that hang loose from the end of the texture, tell me, just how was the story finished? Did Barabbas catch sight of the throng wending their way to Calvary's hill? Did he hear the hissings and the jeerings of the multitude, and see yon lovely Man, in robes of white, fall beneath the burden of the cross? Did he run, perhaps, to the old cottage home, and clasping his amazed wife and little boy by the hand, cry:

"Oh, come with me, and let us go and see the man that is dying in my place. Today was the day set for my execution. Today I was to be

---

57. This sermon is an early example of McPherson's narrative style of preaching that would become famous in her elaborate illustrated sermons years later. Already, her tendency to expand on and embellish the biblical text in order to draw her audience emotionally and imaginatively into a story is evident as she describes the dramatic conversion of Barabbas based on the brief mention of him in the Scriptures. See Aimee Semple McPherson, "Barabbas," *Bridal Call Pentecostal Monthly* 2, no. 5 (October 1918): 3–8.

hanged upon the cross and die a felon's death, but another man, an innocent man, is dying, dying for me. Oh, come and let us go and look upon His face that we may fathom the mystery of such love."

And did they push their way together through the throng and up the hill, ne'er stopping till they reached the foot of the cross, where sobbing women mourned the grief of Him who bore our sorrows? And as Barabbas gazed into that face most fair, and saw the nails, and the blood drops streaming down from brow and hands and feet, as he looked into those eyes of deep, unutterable love, and heard the words:

"Father, forgive," falling from those anguished lips, did he cry:

"Oh, Jesus, thy love has won my heart! Yonder are the two thieves, one on the right, one on the left, but there is the middle cross, the cross upon which I should have died." And stooping down, did he take his little son up in his arms, and pointing to the cross did he sob in his ear:

"Oh, Sonny, look, that is the cross your Papa should have died upon; that is the place where I should have hung, the death I should have died, but yon lovely Man, whom they call Jesus, is dying in Papa's place. Oh, wife and son and Oh, my heart, let us ever love and live and work for this Jesus who gave Himself for me?"

As Barabbas gazed steadfast into the eyes of Jesus, did the face of the Lord turn toward him? Did their eyes meet, and was there a look of understanding exchanged between the two that broke Barabbas' heart and held him captive by the chains of love forever? Did he fall upon his knees, crying:

> "Jesus, how can I ever thank you?
> Drops of grief could ne'er repay
> The debt of love I owe;
> Here, Lord, I give myself to Thee,
> 'Tis all that I can do." ♦

BIBLIOGRAPHY

Albrecht, Daniel E. *Rites in the Spirit: A Ritual Approach to Pentecostal/Charismatic Spirituality*. Sheffield: Sheffield Academic, 1999.

Alexander, Kimberly Ervin Alexander. "Restoration, Accommodation, and Innovation: The Contributions of Aimee Semple McPherson." Pages 246–55 in *From Aldersgate to Azusa Street: Wesleyan, Holiness, and Pentecostal Visions of New Creation*. Edited by Henry H. Knight III. Eugene, OR: Pickwick, 2010.

Barfoot, Chas H. *Aimee Semple McPherson and the Making of Modern Pentecostalism*. London: Equinox, 2011.

Blumhofer, Edith L. *Aimee Semple McPherson: Everybody's Sister*. Grand Rapids: Eerdmans, 1993.
_____. "Reflections on the Voice of Aimee Semple McPherson." *Pneuma* 17 (Spring 1995): 21–24.
Booth, Catherine. *Papers on Practical Religion*. London: International Headquarters, 1891.
Epstein, Daniel Mark. *Sister Aimee: The Life of Aimee Semple McPherson*. New York: Harcourt, 1993.
Fish, Thomas. "Sister Aimee's Dutch Swan Song: A Study of the Illustrated Sermon," *Journal of Religion and Theatre* 8 (Fall 2009): 48–71.
Friesen, Aaron T. "Pentecostal Antitraditionalism and the Pursuit of Holiness: The Neglected Role of Tradition in Pentecostal Theological Reflection." *Journal of Pentecostal Theology* 23 (2014): 191–215.
_____. "Classical Pentecostal Liturgy: Between Formalism and Fanaticism." Pages 53–68 in *Scripting Pentecost: A Study of Pentecostals, Worship and Liturgy*. Edited by Mark J. Cartledge and A. J. Swoboda. London: Routledge, 2016.
Johansson, Calvin M. "Music in the Pentecostal Movement." Pages 49–70 in *The Future of Pentecostalism in the United States*. Edited by Eric Patterson and Edmund Rybarczyk. Lanham, MD: Lexington, 2007.
Krejci, Michelle. "Give the Winds a Mighty Voice: Aimee Semple McPherson and Her Radio Voice." Pages 209–30 in *Delivering the Word: Preaching and Exegesis in the Western Christian Tradition*. Edited by William John Lyons and Isabella Sandwell. London: Routledge, 2014.
Maddux, Kristy. "The Feminized Gospel: Aimee Semple McPherson and the Gendered Performance of Christianity." *Women's Studies in Communication* 35 (2012): 42–67.
_____. "The Foursquare Gospel of Aimee Semple McPherson." *Rhetoric and Public Affairs* 14 (Summer 2011): 291–326.
McPherson, Aimee Semple. *Aimee Semple McPherson: The Story of My Life*. Waco, TX: Word, 1973.
_____. "Barabbas." *Bridal Call Pentecostal Monthly* 2, no. 5 (October 1918): 3–8.
_____. "The Five Hundred Room." *Bridal Call Foursquare* 8 (October 1924): 21–22.
_____. "Foursquare!" *Sunset Magazine* 58 (February 1927): 15–16 (80–82).
_____. "If Angelus Temple Could Speak." *Bridal Call* 6 (February 1923): 11–19.
_____. "A Lesson in Homiletics." Unpublished notes in Foursquare Archives.
_____. "Lost and Restored." *Bridal Call* 1 (April 1918): 1–11.
_____. *The Story of My Life*. Los Angeles: Echo Park Evangelistic Association, 1951.
_____. *This Is That: Personal Experiences, Sermons and Writings*. Los Angeles: Bridal Call Publishing House, 1919.
Payne, Leah. *Gender and Pentecostal Revivalism: Making a Female Ministry in the Early Twentieth Century*. New York: Palgrave Macmillan, 2015.
_____. "'Pants Don't Make Preachers': Fashion and Gender Construction in Late-Nineteenth and Early Twentieth Century American Revivalism." *Fashion Theory* 19, no.1 (2015): 83–113.
_____. "Pentecostal Preachers in North America: 1890–1930." Pages 15–31 in *Scripting Pentecost: A Study of Pentecostals, Worship and Liturgy*. Edited by Mark J. Cartledge and A. J. Swoboda. London: Routledge, 2016.
Pope-Levison, Priscilla. *Building the Old Time Religion: Female Evangelists in the Progressive Era*. New York: New York University Press, 2014.
Ray, Donna E. "Aimee Semple McPherson and Her Seriously Exciting Gospel." *Journal of Pentecostal Theology* 19 (2010): 155–169.
Robeck, Cecil M. "Aimee Semple McPherson." Pages 856–68 in *The New International Dictionary of Pentecostal and Charismatic Movements*. Edited by Stanley M. Burgess. Grand Rapids: Zondervan, 2002.
Smith, James K. A. *Thinking in Tongues: Pentecostal Contributions to Christian Philosophy*. Grand Rapids: Eerdmans, 2010.
Sutton, Matthew Avery. *Aimee Semple McPherson and the Resurrection of Christian America*. Cambridge: Harvard University Press, 2007.
Van Cleave, Nathaniel M. *The Vine and the Branches*. Los Angeles: International Church of the Foursquare Gospel, 1992.
Wacker, Grant. *Heaven Below: Early Pentecostals and American Culture*. Cambridge: Harvard University Press, 2001.
Yong, Amos. "Reading Scripture and Nature: Pentecostal Hermeneutics and Their Implications for the Contemporary Evangelical Theology and Science Conversation." *Perspectives on Science and Christian Faith* 63 (March 2011): 3–15.

W. A. Criswell

Expositing the Whole Counsel of God—from Genesis to Revelation

DAVID L. ALLEN

The endeavor to encapsulate W. A. Criswell's lifetime legacy of preaching in one short article is a bit like attempting to dam up Niagara Falls with toothpicks. When the history of twentieth century Southern Baptist preaching is written, Criswell's name will stand among the top of the list. W. A. Criswell (1909–2002) is a man who preached for more than three-quarters of a century and who served as senior pastor and pastor emeritus for more than half a century at the historic First Baptist Church in Dallas, Texas. From behind the beautiful red-velvet-topped carved oak pulpit, his expository preaching ministry became world renowned.

HISTORICAL BACKGROUND

On December 19, 1909, in Eldorado, a sleepy Oklahoma day was disturbed by the newborn cries of W. A. Criswell (he was never called anything other than W. A. by his parents; his father's name was Wallie Amos). Not long after, the Criswell family moved to the Texas Panhandle town of Texline.

Criswell was converted to Christ at age ten, but the desire to be a preacher antedated even his conversion. He explained his call to the pastorate saying, "I'm sure that desire came directly from God, but just when it started or exactly why I'm still not sure. I just know that even before I was saved, the Lord planted it deep in my heart that I would be a pastor—not an evangelist, not a missionary, but a pastor. My father didn't want me to be a preacher. My mother didn't want me to be a preacher. But somehow I knew that in spite of everything and everybody, a preacher I would be."[1]

After attending high school in Amarillo, Criswell began his studies at Baylor University in Waco, Texas. Encouraged by a favorite professor to study the

---

1. W. A. Criswell, *Standing on the Promises: the Autobiography of W. A. Criswell* (Dallas: Word, 1990), 26.

great works of literature, he majored in English. Dr. Henry Trantham, Criswell's Greek professor, instilled in the young preacher a desire to become proficient in the use of the Greek New Testament.[2] His linguistic ability in the pulpit was due in no small measure to studies in language and classical literature during his Baylor years.

In the course of his sophomore year, Criswell assumed his first pastoral position at the Marlow Baptist Church near Waco, preaching three Sundays a month. Shortly thereafter, he began preaching one Sunday a month at the Pecan Grove Baptist Church near Gatesville, Texas. He also held part-time pastorates at Devil's Bend and Pulltight, Texas. From 1928–1931, he preached in Marlow, Texas, White Mound, Texas, and Pecan Grove, Texas. Throughout his college years at Baylor, Criswell not only gained the academic training that was to become foundational for his later ministry, but also practical pastoral experience.

After graduation in 1931, Criswell went on to The Southern Baptist Theological Seminary in Louisville, Kentucky. There he studied under the great A. T. Robertson and W. Hershey Davis, who instilled in him a love for the Greek New Testament. During this period, he also pastored two churches part-time. By 1937, he had earned a master of theology and a PhD.

Upon graduation, he accepted the call to pastor his first full-time church, the First Baptist Church of Chickasha, Oklahoma, serving there until early in 1941. Toward the end of his tenure as pastor, Criswell felt he was "beginning to run dry" in his preaching. On Mondays and Tuesdays, he would pace the floor trying to find new topics to preach the following Sunday.[3] Although the church did well, Criswell began to sense a restlessness in his spirit.

Not long after, he received the call to become the pastor of the First Baptist Church of Muskogee, Oklahoma. It was not until Criswell arrived in Muskogee that he felt he really learned to preach.[4] Before this time, he was by his own admission a topical preacher. He was gifted the library and sermon notes of his predecessor Dr. A. N. Hall by Mrs. Hall after her husband's death. It was through these resources that he was led to a discovery that would change his preaching from that time forward. From these sermon notes, Criswell learned that Hall had preached through virtually the whole Bible, text by text. He shared: "Why should I struggle to think up topics for my sermons . . . when I could let inspiring and informative texts speak for themselves? . . . Suddenly, I found myself really

---

2. Robert A. Rohm, *Dr. C: The Visionary and Ministry of W. A. Criswell* (Chicago: Moody, 1990), 51–52.
3. Criswell, *Standing on the Promises*, 157.
4. Ibid., 158. See also Bill Keith, *W. A. Criswell: The Authorized Biography* (Old Tappan, NJ: Revell, 1973), 55; Matthew McKellar, "An Evaluation of the Elements of Persuasion in the Favorite Messages of W. A. Criswell as Contained in the Book *With a Bible in My Hand*" (PhD diss., Southwestern Baptist Theological Seminary, 1991), 40–41.

proclaiming the Word, book by book, text by text, cover to cover from Genesis to Revelation. I felt new power. Instead of pacing the floor, stressed and anxious, trying to find some new topic to preach, I was pacing the floor with excitement, caught up in the might and majesty of God's Word."[5]

Three years later at the age of thirty-four, on October 6, 1944, W. A. Criswell preached his first sermon as the pastor of First Baptist Church of Dallas, Texas. Over the next fifty-plus years, he would exert a profound influence in his church, the city of Dallas, his Southern Baptist denomination, and even the world.

Preaching Ministry

The kaleidoscopic career of W. A. Criswell furnishes the backdrop to his preaching ministry. He was a pastor and church builder. This was his heart. He had opportunity to be president of more than one university, but his love for the pastorate precluded academic administration. He was the author of fifty-four books. Many of them were expositional sermons on various books of the Bible, such as the now famous *Expository Sermons on Revelation*. He was a denominational leader who served two terms as president of the Southern Baptist Convention. As the key figure who identified the liberal drift in the Convention, he furnished the inspiration for a groundswell of grassroots Southern Baptists to bring their Southern Baptist Zion—as he loved to call it—back to her theologically conservative roots. Who can forget his famous sermons preached at the Southern Baptist Convention Pastor's Conference in 1985 and 1988 respectively, entitled, "Whether We Live or Die" and "The Curse of Liberalism"? In the words of the Winthrop Praed poem "The Vicar," when Criswell preached, "he 'stablish'd truth and startled error."

Bill Keith described Criswell's preaching as a blend of "humor, homely anecdote, snippets of poetry, and straight-from-the-shoulder biblical literalism into a firm foundation on which he erects the superstructure of the message."[6] Russ Bush characterized it as "deep, forceful, and full of doctrine, and it arises out of long hours of study and prayer."[7] C. Richard Wells, president of the Criswell College and a former homiletics professor himself, noted three things that distinguished Dr. Criswell's preaching: his biblical scholarship, understanding of culture, and oratorical skills.[8] With these assessments, all would concur. Probably no one knew him any better than Paige Patterson, who served as president of

5. Criswell, *Standing on the Promises*, 160.

6. Keith, *W. A. Criswell: The Authorized Biography*, 77–78.

7. L. Russell Bush III, "W. A. Criswell," in *Baptist Theologians*, eds. Timothy George and David S. Dockery (Nashville: Broadman & Holman, 1999), 454.

8. "Criswell's Biblical Focus Became a Model for Many," *Dallas Morning News*, Religion Section, (19 January 2002), 3G.

the Criswell College and as associate pastor at the church for seventeen years. "In a sermon's tapestry Criswell would weave together the history of a doctrine, exegete a pivotal text, and apply it to the contemporary milieu in a memorable manner."[9] In a paper presented to the Evangelical Theological Society, Patterson noted how Criswell could "tell the congregation about a perfect periphrastic construction in Greek and have the whole congregation laughing and crying at the same time and garner three professions of faith and sixteen rededications out of an optative mood."[10] Criswell's versatility, knowledge of the original languages, and oratorical skill were marshaled in impressive array Sunday by Sunday in his sermons.

His preaching was often a verbal pyrotechnic extravaganza. Many Sundays were homiletical Fourths of July. Such was the case with the first sermon I ever heard Dr. Criswell preach. I'll never forget the experience. I had just arrived in Dallas to study at Criswell College and attended the morning worship service on August 10, 1975. On that day, Criswell preached what is now considered one of his most famous sermons, "Death in Détente." Coming at a strategic and strained time in American-Soviet relations, this sermon was delivered with such impact, warning of the danger of compromise with an evil empire, that its repercussions were heard all the way to Washington. In fact, it was printed in a pamphlet and distributed to members of Congress and actually made its way to the Oval Office where it effectively contributed to the shaping of American foreign policy during the Reagan years.[11]

THEOLOGY OF PREACHING

Criswell was committed to the biblical text. Because of this, and because of the context in which he preached, there are a couple theological conversations that need to be highlighted in order to understand him as a pastor, preacher, and theologian. These were the doctrine of inerrancy and an exalted view of Christ.

Doctrine of Inerrancy

The foundation of Criswell's preaching was his unswerving commitment to the inerrancy of Scripture. Criswell had witnessed firsthand the debilitating effects of liberalism on the mainline Protestant denominations in the first half

---

9. Paige Patterson, "W. A. Criswell," in *Theologians of the Baptist Tradition*, eds. Timothy George and David Dockery (Nashville: Broadman & Holman, 2001), 253. This, along with Patterson's other article on Criswell, "The Imponderables of God," in *Criswell Theological Review* 1 (Spring 1987): 237–53, are must-reads.

10. Cited in Patterson, "W. A. Criswell," 253.

11. A point well made by Paige Patterson at Criswell's funeral service.

of the twentieth century. He was also keenly aware of its negative impact on some of the seminaries of the Southern Baptist Convention.

Sprinkled throughout his sermons are references to "the infallible and inerrant word of God." In 1964, Criswell preached nine sermons on the Bible as the Word of God. These sermons were collected and published as *The Bible for Today's World* in 1965.[12] One of his most well-known, and controversial, books was published in 1969, entitled *Why I Preach That the Bible Is Literally True*.[13] Here Criswell articulated his clarion affirmation and defense of the inerrancy of Scripture. The book appealed to an eclectic mix of personal experience and historical legal evidence to support his view of inerrancy.

In 1980, Criswell preached a sermon in which he summarized the essential elements of his position in a sermon that contained the same title. A summary of these elements includes the following: (1) the Bible's universal appeal in whatever language into which it is translated; (2) the Bible's unparalleled influence on human life and culture; (3) the authority of the Bible is confirmed by the authority of Jesus Christ; (4) archaeological affirmations; (5) reliability of the manuscripts; (6) discovery of the Dead Sea Scrolls; (6) the unity of the Bible.[14]

Criswell's confidence in the inerrancy of the Word of God was instilled in him from an early age. He spoke of those pastors that he heard preach as a young boy: "They left upon me the impression of the reality of God and the glory of Christ and the truth of the Bible and the genuineness of our experience with the Lord and trusting Him and believing in Him. All of the things that I now believe and preach are those things that I first listened to from those men."[15]

Christology

Criswell's sermons had an overtly christocentric focus. Criswell was not only a student of the Word, but also a great student of history. He was extremely well-read in a wide array of disciplines. One area of study in particular made an immense impression on Criswell and his christocentricism, and that was his study of Charles Haddon Spurgeon. Spurgeon was a hero to Criswell, and in many ways Criswell modeled his ministry after Spurgeon's. Criswell cites Spurgeon's influence in his chistocentric preaching: "There is one great theme of the Word of

---

12. W. A. Criswell, *The Bible for Today's World* (Grand Rapids: Zondervan, 1965).

13. W. A. Criswell, *Why I Preach that the Bible Is Literally True* (Nashville: Broadman, 1969), 44–52. See also W. A. Criswell, *Criswell's Guidebook for Pastors* (Nashville: Broadman, 1980), 73–79.

14. W. A. Criswell, "Why I Preach the Bible Is Literally True," Criswell Bible Institute Chapel, October 14, 1980. https://www.wacriswell.com/sermons/1980/why-i-preach-the-bible-is-literally-true/?keywords=Why+i+preach+the+bible+is+literally+true.

15. Quoted in Hochul Song, "A Critical Examination of W. A. Criswell's Sermons from Acts in Comparison with His Theory of Preaching" (Unpublished PhD diss., New Orleans Baptist Theological Seminary, 2011), 68.

God. The theme is constant from beginning to end. That theme is Jesus. He is on every page, in every event, in every type, in every book. Someone once asked the famed Charles Haddon Spurgeon of the Metropolitan Tabernacle in London, 'Why do all of your sermons sound alike?' Spurgeon replied, 'Because I take a text and make a beeline to the cross.' The entire Bible presents Jesus, and the man who wants to proclaim Christ must do so by preaching from all the Word of God."[16]

The first and last entry in his pastoral ledger illustrate the christocentric focus of Criswell's preaching. The first entry is actually his "trial" sermon preached to the church before he was called to be the pastor. It is dated August 27, 1944. The text is 1 Corinthians 1:18, and the title is "Christ the Power of God." The last entry concludes with the week of pre-Easter services in 1995, which Criswell had instituted annually years earlier. This was a series of sermons preached at noon Monday through Friday prior to Easter Sunday at First Baptist Church. The sermon is entitled "Jesus Is the Coming King."[17] His preaching was thoroughly biblical and Christ centered. Consequently, Criswell's preaching was thoroughly evangelistic. He believed in the necessity of publically calling people to Christ at the conclusion of his sermons. He employed the altar call regularly in his preaching.

METHODOLOGY FOR PREACHING

Criswell's own views on preaching can be found primarily in his *Guidebook for Pastors*.[18] He states: "A sermon is not a theological essay. It is designed to move the heart and the will of the people as well as to instruct them in the way and in the faith. A sermon ought to be like the epistles of Paul. The apostle wrote of great doctrinal truth and teaching, then he closed with wonderful application. . . . There are many different kinds of preaching, but the heart of it all is to preach the Christ of the Bible, the Word of God incarnate, spoken and written."[19]

Speaking of his early preaching as a young man and comparing it with his later years at First Baptist Church in Dallas, Criswell said:

> When I first began to preach as a teenager . . . I preached about what-
> ever fell by chance into my mind. I preached according to whatever some

---

16. Ibid., 90.

17. This was not the last sermon Criswell ever preached, as he occasionally preached—health permitting—at the church, conference, or other setting. The last time I heard him speak was from a wheelchair in chapel to the students of Criswell College in 2001.

18. Criswell, *Criswell's Guidebook for Pastors*. See especially 27–57, the chapter entitled "The Pastor in the Pulpit." This is a must-read for all preachers.

19. Ibid., 41.

incident or event or saying would suggest. That is about as poor a way to prepare a sermon as could be found in all the world. . . . If I had my ministry to do over again, I would from its very beginning preach the Bible and nothing but the Bible. I would go through book after book of the Bible. If I could not find a message in a verse, I would take a paragraph. If I could not find a message that moved my heart in a paragraph, I would take a chapter.[20]

In 1946, Criswell began a preaching tour through the entire Bible. He began with Genesis. Seventeen-and-a-half years and a few thousand new members later, he finished Revelation. When he announced his intention to preach through the Bible, the naysayers emerged from within the church. "You'll kill the church!" some warned. "People won't come," moaned others. "What will you do when you get to the book of Numbers," asked some. As Criswell often put it, "You never heard such lugubrious prognostications in all of your life." During those years, FBC needed no ecclesiastical undertakers; in fact, her ministries flourished. Under Dr. Criswell's preaching, FBC became the prototype for the megachurch, with her membership rolls swelling to over twenty-five thousand by the mid-1980s.[21] In an era when preaching in the mainline denominational churches was afflicted with nervous prostration, Criswell proved you could still build a great church on the preaching of the Bible as the inerrant Word of God.

Unlike many modern preachers, Criswell never endured the disgrace of having his sermons received with blank stares and feelings of boredom. W. A. Criswell presented his people with a steady diet of expositional preaching combined with a rhetorical eloquence that kept people on the edge of their seats. His knowledge of history, the arts, literature, and human nature was only eclipsed by his knowledge of Scripture. Criswell's sermons were always lightly sprinkled with quotes and illustrations from these other sources, which enhanced his powerful exposition and application of the Bible.

Criswell's thorough sermon preparation was obvious to all.[22] In fact, it was his trademark to spend the morning hours in study and sermon preparation at home before he ever went to the church office. During the "School of the Prophets" (an annual pastors' conference sponsored by Criswell and the First Baptist Church), in his *Guidebook for Pastors*, and in conferences and other settings, Criswell never tired of challenging young preachers to save their morning hours

---

20. Criswell, *Why I Preach That the Bible Is Literally True*, 86–87.
21. See Patterson, "W. A. Criswell," 236.
22. Leon McBeth, *First Baptist Church of Dallas: A Centennial History* (Grand Rapids: Zondervan, 1968), 332.

for study and sermon preparation. As James Bryant put it, "No man ever entered the pulpit more consistently prepared than did Criswell."[23]

One of the most amazing things is the record Criswell kept of every sermon preached from the day he became pastor at First Baptist Church in Dallas in 1944 until a final entry in 1995. The sermons are recorded in an old church ledger with page headings like "Record of Baptisms," "Record of Members Received," and "Record of Marriages." Each page has ruled lines and columns, thirty lines to a page. Scrawled on the top left of the first page in hieroglyphics that would take the CIA's best code breakers roughly a week to decipher are the words, "I was called to be pastor of the 1st Bap. Ch. Dallas Wednesday, Sept. 27, 1944." Criswell's sermon ledger is 147 pages long and contains roughly four thousand sermons, recorded line by line, thirty to a page. He would first list the text, then the sermon title, followed by "a.m." or "p.m." to designate morning and evening service, then the date listed by month, day, year.

Criswell's preaching has been the subject of numerous dissertations.[24] Of these, Matthew McKellar gives the most in-depth analysis and evaluation.[25] Perhaps McKellar's most significant conclusion, however, lies in the relationship of Criswell's preaching to biblical authority: "One does not have to capitulate at the point of biblical authority in order to be persuasive as a preacher to contemporary hearers. Criswell's sermons reflect the perspective that biblical exposition energized by the Holy Spirit has a supernaturally persuasive value which transcends all human efforts to persuade."[26]

Criswell's preaching reflects a mastery of correct use of grammar. Poor grammar never detracts from the persuasion of his sermons. He also excelled at

---

23. James Bryant, "The Legacy of Dr. W. A. Criswell in Pastoral and Denominational Leadership," *Shophar*, special tribute edition, n.d., 9.

24. Harold T. Bryson, "The Expository Preaching of W. A. Criswell in His Sermons on Revelation" (ThM Thesis, New Orleans Baptist Theological Seminary, 1967); James Towns, "The Rhetoric and Leadership of W. A. Criswell as the President of the Southern Baptist Convention: A Descriptive Analysis through Perspective and Public Address" (PhD diss., Southern Illinois University, 1970); Craig Roberts, "W. A. Criswell's Choice and Use of Illustrations" (ThM Thesis, Dallas Theological Seminary, 1976); Gray Allison, "The Preaching of W. A. Criswell: A Critical Analysis of Selected Messages" (ThD diss., Mid-America Baptist Theological Seminary, 1990); and McKellar, "An Evaluation of the Elements of Persuasion."

25. Bryson deals capably with the sermons on Revelation; Gray Allison analyzes only three of Criswell's most famous sermons: "The Scarlet Thread Through the Bible," "The Infallible Word of God," and "Whether We Live or Die." McKellar evaluates the use of persuasion from the book *With a Bible in My Hand,* a collection of sixteen of the favorite sermons of Criswell ranging over a period of nearly sixty years. Five evaluative criteria, taken from Kenneth Burke and Robert Oliver, are used to evaluate the introduction, explanation, illustration, application, and conclusion portions of Criswell's sermons. McKellar discovered that Criswell's most effective use of persuasion occurred in the expositional portion of the sermon. Persuasive techniques were found to be least effective in the introduction and conclusion portion of the sermon. See Kenneth Burke, *A Grammar of Motives* (New York: Prentice Hall, 1952); Kenneth Burke, *A Rhetoric of Motives* (Los Angeles: University of California Press, 1974); and Robert Oliver, *The Psychology of Persuasive Speech,* 2nd ed. (New York: Longmans, Green, 1957). The five evaluative criteria include: action verbs, identification terms, ultimate terms, interest-gaining techniques, and figures of speech.

26. McKellar, "An Evaluation of the Elements of Persuasion," 176–77.

explaining a biblical text without the use of technical theological jargon.[27] His use of the elements of persuasion made Criswell virtually peerless in his ability to make relevant biblical exposition. Criswell's oratorical style actually had more in common with the nineteenth century than with the twentieth century, yet contemporary audiences flocked to hear him preach. He had a reputation of being "a Holy-roller with a PhD," whose sermons invaded the open windows of anyone anywhere within five miles of his preaching.[28] Vividness of language, his use of strong, active verbs, and a regular use of the first person plural instead of the second person, all combined to create a bond between himself and his hearers. Concreteness, repetition, and alliteration, combined with a superb ability to make use of figures of speech turned the ear into an eye for Criswell's listeners.

Criswell was also a master at the use of gestures during a sermon. Often, he would combine gesticulation with his words in such a way that the total effect could virtually mesmerize some. His sermons were also energized by his illustrations. McKellar notes that Criswell used "action verbs, interest-gaining techniques, and figures of speech with notable frequency and effectiveness" in his use of illustrative material.[29]

With respect to sermonic structure, Criswell usually maintained the priority of content over structure, with the result that his audience was not "distracted" by overly analytical or artificial outlining. Bush perceptively notes that most of Criswell's sermons have three major parts in terms of outline: the biblical illustration of the subject at hand and the illustration of the truth in human history, followed by the application to daily life.[30]

Criswell violated virtually every homiletical rule in the book when it came to sermon introductions. In short, he scarcely ever had an introduction, as his sermons began like a vertical leap off the proverbial ledge into the waters below. Criswell seldom commenced a sermon with any reference to the hearers and their context. Rather, he started with the "then" of the text and not the "now" of the reader. Criswell seldom used any modern-day illustrations or felt the need to connect to the audience in his sermon introductions.

Criswell also made effective use of pause, rate, vocal variation, etc., in his preaching. His voice would rise to a shout and then fall to a whisper.[31] These matters of delivery merged with his expository content created an effective

---

27. Criswell did, however, employ a significant amount of traditional religious language in his sermons, assuming a knowledge in his audience that might not always have been there.

28. See Bush, "W. A. Criswell," 450.

29. McKellar, "An Evaluation of the Elements of Persuasion," 164.

30. Bush, "*W. A. Criswell*," 464, footnote 35, and 465, footnote 41. McKellar, "An Evaluation of the Elements of Persuasion," 163–64. See also Criswell's approach to sermon preparation in his *Guidebook*, 73–79.

31. McBeth, *First Baptist Church of Dallas*, 332.

combination, like the one-two punch of a skilled pugilist. Criswell's use of illustrations is ably treated in a master's thesis by Craig Roberts. Roberts spent an entire calendar year (Nov. 1974–Nov. 1975) listening to and evaluating Criswell's Sunday morning sermons in terms of his choice and use of illustrations.[32] In forty sermons, Criswell made use of 335 illustrations, an average of 8.4 per sermon. Of these, roughly 20 percent were biblical illustrations. Roberts drew three conclusions: (1) Criswell's main sources for illustrations were the Bible and his personal experiences; (2) he preferred the use of story or anecdote; and (3) he used illustrations primarily to persuade.[33]

McKellar notes in his evaluation of Criswell's preaching that application was often minimized by a lack of specificity.[34] Although McKellar's conclusion here appears to be accurate for the sermons studied, it might be somewhat premature given the small sample of only sixteen sermons. Russ Bush notes that in Criswell's later years, due to the burdens of a rigorous study schedule, application became more and more the content of the sermon.[35] Nevertheless, his sermons always made some application of the text, usually more toward the conclusion.

Perhaps one of the most important points to note about Criswell's preaching is the correlation of *logos*, *pathos*, and *ethos* (to put it in Aristotelian rhetorical terms). His messages had content, but his audience viewed him as credentialed, believable, and genuine. Indeed, he was to some almost larger than life. His sermons had passion—something drastically lacking in much of contemporary preaching. Criswell preached "to hearts as well as to heads."[36] I was privileged to sit under his preaching for eighteen months in 1975–1976 while in college. The thing I remember the most about his preaching was his passion—for Jesus, for the Word, for people, and for lost souls. Jerry Vines said of him, "W. A. Criswell is still a heart preacher, even in his nineties."[37] This trait contributed heavily to his influence and effectiveness.

CONTRIBUTIONS TO PREACHING

Criswell's influence on other pastors, both within the Baptist world and beyond, is enormous. In 1971, Criswell began an annual weekly seminar for pastors, "The

---

32. Roberts, "W. A. Criswell's Choice and Use of Illustrations."

33. Ibid., 31.

34. McKellar, "An Evaluation of the Elements of Persuasion," 170. Application contemporizes, personalizes, and particularizes the exposition for the hearer.

35. Bush, "W. A. Criswell," 465, footnote 41.

36. McBeth, *First Baptist Church of Dallas*, 332.

37. Jerry Vines and Jim Shaddix, *Power in the Pulpit: How to Prepare and Deliver Expository Sermons* (Chicago: Moody, 1999), 349.

School of the Prophets." Pastors came to the campus of First Baptist Church in Dallas to learn the church growth methods Criswell employed. There his views on preaching were learned by young pastors,[38] some of whom now fill pulpits among the largest churches in America. Rick Warren, pastor of the world-renowned Saddleback Community Church in California, attributes his inspiration to Dr. Criswell. Warren refers to Criswell as the pioneer of the megachurch movement, as well as the inspiration for his own ministry.[39]

Dr. Criswell's visionary leadership led to the founding of The Criswell College in 1971, with two main purposes in mind: (1) to stand for the inerrancy and infallibility of Scripture; and (2) to train men of God for the pastoral ministry and especially in the art of expository preaching[40]

Criswell's lifetime preaching legacy influenced future generations of preachers in several significant areas. First, Criswell regularly emphasized the need of the pastor to devote their morning hours to study and sermon preparation, preferably at home.[41] This longtime habit of Criswell influenced many during the decades of the sixties, seventies, and eighties, who are now preaching and teaching worldwide.

Second, from the beginning of his ministry at age seventeen, Criswell preached without notes. This choice undoubtedly contributed to his effectiveness in the pulpit and his influence on many who preach without notes because of his example.

---

38. First Baptist Church no longer sponsors the annual "School of the Prophets," but a very similar conference is now sponsored annually by the First Baptist Church of Jacksonville, Florida.

39. Rick Warren, *The Purpose Driven Church: Growth Without Compromising Your Message & Mission* (Grand Rapids: Zondervan, 1995), 25–27. Criswell wrote the Foreword to Warren's book.

40. At first called the Criswell Bible Institute (so named by the founding committee against Dr. Criswell's wishes), today Criswell College offers fully accredited degrees at the bachelor and master's level, and has an alumni base of over 1,400. The student body is both gender and ethnically diverse, with men and women from the United States and thirty-six other countries around the world presently studying at Criswell College. The influence this small college has had in Southern Baptist denominational life over the past thirty years is remarkable. Of course it was Paige Patterson, its president from 1975–1992, who was one of two key architects of the conservative resurgence in the SBC. Furthermore, from her professorial ranks have come dozens of people whose teaching careers began at Criswell College and who now teach on the faculties or serve in an administrative capacity at the six seminaries owned by the Southern Baptist Convention. In addition, at least one Criswell College graduate has served or is presently serving on each the Boards of Trustees for these institutions as well as most other Convention boards and agencies. In virtually every case, those graduates have played a major role in the turning of the seminaries/agencies to a more conservative stance. Like Bethlehem of Micah 5:2, Criswell College may be small among the SBC institutions, yet has exerted a profound influence in inverse proportion to its size.

In 1999, with the inauguration of "The Jerry Vines Institute of Biblical Preaching" at Criswell College, the legacy of Criswell's commitment to expository preaching and his desire to train people for this task continues through seminars and workshops on expository preaching. These are offered both on off campus in churches, local Baptist associations, and state conventions. The institute has now been invited to Nigeria to train local pastors.

41. Criswell, *Standing on the Promises*, 233–34. See also McKellar, "An Evaluation of the Elements of Persuasion," 44; Rohm, *Dr. C*, 112–14.

Third, Criswell influenced forthcoming generations of preachers to use the expository method of preaching.[42] Perhaps more than any other preacher in the last half of the twentieth century, W. A. Criswell fostered the expositional preaching of the Bible. Adrian Rogers, pastor of the great Bellevue Baptist Church in Memphis, said to him, "You have been my hero since I have been a young preacher."[43] Carl F. H. Henry, dean of evangelicals, wrote of Criswell: "More and more he became for countless pastors the voice of evangelical theology at the pulpit and Bible conference level. His ministry and his influence has extended far beyond Baptist life into the larger Christian community. To the evangelical world, he remains the living symbol of proclamation in the expository tradition, and of biblical theology articulated so relevantly that the man in the street and the minister in the pew must alike come to terms with it."[44]

Such sentiments could be multiplied a thousandfold. He was a fiery prophet, bold like a lion but gentle as a lamb, often weeping during his sermons over the many lost souls.

Fourth, through his expository preaching ministry and his study of Scripture, Criswell became a committed premillennialist during his tenure as pastor at Muskogee, Oklahoma.[45] After World War I, postmillennialism as an eschatological position waned in influence. In the aftermath of World War II, amillennialism came to ascendancy in Southern Baptist views. Criswell's espousal of premillennialism became increasingly influential on Southern Baptist pastors after 1944. Indeed, this "move" toward a premillennial eschatology in the SBC would, among other factors, be a "major contribution" of Criswell's preaching.[46]

Fifth, despite the significance of Criswell's influence through his expository preaching and premillennialism, the most powerful influence he exerted within his own denomination and beyond was through his unswerving commitment to the inerrancy and infallibility of the Scriptures. In his preaching and writing, he inveighed against the liberalism he thought had infected Protestantism as well as his own beloved Southern Baptist "Zion."

He became the "sometime unwillingly and often unwittingly" patriarchal champion of biblical inerrancy in the SBC, the stack pole around which others united to produce the single largest shift of a denomination back to her orthodox roots in the history of the Christian church.[47] As O. S. Hawkins stated at

---

42. Patterson, "The Imponderables of God," 245.

43. Adrian Rogers, Letters of Appreciation, *Criswell Theological Review* 1, no. 2 (1987): 230–31.

44. Carl F. H. Henry, "A Voice for God," *Criswell Theological Review* 1, no. 2 (1987): 235–36.

45. Patterson, "W. A. Criswell," 23. Bush noted Criswell "is dispensational, but he is not a dispensationalist." (Bush, *W. A. Criswell*, 454.)

46. Patterson, "The Imponderables of God," 248.

47. Bryant, "Legacy," 9. In addition to Criswell's sermons, see his *Why I Preach That the Bible Is Literally*

Criswell's funeral, "He was our standard bearer. Let those who one day may be prone to rewrite history and temper his influence, let them know that what Spurgeon was to the Downgrade Controversy in nineteenth-century England, he was, much more, to twentieth-century American Christianity."[48]

Criswell has often been compared to his favorite preacher, Charles Haddon Spurgeon, the famed London Baptist pastor of the nineteenth century. There are a number of similarities between the two. Both were, generally speaking, Bible expositors; both built great churches; both founded schools to train preachers; and both were embroiled in doctrinal controversy in their denominations in the later years of their ministries. There is, however, at least one difference. Spurgeon's warnings went unheeded in the Baptist denomination in England, and the result was disastrous. Criswell's warning, however, was taken up by grassroots Southern Baptists and resulted in the recapturing of a denomination and her six theological seminaries for biblical orthodoxy.[49]

Dr. Criswell's homiletical influence is seen in the number of times he is referenced in dictionaries, books, and articles on preaching. He garners references in the *Dictionary of Baptists in America* and in the *Twentieth-Century Dictionary of Christian Biography*.[50] He authored a chapter on the infallible Word of God in

---

True. For the history of the conservative resurgence within the SBC, which began officially in 1979, consult Jim Hefley, *The Truth in Crisis*, 5 vols. (Hannibal, MO: Hannibal, 1986–1990); Paul Pressler, *A Hill on Which to Die: One Southern Baptist's Journey* (Nashville: Broadman & Holman, 1999); and Jerry Sutton, *The Baptist Reformation: The Conservative Resurgence in the Southern Baptist Convention* (Nashville: Broadman & Holman, 2000).

48. Audio of W. A Criswell Funeral Services, recorded 2002.

49. The mention of the name "W. A. Criswell" in Southern Baptist circles has often brought one of two reactions: "pucker or duck." Because of his strong stand on the inerrancy of the Bible, most people of the SBC have loved him; but many of a more liberal stripe within the denominational leadership despised him for it. Some believe this is why he was ignored in the multivolume *A Treasury of Great Preaching* (Clyde Fant and William Pinson, eds., *A Treasury of Great Preaching*, 13 vols. [Dallas: Word, 1995].) This set was originally published in 1971 under the title *20 Centuries of Great Preaching* by the editors, both of whom were Southern Baptists, but who also were theologically moderate (Pinson) and liberal (Fant). In an article appearing in the *Dallas Morning News* shortly after Criswell's death, John Holbert, a professor of preaching at Southern Methodist University's Perkins School of Theology was quoted as saying: "In the limited world in which he preached, he was judged to be quite extraordinary, but in the broader Christian world, that's not something people would say." ("Criswell's Biblical Focus Became a Model for Many," *Dallas Morning News*, Religion Section [19 January 2002], 1G.) Thomas Long, professor of preaching at Candler School of Theology in Atlanta is also quoted as saying: "His theology was too narrow, his rhetorical appeal too regional and his influence too limited to a particular subset within his denomination." Ibid. The facts speak otherwise. These comments, on the order of "damning with faint praise," appearing less than two weeks after his death, remind me of two Chihuahuas barking on the heels of a Great Dane. Others, both within and without the Baptist world, viewed him differently. "Certainly he would be on anyone's list of the 20 outstanding preachers of the 20th century" Ibid. So said Dr. Haddon Robinson, a non-Baptist, distinguished professor of preaching at Gordon-Conwell Theological Seminary. Helen Parmley, former longtime religion editor of the *Dallas Morning News* said of Criswell: "As an expository preacher—one whose sermons move systematically from one Bible verse to the next—he was without peer. He was widely recognized as one of the most influential preachers of the 20th century." Helen Parmley, "Preacher Made a Big Impression," *Dallas Morning News* (12 January 2002), 1G.

50. "Criswell is considered one of the most influential fundamentalist ministers in the latter half of the twentieth century." M. G. Toulouse, "Criswell, W. A." *Dictionary of Baptists in America*, ed. Bill Leonard

a collection of essays honoring the great expository preacher Stephen Olford,[51] as well as a chapter on preaching the Old Testament in *Tradition and Testament*.[52] Harold Bryson mentions Criswell's seventeen-year preaching tour through the Bible along with his famous sermons on the book of Revelation.[53] Wayne McDill, professor of preaching at Southeastern Baptist Theological Seminary and homiletics author, recounts the first time he and his wife heard a sermon by W. A. Criswell. McDill's college pastor, Brother Bill, was a dynamic preacher, the likes of whom McDill said he had never heard in his nineteen years of life. After college, he and his wife moved to Fort Worth, Texas, to attend seminary.

> One Sunday we drove the twenty miles to downtown Dallas to attend worship at the renowned First Baptist Church. There we heard a sermon by W. A. Criswell. I was amazed. The sermon was marvelous. It was animated, passionate, and strongly biblical, with a dramatic flair and a tremor of emotion in the voice. He preached just like Brother Bill. How could two pastors preach in such an identical way? We were perplexed for only a moment, then looked at one another knowingly as we remembered that Brother Bill had grown up in Dallas. He had apparently so admired Dr. Criswell that he copied his style of preaching.[54]

Warren Wiersbe mentions the fact that Criswell, unlike Spurgeon and Criswell's own predecessor, George Truett, expounded Scripture book by book during his long tenure as pastor of First Baptist Church.[55] Jerry Vines acknowledges his own debt, as well as that of the Southern Baptist denomination, to Criswell for breaking ground in the area of expository preaching.[56]

Vines said Criswell "has gained international recognition as a Bible expositor. . . . His books are veritable storehouses of information and guidance for the

---

(Downers Grove, IL: InterVarsity Press, 1994), 98; "Described as one of the greatest preachers of the twentieth century, he is known for dynamic expository preaching without notes." Norman Ericson, "Criswell, W. A.," *Twentieth Century Dictionary of Christian Biography*, ed. J. D. Douglas (Milton Keynes: Paternoster, 1995), 113.

51. David L. Olford, ed. *A Passion for Preaching: Essays in Honor of Stephen F. Olford* (Nashville: Thomas Nelson, 1989). Criswell also has other articles dealing with aspects of preaching.

52. Criswell, "Preaching from the Old Testament," in *Tradition and Testament*, ed. by J. S. Feinberg, (Chicago: Moody, 1981), 293–305.

53. Harold T. Bryson, *Expository Preaching: The Art of Preaching Through a Book of the Bible* (Nashville: Broadman & Holman, 1995). Bryson did his master's thesis on "The Expository Preaching of W. A. Criswell in His Sermons on the Revelation" (New Orleans Baptist Theological Seminary, 1967). Bryson held the J. D. Grey chair of preaching at New Orleans Baptist Seminary and later became professor of preaching and director of the Institute of Christian Ministry at Mississippi College.

54. Wayne McDill, *The Moment of Truth: A Guide to Effective Sermon Delivery* (Nashville: Broadman & Holman, 1999), 113.

55. Warren Wiersbe, *The Dynamics of Preaching* (Grand Rapids: Baker, 1999), 116.

56. Jerry Vines, *A Practical Guide to Sermon Preparation* (Chicago: Moody, 1985), xiv.

preacher who would preach expositorily. His volumes on Revelation are among the finest. His word study is excellent, and his interpretation is clear and concise. Though a clearly discernable outline often does not appear, the preacher will learn much about expository preaching by a careful study of his work."[57]

In an interview, Criswell was asked to describe the greatest contributions God had enabled him to make to the kingdom of God. His response:

> I would think it is my emphasis on preaching the Bible.... I do not know whether this is correct or not, but I read often the observation that it was my ministry here in Dallas that turned preachers to preaching the Bible. It is said that preachers just preached subject sermons before but that when I started preaching here as I did, that became a model and a pattern for countless numbers of other pulpiteers to preach the Word of God. If that is true, I say "Praise God that I could do such a thing as that![58]

Criswell clearly viewed his greatest contribution to be in the area of his influence on other preachers to preach the Bible in an expositional fashion.

CONCLUSION

As the author of Hebrews 11:4 noted about Abel, "[He] still speaks, even though he is dead," so the influence of W. A. Criswell's preaching ministry continues. It continues in his fifty-four books; it continues in the school he founded known as The Criswell College, which exists to train kingdom leaders and kingdom preachers for the glory of God; it continues in the recently released Criswell Legacy Project;[59] it continues in the countless preachers filling pulpits around the world whose expositional approach to preaching was somehow encouraged by W. A. Criswell. Mac Brunson, while pastor of First Baptist Church in Dallas, said it succinctly during Criswell's funeral service: "W. A. Criswell in our day was God's man to fortify the truth for the future."[60]

The Lord has many servants, but few soldiers. Dr. Criswell was a soldier of Jesus Christ, committed to the Scriptures and his calling to proclaim them, which started when he was just seventeen years old. Were he here today to express

---

57. Vines and Shaddix, *Power in the Pulpit*, 41.

58. Paige Patterson, "Interview with Dr. W. A. Criswell," *The Church at the Dawn of the 21st Century: Essays in Honor of W. A. Criswell*, eds. Paige Patterson, John Pretlove, and Luis Pantoja (Dallas: Criswell Publications, 1989), 15.

59. The W. A. Criswell Sermon Library can be found at www.wacriswell.com where more than two thousand of his sermons are archived to be downloaded by listeners.

60. Audio of W. A. Criswell Funeral Service.

a word about it all, I think I can envision the gleam in his eye and hear that inimitable voice, speaking with Criswellian pause and inflection, the words of the great Reformer Martin Luther before his death: "I simply taught, preached, wrote God's Word . . . otherwise I did nothing . . . the Word did it all."

Sermon Excerpt
The Scarlet Thread through the Bible[61]

So what I pray for is you all just be comfortable now. Be seated in comfort and listen with your head as well as with your heart. And we are going to preach clear through the Bible beginning at Genesis and closing climactically in the Revelation. And I have a text for the whole message in Leviticus chapter 17 verse 11 (KJV):

For the life of the flesh is in the blood: and I have given it to you upon the altar to make an atonement for your souls: for it is the blood that maketh atonement for the soul.

And using that as a background text we are going to speak of The Scarlet Thread Through The Bible—the blood of atonement from beginning to end. . . .

Wonderful! Beautiful! But in the middle of the garden there was a tree. And the Lord interdicted the fruit of that tree lest they be like Lucifer had been, wise in their own eyes and covetous [Genesis 2:17]. So Satan came into the garden of Eden where the Lord had placed the man and his wife, beautiful. In the cursing of Satan he became a serpent, but he was beautiful to begin with. And he could talk to the woman, and he enticed her to take of the forbidden fruit. And when Adam saw that his wife had partaken of the forbidden fruit, rather than live by himself he also ate of that tree, that he might die with his wife rather than live without her [Genesis 3:1–6].

And when the two had partaken of the interdicted fruit they looked at themselves, and their eyes were opened, and they were naked, and they were conscious of their sin and of their shame. So they took fig leaves and sewed them together to cover their sin, and their shame, and their nakedness [Genesis 3:7]. . . .

---

61. W. A. Criswell, "The Scarlet Thread through the Bible." Sermon on Leviticus 17:11, December 31, 1995. https://www.wacriswell.com.

And when the Lord looked upon them, He looked upon those fig leaves to cover their shame, and sin, and nakedness, and the Lord said, "Not enough." And God took one of the innocent animals He had created in the garden, and He slew that animal and poured out its blood on the ground, and the earth drank it up. And with a coat of skins He covered the nakedness and shame of our first parents [Genesis 3:21]. And that is the beginning of the scarlet thread through the Bible; the pouring out of blood of atonement, of covering. . . .

The scarlet thread through the Bible.

And I have time to close with a personal testimony. So being reared in a little town of about three hundred people, in a little white cracker box of a church house, the preacher holding the revival meeting, stayed in our home. And at night around the table he would talk to me about the Lord.

I asked the teacher at the school if I could be dismissed to attend the morning service. She acquiesced. And it just happened to be that, when I went to the church house, I sat right back of my sainted mother. And when the preacher had preached his sermon and made appeal, they were singing:

> *There is a fountain filled with blood*
> *Drawn from Emmanuel's veins;*
> *And sinners plunged beneath that flood*
> *Lose all their guilty stains.*
>
> *The dying thief rejoiced to see*
> *that fountain in his day;*
> *And there may I though vile as he,*
> *Wash all my sins away.*

["There Is a Fountain Filled with Blood," William Cowper]

And my mother, while they were singing that song, turned around and said to me, "Son, today would you give your heart to the Lord Jesus? Would you let Jesus come into your heart?"

And I said, with many tears, "Yes, mother. Yes." And I stepped out in the aisle and couldn't even see the preacher for crying.

You know, that's one of the strangest things, from that day until this, the gospel message, the atoning grace of the Lord, brings tears to my eyes. I cannot preach the Lord Jesus without crying. I cannot do it. I prayed to God, "Lord, take these tears away from me." And the Lord has said "No. No that's you. That's you." So I just cry and praise the Lord, how good He is and will be unto me.

So may I close? I come to the end of the Apocalypse, and how gloriously does it close! Revelation 22, verses 17 and [20]:

And the Spirit and bride say, Come. And let him who hears say, Come. And let him that is athirst come. And whosoever will, let him take the water of life freely. . . . He which testifieth these things saith, Surely, surely I come quickly. Amen. Even so, come, Lord Jesus. ♦

BIBLIOGRAPHY

Allison, Gary. "The Preaching of W. A. Criswell: A Critical Analysis of Selected Messages." ThD diss., Mid-America Baptist Theological Seminary, 1990.

Bryant, James. "The Legacy of Dr. W. A. Criswell in Pastoral and Denominational Leadership." *Shophar*, special tribute edition, n.d.

Bryson, Harold T. *Expository Preaching: The Art of Preaching Through a Book of the Bible.* Nashville: Broadman & Holman, 1995.

_____. "The Expository Preaching of W. A. Criswell in His Sermons on Revelation." ThM thesis, New Orleans Baptist Theological Seminary, 1967.

Burke, Kenneth, *A Grammar of Motives.* New York: Prentice Hall, 1952.

_____. *A Rhetoric of Motives.* Los Angeles: University of California Press, 1974.

"Criswell's Biblical Focus Became a Model for Many," *Dallas Morning News,* Religion Section. 19 January 2002.

Criswell, W. A. *Criswell's Guidebook for Pastors.* Nashville: Broadman & Holman, 1980.

_____. "Preaching from the Old Testament." Pages 293–305 in *Tradition and Testament.* Edited by J. S. Feinberg. Chicago: Moody, 1981.

_____. *Standing on the Promises: The Autobiography of W. A. Criswell.* Dallas: Word, 1990.

_____. *The Bible for Today's World.* Grand Rapids: Zondervan, 1965.

_____. *Why I Preach That the Bible Is Literally True.* Nashville: Broadman, 1969.

Ericson, Norman. "Criswell, W. A." *Twentieth-Century Dictionary of Christian Biography.* Edited by J. D. Douglas. Milton Keynes: Paternoster, 1995.

Fant, Clyde, and William Pinson, eds. *A Treasury of Great Preaching,* 13 vols. Dallas: Word, 1995.

Hefley, Jim. *The Truth in Crisis,* 5 vols. Hannibal, MO: Hannibal, 1986–1990.

Henry, Carl F. H. "A Voice for God." *Criswell Theological Review* 1, no. 2 (1987): 235–36.

Keith, Bill. *W. A. Criswell: The Authorized Biography.* Old Tappan, NJ: Revell, 1973.

Letters of Appreciation, *Criswell Theological Review* 1, no. 2 (1987): 230–31.

McBeth, Leon. *First Baptist Church of Dallas: A Centennial History.* Grand Rapids: Zondervan, 1968.

McDill, Wayne. *The Moment of Truth: A Guide to Effective Sermon Delivery.* Nashville: Broadman & Holman, 1999.

McKellar, Matthew. "An Evaluation of the Elements of Persuasion in the Favorite Messages of W. A. Criswell as Contained in the Book *With a Bible in My Hand.*" PhD dissertation, Southwestern Baptist Theological Seminary, 1991.

Olford, David L. ed. *A Passion for Preaching: Essays in Honor of Stephen F. Olford.* Nashville: Thomas Nelson, 1989.

Oliver, Robert. *The Psychology of Persuasive Speech.* 2nd ed. New York: Longmans, Green, 1957.

Parmley, Helen. "Preacher Made a Big Impression." *Dallas Morning News.* 12 January 2002.

Patterson, Paige, "W. A. Criswell," in *Theologians of the Baptist Tradition.* Edited by Timothy George and David Dockery. Nashville: Broadman & Holman, 2001.

_____. "The Imponderables of God." *Criswell Theological Review* 1 (Spring 1987): 237–53.

Patterson, Paige, "Interview with Dr. W. A. Criswell." *The Church at the Dawn of the 21st Century: Essays in Honor of W. A. Criswell*. Edited by Paite Patterson, John Pretlove, and Luis Pantoja. Dallas: Criswell Publications, 1989.

Roberts, Craig. "W. A. Criswell's Choice and Use of Illustrations" ThM thesis, Dallas Theological Seminary, 1976.

Rohm, Robert. *Dr. C: The Visionary and Ministry of W. A. Criswell*. Chicago: Moody, 1990.

Pressler, Paul. *A Hill on Which to Die: One Southern Baptist's Journey*. Nashville: Broadman & Holman: 1999.

Sutton, Jerry. *The Baptist Reformation: The Conservative Resurgence in the Southern Baptist Convention*. Nashville: Broadman & Holman, 2000.

Toulouse, M. G. "Criswell, W. A." *Dictionary of Baptists in America*. Edited by Bill Leonard. Downers Grove, IL: InterVarsity Press, 1994.

Towns, James. "The Rhetoric and Leadership of W. A. Criswell as the President of the Southern Baptist Convention: A Descriptive Analysis through Perspective and Public Address." PhD diss., Southern Illinois University, 1970.

Vines, Jerry. *A Practical Guide to Sermon Preparation*. Chicago: Moody, 1985.

Vines, Jerry and Jim Shaddix. *Power in the Pulpit: How to Prepare and Deliver Expository Sermons*. Chicago: Moody, 1999.

Warren, Rick. *The Purpose Driven Church: Growth Without Compromising Your Message & Mission*. Grand Rapids: Zondervan, 1995.

Wiersbe, Warren, *The Dynamics of Preaching*. Grand Rapids: Baker, 1999.

Gardner C. Taylor
Preacher Laureate

ALFONZA W. FULLWOOD
ROBERT SMITH JR.

In American Protestantism, Taylor's popularity soared for over fifty years. A great orator, pastor, and the consummate preacher, teacher, theologian, poet, and civil rights activist, Gardner C. Taylor (1918–2015) was known for his preaching that defined eloquence and entranced thousands who heard him preach the gospel of Christ. Widely viewed as one of America's greatest preachers of the twentieth and early twenty-first centuries, he is a towering preaching figure and homiletical model. Known as the pulpit king, a preaching exemplar, poet laureate of American Protestantism, and legend among preachers, he continues to influence preachers of every race and tradition in America.

HISTORICAL BACKGROUND

Gardner C. Taylor was born in Baton Rouge, Louisiana, on June 18, 1918, as the only child of the Reverend Washington Monroe Taylor and Selina Gresell Taylor. He was the grandson of former slaves and grew up in the segregated South of the early twentieth century. At the time of Gardner's birth, Washington, a prominent Baptist preacher in his own right, served as the eminent pastor of Mount Zion Baptist Church of Baton Rouge. Mount Zion, distinguished as one of the largest congregations in the city, had many members who were former slaves.[1] While Washington did not finish high school, he distinguished himself as a skillful and influential preacher of his time. In doing so, he left behind a trail of outstanding service and leadership accomplishments beyond Baton Rouge. These accomplishments catapulted him into national prominence as a Christian

---

1. Gerald Lamont Thomas, *African American Preaching: The Contribution of Gardner C. Taylor* (New York: Peter Lang, 2004), 62–63. Background information on Taylor is according to Thomas's work. For other sources see C. Eric Lincoln and Lawrence H. Mamiya, *The Black Church in the African American Experience* (Durham: Duke University Press, 1990); Leroy Fitts, *A History of Black Baptists* (Nashville: Broadman, 1985).

leader at a very critical period in America pertaining to the plight of African Americans.[2]

It would be safe to assume that Washington exposed young Gardner to the best of African American preaching. Due to his father's leadership in both the state and national convention, young Gardner saw and heard the melodious voices of great preachers who were invited to "tell the story" in the Mount Zion pulpit.[3] In 1931, Washington died, leaving thirteen-year-old Gardner in the care of Selina. More importantly, he left behind a legacy of outstanding and prominent Christian leadership. Exposure to such prominence played an important role in shaping young Gardner's life and in his preaching ministry.

Selina taught school at the Perkins Road School for Negroes, having secured the position to fill the financial void occasioned by the death of her husband. Selina held a passion for the English language in a way that enriched Taylor's eloquent vocabulary. Selina held an unrelenting determination to shape her precocious son for success. But the notion that "it takes a village to raise a child" is clearly evidenced by the investment her sister Gert and the Mount Zion church made in the maturation, education, and discipleship of young Taylor.[4] Although he did not enjoy the advantages of a privileged life, still, under the surrogate covering of the "village," he showed remarkable aptitude and academic promise.[5] His intellectual brilliance was confirmed in the mid-1920s when he achieved the highest score on an IQ test ever recorded in the state among white or black students.[6] Therefore, it is of no surprise that he graduated valedictorian of his class in high school and was also captain of the football team.

Taylor received a football scholarship to attend Leland College, a black Baptist college in Baker, Louisiana, twelve miles from Baton Rouge. While attending Leland, Taylor exhibited exceptional skills and qualities of oral speech. Naturally, his parents' linguistic feel for the power of words gave this young prodigy his natural affinity toward eloquence, which became the hallmark of

2. In the earlier twentieth century, the black church under the leadership of visionary leaders such as Washington Taylor assumed the task of turning back the tide of social and economic inequalities in America. Washington evidenced such a legacy of leadership by ascending to presidency of the Louisiana State Baptist Convention and vice president at large of the National Baptist Convention, U.S.A., Inc. Even more, his prominence is symbolized in his delivering the eulogy of Elias Camp Morris. Morris served as the first president of the National Baptist Convention U.S.A., Inc.

3. It would be safe to assume that one of the great preachers young Taylor heard at Mt. Zion was Morris Elias Camp, the first president of the National Baptist Convention, U.S.A., Inc. Morris and Washington Taylor were contemporaries who served as major leaders of the convention. The inference heightens when one considers the fact that Taylor eulogized Morris.

4. See E. Franklin Frazier and C. Eric Lincoln, *The Negro Church in America and the Black Church Since Frazier* (New York: Schocken, 1974), 5–6.

5. Thomas, *Contribution*, 83–84.

6. Ibid., 85–86.

his preaching.[7] He engaged in class debates, which became an incubator that fueled his rhetorical passion and genius. Invariably, his passion for rhetorical discourse sparked a flame to become a criminal lawyer.[8] He gained entrance into the University of Michigan Law School. Such an acceptance represented historic milestones. No African American had ever been admitted to the Louisiana State Bar.[9] Taylor accepted the challenge in the face of uncertainty. However, before entering law school, an incident occurred that had far-reaching implications on his life.

Like Paul of Tarsus on the road to Damascus, Taylor's personal itinerary was preempted by a divine call to preach the gospel of Jesus Christ. While a student at Leland College, Taylor enjoyed the honor of chauffeuring the president of the college, James A. Bacoats, who also succeeded Taylor's father as pastor at Mount Zion. One afternoon, en route to the college, Taylor had a near-death experience caused by a car accident. It took the life of one white individual and seriously injured another. Concerning this incident, Taylor later noted, "My quick brush with death that afternoon, either from the accident or at the hands of the mob, turned imperiously toward consideration of the meaning of my life and the ultimate purpose of human existence."[10] Taylor experienced a spiritual transformation and heard his call to preach. Upon the recommendation of Dr. Bacoats, he went to the Oberlin Graduate School of Theology.

Oberlin School of Theology, as early as 1937, was noted for its liberal stance with regard to racial equality.[11] Charles Grandison Finney, great revivalist, educator, theologian, and social reformer related to the abolitionist movement, accepted the presidency of Oberlin with the provision that the admittance policy was without regard to race, creed, or color. For this reason, the school received notoriety for its strong antislavery stance. Notwithstanding, the school had only graduated seven African American students at the time Taylor enrolled in 1937.[12] Taylor's matriculation at Oberlin exposed him to classical theology and the roster of great preachers such as Andrew Blackwood, Alexander Maclaren, F. W. Robertson, Frederick Norwood, Clarence Macartney, and Charles Spurgeon. While at Oberlin in 1941, Taylor met and married Laura Bell Scott, also a student at Oberlin.

---

7. Gardner C. Taylor, *How Shall They Preach: The Lyman Beecher Lectures and Five Lenten Sermons* (Elgin, IL: Progressive Baptist Publishing House, 1977), 13.

8. Ibid., 87.

9. Timothy George, "Introduction: Honor to Whom Honor Is Due," in *Our Sufficiency Is of God: Essays on Preaching in Honor of Gardner C. Taylor,* eds. Timothy George, James Earl Massey, and Robert Smith Jr. (Macon, GA: Mercer University Press, 2010), xiii.

10. Ibid., xiv.

11. Ibid.

12. Ibid.

Taylor received a call to serve at the Bethany Baptist Church in Elyria, Ohio, from 1938–1941. Three other pastorates followed, including Beulah Baptist Church in New Orleans from 1941–1943, Mount Zion Baptist Church in Baton Rouge from 1943–1948, and the Concord Baptist Church of Christ, Brooklyn, New York, from 1948–1990. When Taylor arrived in Brooklyn, the five thousand members of Concord were already well-established as one of the most nationally recognized congregations in the country.[13] Under Taylor's leadership, the congregation grew to fourteen thousand members.[14]

The prominence of Taylor inspired a constituency that summoned him to further effect change, electing him to serve on the city of New York's Board of Education and the Citywide Committee for Integrated Schools. They also asked Taylor to consider running for Congress, but he decided to focus his commitment on his ministry.[15] After forty-two years, he retired from Concord in June of 1990 but did not retire from preaching. He continued to "fill pulpits, give lectures and provide keynote addresses at churches and educational institutions across the country" until his health prevented him continuing.[16]

Taylor represented the culmination of a rich heritage of African American preaching. Like nineteenth-century African American preachers, he shaped the moral consciousness of America on race dilemmas and social justice issues. The conditions of the time also gave impulse to and shaped his preaching. It was a time of social upheaval. Taylor's influence emerged at a crucial period in the history of the country. Civil rights activists, inspired by the leadership of Martin Luther King Jr.—who was mentored by Taylor—mobilized the community. Taylor's preaching and ministry were grounded in a social action and social justice homiletic. As a civil rights leader, he used the black church as a vehicle to address the issues of social and economic injustice.

The period during the 1950s and 1960s represented a crucial moment in history for the black church relative to the civil rights movement in America.[17] Taylor led the effort in raising money in the North to support the movement. And he played a central role in pushing the National Baptist Convention, USA, Inc. to assume a more active role in the struggle for social justice.[18] This convention represented the "largest African American denomination. It is also considered the largest organization of African Americans in existence."[19] The social

---

13. Ibid., xiv–xv.
14. Ibid.
15. Thomas, *Contribution*, 99.
16. Edward Gilbreath, "The Pulpit King: The Passion and Eloquence of Gardner C. Taylor, a Legend among Preachers," *Christianity Today* (11 Dec 1995): 26.
17. Lincoln and Mamiya, *The Black Church*, 196–235.
18. Ibid., 30–32.
19. Ibid.

justice issues became the impetus behind different sociopolitical ideologies in the Convention. The ideological differences led to a national leadership divide within the Convention. Taylor and Martin Luther King Jr. pushed for a more aggressive social action agenda and attempted to seize control of the leadership of the Convention. Their action led to a separation in the Convention along conservative and liberal lines.[20] Taylor worked tirelessly for social and economic changes in America, but his efforts were not limited to civil rights for African Americans. He also addressed broader social issues, such as abortion, noting: "All of life is sacred. It is no more permissible to destroy life six months before birth than five years after birth. Many people claim that they are interested in human life and fight for the child's right to be born. But the same people are often nowhere to be found when the child's body is stunted by poor nutrition and its mind is affected by poor education."[21]

As seen, Taylor demonstrated a sociopolitical and pastoral stance that covered the moral issues and cultural changes that were occuring in America.

Taylor influenced pulpits across America with regard to his homiletical performance. He received invitations to preach at most leading pulpits. Many seminaries also sought to expose their students to his homiletical genius.[22] For the most part, it is felt that Taylor "is one of the first [African American preachers] whose influence crossed over into the realm of white homiletics and white preachers."[23] Such a claim is evidenced in his ability to move in and out of diverse Protestant circles—both mainline and conservative."[24] This broad appeal across various experiences symbolized his homiletical influence.

THEOLOGY OF PREACHING

Taylor is widely viewed as a skillful practitioner of preaching the gospel of Christ. To a lesser degree, he is known as a homiletical theorist in the technical

---

20. Ibid., 30–38. Taylor and King opposed the reelection of the social conservative J. H. Jackson, who served the Convention for twenty-nine years as its president, largely because he blocked the participation of the Convention as an institution in the Civil Rights movement and the Southern Christian Leadership in particular. Jackson had declared that the conventions were "inadvisable and injurious to the cause of racial advancement, and harmony."

21. Gardner C. Taylor, *Lectures, Essays, and Interviews*, vol. 5 of *The Words of Gardner Taylor,* comp. Edward L. Taylor (Pennsylvania: Judson, 2001), 85–86.

22. Taylor taught at Union Baptist Seminary in New Orleans, Colgate Rochester Divinity School (1969–1972), Union Theological Seminary (1973–1974), and Harvard Divinity School (1975–1976). After retirement, Taylor moved to Raleigh, North Carolina, and taught at Shaw University Divinity School (2006–2010). During this season at Shaw, the primary author of this chapter was privileged to coteach a preaching course with Taylor.

23. Gilbreath, "The Pulpit King," 27

24. Ibid., 28.

sense. As a profound Christian thinker, he shared his thoughts concerning the nature of preaching and the preacher.[25] For example, his Lyman Beecher Lectures on Preaching and other publications of articles and essays revealed his homiletical insight. He dealt little with the technical and mechanical details of homiletics, but he offered general perspectives on the preacher and preaching. O. C. Edwards noted, "In his lectures, Dr. Taylor is like Phillip Brooks, in that he does not so much seek to instruct in the mechanics of homiletics as he does to provide a spiritual perspective on the preaching task."[26] To this, Taylor offered thoughtful perspectives that proved useful to the preaching ministry. In many ways, these publications revealed a basic theology of preaching. In view of this, there are five factors that informed Taylor's understanding of preaching.

First, Taylor used an interdisciplinary approach that informed his assumptions about preaching. He brought a depth of learning in other disciplines to his preaching. Many saw him as a student of American and world history. Others saw him as a student of poetry, a social critic, a civil rights activist, a political leader, and a student of cultural studies. James Earl Massey noted, "He has a firm understanding of the best of both African American and Anglo-Saxon culture."[27] Yet, other areas of exposure were literature, prose, and theater.

The second factor was his depth of knowledge of the history of Christian preaching. He studied the great preachers and theologians of history. In his writings and sermons, he frequently cited names and words of those figures who made an enduring contribution. In fact, he credited those preaching figures for his own preaching performance and legacy.[28] Taylor noted, "Any preacher greatly deprives himself and herself who does not study the recognized masters of the pulpit discourse, not to copy them but rather to see what has been the way in which they approached the Scripture, their craftsmanship."[29] Timothy George suggested that Taylor's knowledge of others from previous eras was so thorough that he gave the impression that he was their contemporary.[30]

The third factor involved "linguist decorum," or a strong use of language for rhetorical results. (This area will be explored further in a section below.) Fourth, Taylor held to an existential view embedded in his preaching assumptions. On one hand, he maintained that sermons may come from newspapers such as the

---

25. For more detailed information on Taylor's theology of preaching, see Alfonza W. Fullwood, "A Study of Gardner C. Taylor's Theology Of Preaching as a Decisive Factor Shaping His Theory of Preaching: Implications for Homiletical Pedagogy" (PhD diss., The Southeastern Baptist Theological Seminary, 2012).

26. O. C. Edwards Jr., *A History of Preaching*, 2 vols. (Nashville: Abingdon, 2004), 1:715.

27. Gilbreath, "The Pulpit King," 27.

28. For more information on Taylor's breadth of learning, see Fullwood, "A Study of Gardner," 178–81.

29. Taylor, *How Shall They Preach*, 63–64.

30. George, "Introduction," xix.

New York Times. On the other hand, he advised against preaching "exclusively from the morning press."[31] Still, he expressed concerns about preaching "exclusively from Scripture."[32] This is not to say that he did not hold a high view of Scripture. Nor does it mean that he allowed other sources to supplant Scripture. For him, Scripture was not the only authority that spoke to the meaning of life. To this point, extrabiblical material becomes a source of encounter with God."[33] These views show an existential strand of thought or leanings in the way Taylor did his preaching. Fifth, and related to the fourth factor, is a distinct epistemology at work. More specifically, there were sociocultural factors and historical experiences that shaped Taylor's assumptions and understanding of preaching. What is more, it formed a distinct hermeneutic that guided the way Taylor approached Scripture.[34] It is important to clarify, though, that he was not unique concerning a distinct epistemology functioning in the backdrop of his preaching practice. Typically, this is true in the African American preaching tradition. Its cultural context for preaching forms the template for preaching practice.[35] With that said, these five factors are important sources that brought a certain quality and character to Taylor's preaching. And while all of these areas informed the way he preached, language seemed to hold the dominant influence.

The Role of Language in Taylor's Theology of Preaching

Language functioned at the core of Taylor's theology of preaching. It was not simply a linguistic and aesthetic exercise. He believed that language is a means that "excites, electrifies, elevates and edifies."[36] Therefore, for him, success in the pulpit depended on use of language. Taylor felt that "language is the only weaponry that a preacher has."[37] There were several reasons that formed the basis for how he understood the nature of language and how it functioned in the sermon.

First, Taylor believed, "One key to the pulpit is language. I think our preachers ought to seek to clothe the gospel in as worthy a language as they can find for it."[38] Second, Taylor believed that language should not be pedestrian but should "fire the imagination."[39] It should be gripping and have an "added sense of

---

31. Avery Lee and Gardner C. Taylor, *Perfecting the Pastor's Art: Wisdom from Avery Lee and Gardner Taylor* (Pennsylvania: Judson, 2005), 39.

32. Ibid.

33. Fullwood, "A Study of Gardner," 37.

34. Cleophus J. LaRue, *The Heart of Black Preaching* (Louisville: John Knox, 2000), 1.

35. See Henry H. Mitchell, *Black Preaching: The Recovery of a Powerful Art* (Nashville: Abingdon, 1990).

36. Gardner C. Taylor, "Preaching and the Power of Words," in *Communicate with Power: Insights from America's Top Communicators*, ed. Michael Duduit (Grand Rapids: Baker, 1996), 207.

37. Lee and Taylor, *Perfecting*, 42.

38. Taylor, "The Power of Words," 208.

39. Ibid., 210.

majesty, life, the glory of its possibilities, and the greatness of the glory of God."[40] Third, Taylor said of language, "It's saying something, but it's saying something in a glorious way."[41] Fourth, Taylor asserted, "I think that we need to recover a sense of preaching as an art form, one that features grand and piercing language, language that wrestles with and grips the hearer."[42] To add, Taylor noted that the "preacher ought to try to bring the people before the presence of God and within sight of the heart of Christ. No sermon can do more. None should want to do less."[43] Experientially or existentially ushering people into the presence of God formed his preaching purpose. Some observers call it "sacred eloquence" in the service of the gospel of Jesus Christ.[44] Language also carried hermeneutical assumptions. He believed a "single word" has the potential to "lift up" the hearers.[45] For this reason, Taylor thought language carried a power of its own. In his view, language evokes presence, meaning, and encounter. Therefore, for him, it helps the preacher in the task of addressing the meaning and purpose of life. In a sermon entitled "Embracing Hope," Taylor employed this type of poetic elegance: "Belief beyond despair is hope. In the midst of wickedness and weakness, we must hope. Hope in the midst of faults and failures, hope in the midst of disaster. When facing death with its foul despair, hope. Not allowing this mean world to have the last word, hope. If you are facing illness and need healing, hope. When all the world's dark disasters come, every enemy stands against us, every stormy wind blows, every troubled time seems near, hope! Youth and energy may pass, friends fail, troubles rise, scenes fail, comrades die, health may fail, but hope."[46]

Taylor's vivid, attractive, and engaging language, expressed in the richness of poetic diction, lifted and inspired listeners in ways that filled their lives with hope. In his sermon "Laodicea, Part III: The Door of the Soul," Taylor used language such as "on the very edge of hell, hanging over that bottomless abyss of endless nothingness . . ."[47] He used imagery to depict the waning of life: "My shadow is already behind me, the sign that the sun is far, far along."[48] Here, as

---

40. Ibid.
41. Ibid.
42. Ibid.; Lee and Taylor, *Perfecting*, 43.
43. Gardner C. Taylor, "Shaping Sermons by the Shape of Text and Preacher," in *Preaching Biblically: Creating Sermons in the Shape of Scripture*, ed. Don M. Wardlaw (Philadelphia: Westminster, 1983), 142.
44. Martha J. Simmons and Brad R. Braxton, "What Happened to Sacred Eloquence?" in *Our Sufficiency Is of God: Essays on Preaching in Honor of Gardner C. Taylor*. Edited by Timothy George, James Earl Massey, and Robert Smith Jr. (Macon, GA: Mercer University Press, 2010), 281.
45. Lee and Taylor, *Perfecting*, 43.
46. Gardner C. Taylor, *Faith in the Fire: Wisdom for Life*, ed. Edward Taylor (New York: Smiley, 2011), 69.
47. Gardner C. Taylor, *Special Occasion and Expository Sermons*, vol. 4 of *The Words of Gardner Taylor*, comp. Edward L. Taylor (Pennsylvania: Judson, 2001), 253.
48. Ibid.

typified in his preaching, Taylor closed his sermon with eschatological hope. For instance, he explained: "Measured by almost any gauge, preaching is a presumptuous business. If the undertaking does not have some sanctions beyond human reckoning, then it is, indeed, rash and audacious for one person to dare to stand up before or among other people and declare that he or she brings from the Eternal God a message for those who listen which involves issues nothing less than those of life and death."[49]

Taylor understood preaching as a divine mandate entrusted to those who are called to preach. Once again and as stated earlier, Taylor's thoughts are, at the core, a theology of preaching. It revealed streams of a theological anthropology underpinning.

Social Justice in Taylor's Theology of Preaching

As stated above, Taylor stood in the tradition of nineteenth-century African American preachers. They used the pulpit to address social justice issues in America. They viewed the pulpit and the sermon as tools to create a new community for African Americans.[50] In similar ways, Taylor continued in this tradition. He used his pulpit to give voice to those who were on the margins of life. Many of his sermons addressed civil rights concerns in America. His six-volume sermon collection, *The Words of Gardner Taylor,* is laden with instances of addressing issues of race relations. He sought to bring the gospel message to bear on the social injustices in America. Taylor noted, "The goal of social change for the Christian is to honor God. It was he who commanded humankind to have dominion over the earth, not over each other."[51] He further articulated his conviction, "To deny our oneness through war, or racism or poverty, or any other fragmentation of humanity, is to cast doubt upon God's wisdom in creating of one blood all nations of men."[52] Taylor held a strong record in civil rights involvement, working to achieve its goals of fair play and social equality. His many "civil rights arrests" served as further proof of his social justice involvement."[53] But his social justice message extended beyond pulpits in America. It reached across the Atlantic in other countries as well.

He preached on social justice issues in international and intercultural circles. Specifically, volume four of his sermon collection shows several social justice

---

49. Ibid., 24.
50. Nineteenth-century African American preachers noted for their use of the pulpit to address social justice issues include, among others, Richard Allen, Daniel Alexander Payne, Henry Highland Garnet, Alexander Crummell, and Samuel Ringgold Ward.
51. Taylor, *Special Occasion and Expository Sermons,* 82.
52. Ibid.
53. Taylor, *How Shall They Preach,* 41.

sermons preached at the Baptist World Alliance. In 1970, in Tokyo, Japan, he preached about the "Goals of Social Change." In 1960, in Rio de Janeiro, Brazil, he delivered a sermon entitled "The Minister's Role in Today's World." Taylor also accepted an invitation to preach in Johannesburg, South Africa, during the height of the apartheid struggle.[54] All of this shows that Taylor did not separate social justice and the human predicament from the gospel he preached.

Taylor was not a politician in the sense of seeking political office. Yet and still, he "considered political issues to be subject to theological reflection."[55] Taylor argued, "At any rate, the preacher has no warrant to speak to our social ills, save in the light of God's judgment and God's grace."[56] He was concerned that the church focused "more on personal prosperity than on issues such as poverty and injustice."[57] Taylor noted, "I think the church today in America partakes of the contemporary disease of 'Let me alone. I want to get along and I don't want to be bothered with too many things.'"[58] He continued, "When the pulpit becomes an echo of the pew, it loses, I think, almost all of its reasons for existence."[59] Here, again, Taylor focused on social justice. He carefully measured and tempered social justice by the mandates of the gospel and theological reflection. In so doing, he grounded his social justice sermons and christological themes. What this shows is that Taylor believed social justice issues were fundamentally a doctrinal issue.

Forward-Looking Christology in Taylor's Theology of Preaching

Taylor held a strong christological focus concerning the power of the cross. These christological themes were also at work in the backdrop of his preaching theology. For him, the gospel of the cross transcended racial, cultural, and social boundaries. He believed that the solution to the race and class divide in America rested in the cross. He argued this point, "There is power in the cross to bridge the chasm between human beings, to bring people of diverse backgrounds together. To unite them on that hill where manna from eternity falls."[60] Taylor held no ambiguity about the primacy of Christ in preaching. Such a conviction was firmly revealed when he noted, "And, preacher, no matter what skills you have, no matter what histrionics you may enter, no matter what eloquence you

54. Ibid., 41–42.

55. L. Susan Bond, *Contemporary African American Preaching: Diversity in Theory and Style* (St. Louis: Chalice, 2003), 53.

56. Taylor, *How Shall They Preach*, 84.

57. Kim A. Lawton, "Gardner Still a Preaching Exemplar," *Christian Century* 123, no. 21 (October 2006): 16.

58. Ibid.

59. Ibid.

60. Taylor, *Special Occasions and Expository Sermons*, 35

may possess, no matter what gestures you may make, if you don't have the cross, if you don't have Jesus Christ at the center, your preaching is as sounding brass."[61] Taylor continued to urge preachers in a compelling tone, "We ought to preach the cross not only at the Passion season. The devil has driven us from our central place. Calvary ought to be in all our sermons, explicit or implicit."[62] For Taylor, a sermon that fails to make Christ prominent is a sermon that lacks the gospel.

Taylor also held a strong eschatological view, and such themes were recurring in his sermons. He concluded a sermon in typical eschatological fashion where Christ returns to the earth to establish his eternal kingdom of righteousness and justice among all nations and communities.[63] He saw this day as a new ordering of society into one family, free of those sinful properties that caused an unjust society. He noted, "There is a new world a-coming, cleansed of pride and prejudice. New world a-coming, purged of struggles and war's red strife. New world a-coming, a family of God."[64] Taylor's eschatological vision included a community where the common bond between people was not cultural but Christ who reigns in their heart. Taylor exclaimed:

> God is going to win, and we who enlist in this army is going to win because we are his and he is ours. When our warfare is over, we shall claim the triumph, and we shall go stately sweeping to the great coronation, waving palms of victory in our hands, and shouting "we have overcome the evil one." We shall march on through floods and flames, through sufferings and sorrows, until the great victory banquet of the Lamb. We shall come up from every side, from the north, south, east and west carrying our crosses, bearing our burdens, weeping our tears, suffering our sorrows, limping with our hurts and nursing our wounds. When the journey is past, we shall live, love, learn, and labor in that sunlit land where the flowers never fade, the day never dies, and the song never stills.[65]

He assured his listeners that God is ultimately in control of the events of a new world. To him, this new world is absent of evil and clothed with God's glory. He did not leave his listeners in hopelessness. Rather, he reminded them that God took them to a reality of peace and immeasurable joy.

---

61. Taylor, *Lectures, Essays, and Interviews,* 117.
62. Ibid., 116–17.
63. Taylor, *Special Occasion and Expository Sermons*, 34.
64. Ibid.
65. Gardner C. Taylor, *50 Years of Timeless Treasures,* vol. 6 of *The Words of Gardner Taylor,* comp. Edward L. Taylor (Pennsylvania: Judson, 2002), 245.

METHODOLOGY FOR PREACHING

Taylor's use of language to achieve his sermon's purpose was arguably the most dominant of the five factors shaping his theology of preaching. Out of all of this, the question is: how did his theology of preaching affect his preaching method? Simply put, the preaching assumptions he held cannot be separated from the method he used. In view of this, there is little explicit consideration, on his part, concerning his methodological preference. Concerning his publications, he offered little insight concerning an explicit preaching methodological preference or designation. In his Lyman Beecher Lectures on Preaching, he shared little insight relative to the value of homiletical methods. That is to say, he did not address the technical aspects of a preaching method.[66] The only consideration available is his published sermons, and from these sermons clues are given. An examination of his six-volume collection of sermons reveals specific methodological preferences. Generally, he followed a distinct and identifiable narrative structure or method. And to a lesser extent, he adhered to a rational-deductive theological proposition characteristic of expository preaching. Many of his sermons took his listeners on a journey of discovery or a quest for meaning intended to usher them into the presence of God. This approach showed a stream of theological anthropology that informed his preaching methodology.

Moreover, his choice of narrative method over deductive proposition was not a methodological preference owing to preaching classes at Oberlin. Such a preference represented the influence of the cultural roots of black preaching. This cultural identity was embedded in the practices of the African American pulpit tradition. Thus, Taylor was indebted to the entire "cloud of witnesses" that preceded him.[67]

The African American style of the narrative method is a culturally learned practice, nurtured by community norms and verbal customs, occurring outside of the academy.[68] These are culturally and historically conditioned factors related to storytelling form.[69] Taylor drew "upon the stories of Scripture" and his

---

66. Bond, *Contemporary*, 61.

67. The African American preaching tradition was informed by a strong oral tradition indigenous to Africa's way of transmitting history. See Olin P. Moyd, *Sacred Art: Preaching and Theology in the African American Tradition* (Pennsylvania: Judson, 1995), 43. Also see Mitchell, *Black Preaching*, 69–70.

68. See Kendra Fullwood, "The Extracurriculum of Two Black Preachers: A Descriptive Study of Culturally Learned Practices." (PhD diss., University of Kansas, 2014).

69. Richard L. Eslinger, *The Web of Preaching: New Options in Homiletic Method* (Nashville: Abingdon, 2004), 103–4; James H. Cone, *God of the Oppressed* (New York: Seabury, 1975), 90; Valentino Lassiter, *Martin Luther King in the African American Preaching Tradition* (Cleveland: Pilgrim, 2001), 13–42.

cultural context.[70] In this sense, his context called upon him to "know and tell the story but also to weave the biblical story to the listener's story."[71]

Taylor's narrative development functioned as his exposition.[72] It set a sermonic course of movement, which applied points of meaning in the narrative structure. Still, Taylor's preaching method converged also with the deductive-proposition method. Volume four of Taylor's preaching collection consists of sixteen expository sermon series. These sermons are completely uncharacteristic and atypical of the other sermons in the six-volume collection. Hence, Taylor showed diversity in his preaching method, using narrative and expository methods as they suited his preaching motive and context.[73]

CONTRIBUTIONS TO PREACHING

Taylor mirrored a distinct cultural practice in his preaching style. He also showed intercultural practice that should be understood as multicultural as opposed to monocultural.[74] He did not represent "something inimitable, belonging to particular cultures and heritages, unique unto itself as a dialogue partner."[75] So the question is this: what was Taylor's contribution in the area of preaching, and what were the pedagogical implications useful in the African American context and the white Protestant pulpit in America? In answer to this question, noted preaching scholar James Earl Massey stated that Taylor possessed one of the best working vocabularies of any minister alive.[76] Massey offered a criterion for measuring great preaching, noting, "He [Taylor] has a firm understanding of the best of both African American and Anglo Saxon culture."[77] He continued, "The best preaching is that which can go beyond one's self and one's own culture to touch others who are from different backgrounds—and that's what Dr. Taylor does."[78]

Another aspect of Taylor's contribution lies in his "holistic grasp of the gospel." It was symbolized in his own "church that served as a model for urban

---

70. Ibid.

71. The black context for preaching is described in works of Henry Mitchell. Mitchell maintained that to understand black preaching one must understand the "setting in which Black preaching takes place." The character of that setting reflects "patterns traceable to West African culture." See Mitchell, *Black Preaching*, 100.

72. See Calvin Miller, *Preaching: The Art of Narrative Exposition* (Grand Rapids: Baker, 2006), 20–22. Miller argues the case that narrative preaching brings Scripture to life through devices such as metaphor and image. He essentially believes that narrative is a legitimate form of exposition.

73. See Taylor, *Special Occasion and Expository Sermons.*

74. See Mitchell, *Black Preaching*, and William H. Pipes, *Say Amen, Brother! Old-Time Negro Preaching: A Study in African Frustration* (Detroit: Wayne State University, 1992).

75. Paul Scott Wilson, *Preaching and Homiletical Theory* (St. Louis: Chalice, 2004), 115.

76. Gilbreath, "The Pulpit King," 26.

77. Ibid.

78. Ibid.

congregations across the nation with its commitment to community outreach and development."[79] Yet another area of his contribution was his social activism. During the civil rights period, he played a critical role in influencing legislation mandating social change in America. Notwithstanding, out of all of these accomplishments, "the world will likely see his oratorical gifts as his defining quality."[80] Taylor was one of the most profound Christian preachers of his time.

CONCLUSION

Taylor's preaching ministry was too prolific to cover in one short essay. The information provided is simply a window one looks through to get a glimpse of the width and depth of his enduring contribution in the history of Christian preaching. He was one of the most celebrated preachers in the twentieth century and yet carried this badge of honor with a profound sense of humility. It would be a disservice to his preaching legacy if it were to become only a trophy of aesthetics to admire instead of an academic curriculum to study for pedagogical or instructive purposes in seminaries across the country. With this said, there is no better way to end this essay than with a quote from such a deep and profound Christian thinker as Taylor: "One of our chief problems as preachers is finding enough inner security, by God's grace, to do our work without being intimidated by the society around us, and without trying to court the favor of people who are in power."[81]

Sermon Excerpt

His Own Clothes (Mark 15:20)[82]

There are still many who put cloaks of imitation honor and false respect on the Lord Jesus as surely as those soldiers put their old scarlet robe on the Savior. Such do not mean their patronizing words of respect about the Lord Jesus. You can hear them now and again. One says, "I respect and honor Jesus. His golden rule is enough religion for anybody to live by. I admire his life and believe it to be a thing of beauty. His ethics are splendid principles of conduct and human relations."

79. Ibid
80. Ibid.
81. See online: http//www.bcnn1.com /gardnerctaylor/
82. Sermon taken from Gardner C. Taylor, *Quintessential Classics, 1980–Present*, vol. 3 of *The Words of Gardner C. Taylor*, comp. Edward L. Taylor (Pennsylvania: Judson, 2001), 116–21.

As for his church and all of that, these smart people are very lofty: "It is all right for those who need it, but I do not go to church. I do not feel the need of it, really." And so saying, they feel they have delivered themselves of something very profound and, if not profound, then chic and fashionable. Well, I had a dog, a blooded Doberman pinscher, who never went to church either. I feel like answering such glib dismissal of the church for which Christ died by saying, "My dog did not go to church either. He never felt the need of it because he was a dog. Now, what is your reason?"

There are still others who put garments of mock royalty on the Lord and who call his name but who feel no deep loyalty to him, no crowning and controlling love for the Lord, who has done so much for us. You may see them now and again in church, now and then among the people of Christ. They throw their leftovers at the Lord who made us all, as one would toss scraps to a pet dog. They are neither hot nor cold, and to such the word of the Revelation applies, "I will spue thee out of my mouth" (3:16, KJV). ◆

BIBLIOGRAPHY

Bond, L. Susan. *Contemporary African American Preaching: Diversity in Theory and Style*. St. Louis: Chalice, 2003.

Brown, Teresa Fry L. "Poetic Persuasion: A Master Class on Speaking Truth to Power." Pages 260–71 in *Our Sufficiency Is of God: Essays on Preaching in Honor of Gardner C. Taylor*. Edited by Timothy George, James Earl Massey, and Robert Smith Jr. Macon, GA: Mercer University Press, 2010.

Cone, James H. *God of the Oppressed*. New York: Seabury, 1975.

Demaray, Donald E. "The Magic of Music and Metaphor: Preaching and the Arts." Pages 45–61 in *Our Sufficiency Is of God: Essays on Preaching in Honor of Gardner C. Taylor*. Edited by Timothy George, James Earl Massey and Robert Smith Jr. Macon, GA: Mercer University Press, 2010.

Edwards, O. C., Jr. *History of Preaching*. 2 vols. Nashville: Abingdon, 2004.

Eslinger, Richard L. *The Web of Preaching: New Options In Homiletic Method*. Nashville: Abingdon, 2002.

Fitts, Leroy. *A History of Black Baptists*. Nashville: Broadman, 1985.

Frazier, E. Franklin, and C. Eric Lincoln. *The Negro Church in America and The Black Church Since Frazier*. New York: Schocken, 1974.

Fullwood, Alfonza W. "A Study of Gardner C. Taylor's Theology of Preaching as a Decisive Factor Shaping His Theory of Preaching: Implications for Homiletical Pedagogy." PhD diss., The Southeastern Baptist Theological Seminary, 2012.

Fullwood, Kendra L. "The Extracurriculum of Two Black Preachers: A Descriptive Study of Culturally Learned Practices." PhD diss., University of Kansas, 2014.

George, Timothy. "Introduction: Honor to Whom Honor Is Due." Pages ix–xxxii in *Our Sufficiency Is of God: Essays on Preaching in Honor of Gardner C. Taylor*. Edited by Timothy George, James Earl Massey, and Robert Smith Jr. Macon, GA: Mercer University Press, 2010.

Gilbreath, Edward. "The Pulpit King: The Passion and Eloquence of Gardner C. Taylor, a Legend among Preachers," *Christianity Today* (11 December 1995): 26.

Lassiter, Valentino. *Martin Luther King in the African American Preaching Tradition*. Cleveland: The Pilgrim, 2001.

Lawton, Kim A. "Gardner Still a Preaching Exemplar," *Christian Century* 123, no. 21 (October 2006): 16.

Lee, Avery, and Gardner C. Taylor. *Perfecting the Pastor's Art: Wisdom from Avery Lee and Gardner Taylor.* Pennsylvania: Judson, 2005.

Lincoln, C. Eric., and Lawrence H. Mamiya. *The Black Church in the African American Experience.* Durham: Duke University Press, 1990.

McClure, John. *Preaching Words: 144 Key Terms in Homiletics.* Louisville: Westminster John Knox, 2007.

Miller, Calvin. *Preaching: The Art of Narrative Exposition.* Grand Rapids: Baker, 2006.

Mitchell, Henry H. *Black Preaching: The Recovery of a Powerful Art.* Nashville: Abingdon, 1990.

Moyd, Olin P. *The Sacred Art: Preaching and Theology in the African American Tradition.* Pennsylvania: Judson, 1995.

Pipes, Williams H. *Say Amen, Brother!: Old-Time Negro Preaching: A Study in African Frustration.* Detroit: Wayne State University Press, 1992.

Proctor, Samuel D., Gardner C. Taylor, and Gary V. Simpson. *We Have This Ministry: The Heart of the Pastor's Vocation.* Pennsylvania: Judson 1996.

Simmons, Martha J., and Brad R. Braxton. "What Happened to Sacred Eloquence?" Pages 272–300 in *Our Sufficiency Is of God: Essays on Preaching in Honor of Gardner C. Taylor.* Edited by Timothy George, James Earl Massey, and Robert Smith Jr. Macon, GA: Mercer University Press, 2010.

Taylor, Gardner C. *Special Occasion and Expository Sermons.* Vol. 4 of *The Words of Gardner C. Taylor.* Compiled by Edward L. Taylor. Pennsylvania: Judson, 2001.

———. *Lectures, Essays and Interviews.* Vol. 5 of *The Words of Gardner C. Taylor.* Compiled by Edward L. Taylor. Pennsylvania: Judson, 2001.

———. *50 Years of Timeless Treasures.* Vol. 6 of *The Words of Gardner C. Taylor.* Compiled by Edward L. Taylor. Pennsylvania: Judson, 2002.

———. "Preaching and the Power of Words." Pages 206–15 in *Communicate with Power: Insights from America's Top Communicators.* Edited by Michael Duduit. Grand Rapids: Baker, 1996.

———. *Quintessential Classics 1980–Present.* Vol. 3 of *The Words of Gardner C. Taylor.* Edited by Edward L. Taylor. Pennsylvania: Judson, 2001.

———. *How Shall They Preach: The Lyman Beecher Lectures and Five Lenten Sermons.* Elgin, IL: Progressive Baptist Publishing House, 1977.

———. "Shaping Sermons by the Shape of Text and Preacher." Pages 137–52 in *Preaching Biblically: Creating Sermons in the Shape of Scripture.* Edited by Don M. Wardlaw. Philadelphia: Westminster, 1983.

———. *Faith in the Fire: Wisdom for Life.* Edited by Edward L. Taylor. New York: Smiley, 2011.

Thomas, Gerald L. *African American Preaching: The Contribution of Dr. Gardner C. Taylor.* New York: Peter Lang, 2004.

Wardlaw, Don M., ed. *Preaching Biblically.* Philadelphia: Westminster, 1983.

Wilson, Paul Scott. *Preaching and Homiletical Theory.* St. Louis: Chalice, 2004.

Billy Graham
Evangelist to the World

JOHN N. AKERS

Throughout the history of the Christian church, some individuals have been called and gifted by God to be evangelists. Often facing cultural, ecclesiastical, and social barriers, these evangelists sought to build up the church by reaching out to those to whom Jesus Christ was unknown or unacknowledged, and urging them to commit their lives to him. Most have labored in obscurity, but occasionally an evangelist has been given unexpected public recognition and influence. Such was the case with Billy Graham (1918–2018) who, during over sixty years of public ministry, spoke face-to-face to more people than any other person in history.

HISTORICAL BACKGROUND

William Franklin "Billy" Graham Jr. was born on a dairy farm outside the city of Charlotte, North Carolina, on November 7, 1918. He was the first of four children born to Frank and Morrow Graham, and in addition to attending local schools, began working on the family's farm at an early age. His parents were of Scottish heritage and were active in the Associate Reformed Presbyterian Church in Charlotte. Billy dutifully attended church with them, but it was not until a well-known evangelist, Dr. Mordecai Ham, came to Charlotte for an extended series of citywide meetings that Graham, around his seventeenth birthday, became convicted of his need for God's forgiveness and publicly made a commitment of his life to Jesus Christ.

Although he dreamed of becoming a professional baseball player, Billy assumed he probably would follow in his father's footsteps and become a farmer. After his conversion, however, he felt a need for further education (particularly in the Bible), and after high school he enrolled briefly in Bob Jones College in Tennessee, then transferred to Florida Bible Institute (FBI) near the city of Tampa. FBI proved to be a positive experience for him; not only did he gain a deeper understanding of the Bible through his classes there, but he also met a number of prominent preachers and evangelists who visited the school during the winter months.

While at Florida Bible Institute, Graham sensed God was calling him to become a preacher. At first he resisted, and only after a period of deep spiritual struggle did he commit himself to that calling. Almost immediately, he began accepting invitations to speak in local churches and also preached on street corners, in trailer parks, and at other public venues. During his student days at FBI, he was ordained as a Southern Baptist minister.

Upon graduation, he enrolled in Wheaton College, a respected Christian liberal arts institution outside Chicago. There he majored in anthropology, which greatly broadened his understanding of world cultures. While at Wheaton, he met his future wife, Ruth McCue Bell, who had grown up in China as the daughter of Presbyterian medical missionaries. They were married upon graduation in 1943, and he was called to become pastor of a small Baptist church in nearby Western Springs, Illinois. His burden for evangelism continued to grow, however, and in 1945 he resigned from the church to become the first evangelist for Youth for Christ (YFC), a recently formed nondenominational evangelistic organization. During the next few years, Graham traveled extensively with YFC, both in the United States and Great Britain. Although he was largely unknown to the general public, his reputation as a gifted and dynamic young evangelist grew steadily.

The turning point in Graham's public ministry occurred in 1949, when several hundred churches in the Los Angeles, California, area invited him to hold a united evangelistic campaign. At first, the meetings—held in a large tent—attracted little interest outside the sponsoring churches, but the conversion of several well-known local personalities (including a popular radio broadcaster, an Olympic athlete, and a gangster) suddenly made the Los Angeles campaign front-page news across the nation. Invitations to hold similar citywide evangelistic campaigns poured in, and from that point until his formal retirement in 2005, Graham held over four hundred major campaigns in stadiums and other large venues across the world. It has been estimated that during his long career Billy Graham spoke face-to-face to nearly 215 million people, with hundreds of millions more being reached through television, video, film, and webcasts.

Quick to take advantage of new developments in communications technology, Graham became a pioneer in the use of radio, television, film, and the internet for extending the message of the gospel. He also authored over thirty books, as well as a daily column appearing in over two hundred newspapers. Although he was personally acquainted with every American president since Harry

Truman (as well as a number of other world leaders), he always stressed that most of his time was spent with ordinary people. He saw himself as part of a long line of evangelists—Assisi, Luther, Whitefield, Wesley, Booth, Moody, Sunday, and a host of others. "I am only one in a glorious chain of men and women God has raised up through the centuries to build Christ's church and to take the Gospel everywhere."[1]

Billy Graham died on February 21, 2018, at the age of ninety-nine years old. Al Mohler, President of The Southern Baptist Theological Seminary wrote a fitting epilogue upon the passing of Dr. Graham: "An epic era of evangelical history has come to an end. Billy Graham was not only a titanic figure in evangelicalism, but in world history and perhaps represents the last of a kind. He dominated 20th century American evangelicalism and remained a major figure on the world stage throughout most of the 20th century in a way that we can envision no evangelical leader in our times."[2]

THEOLOGY OF PREACHING

Central to Billy Graham's thinking was the conviction that he had been called by God to be an evangelist—specifically, a preaching evangelist. This he saw not only as a divine calling, but also as a spiritual gift given to him by the Holy Spirit. Foundational to this conviction was Paul's statement in Ephesians 4:11–12, to which he often referred: "And he gave some, apostles; and some, prophets; and some, evangelists; and some, pastors and teachers; For the perfecting of the saints, for the work of the ministry, for the edifying of the body of Christ" (KJV).[3] He realized the gift of the evangelist had been neglected (and even denigrated) during much of the church's history, but he was convinced that "the gift of the evangelist is just as valid and crucial for the church today as it was in New Testament times."[4] Although he seldom spoke of it publically, he deeply hoped his ministry would reawaken the broad church to the legitimacy and urgency of the evangelist's calling.

---

1. Quoted in Russell Busby, *Billy Graham: God's Ambassador* (New York: Time-Life, 1999), 18.

2. Al Mohler, "Mohler on Graham: 'An Epic Era of Evagnelical History Has Come to An End," Southern News. http://news.sbts.edu/2018/02/21/mohler-graham-epic-era-evangelical-history-come-end/.

3. The quotation is from the King James Version of the Bible, which was the basis of Graham's early Bible study. Later he became an advocate for new translations and paraphrases as they became available, and encouraged their wide distribution so the Bible could be understood by as many as possible.

4. Billy Graham, *A Biblical Standard for Evangelists* (Minneapolis: Billy Graham Evangelistic Association, 1984), 31. This volume is Graham's commentary on the affirmations concerning evangelism made by participants in the 1983 International Conference for Itinerant Evangelists, held in Amsterdam. This was one of several international conferences on evangelism sponsored by Billy Graham to encourage and train evangelists from across the world.

By embracing his own calling as an evangelist, Graham was in no way dismissing the importance of those who had been called to other types of ministry. His own experience as a pastor—although brief—had helped him understand the crucial role of the local church; his term as a college president gave him a lifelong concern for Christian education.[5] Central to his support for other types of ministry was his conviction that the preaching of the Word of God was essential to both the conversion and spiritual growth of the believer. Graham's understanding of the importance of preaching never caused him to ignore or denigrate other aspects of the church's calling. Worship, he knew, must be an integral part of the church's calling; without it the church turns inward and becomes little more than another social organization. The church is also called to express Christ's love by acts of mercy, reconciliation, and service. "We must have a burden for the needs of people that goes beyond just 'concern' and results in action," he wrote. "We must be concerned with human suffering wherever it is found because God is concerned about it."[6]

Nevertheless, Graham was convinced that among all the things that God has called his people to do, priority must be given to evangelism. Relatively few individuals, he knew, had been given the spiritual gift of evangelism, but every Christian was called to be a witness for Christ, both by their words and their deeds. "We are stewards of the Gospel. Some think that only ministers are to preach, but that is wrong. Every Christian is to be a witness; every follower of Christ is to be a witness."[7] Nor should pastors neglect their responsibility to make evangelism an inherent part of their preaching. When speaking to pastors Graham often echoed Paul's command to Timothy: "Preach the word. . . . Do the work of an evangelist" (2 Tim 4:2, 5).

Foundational Principles for Preaching

Billy Graham's understanding of the importance of preaching rested on at least five foundational principles. The first was his conviction that the Bible, and the Bible alone, was the authoritative and inspired Word of God. As such, the Bible must be both the source of the evangelist's message and the authority for his or her calling. Apart from the Bible, the evangelist has no message; for only

---

5. From 1948 to 1952, Graham served as president of Northwestern Schools in Minneapolis, Minnesota, which included a liberal arts school, a Bible college, and a seminary. In his autobiography he recounts his reluctance to accept the position and his subsequent struggles to balance his commitment to evangelism with his responsibilities as president. Billy Graham, *Just As I Am: The Autobiography of Billy Graham*, 2nd ed. (San Francisco: HarperOne, 2007), 112–22. Graham later served on the Board of Trustees of Fuller Theological Seminary and Wheaton College, and helped found Gordon-Conwell Theological Seminary.

6. Graham, *A Biblical Standard for Evangelists*, 115–16.

7. Joan Winmill Brown, ed., *Day by Day with Billy Graham: A Daily Devotional* (Minneapolis, World Wide Publications, 1976), selection for September 26.

through it do we learn the truth of humanity's alienation from God because of sin. And only through it do we learn of the possibility of God's forgiveness and salvation through Christ's death and resurrection. To the thousands of evangelists gathered for the 1986 International Congress for Itinerant Evangelists, held in Amsterdam, The Netherlands, Graham declared, "Biblical evangelism is committed to the full and final authority of Scripture alone."[8]

Graham's commitment to the authority and inspiration of the Bible did not come easily, however. As a young man, he had accepted without question the Bible's divine origin and authority. However, as he approached the 1949 Los Angeles Crusade, his mind and heart were thrown into turmoil due to the arguments of one of his closest friends—a fellow evangelist who dismissed Graham's belief in the Bible as naïve and uninformed, and asserted that modern scholarship had proved the Bible must be approached as a book of human, not divine, origin. Graham knew the issue was crucial, affecting not only his calling as an evangelist but the validity of the gospel. "I had to have an answer. If I *could not* trust the Bible, I could not go on . . . I would have to leave pulpit evangelism."[9] In what turned out to be one of the greatest spiritual struggles of his life, Graham reaffirmed his commitment to the Bible as God's Word and from that point on the Bible became the foundation of his life and ministry.

> One night after the meetings he went off by himself, placed his open Bible on a tree stump, and knelt in prayer. He later wrote, "The exact wording of my prayer is beyond recall, but it must have echoed my thoughts. . . . 'Father, I am going to accept this as Thy Word—by *faith!* I'm going to go beyond my intellectual questions and doubts, and I will believe this to be Your inspired Word.' When I got up from my knees . . . I sensed the presence and power of God as I had not sensed it in months. Not all my questions were answered, but a major bridge had been crossed. In my heart and mind I knew a spiritual battle in my soul had been fought and won.[10]

The second foundational principle undergirding Graham's preaching was his belief that the gospel was true, and therefore could be proclaimed with full confidence in its veracity. If the Bible was true, then the message it contained must also be true—and the heart of that message was the good news concerning

---

8. Billy Graham, "The Gift and Calling of the Evangelist," in *The Calling of an Evangelist: Papers From The Second International Congress for Itinerant Evangelists*, Amsterdam, The Netherlands, 1986, ed. James D. Douglas (Minneapolis: World Wide Publications, 1987), 18.

9. Graham, *Just As I Am*, 139.

10. Ibid.

Jesus Christ. "Our authority is not based upon our experiences, or upon our traditions, or upon the latest ideas of philosophers or politicians. Our authority and our message are solely based on what God has revealed to us in His Word, the Bible."[11] Repeatedly, Graham warned people against confusing their feelings with the historical facts of Jesus's life, death, and resurrection. Our feelings can change and mislead us, he pointed out, but the truth of the gospel never changes and never deceives. "The work of Christ is a fact, His cross is a fact, His tomb is a fact, and His resurrection is a fact. . . . Trusting in Him for your eternal salvation is trusting in a fact."[12]

A third foundational principle in Graham's view of preaching was the relationship between biblical preaching and the work of the Holy Spirit. Apart from the Holy Spirit—the third person of the triune God—the evangelist is powerless; only the Holy Spirit can convict individuals of their sin and their need of a Savior, and only the Holy Spirit can convince them of the truth of the gospel. Furthermore, only the Holy Spirit can draw people to Christ and give them the spiritual rebirth of which the Bible speaks.[13] Because of his conviction that the Holy Spirit was crucial for effective evangelism, Graham made prayer a central part of every campaign, including the organization of hundreds of prayer meetings in the area. When asked to explain why a campaign was successful, his reply was always the same: "Prayer . . . prayer . . . and prayer!"

If the Holy Spirit is critical in conversion, however, he is just as critical in the preaching of the gospel. Admittedly, all preaching is a human enterprise, but in God's providence biblical preaching also is a divine activity. In other words, the preaching of the gospel is inextricably linked with the work of the Holy Spirit; Word and Spirit unite to accomplish God's purposes. Graham stated his understanding of the connection between the Word of God and the Holy Spirit in this way: "I believe effective preaching must be biblical preaching. . . . The Word is what the Spirit uses. . . . When we preach or teach the Scriptures, we open the door for the Holy Spirit to do His work. God has not promised to bless oratory or clever preaching. He has promised to bless His Word. . . . God the Holy Spirit can take the humblest preaching or the feeblest words of our witness to Christ, and transform them by His power into a convicting word in the lives of others."[14]

---

11. Graham, "The Gift and Calling of the Evangelist," 18.

12. Billy Graham, *Peace with God: The Secret of Hapiness*, rev. ed. (Waco, TX: Word, 1984), 148.

13. Although he was reluctant to criticize other evangelists, Graham privately expressed concern over those who relied on emotionalism or coercive tactics, or promised prosperity or health to their supporters; they were in danger of substituting human methods for reliance on the Holy Spirit. Affirmation VI of The Amsterdam Affirmations declares, "In our proclamation of the Gospel we recognize the urgency of calling all to decision to follow Jesus Christ as Lord and Savior, and to do so lovingly and without coercion or manipulation."

14. Billy Graham, *The Holy Spirit: Activating God's Power in Your Life* (Dallas: Word, 1988), 47, 54.

On a practical level, this meant that Graham drew his preaching from the Scriptures and included frequent quotations from the Bible in his preaching. His oft-repeated phrase, "The Bible says," permeated every sermon and became closely identified with both his spoken and written works. Even an obscure or offhand quotation from the Bible, he came to realize, could be used by the Holy Spirit to speak to someone in spiritual need. The Bible also had the power to reach across every kind of cultural barrier. "I have had the privilege of preaching the Gospel on every continent [and] in most of the countries of the world. And I have found that when I present the simple message of the Gospel of Jesus Christ, with authority, quoting from the very Word of God—He takes that message and drives it supernaturally into the human heart."[15]

A fourth foundational principle in Graham's understanding of the importance of preaching can be stated simply: Before people can respond to the gospel, they must hear the gospel. Preaching, therefore, is a crucial link in God's plan of salvation.

Graham was well aware that God used a vast variety of methods to communicate the truth of the gospel to a lost world. He was also aware that in rare instances God could even break through the barriers of culture and geography to reveal himself in supernatural ways to individuals who otherwise had no access to the preaching of the Word. But regardless of the method, the message was the same: the life, death, and resurrection of Jesus Christ for our salvation.

Nevertheless, the preached Word was essential if the world was to hear of Christ and his offer of salvation. Graham frequently returned in his thinking to Paul's words to the Christians in Rome: "How, then, can they call on the one they have not believed in? And how can they believe in the one of whom they have not heard? And how can they hear without someone preaching to them? And how can anyone preach unless they are sent?"[16] There is an urgency to the gospel, and therefore there is an urgency to its preaching. "You may be speaking to some who will hear the Gospel for the last time," he reminded his fellow evangelists. "Preach with the urgency of Christ."[17]

The fifth and final principle for Graham's preaching follows logically from the fourth principle: The evangelist is under divine orders. God has commanded that his gospel must be preached to the ends of the earth, and those orders are to be obeyed, regardless of circumstances, opposition, discouragement, or human frailty.

---

15. Busby, *God's Ambassador*, 11.
16. Rom 10:14–15.
17. Billy Graham, "The Evangelist and His Preaching," in *The Work of an Evangelist: Papers from the International Conference for Itinerant Evangelists, Amsterdam, The Netherlands, 1983*, ed. James D. Douglas (Minneapolis: World Wide Publications, 1984), 98.

Faced with a world that was lost and alienated from God, an evangelist could only respond in obedience to God's sovereign command. "We engage in evangelism today not because we want to, or because we choose to, or because we like to, but because *we have been told to*. We are under orders.... We have no choice."[18]

When urged by some to run for the American presidency, Graham replied that preaching the gospel is "the greatest service I can render to God and to the world in this critical period of history."[19] In an interview with *Parade* magazine, he stated, "Our task is to do all we can—not to sit and wait."[20] More direct were Graham's words to his fellow evangelists: "The Great Commission is still in effect. Christ's command has not changed, and neither has God's great plan of redemption.... Even if we had no other reason to go and proclaim the Gospel, the command of Christ would be enough."[21]

Foundational Principles for Living

Our concern in the previous section has been to outline five theological principles that undergirded Billy Graham's understanding of his preaching. Any discussion of his principles would be incomplete, however, without noting at least briefly what might be called his "foundational principles for living." In Graham's view, the principles by which he lived were inextricably linked with the principles by which he preached. Both were rooted in the Bible, and both were essential to his effectiveness as a preacher. The Bible, he firmly believed, not only taught us what to believe but also how to live. He often spoke of his practice of reading a chapter from the book of Proverbs every day, finding in it practical guidance for life's challenges.

Graham would have denied that his foundational principles for living were only for evangelists; they applied to every believer. Nevertheless, in his view they had special relevance to those who were called to ministry, and especially preaching evangelists. "We must remember that we communicate the Gospel by our lives as well as our lips," he reminded his fellow evangelists. "We live before a watching world, a world that is waiting to see if what we say is lived out in our lives.... The devil will do all he can to blunt the effectiveness of those who have been called of God to preach the Gospel."[22] Although a detailed analysis of these

---

18. Graham, "The Gift and Calling of the Evangelist," 17.
19. "Billy Graham Not Interested in Job at White House," *Associated Press* (reprinted in The Independent Record, Helena, Montana, February 3, 1964). The suggestion had come only months after the assassination of President John F. Kennedy.
20. Colin Green, "The Rev. Billy Graham reflects on his faith, his country and his life," *Parade Magazine*, (20 October 1996): 4.
21. Graham, *A Biblical Standard for Evangelists*, 26–27.
22. Billy Graham, "Preaching the Word—Reaching the World," in *The Calling of an Evangelist: Papers from the Second International Conference for Itinerant Evangelists, Amsterdam, The Netherlands, 1986*, ed. James D. Douglas (Minneapolis: World Wide Publications, 1987), 134.

principles is beyond the scope of our present study, they may be summarized under the following five headings.

First, the evangelist is called to a life of integrity and moral purity. During Graham's formative years, the novel *Elmer Gantry* by Sinclair Lewis harmfully influenced the views of many people concerning all evangelists because of the negative image of the novel's protagonist, a corrupt evangelist. Graham was determined to do all he could to overcome that image and worked strenuously to avoid any appearance of dishonesty or immorality. As one historian has written, "Even in an era of rampant political and televangelist scandals, no one has seriously challenged Graham's personal integrity. That must surely be remembered as one of his most significant contributions to religion in the 20th century."[23]

Second, the evangelist is called to a life of accountability and transparency. Not only should an evangelist be morally pure, but they should also have individuals around them to whom they are accountable. One of Graham's oft-perceived strengths was his ability to surround himself with a team of men and women who could give him advice and, if necessary, correction. Less visible, but in some ways more important, was his board of directors (drawn mainly from the world of business), who oversaw the finances of his work and determined the policies and procedures.

Third, the evangelist is called to live a life of compassion and understanding. For Graham, this included special attention to parts of the world that were impoverished or stricken by disaster; only the gospel could bring lasting hope and transformation. He also sought to understand his critics and learn from them instead of striking back or condemning them. Also, compassion should permeate the evangelist's preaching: "Even when your message includes the fact of judgment and hell, your hearers should realize that both God and His messenger speak from a broken heart."[24]

Fourth, the evangelist is called to a life of humility and wisdom. Evangelists, Graham knew, were especially vulnerable to pride, and the more visible they were, the greater the danger. He said, evangelists "need to be wary of the guile of the enemy, who usually attacks along three lines: money, morals and/or pride. . . . The devil has never changed and is always seeking that opportune moment to entrap us."[25]

Finally, the evangelist is called to a life of vision and boldness. Throughout his ministry, Graham always looked for opportunities to preach in places with limited Christian witness. He returned repeatedly to countries that historically had

---

23. Randall Balmer, "He brought modern man to that old time religion," *St. Louis Post-Dispatch* (9 October 1999), 26.

24. Graham, "Preaching the Word—Reaching the World," 133.

25. Billy Graham, "The Evangelist in a Changing World: It's a New Day," in *Equipping for Evangelism: Papers from the North American Conference for Itinerant Evangelists, 1994,* ed. Charles G. Ward (Minneapolis: World Wide Publications, 1996), 23.

strong Christian ties but were now in the grip of militant secularism. Major non-Christian nations like India also were of special concern to him. Many strongly urged him not to accept invitations to preach in communist Eastern Europe and the Soviet Union, fearing he would be used for propaganda purposes. He countered by pointing out that the Great Commission did not exclude the communist world. When asked by a reporter if he was aware the Soviet government had been using him for propaganda purposes, he replied, "Yes, I am aware of this, but I have been using them for my propaganda, and my propaganda is more powerful."[26]

METHODOLOGY FOR PREACHING

Billy Graham probably would have been the first to insist that no one should seek to imitate his preaching methods or follow his pattern of sermon preparation. "I am not a great preacher," he said, "and I don't claim to be a great preacher. I've heard great preaching many times and wished I was one of those great preachers. I'm an ordinary preacher, just communicating the Gospel in the best way I know how."[27] Nevertheless, future generations of preachers undoubtedly will study Graham's preaching and, regardless of his self-effacing claim, profit from both his theological understanding of preaching and his preaching methodology. In this section, we will examine three aspects of his methodology.

Personal Preparation

The first dimension of Graham's preaching methodology was his personal preparation—his process for gaining a broad understanding of the context in which he would be preaching. As a traveling evangelist, he constantly faced new audiences, and he worked diligently to adapt his message to each context.

The answer for him was to learn as much as possible about the audience he would be facing and adjust his approach to their situation. For example, before going to a city for a major evangelistic campaign, Graham would be briefed on the area by local residents and members of his preparatory team. He also would start reading the city's newspapers, trying to get a feel for the area's social or racial problems and looking for any examples of civic pride that might be used as illustrations.

A careful examination of his sermon notes demonstrates this process. Many sermons were repeated from city to city, but the sermon notes were never the same. Instead, interspersed in the basic outline would be a number of comments

---

26. Busby, *God's Ambassador*, 138.
27. Ibid., 23.

about specific local events or groups that would help bridge the gap with his audience (e.g., the success of a local sports team, for instance, or complimentary references to a city's progress).[28]

Sermon Preparation

The second dimension of Graham's preaching methodology was his actual sermon preparation. As a student, Graham avidly read sermons from noted preachers and evangelists and even memorized some of them; they formed the basis of his first evangelistic messages. Similarly, he read widely from evangelists of the past, but he developed his own sermons, drawing on passages of Scripture that could be used to preach the gospel. Many were based on biblical characters, while others drew on topics that spoke to the inner needs of his audience (loneliness, the family, marriage, etc.). Messages on *The Hour of Decision* radio program often used recent items in the news as their starting point—a political crisis, the threat of nuclear war, drugs, alcohol, etc. Whatever the initial theme, however, Graham always related it to the deeper truths of the gospel.

Illustrations were of major importance to Graham. They were usually brief but easily understandable for his audience. This was especially important whenever he preached one of his prior sermons. He said to those gathered for the third (and final) International Conference for Itinerant Evangelists, "I'm always searching for new ways to approach the same message. For example, let's say that I preached a message 40 years ago. I can still preach that same message today but I need a new outline, I need new illustrations. I'm always asking my team members and my friends to please help me with these illustrations. I like to use illustrations that are fresh and up-to-date."[29] Almost every sermon went through several drafts, and even during a meeting's preliminaries, Graham could be seen on the platform, writing in new ideas or illustrations.

As he prepared, Graham had what might be called a "mental grid" through which he viewed every message. Regardless of the cultural or social background

---

28. Billy Graham's sermon notes can be accessed online through the archives of the Billy Graham Center of Wheaton College (https://www.wheaton.edu/academics/academic-centers/billy-graham-center/resources/recommended-resources-for-evangelism/billy-graham-center-archives/sermons-of-billy-graham/). Graham seldom preached from a full manuscript, however, and most of his sermon notes are quite brief. An exception was the weekly broadcast of *The Hour of Decision*; because of the need for precise timing, he used a full manuscript. A number of videos of his preaching can be accessed through the website of the Billy Graham Evangelistic Association, at billygraham.org/videos/. Transcripts of his actual sermons are not currently available, but most issues of *Decision Magazine* included an edited version of a Billy Graham sermon; copies can be accessed at billygraham.org/decision-magazine/. Manuscripts of sermons preached on *The Hour of Decision* are not currently available. All sermon material is under copyright, with limited access for downloading.

29. Billy Graham, "How to Reach People Effectively," *The Mission of the Evangelist: Papers from Amsterdam 2000, A Conference for Preaching Evangelists*, ed. William Conrad (Minneapolis: World Wide Publications, 2001), 103.

of his hearers, he was convinced that human nature across the world was essentially the same. All people experienced loneliness, guilt, and a fear of death, and all people had within them a sense of emptiness or quest for meaning and purpose. The gospel spoke to each of these, and this provided an opening for the evangelist to speak to the hearts and minds of his listeners.[30]

The Task of Preaching

The third aspect of Billy Graham's methodology was the preaching itself. As a young man, his preaching was dynamic and physically vigorous; later, he moved away from this, realizing that it was not necessary and could even be a barrier to some people. Preaching to a large crowd, often sitting hundreds of feet away from him, required special attention to his speech; short sentences, simple language, and clear intonation were essential. In addition, he urged evangelists to "communicate the Gospel with authority . . . with simplicity . . . with repetition . . . with urgency (and) for a decision."[31] Eye contact was also important; any reference to his sermon notes needed to be brief.[32]

More important to Graham than his presentation, however, was the content of his messages. Method and message must be linked in his view; they could not be separated. As an evangelist, he was called to preach the gospel, but what exactly did this mean in terms of a message's actual content?

LINKING METHOD AND THEOLOGY

In Billy Graham's understanding, the gospel was centered in what God had done for us in Jesus Christ, the incarnate Son of God, who was sent by the Father to become the final and complete sacrifice for human sin. "At the heart of [the] Good News is Jesus Christ and the love and forgiveness He gives," he wrote. "He is God in human flesh, and the story of His life, death, and resurrection is the only Good News the world will ever hear."[33]

Reality of Sin and Consequences

As a result, in almost every evangelistic sermon, Graham sought to include four elements. First, he stressed the reality and consequences of sin. "We need to

---

30. Graham elaborated on these points in his message to the evangelists at Amsterdam 83 Conference? "The Evangelist and His Preaching," in *The Work of an Evangelist*, 95–100.

31. Ibid., 97–98.

32. For an academic analysis of his speaking style and communication techniques, see Donald Allen Waite, "The Evangelistic Speaking of Billy Graham, 1949–1959," PhD thesis, Purdue University, 1961.

33. Billy Graham, *Storm Warning: Whether Global Recession, Terrorist Threats, or Devastating Natural Disasters, These Ominous Shadows Must Bring Us Back to the Gospel*, rev. ed. (Nashville: Thomas Nelson, 2010), 81.

emphasize that all are sinners and stand under the judgment of God. . . . People must be aware that they have broken God's law before they can realize their need."[34] In the face of human pride and pretense, the evangelist must stress the fact of humanity's rebellion against the holy and loving God who made them. "Never lose sight of the seriousness of sin," he declared. "This is why our greatest need is not economic or political or educational in nature; it is spiritual. *Our greatest need is to have our sins forgiven and our old sinful nature exchanged for a new one.*"[35]

Accomplishment of God through Christ

The second element in the evangelist's message must be the declaration of what God has done through Jesus Christ to provide the way for our sins to be forgiven. Jesus was God in human flesh, and as such, he was without sin. When he died on the cross, however, all our sins were transferred to him, and he took upon himself the judgment and hell that we deserve. "God's justice demands that sin must be punished; if it isn't, there is no right and wrong, and God is not just. But instead of us having to bear the condemnation we deserve, Christ took upon Himself our guilt and our punishment. He substituted Himself for us."[36]

Jesus's death on the cross, therefore, must be a central part of the evangelist's message. Graham often recounted an incident early in his ministry that enforced this truth in his mind. He was in Dallas, Texas, for a series of meetings in the city's famous Cotton Bowl stadium, and one night he sensed his message had lacked spiritual impact. Afterward, he expressed his concern to a close friend, who bluntly replied, "Billy, you didn't speak about the Cross. How can anyone be converted without having at least one single view of the Cross where the Lord died for us?" Graham realized his friend was correct, and he resolved never to preach again without stressing the importance of Christ's death.[37]

The good news of the gospel did not end with the cross, however. It also included Christ's resurrection. The resurrection confirmed Christ's atoning work on the cross, and by his resurrection Christ conquered death and hell and Satan forever. Furthermore, because of the resurrection we can have the hope of life after death in heaven. "In the resurrection of Jesus Christ, we have the answer to the great question of the ages: 'If mortals die, can they live again?'

---

34. Graham, *A Biblical Standard for Evangelists*, 51.

35. Billy Graham, *The Journey: How to Live by Faith in an Uncertain World* (Nashville: W Publishing Group, 2006), 39, 45.

36. Ibid., 49. It should be noted that substitution was not the only image Graham used to describe the atoning work of Christ. Other biblical images he used included sacrifice, redemption, and conquest.

37. Graham frequently referred to the incident, especially when speaking to pastors. It is recounted in Graham, *Just as I Am*, 243.

The Bible teaches that because Christ lives, we shall live also. The greatest truth that you can ever hear is that Jesus Christ died but rose again, and that you too will die but can rise again into newness of life."[38]

It is in the cross that we see both the justice and the love of God. God's justice must be satisfied, and this was accomplished in the most profound way imaginable through Christ's death for us. However, the cross also was the ultimate expression of God's love for the human race. In his later years, Graham acknowledged that he probably had stressed the judgment of God too much in his early ministry. Later, however, he sought to put more stress on the love of God; virtually every crusade in his final decades of preaching included a sermon on John 3:16. "Everything you've ever done, everything you've ever thought, all the thoughts and intents of your heart are someday going to be exposed at the judgment. There is a day of judgment coming! . . . But the Bible also teaches that God is a God of love. He loves you. He loves every one of us, and He loves us so much that He gave His Son to die on the cross."[39]

The Call to Decision

The third element in a typical evangelistic sermon by Billy Graham was the call to decision. This was often the most memorable part for many listeners, as hundreds and perhaps thousands streamed forward at his invitation to some type of spiritual decision. In other contexts, in restricted access countries, for example, less overt expressions of commitment would be used.

Regardless of the method, Graham was absolutely convinced that the gospel demanded decision; it was not simply something to be pondered or admired but to be personally accepted and believed. Nor was this a mere intellectual assent; inherent in the gospel message was the demand for personal repentance and commitment. Typical was the closing invitation of one of his sermons during the 2005 New York Crusade: "I'm asking you tonight to come and be born into God's family. . . . He'll bring a peace and a joy to your heart that you've never known. He'll fill the void that's in your heart. Some of you have been looking for something for years. Others of you are young. But no matter who you are, you are searching for peace and meaning and a purpose in life. What do you have to do? By faith open your heart to Christ and say, 'Lord Jesus, come into my heart'— and He will. . . . Come now and give your life to Christ."[40]

---

38. Billy Graham, "The Greatest News Ever Heard," *Decision Magazine* (April 1995). This was an edited version of a sermon broadcast on *The Hour of Decision*, the radio ministry of the Billy Graham Evangelistic Association.

39. Billy Graham, "The Love of God." Sermon on John 3:16 reprinted in *Decision Magazine* (March 2015).

40. Billy Graham, *The Last Crusade* (New York: Berkeley Praise, 2005), 56–59. This was Graham's final series of public meetings, although he would make occasional appearances at other events.

The Call to Discipleship

The final element in the gospel's message was the call to discipleship. To believe in Christ was to follow him, and this meant turning from old ways of living and embracing his call to become his disciple. "We must emphasize the cost of coming to Christ and following Christ," he urged his fellow evangelists. "Let us always remember that Christ calls men and women not only to trust Him as Savior, but also to follow Him as Lord."[41]

CONTRIBUTIONS TO PREACHING

Undoubtedly, it is too soon to evaluate Billy Graham's full contribution to preaching, nor is it possible to say exactly what his long-term impact on preaching may be. Beyond question, however, his example encouraged countless preachers to reevaluate their preaching and become more diligent in presenting the gospel message with clarity and confidence.

Historian Randall Balmer may be right in his judgment that "there will never be another Billy Graham."[42] Societies change, communications change, and times change. What happened in one generation may not be repeated in the next. But the gospel is timeless, and there will always be those who, by the grace of God, are called and equipped by him to declare its truths to their generation. The gospel that motivated and shaped Billy Graham will motivate and shape them as well, and through them, bring new generations to Christ and his kingdom.

Sermon Excerpt

Things That Never Change[43]

Millions are hoping against hope that the coming year will be better than the last. They want to feel that beneath the swirling tides of change there are some things they can count on. But is there anything changeless to which you and I can look for certainty, hope, and help? There definitely is!

---

41. Graham, *A Biblical Standard for Evangelists*, 52–53. To one interviewer he admitted, "This is where I think I failed in my earlier ministry—I didn't emphasize enough what it costs to follow Christ." James Michael Beam, "I Can't Play God Anymore," *McCall's* (January 1978): 156.

42. Balmer, "He brought modern man," 26.

43. "Things that Never Change," © Billy Graham Evangelistic Association. Used by permission.

First of all, God has not changed. He is and ever will be the sovereign Lord who controls the universe. For two thousand years, tyrants have shaken their fists in the face of God, declaring that they were the rulers of this earth. But God's Word affirms, "He that sitteth in the heavens shall laugh: the Lord shall have them in derision."

Secondly, God's attributes never change. His holiness has not changed. It is still wrong to lie, it's still wrong to steal, it's still wrong to murder, it's still wrong to commit sexual immorality, it's still wrong to tolerate social injustice. Nor has the love of God changed. Love is one of God's greatest attributes. It reaches out to you tonight. God is saying He loves you with an everlasting love. The Bible says, "God is love." God loved us so much that He did not spare His own Son but sent Him to the Cross. No matter what your condition may be tonight, God loves you.

Thirdly, man hasn't changed. God created the first man and woman perfect. But Adam and Eve rebelled against God. Since that fateful hour in the Garden of Eden all men and women have been separated from God by the disease called sin. As a result of their sin, men's needs are the same. They still need peace of mind. They still need forgiveness. They still need hope. They still need cleansing from guilt. They still need to find meaning and fulfillment in life. And they can find these only in God. What Augustine said hundreds of years ago applies to you tonight: You were made for God, and your soul is restless till it finds its rest in Him.

Fourthly, the way of salvation never changes. It is to the Cross of Christ you and I must come to have the guilt of sin and its stain washed away. Jesus said, "I am the way, the truth, and the life: no man cometh unto the Father, but by me."

Fifthly, the promises of God haven't changed. Jesus said, "Come unto me, all ye that labour and are heavy laden, and I will give you rest." That includes you. He will not only save you, He will help you. His promises never change.

The tragedy is that we have turned our backs on God. The darkness of our civilization, with its materialism, its humanism, and its secularism, is ominous and frightening. But God still loves you. He still calls for you to respond in personal faith to Jesus Christ His Son. Wouldn't it be wonderful to know that all your guilt is gone, to have the absolute certainty of eternity before you? By faith put your hand into Christ's hand tonight. ♦

BIBLIOGRAPHY

Brown, Joan Winmill, ed. *Day by Day with Billy Graham: A Daily Devotional*. Minneapolis: World Wide
    Publications, 1976.
Busby, Russell. *Billy Graham: God's Ambassador*. New York: Time-Life, 1999.
Graham, Billy. *A Biblical Standard for Evangelists*. Minneapolis: Billy Graham Evangelistic Association, 1984.
_____. "The Evangelist and His Preaching." Pages 95–100 in *The Work of an Evangelist: Papers from
    the International Conference for Itinerant Evangelists, Amsterdam, The Netherlands, 1983*. Edited by
    James D. Douglas. Minneapolis: World Wide Publications, 1984.
_____. "The Evangelist in a Changing World: It's a New Day." Pages 15–25 in *Equipping for Evange-
    lism: Papers from the North American Conference for Itinerant Evangelists, 1994*. Edited by Charles G.
    Ward. Minneapolis: World Wide Publications, 1996.
_____. "The Gift and Calling of the Evangelist." Pages 15–18 in *The Calling of an Evangelist: Papers
    from the Second International Conference for Itinerant Evangelists, Amsterdam, The Netherlands,
    1986*. Edited by James D. Douglas. Minneapolis: World Wide Publications, 1987.
_____. "The Greatest News Ever Heard." *Decision Magazine* (April 1995).
_____. *The Holy Spirit: Activating God's Power in Your Life*. Dallas: Word, 1988.
_____. "How to Reach People Effectively." Page 103 in *The Mission of the Evangelist: Papers from
    Amsterdam 2000, A Conference for Preaching Evangelists*. Edited by William Conard. Minneapolis:
    World Wide Publications, 2001.
_____. *The Journey: How to Live by Faith in an Uncertain World*. Nashville: W Publishing Group, 2006.
_____. *Just As I Am: The Autobiography of Billy Graham*. 2nd edition. San Francisco: HarperOne, 2007.
_____. *The Last Crusade*. New York: Berkeley Praise, 2005.
_____. "The Love of God." *Decision Magazine*. (March 2015).
_____. *Peace with God*. Rev. ed. Waco, TX: Word, 1984.
_____. "Preaching the Word—Reaching the World." Pages 131–34 in *The Calling of an Evangelist:
    Papers from the Second International Conference for Itinerant Evangelists, Amsterdam, The Netherlands,
    1986*. Edited by James D. Douglas. Minneapolis: World Wide Publications, 1987.
_____. *Storm Warning: Whether Global Recession, Terrorist Threats, or Devastating Natural Disasters,
    These Ominous Shadows Must Bring Us Back to the Gospel*. Nashville: Thomas Nelson, 2010.
Martin, William. *A Prophet with Honor: The Billy Graham Story*. Updated ed. Grand Rapids: Zondervan, 2018.
Pollock, John. *Billy Graham: The Authorized Biography*. New York: McGraw Hill, 1966.
_____. *Billy Graham: Evangelist to the World*. San Francisco: Harper & Row, 1979.
Wacker, Grant. *America's Pastor: Billy Graham and the Shaping of a Nation*. Cambridge: Belknap/Harvard
    University Press, 2014.
Waite, Donald Allen. "The Evangelistic Speaking of Billy Graham, 1949–1959." PhD thesis, Purdue
    University, 1961.

Martin Luther King Jr.
Preaching a Prophetic Dream of Social Justice as Kingdom Work

ALFONZA W. FULWOOD
DENNIS R. MCDONALD
ANIL SOOK DEO

In 1903, W. E. B. Du Bois noted, "The preacher is the most unique personality developed by the [African American] on American soil. A leader, a politician, an orator, a 'boss,' an intriguer, an idealist—all of these he is, and ever, too, the centre of a group of men, now twenty, now a thousand in number." Martin Luther King Jr. (1929–1968), more than any other African American preacher before or after him, embodied Du Bois's description. History views him as a social activist, agitator, ritual leader, political organizer, charismatic figure, world statesman, theologian, "a first citizen of the world," social ethicist, personalistic philosopher, orator, priest, and prophet, but he was preeminently a Baptist preacher. Although he had many detractors, he won the respect and admiration of presidents, vice presidents, senators, congressmen, governors, popes, and other religious leaders in America and throughout the world. Like the prophets of the Old Testament, he converted the public square into his pulpit and proclaimed, "Let Justice roll on like a river, righteousness like a never-failing stream" (Amos 5:24, NKJV). King awakened the moral conscience and influenced an entire nation, changing the course of history concerning the dignity and humanity of all of God's children. He was assassinated at the young age of thirty-nine, yet in his brief life, he accomplished more than other great leaders who lived to be twice his age. Many of his admirers believed he was the most eloquent preacher and the most important figure of the twentieth century. The world has produced two great reformers: the first was in Europe during the sixteenth century, and the second reformer was in North America during the twentieth century. Both of these men were preachers, theologians, pastors, revolutionaries—and named Martin Luther.

461

HISTORICAL BACKGROUND

Martin Luther King Jr. was born in Atlanta, Georgia, on January 15, 1929, to Martin Luther King Sr. and Alberta Williams King.[1] Young Martin was, in many ways, destined to be a preacher. He came from a rich and fruitful family where members championed a preaching legacy of black consciousness. In 1846, Willis Williams, Martin Luther King Jr.'s great-grandfather, was an advocate of social justice at Shiloh Baptist Church, located just outside of Atlanta, Georgia. From the union of Williams and Creecy came A. D. Williams, Martin's maternal grandfather. A. D. became the pastor of Ebenezer Baptist in Atlanta in 1894. A. D. Williams grew in his social consciousness regarding black people and their plight concerning southern segregation. This familial and ancestral background would come to impact Williams's son-in-law, Martin Luther King Sr. Author Garth Baker Fletcher comments on A. D. Williams's influence on King Sr. and ultimately Martin Luther King Jr: "Williams believed and practiced political protest as the necessary way for Negroes. . . . This ability of the Williams-King family to make positive difference in the dignity of Negroes was an important part of the environment within which Martin Luther King, Jr. grew up."[2] The political dissent of his father and grandfather laid the groundwork that gave impetus to King Jr.'s vision for social justice and his preaching ministry.[3]

King Jr. showed signs of unusual intelligence at an early age. His parents found a way to enroll him in school at the age of five. He was talkative and told his class that he was only five. School administration sent him home because he was one year younger than the legal requirement.[4] His academic ability exceeded his peers, which allowed him to skip two grades while attending Booker T. Washington High School. At the age of fifteen he began his college career at Morehouse College, a distinguished historically black college in Atlanta.[5] Both his father and grandfather were graduates of the school. Martin seriously thought

---

1. The authors would like to thank James Earl Massey Jr., who assisted with reviewing the final draft of this chapter.

2. Garth Baker-Fletcher, *Somebodyness: Martin Luther King, Jr., and the Theory of Dignity* (Minneapolis: Fortress, 1993), 6.

3. Martin Luther King Sr., affectionately called 'Daddy King,' was the pastor of Ebenezer Baptist Church in Atlanta, Georgia, for forty-four years. In his own right, he was a prominent civic leader with a proven record of social and political activism, protesting discriminatory practices in the city of Atlanta. King Sr. was born Michael King and his son was named Michael King Jr. In 1934, King Sr. attended the World Baptist Alliance in Europe which convened in Berlin. He toured other areas of historic biblical significance including Palestine and the Holy Land. As a result of this experience, he gained a deeper and more profound appreciation for the gospel ministry. Profoundly affected by the experience in Europe, he changed his name and his eldest son's to Martin Luther King.

4. Jerry Tallmer, "A Man with a Hard Head," in *Martin Luther King, Jr.: A Profile*, ed. C. Eric Lincoln (New York: Hill & Wang, 1970), 4.

5. Morehouse College (formerly Augusta Institute) was one of five colleges started under the leadership

about pursuing a career in medicine or law. Instead, he chose the preaching ministry, largely due to the influence of his father and Benjamin Mays, president of Morehouse College. King Jr. received a BA degree in 1948 and pursued his theological studies at Crozer Theological Seminary in Pennsylvania. He was one of only six African American[6] students in the program, and the first African American elected as president of his senior class. Not surprising, the school named him valedictorian of his class. He earned a BD degree and received several academic honors. Having received a graduate scholarship to pursue doctoral studies to a school of his choice, he entered a graduate program at Boston University and earned a PhD degree in systematic theology in 1955.[7]

While studying at Boston University—a unique melting pot for theological ideas—the young Dr. King met Coretta Scott (1927–2006), a young singer from Marion, Alabama, who was studying at the New England Conservatory of Music. Like Martin, preaching was in her bloodline. Her grandfather had been a preacher, but her father was a businessman. Dr. King and Coretta were married by King Sr. in 1953, and settled in Montgomery, Alabama. They had four children: Yolanda Denise King (1955–2007), Martin Luther King III (born 1957), Dexter Scott King (born 1961), and Bernice Albertine King (born 1963).

Public Ministry

King accepted the invitation to serve as pastor of the Dexter Avenue Baptist Church in Montgomery, Alabama, in 1954, at the young age of twenty-six. The Dexter Avenue church was an upper-middle-class congregation with many members who matched well with King's scholarly background. A commodious parsonage was provided, and the church paid him the highest salary of any African American in the city.[8] At this juncture in his life, an event occurred which placed America on an inevitable collision course with a prophet with a dream of social and political reform—his life summoned by the events of the "continued rise of African American expectations and protest."[9] What happened next in connection with events of protest thrust him into the helm of leadership, which transcended family, Dexter Avenue, and Montgomery, Alabama.

---

of Elias Camp Morris, who was elected the first president of the National Baptist Convention, a position he held for twenty-seven years.

6. The term "African American" will be used interchangeably with the term "black" based on time periods and developments in America.

7. Tallmer, "A Man with a Hard Head," 4. King's dissertation title was "Comparing the Religious Views of Paul Tillich and Henry Nelson Wieman."

8. Ibid., xviii.

9. David Levering Lewis, "Martin Luther King, Jr., and the Promise of Nonviolent Populism," in *Black Leaders in the Twentieth Century*, eds. John Hope Franklin and August Meier (Chicago: University of Illinois Press, 1982), 277–78.

In 1955, an African American seamstress named Rosa Parks, riding a seg-regated bus, refused to give up her seat to a white passenger. Law enforcement arrested her for breaking Alabama's Jim Crow segregation laws that made Afri-can Americans second-class citizens. Parks's act brought about a series of events that began with the Montgomery Bus Boycott. Her action inspired the entire African American community in the city to protest. Leaders of the African American community organized the Montgomery Improvement Association to steer the boycott and elected Martin Luther King Jr. as president.[10] The boycott was successful and lifted King to national prominence. Now emboldened and preoccupied with issues regarding civil rights, he had little time available to ful-fill his pastoral duties at Dexter Avenue. In 1960, he made a decision to leave the church, telling his congregation while giving his resignation, "History has thrust something upon me from which I cannot turn away."[11]

Martin Luther King Jr. used the success of the boycott for leverage with other issues created by the long history of social inequality in America. The civil rights movement accelerated, and King galvanized wide support not only from the South but also by the media across the United States. In 1957, a group of African American preachers across denominational lines founded the Southern Christian Leadership Conference (SCLC) and they elected him as its president.[12] Interestingly, King had long explored various intellectual quests for a method to eliminate social ills."[13] Considering several ethical and social theories, he resolved that the "method of nonviolence was one of the most potent weapons available to oppressed people in their struggle for freedom."[14] For him, "nonviolence became more than a method for which [he] gave intellectual accent; it became a commit-ment to a way of life."[15] In practical terms, he employed a method of nonviolent direct action (protest). His intent was to cause a crisis. When a crisis occurred, it created an opportunity for negotiation. King's philosophy of nonviolence spread to African American colleges across the country and gave rise to the nonviolent student movement.[16]

Although Martin Luther King Jr. received national prominence for leading

10. Jim Crow laws prevented African Americans from sitting in the same row as whites. See Adam Fairclough, *Martin Luther King, Jr.* (Athens: University of Georgia Press, 1990), 17.

11. Robert Jakoubek, *Martin Luther King, Jr.: Civil Rights Leader* (Danbury, CT: Chelsea, 1989), 39. See a report of King's ministry at this church, Zelia S. Evans and J. T. Alexander, eds., *The Dexter Avenue Baptist Church: 1877–1977* (Montgomery: Dexter Avenue Baptist Church, 1978), especially pages 68–144.

12. Richard Lischer, "King, Martin Luther," in *Concise Encyclopedia of Preaching*, eds. William H. Willimon and Richard Lischer (Louisville: Westminster John Knox, 1995), 288–90.

13. James M. Washington, ed., "Pilgrimage to Nonviolence," *A Testament of Hope: The Essential Writings of Martin Luther King, Jr.* (San Francisco: Harper & Row, 1986), 37.

14. Ibid., 38.

15. Ibid.

16. Ibid., 43–53.

a movement that arguably changed the course of history, it came at great sacrifice and cost. On January 30, 1956, a bomb exploded, destroying a part of his house. He constantly received death threats, and his family lived in the shadows of danger. Southern whites viscerally attacked him, labeling him a communist, among other things. Southern governors, including other elected officials and law enforcement officers, viewed him and the civil rights movement as breakers of "law and order."[17] Law enforcement officers arrested and jailed him twenty-nine times. During the many protest marches, his detractors spit on him and threw objects at him, sometimes nearly knocking him to the ground.[18] Radical and militant African American groups such as the Black Power movement rejected his nonviolent-resistance method. Some African American clergy opposed his political and social activism, believing that his action went beyond the nature and purpose of the church and the pulpit. Even the National Baptist Convention U.S.A., Inc. (NBC), led by its fundamentalist president J. H. Jackson and a huge part of his constituency, rejected King's social action, protesting that it hurt the cause of race relations and progress for African Americans.[19] The political ideological differences within the convention caused a great divide that split the convention. Thus, the Progressive National Baptist Convention (PNBC) was founded under the leadership of Martin Luther King Jr. and Gardner C. Taylor, legendary pastor of Concord Baptist Church in New York. Most of the younger and more educated ministers in the northern states who held a "black consciousness" view joined the progressive convention.[20] Moreover, King arguably gave up the comfort of a modest middle-class life as a pastor. Finally, he paid the ultimate sacrifice with his life. On April 4, 1968, at the young age of thirty-nine, while standing on the balcony of the Lorraine Motel in Memphis, Tennessee, he was assassinated by a gunshot fired by James Earl Ray.

The day before his death, King spoke in support of striking sanitation workers at Mason Temple in Memphis. It was his famous "I've Been to the Mountaintop" speech. During the delivery of the speech, he hinted about his death and mortality as if he knew it was imminent. A master of the African American preaching tradition, King aroused the crowd with his oration and cadence, saying:

---

17. See Michelle E. Alexander, *The New Jim Crow: Mass Incarceration in the Age of Colorblindness* (New York: The New Press, 2011), 140–158. Also see Lionel Lokos, *House Divided: The Life and Legacy of Martin Luther King* (New Rochelle: Arlington, 1968), 299–499.

18. See Jakoubek, *Martin*, 128.

19. See C. Eric Lincoln and Lawrence H. Mamiya, *The Black Church in the African American Experience* (Durham: Duke University Press, 1990), 196–239.

20. See Alfonza W. Fullwood, "A Study of Gardner C. Taylor's Theology of Preaching as a Decisive Factor Shaping His Theory of Preaching: Implications for Homiletical Pedagogy" (PhD diss., Southeastern Baptist Theological Seminary, 2012), 141–43.

I don't know what will happen now. We have got difficult days ahead. But it doesn't matter with me because I've been to the mountaintop. Like anyone else, I would like to live a long life. But I'm not concerned with that. I just want to do God's will and He has allowed me to go up the mountain. I see the promised land. I may not get there with you, but I want you to know tonight that we as a people will get to the promised land. I am happy tonight that I am not worried about anything. I'm not fearing any man. Mine eyes have seen the glory of the coming of the Lord.[21]

King's death caused African Americans unrest throughout the country, resulting in riots, burnings, injuries, and loss of life.[22] Literally thousands of admirers paid their respect to this fallen crusader of justice and peace when he was laid to rest on April 9, 1968. Many federal and state officials and dignitaries came to Atlanta for King's funeral. His death attracted as much attention as did his dream to change America.[23]

While King's efforts to fulfill his dream of equality and fair play cost him so much, he was recognized for his work to reshape this nation's moral character. He received hundreds of awards and honors for his effort to bring human dignity to all Americans. Most notable was the Nobel Peace Prize in 1964 at the age of thirty-five, which made him the youngest to ever receive the award. Others included: Man of the Year, awarded by *Time* magazine in 1963; Who's Who in America; National Newspaper Publisher's Russwurm Award in 1957; and the Presidential Medal of Freedom (posthumously) in 1977. Furthermore, some major federal legislation was passed and Supreme Court decisions handed down because of the influence of King, including: the Civil Rights Act of 1964, banning discrimination in employment and public accommodation; the Voting Rights Act of 1965, restoring and protecting the right to vote; and the Fair Housing Act of 1966, banning housing discrimination relative to sales and rentals. His challenge to America with regard to the dignity of all people of every race held far-reaching future implications. His efforts paved the way for black progress in America, especially in the South. For sure, these gains represented the fulfilment of a dream of a Baptist preacher. He not only used the church but the public square as a pulpit to resound the words of the prophet Amos, "Let justice roll down like water and righteousness like a mighty stream" (Amos 5:24).

From the time Martin Luther King Jr. led the Montgomery Bus Boycott in

---

21. Coretta Scott King, *The Words of Martin Luther King, Jr.* (New York: New Market, 1958), 94.
22. Lischer, "King, Martin Luther," 288–90.
23. See Dr. Mervyn A. Warren, *King Came Preaching: The Pulpit Power of Dr. Martin Luther King Jr.* (Downers Grove, IL: InterVarsity Press, 2001), 43.

1954, his message focused on improving the plight of African Americans in the United States. However, in 1968, his "speaking truth to power" broadened to include other concerns that went beyond the issue of African American ethnic equality. He began functioning as a voice for the poor, and his reading of the Old Testament prophets led him toward alliances with Jewish-American leaders. Moreover, he addressed the militarism of the United States, calling the war in Vietnam unjust. Such concerns were not African American issues but issues for all Americans, irrespective of race. But none of these issues in and of themselves or collectively make what King accomplished extraordinary without viewing the history and context of what the Jim Crow system looked like in the Deep South where he grew up. More specifically, the particular area of Montgomery, where the Rosa Parks incident launched the social justice vision of King, was immensely important.

Social and Political Context

To appreciate the significance of King's social justice vision that reshaped the moral character of a nation, it is important to understand the social and political context, or backdrop, of the time. The 1950s was an increasingly tumultuous period in America, especially in the South. Several situations were in play simultaneously, creating the perfect storm. First, Jim Crow was based on a theory of white superiority and African American inferiority, creating inhumane conditions for an entire community. Continued "justification and defense" of such a system carried enormous economic and political implications.[24] Second, African Americans were constantly subjected to racial terror heightened by acts of lynching as a means of social control. Such acts of human atrocity can be traced to slavery, the Civil War, and the Reconstruction period.[25] Third, and even more consequential, the United States Supreme Court began to make rulings against segregation. In 1954, the court's decision in the case of Brown v. Board of Education ruled that separate educational facilities were inherently unequal. They believed that segregation was a denial of the equal protection of the law. Fourth, African American apathy waned and expectation and protest grew, resulting from a rise in "black consciousness" and self-identity, stirred by strong voices from African American pulpits. And fifth, the African American community, under the leadership of the civil rights groups, was mobilized and "demonstrated before the court and world opinion the urgent need for change."[26]

---

24. See C. Vann Woodward, *The Strange Career of Jim Crow* (New York: Oxford University Press, 1957).

25. Washington, *A Testament of Hope,* xix.

26. Washington, "Nonviolence: The Only Road to Freedom" in *A Testament of Hope,* 54.

Keep in view that in 1954, Montgomery, Alabama, held the distinction of being the most segregated city in the South. The city was called "the cradle of the confederacy" and was the confederacy's first capital.[27] Of Montgomery's 120,000 citizens, 48,000 were African Americans. Often their houses had no electricity or running water and were located on dirty, unpaved streets. The African American community relied on city buses to handle their transportation needs. Conditions which the community faced were the consequences of economic injustices. Over half of the African American men and women were domestic workers. Restrooms and drinking fountains were marked "whites only" and "colored only," and people of different colors could not ride in the same taxi together.[28] The segregation of public transportation and restaurants created much resentment and unrest. Even worse, segregation also caused a widespread sense of "apathy" in terms of African Americans' acceptance of their situation.[29] However, Montgomery was not unlike other Southern cities where segregation was a way of life. Little was done to bring about the changes ordered at the federal level. Supreme Court decisions had little effect in Montgomery and other Southern states.[30]

Up to this point, little has been said concerning the theology that informed Martin Luther King Jr.'s social justice dream. Nor has there been any attention given to his theology of preaching and how it shaped his homiletical method. Even more important is the question whether his homiletical method and style of delivery represented a departure from or "pivotal marker" of the rich and fertile preaching heritage of the black church. And, if a departure or marker, how has it influenced the way African American preaching is done today? These areas will be examined and questions will be answered next.

THEOLOGY OF PREACHING

At first glance, Martin Luther King Jr.'s curriculum vitae looks like one of a political official. One can easily come away thinking he was an elected public official representing his African American constituency. Or, at best, one would come away with the impression that he relegated preaching and the black church as secondary. However, nothing could be further from the truth. His preaching skills stirred the heart and the moral conscience of a nation. The African

---

27. Ibid.
28. Richard Lischer, *The Preacher King: Martin Luther King Jr. and the Word That Moved America* (New York: Oxford University Press, 1995), 72–73.
29. Jakoubek, *Martin*, 41.
30. Montgomery showed no intent or desire to comply. The court attempted to end segregation, but it failed to give or recommend an implementation plan to achieve full integration. See Ibid.

American church functioned as the "womb" of black culture and the civil rights movement.[31] Churches became key centers in unifying and rallying the community. They became major points of mobilization for thousands of demonstrators and meetings.[32]

Martin Luther King Jr. saw himself as a preacher of the gospel of Jesus Christ. This is evident in his own words concerning his preaching pedigree: "I am . . . the son of a Baptist preacher, the grandson of a Baptist preacher, and the great grandson of a Baptist preacher. The church is my life and I have given my life to the church."[33] King did not give his life to civil rights but to the church as a gospel preacher. He saw himself as a preacher who was a voice of the black church. In fact, it troubled him that people saw him as a civil rights leader more than a preacher.[34] On another occasion he noted, "I am fundamentally a clergyman, a Baptist preacher."[35] For this reason, he constantly reminded people that he was a preacher. Nonetheless, the civil rights movement exposed the nation and the world to one of the most eloquent preachers of the twentieth century.[36] Executing his brilliant oratory, "he routinely cited the Bible as the authority for his social activities, and cast the civil rights movement in the light of biblical events and characters."[37] Before a national audience, King articulated his social and political message in a homiletical fashion. O. C. Edwards refers to the preaching of King as a "homiletical epiphany" and "the emergence of African American preaching in majority consciousness."[38] King moved the classical homiletic of the African American preacher beyond the black church context. Through the vehicle of news media coverage, the rest of America was exposed to and experienced the homiletic "performance" and "power" of the preaching tradition long known within the African American church.[39]

King's homiletical style was not a departure from the roots and heritage of the African American preaching tradition. The way he preached represented the homiletical style that gave African American preaching its distinctiveness.[40] As with most African American preachers, he imitated the tradition that birthed him. But his social and political message represented a pivotal marker for social

---

31. Lincoln and Mamiya, *The Black Church*, 17.
32. Ibid., 211–12.
33. Warren, *King Came*, 15.
34. See Clyde E. Fant and William M. Pinson Jr., *20 Centuries of Great Preaching: An Encyclopedia of Preaching*, 12 vols. (Waco: Word, 1971), 12:358.
35. Lischer, *Preacher*, 3.
36. O. C. Edwards, "History of Preaching," in *Concise Encyclopedia of Preaching*, ed. William H. Willimon (Louisville: Westminster John Knox, 1995), 224–25.
37. Lischer, *Preacher*, 4.
38. O. C. Edwards Jr., *A History of Preaching*, 2 vols. (Nashville: Abingdon, 2004), 1:703.
39. Ibid., 1:704.
40. Mitchell, "African American Preaching," 7–8.

justice preaching in the public square. Still, the social relevance of the black church tradition nurtured and informed his social gospel homiletic.

African American church historian Henry H. Mitchell noted that the social relevance of the black church is not a "new phenomenon." [41] Since the nineteenth century, the black church and the African American preacher in particular, played a significant role in shaping social, political, and economic reform.[42] Even before the Civil War, most of the abolitionists were the great black orators of that time.[43] They laid the groundwork, becoming a precursor of King's social equality dream. They passed the baton of homiletical genius to ensuing generations of preachers such as King.

More than any other African American preacher, King's homiletical style revealed a deeper insight into the power of the pulpit and the social relevance of the gospel.[44] In many ways, he "modeled a new role for the black preacher and a new militancy for the black church in the South."[45] How is it that a nation was "so profoundly affected by a minister of a little black church in Montgomery, Alabama?"[46] Arguably it was his preaching DNA that accounted for his influence on America. He became the "heir apparent" to a rich preaching legacy of protest that began with the "invisible institution" situated on the slave plantations of the South.[47]

An understanding of King's theology of preaching begins with an understanding of his theology. His early exposure was to the fundamentalist leanings of his father. Later he was exposed to the liberal theology of Crozer and the Boston School of Theology. While he found liberal theology useful, he held concerns with its theological anthropology or doctrine of humanity. Specifically, liberalism went too far with the natural goodness of human beings. As an option, he considered the neoorthodoxy of Karl Barth, Emil Brunner, Reinhold Niebuhr, and Paul Tillich. Yet and still, he pushed back on aspects of neoorthodoxy because "it did not provide an adequate answer to basic questions" concerning humanity.[48] King explained:

---

41. Ibid.
42. Lewis, "Promise," 277.
43. Mitchell, "African American Preaching," 7.
44. Edwards, "History of Preaching," 224–25.
45. Lischer, "King, Martin Luther, Jr.," 290.
46. Ibid.
47. Mitchell, "African American Preaching," 4. The "invisible institution" was a secret and illegal gathering of slaves, usually led by a slave folk preacher for the creation of their own worship experience that met their existential needs. These meetings occurred late at night in slave huts, brush harbors, down by the creek, and under trees, removed from detection of the master. Mitchell referred to the "invisible institution" as the "underground church" that met for its own African adaptation of Christianity.
48. Warrren, *King Came*, 18–19.

So although liberalism left me unsatisfied on the question of the nature of man, I found no refuge in neo-orthodoxy. I am now convinced that the truth about man is found neither in liberalism nor in neo-orthodoxy. Each represents a partial truth. A large segment of Protestant liberalism defined man only in terms of his essential nature, his capacity for good; neo-orthodoxy tended to define man only in terms of his existential nature, his capacity to evil. An adequate understanding of man is found neither in the thesis of liberalism nor the antithesis of neo-orthodoxy, but in a synthesis which reconciles the truths of both.[49]

King found himself close to the middle of two extremes, taking a moderate position on liberalism and neoorthodoxy. As will be shown in his theology of preaching, his theological stance served his social gospel preaching.

FROM THEOLOGY TO METHODOLOGY

King held specific assumptions regarding what to preach and how to preach, based on his desired outcomes. For the most part, seven factors drove the way he structured and delivered his sermons, which make up the basis for his homiletical theology. These factors hold implications on form, structure, method, rhetoric, and theology. First, King's preaching pedigree was a decisive factor in the way he preached. He was exposed to both the paternal and maternal preaching legacies of his father and grandfather. He was also surrounded with a "cloud of witnesses" of great black preachers in Atlanta and beyond. They modelled the best of black preaching, "demonstrating the compatibility of academic learning and homiletical eloquence."[50] King received his theological training, including several preaching courses, in white seminaries. But he did not preach like his white counterparts who took the same courses with him.[51] What gave his preaching its distinctiveness was not just related to seminary experience but the cultural expression and communication style of the black preaching tradition he inherited.[52] He exhibited a hybrid model, that is, the bringing together of two traditions. He combined the best of what William H. Pipes called "old-fashioned

49. Ibid.
50. King Jr. was exposed to a rich fraternity of skilled preachers such as William Holmes Boarders of Wheat Street Baptist Church, known for the richness of his poetic imaginative expressions, and Benjamin Mays. Others were Howard Thurman, Mordecai Johnson, Vernon Johns, Gardner C. Taylor, and J. Pius Barbour. See Mitchell, "African American Preaching," 288.
51. Ibid., 2.
52. Ibid.

negro preaching" traits and academic homiletics.[53] Despite all of his superb academic rigor and exposure, it did not eclipse the "folk preaching" impulse of the South that flowed through his veins.

The second factor that influenced King's homiletical assumptions and preaching practice was his exposure to personalist and liberal theology. King was exposed to personalism at Crozer. Professor George W. Davis introduced him to Edgar Sheffield Brightman's theology of personalism.[54] After completing his studies at Crozer, King went to Boston University, where he delved more deeply into personalism under the teaching of Brightman and L. Harold DeWolf.[55] Not surprisingly, they had an influence on King's philosophical and theological development.[56] King himself confessed, "Both men greatly stimulated my thinking. It was mainly under these teachers that I studied personalistic philosophy—the theory that the clue to the meaning of ultimate reality is found in personality."[57] He continued: "This personal idealism remains today my basic philosophical conviction."[58] It was, therefore, this idea of inherent value and worth, the notion of "a moral order and the social character of human existence" that reinforced King's "ethical consciousness."[59]

The themes of human dignity for all and the inherent decency of humanity in spite of the evil of some, were woven into King's speeches and sermons. This explains King's philosophy of never causing injury to another person in spite of the injury inflicted on him. He noted, "But we must never forget that there is something within human nature that can respond to goodness, that man is not totally depraved; to put it in theological terms, the image of God is never totally gone."[60] He crafted his sermons in this way and appealed to the moral consciousness of America based on his personalist underpinnings.

The third factor that infused the homiletical assumptions of King was his drawing from a corpus of "Negro spirituals," songs, narratives, poetry, and

---

53. See William H. Pipes, *Say Amen, Brother! Old-Time Negro Preaching: A Study in American Frustration* (Detroit: Wayne State University Press, 1992); and Frank A. Thomas, *Introduction to the Practice of African American Preaching* (Nashville: Abingdon, 2016), 4.

54. Personalism is a dominant and central theme espoused in some branches of liberal theology. This idea essentially holds that humanity is made in the image of God, therefore the essence of human life is the personal dimension that elevates humanity above all other forms of life. Thus, a human being is treated qualitatively better than other forms of animal life. Essentially personalism asserts the worth, value, and inherent dignity of humanity. This explains the usefulness of such a philosophy that grounds King Jr.'s theology and his views on segregation.

55. William D. Watley, *Roots of Resistance: The Nonviolent Ethic of Martin Luther King, Jr.* (Pennsylvania: Judson, 1985), 31–32.

56. Ibid.

57. Martin Luther King, Jr., *Stride Toward Freedom: The Montgomery Story* (New York: Harper & Row, 1958), 82.

58. Ibid.

59. Watley, *Roots of Resistance*, 31–32.

60. Washington, "Love, Law and Civil Disobedience," in *A Testament of Hope*, 48.

testimony. Lodged in these genres was the African American story of "how they made it over." This body of collective memory and experience provides a window into the belief systems of African Americans about God, suffering, and an eschatological hope of a better day. As Thabiti M. Anyabwile notes: "One has to look not in the academy but in sermons, slave narratives, political speeches and popular writings for traces of the early beliefs of African Americans since the 1700s."[61] For King, these sources represented a treasure chest of information—a homiletical inventory of material. With homiletical skill and precision, he wove them into the biblical narratives and freedom motif of the Bible. In many of his sermons, he evoked what Richard Lischer calls "skillful manipulation of memorized set pieces organized in classical fashion around topics that he inserted as needed into any sermon or speech."[62] For instance, during the March on Washington, King stood before the Lincoln Memorial. In his "I Have a Dream" speech, he cited a portion of a hymn ingrained in the memory of African Americans. In the homiletical cadence of the African American preaching tradition, he reminded his audience of some 250,000 people about longing for freedom. In the nation's hearing, he cited what happens when "freedom rings." In the climax of his speech, he shouted words of the African American spiritual, "Free at last! Free at last! Thank God almighty, we are free at last."[63]

The fourth factor that shaped King's homiletical assumptions was patriotism. He devoted portions of his sermons and speeches to the patriotic tradition such as the Federal Constitution and the Bill of Rights, the Declaration of Independence, and the Emancipation Proclamation. Such devotion, flowing from his liberal education, moved him away from a pie-in-the-sky and otherworldly theology prevalent in some black religious fundamentalist thought. Embedded in his sermons were the principles and the spirit of a nation that was founded on the idea of freedom as an "inalienable right, among these life, liberty, and the pursuit of happiness." In sermonic fashion, he constantly cited the words of the founding fathers and the framers of the Constitution. In the famous "I Have a Dream Speech," King exclaimed, "I have a dream that one day this nation will rise up and live out the true meaning of its creed: we hold these truths to be self-evident; that all men are created equal."[64] Further into the speech, he again drew from another important source with a resounding voice, "My country 'tis of thee, sweet land of liberty, of thee I sing. Land where my fathers died, land of

---

61. Thabiti M. Anyabwile, *The Decline of African American Theology: From Biblical Faith to Cultural Captivity* (Downers Grove, IL: IVP Academic, 2007), 17.
62. Lischer, "King, Martin Luther, Jr.," 289.
63. King, *The Words*, 98.
64. Ibid., 95.

the pilgrim's pride, from every mountain, let freedom ring."[65] In Memphis, the day before his martyrdom, closing out his speech in "ecstatic climax," he drew from a patriotic hymn, "My eyes have seen the glory of the coming of the Lord."[66] These patriotic pieces were reoccurring themes in King's sermons and speeches.

The fifth factor is the rhetorical assumptions that shaped King's understanding of preaching as the power of language.[67] These rhetorical assumptions that underlie his preaching lifted the effectiveness of his sermonic delivery; Martin Luther King Jr. elevated the use of rhetorical devices in his preaching. He routinely peppered his sermons with such devices for persuasive theological and sociopolitical arguments. One of his foremost "rhetorical strategies was to locate his appeal within the context of cherished religious, cultural, and patriotic traditions."[68] He quoted the "Old Testament and John Donne, Paul and Socrates, Aquinas and Emerson, Shakespeare and Jefferson, Hymn-writers and Paul Tillich."[69] Even he acknowledged that "eloquent statement of ideas is his greatest talent, strongest tradition, and most constant interest."[70]More likely than not, King's studies at Crozer influenced his strong use of rhetorical tools. He took nine courses in homiletics while he was a student at Crozer. Robert Keighton was his principal instructor. "Keighton brought to the classroom a preoccupation with style and the classical forms of argument."[71] He drew on Augustine's view that religion was about public persuasion. He exposed King to the "shorthand prescription of oratory, proving, painting and persuasion."[72] These streams of metaphoric and "poetic cadence" were intentional homiletical strategies that King executed. Lischer and Valentino have pointed out five dominant forms of sermonic repetition found in King's preaching.[73]

Within each sermon series, King used metaphor and imagery that favored his audience. Not only did he use metaphorical language, but he used it with a poetic rhythm, which delighted his audience. Examples of metaphoric images include but are not limited to "the iron feet of oppression," "the dark chambers

---

65. Ibid., 96.

66. Ibid., 94.

67. Lischer, "King, Martin Luther, Jr.," 289.

68. Keith D. Miller, "Martin Luther King, Jr. Borrows a Revolution: Argument, Audience, and Implications of a Secondhand Universe," *College English* 48, no.3 (1986): 249.

69. Ibid.

70. L. D. Reddick, *Crusader without Violence: A biography of Martin Luther King, Jr.* (New York: Harper & Brothers, 1959, 11.

71. Keighton taught his preaching students the power and effectiveness of argument and the use of a sermon outline that was useful in achieving persuasion. He taught King the skill of climbing through arguments of increasing power toward the conclusion the preacher hoped to make convincing. See http://delanceyplace. blogspot.com/2006/03delanceyplace18.html

72. Lischer, *Preacher*, 39–71.

73. These five forms are alliteration, assonance, anaphora, epistrophe, and amplification. For a further explanation of these forms, see Lischer, *Preacher*, 128–29.

of pessimism," "the dark and desolate valleys of despair," and many others which were fixtures in King's speeches and sermons.[74] King stitched together ideas with images of something material so his reader or listener could have a mental picture. His vocal talents were musical yet couched in rhetorical devices that caused his listeners to be more receptive and anticipatory. He effectively represented the African American tradition of colorful, lively, and picturesque sermonic imagination.

The sixth factor that drove King's homiletical assumptions was his use of voice. Preaching in the black church is an "acoustic affair," where stylistic sound became part of the "interpretative method."[75] He argued, "A sermon is not an essay to be read but a discourse to be heard. It should be a convincing appeal to a listening congregation. Therefore, a sermon is directed toward the listening ear rather than the reading eye."[76] The written form of King's sermon cannot "adequately convey the pathos of King, Jr.'s voice."[77] King used his voice like a string instrument, utilizing a range of cadences, tones, or melodies carried by his low, mid, and high range baritone. This "homiletical musicality" embedded in his delivery represented a long-standing homiletical birthright of his preaching tradition.[78] As Olin P. Moyd explained, "Style is a part of the immaterial context of African American preaching."[79] Style as related to musicality also represents a "cultural identity" that carries celebrative and experiential value but meaning as well.[80] However, if tone of voice trumps rational content of the sermon, arguably, it goes against homiletical practice in North America. This idea is especially true in Reformed evangelical thinking, where *logos* reigns in supremacy over *pathos*. King held the two not in competition but in cooperation with one another, creating a sermonic symphony. Lischer called King's voice synthesizing (musicality) a 'meaning' that "transcends cognitive analysis."[81]

Finally, King's use of Scripture represented the seventh factor relative to

---

74. Marvin A. Warren discusses eighteen such elements of figure of speech and rhetorical devices in King's language: alliteration, anachronism, anaphora, asyndeton, comparison, contrast, enantiosis, epiphonema, erotesis, the historical present, irony, metaphor, oxymoron, paramonasia, prolepsis, restatement, simile, and synecdoche. See Warren, *King Came*, 145–51.

75. Dale P. Andrews, *Practical Theology for Black Churches: Bridging Black Theology and African American Folk Religion* (Louisville: Westminster John Knox, 2002), 19–20. "Acoustic affair" comes from an idea of Davis L. Larsen. See Davis L. Larsen, *The Anatomy of Preaching: Identifying the Issues in Preaching* (Grand Rapids: Kregel, 1989), 190.

76. Martin Luther King, Jr., *Strength to Love* (New York: Harper & Row, 1963), x.

77. Lischer, *Preacher*, 134.

78. Musicality is a term coined by Evans E. Crawford concerning the way the preacher uses timing, pause, inflection, pace, and other qualities as a way of "awaking such a response" relative to audiences." See Evans E. Crawford and Thomas H. Troeger, *The Hum: Call And Response in African American Preaching* (Nashville: Abingdon, 1995), 16.

79. Olin P. Moyd, *The Sacred Art: Preaching and Theology in the African American Tradition* (Pennsylvania: Judson, 1995), 88.

80. Henry H. Mitchell, *Blacking Preaching: The Recovery of a Powerful Art* (Nashville: Abingdon, 1990), 89.

81. Lisher, *Preacher*, 134.

the manner of how he did his preaching. His theology of Scripture determined how the biblical text actually functioned in his sermon. He was careful to select certain passages and themes to serve his preaching purpose. Predictably, he frequently drew from Exodus and other freedom motif biblical events. King used primarily two interpretative approaches to Scripture aimed to achieve a desired end. First, he used a typological approach of identification, continuation, and continuity. Biblical characters such as Moses and the people of Israel were relived in the experience of African Americans seeking freedom from oppression.[82] He was able to move from biblical characters and events to contemporary and current problems of race by way of typology. In his sermon "The Birth of a New Nation," he inserted a liberation typology, "We find ourselves breakin' a-loose from an evil Egypt, trying to move through the wilderness toward the promised land of cultural integration." He appropriated biblical characters and events in a way that they became existentially relevant to the plight of African Americans.

The second interpretative approach King used was an allegorical method, which allowed him to affix a different meaning unrelated to the historical-cultural and theological interpretation. For example, in his sermon "The Three Dimensions of a Complete Life," he did not literally interpret but rather figuratively discussed the dimensions of an individual's life. He noted: "The length of life is the inward drive to achieve one's personal ends and ambitions, as inward concern for one's own welfare and achievement."[83] He continued allegorically, "The breadth of life is the outward concern for the welfare of others. The height of life is the upward reach for God."[84] Even in this sermon, there is a personalist assumption relative to high ideas concerning the potential of the individual. These two interpretative approaches represented a way to spiritualize the text for an existentially relevant application. While King's use of Scripture borders on an existential hermeneutic, he believed in the authority of Scripture, for he constantly used Scripture as his primary source.[85]

METHODOLOGY FOR PREACHING

King used several homiletical methods that revealed his theology. These methods were not by chance but directly related to what he desired to achieve in his

---

82. Warren, *King Came*, 53.

83. King, Jr., *Strength to Love*, 69.

84. Ibid.

85. King Jr. continually used the authority of Scripture, both Old and New Testaments, to challenge the social order of America. In his sermons and speeches, he cited and quoted Scripture as a source of authority, especially when dealing with the themes of love, forgiveness, mercy, peace, and justice. See Lassiter, *African American Preaching Tradition*, 52–61.

preaching agenda. In other words, whatever King assumed about the purpose for his preaching determined his method of preaching. His homiletical method served his preaching aim. He dedicated his preaching purpose to address social justice issues that had become a part of the fabric of American culture.

The dominant method King used was the topical method, which provided greater latitude and flexibility. Such a freedom allowed him to begin the sermon with issues of the community. He moved from community issues or topics to the text as opposed to moving from text to community issues. This method is quite different than the textual or expository approach where the text guides the sermon title, idea, and structural matters. King allowed the important and critical issues of the community to guide his sermon title, idea, points, and/or structure. To state it another way, "Instead of following the contours of the biblical text, the topical sermon identified and organized an important idea."[86]

Structurally, King typically followed an outline that divided the topic into three sections or divisions.[87] This method was traditionally known as a classification outline. An example of this outline is his sermon entitled "On Being a Good Neighbor," based on the text of Luke 10:29. The sermon focused on the notion of altruism existing on three levels, including universal altruism, dangerous altruism, and excessive altruism. Another example is his sermon (cited above) entitled "Three Dimensions of a Complete Life," based on Revelation 21:16. King divided the topic into three sections. Divisions included: length of life is the person's inward drive; breadth of life is the person's outward concern for others; and height of life is the person's upward reach for God.[88] This methodological strategy served his personalist theology. From a structural standpoint, King's body of sermons and speeches generally followed this topical outline.

King used various argumentative forms in the execution of the topical method. The most common persuasive argument form was the Hegelian thesis-antithesis-synthesis approach.[89] Many of his sermons established two ideas in contrast, which for all practical purposes represented the thesis and antithesis. Then he resolved the tension by offering a third option, which represented the synthesis. King utilized this argumentative strategy as seen in the two sermon examples above, and especially evident in the sermon "Three Dimensions of a

---

86. Lischer, *Preacher*, 65.

87. King Jr.'s topical sermon outline followed the Halford E. Luccock outline format. See Halford E. Luccock, *In the Minister's Workshop* (Nashville: Abingdon-Cokesbury, 1944), 118–47.

88. See King Jr.'s seventeen published sermons, which followed the classification outline of Luccock relative to the topic driving the structure of the sermon. King, Jr., *Strength to Love.*

89. The Hegelian method, from the 1800s German Idealist philosopher, is a method of logic based on the concept of advancing contradictory arguments of thesis, antithesis, and seeking their resolution by synthesis. In this sense the sermon takes on two opposing positions, finding resolution between the two to create the third and ideal position. He argues that truth is found not in the thesis or antithesis but in an emergent synthesis.

Complete Life." He proposed two value dimensions, but they hold tension. His third dimension had to do with the pursuit of God, which is far better than the first two dimensions. He resolved the tension between two positions. Yet a third sermon reflects similar design of persuasive argument. It is entitled "A Tough Mind and a Tender Heart" (cited earlier) based on Matthew 10:16. In this sermon, King proposed two opposites each relating to the struggle for freedom. The two opposites included the need for a "tough mind" and a "tender heart." His third point (synthesis) dealt with the need for "nonviolent resistance." And the first two opposites were found useful to implement the resistance. However, he maintained that the "tough mind" must not lead to violence and the "tender heart" must not lead to "complacency and do-nothingness."[90] Although King favored the topical method, in no way did he jettison his beliefs and use of Scripture with respect to his sermons. In most of his sermons, he delved right into the preaching passage, making thoughtful comments. He included comments about the historical, cultural, and theological contexts as part of the introduction. And he intermittently drew from the biblical text in the actual development of his topic outline.[91]

CONTRIBUTIONS TO PREACHING

Martin Luther King Jr.'s life and preaching influenced a nation and, in some regards, the world. Arguably, people all over the world have benefited in some way from his message of dignity for all humanity. Nonetheless, an important observation concerning King is the impact he had on the African American church and community. Even more important is the influence he had on African American preachers across the country and those who worked closely with him in achieving the goals of the Southern Christian Leadership Conference. These pulpit leaders were, themselves, transformed from the traditionalism and somewhat other-worldly outlook often held by the African American church.

Martin Luther King Jr. elevated the social relevance of the African American church and African American preaching. He "brought a new image, a fresh message, and a renewed zeal to the black pulpit."[92] The Progressive National Baptist Convention was founded by a constituency of African American preachers who committed themselves to the aggressive social action agenda of King. Today that Convention remains committed to its agenda. King's legacy also included

---

90. See King, Jr., *Strength to Love*, 1–7.
91. Ibid., 1–142.
92. Lewis V. Baldwin, *There Is a Balm in Gilead: The Cultural Roots of Martin Luther King, Jr.* (Minneapolis: Fortress, 1991), 330.

numerous African American preachers who were catapulted to national prominence as they continued to build on his legacy. These preachers held local, state, and national political offices. These include preachers such as John Lewis, Hosea Williams, Andrew Young, Walter E. Fauntroy, William Gray, and Floyd Flake, to name a few. Other ministers continued to build on King's legacy through their own ministries and political and religious organizations. These preachers include Jesse Jackson, C. T. Vivian, Wyatt T. Walker, and Fred Shuttlesworth, and many others. These are but a few noted preachers who fused religion and politics. Like Martin Luther King Jr., and because of him, they saw no difference between preaching the gospel and addressing social justice concerns.

Martin Luther King Jr. did not technically hold strands or streams of black theology in his preaching. Nor did he advocate a black nationalist view. For an example, he agreed with the political and social agenda of the Black Power movement, but he condemned their revolutionary violence and separatist ideals.[93] King held to a "communitarian" philosophy that included themes of "love, nonviolence, forgiveness, reconciliation, freedom, justice and humanity."[94] However, his social justice preaching influenced a rise in "black consciousness" that impacted black theologians and the black theology movement in America.[95]

As seen, the baton of King's legacy is carried on by the African American church, preachers, theologians, and activist organizations. It was the same baton that the black church tradition passed on to him. But his legacy does not only continue in the African American community. The measure of his impact in America is not complete because the depth of his vision continues to shape the sociopolitical and religious landscape. Martin Luther King Jr. belongs to the world because his ideas transcend race, gender, religion, and geographical boundaries. But he remains a prodigy and product of the black church and culture.

King's homiletical gift elevated black preaching in a way that academic homiletics began serious consideration of this "proclamation phenomenon." King "modelled a new role for the black preacher."[96] He changed African American preachers' perception of preaching and expanded their understanding of doing ministry. This new role provided a template for a "social gospel homiletic" and the church as a "social action ministry" that does not separate pulpit preaching from public policy issues and concerns of a nation and the world. In this sense, today's black church and black preaching embody the prophetic voice of King.[97]

---

93. Washington, "Black Power Defined," in *A Testament of Hope*, 303–12.
94. Baldwin, *Balm in Gilead*, 338.
95. Washington, "The Rising Tide of Racial Consciousness," in *A Testament of Hope*, 145–51.
96. See Lewis, "Promise", 277.
97. Baldwin, *Balm in Gilead*, 3.

CONCLUSION

As previously indicated, Martin Luther King Jr.'s impact on America cannot be fully assessed. The initial thrust of his prophetic ministry focused on a constituency of African Americans. The national attention and prominence of his message of love and human rights for all citizens gained traction, drawing support across racial and religious lines.[98] In addition, other groups who felt that their civil rights were infringed upon, benefited from King's moral voice. Homiletically speaking, King represented a treasure chest for all ethnic preachers: Protestants and non-Protestant. He was effective in what Jared E. Alcantara called "Crossover Preaching" or "Intercultural-Improvisational Homiletics."[99] He had the ability to reach white audiences, the educated and the uneducated, and the rich and the poor. In preaching or speaking events, he applied a homiletical style based on the cultural situation of the audience.[100] His intellectual development was immersed in white Western philosophy and theology, but his call for social change was immersed in and emerged from the black church. Thus, his preaching qualities coupled with his national and international prominence support a reasonable argument that he was, arguably, the most important figure in the twentieth century.

Sermon Excerpt

Loving Your Enemies[101]

To our most bitter opponents we say: "We shall match your capacity to inflict suffering by our capacity to endure suffering. We shall meet your physical force with soul force. Do to us what you will, and we shall continue to love you. We cannot in all good conscience obey your unjust laws, because noncooperation with evil is as much a moral obligation as is co-operation with good. Throw us in jail, and we shall still love you.

---

98. J. Deotis Roberts, *Bonhoeffer & King: Speaking Truth to Power* (Louisville: Westminster John Knox, 2005), 96.

99. See Jared E. Alcantara, *Crossover Preaching: Intercultural-Improvisational Homiletics In Conversation With Gardner C. Taylor* (Downers Grove, IL: InterVarsity Press, 2015).

100. Baldwin pointed out that King Jr. switched from "folk idioms" to "reason argument" and cited "Euro-American authorities" when he preached to a white audience. Baldwin, *Balm in Gilead*, 290.

101. King Jr., *Strength to Love*, 40–41. © 1963 Dr. Martin Luther King Jr. © renewed 1991 Coretta Scott King. Reprinted by arrangement with The Heirs to the Estate of Martin Luther King Jr., c/o Writers House as agent for the proprietor New York, NY.

Bomb our homes and threaten our children, and we shall still love you. Send your hooded perpetrators of violence into our community at the midnight hour and beat us and leave us half dead, and we shall still love you. But be ye assured that we will wear you down by our capacity to suffer. One day we shall win freedom, but not only for ourselves. We shall so appeal to your heart and conscience that we shall win you in the process, and our victory will be a double victory.

Love is the most durable power in the world. This creative force, is beautifully exemplified in the life of our Christ, is the most potent instrument available in mankind's quest for peace and security. Napoleon Bonaparte, the great military genius, looking back over his years of conquest, is reported to have said: "Alexander, Caesar, Charlemagne and I have built great empires. But upon what did they depend? They depended on force. But centuries ago Jesus started an empire that was built on love, and even to this day millions will die for him." Who can doubt the veracity of these words. The great military leaders of the past have gone, and their empires have crumbled and burned to ashes. But the empire of Jesus, built solidly and majestically on the foundation of love, is still growing. ♦

BIBLIOGRAPHY

Alcantara, Jared E. *Crossover Preaching: Intercultural-Improvisational Homiletics in Conversation with Gardner C. Taylor.* Downers Grove, IL: InterVarsity Press, 2015.

Alexander, Michelle E. *The New Jim Crow: Mass Incarceration in the Age of Colorblindness.* New York: The New Press, 2011.

Andrews, Dale P. *Practical Theology for Black Churches: Bridging Black Theology for African American Folk Religion.* Louisville: Westminster John Knox, 2002.

Anyabwile, Thabiti M. *The Decline of African American Theology: From Biblical Faith to Cultural Captivity.* Downers Grove, IL: IVP Academic, 2007.

Baker-Fletcher, Garth. *Somebodyness: Martin Luther King, Jr., and the Theory of Dignity.* Minneapolis: Fortress, 1993.

Baldwin, Lewis V. *There Is a Balm in Gilead: The Cultural Roots of Martin Luther King, Jr.* Minneapolis: Fortress, 1991.

Crawford, Evans E., with Thomas H. Troeger. *The Hum: Call And Response in African American Preaching.* Nashville: Abingdon, 1995.

Edwards, O. C., Jr. *A History of Preaching.* 2 vols. Nashville: Abingdon, 2004.

_____. "History of Preaching." Pages 224–225 in *Concise Encyclopedia of Preaching.* Edited by William H. Willimon. Louisville: Westminster John Knox, 1995.

Fant, Clyde E., Jr. and William M. Pinson, Jr. *Marshall to King.* Vol. 12 of *20 Centuries of Great Preaching: An Encyclopedia of Preaching.* Waco: Word, 1971.

Fullwood, Alfonza W. "A Study of Gardner C. Taylor's Theology of Preaching as a Decisive Factor Shaping His Theory of Preaching: Implications for Homiletical Pedagogy" PhD diss., Southeastern Baptist Theological Seminary, 2012.

Jakoubek, Robert. *Martin Luther King, Jr.: Civil Rights Leader.* Danbury, CT: Chelsea, 1989.

King, Coretta Scott. *The Words of Martin Luther King, Jr.* New York: New Market, 1958.

King, Martin Luther, Jr. *Strength to Love.* New York: Harper & Row, 1963.

_____. *Stride Toward Freedom: The Montgomery Story.* New York: Harper & Row, 1958.

Larsen, David L. *The Anatomy of Preaching: Identifying the Issues in Preaching.* Grand Rapids: Kregel, 1989.

Lassiter, Valentino. *Martin Luther King in the African American Preaching Tradition.* Cleveland: Pilgrim, 2001.

Lewis, David L. "Martin Luther King, Jr., and the Promise of Nonviolent Populism." Pages 277–78 in
    Black Leaders in the Twentieth Century. Edited by John Hope Franklin and August Meier. Chicago:
    University of Illinois Press, 1982.

Lincoln, C. Eric, and Lawrence H. Mamiya. *The Black Church in the African American Experience.*
    Durham: Duke University Press, 1990.

Lischer, Richard. *The Preacher King: Martin Luther King, Jr. and the Word That Moved America.* New
    York: Oxford University Press, 1995.

_____. "King, Martin Luther Jr." Pages 288–90 in *Concise Encyclopedia of Preaching.* Edited by
    William Willimon and Richard Lischer. Louisville: Westminster, 1995.

Lokos, Lionel. *House Divided: The Life and Legacy of Martin Luther King.* New Rochelle: Arlington, 1968.

Miller, Keith D. "Martin Luther King, Jr. Borrows a Revolution: Argument, Audience, and Implications of
    a Secondhand Universe." *College English* 48, no. 3 (1986): 249.

Mitchell, Henry H. "African American Preaching." Pages 2–9 in *Concise Encyclopedia of Preaching.* Edited
    by William Willimon and Richard Lischer. Louisville: Westminster, 1995.

_____. *Black Preaching: The Recovery of a Powerful Art.* Nashville: Abingdon, 1990.

Moyd, Olin P. *The Sacred Art: Preaching and Theology in the African American Tradition.* Pennsylvania:
    Judson, 1995.

Pipes, Williams H. *Say Amen, Brother! Old-Time Negro Preaching: A Study in African Frustration.* Detroit:
    Wayne State University Press, 1992.

Reddick, L. D. *Crusader without Violence: A Biography of Martin Luther King, Jr.* New York: Harper &
    Row, 1959.

Roberts, Deotis, J. *Bonhoeffer & King: Speaking Truth to Power.* Louisville: Westminster John Knox, 2005.

Tallmer, Jerry "A Man with a Hard Head," in *Martin Luther King, Jr.: A Profile.* Edited by C. Eric Lincoln
    (New York: Hill & Wang, 1970)

Thomas, Frank A. *Introduction to the Practice of African American Preaching.* Nashville: Abingdon, 2016.

Warren, Mervyn A. *King Came Preaching: The Pulpit Power of Dr. Martin Luther King, Jr.* Downers
    Grove, IL: InterVarsity Press, 2001.

Washington, James M., ed. *A Testament Of Hope: The Essential Writings of Martin Luther King, Jr.* San
    Francisco: Harper & Row, 1986.

Watley, William D. *Roots of Resistance: The Nonviolent Ethic of Martin Luther King, Jr.* Pennsylvania:
    Judson, 1985.

Willimon, William H., and Richard Lischer, eds. *Concise Encyclopedia of Preaching.* Louisville: Westminster
    John Knox, 1995.

Woodward, Vann C. *The Strange Career of Jim Crow.* New York: Oxford University Press, 1957.

Adrian Rogers
Faithfulness to the Word of God

DANIEL L. AKIN
BILL CURTIS

Adrian Rogers (1931–2005) pastored Bellevue Baptist Church in Memphis, Tennesee (1972–2005), and was elected president of the Southern Baptist Convention three times (1979–1980; 1986–1988). He was one of the most popular preachers in America in the latter half of the twentieth century. His powerful presence in the pulpit was used by God to usher in the Conservative Resurgence in the Southern Baptist Convention and return it to its orthodox, evangelical roots as churches committed to the Word of God.

HISTORICAL BACKGROUND

Adrian Rogers was one of the most popular and influential preachers and pastors of the latter half of the twentieth century. He was known for expository preaching, evangelistic passion, love for the nations, and his uncompromising commitment to the Bible as the infallible and inerrant Word of God. His ministry spanned over fifty years, and he was pivotal in the Conservative Resurgence within the Southern Baptist Convention.

Adrian Rogers trusted Jesus as his Lord and Savior at the age of fourteen. At a revival crusade, he followed his father who went forward first in receiving Christ. Reflecting on that night Adrian said, "My father's going forward astounded me. I did not know he was thinking about it. To that point everything the preacher had said seemed to pertain to other people. But at that moment my father stepped forward, the message became personal. I was immediately smitten by God's Spirit and knew I needed to do the same thing as my father. When he stepped forward, I did also and made a profession of my faith in Christ. . . . I believe an eternal change took place in those moments, and I became a new creature in Christ."[1]

---

1. Joyce Rogers, *Love Worth Finding: The Life of Adrian Rogers and His Philosophy of Preaching* (Nashville: Broadman & Holman, 2005), 13–14.

God's grace began a work that redirected the strength and leadership that Rogers often misused as a young man: "He had gained a reputation of being one of the toughest kids in his school. He would challenge others to a fight just for an expression of what must have been an inner turmoil. He had challenged his classmates one by one to a dual of fisticuffs."[2] All of this changed after Roger's conversion. Little did he or his high school sweetheart, Joyce, know, but God was preparing to use Adrian's strength and leadership as a positive force in his spiritual kingdom.

At first, Rogers experienced trepidation in ministry settings, even declining an invitation to pray in Sunday school as a young teen because of feelings of inadequacy. Quickly, however, these anxieties subsided as Rogers began to feel a calling on his life to pastoral ministry. In an interview with John Brunet, Rogers recalled one night on a football field and the moment he surrendered himself to be used by God in ministry: "Kneeling did not seem good enough or humble enough, so I laid down prostrate in the grass and said, 'Father, I want you to use me.' That did not seem humble enough so I took my finger and made a hole in the dirt and put my nose down in that hole. I called out, 'Lord, I am as low as I know how to get, I want you to use me.'"[3]

As a junior in high school, Rogers publically answered the call to preach one night during a retreat at Ridgecrest Baptist Assembly. Rogers described the meaning and nature of this calling: "To me, preaching and the ministry is not something I 'surrendered to.' Preaching is something I submitted to willingly and gladly. I was thrilled and honored that God would call me to preach. I am still amazed that God would use me and grateful that He does."[4]

Rogers married Joyce on September 21, 1950, during their freshmen year of college. The newlywed couple took their first pastorate when Rogers was nineteen, at the First Baptist Church of Fellsmere, Florida, in 1951.[5] The early years of ministry and seminary were humble beginnings for the Rogers family. He and Joyce were hit with an incredible personal tragedy in the loss of their baby boy, Philip, who died due to sudden infant death syndrome (SIDS).[6] All the while, their own testimony pointed to God's provision and blessing. Joyce Rogers wrote of this time, "We discovered that Christ within us was sufficient to meet every challenge we face and that He is always sufficient to give comfort as we walk through the valley of sorrow."[7]

2. Ibid., 3.

3. Adrian P. Rogers, interviewed by Dennis John Brunet, "A Critical Examination of the Homiletical Philosophy and Practice of Adrian P. Rogers" (PhD diss., New Orleans Baptist Theological Seminary, 1994).

4. Rogers, Love Worth Finding, 18–19.

5. Ibid., 28. Rogers was ordained on May 8, 1951. His salary was twenty-five dollars a week.

6. Ibid.

7. Ibid., 43–44.

Every church Rogers was called to pastor was blessed by God and grew tremendously. While these times were not without challenges, God was using these trials to craft a man of conviction who would not compromise for a great work that lay ahead. These lessons and the resulting maturity would become obvious as Rogers eventually became pastor of the historic Bellevue Baptist Church in Memphis, Tennessee. John Brunet provides the record and a brief perspective of his pastorates: "Ministerial success was a determining factor which influenced Rogers's homiletical philosophy and practice. From the Waveland pastorate (following Fellsmere), Rogers became pastor of Parkview Baptist Church in Fort Pierce, Florida. During his seven year ministry at Parkview, church membership nearly quadrupled from 484 to 1,338. In 1965, Rogers accepted the call to pastor First Baptist Church of Merritt Island, Florida. During his eight-year ministry, church membership grew from 1,153 to 4,037. Rogers became pastor of Bellevue Baptist Church of Memphis, Tennessee in September 1972."[8]

At Bellevue, Rogers's preaching and leadership was used by God to bring incredible growth. During his time at Bellevue, the church grew from around nine thousand members to well over twenty thousand.[9]

Adrian Rogers served as president of the Southern Baptist Convention (1979–1980 and 1986–1988) during the height of the Conservative Resurgence, or the "Battle for the Bible." During this time in office, Rogers was instrumental in helping the Southern Baptist Convention (SBC) return to its theologically conservative roots. Rogers joined other men to navigate the most significant debate in the history of the SBC, one of the largest Protestant denominations in the world. This was a time of serious contention among Baptists and evangelicals, due to the infiltration of theological liberalism and neoorthodoxy that had spread throughout SBC seminaries and churches. The stakes were high. Not only did Rogers's leadership have a significant impact on the debate over the doctrine of inerrancy, he modeled biblical conviction and compassion that caused even those who disagreed with him to respect him for his integrity.

During the Conservative Resurgence, Rogers was asked to serve on the "Peace Committee." Rogers and the other committee members were charged with reaching a compromise between liberal and conservative Baptists on theological doctrines. At one point in their meetings, Rogers was approached by a lawyer who represented the moderate side, or the liberal Baptists. It was during this conversation that Rogers made a famous statement that in so many ways defines the man he was. Of that event Joyce Rogers wrote, "A successful lawyer who represented

---

8. Brunet, "A Critical Examination," 41.
9. Ibid.

the moderate faction pulled Adrian aside and said, 'Adrian, if you don't compromise, we will never get together.'"[10] Joyce noted her husband's reply, "I'm willing to compromise about many things, but not the Word of God. So far as getting together is concerned, we don't have to get together. The Southern Baptist Convention, as it is, does not have to survive. I don't have to be the pastor of Bellevue Baptist Church. I don't have to be loved; I don't even have to live. But I will not compromise the Word of God."[11] This one statement summarizes the tremendous conviction Rogers held for the inerrancy of the Bible and helps one understand, at least in part, why he was such a powerful preacher of the Word of God.

Adrian Rogers announced his retirement to the Bellevue congregation on September 12, 2004. He had served Bellevue for thirty-two years. He would officially retire in the spring of 2005. He had planned to stay in Memphis and continue to minister through the Adrian Rogers Pastor Training Institute, Mid-America Baptist Theological Seminary, and his ministry Love Worth Finding.[12] In God's mysterious providence, he would be diagnosed with cancer shortly after his retirement. He went to be with his Lord Jesus on November 15, 2005. More than ten thousand people attended his funeral. The service was carried live on local Memphis television stations and streamed around the world. Tributes, too numerous to list and recount, poured in from around the world.

Dr. Rogers was a lion in our midst—the man God used to serve as leader and voice for a great resurgence of biblical Christianity. He was a man of tremendous gifts, whose booming voice was matched by a gift for words and a powerful delivery. He dominated the pulpit as few people ever have, preaching the Word and calling sinners to faith in the Lord Jesus Christ. He was a modern-day "Prince of Preachers," whose personal example served to encourage thousands of others to greater faithfulness in preaching the Word of God.

THEOLOGY OF PREACHING

In exploring Adrian Rogers's theology of preaching, I must first clarify that his theology was not only a theology of preaching, but his theology was for preaching, his theology was in his preaching, and it was by his theology that he approached the task of preaching. For him, theology was not just an aspect of preaching; it was wholly and thoroughly a part of his posture as he approached the pulpit.[13]

---

10. Ibid., 109.

11. Ibid., 110–11.

12. Ibid., 211.

13. In each volume of the *Christ-Centered Exposition Commentary* series, edited by David Platt, Tony Merida, and Daniel Akin, the inside cover reads, "Dedicated to Adrian Rogers and John Piper. They have taught us to love the gospel of Jesus Christ, to preach the Bible as the inerrant Word of God, to pastor the

Rogers's theology of preaching can be described as christocentric, with accompanying components of evangelism, disciple making, and worship. According to Rogers, "The man of God must preach the Christ of Scripture. The preacher must ask himself, 'Where is Jesus in this sermon?' I believe in all of the Bible you will find Jesus. The Bible has but one hero, one villain, and one theme. The hero is Jesus, the villain is Satan, and the theme is 'Jesus saves.' Somehow, somewhere, in some way, that theme is present all through the Bible. Christ is in all the Scriptures, and the Scriptures testify of Christ; Jesus is the message of the Bible and, thus, He must be the message of the preacher."[14]

To preach Jesus is to preach the gospel. However, to preach the gospel is not to neglect discipleship, an absolute essential to building the body of Christ. Rogers clarified, "Yes, preach the gospel. However, preachers who are constantly preaching, 'Hell is hot, heaven is sweet, sin is black, judgment is sure, and Jesus saves' are emptying their churches because they are not feeding their sheep."[15] Thus, the essence of this Christ-centered focus for preaching is that people should "become more like Christ."[16]

Rogers preached with a drive to make disciples, but he argued that "the preacher's love for souls" is not "the great key to ensure ministerial success."[17] He wrote, "Rather I believe the great key for ministerial success to be the preacher's personal love for Jesus Christ. A love for Jesus is a greater motivator than a love for people. The motivating factor behind ministry should be the preacher's desire to do something for Christ. The preacher should say in his heart, I want to preach for Him. I want to obey Him. I want to be pleasing to Him."[18]

Church for which our Savior died, and to have a passion to see all nations gladly worship the Lamb." The reason for this dedication is simple: both men, without apology or compromise are committed to the Word of God. This foundation is built on a robust theological commitment to: (1) the inerrancy, infallibility, authority, and sufficiency of the Bible; (2) the triune God who is omnipotent, omniscient, and omnipresent; (3) God as Creator and reject naturalistic evolution as nonsense; (4) both the dignity and depravity of humanity; (5) the full deity, perfect humanity, and sinlessness of Jesus the Son of God; (6) the penal substitutionary nature of the atonement as foundational for understanding the cross work of our Savior; (7) the good news of the gospel as the exclusive and only means whereby any person is reconciled to God; (8) the biblical nature of a regenerate church witnessed in believer's baptism by immersion; (9) salvation by grace alone through faith alone in Christ alone for the glory of God alone; (10) the understanding that reception of the Holy Spirit is at the moment of regeneration/conversion and that the blessing of spiritual gifts are for the building up of the body of Christ; (11) the literal, visible, and historical return of the resurrected and glorified Lord Jesus Christ to this earth when he will manifest fully his kingdom; (12) the reality of an eternal heaven and an eternal hell with Jesus as the only difference; (13) a "sanctity of life" ethic from conception to natural death; (14) the sanctity of heterosexual marriage, the goodness of sex in marriage, and the gift of children; and; (15) the complementary nature of male/female relationships rejoicing in the divine ordering of them for the home and the church. This list could go on, and because of this theological commitment, Rogers (and Piper) are two "warriors of the faith" and role models worthy of consideration and emulation in the pattern of 1 Corinthians 11:1.

14. Rogers, *Love Worth Finding*, 186–87.
15. Ibid., 187.
16. Ibid., 188.
17. Ibid.
18. Ibid.

Rogers's theology of preaching produced a fundamental expectation of transformation through the preaching event, and this expectation was based on his confidence in the total truthfulness of the Scriptures.

Rogers was thoroughly conservative theologically. This was nowhere more evident than in his commitment to the doctrine of biblical inerrancy, which provided the foundation on which his theology of preaching was built. The SBC Conservative Resurgence revolved primarily around this one critical doctrine. In a testimony to his lifelong commitment to biblical inerrancy, which was so critically important to his theology of preaching as well as his pastoral and denominational leadership, Adrian Rogers was appointed as the chairman of the Baptist Faith and Message Study Committee (1999–2000), and the 2000 BFM is dedicated in his honor. This document changed the statement on the Scriptures to include one new, famous phrase: "Therefore, all Scripture is totally true and trustworthy."[19] With this statement, the future of the SBC was changed, as the affirmation of biblical inerrancy became required to teach in SBC seminaries and to serve in SBC agencies. Under the capable leadership of Adrian Rogers, the SBC had returned to its historic traditions.

METHODOLOGY FOR PREACHING

Adrian Rogers wasn't just a preacher; he was scholar pastor. As such, he saw his work in the pulpit as one of a craftsman, and he spent his whole life honing his skills. His dynamic orations were built on a simple yet robust methodology. We will examine it in four parts.

First, Adrian Rogers was authentic in his private life. For Rogers, dynamic preaching was the result of dynamic devotion. As you might imagine, prayer was the bedrock of his proclamation. He said, "Prayer is the secret of fruitfulness in ministry. I would say that my life does not so much consist of long prayers, but rather, of much praying. The most valuable contribution a preacher can make is not when he is before his people talking about God, but when he is before God talking about his people."[20] Rogers also incorporated reading in his times of personal devotion. And though he used numerous sources, he preferred to read devotional material that coincided with his preaching calendar.[21] Further, he understood that preaching was powerless without the work of the Holy Spirit. He said, "A man does not prepare in the flesh and preach in the Spirit. He must prepare in the Spirit in order to preach in the Spirit. The Holy Spirit

---

19. LifeWay Church Resources, Nashville: 2000.
20. Rogers, *Love Worth Finding*, 193.
21. Ibid., 193–94.

not only must stand with him when he preaches, but He must sit with him when he studies."[22]

Second, Adrian Rogers was intentional about his sermon planning. Rogers favored a textual-thematic approach to expository preaching, although he regularly taught through books of the Bible too. He said, "I really cannot give a scientific explanation of how I go from one subject to another, except by intuition, hunch, or materials that seem to appear before me that pique my interest. I may interrupt a series of messages for a special occasion message, and I do place emphasis on holidays and special occasions, because those times carry life and joyful expectation, which provides a unique launching pad for ideas and communication."[23] To assist with his sermon planning, Rogers kept an exhaustive catalog of sermon ideas and exegesis. He had a file for every chapter in the Bible. Of course, he developed this approach in the years before computers made everything accessible with just the touch of a button. He said, "When I begin my exegesis of a passage, I draw from my files all the materials I have that is related to that text. . . . Thus, when I prepare, I have available my library, my files, and of course, my memory of the subject. After I have assembled all of the material, it requires between four and eight hours to complete a sermon. I have hardly ever preached a message that I felt was fully ripe, fully mature before I picked it."[24]

Third, Adrian Rogers was diligent in his sermon preparation. For Rogers, good preaching began with good hermeneutics. Rogers identified three specific questions that served as the hermeneutical foundation for his exegesis. First, he asked, what did the text mean then? Because Rogers was an inerrantist, he believed that the authors uniquely wrote everything that God intended. As a result, authorial intention was the key for unlocking the meaning of the text. Second, he asked, what does the text mean now? In this sense, Rogers was wrestling with the two horizons: that of the biblical world and that of the modern world. While the authors' intended meaning always remains unchanged, its applications could be different when transferred into different cultural contexts. Rogers wanted to be sure that the eternal truths of Scripture were properly explained and applied for his people. Third, he asked, what does the text mean to me personally? Here, Rogers wanted to grasp the Bible's truths for his own heart and life first. He said, "If you are teaching what it meant then, you may be a preacher. If you preach what it means now, you may be a preacher. But if you preach what it means to you personally, you become a prophet and a powerful preacher."[25]

22. Ibid., 198.
23. Ibid., 194.
24. Rogers, *Love Worth Finding*, 203.
25. Ibid., 198–99.

This kind of preaching would be "biblical in content, applicable, pertinent, and understandable."[26] For Rogers, the goal of this kind of preaching was life change.

As he began answering those questions during his exegetical work, he kept the end goal in mind, to "confront, convict, convert and comfort men and women through the preaching of biblical concepts. . . . Preaching is more than the dissemination of truth. It is not primarily information, but transformation. . . . An effective sermon moves toward effective action. If there is no call to action, there has been no sermon preached, only a lesson rendered."[27] Consequently, Rogers struck a wonderful balance between explanation and application.

Adrian Rogers understood the concept of preaching to human needs before most people had even heard of the concept. He said, "To be effective, the pastor must preach to the needs of his people. If the preacher does not apply the spiritual truth of the text to the day in which his audience lives, the preaching becomes an exercise in futility and the church becomes a glorified country club."[28] To accomplish this, Rogers developed his messages with great attention to explanation, illustration, and application. At the level of application, of course, was where the message either succeeded or failed. The preacher must "illustrate that truth and show how that truth can be applied and worked out in contemporary living. Then he must call upon his people to act upon that truth."[29] Rogers was a master at this process.

Rogers constructed a sermon outline at the end of his exegetical work, but he resisted the use of sermon manuscripts. He said, "I do not write out my sermons in manuscript form. However, upon completion of the sermon, I do write out a full outline that contains points, sub-points, and illustrations."[30] Rogers developed his outlines in keeping with the tradition of classical expository preaching. He said, "I would describe the process of outlining the text as dividing the sermon into logical bite-size parts that adhere to the central theme of the text. The goal is for each division to stand-alone and to lend credence to the theme. I outline the passage according to the natural divisions found within the text."[31] Rogers, like many from his era, believed in the value of alliteration. He said, "I make extensive use of alliteration in my sermon outline. Alliteration is helpful" for the listener.[32] At the same time, however, he believed that forced alliteration was counterproductive and "should never be used."[33]

---

26. Ibid., 194.
27. Rogers, *Love Worth Finding*, 194–95.
28. Ibid., 202.
29. Ibid.
30. Ibid.
31. Rogers, *Love Worth Finding*, 200.
32. Ibid., 202.
33. Ibid., 203.

Rogers believed that a well-developed outline was a preacher's friend. It allowed the preacher to stay on task and avoid needless discursive dialogue, while assisting the listener to best understand the truth of the message. Further, Rogers believed that a well-constructed outline helped the message maintain a pace that was conducive to maximum impact. He understood that preachers must practice to develop the skill of writing substantive sermon outlines. He noted, "Preachers should reject forced, artificial outlines and master the art of developing strong outlines based upon the natural flow of the text."[34]

The heart of Rogers's outlines was contained in the persuasive elements he used. Again, he followed classical expository forms to create these. He began by crafting strong division statements. The number of statements was based on the length and content of the biblical passage under consideration. Rogers wanted the points of his sermon to be strong enough that his listeners could easily follow along.[35] Together with his development of strong division statements, he also worked hard to develop strong transitional statements between the individual divisions, because they created "a smooth flow from one part of the sermon to the next."[36]

Next, Rogers explained the text so that his listeners could fully understand its meaning and the relationship between the individual sermon divisions and the central idea of the text. He said, "I begin sermon preparation with a specific text and allow the exegesis of the text to determine the sermon's theme. There is more than one theme that can be drawn from any text, but . . . the theme should be incipient in the text. It is important to allow the Bible to speak for itself and not try to read some thematic idea into the passage."[37] It was this exegetical material that Rogers shared as he explained a text.

Following the explanation, Rogers utilized illustrations to help his listeners "see" how the truth of the text connected with their own lives. As a result, he looked everywhere for helpful illustrations. He said, "Everything is grist for the preacher's mill. I cannot give you a specific source from where I get my general sermon material, for the source comes from life itself. . . . I gather material from everywhere just by keeping my eyes and ears open."[38] Indeed, Rogers believed that nonbiblical illustrations were some of the best because people become very attentive when contemporary issues are connected to biblical truth.[39]

Adrian Rogers also understood the significance of using cross-referencing to support the central idea of the text. While he did not address the topic at length,

34. Ibid., 201.
35. Rogers, *Love Worth Finding*, 200.
36. Ibid., 205.
37. Ibid., 197.
38. Ibid., 195.
39. Ibid., 201.

he utilized other Scriptures often in his preaching. He said, "It is a beautiful thing to bring many other scriptures that strengthen the truth of the text."[40]

As we noted earlier, Rogers spent considerable time planning and preparing for the application areas of his sermons. He used application in conjunction with every sermon division. The application was where the text was applied to both personal and social needs. "When a pastor prepares a sermon, he must, in reality, or through his creative imagination, focus upon human needs, hurts, and failure."[41] Rogers made this a priority because of his theology of preaching. He said, "For the preacher to be effective, he must be able to exegete two books: God's Book and the book of human nature. I am the middle man between the Word of God and the congregation, for I must understand how to take that which is immutable, the Word of God, and apply it to that which is transitory, the human event. If the preacher does not apply the Word of God to the human event, he is only a gadfly hobnobbing with his congregation."[42] Application was the critical part of the sermon for Rogers.

Like many expositors, Adrian Rogers waited to write his introduction until his exegesis and sermon outline were complete. He said, "I believe the introduction should be constructed after the preacher has prepared his sermon, because you cannot know what you are introducing until you have prepared the sermon."[43] Rogers believed the introduction was one of the most important parts of the sermon because the audience often was either captured or lost during those few minutes.

As a rule, Rogers used the "Hey! You! Look! Do!" model to craft his introductions. As a result, his introductions were built to capture attention, identify the human need element in the message and connect it to the listener, provide some information about the topic at hand, and foreshadow the life-change that the sermon should produce in the listener.[44] In this way, he was able to capture the audience's attention from the very beginning of the sermon.

It took time to develop this strategy every week, however. He said, "The introduction requires creative thought on the part of the preacher. It must be a clear, concise opening statement. The introduction is where the preacher must focus the purpose of the sermon. He must decide what is the best way to get interest for the message. And, he must show them how the truth contained in the message will be applicable to their lives. The objective to be achieved through

---

40. Rogers, *Love Worth Finding*, 200.
41. Ibid., 196.
42. Ibid., 198.
43. Ibid., 203–4.
44. Rogers, *Love Worth Finding*, 204.

the introduction is to make people determine that they will pay attention and hear what the preacher has to say."[45]

Similarly, Rogers waited to construct the conclusion until the end of his sermon preparation, and he believed that it was as critically important as the introduction. Yet he believed that it was one of the most underdeveloped parts of most preachers' sermons. He said, "I consider the conclusion vitally important to achieving success in preaching. It is the drawing of the net."[46] He developed his conclusion by answering two questions: "1) What do I desire the people to do concerning this sermon? 2) How will I move them to act upon the applied truth of the sermon?"[47]

To accomplish this, Rogers would restate the important points in the sermon, use a dramatic illustration, and issue a strong challenge to the congregation. He said, "The conclusion need not be long to be effective, for in most instances, brevity is a virtue. The preacher should avoid rehashing the sermon or introducing some new thought during the conclusion. . . . I would maintain a clear distinction between the conclusion and the invitation. By having the congregation pray with heads bowed, I transition from the conclusion to the invitation."[48]

Like the introduction and conclusion, Rogers waited until the end of his sermon preparation to give a sermon its title. He said, "The sermon title is best expressed in some rhythmic or alliterative form which catches the ear of the listener. . . . It should reflect clearly the message of the text and should communicate what is to be found in the sermon. The primary purpose of the title is to be descriptive of the biblical truth."[49] By waiting to write the introduction, conclusion, and sermon title until the end of his exegesis and sermon preparation, Rogers guarded against letting a title shape the sermon rather than letting the text shape the sermon.

The goal of Adrian Rogers's preaching was to produce heart transformation in his listeners. The invitation is where Rogers hoped this transformation would make itself apparent. Interestingly, he did not prepare for the invitation like he did for his sermon. He said, "I have three or four varieties of invitations that I use and feel natural in giving without much preparation. I depend upon the inspiration of the moment rather than upon preparation for the delivery of the invitation. . . . The invitation I deliver in a simple style that flows naturally. I generally tell people what it means to be saved and how they can be saved. . . .

---

45. Ibid.
46. Ibid., 205.
47. Rogers, *Love Worth Finding*, 205.
48. Ibid., 206.
49. Ibid., 196.

I follow the same pattern for church membership and transfer of membership."[50] Rogers knew that his members might find this repetition tedious, but he was undaunted. He said, "The invitation must be extremely plain and clear to the person who is in the audience for the first or second time. Many times, preachers deliver invitations that are so vague that an unsaved man would not have the foggiest idea what he is expected to do. I believe that the preacher's effectiveness in the invitation is linked to his clarity, explanation, and . . . convictional delivery."[51]

Rogers became well-known around the world because of his skill in handling the Scriptures. Yet he wasn't famous for his time in the study. He was famous for his outstanding voice and communication skills. He was a master at bringing a sermon to life. As we've noted, Rogers's biblical preaching was the process of "applying the truth of the Bible to the human situation and calling for action."[52] He acknowledged the power of God at work through the calling, anointing, and divine unction on the preacher of God, but he also gave attention to God's use of the preacher in this task. He wrote, "The gospel message cannot be separated from the God-called messenger. . . . Truth on paper is not the same as truth in human flesh."[53] In this context, Rogers believed rhetoric was an important component in the preaching event; one could even say he believed it was essential. He wrote about the power and value of rhetoric in the proclamation of the Scriptures:

> I encourage preachers to be trained in the art of rhetoric. The preacher ought to study words. He should be a lover of words, logic, and beauty. The preacher ought to be a lover of order, and rhetoric will help him accomplish that purpose. His rhetoric ought to go beyond his words and extend into his voice and facial expressions. He should master a rhetoric that enhances his ability to communicate the Word of God. I'd describe much of contemporary preaching as throwing mud at a wall, hoping some of it will stick. Preachers need to not only say things; they need to say things with a barb on them so the message will stick. It might help to relate the art of rhetoric to architecture. Good architecture, like good preaching, is not just an arrangement of beautiful materials. It is a beautiful arrangement of materials. The preacher has an obligation to make his words powerful, as well as beautiful. The Bible says, "Let your speech be always with grace, seasoned with salt" (Col. 4:6a, KJV). That is, make it palatable. Preaching is not

---

50. Rogers, *Love Worth Finding*, 206–7.
51. Ibid., 207.
52. Ibid., 185.
53. Ibid.

simply reciting words or composing a speech. One of the reasons I enjoy preaching from the King James Version of the Bible is because the translators endeavored not only to keep the objectivity and the truth of the Word, but they also endeavored to keep the rhetoric and beauty of the Word.[54]

Rogers modeled a unique, God-given ability to navigate seamlessly between great preparation and great delivery. Yet even for him, his skills reflected a lifetime of labor in the laboratory that is the pastor's study. He remains an inspiration to preachers everywhere who long to handle God's Word with equal skill and grace.

CONTRIBUTIONS TO PREACHING

Adrian Rogers was a giant in the history of Southern Baptist preaching. He was used of God to reach thousands of people with the gospel through the growth of his preaching and teaching ministry at Bellevue Baptist Church in Memphis, Tennessee. He was instrumental in the training of preachers through his support of Mid-America Baptist Theological Seminary. And he was invaluable to the Southern Baptist Convention during his years as convention president in the midst of the Southern Baptist Conservative Resurgence.

Perhaps his greatest contribution to preaching was the consistency of exposition that he modeled during his ministry. He not only blessed his own church, but through Love Worth Finding ministries, his legacy of preaching continues to touch people around the world even years after his death. Further, he remains a role model for the thousands of preachers who knew him—or knew about him—because he was the same man outside the pulpit as he was when he was he was preaching.[55] He loved his wife, his children, his friends, his denomination,

---

54. Rogers, *Love Worth Finding*, 171–72.

55. Daniel Akin, a coauthor of this chapter and the president of Southeastern Baptist Theological Seminary, knew Dr. Adrian Rogers well. He shares the following story about Dr. Rogers's influence on his life. "Dr. Rogers always made time for others. It did not matter who they were. The last time he was at Southeastern Seminary, he impressed this truth on me in a manner that has left a permanent imprint on my life. Following his message in chapel, people lined up by the dozens to speak to him. I knew this would happen. This started at about 11:00 a.m. At 11:45 a.m. the line was still long. I went to his wife, Joyce, to gain her assistance in graciously pulling him away. I should have listened more carefully when she said, 'If you want to get him, then you go ahead. I am staying here!' Not listening, I walked up and touched his arm and attempted to begin nudging him away. I will never forget what he said, gently but firmly. 'Little Danny, when I am ready to leave I will let you know.' In the voice of a squeaky mouse I responded and said, 'OK,' then scurried back to a pew and sat there like a little boy who had just gotten his knuckles rapped with a ruler! At 12:15 p.m. I walked back up as the last person in line approached. It was a small gray-headed lady in her eighties. She approached Dr. Rogers and said, 'I have heard you preach for years, but I never thought I would get to meet you. I just want to touch your cheek.' She reached up and placed her wrinkled hand on the cheek of this great servant of Christ. He gently placed his hand over hers, bent over, and gave her a kiss on her cheek. With sweet tears running down

and his church. He was gracious to everyone—even those who treated him like an enemy. And he demonstrated how to finish one's life and ministry well, even as disease overtook him at the young age of seventy-four. Finally, he modeled what it meant to love Jesus with all one's heart. He never recovered from his salvation experience, and he loved to share the gospel with anyone who would listen. And that, perhaps, is his greatest contribution to his legacy of preaching.

Sermon Excerpt

How to Be a Faithfully Committed Disciple of Jesus Christ (Luke 14:25–35)[56]

Introduction

A disciple is someone who learns from his master. The word "disciple" means learner. When we learn from our teacher, then we will be like our teacher. Jesus' commands can be summed up in two phrases, "Come unto Me," and "Come after Me."

We sing, "It pays to serve Jesus, it pays every day." And it does. May I also say that it costs to serve Jesus, it costs every day, it costs every step of the way. Salvation is free but discipleship costs. The curse of today's Christianity is this—we have made discipleship too easy. We have an easy, flabby, air-conditioned, upholstered faith. . . .

When you come to be a disciple, you need to come with your eyes wide open. You are called not to share His popularity but His unpopularity. . . . To be a follower of Jesus may not bring you medals. It may bring you scars. . . . What is the cost of true discipleship?

I. Disciples Must Worship at Any Cost

1. At the cost of personal relationships. "Hate not his father . . ." This does not mean that we are not to love our parents. Jesus would never cause us to break the commandment that tells us to honor father and mother. To love Jesus causes us truly to love others more.

---

her face, she turned and walked away. As she did, Adrian looked at me and said, 'Now we can go.' Words are not adequate to express the lesson he taught me that day."

56. The following excerpt is used with permission of the Pastor Training Institute. It is the typed manuscript of what Rogers took with him into the pulpit.

The word "hate" as it is used by Jesus means to make a clear choice (Matthew 6:24; 10:37–38). There are times when you must make a choice. Those of us who put our children on airplanes to live on foreign soil to preach the Gospel know something of this.

2. At the cost of personal reputation. "His own life." This is not talking about self-denial but denial of self. There is a difference. You can deny yourself things without denying yourself. . . . Churches today have become self-service cafeteria lines. Self-esteem seems to be the main goal. We are told how to be fulfilled. The flesh is promised pleasures, pride and glory. . . .

3. At the cost of personal realization. "Bear his cross." When you come to Jesus as a disciple, you have made your last independent decision. A jewelry store had a sign in the window, "Crosses—Half Price." There are no true half price crosses. . . .

II. Disciples Must Work at Any Cost

Discipleship is a life of building. A crucifixion to the old world is followed by a construction of a new life. . . .

1. The life we build must be spiritually conceived. Rather than asking God to bless what you are doing, pray and ask God that you might do what He is blessing. Let God be the architect of your tower. . . .
2. Your life should be sacrificially constructed. . . .
3. Your tower should be steadfastly completed. . . . ◆

BIBLIOGRAPHY

Primary Sources

Rogers, Joyce. *Love Worth Finding: The Life of Adrian Rogers and His Philosophy of Preaching.* Nashville: Broadman & Holman, 2005.
The Adrian Rogers Legacy Collection. WORDsearch Corp.
Rogers, Adrian. Adrian Rogers Legacy Library. Memphis: Rogers Family Trust, 2010.

Secondary Sources

Ammerman, Nancy Tatom. *Baptist Battles: Social Change and Religious Conflict in the Southern Baptist Convention.* New Brunswick: Rutgers University Press, 1990.
Fletcher, Jesse C. *The Southern Baptist Convention: A Sesquicentennial History.* Nashville: Broadman & Holman, 1994.
Hefley, James C. *The Truth in Crisis.* 6 Vols. Richmond, VA: Hannibal, 1996.
Pressler, Paul. *A Hill on Which to Die: One Southern Baptist's Journey.* Nashville: Broadman & Holman, 1999.

Sutton, Jerry. *The Baptist Reformation: The Conservative Resurgence in the Baptist Convention*. Nashville: Broadman & Holman, 2000.

Dissertations

Burnet, Dennis John. "A Critical Examination of the Homiletical Philosophy and Practice of Adrian Rogers." PhD diss., New Orleans Baptist Theological Seminary, 1994.

Cummings, Ricky C. "A Critical Examination of the Old Testament Evangelistic Preaching of Adrian P. Rogers." PhD diss., New Orleans Baptist Theological Seminary, 2013.

Hight, Timothy A. "A Comparative Homiletical Analysis of Selected Southern Baptist Convention Presidents from 1979 through 1989." ThD diss., Mid-America Baptist Theological Seminary, 1991.

Jacumin, Charles Martin. "A Theological and Historical Analysis of the Southern Baptist Convention Peace Committee, 1985–1987." PhD Diss., Southeastern Baptist Theological Seminary, 2008.

Montalbano, Michael Pete. "A Critical Comparison of the Preaching of Robert G. Lee, Ramsey Pollard, and Adrian Rogers." ThD diss., Mid-America Baptist Theological Seminary, 1993.

Nolen, Michael Wayne. "A Critical Evaluation of the Historiography Surrounding the Southern Baptist Convention Controversy, 1979–1996." PhD Diss., Deerfield, IL: Trinity Evangelical Divinity School, 1997.

O'Brien, Michael. "A Biblical Foundation of Integrity As Modeled By the Life of Adrian Rogers." DMin diss., Southeastern Baptist Theological Seminary, 2012

Yelton, Johnny Derrick. "The Evangelistic Emphasis in the Pastoral Preaching of Adrian P. Rogers." PhD Diss., Louisville: The Southern Baptist Theological Seminary. 2013

Articles

"Adrian Rogers Undergoing Cancer Tests in Houston." *Baptist Press*. June 15, 2005. http://www.bpnews .net/20989/adrian-rogers-undergoing-cancer-tests-in-houston.

Ellsworth, Tim. "Adrian Rogers: The 'Prince of Preachers' Retires." *SBC Life*. March 2005. http://www .sbclife.net/Articles/2005/04/sla8.

_____. "At Bellevue, Thousands Say Goodbye to Adrian Rogers." *Baptist Press*. November 18, 2005. http://www.bpnews.net/22105/at-bellevue-baptist-thousands-say-goodbye-to-adrian-rogers-til -heavenly-reunion.

Foust, Michael. "Adrian Rogers Announces Retirement from Bellevue." *Baptist Press*. September 14, 2004. http://www.bpnews.net/19083/adrian-rogers-announces-retirement-from-bellevue-baptist.

_____. "Adrian Rogers, Longtime Bellevue Pastor and Leader in Conservative Resurgence, Dies." *Baptist Press*. November 15, 2005. http://www.bpnews.net/22069/adrian-rogers-longtime-bellevue -pastor-and-leader-in-conservative-resurgence-dies.

_____. "In His Final Days, Adrian Rogers Told Those Gathered around Him, 'I Am at Perfect Peace.'" *Baptist Press*. November 16, 2005. http://www.bpnews.net/22079/in-his-final-days-adrian -rogers-told-those-gathered-around-him-i-am-at-perfect-peace.

Marus, Robert. "Adrian Rogers to Retire but Remain at Bellevue." *Baptist News Global*. September 16, 2004. https://baptistnews.com/archives/item/1363-update-adrian-rogers-to-retire-but-remain-at -bellevue.

SBC Peace Committee. "Committee Proceedings, 1985–1988." Tape #1–145. AR 629 Tape Collection of the Southern Baptist Convention.

Tomlin, Gregory. "Special Memories of Rogers Recounted by Southern Baptist Convention Presidents." *Baptist Press*. November 17, 2005. http://www.bpnews.net/22091.

"Two Pastors Pay Tribute to Fellow Shepherd Adrian Rogers." *Baptist Press*. November 22, 2005. http:// www.bpnews.net/22129.

Books by Adrian Rogers

Rogers, Adrian. *Adrianisms: The Wit and Wisdom of Adrian Rogers*. 2 vols, 2006, 2007.

_____. *The Passion of Christ and the Purpose of Life*. Wheaton, IL: Crossway, 2005.

_____. *What Every Christian Ought to Know*. 2005.

_____. *Family Survival in an X-Rated World*. 2005

_____. *Unveiling the End Times in Our Time: The Triumph of the Lamb in Revelation*. 2004, 2013.

_____. *Standing for Light and Truth*. 2003

_____. *The Nature of Hope*. 2003.

_____. *The Incredible Power of Kingdom Authority: Achieving Victory through Surrender*. 2003.

_____. The Incredible Power of Kingdom Authority: Getting an Upper Hand on the Underworld. 2002

_____. The Wonder of It All. 2001

_____. God's Wisdom Is Better than Gold. 2001

_____. The Lord Is My Shepherd. 1999.

_____. Judges. 1998.

_____. Ruth. 1998.

_____. God's Hidden Treasure. 1997.

_____. A Family Christmas Treasury. 1997.

_____. Believe in Miracles but Trust in Jesus. 1997.

_____. A Future for the Family. 1996.

_____. Ten Secrets for a Successful Family. 1996.

_____. The Power of His Presence. 1995.

_____. Mastering Your Emotions. 1988.

_____. God's Way to Health, Wealth, and Wisdom. 1987.

_____. The Secret of Supernatural Living. 1982.

E. V. Hill

Preaching God's Word for Spiritual and Social Transformation

DANTE D. WRIGHT I

Preaching with boldness, imagination, and clarity—these words only begin to describe the ministry of Edward Victor Hill (1933–2003), an African American evangelical who has impacted his neighborhood, his city, his nation, and his world. To talk about evangelical preaching and ministry without talking about E. V. Hill would greatly diminish the role of a cross-cultural evangelicalism that impacts the church and government for social transformation. It is essential to see E. V. Hill as a model for applicational preaching that touches the urban neighborhood, the affluent neighborhood, and the upper echelons of government and international organizations.

HISTORICAL BACKGROUND

Edward Victor Hill was born in Columbus, Texas, on November 10, 1933. His parents were William and Rosa Hill. He was one of five children born in Texas during the middle of the Great Depression.[1] Hill was not born into an affluent family, but rather into poverty and off the beaten path of life. When Hill was just the tender age of a year and a half, his father walked out on his mother because of his struggle to support the family financially. The abandonment of his father forced his mother to become the primary provider for the family. She worked multiple jobs to try and make ends meet. His mother's difficult work schedule left him and his siblings alone to care for themselves.[2]

In his book *A Savior Worth Having*, Hill described the struggles his mother had to endure to provide for the family: "She moved with her four children to San Antonio, Texas. She got a job making $12.50 a week. Out of that [she] had

---

1. Martha Simmons and Frank A. Thomas, eds., *Preaching with Sacred Fire: An Anthology of African American Sermons, 1750 to Present* (New York: Norton, 2010), 700.

2. E. V. Hill, *A Savior Worth Having* (Chicago: Moody, 2002), 10.

to come up with rent. Most of the food we had as children was leftovers from the White people's table where Mother worked."[3]

Aaron and Ella Langdon's relatives lived next door to the Hills and eventually recognized the need of E. V. and his family. They offered to assist his mother by providing for some of the children. His mother replied to their kind offer, "'Don't ask me to give my children away.' And they said, 'Just drop us a line whenever you want them back and we'll send them back to you right away.' Rosa Hill reluctantly agreed to the Langdons' request,"[4] according to Edward Hill II.

Hill recalled the first time he met the Langdons:

> One day I was playing out in the yard when some elderly people came up and said, "Who is this boy who is so underfed? I had a great big head and a distended stomach, from malnutrition. Some said, "That's Miss Hill's boy." "Where is Miss Hill?" "She's working." "Who takes care of the children when she's gone?" "They take care of themselves." So they waited until mother came home. They said, "We're the Langdons. We live out in the country. Our sister lives next door to you. She's ill; we come up every two weeks to see her. All our children are grown and gone. We live alone, and we have plenty. We'd like to take this boy and girl (my sister) to the country where they could play." Then and there I heard the word *plenty*. It stuck in my ear. I had never been around a place where there was plenty.[5]

Years later, Hill's son, Edward II recalled his father saying, "Momma Langdon was a rough, tough lady who knew how to raise boys."[6] Aaron and Ella Langdon eventually became known as Poppa and Momma; however, Hill's birth mother was always referred to as "mother." Hill used these differentiations to help his audience understand and identify whom he was talking about when articulating the narrative of his life.

The Langdons took Hill to live with them in their "land of plenty" in Seguin, Texas. However, to Hill's disappointment, his understanding of a "land of plenty" turned out to be quite different than reality. In his sermon "How to Pick a Savior," Hill described his new home: "The plenty turned out to be a two-room log cabin. I was looking for a great big old house. The plenty turned out to be wild rabbit, squirrel, hickory nuts and wild berries."[7] Hill never experienced

---

3. Ibid., 40.
4. E. V. Hill II, *Dr. E. V. Hill Interview*, March 26, 2016.
5. E. V. Hill, *A Savior Worth Having*, 41.
6. E. V. Hill II, Dr. E. V. Hill Interview.
7. Hill, *A Savior Worth Having*, 41.

"plenty" the way he had imagined. Hill soon realized his new life brought with it an unimaginable struggle. He stated, "I had to pick cotton during the summer, and shake peanuts and pull corn. Sometimes we would kill a hog and put it in the smokehouse and get some syrup."[8]

"As for clothing, I had lots of hand-me-ups given to me."[9] The land of plenty also introduced Hill to the ugliness and depravity of racial inequality, racial hostility, and racial segregation. He reflected on this upbringing, saying, "I was born amidst hatred and discrimination. I saw all of the evils and I grew up not only hating White people, but I hated them with what I felt was the sanction of the Holy Ghost."[10] Hill's hatred and anger toward white America is outlined in his contribution to the book entitled *Seven Black Preachers Tell What Jesus Means to Me* and is stated as follows:

1. First of all, the white man was a hypocrite. He talked equality in the Declaration of Independence, and piously in the churches across the land, but lived with partialities in his daily life.
2. Secondly, he was selfish and egotistical. He had designed and perpetuated a system that favored his own skin color and short-circuited mine. And I resented the white people's belief that the Negro was just trying to become white. Such self-centeredness on the part of the white man was detestable to me.
3. Third and most important, I hated the white man because he gave me a position beneath my capabilities. The frustrating roadblocks: "You can't eat in my kitchen"; "You can't drink from my fountain"; "You can't go to my school"; "You can't handle my job"; "You can't urinate in my pot"; were constantly there to remind me of my "white-people imposed" position. A position they would not let me bypass. I could not bypass![11]

Momma constantly reminded Hill that in the game of life, he would always be faced with two strikes against him, namely, that he was poor and that he was a colored man. She was trying to impress upon him that he only had one swing to hit a home run in the game of life. However, Hill's new family helped him with this swing by providing security and stability that had been lacking in his life.

---

8. Ibid.
9. Ibid., 42–43.
10. Ibid., 98–99.
11. Emmanuel L. McCall Sr. et al., *Seven Black Preachers Tell What Jesus Means to Me* (Nashville: Broadman, 1971), 101.

Specifically, Poppa filled the void in young Hill's life after his father abandoned the family and left him feeling unwanted and unloved.

Hill found joy in having a man in his life that loved him, spent time with him, taught him, and demonstrated true manhood for him. The security of having a father in his life came to a crashing end when Hill, at the age of eleven, experienced the most devastating loss of his young life. Hill described this time in his sermon "An Emotional Hope" when he said, "At age eleven I woke up one morning and found Poppa dead in his rocking chair."[12] This shocking and unexpected death of Poppa in 1944 left Hill devastated and lonely. However, Hill found comfort, hope, and strength through the pain of Poppa's death when he united with and was baptized at the Sweet Home Baptist Church of Seguin, Texas, under the preaching and pastoral leadership of Reverend Mayes.

After he was saved, Hill's life began to flourish spiritually and academically. In junior and senior high school, he was president of the Sweet Home School student body and president of Area Three of the New Farmers of America. During this period, he also served as the vice president of the Texas New Farmers of America and president of the regional 4-H Club. Hill expanded his Christian service during his time by working as president of local, district, and state Baptist youth organizations.[13]

The persistent pushing of Momma night and day paid off for young Hill. Graduating from high school was no longer an improbability. Hill said, "When I was in the ninth grade, Momma got up in prayer meeting and announced, 'My boy is gonna finish high school.' Well, in that community, few Negro boys finished high school. Maybe you got to the tenth grade, but then you were hired out by a White farmer."[14] The deacons and leaders in the community warned Momma not to become overconfident about Hill's academic future. Momma told them with no uncertainty, "He's gonna finish his school."[15] Later in life, Hill recalled this time of life, saying, "And so I finished high school—president of my class, valedictorian, and highest academic student in my class. By the way, I was the only student in my class."[16]

After Hill graduated from high school, Momma encouraged him to go to college. By faith and the grace of God, Momma sent her son off to Prairie View College in Texas in the fall of 1951, with five dollars, his clothing, and these

---

12. Hill, *A Savior Worth Having*, 42.
13. John H. Pace Jr., "The Use of Application in the Preaching of Dr. E. V. Hill: Building a Bridge From the Biblical Text to Contemporary Life in African American Preaching" (PhD diss., New Orleans Baptist Theological Seminary, 2007).
14. Hill, *A Savior Worth Having*, 45.
15. Ibid.
16. Ibid.

penetrating words, "Now go on to school, the Lord will make a way. . . . I'll be praying for you."[17] God listened to Momma's prayers and sovereignly intervened to provide for Hill via the generosity of Dr. Drew, the president of his college.[18]

The year of 1951 proved to be a year of changes for Hill. He moved to college, recognized God's call to preach, and was licensed as a preacher. At Prairie View, Hill became the "leader of the National Baptist Student Union, which included the responsibility of preaching at the Tuesday night prayer meeting that he grew to an average weekly attendance of about 1,100."[19] Hill's maturation continued to provide him leadership and ministerial opportunities. He was "elected president of the National Baptist Youth Convention of America. Then, in 1954, he was Ordained as a Baptist Minister by the Greater Mount Zion Missionary Baptist Church in Austin, Texas. He received a call to his first pastorate at Friendly Will Missionary Baptist Church, Austin, Texas. Further, he was named the director of youth for the General Baptist Convention of Texas."[20] Hill graduated from college in 1955 in the top ten of his class.

In 1955, Hill transitioned churches and accepted the pastorate of Mount Corinth Missionary Baptist Church in Houston, Texas, one of Houston's oldest and most revered African American congregations. Under Hill's leadership, the church's influence expanded to reach the entire state of Texas. In six years, the church expanded from 214 to 1,100 members and was praised for having one of the largest youth ministries in America.[21] Hill's leadership positioned the church to shape the landscape of "social, political and civic endeavors."[22] Hill fought against the unjust Texas law that criminalized establishing the National Association for the Advancement of Colored People (NAACP) in the state by organizing the Freedom Fund of Texas at Mount Corinth in order to overturn the law. Hill served as an "original Board member of the Southern Leadership Conference" and it is said that Hill even "nominated Martin Luther King Jr. as its first president."[23] Due to his tireless work in the church and in society, Hill received

---

17. Hill, *A Savior Worth Having*, 46.

18. In a sermon by Hill, he recounted going to college without knowing how he would fund his education. As he stood in the cashier's line, he began to get nervous because he knew he could not pay for his college tuition with the money he had. As he remembered Momma's words, "I'll be praying for you," something truly amazing happened: "Dr. Drew touched me on the shoulder and he said, 'Are you Ed Hill?' I said, 'Yes.' 'Are you Ed Hill from Sweet Home?' 'Yes.' 'Was your principal R.V. Arnold?' 'Yes.' 'Have you paid yet?' 'Not quite.' 'We've been looking for you all morning and we were hoping we would get to you before you paid so we wouldn't have to go through the ordeal of refunding you.' I said, 'Well what do you want with me?' 'We have a four-year scholarship that will pay your room and board, your tuition and give you thirty-five dollars a month to spend.'" Simmons and Thomas, *Preaching with Sacred Fire*, 707–8.

19. Pace, "The Use of Application," 26.

20. Hill, *A Savior Worth Having*, 171.

21. Ibid., 171–72.

22. Pace, "The Use of Application," 26.

23. Ibid.

an "honorary Doctor of Law degree from Union Baptist Theological Seminary in Houston."[24] By this time in Hill's life, he was quickly emerging as a leader in church life and in the community, both socially and politically.

Hill experienced another life change when "on August 29, 1955, he married Jane Edna Coruthers of Prairie View, Texas. They were married for thirty-two years and had two children, Norva Rose Hill (Kennard) and Edward Victor Hill II. Hill dearly loved Jane, whom he affectionately called, 'Baby.'"[25] They were a unique couple in that they came "from very different worlds. Jane's father was a professor and she was well educated, receiving a Master's Degree in Nursing and a PhD in Psychology."[26] Sadly, "on October 29, 1987 Jane passed away and Dr. Hill remained alone for four years until he was remarried to LaDean Donald on March 7, 1992."[27]

In January 1961, Hill began pastoring the historic Mount Zion Baptist Church located in the Watts community of Los Angeles, California. "Mount Zion was a church plant that started in 1892 by Second Baptist Church of Los Angeles. The church was primarily planted for African Americans from the Southern United States who had relocated to Los Angeles."[28] The mission effort of the Mount Zion Baptist Church was the famous Lord's Kitchen, which served thousands of meals to the poor and homeless per week, as well as supplied resources to various food pantries across the city.[29] Hill's ministry to the poor and marginalized, his shepherd's heart, and his Christ-centered preaching catapulted him to statewide recognition. These incalculable gifts then opened the door for Hill to be elected to the California State Baptist Convention (NBC USA Inc.). Hill also served as the cochairman of the Baptist World Alliance. In addition to his honorary doctorate from Union Baptist Theological Seminary, Hill received an honorary doctoral degree from Oral Roberts University. He also taught as an associate professor of evangelism at the Billy Graham Evangelistic Association and served on its board of directors.[30]

In politics, Hill was staunchly committed to civil rights and "was intentional about race reconciliation."[31] However, at some point his political allegiances shifted from the Democratic Party to the Republican Party, becoming one of the most influential African American conservative voices in the country.[32] As a

---

24. Ibid.
25. E. V. Hill II, Dr. E. V. Hill Interview.
26. Ibid.
27. Hill, *A Savior Worth Having*, 173.
28. Pace, "The Use of Application," 27.
29. Ibid.
30. Ibid., 28.
31. E. V. Hill II, Dr. E. V. Hill Interview.
32. Hill was summoned to Washington, DC, by six presidents as they sought advice on his concept of reconciliation. This information is found in Hill's sermon entitled, "A Savior Who Gives Us Privileges." Hill, *A Savior Worth Having*, 134–35.

result, he was offered a prestigious governmental post in the Reagan administration.[33] However, he turned this down, because he "could not give up his calling as a minister of the gospel of Jesus Christ."[34]

Modern history has hailed Hill as one of the nation's greatest preachers of the gospel from both black and white pulpits. In his role, he transcended traditional ministerial circles of influence as he was one of the first African American pastors to preach regularly on TBN, a "mainly [white] charismatic Christian television station."[35] In a tribute to E. V. Hill from the Mount Zion Baptist Church where he pastored for forty-two years, it was stated, "He was considered one of the most significant preachers of the twentieth century."[36]

MINISTRY CONTEXT

It is important to understand the uniqueness of the black church experience and why the black church exists to better understand the ministry context of E. V. Hill. According to Kelly M. Smith, in the book *Social Crisis Preaching,* "The Black church in America was called into being as a response to adverse social circumstances and crisis. It became clear immediately that there was no discontinuity between the evil in White society generally and the social evil that manifested itself in the churches."[37] The evil in white society that the author was describing toward African Americans was evident in a multiplicity of ways, including slavery, racism, segregation, unfair and unjust laws, lack of educational opportunities, fair housing laws, etc. "The Black church did and does facilitate Black people's search for truth about themselves. The Christian faith transfers Blacks from the status of nonpersons to the level of sombodiness."[38] This embodies the ministry context of E. V. Hill who was a black man who rose from obscurity to a level of national and international notoriety as he preached a Christ-centered message that provided salvation, hope, and reconciliation for humanity. Hill's purpose for ministry was to bring others into the "third world." As he put it: "For the emphasis in life is neither the black world or the white world, but the kingdom of God! This is something all races must work together for."[39]

---

33. Pace, "The Use of Application," 29.

34. Ibid.

35. Funeral Program: A Memorial Assembly in Loving Memory of Pastor Edward Victor Hill. Friday, March 7, 2003 & Saturday, March 8, 2003. "He was among the first Negro Baptist to preach on the Trinity Broadcasting Network, a mainly charismatic Christian station, which began a love relationship that endured decades."

36. "Tribute to Dr. E. V. Hill," Mt. Zion Missionary Baptist Church, http://www.mtzionla.org/mt-zion-missionary-baptist-church-dr-edward-hill-tribute.php.

37. Kelly M. Smith, *Social Crisis Preaching* (Macon, GA: Mercer University Press, 1984), 9.

38. Ibid.

39. McCall et al., *Seven Black Preachers,* 103.

Edward Victor Hill faithfully served the Mount Zion Missionary Baptist Church for forty-two years. His tenure at Mount Zion Missionary Baptist Church was the last and longest of his illustrious pastoral ministry. "A change of geographical and political scenery came when Hill took over the pastorate of the Mount Zion Baptist Church in Los Angeles. Hill, who had received the nickname 'Hellraiser' for his civil rights work in Houston, claimed that he had left that and his liberal-Democrat tendencies in Texas. [He now embraced] the label of 'conservative Republican.'"[40]

Mount Zion Missionary Baptist Church, located in the Watts community of Los Angeles, has been described as an "island of Black poverty surrounded by middle class White suburbs."[41] This economically plagued and racially "isolated community generated resentment against insufficient hospitals, schools and frequent incidents of police brutality."[42] Racial tension and community unrest meant that Watts was continually on the verge of explosion.

During his early years in Watts, Hill was encouraged to meet his congregation where they were by his friend Dr. Martin Luther King Jr., who stated, "Only a dry as dust religion prompts a minister to extol the glories of heaven while ignoring the social conditions that cause men an earthly hell."[43] As long as the black church has been in existence, "the black preacher has been burdened and blessed with the responsibility of leading black people in the most intimate and critical experiences of their lives."[44] Addressing his congregation, Hill did a compare and contrast of the pastoral responsibilities of an African American pastor and an Anglo-American pastor, suggesting "that white pastors have fewer responsibilities. They merely marry, bury the dead, baptize and preach. Their boards take care of other matters. The black pastor, he stated, 'is considered a community leader, and every aspect of politics, education, civil rights, feeding people, fighting battles, organizing economic opportunities for black people, housing—all of that is considered part of being a good [black pastor]."[45]

Hill understood and accepted this all-encompassing responsibility as a black pastor and community leader. It is because of such responsibility that E. V. Hill's ministry during this time in history had to be multipurposed. "We preach so that souls will be saved, so that social structures will be challenged, so that

---

40. M. Shawn Copeland, "Race and the Vocation of the Christian Theologian," *Spiritus* 2, no. 1 (2002): 19.
41. Kate Meakin, "Watts, Los Angeles (1903-)," The Black Past: Remembered and Reclaimed. http://www.blackpast.org/aaw/watts-los-angeles-1903.
42. Ibid.
43. Martin Luther King, Jr., *Why We Can't Wait* (New York: Harper & Row, 1964), 65.
44. H. Beecher Hicks Jr., *Images of the Black Preacher: The Man Nobody Knows* (Pennsylvania: Judson, 1977), 8.
45. "Time Has Told the Story: E. V. Hill," *Fundamental Journal* 7, no. 2 (1988): 22–23.

congregations will be instructed, so that communities will be formed and so on."[46] The voice of E. V. Hill heralded the concerns, complaints, pains, and cries of the black community. Hill became a voice for his people and their communities, not only in the Watts community but across the United States.

Hill led the Mount Zion Missionary Baptist Church through some of the most tumultuous times in their church history, such as the Watts riots and the financial crisis of the church. He displayed tremendous faith as he was plagued by the burden and injustices of the Watts community, but blessed with the responsibility of leading this church. Hill was a visionary leader, teacher, mentor, conservative evangelical, civil rights activist, and an agent of the Lord who was powerfully used to transform the lives of people in need. He was a forward-thinking man who had the innate ability to envision what others could not see, understand, or comprehend.

It was during the summer of 1965 that Hill's faith and pastoral leadership were being severely challenged because "the Watts area of Los Angeles was being rioted by thousands of earnest young blacks."[47] For weeks, the news media played a major role in portraying racial stereotyping that contributed to "creating social fear of specific urban social spaces."[48] This horrific event left the area of Watts in physical as well as spiritual shambles. According to Hill, "It left many frightened and disillusioned. It left the Christians of Watts on their knees! Lord, this isn't helping your cause. This isn't helping our people. We're waiting on you now, Lord. Show us what to do. If you have the faith, God has the power! As one minister put it, 'Let's make Watts burn again! This time for God!'"[49]

In June of 1966, ten months later, after one of America's most horrific events, an amazing and miraculous event occurred in the life of the Watts community, the church, and in the leadership of Pastor E. V. Hill. It was God's response to the prayers of the righteous. Hill said, "The first summer after the riot we enrolled 902 in Bible School with more than 200 professed decisions for Christ. The second summer after the riot we enrolled 4,928 in Bible School with more than 500 'new faiths' reported. Twenty-eight local churches and twenty-two mission stations were left glowing with the thrill of the presence and power of God. And God is still at work in tremendous ways. If you have the faith, God has the power!"[50]

---

46. L. Susan Bond, *Contemporary African American Preaching: Diversity in Theory and Style* (St. Louis: Chalice, 2003), 8.

47. McCall et al., *Seven Black Preachers*, 103.

48. Sorin A. Matei and Sandra Ball-Rokeach, "Watts, the 1965 Los Angeles Riots, and the Communicative Construction of the Fear Epicenter of Los Angeles" https://www.researchgate.net/publication/233245184, 304.

49. McCall et al., *Seven Black Preachers*, 104.

50. Ibid.

Another serious challenge Hill faced as the spiritual leader of the Mount Zion Missionary Baptist Church was its financial crisis and a dwindling membership. "Upon arriving at Mount Zion, the church was on the brink of foreclosure. Hill's solution was to disband all the church organizations, dismiss all the church officers, and restructure the church entirely."[51] In addition to this, "Every church debt and a looming $151,000 lawsuit was settled within the first six months of his tenure."[52] Over the course of his ministry at Mount Zion, the church saw approximately ten thousand professions of faith and three thousand baptisms.[53] His visionary leadership resulted in numerical, spiritual, and financial growth in both the church and the community.

Due to Hill's organizational success and theological conservatism, new doors of ministry opened to him. "The church soon bought two additional parcels of land, and became a mission sanctuary for the community of Watts."[54] The church started "the Fragment Center, which was a clothing and appliance service center to serve the community. The church also started the Lord's Kitchen, which served breakfast, lunch, and dinner for only fifty cents a meal."[55] The Lord's Kitchen was so successful that reportedly, "at the time of Hill's death, more than two million meals had been served."[56] He traveled and spoke extensively, "receiving up to 600 invitations a year. However, the church did not suffer, nor did they oppose his traveling because they were so proud of him."[57]

E. V. Hill's ministry continued to expand as he crisscrossed the country and was sought out by those in affluent circles and high political office. Hill had a way of knowing how to interact with and relate to people from all walks of life. He could sit and interact with the homeless and downtrodden and yet mingle with the middle class, upper class, and even national dignitaries. He was a "sought-after preacher in numerous churches throughout the Southern Baptist Convention and other denominations" and was a featured speaker at the Promise Keepers conferences.[58] Hill was a speaker at Billy Graham's Schools of Evangelism, his good friend Jerry Falwell's Super Conference, and Moody Bible Institute's Pastors' Conference and Founder's Week.

He was asked by President Nixon to offer the inaugural prayer at Nixon's second inaugural ceremony and hosted President George H. W. Bush at Mount

51. Pace, "The Use of Application," 27.
52. E. V. Hill II, Dr. E. V. Hill Sr. Interview.
53. Hill, *A Savior Worth Having*, 174.
54. E. V. Hill II, Dr. E. V. Hill Sr. Interview.
55. Ibid.
56. Ibid.
57. Ibid.
58. Pace, "The Use of Application," 29–30.

Zion.[59] On the international level, Hill traveled across the world preaching and speaking in one venue after another. He was a speaker at Billy Graham's Amsterdam 1983 Conference. He also spoke in China, Israel, Switzerland, Stockholm, India, and Russia.[60] Although Hill maintained a hectic schedule, his personal success did not hinder him from preparing others for the harvest: "A further indication of [E. V. Hill's] success was the call and ordination of 145 'Sons of Zion'[61] or ministers into God's vineyard, including the current pastor of Mount Zion, his son, Edward Victor Hill II."[62]

E. V. Hill's message was not limited to Mount Zion Missionary Baptist Church and the local community. His prophetic voice, boldness, influence, and tenacity were seen and heard from Watts to the White House in his fight to achieve social justice for humanity. He helped to champion the cause of black Americans as he fought for racial parity and justice for all US citizens. God provided E. V. Hill a worldwide platform from which he preached God's Word for spiritual and social transformation.

THEOLOGY OF PREACHING

The theology of E. V. Hill's preaching helps to capture the heart of his overall preaching ministry. The twenty-three sermons recorded in the books *A Savior Worth Having* and *Victory in Jesus* display three prominent theological elements: the preeminence of Jesus, a high view of Scripture, and a view of salvation. The following is a discussion of these three elements as the shape of E. V. Hill's preaching ministry.

One of the highlights of Hill's preaching was the embedded theology throughout his sermons, particularly of God and Jesus.[63] In one such sermon entitled "In the Name of Jesus," Hill is recorded as saying, "How can you preach a sermon without Jesus? He's the subject and the center, He's the introduction, He's the argument, and He's the conclusion. How can you preach a sermon without Jesus?"[64] Hill's understanding of a well-crafted sermon was one that presents Jesus through every aspect of the sermon: introduction, body, and conclusion. When preaching about Nicodemus, Hill made the claim that divine knowledge

---

59. Ibid.

60. A. Louis Patterson, "Living Legend Dr. E. V. Hill," 2002 International Conference on Expository Preaching, July 8–12, 2002, Dallas, Texas.

61. Funeral Program: A Memorial Assembly in Loving Memory of Pastor Edward Victor Hill, 2003.

62. Ibid.

63. The combination of God/Jesus in this portion of the chapter is not meant to disregard Trinitarian theology; rather it is meant to show Hill's use of God and Jesus in his sermons.

64. Hill, *A Savior Worth Having*, 30.

is an act of divine revelation that can only come from God. He makes this point by stating, "God has been the soul of my understanding. I am not a theologian. But sometimes I preach to theologians. I am not a graduate of a seminary, but I teach in a seminary. I have never had instructions on how to pastor, but I instruct pastors. They call on me from all over the world to instruct, for I got it from revelation. God revealed it to me."[65] What this quote reveals about E. V. Hill is his commitment to utter reliance on God, through Jesus Christ, to reveal the truth of Scripture and to be the subject of the preached Word.

Hill embodies what Cleophus LaRue and Francis Landry Patton, associate professors of homiletics at Princeton Theological Seminary and renowned black homiletics scholars, say about the sovereignty of God in black preaching. LaRue says, "Powerful Black preaching speaks forth the things of God. . . . Each sermon should concern itself with God's essence and actions—God's divine initiative and revelatory activity, especially as that activity is manifested through the work and person of Jesus Christ."[66] God is held in ultimate regard as theologically necessary in preaching, and Hill holds that Scripture ought to be the primary text from which the word of God is heard. The black church tradition believes that "biblical preaching, defined as preaching that allows a text from the Bible to serve as the leading force in shaping the content and purpose of the sermon, the type of preaching considered to be most faithful to traditional understandings of the proclaimed word."[67]

After hearing Hill's sermons, Dante Wright is immediately drawn to Hill's use and command of Scripture. "His theological position on Scripture is that Scripture must be used to display the power of God. Hill consistently referenced Scripture as he formed his application and explanation. Drawing on the tradition of Black preaching, he draws his hearers to the biblical story in order to orient them to God's truth."[68]

Finally, Hill's theology concerning salvation is compelling in that Hill understood salvation as reaching far beyond one's conversion and being holistic in nature. It is holistic in that Hill believed salvation extended to include not only one's conversion decision, but one's lifestyle as a Christian: their talk, their walk, and their overall life in Christ.

While preaching in Lausanne, Switzerland, E. V. Hill presented his conception of salvation and the church's role in presenting the gospel. Hill used a baseball diamond as his illustration:

65. E. V. Hill, *Victory in Jesus: Running the Race You Were Meant to Win* (Chicago: Moody, 2003), 10.
66. Cleophus LaRue, *The Heart of Black Preaching* (Louisville: Westminster John Knox, 2000), 115.
67. Ibid.
68. J. A. Smith Interview.

In the gospel, there is a first base. First base in the gospel is reconcilia-tion to God through Jesus Christ. . . . Second base is where people who are reconciled to God form a visible brotherhood. . . . A relevant church has a second-base movement that encourages love and fellowship and the manifestation of the fruit of the Spirit. . . . People reconciled to God and to each other . . . must proceed to third [base], where, motivated by Jesus' love, filled with agape, we seek to feed the hungry, clothe the naked, bind up the wounded, touch the untouched, heal the brokenhearted, free the captives of unjust circumstances and discrimination, bring close those who are far off, and shelter those without a home. . . . The gospel must have a home base. The gospel must tell all men that by and by they've got to go home.[69]

Hill maintained a holistic view of the gospel and salvation. While Hill wholeheartedly believed one must experience the reconciling power of Jesus Christ before you can run to the other bases, he also believed you could not neglect the other three bases. For Hill, spiritual transformation opens the door for social transformation. Reconciliation with God must lead to reconciliation with all people regardless of race, which must lead to empathizing with and alle-viating the pain of all people. While all of these bases are important, none of them are the end goal. Heaven, a tangible place for the righteous, is home plate. We move from the temporary to the permanent, but while we are moving, Hill believed we must touch all the bases. The base analogy is a snapshot of the spiri-tual transformation in the life of E. V. Hill.

Prior to Hill's true spiritual awakening, he had always believed there was "the negro world and there was the white world."[70] But God revealed to him there was "a third world, the Christian world." Hill described the third world as "a place where men of every color, every race, and every language love one another, stand by one another, and sacrifice for one another whatever the cost! It is a by-product. It is a symptom. It is an experience. It is the love of God produced in a man to the extent that the color of a man's skin makes no difference. It is a result of allowing Jesus Christ to be 'top priority' in a man's life."[71]

The theology of Hill's preaching was an all-inclusive Christ-centered mes-sage that did not violate the Great Commission by preaching only to one's cul-ture context.

---

69. Hill, *Victory in Jesus*, 86.
70. McCall et al., *Seven Black Preachers*, 100.
71. Ibid., 100–101.

METHODOLOGY FOR PREACHING

It has been said that "Edward Victor Hill mastered the folk preaching style."[72] Hill's preaching methodology does not offer scholars much technical or homiletical insight. In his two books of sermons, *A Savior Worth Having* and *Victory in Jesus*, he included twenty-three messages that displayed a high view of Scripture with masterful storytelling and outstanding application. Hill's methodology of preaching would not be that of an expositor, but that of a textual preacher (a textual preacher is one who preaches a sermon based on one or two verses from the Bible), who had the characteristics of a middle-style preacher. Hill's middle, or persuasive, style of preaching was "interesting and energizing.... Aspects such as descriptive language, vivid words, and sensory imagery mark evocative language. The persuasive style also employs analogy, example, and other figures of speech."[73] The methodology of Hill's preaching focused on taking the biblical text and using sound biblical exegesis to appeal to the listening audience's intellect and imagination, and to persuade them to have a new life in Christ. "The biblical text and the African American experience are the Black preacher's main tools for expounding on the Word of God. The text and context of the people and the preacher work together to form and guide the sermon."[74]

Richard Lischer gives a threefold description of the art form of African American preaching based on his observation and study of Martin Luther King Jr.'s preaching: "(1) Proving—An appeal to the intellect, (2) Painting—An appeal to the imagination, and (3) Persuading—An Appeal to the heart."[75] Hill's methodology was not built on Lischer's definition; however, one can see strong similarities between Hill's practice and Lischer's homiletical description of the task of preaching. It must further be noted that black preaching during Hill's time was a folk tradition. The folk tradition of black preaching was passed down from generation to generation. It was not until Henry Mitchell's groundbreaking writings in the 1970s on African American homiletics, *Black Preaching* and *The Recovery of Black Preaching*, that there was a written methodology on black preaching. For the purposes of this study, the following three Ps of the black preaching tradition that Hill utilized in his preaching come from Lischer's study of Dr. Martin Luther King Jr.'s preaching.

72. Simmons and Thomas, *Preaching with Sacred Fire*, 700.
73. William H. Kooienga, *The Craft of Preaching: Elements of Style for Preaching* (Grand Rapids: Ministry Resources Library, 1989), 56–57.
74. James H. Harris, *The World Made Plain: The Power and Promise of Preaching* (Minneapolis: Ausburg Fortress, 2004), 131.
75. Richard Lischer, *The Preacher King: Martin Luther King, Jr. and the Word that Moved America* (New York: Oxford University Press, 1995), 38.

Proving (and Preaching) Christ unto Transformative Understanding

The brilliance of E. V. Hill's preaching began with his methodology of proving the text: "Despite the ambivalent relationship between black peoples and the Bible historically, the Bible plays an important role in the ministry of preaching, as the spirituals demonstrate. Spiritual preaching necessitates conversation with Scripture even if one eventually closes it as did the old-time preachers. In preaching, one 'must contend with the Bible.' A preacher wrestles with the biblical text until God pours out a blessing. 'What one needs to get the preaching job done comes with some kind of encounter with Scripture.'"[76]

"The black preacher often used the best of biblical scholarship to add living details that would not otherwise be evident to the laity. The fresh insights are used to enhance the gripping realism of a message."[77] Proving the text for E. V. Hill meant convincing the audience that Christ was sufficient and that the Bible was to be revered, preached, and believed. Joseph Stowell stated that "Dr. Hill argues without apology that our Savior is above all others, He is Supreme, all-sufficient, a restorer of the soul, and singularly able to save."[78]

Hill's high view of Scripture caused some scholars to view him as proclaiming "an extremely conservative, no-nonsense, back-to-basics type of Christianity."[79] Hill was a conservative evangelical who believed in biblical inerrancy. Thabiti Anyabwile, in his book *Reviving the Black Church: A Call to Reclaim a Sacred Institution,* described the faith tradition behind E. V. Hill's evangelical view of the Bible this way: "In summary, the earliest African American Christians held an evangelical view of the Bible. They believed the Scriptures to be inspired by God, to have authority over the people and the life of faith, and to be sufficient for discerning how one should live—even in the midst of wickedness and oppression perpetrated against them by White professing Christians."[80]

In his methodology of proving that the Bible was sufficient for all of people's needs, Hill did not speak in an abstract or pretentious way. "Hill spoke and preached God's truth in a very practical way. He preached in such a profound way that the gospel message he proclaimed was intellectually high enough to reach the mind of a giraffe, yet simple enough that the sheep could eat at the same time."[81] Hill was the type of preacher who could take deep biblical truths and

---

76. Luke A. Powery, *Dem Dry Bones: Preaching, Death, and Hope* (Minneapolis: Fortress, 2012), 112.

77. Henry H. Mitchell, *Black Preaching: The Recovery of a Powerful Art* (Nashville: Abingdon, 1990), 61.

78. Hill, *A Savior Worth Having,* 12.

79. Simmons and Thomas, *Preaching with Sacred Fire,* 701.

80. Thabiti Anyabwile, *Reviving the Black Church: A Call to Reclaim a Sacred Institution* (Nashville: Broadman & Holman, 2015), 19.

81. J. Alfred Smith Sr., interview by Dante D. Wright I. J. Alfred Smith Sr. Interview on E. V. Hill (March 22, 2015).

relay them to the common person. The gospel message Hill preached allowed the intelligentsia, potentates, the Crips and the Bloods to eat with ordinary people at the same time. E. V. Hill's methodology of proving the biblical text was not an exhaustive exegesis of one passage of Scripture. Hill consistently utilized the technique of referencing several biblical passages that reinforced and established biblical truth that would connect the listening audience to the ancient text, the present, and the future.

In his sermon entitled "What Is Your Life," based on James 4:14, Hill referenced and expounded on several passages of Scripture from the Old Testament to the New Testament, to argue his main point, "What is your life?" Hill used these additional passages to argue and emphasize the point that "true meaning in life is doing the work that God has destined for one to do in relationship with Him."[82] Hill's methodology of proving the text was done differently from traditional homiletics in that he did not use the focal text to do exhaustive exegesis on it to bring out the biblical meaning. Rather, in his proving, he used multiple passages of Scripture to illustrate and expand the biblical knowledge of his hearers to live out the meaning found in James 4:14. Hill's preaching reminds us "that the sermon is not a verbal essay, but an oral performance of Scripture that includes the whole congregation."[83]

Painting Pictures with Words for Imaginative Application

David Buttrick sagaciously suggested that "many a promising sermon is stultified because it is woven of concepts rather than pictures."[84] Maurice Watson further expounds how painting pictures with words is used in black preaching: "Spiritual imagination as a purposeful, methodological consideration for preaching represents one major ingredient to the secret of back preaching. The ability to paint pictures with words, to describe in great detail the landscape, emotions, and nuances of Scripture is first and foremost a spiritual practice that takes discernment of both ancient and contemporary realities."[85]

In black preaching, when the spiritual connects with imagination, you find a preacher with a spiritual, sanctified imagination. Watson described the experience of sanctified imagination as "the wedding between homiletical creativity and hermeneutical accuracy. . . . This wedding takes place between the cardiological,

---

82. E. V. Hill, *"What Is Your Life?"* (Los Angeles: Mount Zion Missionary Baptist Church-Pastor Hill's Tape Ministry #8627, date unknown), audiocassette.

83. Mike Graves, ed., *What the Matter with Preaching Today?* (Louisville: West Minster John Knox Press, 2004), 127.

84. Warren Wiersbe, *Preaching and Teaching with Imagination* (Grand Rapids: Baker, 1994), 14.

85. Beeson's Pastor's Conference held at Samford University, Birmingham, Alabama, on July 18–22, 2011.

the heart, and the cerebral, the brain."[86] It is through spiritual imagination, a canvas of sorts, that the truth comes alive. E. V. Hill assumed this role of a painter and illustrator of God's Word. He consistently used his words to paint pictures of Scripture and to define its practical meaning. Using his rich palate of words and phrases, he painted with sayings, stories, analogies, metaphors, figures of speech, contrast and comparison, historical references, and illustrations. Hill's imaginative preaching is seen in one of his most celebrated sermons entitled, "When God Was at His Best," from Genesis 1:1, "In the beginning God created the heavens and the earth."[87] An excerpt of that sermon is as follows:

> As a matter of fact, if you noticed, I didn't even open my Bible, because when God was at His best was not when He made the heavens and the earth, it was not when He put the sun in place, it was not when He put the moon in place, and it was not when He raised Lazarus from the dead! It wasn't even when He raised Christ from the dead. When God was at His best was in the Sweet Home community. Now Sweet Home is eleven miles south of Seguin. Seguin is twenty-seven miles west of San Antonio. You go down the San Antonio/Houston freeway and you get the Sweet Home cutoff, you turn right, you go down eleven miles to Burland on the highway, and then a dirt road cuts off to your left. That's going where the colored folks live. That's Sweet Home. And it was in Sweet Home when I was eleven years old walking down Grandma Jody's lane that this great big old God, who created the heavens and the earth, this great big old God who made man with all his brilliance, this great big old God who called Lazarus from the dead, this great big old God who made the waters still, He heard my cry.
>
> And He came, this great big old God, dwarfed Himself again and came and entered my heart and saved me. Now, that's when God was at His best. When He save my soul. A little old country boy, a little old semi-orphan boy with nothing but a two-room cabin to live in, insignificant to everybody who saw him. They prophesied that he'd never be anything, and I wish they could wake up from the dead now and see me wherever I am. It was when He entered my heart and saved my soul, and I've been saved for fifty-six years! He did a good job. I haven't had to call Him back to repair anything, I'm saved! I don't believe in saved Monday, lost Tuesday. I've been saved! God was at His best! And I want to go further; God is at His best at saving souls.[88]

86. Beeson's Pastor's Conference.
87. Gen 1:1, ESV.
88. Hill, *A Savior Worth Having*, 60–61.

As seen in this excerpt, Hill was skilled at capturing people's senses for the purpose of spiritual transformation through God's Holy Word. "To preach biblically means much more than to preach the truth of the Bible accurately. It also means to present that truth the way the biblical writers and speakers presented it, and that means addressing the imagination."[89] His gift of illustration enabled him to use his words and hang pictures in the gallery of the listening audience's mind. Hill had the innate ability through the power of the Holy Spirit to "instruct some person on how to live, inspire some person to go on living with hope, despite troubles and strain, give insight into problems and possibilities within and beyond those problems . . . to liberate the hearer's spirit."[90]

Persuading the Congregation for Effective Transformation

E. V. Hill's textual preaching always led him to faithfully prove the text, to paint a picture of the text, and successfully argue the text. However, the true brilliance of his preaching is seen in his ability to persuade the listening audience to apply the Word of God in their daily lives. This is foundational in African American preaching. "African American preachers use application throughout the entirety of the sermon, with the purpose of biblical exegesis being to explain intimately and immediately how the teachings of God's Word impact lives, from salvation, to Christian growth and service, and to the questions and needs of daily life."[91]

Hill's art of persuasion was as a precise tornado, filled with plenty of energy, plenty of enthusiasm, and lots of wind and movement, heading toward a precise target that led the hearers to the saving power of Jesus Christ. Al Fasol said, "Explanation is necessary in a sermon because that is where feeding from the Word occurs. Application is important to either alert or verify for the congregation how the sermon's biblical text applies to our lives here and now."[92]

Hill's true aim in his textual preaching was not merely to fill the mind with biblical insight but to give life application. The job of a faithful proclaimer of God's Word is to preach to the hearer's head, heart, and will. Dr. J. Alfred Smith, a contemporary of Hill, called him "the king of life application."[93] Smith has suggested that "the greatest strength of E. V. Hill's preaching was his great ability to give insightful and life-changing application during the preaching moment. Hill's application touched three categories of human needs: felt needs, hidden

---

89. Wiersbe, *Preaching and Teaching*, 36.
90. Bond, *Contemporary African American Preaching*, 79.
91. Pace, "The Use of Application," 74.
92. Al Fasol, interview by Dante D. Wright I. *Al Fasol Interview on Preaching* (December 5, 2015)
93. J. Alfred Smith Sr. Interview.

needs and spiritual needs."[94] Hill believed that if the people were to hear from heaven, then he must "show how the ancient words of the Bible offered guidance for living."[95] The methodology of his preaching shows that application was used throughout his sermons, and not merely used as an appendix or an add-on to the sermon. It was, in fact, the heartbeat of his sermons. In studying Hill's methodology for application, we see he utilized three kinds of sermon applications: "(1) Interrogative application, which asks a question, (2) Indicative application, which points out who God is, or more simply stated, it defines the truth to be believed, and (3) Imperative application, which is an application that directs the listener to take action."[96]

Hill crafted his application by asking probing questions of the people, by showing the congregation who they are in Christ, by encouraging the hearer to believe what God says about them, and by presenting clear ways to take action once the message was understood.

John Pace performed detailed research on Hill's use of application in his sermons. After analyzing over seventy sermons, Pace discovered that "the majority (67 percent) of the instances of application are found in the body of the sermons . . . and Hill's approach is to employ application constantly throughout the sermon."[97] The result of this approach is that the hearer of the sermon was constantly introduced to actions they could take to implement the teachings of the text. By the conclusion of the sermon, Hill had given multiple ways to incorporate Scripture into their lives. Hill's preaching was extremely concerned about applications, and this bore incredible fruit.

The centrality of application in Hill's preaching helps hearers construct a biblical worldview centered on life with Christ as Savior. Hill's application acts as a guide to better living, better faith, and better focus on the kingdom of God. Hill preached, persuading believers to respond to a call to action that was taught through the biblical text. Through application, the church helped the poor, they helped the elderly, they encountered and welcomed gang members, and they saw true life change. Hill pushed application past the preaching moment into the living moment. Hill's application achieves what David Veerman describes as application that "helps people know what to do or how to use what they have learned."[98]

94. Ibid.

95. Paul S. Wilson, *The New Interpreter's Handbook of Preaching* (Nashville: Abingdon, 2008), 176.

96. Awbrey, Ben. "Style & Application in Expository Preaching." Lecture, Application in Expository Preaching, Midwestern Baptist Theological Seminary, Kansas City, Kansas, June 6–8, 2017.

97. Pace, "The Use of Application," 101.

98. David Veerman, "Apply Within," in *The Art and Craft of Biblical Preaching: A Comprehensive Resource for Today's Communicators*, eds. Craig Brian Larson and Haddon Robinson (Grand Rapids: Zondervan, 2005), 285–286.

CONTRIBUTIONS TO PREACHING

It is very rare in life that we are able to behold someone who already belongs to the ages. If we are fortunate, maybe this occurs once or twice in our lifetime. Before his journey into God's eternal rest, the place of Edward Victor Hill was secured in the history of preachers. His life and ministry will not be a lost footnote in time. When future generations of the church take note of twentieth-century preaching, they will note stalwarts such as Billy Graham, Martin Luther King Jr., and Gardner Taylor. Historians will also speak of E. V. Hill and recognize the great calling placed on his life and the great ministry that was brought forth from his pulpit through the power and anointing of the Holy Spirit.

There are two major contributions E. V. Hill left: (1) a great legacy for the art and science of African American preaching, especially with regard to how his high view of Scripture and Christ-centered theology were painted into pictures for life application and (2) his innate ability to appeal to a cross-cultural audience for both spiritual and social transformation.

In his book *Images of the Black Preacher,* H. Beecher Hicks Jr. said, "We must begin now preserving something of the great preaching tradition and heritage of Black people. The contribution of Black pulpit giants has only been spasmodically recorded and not at all preserved for our posterity."[99] It is because of the preaching prowess of E. V. Hill and other noted African American preachers that the preaching tradition of African Americans will no longer rest in the deep freezer of eternity.

Hill's preaching provides a plethora of insight into the art and science of black preaching, but his preaching is not only educational for those aspiring to serve in historically Black churches. As one examines Hill's preaching, it is imperative not to label him simply as a black preacher, for Hill himself said in his sermon "If the Foundations Be Destroyed," "When I moved to Los Angeles, I refused to preach a Black gospel (I refused to even use the word). I'm still a Negro. I'm proud of the fact that my great-grandfather was a Negro. I know that Black is an adjective and I'm not an adjective, I'm a noun: as a matter of fact, I'm a proper noun. You say Black, you've got to say something, and it's that something that disturbs me."[100]

Hill was a gifted African American preacher who was raised in the African American experience. Yet he was often frustrated by the term *black* as attributed to his personhood. He recognized his personhood as Negro, a proper noun,

---

99. Hicks, *Images of the Black Preacher,* 118.
100. Hill, *Victory in Jesus,* 62.

and not as black, an adjective used to describe the color of some object. African American preaching at its finest allows for the preacher to locate their personhood in the gospel truth without having to lower themselves to mere descriptive sidenotes.

While today the terms African American and black may be argued as synonymous, E. V. Hill challenged us to preach to the person and not the description. Black preaching can be summed up as the ability to preach in such persuasive fashion that the downtrodden realize their personhood in Christ and dismiss the indoctrination that they are merely sidenotes. Hill's preaching was a light that shone brightly on the rich historical tradition of African American preaching. Through Hill's tireless preaching ministry, he has made it so black preaching can no longer be cast aside as unworthy of homiletical and theological reflection. African American preaching has made an impact on the history of preaching, and others are finally taking notice of and accepting African American preaching as the true preaching art and science form it is.[101]

Hill's second contribution was his ability to appeal to a cross-cultural audience with both spiritual and social transformation. As stated in *Crossover Preaching*: "Crossover speakers not only show adeptness at crossing over racial, cultural, and ecclesial difference in lecturing and preaching, but they show adeptness at performing improvisation and intercultural competence."[102] Hill's preaching on racial reconciliation had a dual approach like the apostle Paul's message in 2 Corinthians 5:17–20.[103] Hill was an exemplar of one who lived out the ministry *and* the message of reconciliation. Hill's dual approach in preaching the gospel offered believers *spiritual* hope and *social* transformation. Hill used his prophetic voice to always fight injustice with God's justice. Hill

---

101. Several modern homileticians explicitly encourage students and pastors alike to learn from the rich history of black preaching. On this Paige Patterson once commented, "When it comes to rhetoric, the best Anglo preachers on their best days don't preach as well as a good black preacher on his worst day." David Van Biema, "America's Best: Spirit Raiser," *Time* 158, no. 11 (17 September 2001), 53; David Buttrick has said, "I have been influenced by the Black homiletic tradition. All things considered, it is probable that the finest preaching in America today is Black." David Buttrick, *Homiletic* (Philadelphia: Fortress, 1987), 469; Leander Peck has said, "One could show rather easily that preaching has lost its centrality in most mainline white Protestant churches, although it has never lost its place in black Protestantism." Leander Peck, *The Bible in the Pulpit* (Nashville: Abingdon, 1978), 15; and Richard Lischer, in a *Time* magazine feature said, "They remind us that the sermon is not a verbal essay but an oral performance of Scripture that includes the whole congregation." David Van Biema and Nadia Mustafa, "How Much Does Preaching Matter?," *Time* 158, no. 11 (17 September 2001), 53.

102. Jared E. Alcantara, *Crossover Preaching: Intercultural-Improvisational Homiletics in Conversation with Gardner C. Taylor* (Downers Grove, IL: IVP Academic, 2015), 68.

103. 2 Corinthians 5:17–20 (ESV), "Therefore, if anyone is in Christ, he is a new creation. The old has passed away; behold, the new has come. All this is from God, who through Christ reconciled us to himself and gave us the *ministry of reconciliation*; that is, in Christ God was reconciling the world to himself, not counting their trespasses against them, and entrusting to us the *message of reconciliation*. Therefore, we are ambassadors for Christ, God making his appeal through us. We implore you on behalf of Christ, be reconciled to God." (Emphasis added.)

was "a compassionate minister to both poor of spirit and those poor in worldly goods."[104] He refused to separate these two tasks of preaching for spiritual *and* social transformation.

CONCLUSION

E. V. Hill represents what W. E. B. Du Bois asserted regarding the black preacher: "The Preacher is the most unique personality developed by the Negro on American soil."[105] Hill was a man who was revered from the church house to the White House, from the African American context to the Anglo-American context, from the down-and-out to the highfalutin people and potentates. However, the Mount Zion Missionary Baptist Church of Los Angeles, California, is the place where the genius of Hill was birthed and gained national attention. From the pulpit of Mount Zion Missionary Baptist Church, Hill was an exemplar of what H. Beecher Hicks Jr. described in his book *Images of the Black Preacher*: "The black preacher is expected to be the leader in the black church. He is head of the church family, the husband in the romantic relation, and in a spiritual sense the father/parent of every person in the church. Primarily black people see in his leadership the symbols of strength and accomplishment when all around them are symbols of weakness and miserable failure."[106]

As a conservative evangelical with a prophetic voice for the nation, Hill's sermons were rooted in the infallible Word of God. "Like every Christ-commissioned preacher, the Black Christian preacher has had to preach the gospel, but he has also had to work actively against the social forces that undermine human dignity and make the gospel seem only a wealth of words."[107]

The influence and uniqueness of E. V. Hill's preaching belong not only to his time but to all times. It would be wise for preachers and scholars to study his deep reverence for the biblical text, his innate ability to tell the biblical story and give insightful application, and his ability to preach the gospel cross-culturally. Regardless of the risk or personal cost, E. V. Hill crossed racial, social, political, and economic barriers. His unique and vivacious personality, his robust dependence on the Word of God, and his incredible preaching prowess has left him to be remembered and recognized as one of the most gifted preachers, activists, and leaders of the twentieth century.

---

104. Simmons and Thomas, *Preaching with Sacred Fire*, 701.
105. W. E. B. Du Bois, *Booker T. Washington, W. E. B. Du Bois, Frederick Douglass: Three African American Classics* (New York: Dover, 2007), 282.
106. Hicks, *Images of the Black Preacher*, 95.
107. Bond, *Contemporary African American Preaching*, 67.

Sermon Excerpt
What's in a Name (Acts 4:7, 10, 12)[108]

What's in a Name?

Of all the names on earth today, one name is more powerful than any other. Christians know it has the power to change lives, save lost souls, heal sick bodies, and secure eternity. It is the name of our beloved Savior, Jesus.

I was reared in a log cabin; Momma and I came up together. Papa passed on when I was eleven. Momma and I battled through. Then Momma passed on, and every so often when I am privileged to speak in one of the great venues of Christendom, I ask the Lord, "Lord, let Momma see me here!" (I realize theologically it's not quite possible—but I didn't go to seminary, so I can take this liberty.)

One of the great thrills of my life was preaching in Moscow several years ago—just a couple of blocks from Lenin's Tomb, in the heart of Moscow. I was speaking to about 6,000 preachers (I suspect old Lenin was turning over in his grave) about this wonderful Jesus. For now, even in Moscow, the name of Jesus can be publicly spoken. Who would have thought four or five or ten years ago that the name "Jesus" could be uttered freely on the streets of the former Soviet Union? Tragically, while in Russian public schools He can be read about and discussed freely, in our own public schools, it is forbidden to speak His name.

Who Needs a Savior?

Wherever you go, no matter what class—whether it's politicians, seminarians, professors, teachers, or even with people whose homes are breaking up—the heart's plea is, "I need a savior." Even the brightest minds need a savior.

One of the members of the Mount Zion church where I pastor, holds a double master's degree in Law and Finance. He left my church and went to another group that dealt with the mind, for he said he wanted to go to a place that fed his mind. He complained that the average preacher was too simple in his presentation, that he needed someone who would deal with his mind.

---

108. Hill, *A Savior Worth Having*, 13–23.

So I told him, "I'll be praying for you." Then I added, "Incidentally, you are not my attorney anymore."

He replied, "Why? Are you prejudiced because I'm leaving your church?"

Then I said, "No, I just don't want an attorney who doesn't know the difference between stepping up and falling down."

Then one Sunday I was preaching my National Children's Day sermon. And I was speaking on Billy (my rabbit). Billy was a wonderful rabbit, and I was telling the children about Billy. At invitation time, here comes this double-master fellow down the aisle. He says, "Pastor, that's the greatest sermon I've ever heard you preach!" Even someone with a double master's degree needs a savior. ◆

BIBLIOGRAPHY

"American Preaching: A Dying Art." *Time* 114, no. 27 (31 December 1979). http://time-proxy.yaga.com

Alcantara, Jared E. *Crossover Preaching: Intercultural-Improvisational Homiletics in Conversation with Gardner C. Taylor.* Downers Grove, IL: IVP Academic, 2015.

Al Fasol, interview by Dante D. Wright I. *Al Fasol Interview on Preaching* (December 5, 2015)

Anyabwile, Thabiti. *Reviving the Black Church: A Call to Reclaim a Sacred Institution.* Nashville: Broadman & Holman, 2015.

Beeson's Pastor's Conference held at Samford University, Birmingham, Alabama, on July 18–22, 2011.

Bond, L. Susan. *Contemporary African American Preaching: Diversity in Theory and Style.* St. Louis: Chalice, 2003.

Broadus, John. *On the Preparation and Delivery of Sermons.* Birmingham: Solid Ground Christian Books, 2005.

Buttrick, David. *Homiletic.* Philadelphia: Fortress, 1987.

Curry, Erin. "E. V. Hill Remembered as a Conservative African American Pastor, Civil Rights Leader." *Baptist Press* (26 February 2003). http://www.bpnews.net/15322.

Evans, Tony. *Theology You Can Count On.* Chicago: Moody, 2008.

Fasol, Al. *Essentials for Biblical Preaching: An Introduction to basic Sermon Preparation.* Grand Rapids: Baker, 1989.

"Funeral Program: A Memorial Assembly in Loving Memory of Pastor Edward Victor Hill." Los Angeles, March 2003.

Graves, Mike. *What's the Matter with Preaching Today?* Louisville: West Minster John Knox, 2004.

Hendricks, Howard. *Living by the Book.* Chicago: Moody, 1991.

Hicks Jr., H. Beecher. *Images of the Black Preacher: The Man Nobody Knows.* Pennsylvania: Judson, 1977.

Hill, E. V. *A Savior Worth Having.* Chicago: Moody, 2002.

_____. *Victory in Jesus: Running the Race You Were Meant to Win.* Chicago: Moody, 2003.

Hill II, Edward Victor, interview by Dante D. Wright I. A Chat with Dr. E. V. Hill's Only Son (March 10, 2015).

Hoyt, Carlos R. "The Pedagogy of the Meaning of Racism: Reconciling a Discordant Discourse." *Social Work* 57, no. 3 (July 2012): 225–34.

Hughes, Jack. *Expository Preaching with Word Pictures: With Illustrations from the Sermons of Thomas Watson.* Fearn, Scotland: Christian Focus, 2001.

LaRue, Cleophus. *I Believe I'll Testify.* Louisville: Westminster John Knox, 2011.

_____. *The Heart of Black Preaching.* Louisville: Westminster John Knox, 2000.

Lischer, Richard. *The Preacher King: Martin Luther King, Jr. and the Word that Moved America.* New York: Oxford University Press, 1995.

McCall, Emmanuel, et al. *Seven Black Preachers Tell What Jesus Means to Me*. Nashville: Broadman, 1971.

Mitchell, Henry. *Black Preaching: The Recovery of a Powerful Art*. Nashville: Abingdon, 1990.

Pace, John H., Jr. "The Use of Application in the Preaching of Dr. E. V. Hill: Building a Bridge from the Biblical Text to Contemporary Life in African American Preaching." PhD diss., New Orleans Theological Seminary, 2007.

Patterson, A. L. "Living Legend (Dr. E. V. Hill)." Comp. Dove Conference Services. 2002.

Peck, Leander. *The Bible in the Pulpit*. Nashville: Abingdon, 1978.

Simmons, Martha, and Frank A. Thomas. *Preaching with Sacred Fire: An Anthology of African American Sermons, 1750 to the Present*. New York: Norton, 2010.

Smith, Kelly M. *Social Crisis Preaching*. Macon, GA: Mercer University Press, 1984.

Smith, Robert. *Doctrine that Dances*. Nashville: Broadman & Holman, 2003.

Van Biema, David. "America's Best: Spirit Raiser." *Time* 158, no. 11 (17 September 2001): 53.

Van Biema, David, and Nadia Mustafa. "How Much Does Preaching Matter?" *Time* 158, no. 11 (17 September 2001): 53.

Veerman, David. "Apply Within." Pages 283–288 in *The Art and Craft of Biblical Preaching: A Comprehensive Resource for Today's Communicators*. Edited by Craig Brian Larson and Haddon Robinson. Grand Rapids: Zondervan, 2005.

Wiersbe, Warren. *Preaching and Teaching with Imagination*. Grand Rapids: Baker, 1994.

Wilson, Paul S. *The New Interpreter's Handbook of Preaching*. Nashville: Abingdon, 2008.

Jerry Falwell
Preaching Dynamic Faith

EDWARD E. HINDSON

A Baptist pastor, educator, and social activist, Jerry Falwell (1933–2007) founded one of the largest churches of the twentieth century and the world's largest evangelical Christian university. He was also a lightning rod in American politics, galvanizing evangelical pastors to support conservative causes. He was voted America's "Man of the Year" in 1979 by *Good Housekeeping* magazine. Although often remembered by those looking in from the outside as a political activist, Jerry Falwell was first and foremost a pastor and preacher. His sermons were filled with words of encouragement, practical application, calls to action, and a belief that dynamic faith could move mountains.

HISTORICAL BACKGROUND

Jerry and his twin brother, Gene, were born in Lynchburg, Virginia, on August 11, 1933. Their father, Carey Falwell, was a businessman, a bootlegger, an alcoholic, and an avowed atheist. Carey had shot and killed his brother Warren in self-defense and eventually drank himself to death. Their mother, Helen, has been described as "a saint in the midst of a rough and rowdy family of southern rebels."[1] It was this rough-and-tumble background that galvanized young Jerry Falwell with strength and courage.

The Falwell family traced their roots in Virginia to the early 1600s. Jerry's great-great-grandfather, Hezekiah Falwell, arrived in Lynchburg in 1850. In 1914, Jerry's grandmother, Martha Falwell, died from a crippling disease. As a result, his grandfather turned his back on God and his bitterness affected his son Carey. Jerry's father, Carey Falwell, adamantly rejected God until he made a profession of faith on his deathbed when he was succumbing to cirrhosis of the liver. Years later, Jerry heard the story from Frank Buford, who was there when

---

1. Macel Falwell, *Jerry Falwell: His Life and Legacy* (New York: Howard, 2008), 4.

his father finally accepted Christ two weeks before he died.[2] Jerry explained that his compelling desire to share the gospel with as many people as possible was the fact that no one—to his knowledge—had ever dared to share the gospel with his father until his dying moments.

Having lost his father at an early age, Jerry often roamed the hills near their family home. Even before his conversion, Jerry was drawn to a particular mountain. "Someday I'm going to own that mountain," he told himself, long before purchasing the five thousand acres that would eventually house Liberty University.[3]

After high school, Jerry enrolled at the local Lynchburg College as a math major. In the meantime, his widowed mother continued to pray for her son's conversion as she blared the preaching of Charles Fuller and the *Old Fashioned Revival Hour* on the radio for Jerry to hear. Convicted by Fuller's message, Jerry decided to attend the evening service at the local Park Avenue Baptist Church on January 20, 1952. That night, nineteen-year-old Jerry went forward to profess his faith in Christ, and his life was dramatically changed. Within three months, he felt a call to the ministry. That fall, he transferred to Baptist Bible College in Springfield, Missouri, graduating *summa cum laude* in 1956. A brilliant student, Jerry quickly memorized hundreds of Bible verses, his theology textbook, and most of the notes in the *Scofield Bible*.[4] He was also influenced by several books on prayer and faith.[5] His balanced theology was influenced by a strong commitment to the inerrancy of Scripture, the deity of Christ, the centrality of the gospel, and the importance of the local church.

Returning to Lynchburg after graduation, Jerry founded the Thomas Road Baptist Church in his hometown with thirty-five charter members in 1956. Jerry's love for Christ and for people motivated him his entire life. He knocked on a hundred doors a day, inviting people to the church. Two years later he married Macel Pate. She would say of her husband that he never gave up on people because his mother never gave up on him.[6] "We all need to know that God loves us . . . that in Christ God has forgiven our sins and our failures . . . and that through Christ we can begin again," he proclaimed.[7]

---

2. Ibid., 22.

3. Ibid., 23.

4. Scofield's dispensational annotations and the influence of Noel Smith, Jerry's theology professor, gave him a love for the promise of the rapture and the premillennial hope, both of which shaped his views about Israel and the Jewish people. See Merrill Simon, *Jerry Falwell and the Jews* (Middle Village, NY: Jonathan David, 1984), 20–21.

5. Some of the authors most influential in this area were E. M. Bounds, Andrew Murray, and Oswald Chambers.

6. Macel Falwell, *Falwell: His Life and Legacy*, 17.

7. Ibid., 43.

Within a few weeks, Falwell launched the *Old-Time Gospel Hour* radio broadcast, and by the end of the year, he began a telecast with the same name on the local ABC affiliate in Lynchburg. Television made him an instant celebrity in those early days of religious broadcasting.[8] In the meantime, the Thomas Road Baptist Church grew rapidly and built a three-thousand-seat Jeffersonian, octagonal sanctuary in 1968. It was one of the largest and most impressive church buildings of its time and drew national attention. Within Falwell's lifetime, the church grew to over twenty thousand members. By 1970, Falwell was preaching the evangelical gospel to millions through his national telecast, the *Old-Time Gospel Hour.*[9]

In 1971, Falwell founded Lynchburg Baptist College (renamed Liberty University in 1985) with the goal of training a projected five thousand pastors, missionaries, and Christian workers. Propelled by the popularity of his telecast, the school grew rapidly from 124 initial students to become the largest evangelical Christian school of higher education in the world. Falwell would later set a goal of fifty thousand future students. Today, Liberty University is fully accredited by the Southern Association of Colleges and Schools Commission on Colleges to award associate, bachelor's, master's, specialist, and doctoral degrees in a variety of disciplines, including law, medicine, and divinity. They have a total enrollment of over one hundred thousand residential and online students.

In 1979, Falwell formed the Moral Majority organization, rallying conservative pastors nationwide to urge their congregations to register to vote in the upcoming election in 1980. Despite coming from a Southern family of lifelong Democrats, Falwell believed the Republican agenda of the time better suited the Christian values that he espoused. Like many in the South, Jerry became disillusioned with President Carter's liberal policies, despite his born-again profession. As a result, Falwell led a vigorous campaign to unseat Carter and elect Ronald Reagan as president. It is estimated by Falwell's staff that he logged more miles than Reagan and Carter combined, often appearing in more than three cities a day, attempting to "get out the vote."

Falwell's political agenda was driven by his biblical beliefs in the sanctity of life, the importance of the family, opposition to abortion-on-demand, gay marriage, illegal drugs, and pornography. He was strongly committed to the right of the State of Israel to exist in its biblical homeland. He also believed that a strong

---

8. Falwell's *Old-Time Gospel Hour* became the most watched religious telecast of the late 1970s and early 1980s. See Dinesh D'Souza, *Falwell Before the Millennium: A Critical Biography* (Chicago: Regnery Gateway, 1984), 143–56.

9. Ibid.

national defense was the best deterrent to war.[10] At the same time, he remained committed to spiritual revival, church planting, and Christian education—not politics—as the greatest means to turn America back to God. In 1982, *U.S. News and World Report* named Jerry Falwell as one of the twenty most powerful and influential people in America.

MINISTRY CONTEXT

Jerry Falwell was born during the Depression, grew up during World War II, and spent his collegiate years during the Eisenhower presidency. In almost every way, he was a product of the mid-twentieth century. His family was affluent by the standards of the time. When he left home to study for the ministry in 1956, he drove a brand-new Buick and had four thousand dollars cash in his pocket. Unlike some televangelists who grew up poor and later overindulged on their success, Falwell remained unaffected by the lure of money, which had such a devastating effect on his father. Falwell drove a truck as his personal vehicle, wore black suits, white shirts, and usually a red tie. Known for his generosity, he gave away money, scholarships, and favors to thousands of people. Affable and personable, he was even liked by most of his opponents, including Phil Donahue and Ted Kennedy.[11]

Falwell was intellectually brilliant but undereducated. His entire ministry was based on his three-year Bible college education. In many ways, his personal life and experiences were very similar to the two great preachers of the nineteenth century whom he admired most: D. L. Moody and Charles Spurgeon, neither of whom had significant *formal* education, yet founded schools and greatly influenced their generation.

Theologically, Falwell was committed to what he believed were the basic fundamentals of the Christian faith, which included premillennial eschatology, the necessity of a born-again experience, the importance of prayer, great personal faith, evangelistic soul-winning, and practical local church ministry. For him, faith meant "taking God at His word no matter how bleak the circumstances appear to be" and "standing on God's integrity and acting on His promises even if you have to act or stand alone." [12] He often added, "Nothing of eternal consequence is ever obtained without prayer," which he viewed as "the most dynamic force available to any human being."[13] Therefore, he believed "a Christian must

---

10. Jerry Falwell, Ed Dobson, and Ed Hindson, *The Fundamentalist Phenomenon* (Garden City, NY: Doubleday, 1981), 189–90.

11. Jerry Falwell, *Strength for the Journey: An Autobiography* (New York: Simon & Schuster, 1987), 377–88.

12. Jerry Falwell, *Keys to Daily Living: A Practical Guide to Life* (Milwaukee: Ideals, 1981), 4, 13.

13. Ibid., 8.

take his or her stand for the truth, no matter what it costs. It is more important to be right than popular."[14]

Undaunted by criticism, obstacles, or objections, Jerry Falwell was a spiritual giant, a man's man, and a leader's leader. He amassed a huge staff, managed an enormous ministry, raised millions of dollars, motivated thousands of pastors, and undoubtedly left his mark on his generation. Despite America's moral erosion and spiritual drift, Jerry remained a major voice for biblical truth and morality during his lifetime.

Jerry Falwell was "a man standing at a crossroads of history," blessed with a personal charisma and powerful influence.[15] Upon his conversion, he entered the fundamentalist milieu which, by the mid-twentieth century, was reacting to the wave of theological, social, and political liberalism that had been sweeping mainline Protestants away from what he viewed as America's spiritual heritage. Dinesh D'Souza remarked, "Falwell has not only been able to tap into fundamentalist alienation and frustrations . . . but also to attract followers among the majority of American Christians and Jews worried about the slide of their society."[16]

At the same time, Falwell was committed to evangelism and church growth. By 1970, his church had been identified as one of the largest and fastest growing churches in America.[17] At a time when few evangelical churches grew beyond one thousand members, Falwell set his sights on multiple thousands. By 1972, he held a Sunday school rally in Lynchburg that attracted a reported nineteen thousand people with over one thousand professions of faith. His church was rapidly becoming one of America's original megachurches. To this day, close to ten thousand people a week worship at the Thomas Road Baptist Church under the ministry of Falwell's son Jonathan.[18]

God called a gifted and unusual young man from a very obscure community in the foothills of the Blue Ridge Mountains to touch the world. Today, Lynchburg, Virginia, is a key destination on the evangelical map. Church leaders, politicians, musicians, artists, publishers, and authors from every spectrum of the evangelical world visit the campus of Liberty University, led by his son Jerry Falwell Jr. With nearly fifteen thousand students in residence and over ninety-five thousand students online, Liberty University—perhaps Jerry's greatest legacy—has become a world-class university with a global outreach as a result of one man's vision to make a difference.

---

14. Ibid., 27.

15. D'Souza, *Falwell Before the Millennium*, 23.

16. Ibid., 32.

17. Elmer Towns, *America's Fastest Growing Churches* (Nashville: Impact, 1972); John Vaughn, *The World's 20 Largest Churches* (Grand Rapids: Baker, 1984), 117–24.

18. Jonathan Falwell, *Innovate Church* (Nashville: Broadman & Holman, 2008); cf. also "Largest Churches in America, 2015" *Outreach* (Nashville: Lifeway Research, 2015), centerpiece.

THEOLOGICAL CONTEXT

"I'm a Christian," Jerry Falwell would often say, "and that's all that really matters." His optimistic outlook on life tempered his fundamentalist training. Despite his conservative theology, he avoided the extreme separationism that marked most fundamentalists. He plowed ahead in the ministry with unswerving faith, constant prayer, and incredible personal energy. In many ways, he was a blend of theologies. He clearly rejected limited atonement but strongly affirmed the security of the believer and the sovereignty of God. He was definitely a Baptist in polity and an evangelical in spirit. He advocated "co-belligerence" with other faiths on matters of social policy and political engagement.

Early in his ministry, Falwell was also influenced by "deeper life" ideas he gleaned from reading authors like Oswald Chambers, A. W. Tozer, R. A. Torrey, and E. M. Bounds. He was also impressed with the biography of George Müller. Jerry was attracted to the importance of faith and prayer in these works. He said, "Those who have learned to pray have learned to receive things from God, to live in the supernatural, and to be used of God to bless others."[19]

By the second decade of his ministry, Falwell developed a passion for reaching his city and the nation for Christ. He said, "I believe in radio, television, and the printed page. Our principle of saturation evangelism means simply preaching the gospel to every available person, at every available time, by every available means."[20] He saw this as the primary objective of every local church, which he believed was called of God to "win their city to Christ."[21] By the early 1970s, Falwell was preaching at pastors' conferences nationwide, challenging other pastors to do what he had done in his hometown of sixty thousand people. Falwell outlined his ingredients for a successful soul-winning church by highlighting the following pastoral practices: (1) preach the gospel with power, (2) be willing to pay the price, (3) build great congregations of believers, (4) everything must be bathed in prayer, and (5) penetrate the entire community.[22]

By 1975, Jerry began to turn his vision for his hometown to America as a whole. He launched a series of "I love America" rallies that took him to the steps of forty-five state capitols. His powerful message calling America back to God resonated with the American bicentennial fervor that was sweeping the nation by 1976. At the same time, however, he began to receive criticism for his

---

19. Falwell, *Keys to Daily Living*, 8.

20. Rod Dempsey, "The Ministry Methods of Jerry Falwell," *Eruditio Ardescens* 1, no. 1 (2013) at http://digital commons.liberty.edu/jlbts/vol.1/iss1/2.

21. Jerry Falwell, *America Can Be Saved* (Murfreesboro, TN: Sword of the Lord, 1979), 100.

22. Ibid., 102–7.

conservative views. He believed that most of those who condemned him for his involvement in politics were simply hypocritical. "If I called for the nationalization of major oil companies, every liberal in the country would be for me," he said. "But because I stand for the family, for patriotism, and against abortion, all these people say I am a threat to the Bill of Rights."[23]

The evangelical shift in voting patterns from 1976 to 1980 and beyond has been largely credited to Falwell's influence within evangelical churches.[24] He worked tirelessly to urge politicians in both major parties to defend what he believed were the biblical and conservative values and found his message was more receptive to Republican candidates like Ronald Reagan, George H. W. Bush, and George W. Bush.

Falwell eventually closed the Moral Majority organization to focus on his primary responsibilities as pastor of the Thomas Road Baptist Church and chancellor of Liberty University. From about 2000 on, he referred to this time as his "fourth quarter ministry," leaving behind one of America's largest churches and the world's largest evangelical university.

METHODOLOGY FOR PREACHING

Jerry Falwell exuded the gift of exhortation and excelled at personal and practical application. By no means was he an expository preacher; instead, his preaching was a blend of prophetic declarations and pragmatic applications. He once preached chapter by chapter through Proverbs, focusing on what he called "wisdom for living."[25] He often highlighted key ideas that he believed would help people live successful Christian lives. Balancing his view of God's sovereignty and people's responsibility, he said, "the Book of Proverbs is the most concise blueprint for successful living to be found in the sixty-six books of the Bible."[26] Within these sermons, Falwell outlined biblical advice for wisdom, success, parenting, leadership, and right living.

Falwell's practical application of familiar biblical stories can be seen in his series *Champions for God*.[27] Each sermon was a character study on leading figures of the Bible: Abraham, Moses, Joshua, David, Elijah, Elisha, Daniel, Nehemiah,

---

23. Dinesh D'Souza, "Jerry Falwell Is Reaching Millions and Drawing Fire," *Conservative Digest* (Dec. 1986), 9.

24. Ibid., 11. Cf. also A. Cerillo and M. Dempster, "The New Right Activates the Grass Roots," in *Salt and Light: Evangelical Political Thought in Modern America*, by Augustus Cerillo (Grand Rapids: Baker, 1989), 107–43.

25. Jerry Falwell, *Wisdom for Living* (Wheaton, IL: Victor, 1984).

26. Ibid., 18.

27. Ibid., 33. Throughout most of his ministry Falwell would state the same principle as "Champions for Christ."

Esther, John the Baptist, Peter, and Paul. In each example, he found principles for practical Christian living. "God wants you to be a champion," he said. "God wants you to be an overcomer who attains the very best you can for His glory." He viewed spiritual champions as those who are single-minded in purpose, willing to endure hardship, work long hours, and who train others to do the same.

His sermons were laced with everything from biblical examples and personal stories to quotes from Christian leaders. He was especially fond of D. L. Moody's story of a preacher saying, "It yet remains to be seen what God can do with one man who is wholly dedicated to the Lord." Moody responded, "By God's grace, I'll be that man." Falwell took that challenge a step further and added, "I wonder what God could do with an entire church committed to being champions for Christ. I believe we could shake the world for God."[28]

Jerry Falwell's sermons were extremely practical. He generally read his text and went straight to its application. For example, in "Winning the Race That Is Set Before Us,"[29] he began with Hebrews 12:1–2: "Therefore, since we are surrounded by such a great a cloud of witnesses, let us throw off everything that hinders and the sin that so easily entangles. And let us run with perserverance the race marked out for us, fixing our eyes on Jesus, the pioneer and perfecter of faith." Falwell then defined the race as the race to get the gospel to the whole world in our lifetime. "This is our generation," he said, "and the race is on. We must carry out the great commission in our generation."

Throughout his preaching, his tone was always optimistic and encouraging. There were problems to confront, but he was convinced, "God never tells us to do something without providing the means to do it." After commenting on the "cloud of witnesses" (people and angels), he developed the main body of the message around a list of "weights that hinder" Christians from being successful, such as: (1) the weight of discouragement (here, he referred to Moody who was quoted as saying, "I have never known God to use a discouraged person"); (2) the weight of weariness which is caused by a lack of spiritual nourishment; (3) the weight of carelessness which grows in the life of those who fail to discipline their spiritual pursuits; (4) the weight of prayerlessness, which is common, but needs to be fixed in the lives of Christians (Falwell was greatly impacted by Andrew Murray and George Müller, both of whom were richly invested in the discipline of prayer); and lastly, (5) the weight of bitterness (here, Falwell explained that jealousy is the tribute that mediocrity pays to greatness—therefore, Christians cannot allow even a root of bitterness to ruin our ministry). Falwell typically concluded his

---

28. Ibid., 12.
29. Jerry Falwell, "Winning the Race That Is Set Before Us," in *America Can Be Saved*, 123–36.

sermons with a homespun Southern expression, such as, "It is not a matter of whether the rabbit can climb the tree; the rabbit must climb the tree!" His concluding appeal was, "The giants of the past are dead and the next generation may never get here. This is our day and we can do it."

Falwell loved people and it showed in his preaching. He was affable and engaging. He often referred to people in his congregation by name in his sermons. He would emphasize some positive attribute, ability, or contribution they were making to the cause of Christ. "He made you feel like you were his best friend," people often remarked. Because of his photographic memory, he never forgot a name. Because of his love for people, he was able to communicate with his audience as though he was speaking to each one personally. His wife observed, "It was Jerry's love for people that would drive him and motivate his entire Christian life."[30]

It was during his political phase (1975–1992) that Falwell became known for his willingness to point out what he believed was wrong in America and called the nation to repent. For many, these were his most controversial sermons. He admitted he had been wrong in opposing clerical involvement in political, social, and civil causes. The sweeping influence of secularism, relativism, and materialism was causing public awareness of a seismic shift in American values and very few were speaking out against it. Martin Marty observed at the time, "Today's fundamentalist leadership has spotted a powerful vacuum . . . and has become a political force among forces."[31] Nathan Hatch added that Falwell's message, and that of other fundamentalists and evangelicals, resonated with the general public more than the academic elite. He wrote, "If mainline Protestants have taken their cues from secular and academic culture, evangelicals have remained in tune with popular mores."[32]

During the 1980s, Falwell was also significantly influenced by apologist Francis Schaeffer, who believed the Christian conscience that had initially shaped American culture was fading fast and was being replaced by "relativistic values based upon statistical averages, or the arbitrary decisions of those who hold legal and political power."[33] Thus, Falwell's emphasis on political involvement was driven by his belief in biblical truth as the only final, objective authority.

---

30. Macel Falwell, *Falwell: His Life and Legacy*, 19. Sermons of this type were filled with exhortations and encouragement, two of his best qualities.

31. Martin Marty, "Fundamentalism as a Social Phenomenon," in *Evangelicals and Modern America*, ed. George Marsden (Grand Rapids: Eerdmans, 1984), 61.

32. Nathan Hatch, "Evangelicalism as a Democratic Movement," in *Evangelicals and Modern America*, 80–82.

33. Schaeffer's last book before his death was aimed at what he viewed as the growing erosion of the biblical roots of evangelicalism: *The Great Evangelical Disaster* (Westchester, IL: Crossway, 1984), 47. A cobelligerent with Falwell on various social and ethical issues, Schaffer viewed the "New Right" as those Christians who were

Electing conservative politicians was seen by him as a pragmatic obstruction to the liberal juggernaut that he was convinced was ruining America for generations to come. He never really viewed the political process as the solution to America's problems, but he did see it as the best means of leveling the playing field.

The methodology of Falwell's more political sermons usually involved articulating a biblical principle or example and relating it to a contemporary event or situation which he believed violated those principles. In his message on the changing American family, Falwell said, "This is an age of pornography and hedonism unimaginable just a generation ago. Increasing economic pressures combined with skyrocketing divorce, unprecedented levels of abuse and neglect, and rampant sexual promiscuity have created a volatile climate which eats like caustic acid into the fabric of the American home."

Falwell's sermons during this phase of his ministry were often laced with both positive and negative examples of everyone from presidents and world leaders to movie stars and television talk show hosts. Ironically, he actually formed personal friendships with some of his greatest antagonists (Ted Kennedy, Phil Donahue, Alan Dershowitz, and Al Sharpton). Falwell was fully aware that they often used him as a foil to get their message across, because he was using his encounters with them to do the very same thing. "No matter what we talk about, I am always able to get in the gospel," he often announced.

CONTRIBUTIONS TO PREACHING

Jerry Falwell was an expert at contextualizing his sermons by identifying his audience. Thus, he could communicate with a wide variety of listeners from rural to urban settings, from Bible colleges to major universities, from Christian churches to Jewish synagogues.[34]

By the twenty-first century, Falwell often reiterated the basic principles of the gospel and Christian life. In this "back to basics" phase, he often recounted how God led him to plant the church, evangelize the community, and launch the university. "Keep your eye on the goal," he emphasized. "Don't go to extremes, you will end up in the ditch on either side." Neither reformed nor charismatic, Falwell remained a balanced evangelical with a pastor's heart and an evangelist's passion. He did weddings, funerals, and hospital calls until his dying day.

Perhaps Falwell's greatest contribution to the field of preaching was

---

willing to take a stand rather than accommodate liberal secularism. He urged that further accommodation would erode any Christian influence that was still left in society (150).

34. Falwell spoke at Harvard, debated at Oxford, spoke in numerous synagogues, and addressed the Knesset in Israel. See Falwell's *Strength for the Journey*.

challenging pastors to speak out on ethical, moral, and social issues from a biblical worldview. He believed these issues directly influenced the Christian's impact on society and needed to be articulated from the pulpits of a nation's churches.[35] He led hundreds of rallies nationwide, challenging local church pastors to follow his example.[36] The continuing influence of evangelical voters in American politics is a direct result of Falwell's influence in galvanizing their initial entrance onto the political scene since the 1980s.

CONCLUSION

Jerry Falwell was blessed with a photographic memory, incredible faith, indomitable vision, personal courage, and an undaunted work ethic. He was a natural leader—a big man with a booming voice and a captivating personality. His evangelistic preaching articulated his philosophy of "saturation evangelism" which he expressed as "preaching the gospel to everyone, everywhere, by every means possible."[37] In order to do this, he launched the "Old-Time Gospel Hour" telecast in 1956 and by the 1970s, he was one of America's most prominent televangelists, broadcasting "The Old-Time Gospel Hour" from his church in Lynchburg, Virginia, on over four hundred network television stations in America.[38]

A staunch conservative theologically, politically, and socially, Falwell became concerned about America's drift into secularism and political and social liberalism. In 1979, he founded the Moral Majority along with Tim LaHaye, Charles Stanley, and D. James Kennedy and threw his efforts into helping elect Ronald Reagan as president of the United States in 1980 and again in 1984. He forged an informal coalition of evangelicals into what the media dubbed as the "New Right."[39] In 1987, he aligned himself with the Southern Baptist Convention and

---

35. This is illustrated in his sermon "I Love America." Full text in Falwell, *America Can Be Saved*, 21–37.

36. While most of his emphasis was on turning America back to God, Falwell also spoke to pastors in England, Russia, Africa, Haiti, Korea, the Philippines, South America, and the Bahamas. One of his most eventful trips was to the Middle East in 1979, when he met personally with Anwar Sadat of Egypt, King Hussein of Jordan, and Menachem Begin of Israel, seeking peace in the Middle East by urging Egypt and Jordan's acceptance of Israel's right to exist.

37. For details see Falwell, "Spreading the Word," in *Strength for the Journey*, 189–218. This volume is Falwell's autobiography and includes numerous insights into his ministry philosophy.

38. Cf. Ben Armstrong, *The Electric Church* (Nashville: Thomas Nelson, 1979); Jeffrey Haddon and Charles Swann, *Prime-Time Preachers: The Rising Power of Televangelists* (Reading, MA: Addison-Wesley, 1981); and Flo Conway and Jim Siegelman, *Holy Terror* (Garden City, NY: Doubleday, 1982). The latter critically dubbed Falwell, "the prince of the power of the air" (66).

39. Falwell's foray into the American political arena became the major religious story of the 1980s as can be seen from the number of books and articles written on this subject during that decade. For example, see Chuck Colson, *Kingdoms in Conflict* (New York: William Morrow, 1987); Ed Dobson and Ed Hindson, *The Seduction of Power: Preachers, Politics, and the Media* (Old Tappan, NJ: Revell, 1988); Gabriel Fackre, *The Religious Right and the Christian Faith* (Grand Rapids: Eerdmans, 1982); Edward E. Hindson, "Thunder in the Pulpit: The Socio-Political Involvement of the New Right," *Foundations* (April-June 1982): 144–52;

played an active role in the conservative resurgence within the SBC during the 1990s and early twenty-first century.[40]

Sermon Excerpt

Never Quit[41]

The apostle Paul said, "Blessed be . . . the God of all comfort; who comforts us in all our tribulation that we may be able to comfort them which are in any trouble, by the comfort wherewith we ourselves are comforted of God" (2 Cor 1:3–4, KJV).

One reason we're in constant trouble is because most Christians have the wrong view of trouble. Too many Christians think that knowing Christ means deliverance from trouble. There is no such promise in the Bible. Knowing Christ simply means deliverance in trouble, and that's very different. The three Hebrew children were cast into the fiery furnace; they were not delivered from it. But, when they went into the fiery furnace He, Christ, went in with them. He has promised not to deliver us from trouble, but to walk with us through our troubles.

You've heard me hundreds, maybe thousands, of times say, "You do not determine a man's greatness by his talent or wealth, as the world does, but rather by what it takes to discourage him." And that is a fact.

Mr. Moody said, "I've never known God to use a discouraged person." I have a plaque on the wall of my study at home that reads, "Life is filled with glorious opportunities brilliantly disguised as insurmountable problems." Most Christians have a wrong view of trouble. You're never going to get out of trouble. You are either in trouble, you just got out of trouble, or you are about to get into trouble. Trouble is a basic ingredient for spiritual growth.

God does not give us overcoming life, He gives us life as we overcome. The strain is the strength. If there is no strain, there is no strength.

Erling Jorstad, *The Politics of Moralism: The New Christian Right in American Life* (Minneapolis: Augsburg, 1981); John Krater, *Christian on the Right: The Moral Majority in Perspective* (New York: Seabury, 1982); Robert Zwier, *Born Again Politics: The New Christian Right in America* (Downers Grove, IL: InterVarsity Press, 1982).

40. James C. Hefley, *The Conservative Resurgence in the Southern Baptist Convention* (Hannibal, MO: Hannibal, 1991). Hefley notes that Falwell commented of his desire to work with the SBC on world evangelism stating, "I don't believe any of us can do it alone" (81).

41. Personal notes of this author.

Are you asking God to give you life, liberty, and joy? He cannot do that unless you are willing to accept the strain that comes with it. And, the moment you're willing to say, "I accept the strain, I accept the pressure, I accept the trouble," then God will give you the strength. It's not until you put your foot in the water that the water rolls back.

I don't care what you are facing, quitting is never the answer. You can't run from failure. It will follow you until you face it head on. Face your problems. Launch out by faith and win the victory. Be a champion for Christ in every area of your life. ◆

BIBLIOGRAPHY

Armstrong, Ben. *The Electric Church*. Nashville: Thomas Nelson, 1979.

Cerillo, A., and M. Dempster, "The New Right Activates the Grass Roots." Pages 107–43 in *Salt and Light: Evangelical Political Thought in Modern America*. Grand Rapids: Baker, 1989.

Claybough, Gary. *Thunder on the Right: The Protestant Fundamentalists*. Chicago: Nelson-Hall, 1974.

Colson, Chuck. *Kingdoms in Conflict*. New York: William Morrow, 1987.

Conway, Flo, and Jim Siegelman. *Holy Terror*. Garden City, NY: Doubleday, 1982.

Dempsey, Rod. "The Ministry Methods of Jerry Falwell." *Eruditio Ardescens* 1, no. 1 at http://digitalcommons .liberty.edu/jlbts/vol.1/iss1/2.

Dobson, Ed, and Ed Hindson. *The Seduction of Power: Preachers, Politics, and the Media*. Old Tappan, NJ: Revell, 1988.

D'Souza, Dinesh. *Falwell Before the Millennium: A Critical Biography*. Chicago: Regnery Gateway, 1984.

_____. "Jerry Falwell Is Reaching Millions and Drawing Fire." *Conservative Digest* (Dec. 1986).

Fackre, Gabriel. *The Religious Right and the Christian Faith*. Grand Rapids: Eerdmans, 1982.

Falwell, Jerry. *America Can Be Saved*. Murfreesboro, TN: Sword of the Lord, 1979.

_____. *Building Dynamic Faith*. Nashville: Thomas Nelson, 2005.

_____. *Finding Inner Peace and Strength*. Garden City, NY: Doubleday, 1982.

_____. *How to Book*. Lynchburg, VA: Jerry Falwell Ministries, 1999.

_____. *Keys to Daily Living: A Practical Guide to Life*. Milwaukee: Ideals, 1981.

_____. *Listen America*. Garden City, NY: Doubleday, 1980.

_____. *The New American Family: The Rebirth of The American Dream*. Dallas: Word, 1992.

_____. *Strength for the Journey: An Autobiography*. New York: Simon & Schuster, 1987.

_____. *Wisdom for Living*. Wheaton, IL: Victor Books, 1984.

_____, and Elmer Towns. *Church Aflame*. Nashville: Impact, 1972.

Falwell, Jerry, Ed Dobson, and Ed Hindson, *The Fundamentalist Phenomenon*. Garden City, NY: Doubleday, 1981.

Falwell, Jerry, and Elmer Towns. *Stepping Out on Faith*. Carol Stream, IL: Tyndale House, 1984.

Falwell, Jonathan. *Innovate Church*. Nashville: Broadman & Holman, 2008.

Falwell, Macel. *Jerry Falwell: His Life and Legacy*. New York: Howard, 2008.

Haddon, Jeffrey, and Charles Swann. *Prime-Time Preachers: The Rising Power of Televangelists*. Reading, MA: Addison-Wesley, 1981.

Hatch, Nathan. "Evangelicalism as a Democratic Movement." Pages 80–82 in *Evangelicals and Modern America*. Edited by George Marsden. Grand Rapids: Eerdmans, 1984.

Hefley, James C. *The Conservative Resurgence in the Southern Baptist Convention*. Hannibal, MO: Hannibal, 1991.

Hindson, Edward E. "Thunder in the Pulpit: The Socio-Political Involvement of the New Right." *Foundations* (April-June 1982): 144–52.

_____. "Jerry Falwell." Pages 145–46 in *The Popular Encyclopedia of Church History*. Edited by Ed Hindson and Dan Mitchell. Eugene, OR: Harvest House, 2013.

Hunter, James Davidson. *American Evangelicalism*. New Brunswick, NJ: Rutgers University Press, 1983.
_____. *Evangelicalism: The Coming Generation*. Chicago: University of Chicago Press, 1987.
Jorstad, Erling. *The Politics of Moralism: The New Christian Right in American Life*. Minneapolis: Augsburg, 1981.
Krater, John. *Christian on the Right: The Moral Majority in Perspective*. New York: Seabury, 1982.
Liebman, Robert, and Robert Wuthnow, eds. *The New Christian Right*. New York: Aldine, 1983.
Marsden, George. *Fundamentalism and American Culture*. Oxford: Oxford University Press, 1980.
_____, ed. *Evangelicals and Modern America*. Grand Rapids: Eerdmans, 1984.
Marty, Martin. "Fundamentalism as a Social Phenomenon." Pages 56–70 in *Evangelicals and Modern America*. Edited by George Marsden. Grand Rapids: Eerdmans, 1984.
Neuhaus, Richard John. *The Naked Public Square*. Grand Rapids: Eerdmans, 1984.
Neuhaus, Richard John, and Michael Cromartie, eds. *Piety and Politics: Evangelical and Fundamentalists Confront the World*. Washington, DC: Ethics and Public Policy Center, 1987.
Noll, Mark, Nathan Hatch, and George Marsden. *The Search for Christian America*. Westchester, IL: Crossway, 1983.
Schaeffer, Francis. *A Christian Manifesto*. Westchester, IL: Crossway, 1981.
_____. *The Great Evangelical Disaster*. Westchester, IL: Crossway, 1984.
Selvidge, Marla, ed. *Fundamentalism Today: What Makes It So Attractive?* Elgin, IL: Brethren Press, 1984.
Simon, Merrill. *Jerry Falwell and the Jews*. Middle Village, NY: Jonathan David, 1984.
Towns, Elmer. *America's Fastest Growing Churches*. Nashville: Impact, 1972.
Towns, Elmer, and Jerry Falwell. *Capturing a Town for Christ*. Old Tappan, NJ: Revell, 1973.
Vaughn, John. *The World's 20 Largest Churches*. Grand Rapids: Baker, 1984.
Webber, Robert. *Moral Majority-Right or Wrong?* Westchester, IL: Crossway, 1981.
Wood, James, ed. *Religion and Politics*. Waco, TX: Baylor University Press, 1983.
Zwier, Robert. *Born Again Politics: The New Christian Right in America*. Downers Grove, IL: InterVarsity Press, 1982.

J. I. Packer

Teaching Preachers to Preach as Teachers

LELAND RYKEN

BENJAMIN HERNÁNDEZ

J. I. Packer (1926–) is known primarily as a writer, theologian, and professor; however, throughout the majority of his career, he was a preacher dedicating himself to the training of theologically astute church people. Having stood in hundreds, if not thousands, of pulpits and classrooms throughout the world, Packer has been an influential voice in the theory and practice of homiletics from a historically grounded, theological perspective. For Packer, preaching is teaching.

HISTORICAL BACKGROUND

James Innell Packer was born into a lower-middle-class family in Gloucester, England, on July 22, 1926. He received his college education at the Universitiy of Oxford, where he also earned an MA and DPhil from Wycliffe Hall, the permanent Anglican hall that is within the university. Packer was converted just days after arriving at the University of Oxford. His conversion and early Christian nurture occurred through the work of InterVarsity Fellowship, which, in Oxford, was largely led by students of the Plymouth Brethren persuasion. Even though Packer is most notably known as an academician and theologian, he himself has always thought of his calling in terms of the seminary preparation of preachers. According to Packer, seminaries exist for the training of future ministers, and his place as a theologian is to "instruct today and tomorrow's clergy."[1]

During his third year in college, Packer spent a Sunday afternoon listing reasons for entering the ministry and reasons for not doing so. He decided to seek ordination and immediately took steps toward it. Although Packer was converted and nurtured through the work of non-Anglican evangelicals, he has always regarded himself as an Anglican. In 1947, during his undergraduate studies, Packer formally applied for ordination in the Church of England at a

---

1. Leland Ryken, *J. I. Packer: An Evangelical Life* (Wheaton, IL: Crossway, 2015), 359.

three-day selection conference where he was approved.[2] Upon completion of his formal education, Packer served a two-year tenure as an associate pastor and preacher at St. John's Anglican Church in Harborne, a suburb of Birmingham.[3]

Following graduation and his two years as a parish minister, Packer became a lifelong teacher, first in several theological colleges in Bristol, England, and then at Regent College in Vancouver, British Columbia, starting in 1979. In the middle of his teaching career in England, Packer took a decade-long sabbatical (1961–70) to serve as principal of Latimer House in Oxford, a think tank and theological clearinghouse dedicated to bolstering the evangelical influence in the Church of England.[4]

We can draw three primary conclusions from this biographical sketch. The first is that Packer's teaching career has been grounded in a commitment to the institutional church—not as a parish minister but as an academician who regards his primary calling as the theological education of preachers. As a professor, he has trained scores of students preparing for the ministry in the local church. Likewise, his role with Latimer House also was aimed at serving the same institution. Second, in addition to his role as academician, Packer has also been an occasional guest preacher. When he writes about sermons and preaching, he regularly makes statements to the effect that this is how he himself prepares for his own sermons.[5] Third, despite Packer's Anglican loyalty, his preaching career (including both its academic side and his actual preaching) has been cosmopolitan, transdenominational, and international. Packer has found himself speaking and preaching equally in Anglican churches, mainstream evangelical churches, and interdenominational conferences.

THEOLOGY OF PREACHING

In order to understand Packer's theology of preaching, one must appreciate his ties to Anglicanism, his high view of Scripture, and his devotion to Puritan theology. Packer self-identifies as an Anglican, but in terms of theology this does not yield much because in modern times, Anglicanism has been so comprehensive that it has incorporated virtually every theological position imaginable.[6]

---

2. Ibid., 70. Upon leaving the selection conference, Packer had "such as strong sense of calling to the ministry that he resolved that if his request were denied, he would immediately reapply."

3. Ibid., 71.

4. See Ryken, *J. I. Packer*, 98–121 for a thorough treatment of how Packer bolstered the evangelical influence within the Church of England during his time at Latimer House.

5. For a brief discussion on preaching in Packer's own words, see his chapter entitled "Speaking for God," in *Inside the Sermon: Thirteen Preachers Discuss Their Methods of Preparing Messages*, ed. Richard Allen Bodey (Grand Rapids: Baker, 1990), 185–93.

6. For a greater understanding of the nature of Anglican comprehensiveness, see J. I. Packer, *A Kind*

Packer's lifelong loyalty to Anglicanism has been to an ideal of the institutional church. That ideal has included a preference for a liturgical worship in public church services and an extreme loyalty to the English Book of Common Prayer. It should be noted that Packer is critical of the Anglican Church in many ways, having spent a lifetime as a lonely voice for theological renewal within the church.[7] Additionally, until the homosexual lobby gained control of the Western Anglican Church, Packer had strongly defended the principle of comprehensiveness represented by historic Anglicanism, even to the extent of being tolerant of the presence of liberalism as an acceptable price to pay for the advantages of Anglican comprehensiveness.[8]

Anglicanism explains Packer's denominational preference more than his theological position. To qualify that statement, one must note that the creedal gold standard to which Packer most often resorts in his writing and classroom teaching is the *Thirty-Nine Articles* of the Anglican tradition. However, the *Thirty-Nine Articles* fit into a broader theological system, namely the Calvinistic or Reformed tradition. Packer has, from the beginning of his theological thinking, been a Calvinist. He was salvaged from his first theological crisis (the Keswick view of triumphalism) through the aid of John Owen's book *The Mortification of Sin,* while organizing a library that had been donated to the Oxford Christian student organization.[9] Packer writes, "Suffice it to say that without Owen I might well have gone off my head or got bogged down in mystical fanaticism, and certainly my view of the Christian life would not be what it is today."[10] Continuing on in this Reformed vein of Puritanism, Packer completed his dissertation on Richard Baxter's doctrine of redemption. Almost from the start of Packer's theological career, his sphere of greatest influence has been in Reformed evangelicalism. However, the content of his preaching is not so much Reformed as it is what Baxter called "mere Christianity"—the consensus of evangelical belief through the centuries.[11] From this same evangelical tradition comes the heart of Packer's theological foundation for preaching, namely his theology of the Bible, which can just as well be called a theology of the Word or theology of revelation.

of Noah's Ark? The Anglican Commitment to Comprehensiveness (Oxford: Latimer House, 1981). Chapter 2 specifically explores four conceptions of comprehensiveness on which Anglicanism rests.

7. See Ryken, *J. I. Packer,* 305–25, for a thorough discussion of Packer's experience in the Anglican Church.

8. Ibid., 408–9.

9. Ibid., 265–67.

10. J. I. Packer, *A Quest for Godliness: The Puritan Vision of the Christian Life* (Wheaton, IL: Crossway, 1994), 12.

11. Richard Baxter, *The Practical Works of Richard Baxter* (London: Paternoster Row, 1838), 83, 577, 1026. See also C. S. Lewis, *Mere Christianity* (New York: Simon & Schuster, 1996), 6–11.

No doctrinal subject has preoccupied Packer more than the nature and authority of Scripture. This was the subject of Packer's first book, which sold more than twenty thousand copies in its first year (1958) and has never been out of print. This misleadingly titled book, *Fundamentalism and the Word of God*, has been an encouragement to an entire generation of Christians and at its center asks the question of what constitutes the authority for religious belief. Here Packer provides an anatomy of the three major views of authority that Christians through the ages have embraced—Scripture alone, Scripture plus religious tradition, and human reason. This paradigm of authority has resurfaced throughout Packer's career in many of his theological works as the foundation for his thinking.[12]

In *Fundamentalism and the Word of God*, Packer laid out his case for Scripture alone as the authority for religious belief. He argued that the writers of the Bible claim to be speaking God's words. Likewise, Jesus and the apostles regarded the Old Testament as being the very words of God, and because of Jesus's divinity he spoke the words of God and authorized the apostles to do the same. The conclusion of his argument was the evidence of the revere of the early church for these writings of the apostles. Here Packer has gone well beyond simply affirming the authority and reliability of the Bible, and because of his high view of Scripture, he was a leader in the International Council on Biblical Inerrancy. Among modern theologians, Packer has asserted with unusual thoroughness the belief that the words of the Bible are the very words of God saying, "What Scripture says, God says."[13]

This view of the Bible is the theological foundation of Packer's thinking about preaching, as he himself noted when he defined preaching as that which "grounds [itself] on a particular view of the nature of Scripture."[14] If Scripture alone is the final authority for what people must believe, a sermon must be rooted in the text of the Bible. Therefore, if preaching is God's word to the listener, it needs to be more than just the preacher's thoughts on a subject. The preacher is an intermediary who makes the message of the Bible plain to a listener.

Given Packer's high view of Scripture, it is no wonder that he is a proponent of expository preaching. As such, Packer criticizes topical preaching for falling short of Christian preaching. He writes that in topical preaching, "the only authority that [a] sermon can then have is the human authority of a

---

12. Further writings on the nature and authority of Scripture by Packer include, but are not limited to, *God Speaks to Man: Revelation and The Bible* (Grand Rapids: Baker Academic, 1994); *Beyond the Battle for The Bible* (Wheaton, IL: Crossway, 1980); *Truth and Power: The Place of Scripture in The Christian Life* (Wheaton, IL: Shaw, 1996); and *Engaging the Written Word of God* (Peabody, MA: Hendrickson, 1999).

13. J. I. Packer, *Fundamentalism and the Word of God* (Grand Rapids: Eerdmans, 1958), 47.

14. Packer, "Speaking for God," 186.

knowledgeable person. . . . The authority of God revealed is thus resolved into that of religious expertise."[15] For Packer, preaching in the fullest sense is allowing the Word of God to speak for itself. Yet topical preaching often fails in that area because it highlights the wisdom of the preacher and not the revealed authority of God.

For devotees of expository preaching, this is all familiar territory, but elsewhere Packer provides a fresh view of it, namely, that God is really the preacher.[16] Packer writes, "Holy Scripture, the inspired Word (message) of the living God, may truly be described as God preaching. . . . Only as God himself is perceived to be preaching in our sermons can they have genuine spiritual significance, and God will be perceived to speak through us [preachers] only as we are enabled to make plain the fact that it is really the Bible that is doing the talking."[17] Thus, Packer's theological framework for preaching includes a view of the Bible as inerrant as well as infallible, and as the authority to which all Christians must be subservient. Packer believes that the words of Scripture are God's words and, therefore, the foundation of preaching must be thoroughly biblical as opposed to intermittently biblical. Mastery of the very texture of a biblical passage should become the goal for both preacher and listener.

In addition to his high view of Scripture, Packer's theology and ministry practice has also been significantly influenced by Puritan theology. In terms of primary contributing influences on his preaching, Packer observes in a somewhat broad reflection: "John Chrysostom, Augustine, Martin Luther, Hugh Latimer, John Knox, Richard Baxter, John Bunyan, George Whitefield, John Wesley, Jonathan Edwards, Charles Simeon, Robert Murray McCheyne, Charles Spurgeon, John Charles Ryle, Martyn Lloyd-Jones, and Billy Graham [because] . . . their goal in preaching was to become the means of God's encounter with their hearers, and second, that it was by focusing on God's teaching in Scripture that they sought to achieve their purpose."[18]

Packer explicitly states his indebtedness to the Puritans in his book *A Quest for Holiness: The Puritan Vision of the Christian Life*, saying, "The well-being of the church today depends in large measure on a revival of preaching in the Puritan vein."[19] Preaching never stood higher in people's estimation than it did during the Puritan era, and as a Puritan scholar, J. I. Packer echoes this belief. In elaborating his thesis regarding the importance of Puritan preaching, Packer

---

15. J. I. Packer, "Introduction: Why Preach?" in *The Preacher and Preaching: Reviving the Art in the Twentieth Century*, ed. Samuel T. Logan Jr. (Phillipsburg, NJ: Presbyterian and Reformed, 1986), 4.

16. See Packer's discussion on the nature of Scripture in "Speaking for God," 186–87.

17. Ibid.

18. Packer, *Truth and Power*, 159.

19. Packer, *A Quest for Godliness*, 281.

delineates "four axioms [that] underlay all Puritan thought about preaching." Those four axioms are: the primacy of the intellect, the importance of preaching, the life-giving power of Scripture, and the sovereignty of the Holy Spirit.

The first axiom addresses the mind. Puritan preaching is built on the belief that the sermon must affect the listeners through understanding. Packer rightly states, "It follows that every man's first duty in relation to the word of God is to understand it; and every preacher's first duty is to explain it. The only way to the heart that he is authorized to take runs via the head."[20] Additionally, "the minister who does not make it his prime business, in season and out of season, to teach the word of God, does not do his job."[21] At this point it is not difficult to see why Packer views preaching as teaching. Surely it is the didactic nature of biblical exposition, as demonstrated in puritanical preaching, that has profoundly influenced Packer's approach to the pulpit.

The second axiom upholds the sermon as the central part of corporate worship and the weightiest event of the week. For the Puritans, "the sermon was the liturgical climax of public worship."[22] Not only should this be the view taken by the minister but by the congregants as well, for nothing "honours God more than the faithful declaration and obedient hearing of his truth."[23] Given the supreme importance of preaching, sermons are not to be prepared haphazardly. On the contrary, Packer believes it is the duty of the minister to give the utmost attention to sermon preparation. He writes, "If we are not willing to give time to sermon preparation, we are not fit to preach, and have no business in the ministry at all."[24]

The third axiom is an unwavering belief in the Bible as the very Word of God. As such, "The Puritans insisted that the preachers' task is to *feed* their congregations with the contents of the Bible—not the dry husks of their own fancy, but the life-giving word of God."[25] While the modern picture of pastoral work is that of visitation and personal interaction, the Puritans pictured pastoral work chiefly in terms of preaching. The minister's responsibility first and foremost was to ensure that congregants were being fed the truths of Scripture, for that is the true source of spiritual nourishment.

The fourth axiom is the belief that "the ultimate effectiveness of preaching is out of man's hand."[26] In other words, the preacher bears a responsibility to

---

20. Ibid.
21. Ibid.
22. Ibid.
23. Packer, *A Quest for Godliness*, 281.
24. Ibid., 282.
25. Ibid.
26. Ibid., 283.

faithfully teach the Word, but is not the one who convinces congregants of its truthfulness. Rather, it is God who does the work of conversion. Therefore, in Packer's view, the Puritans "would have criticized the modern evangelistic appeal, with its wheedling for 'decisions,' as an unfortunate attempt by man to intrude into the Holy Spirit's province."[27] It is at this point we catch echoes of Packer's book *Evangelism and the Sovereignty of God*, where he has biblically unfolded the relationship between divine sovereignty and human responsibility. Packer views these two truths in terms of antimony. While it may seem that the two stand in contradiction to one another, nothing could be further from the truth. Speaking of the two, Packer writes, "Far from inhibiting evangelism, faith in the sovereignty of God's government and grace is the only thing that can sustain it, for it is the only thing that can give us the resilience that we need if we are to evangelize boldly and persistently, and not be daunted by temporary setbacks."[28] Therefore, Packer upholds the duty that God has placed on his people to share the gospel, while at the same time affirming a high view of God's sovereignty in salvation.

METHODOLOGY FOR PREACHING

When considering Packer's preaching methodology, it would be a mistake to think that his approach is traditional in a strict sense. Rather, there is much in Packer's views on preaching that is nontraditional. For example, when Packer was asked in an interview what advice he would give to young clergy, his reply was that they "have three priorities: teach, teach, teach."[29] The weakening of churches is a result of their failure to teach the confessions and doctrine. In addition to this, Packer also believes the following: (1) "a clergyman can't be a maintenance man" but must challenge the status quo; (2) the proportion of a sermon should be half exposition and half application; and (3) "the preacher is, indeed, half of his sermon." This statement is not intended to endorse the modern personality syndrome of celebrity preachers but is a call for authenticity in preaching and the recognition that their lives validate, enrich, and give evidence to the things that are said behind the pulpit.

For Packer, the sermon begins not with a topic but with a passage from the Bible. But there is a prior question even here, namely, *"What* passage from the

---

27. Ibid.

28. J. I. Packer, *Evangelism and the Sovereignty of God* (Downers Grover, IL: InterVarsity Press, 1991), 10.

29. J. I. Packer. "An Interview with J. I. Packer on Theological Training." *The Gospel Coalition*. 10 January 2010. https://blogs.thegospelcoalition.org/justintaylor/2010/01/09/an-interview-j-i-packer-on-theological-training/

Bible?" Packer answers the question of where sermon messages come from by saying that they come from two main sources—"the known needs of congregations" and "our own experience of being taught and disciplined by God."[30] Packer also believes that "a rounded theological understanding" of God and the Christian life can be an aid to ensuring that one preaches the whole counsel of God, citing Calvin's *Institutes* as "one theological guide that has suggested to me many messages over the years."[31]

Once the passage has been determined, the preacher needs to become a biblical exegete and interpreter. Packer raises the bar very high here and has often linked his zeal for theological education to the task of preaching. A biblically based sermon needs to interpret the biblical text correctly. One of Packer's striking insights too often overlooked is that "a misinterpreted Bible is a misunderstood Bible."[32]

If the preacher must be an exegete, they must also be a theologian. Packer argues for such in an essay entitled "The Preacher as Theologian: Preaching and Systematic Theology."[33] He demonstrates that in order for the preacher to fulfill their task, they must be well-versed in systematic theology as well as the accompanying disciplines of apologetics, ethics, and spirituality.[34] In doing so, the preacher will be able to communicate with accuracy "a God-centered view of this created world and life within it."[35] An interesting sidelight is that Packer makes the unexpected claim that "the preacher, rather than the critical commentator or the academic theologian, is the true interpreter of Scripture."[36] How can this bold claim be true? For Packer, the explanation is that the preacher moves beyond the interpretation of a text to application: "The preacher is the person whose privilege it is to bridge the apparent gap between the Bible and the modern world by demonstrating the relevance of what Scripture says to the lives of those whom he addresses."[37] Packer adds that "commentaries and theologies are resources for this task, but only preachers can fully perform it; and they perform it fully only as they apply their text."[38]

When Packer explains how he goes about mastering the text that has been chosen, he offers his comments as a description of what he himself does, "without

---

30. Packer, *Engaging the Written Word of God* , 314.
31. Ibid.
32. Packer, *Truth and Power*, 137.
33. Packer, *Engaging the Written Word of God*, 283–96.
34. Ibid., 192.
35. Ibid.
36. Ibid., 311.
37. Packer, *Engaging the Written Word of God*, 311.
38. Ibid.

wishing to make rules for anyone else."[39] Packer first "walks round" his text, looking at it in its larger context (the book of the Bible in which it appears and the Bible as a whole). He jots down observations and possible angles of vision. He composes a tentative outline. Only after he completes his outline does he turn to commentaries, which he uses "to fill out the scheme I already have."[40] Packer derives more help from the older commentators and expositors than from modern ones. For illustrations or generalizations, Packer turns to the Bible and everyday events, believing that searching for "exotic illustrations" turns preaching into "a performance remote from life, so that sermon time ceases to be an encounter with God and becomes an entertainment break."[41]

Having mastered a biblical text, a preacher needs to turn the insights into a sermon. One of the constant themes of Packer's writing about preaching over the decades has been that preaching is a form of teaching. In fact, teaching is part of Packer's definition of a sermon. He writes that "sermons must teach."[42] But teaching by itself does not constitute a sermon. Packer believes that "to pass on biblical content, unapplied, is to teach, not to preach," and it produces "a lecture [but] not a sermon."[43] Accordingly, "Preaching is teaching plus—plus what? Plus application of truth to life."[44] Packer believes that preaching is "interpreting God's Word to God's people."[45] Its adequacy is not determined "by the erudition of one's exegesis but by the depth and power of one's application."[46] Packer, a latter-day Puritan, has a whole "science" of application in which he classifies types of application and recipients of application, in the mode of the Puritans.

A modern enthusiast for application, Packer believes that application should be about half of a sermon. He writes, "A good rule of thumb for pastoral sermons . . . is that half the message should be in essence instruction in biblical truth about God and man and half should be in essence specific application of that truth. Observing these proportions, . . . one cannot go far wrong."[47] Packer believes that "the present-day Evangelical pulpit is [not] strong here," being guilty of "doctrinal overload" in which twenty-eight minutes of a thirty-minute sermon are spent "teaching general principles of divine truth."[48] Thus, Packer advo-

---

39. Ibid., 314–315.
40. Ibid., 315.
41. Ibid., 315.
42. Ibid., 234.
43. Packer, *Truth and Power*, 165.
44. Ibid.
45. Ibid.
46. Packer, *Engaging the Written Word of God*, 311.
47. Ibid., 169.
48. Packer, *Engaging the Written Word of God*, 269. On this topic, I (Leland Ryken) would like to note that I find disconnect between Packer's professed homiletic models and the sermons he actually preaches. I have already noted that Packer makes extravagant claims for the Puritans' influence on his thinking about

cates for an approach to application based on three principles. First, "application should constantly focus on the unchanging realities of each person's relationship to God."[49] In other words, the Scriptures must come to bear on our relationship to God Almighty, specifically as it applies to our faith, obedience, and holiness. Second, "application should constantly focus on the person, place, and power of Jesus Christ."[50] Given that Christ is the focus of the Bible, preachers ought to show how Christ is the answer to their deepest needs. Third, "application should constantly search the consciences of the hearers."[51] Whether congregants are unconverted, young Christians, or mature Christians, the sermon is intended to reach as many people as possible.

In view of his professed preaching model, it is surprising that Packer's sermons deal with biblical texts much like a literary critic. Thus, Packer's approach to the Bible in his sermons is a literary approach. When Packer is free to choose his own sermon topic, he does not follow the common practice of many seminary graduates—to gravitate immediately to the most abstractly theological section of the Bible, namely, the Epistles. Instead he gravitates to biblical narratives. Within that sphere, his expertise is narrative preaching and character studies.

Most important of all, Packer's approach to a biblical narrative consists of reliving the text and then building on that explication. Packer does not follow the dominant contemporary model that tends to search for three generalizations and a convenient proof text. Packer's sermons are expository rather than topical, and the foundation on which the doctrine and application is built is what literary criticism calls an explication or close reading of a text.

While visiting Wheaton, Illinois, to attend a Puritan conference, Packer stayed over the weekend to preach in a local Orthodox Presbyterian church. His sermon on Mary and Martha represents the best of his preaching.[52] Most memorable was Packer's entering into the mind of Martha and empathizing with her frustration when Mary ignored any sense of domestic duty. Packer employed a literary method of following the sequence of the story instead of asserting a series of theological generalizations and imposing them on the story in a topical manner.

---

preaching. Additionally, in numerous places Packer has said that he learned "all I have ever known about preaching" from Martin Lloyd-Jones (under whose preaching Packer sat during a year of teaching at Oak Hill College in London before he started his graduate education). The Puritans and Martin Lloyd-Jones were topical rather than expository preachers, and I myself can think of no tradition that has been more guilty of what Packer calls "doctrinal overload" than the Puritans.

49. Packer, "Speaking for God," 188.

50. Ibid, 189.

51. Ibid., 189–190.

52. The published version of this sermon appears in Packer's book (with Carolyn Nystrom) *Never Beyond Hope: How God Touches and Uses Imperfect People* (Downers Grove, IL: InterVarsity Press, 2000), 95–111.

When preaching the Martha and Mary narrative, Packer relived the story so as to bridge the gap between the text and the experiences of the listeners. The end of the sermon contained a section of application, but application was also intermingled throughout the sermon as he relived the text. Packer's sermon did not follow the script of what we have been taught to see in this story. We have been led to see Mary as a heroic ideal and Martha as an unsympathetic foil. Packer's sermon introduced the listeners to the Martha no one knows—a very human figure (one of us) and also a figure of hope and inspiration. In this glorification of the ordinary, the sermon displayed a strong Puritan affinity. Therefore, readers of the published version of this sermon are sure to find themselves very moved by the figure of Martha as she emerges in Packer's analysis of the story.

CONTRIBUTION TO PREACHING

In assessing Packer's contribution to preaching and homiletics, his primary contribution to contemporary thinking about preaching has been more as a theorist than a practitioner. Packer is a professor, theologian, and author. He has preached all over the world, but most people know about his views on preaching by virtue of his essays and interviews. It is for this reason that we can call Packer a teacher of preachers. In many ways, it is difficult to calculate how many preachers and evangelical theologians owe a debt of gratitude to Packer—Alister McGrath, Timothy George, Mark Dever, and Charles Colson are just a few.[53]

Even though Packer has served more as a theorist, this should in no way diminish the respect that we accord him as a practitioner and expert in the field of preaching. As Packer himself has noted, "You can sometimes do a useful job as a coach even when you are not one of the best players."[54] The homiletic theory of most great preachers is something we infer from their sermons. Instead of having to rely on the interpretation of theory and method from the sermons of Packer, he has instead left the church with a small anthology of treasured essays on the subject. Thus, we do not need to infer but are able to explore his approach and contributions in the concrete.

If we place Packer into the landscape of modern preaching, without a doubt the most important contribution of Packer is that he has served as a prophetic voice against the dominant trends in modern evangelical preaching. In other words, he has sought to advocate for preaching that is biblical, expositional, and

---

53. For a more thorough analysis of Packer's influence on evangelicalism, see Timothy George, ed., *J. I. Packer and the Evangelical Future: The Impact of His Life and Thought* (Grand Rapids: Baker, 2009).

54. See Packer, *Truth and Power*, 160.

nonsubmissive to cultural pressures.[55] In this sense, Packer is countercultural, and a large part of his homiletic thrust has been to critique contemporary trends in preaching.[56]

CONCLUSION

For Packer, preaching is teaching. More specifically, preaching is teaching the Word of God. In a *Preaching Today* interview, Packer was asked to respond to a prevalent contemporary view, namely that the sermonic emphasis that has been around since the Reformation is part of the problem with the church today. Packer refused to budge an inch. He defended Calvin's view of preaching as "God's derivative word," based on a conviction that "Scripture should always be preached and listened to, read, reflected on as the word of the God who here and now is saying what Scripture says."[57] Perhaps this is the greatest lesson to be learned from this teacher of preachers—read, hear, and proclaim the Word of God as the words God says.

Sermon Excerpt
Hope When False Priorities Have Betrayed Me[58]

The first thing communicated by Martha's words was that she wanted to be noticed. Jesus' reply to her begins, "Martha, Martha, you are worried and upset about many things." In other words: "Martha, you are noticed. I know what you're doing, and I'm grateful. Don't be in any doubt about that." You and I should bear in mind that our Lord Jesus always knows. He never forgets those who are his. Though we may

---

55. Packer offers his own views on preaching as an antidote to what he regards as the malaise of current preaching. In summary, they are a conviction of the centrality of preaching in a Sunday worship service, a belief that the Bible itself speaks with unique authority and power and therefore should form the chief content of a sermon, a conviction that a sermon must be an exposition of a passage from the Bible and not an address on a topic, and a belief that a sermon must include a high proportion of application of biblical truth to a person's life.

56. Packer, *Engaging the Written Word of God*, 234–37. He elaborates on six contemporary trends to which he attributes the decline of preaching today. In order, they are: "non-preaching in our pulpits" (i.e., lack of application and teaching in sermons); topical rather than expository preaching; low expectations for preaching (i.e., low expectations are self-fulfilling); the cult of personality; concentration on liturgy; and skepticism about the power of speech to communicate significance.

57. J. I. Packer, "J. I. Packer on Preaching as God's Derivative Word." *Preaching Today*. n.p. [cited 23 August 2016]. http://preachingtoday.com/skills/themes/preachingwithauthority/jipackeronpreachingasgods-derivativeword.html

58. This excerpt is taken from the published sermon based on the story of Martha and Mary, and entitled "Hope When False Priorities Have Betrayed Me" in Packer and Nystrom, *Never Beyond Hope*, 95–112.

ourselves forget him, he never in fact forgets us. He is wonderful in that way. Martha's "don't you care?" reminds us of when Jesus was asleep in the storm, and the disciples woke him up with the same words (Mk 4:38); on both occasions "yes, I care" was the answer implied by his response. Out there in the kitchen preparing the meal, or perhaps making up thirteen extra beds somewhere in the building, Martha ought to have been very sure that the Lord Jesus knew of her efforts. But her self-pity has put that certainty out of her mind. The Lord has to remind her that he knows, and he cares.

The second thing Martha had expressed was that she wanted to control Mary's life by hauling her out into the kitchen. To that, Jesus' response is, "Mary has chosen what is good, and it will not be taken away from her. That is to say, Martha, that resenting her absence from the kitchen is an attitude you shouldn't have; hauling her there is something you shouldn't be trying to do. You ought to be glad that Mary has the opportunity to sit here and listen to me and learn from me. You should think of it as your gift to her." In the same way you and I ought to be glad to give someone else the opportunity. This is clearly Jesus' thought as he reminds Martha that Mary is observing life's first priority.

The third thing that Martha had expressed in her words, as was said above, was a desire to manipulate and use Jesus as her tool against her sibling—in other words, her hammer for hitting Mary over the head. On that, Jesus is being quite firm with Martha. "Martha, you must not try to do that." That is what he implies when he says, "Only one thing is needed. Mary has chosen that good thing, and it will not be taken away from her. I am not going to order her into the kitchen." ◆

BIBLIOGRAPHY

Baxter, Richard. *The Practical Works of Richard Baxter.* London: Paternoster Row, 1838.

Lewis, C. S. *Mere Christianity.* New York: Simon & Schuster, 1996

Packer, J. I. *A Kind of Noah's Ark? The Anglican Commitment to Comprehensiveness.* Oxford, UK: Latimer, 1981.

_____. *A Quest for Godliness: The Puritan Vision of the Christian Life.* Wheaton, IL: Crossway, 1994.

_____. "Babel!" Pages 194–200 in *Inside the Sermon: Thirteen Preachers Discuss Their Methods of Preparing Messages.* Edited by Richard Allen Bodey. Grand Rapids: Baker, 1990.

_____. *Engaging the Written Word of God.* Peabody, MA: Hendrickson, 1999.

_____. *Evangelism and the Sovereignty of God.* Downers Grove, IL: InterVarsity Press, 1991.

_____. *Fundamentalism and the Word of God.* Grand Rapids: Eerdmans, 1958.

_____, and Carolyn Nystrom. "Hope When False Priorities Have Betrayed Me." Pages 95–112 in *Never Beyond Hope: How God Touches and Uses Imperfect People.* Downers Grove, IL: InterVarsity Press, 2000.

_____. "Introduction: Why Preach?" Pages 1–29 in *The Preacher and Preaching: Reviving the Art in the Twentieth Century*. Edited by Samuel T. Logan, Jr. Phillipsburg, NJ: Presbyterian and Reformed, 1986.

_____. "J. I. Packer on Preaching As God's Derivative Word." *Preaching Today*. No pages. Cited 23 August 2016. Online: http://www.preachingtoday.com/skills/themes/preachingwithauthority/jipackeronpreachingasgodsderivativeword.html

_____. "Speaking for God." Pages 185–93 in *Inside the Sermon: Thirteen Preachers Discuss Their Methods of Preparing Messages*. Edited by Richard Allen Bodey. Grand Rapids: Baker, 1990.

_____. *Truth and Power: The Place of Scripture in the Christian Life*. Wheaton, IL: Shaw, 1996.

Ryken, Leland. *J. I. Packer: An Evangelical Life*. Wheaton, IL: Crossway, 2015.

Scripture Index

Subject Index